THE NUBI LANGUAGE OF UGANDA

STUDIES IN SEMITIC
LANGUAGES AND LINGUISTICS

EDITED BY

T. MURAOKA AND C.H.M. VERSTEEGH

VOLUME XLV

THE NUBI LANGUAGE OF UGANDA

TUTA SUB AEGIDE PALLAS
· 1 6 8 3 ·

THE NUBI LANGUAGE OF UGANDA

An Arabic Creole in Africa

BY

INEKE WELLENS

BRILL

LEIDEN · BOSTON

2005

This book is printed on acid-free paper.

Library of Congress Cataloging-in-Publication Data

Wellens, Ineke Hilda Werner.
    The Nubi Language of Uganda : an Arabic creole in Africa / by Ineke
Wellens.
        p. cm. — (Studies in Semitic languages and linguistics, ISSN 0081-8461 ;
vol. 45)
    Includes bibliographical references.
    ISBN 90-04-14518-4 (alk. paper)
    1. Nubi language—Uganda. 2. Creole dialects, Arabic—Uganda. I. Title. II.
Studies in Semitic languages and linguistics ; 45.

PM7895.N83W45 2005
492.7'096761—dc22

PM
7895
.N83
W45
2005

2005051329

ISSN   0081-8461
ISBN   90 04 14518 4

PRINTED IN THE NETHERLANDS

CONTENTS

LIST OF TABLES

ABBREVIATIONS

<	reflex of	CONJ	conjunction
><	compared to	CONN	connective
*	unacceptable	CONT	contingent
Ø	zero-marking	COP	copula
1	first person		
1PL	first person plural	DEF	definite (article)
		DEM	demonstrative
1SING	first person singular	DEM DIS	demonstrative distal
2	second person	DEM PROX	demonstrative proximal
2PL	second person plural	DIM	diminutive
2SING	second person singular	DO	direct object
		DIS	distal
3	third person		
3PL	third person plural	EA	Egyptian Arabic
		EAN	East African Nubi
3SING	third person singular	EMPH	emphasizer
AA	Abbéché Arabic	EQUAT	equative
ADJ	adjective	EXIS	existential
ADR	addressee		
ADV	adverb	FEM	feminine
AG	agent	FOC	focus marker
ANT	anterior	FUT	future
ART	article		
AUG	augmentative	GEN	genitive particle
AUX	auxiliary	GER	gerund
C	consonant	H	high pitch/tone
CAUS	causative	HAB	habitual
COLL	collective		
COM	comitative	IMPER	imperative
COMPL	completive	IMPERF	imperfective
COND	conditional	INDEF	indefinite article

INF	infinitive		PAT	patient
INSTR	instrument		p/c	pidgin/creole
INT	interjection		PERF	perfective
INTRANS	intransitive		PL	plural
IRR	irrealis		POSS	possessive
ITER	iterative		POSSee	possessee
			POSSor	possessor
JA	Juba Arabic		PRED	predicate
			PREP	preposition
KA	Kharṭûm Arabic		PRES	presentative
KN	Kenyan Nubi		PROG	progressive
			PRON	pronoun
L	low pitch/tone		PROX	proximal
LD	left dislocation		PUNCT	punctual
LOC	locative			
			Q-word	question word
MASC	masculine			
MOD	modal		RCL	relative clause
			RD	right dislocation
N	noun		RECIP	reciprocal
NE	negative		REDUP	reduplication
NON-PUNCT	non-punctual		REF	referential
			REFL	reflexive
NON-REF	non-referential		REL	relativizer
			REP	repetitive
NP	noun phrase			
NPRO	proper name		S	subject
NUM	numeral		SA	Sudanese Arabic
			ShA	Shukriyya Arabic
O, OBJ	object			
			SING	singular
P	phrase		s.o.	someone
PART	participle		STAT	stative
PART ACT	participle active		STAT P	stative passive
			s.th.	something
PART PASS	participle passive		SUBJ	subjunctive
PASS	passive		SUFF	suffix

SWAH	Swahili	UN	Ugandan Nubi
TA	tense, aspect	V	vowel
TMA	tense, mood, aspect	V	verb
		VOC	vocative
TRANS	transitive	VP	verb phrase
UDA	Ugandan Dialect Arabic	WSA	Western Sudanese Arabic

PREFACE

'Ija ma jako. Aker ma ja lina.[1] Once upon a time, there was a people who entered Uganda from Sudan . . .'. This could be the introduction to a Nubi story being told on a long dark evening. The story of the Nubi, however, actually happened, and the harsh life they endured is reflected in their stories. At present, about 25,000 Nubi live scattered over the towns of Uganda and Kenya. They are distinguished from other tribal groups in East Africa by the refinement of their culture, which is characterized by their adherence to Islam, the colourful garments of the women, their spicy cooking, their fine handcrafts, and, of course, their language.

Nubi has often been called an Arabic creole. Nubi is Arabic, since about 90% of its vocabulary is of an Arabic nature. It is termed a creole, since many of its structural and developmental features resemble those of known creoles. Creole grammars will be referred to since, in some cases, they provide the obvious referential framework for explaining a Nubi feature. Every chapter will be concluded with a brief but critical comparison between Nubi features and those of creole grammars. However, I do not wish to make a definitive judgement about the creole character of Nubi and would rather leave this task to creolists since they are better placed than I am to answer this most delicate question. My intention here is to give a detailed description of the Nubi variety of Uganda. Nubi is a spoken language with hardly any written literature. However, a few individuals, keen on preserving and establishing Nubi as a fully accepted language, are making the effort to establish an orthography and to write down some of the stories.

The material used for this book was collected during two periods of field research in Uganda. In 1993, recordings were made in Bombo

---

[1] A Nubi narrator introduces his story with *'ija 'ma 'jako*. The public answers with *a'ker 'ma 'ja 'lina*. Both expressions are reflections of Arabic expressions.

'ija   'ma   'ja-   ko   -   a(l)-   'ker   'ma   'ja   'li- na.
story   NEG   come-   PRON 2PL   DEF   good   NEG   come   to   PRON 1PL
'The story did not come to you(PL).'—'The good thing did not come to us.'

in the South of Uganda for a period of nine months. More recently, in 1997–1998, recordings were made in the northern, central, and southern parts of Uganda, again for a period of nine months. The material consists mainly of stories, life histories, Nubi history, dialogues, and role playing. The material was transcribed and translated with the assistance of native speakers from North, Central, and South Uganda. Elicitation was conducted with several speakers from the same areas. Native speakers from all age groups and both sexes were included.

This book consists of three parts. The first part is a socio-linguistic introduction against the background of the history of the Nubi people. In the second part, the present-day Nubi of Uganda is presented in detail. Finally, I revert to Nubi history and attempt to reconstruct some language features through a comparative analysis with the Arabic pidgins Turku and Juba Arabic and with the Egyptian and Sudanese Arabic dialects.

We turn first to the history of the Nubi people and their language.

ACKNOWLEDGEMENTS

First and foremost, I wish to thank the Nubi speakers. They are the inspiration for this work. Many, too many to acknowledge individually, have contributed actively by talking and singing into my microphone. I wish to thank them for their enthusiasm and spontaneity. Special thanks go to Muzamil, Sauda, Jalia, and Amina for their assistance in transcribing and discussing the text material and its translation and to Mze Mustafa Khamis, Mze Abu Jere, and Muzamil Musa for the efforts they took in discussing the Nubi language. I definitely hope that this work will add to the pride in their language.

Special appreciation goes to the families of the late Sheikh Khamis Safi and of the late Sheikh Musa Yaru, who offered me their hospitality.

For suggestions on earlier drafts of this work, I wish to thank Manfred Woidich, Carlos Gussenhoven, Jonathan Owens, Pieter Muysken, Xavier Luffin, Peter Flynn, Chris Bulcaen, Edward Haasl and An Van Kiel.

Other individuals also contributed to the preparation of this work. In particular, I think of Marijke Post and Rudi Vermeulen for their logistic support, of Dr. Muranga for his curiosity and interest in my research, and of Cornelia and Hamid Khamis, who introduced me to the Nubi of Uganda.

Finally, special thanks go to Kees Versteegh: it's only because of his ceaseless support that this book 'exists'.

CHAPTER ONE

HISTORICAL AND LINGUISTIC BACKGROUND

1.1. *Historical Framework*

The Nubi language and culture are believed to have originated in southern Sudan. The development of this Arabic creole language, however, is still largely unknown. It has been suggested that a pidgin Arabic was already in use in the Bilād as-Sudān before 1820 (Owens 1996, 125–72). The events that fostered the development of Nubi, however, started around 1820 when northern Arabic speakers moved southward.

To understand the possible theories on the emergence of the Arabic pidgin/creole ancestor of present-day Nubi, it is necessary to consider the related historical events, so I will sketch the history of the Sudan before and after 1820. Furthermore, the relationship between present-day Nubi and Sudanese Nubi provides information about the nature of the Nubi language and its growth.

1.1.1. *The Sudan before 1820*

The Bilād as-Sūdān, the 'land of the blacks', or in short the Sudan, was the name given by the Medieval Muslim geographers to Sub-Saharan Africa. This geographical description thus differs from the modern state of Sudan. From the seventh century onwards, Arab groups penetrated the Sudan, passing through the Upper Nile area or crossing the Red Sea. The nomadic Arab tribes went as far as Lake Chad and beyond. They intermingled with indigenous people, which led to a slow and continuing process of Arabicization and Islamization. Arabic culture and the Islamic religion gradually infiltrated the Christian Nubian kingdoms from the eleventh century onwards until their subjection to Islam and their adoption of the Arabic language and culture in the early fourteenth century. Thereafter, Arab nomads moved freely to the Sahel region of the Bilād as-Sūdān to find grazing areas for their cattle and camels. The Kawahla, Arab camel keepers, had reached as far south as Kordofan by the nineteenth

century. From the sixteenth century onwards, powerful states emerged
in the savannah zone. Among them were the Funj Sultanate with
its capital at Sinnār and the Muslim Sultanate of Dār Fūr. By the
seventeenth century, the Bilād as-Sūdān had become the scene of
long-distance trade. The routes of the central Bilād as-Sūdān were
linked with North Africa via Fezzān. The routes of the eastern Bilād
as-Sūdān, which are more relevant for us, extended to Dār Fūr.
They linked Sinnār in the south with Egypt in the north and Dār
Fūr in the west with Suākin in the east. Shendi, which lay at the
junction of both routes, had become the main centre of commerce
by the early nineteenth century. Although trading activities between
the eastern and central Sudan were not extensive, many Muslim pil-
grims entered Dār Fūr and continued their way eastward. By 1850,
Arabic had become the lingua franca of the entire area.[1]

1.1.2. *The Sudan from 1820 Onwards*

1.1.2.1. *Occupation of the Sudan (1820–39) and Conscription of Black Slaves into the Army*

From 1820 onwards, Muḥammad ʿAlī, Viceroy of Egypt, began sending troops south to conquer the Sudan. His objectives were the sub-
mission of the Shāʾiqīya, an Arabic-speaking tribe dwelling between
ad-Dabba on the Nile and the fourth Cataract, and the annihilation
of the town of al-ʿUrdi near the town of Dunqula,[2] a refuge of the
rebellious Mamluks.[3] Muḥammad ʿAlī was above all attracted by the
supposed wealth of the country: its gold and slaves. Close to Aswān,
training camps were organized for his Niẓām al-Jadīd: Muḥammad

---

[1] Sources: Holt (1961), Adams (1977), and Braukämper (1993, 13–46).

[2] The town of Dunqula or Dongola lies on the Nile, a bit south of the 3rd
Cataract. Its inhabitants and those of the Dunqula province are called Dunqulāwī,
pl: Danāqla.

[3] The Mamluks were originally slave recruits of Turkish origin who were trained
in the army of the Abbasid Khaliefs. In 1260, they managed to take power and
established the Mamluk Empire, which united Egypt and Syria and lasted for about
three centuries. In 1517, they were defeated by the Ottomans, who established the
Ottoman Empire. By 1700, however, the entire ruling class of Egypt consisted again
of Mamluks, who held the power, rather than the Ottoman governor. Although
they aimed at taking the power officially as well, their attempts failed time and
time again. After Muḥammad ʿAlī came into power in Egypt in 1805, he massa-
cred most of their leaders, whereupon the Mamluks sought refuge in al-ʿUrdi.

'Alī's newly formed modern army, modelled on European training methods and discipline. The main problem, however, was the lack of loyal recruits. The solution opted for was the recruitment of black Sudanese men, whether by force or free will. (Gray 1961, Hill 1959, Holt 1961, MacMichael 1967). Their importance for Muḥammad 'Alī is illustrated by his words to Muḥammad Bey Khusraw, commander of his second expeditionary army (23 September 1825): "You are aware that the end of all our effort and this expense is to procure negroes. Please show zeal in carrying out our wishes in this capital matter." (Holt 1961, 33)

Therefore, a force of 4,000 men, consisting of Turkish infantry and cavalry, Arab irregulars from among the Bedouin tribes of Upper Egypt, and a force of Maḡāriba from northwest Africa under the command of the Viceroy's son Ismā'īl, was dispatched to Kordofān and Sinnār.[4] In the course of 1820–21, Kordofān and Sinnār were conquered. Dunqula was captured without difficulty and the Mamluks were defeated. The Shā'iqīya, however, showed more resistance. Eventually subjected, their military worth was praised and rewarded by their enlistment as irregular cavalry, known as *bāshī-buzūq*,[5] under their own chiefs (Hill 1959, Holt 1961). The invading force and the Egyptian administration, although not only of Turkish origin, were referred to as *Turkīya* by the Sudanese during the entire period of their rule (Emin 1919, Gray 1961).

After this conquest, Muḥammad 'Alī's attention went to the main goal of the expedition: the acquisition of gold and slaves. Slaves could be obtained in two ways. Initially, the invaded regions were subjected to very heavy taxation. Since cash was hardly available in those days, slaves owned by the local population were collected instead.[6] The slaves thus passing from Sudanese into Turco-Egyptian hands were mainly meant for conscription into the army. Slave raids, which were organized once or twice a year among the black animist tribes primarily in the Nūba mountains, in the bordering regions

---

[4] *Maḡāriba* is the plural of *Maḡribī*, which refers to an inhabitant of the *Maḡrib* or North Africa.

[5] The Turkish word *bāshī-buzūq* actually refers to irregular cavalry recruited from among Albanians, Circassians, Kurds, and Slavs. In the Sudan, however, its use was extended to irregulars of other origins as well (Hill 1959, Gray 1961)

[6] Even before the Turco-Egyptian occupation, slaves from black animist tribes were held in Islamized northern Sudan (Holt 1961).

to the west as far as the plains of the southern Gazīra, and the area
south of Khartūm between the Blue and the White Nile, were a
more direct way of obtaining them (Gray 1961, Hill 1959, Holt
1961, MacMichael 1967).

The first slave raids, however, did not have the expected results.
Muḥammad ʿAlī had intended to enlist about 20,000 black recruits.
The actual number of captured slaves, however, was much lower.
Even more disappointing was that most of the captive slaves died
while in transit to the training camps of the Niẓām al-Jadīd near
Aswān or after arrival in the camps. Homesickness, adverse climatic
circumstances, and diseases to which the black Sudanese population
was not resistant proved fatal. The slave raids of 1822–23 were more
successful. Approximately 30,000 slaves are believed to have been
taken. In the camps, the surviving recruits were clothed, Islamized,
and given military training (Hill 1959, Holt 1961). According to Hill
(1959), by 1823 the total regiment contained about 3,000 men,[7]
divided into four to five battalions. The officer corps consisted of
Mamluks, while the instructors were of southern European descent.
In 1824, the first five regiments of infantry arrived in the Sudan.
The Jihādīya, as they were called, were the first regular troops consisting of black Sudanese slave recruits who had been trained in
Aswān (Holt 1961).

Since the influx of black slaves for the Niẓām al-Jadīd was still
far from sufficient, from 1824 onwards Muḥammad ʿAlī was obliged
to force conscription upon the Egyptian farmers' sons, which had
devastating consequences for the agricultural and economic development of the country. The Egyptians, however, proved to be better soldiers than had been expected. Thus, Arabic-speaking soldiers
joined the black Sudanese recruits in the military training camps
(Baer 1969). Muḥammad ʿAlī, however, needed more and more slave
recruits, partly for his military operations in Syria and Anatolia,
partly to maintain peace and order in the Sudan itself. From 1826
on, he attempted to raid the tribes of the Upper Nile basin: the
Shilluk, Dinka, Ingassana, and so on (Hill 1959, Holt 1961).[8] From

---

[7] Although 30,000 men were captured, only 3,000 served in the Turko-Egyptian
regiments. What happened to the other 27,000 is not clear. Many must have died,
and others may have ended up as domestic slaves.
[8] These tribes and their languages will be discussed in 7.1.1.2.

1830 onwards, about 3,000 slaves were sent to Egypt annually, a figure which that have become slightly higher in the course of years (Herzog 1957). MacMichael (1967, 23) quotes Pallme who says that: "In the year 1825, . . . the number of slaves which had been led away into captivity was estimated at forty thousand; and in the year 1839 the total number amounted at least to two hundred thousand, without reckoning the thousands stolen by the Bakkara and bought by the Djelabi."[9] Gray (1961) speaks of ten to twenty thousand slaves being brought into Egypt each year by 1838. It seems, however, that the military forces of the Niẓām al-Jadīd were mainly deployed for the occupation of Syria and Anatolia, and only a smaller number of them were sent back to the Sudanese provinces. However, according to Herzog (1957), even before 1840 the number of captured slaves who immediately entered the forces in the Sudan itself was higher than of those who passed through the Egyptian military camps. Holt (1961) adds that in 1835, Muḥammad ʿAlī, forced by his need for more recruits, wished to introduce conscription of Sudanese freemen for military service. Since this policy was not accepted by Sudanese notables and administrative officials, it was agreed that a contribution of a quota of slaves belonging to the local population would be given annually. As mentioned above, from the early days, slaves for agricultural and domestic usage were obtained by the local population mainly from among the Nūba, south of Kordofân. In Kharṭūm, military barracks and a storehouse were constructed for the Jihādīya garrison.

The irregular forces in the Sudan were under the control of the provincial governor in each province. There was no centralized command. The Shāʾiqīya had replaced the former foreign irregulars who had assisted in the conquest of the Sudan and were mainly responsible for tax-collecting and slave-raiding (Hill 1959, Holt 1958).[10]

> Henceforward the military strength of the Turco-Egyptian regime was mainly derived from two sources, the regular *Jihadiyya*, of slave origin, originating from what would now be called the southern Sudan; and

---

[9] The Bakkara, or Baqqāra are Arabic-speaking cattle keepers. Their homeland reaches from a little beyond Lake Chad in the west to the White Nile. Djelabi or *jallāba* were Arabic-speaking petty traders.

[10] MacMichael (1967, 23), however, states that the "force taking part in these slave hunts usually numbered 1000 to 2000 regular troops, 400 to 800 Moghrabin, and 300 to 1000 natives."

the Shaiyqiyya irregulars, serving mainly as cavalrymen under their own chiefs (Holt 1961, 47).

In the meantime, under the administration of Khurshid, Governor-General of the Sudan (1826–38), some Egyptian and black Sudanese soldiers had been promoted into the officer corps. The gradual replacement of Turks by Sudanese in the lower ranks continued until the end of the Turco-Egyptian occupation. In 1852, the Sudan up to the White Nile Basin was garrisoned by a force of 18,000 men, which by 1865 had expanded to 27,000 men of whom about 20,000 were black Sudanese (Gray 1961). According to Hill (1959), however, after a revolt of the Sudanese troops in the same year, the Viceroy reduced the black regiments in the Sudan to three and sent the rest to Egypt. Instead, a mobile force was created consisting of Egyptians, *bāshī-buzūq*, Shā'iqīya, and Albanians, with a battery of field artillery. The Egyptian conquest in the Sudan guaranteed security, which gave merchants the opportunity to establish and increase their trading activities in the area.

1.1.2.2. *Commercial Activities in Southern Sudan: Establishment of Trading Settlements (1840–88)*
Because of the presence of Egyptian military forces in the Sudan, commercial and other activities were greatly stimulated. Migration to the northern territories was facilitated, and the first governmental expeditions to discover the sources of the White Nile were organized from 1839 onwards. Although they did not reach the sources of the Nile, part of the White Nile valley was opened up for trading activities. Thus, small governmental trading expeditions were already proceeding to the newly discovered areas in the 1840s. Muḥammad 'Alī had established a trading monopoly in 1824. According to Holt (1961), at the time of the government monopoly, the major traders based at Kharṭūm had not yet entered the White Nile Basin. *Jallāba* (mainly Danāqla and Ja'alīyīn petty traders) did so and had already managed to establish trading contacts with the Shilluk as early as 1840. Gray (1961) emphasizes the European influence in the White Nile trade and mentions that the European traders, excluded from contacts with the Shilluk by the governmental expeditions and the *jallāba*, concentrated more on the Bari. The traders were mainly interested in ivory, gum arabic, and cattle, and slaves were only occasionally taken and exported in those years (Hill 1959, Holt 1961).

Around 1850, Muḥammad ʿAlī could no longer maintain the trading monopoly as he was compelled by European pressure to introduce a free-market economy. From that time on, trade on the White Nile started to boom. Large Kharṭūm companies sent their Arab agents (among others Turkish, Egyptian, and Egyptian Sudanese) to southern Sudan, where they established *zarības*, fortified thorn-fenced encampments, which were called *daim* or 'camps' followed by the name of the owner or agent. The *zarības* were protected by a private army (mainly consisting of mercenary Danāqla and Jaʿalīyīn, who were called *ʿaskar* (pl.: *ʿasākir*) and provided shelter for the traders and stores for the traded goods. Alliances were made with the surrounding tribal villages, which had to supply the *zarība* with food and services, mainly as porters. In return, the village received the trader's support in intertribal affairs. The latter, however, was turned to the trader's advantage as well, since reprisal raids on other tribes could provide the trader with supplies of ivory and, at a later stage, slaves (Gray 1961, Holt 1961, Schweinfurth 1922).

The slave trade in the White Nile region until then had been conducted sporadically. Slaves were, more incidentally than intentionally, captured during raids for ivory and cattle. The women were sent to Kharṭūm to be sold on the slave market or were taken as concubines in the *zarība*. The men were needed as porters and armed servants (*bazinqir*,[11] *narkuk-* (pl: *narakik*), or *farkha-* (pl: *farukh*)) (Holt 1961, Schweinfurth 1922), and, according to Gray (1961), captured youths received instruction in Arabic and became employed as dragomen (or *targāma*), acting as intermediaries between the traders and the tribal chiefs. From 1860 onwards, the slave trade gained importance due to the dramatic increase of the ivory price in Kharṭūm. The cause of the increase was twofold. The ivory supplies were gradually shrinking, and the growing tribal animosity towards the traders forced the latter to augment their private armies, which greatly increased their trading expenses. The traders needed slaves to sell to their *ʿasākir*, who obtained part of their payment in merchandise, either goods or slaves. The slaves either were kept by the soldiers for their own household (the women as concubines or wives, the

---

[11] Also *bazinger, bazinjar, besinger*. "Some trace the origin of this word to the name of a negro tribe who took service in this capacity, others connect it with Marshal Bazaine, under whom the Sudanese black troops fought in Mexico." (Hill 1959, 140 n.2). Considering the first explanation, one wonders which tribe was involved.

children as their assistants) or were sold to traders to be brought to
the Khartūm slave markets. Thus, although the *zarība* traders themselves were not actively involved in the export of slaves, they played
a key role in the slave trade, and their survival as White Nile traders
depended to a great extent on the continuation and increase of the
slave trade (Gray 1961, Schweinfurth 1922). Relevant for our present concern is that many of the captured black Sudanese slaves
were not transported to the north but were retained in the White
Nile Basin. They only shifted from their animist origins to mainly
Islamic surroundings.

From 1857 onwards, measures against the slave trade were taken
by the successors of Muḥammad ʿAlī.[12] However, because many
traders and government agents were threatened with a loss of income
(MacMichael 1967), the slave trade was continued as before, albeit
more discretely. Moreover, the army was still in need of recruits.
Hill (1959) mentions that, in 1863–64, the Dinka tribes were raided
by opposing tribes reinforced by regular troops. A river police force,
which had been established on the White Nile, managed to take
possession of 3,538 slaves in 1864 but instead of sending them back
to their native villages, they transported them to Khartūm, where
many of them were eagerly accepted as fresh recruits in the army
(Holt 1961). In 1865, the Governor-General of the Sudan himself
sought to increase his army's number with black slave recruits (Gray
1961).

The Baḥr al-Ghazāl was entered by traders from around the mid-
1850s, when the region still lay outside the Turco-Egyptian territory
(Gray 1961, Holt 1961).[13] As in the White Nile Basin where the
Egyptian merchant al-ʿAqqād was in control of nearly all the trade,
the Baḥr al-Ghazāl was actually held by a number of 'merchant
princes' among whom were Idrīs wad Daftār and az-Zubair Raḥma
Manṣūr. The latter was a Jaʿalī-Arab who built his huge *zarība*, called
Daim az-Zubair, in the Baḥr al-Ghazāl in 1856. He had around a
thousand armed men at his service and showed great vigour in his
trading activities. Although initially the main trading object was ivory,
it very soon turned towards slaves and largely surpassed the slave

---

[12] At around 1850, slave raiding was no longer tolerated as a means of gaining
recruits. Slaves could, however, easily be purchased for the purpose of recruitment.
(MacMichael 1967).

[13] The Baḥr al-Ghazāl was officially annexed in 1873 (Holt 1961).

export from the White Nile Basin. For az-Zubair alone, an export of 1,800 slaves annually was not exceptional (Gray 1961). Some of the slaves raided by the traders were taken by the government forces, since their own capacity was too small to raid for slaves successfully. The others were kept in the *zarība* as private slaves.

Through the chain of *zarības*, security was highly augmented in the area, which gave the itinerant *jallāba* the opportunity to travel around freely. For 1874, Schweinfurth (1922) gives an estimate of about 2,000 itinerant *jallāba*, while another 2,000 were residing on a more permanent basis in the Kharṭūm *zarības* in the Baḥr al-Ghazāl. Schweinfurth gives the following figures for the area of the Kharṭūm *zarības* in the Baḥr al-Ghazāl at around 1874 (tables 1 and 2):

Table 1. Population of Baḥr al-Ghazāl *zarības* in 1874

Population groups	Figures
Soldiers recruited from Dunqula, Shā'iqīya, Sinnār, Kordofān, Bedouin tribes, etc. (*'asākir*)	5,000
Black slave soldiers (*bazinqir, farukh* or *narkuk*)	5,000
Idlers looking for free food and accommodation	1,000
Jallāba, Muslim teachers (*fuqahā'*), agents residing in the *zarība*	2,000
Jallāba who are only temporarily in the country in wintertime	2,000
Private slaves of the residential Muslim population	40,000
Total	55,000

Source: Schweinfurth 1922, 507

Table 2. Population in vicinity of Baḥr al-Ghazāl *zarības* in 1874

Tribes	Figures
Bongo	100,000
Mittu (including Madi, Luba, etc.)	30,000
Jur 10,000	
Golo	6,000
Ssere	4,000
Kreish	20,000
Smaller tribes, e.g. Dembo, Bimberri, Manga, etc.	20,000
Total	190,000

Source: Schweinfurth 1922, 507

This means that of a grand total of 245,000 people, approximately 22.5% were living in the *zarība*, whereas 77.5% dwelt in the neighbourhood. If we add up the local population residing in and around the *zarība* (5,000 black slave soldiers + 40,000 private slaves + 190,000 indigenous population = 235,000 of a total of 245,000), then we arrive at a percentage of 96% non-Arabic and 4% Arabic-speaking people. I will come back to this below (1.2.2.1).

At the top of the *zarība* hierarchy were Arabic-speaking Egyptians, Sudanese, and Danāqla traders followed by the 'Nubian' *ʿasākir*, who were mainly Danāqla and Shā'iqīya but among whom could also be found Bedouins and men from Sinnār and Kordofān. Many of these northerners settled permanently in these districts, keeping up their original cultural customs (Holt 1958). The black slaves who were retained in the *zarība* could be subdivided into several groups. The first group consisted of boys from seven to ten years old who were employed to carry the guns and ammunition of the troops, slave or otherwise. Every soldier, whether Dunqulāwī or slave-soldier, had at least one at his service. When reaching the age of ten years old, these boys entered the second group, the so-called *bazinqir*, *farukh* or *narkuk*, all of which refer to slave soldiers. Many of them had been raised in the *zarība*. They were armed and thus formed a kind of black force that had to accompany all forays and expeditions of the Nubian *ʿasākir*, whether commercial or military. In military expeditions, they were actually given the major and hardest tasks (Schweinfurth 1922). The slave-soldiers could amount to half of the armed forces in the *zarība* (see tables 1 and 2). The merchant and the slave troops were dependent upon each other. The loyal *bazinqir* proved to be valuable assets to their master, who in return treated them with affection and let them share in the profits of his raids (Holt 1958). Many natives even voluntarily entered the slave troops, expecting that living conditions in the *zarība* would be less harsh than in their native villages.[14] Consequently, they picked up some cultural elements and were Islamized. Every man had at least one woman slave to do his cooking and so on. Often, these women were married to the men. Schweinfurth considers them the third group, while the fourth group were the slaves, both male and female,

---

[14] Schweinfurth (1922) gives the Niamniam as an example. Entire troops of black people could be recruited from among them.

employed for working the fields (Schweinfurth 1922).[15] The tribes in the environment lived in a vassalage relationship with the *zarība*. They had to provide grain and services. In return, they received some protection and were exempted from slave and cattle raiding.

1.1.2.3. *Interaction between Government and Trading Camps*
During the 1860s, the merchant princes of the Baḥr al-Ghazāl, az-Zubair in particular, became a real threat to the Egyptian government. After an unsuccessful attempt to defeat him, the Khedive Ismā'īl was compelled in 1873 to accept az-Zubair's authority and to offer him the governorship of the Baḥr al-Ghazāl, which henceforth constituted a province. Az-Zubair received the assistance of a small force of regular troops. After some independent actions, which were not agreed to by the government, az-Zubair was detained in Cairo in 1876. In the meantime, in the White Nile Basin, the company of the Egyptian merchant al-'Aqqād and his son-in-law Abū Su'ūd, had, through a strong alliance with the Bari, managed to develop a commercial stronghold controlling about all the stations in the area, the Bari being mainly employed "as porters, herdsmen, and mercenary soldiers" (Gray 1961, 95). In 1869, the Khedive Ismā'īl had engaged the British explorer, Sir Samuel Baker, to extend government control to the territories south of Gondokoro, to organize military posts in the newly acquired regions, and to put a stop to the slave trade. After a battle between Baker and Abū Su'ūd, government control was imposed on the area, and the Danāqla private troops were incorporated as official garrisons. However, they never acted as such but instead rather weakened the government's control of the area (Gray 1961, Hill 1959, Holt 1961). Baker also managed to annex, at least nominally, the areas south of Gondokoro, which were called the Equatorial Province.

In 1873, the English Colonel, Charles George Gordon was appointed governor of the Equatorial Province (1873–76) and attempted to organize the administration in the country.[16] The stations of the slave traders became military posts and administrative centres. Gordon

---

[15] To my understanding, the first group (slave boys), the third group (women), and the fourth group (field workers) together made up the group of 40,000 private slaves, whereas the second group, comprising slave soldiers, amounted to 5,000 men.
[16] See Gray (1961), Hill (1959), Holt (1958, 1961).

was obliged to rely heavily on his Egyptian and Sudanese officials. Some of them, who had already proved their worth during an expedition in Mexico with the French, were indeed most reliable. Others, however, showed very little loyalty. These were mainly political exiles and criminals from Egyptian jails who had been recruited because of a lack of recruits after the abolition of the slave trade (Hill 1959). The same lack of loyalty and enthusiasm was seen with the Danāqla, whom Gordon was forced to employ in many of the civil and administrative posts, since foreign administrators were too expensive. In most of the stations, they outnumbered the regular troops. Franz Stuhlmann gave the following figures for the composition of the garrisons after a reorganization of the stations in 1874 (table 3):

Table 3. Composition of Equatoria Province garrisons in 1874

Stations	Sudanese	Egyptians	Danāqla
Sūbāt, at the confluence of Sūbāt and Nile,	Regular 50	–	–
NāsÑir, on the Sūbāt,	–	–	Irregular 100
Ghaba Schambe	Regular 30	–	150
Makraka	Regular 20	–	Irregular 150
Bor	10	–	100
Lattuka	10	–	100
Lado (headquarters)	10	–	100
ar-Rajjāf	80	–	–
Dufile	10	–	–
Fatiko	250	Regular 100	–
Foweira	100	100	–
Total: 1,470	570	200	700

Source: Franz Stuhlmann 1916, 19.

Table 3 mainly refers to the ethnicity of the garrisons' population. However, it is reasonable to assume that the regular troops consisted mainly of Sudanese and Egyptians and the irregular troops of Danāqla. This is not unlikely since there were 'regular' Sudanese, 'regular' Egyptians, and 'irregular' Danāqla, and nowhere were they listed the other way round. It is also clear that Danāqla were not conscripted in the army on a regular basis. This means that, where Stuhlmann mentions that Lattuka contained 10 Sudanese and 100 Danāqla, it may be interpreted as 10 regulars and 100 irregulars.

Thus, the regular troops (570 Sudanese + 200 Egyptian) outnumbered, although not by very much, the irregular troops, of which there were 700 (i.e., 52% to 48%, respectively). As for language, the Egyptians are the only ones who would have spoken Arabic as their mother tongue. The Danāqla spoke some sort of Arabic, but it is unclear which dialect and at which level. The Sudanese troops most likely consisted of black Sudanese men who had been recruited and trained. It is possible that they had learned a simplified form of Arabic there (see 1.2.2.1). In this period, the results of a continuing process of increasing contact between the stations and the surrounding villages becomes apparent, the villagers being highly attracted to the life at the stations, while the tribal structure had already been weakened through the disrupting contact with the trading communities. Gray (1961, 113) quotes Gordon who talks about "a semi-native semi-arab by contact population of lads and women".

After his return from Equatoria, Gordon was appointed Governor-General of the Sudan in 1877.[17] Immediately, he became concerned with the rebellious actions of az-Zubair's son, Sulaimān, who led a private army of 6,400 slave troops and forces of 9,000 *jallāba* and others. To cut off supplies from Sulaimān, Gordon supported the Baqqāra in harrassing the *jallāba*. The *jallāba*, who had, since the decline of the slave trade, already lost part of their income, were now completely deprived of a livelihood. They took refuge in Kordofān and Dār Fūr, where the Mahdi, the leader of the revolt against the Egyptian administration in the Sudan, was easily able to convince them to join his army (Holt 1961). At the same time, the Italian administrator of the Baḥr al-Ghazāl province, Romolo Gessi was given the task of halting Sulaimān, which he was able to do in 1879, although Rabīḥ, one of Sulaimān's commanders had managed to flee westward and reached Lake Chad, where he was eventually defeated by the French (Gray 1961, Slatin 1896).[18] In 1882, the year

---

[17] In the same year, on 4 August 1877, a convention was signed between Britain and Egypt in which both parties agreed upon the complete prohibition of the public trade in slaves (MacMichael 1967).

[18] According to Tosco and Owens (1993, 177–267), Rabīḥ and his people introduced the p/c Arabic as it was spoken in the southern Sudan to Chad where, in the course of events, it became used among soldiers and officials under the name of Turku. See also 7.1.2.2.

Great Britain succeeded in its occupation of Egypt, 40,000 troops, including many irregulars, were garrisoned in the Egyptian dependencies (Sudan, Eritrean, and Somali districts), while there were approximately 3,000 armed forces in Equatoria and the Baḥr al-Ghazāl (Holt 1958).

In 1877, Emin Pasha became governor of the Equatorial Province.[19] From Emin's appointment until 1880, nearly all transport and communication from the north had been blocked due to the impenetrable vegetation on the Nile, called *sudd*, and the lack of resources in Kharṭūm (Collins 1971, Gray 1961). The province at that time consisted of not much more than a few small isolated stations. Emin, however, managed to extend his influence over the tribal parties. He was greatly assisted by local interpreters, who formed the link between the Danāqla and the governmental garrisons, on the one hand, and the tribal chiefs, on the other In his memoirs, he mentions 30 dragomen in Muggi (Emin 1919, 1922, vol. 3). The contact between the government stations and the native villages thus increased and intensified, and Islam gradually made its way into the tribal societies. Emin reorganized the Province and divided it into several districts, or *idāra*, in which the stations were situated. The administration was in the hands of regular and irregular forces and interpreters.[20] In addition to them, there were the native slave troops, the so-called *bazinqir* (Hill 1959, Emin 1919). Franz Stuhlmann gives figures for the years 1881–82, as they were recorded by Vita Hassan, Emin's secretary (table 4):

Table 4. Composition of Equatoria Province stations 1881–82

District	Stations	Regular *jihādīya*	Irregular *hotteria*	Dragomen *targāma*
Bor	Bor	120	–	40
Lado	Lado, ar-Rajjāf, Bedden	300	–	70
Kiri	Kiri, Chor Aju, Labore, Muggi	70	–	10
Dufile	Dufile, Fabbo, Fatiko, Wadelai	170	–	30
Foweira	Foweira, Fodda	60	–	20

---

[19] Emin Pasha's real name was Eduard Schnitzer, a Silesian Jew, born in 1840.

[20] "Gessi Pasha wrote of these men as *hotteria*, Emin Pasha as *hutteria* and *cotteria*, possibly a corruption of the soldiers' Arabic *awtūrīya*, corrupted in turn from the Turkish *otūrāq*, a local soldier, militiaman" (Hill 1959, 140 n. 1).

Table 4 (*cont.*)

District	Stations	Regular *jihādīya*	Irregular *hotteria*	Dragomen *targāma*
Lattuka	Okello, Tarangole, Obure, Obbo	–	200	20
Fadibek	Labor, Galli, Fadibek	–	170	40
Rol	Ajak, Bufi, Ssajadin, Lessi, Affard, el-Gok-Muchtar	180	–	40
Makraka	Kabadjendi, Wandi, Makraka-sughaira, Gosa, Kallika, Watako, Kudurma, 'Umm-dirfi, Rimo, Korobek, Ganda, Umbimba, Nuguma, Dango, Dango-kebir	60	100	100
Gurguru	Tangasi, Kobbi, Uniboron, Mperia, Rensi, etc.	80	70	30
(Mangbettu)				
Total	1,930 =	990	540	400

Source: Franz Stuhlmann 1916, 25

I shall now relate the numbers of table 4 to those of table 3. Table 3 refers to stations, whereas the numbers in table 4 pertain to entire districts. However, more or less the same areas are involved. Irregular (540) and regular troops (990) together included 1,530 men, i.e. 35% and 65%, respectively. The irregular troops had thus been reduced in 1882 in comparison with 1874, their percentage dropping from 48% to 35%, whereas the regular troops increased from 52% to 65%. Only the Egyptians, who were mainly regular soldiers, were supposedly native speakers of Arabic. From the 1882 figures, however, we do not know the number of Egyptians involved. Emin himself, at the end of 1880, mentioned figures of 1,400 regular soldiers and officers and approximately 200 irregulars, which would mean an even larger increase in the regular troops and therefore a growth of the number of native speakers of Arabic.[21]

Emin thus had managed to establish some control over the Equatorial Province and more or less good relations with the surrounding tribal population. The Mahdi revolt, however, brought an abrupt end to Emin's achievements.

---

[21] Hill (1959) talks about the *idāra* of Rohl, where 455, of whom 96 were Danāqla, were employed, all of them being irregulars.

1.1.2.4. *The Mahdist Revolt and its Aftermath*

The Mahdist revolt, which started in 1882 and reached a climax in 1885 with the fall of Kharṭūm, changed the situation in southern Sudan completely. Except for the area around the White Nile between Lado, Wadelai, and the shores of Lake Albert, which remained under Egyptian control with Emin, the whole of the Sudan was in the Mahdi's hands. Emin had been disturbed by the Mahdists once in 1884. At that time, the Mahdist, Karām Allāh, who had the sympathy of many of Emin's Danāqla and Egyptian officials (Holt 1958), arrived from the Baḥr al-Ghazāl to occupy Equatoria with a force of 5,000 to 8,000 men and told Emin to surrender. Karām Allāh, however, did not continue his conquest, since his army was needed elsewhere (Slatin 1896). Emin and the Equatorial Province were thus left alone for the next few years. However, the Egyptian government had lost all its credibility among the local tribes, who started revolting (Emin 1922, vol. 3, Gray 1961). Emin was thus forced in 1885 to shift the provincial headquarters from Lado to Wadelai and to reduce the troops at the outlying stations of Lado, ar-Rajjāf, and Bedden. However, the first battalion of around 700 armed men, which had been in charge of the northernmost territories, refused to join the evacuation and disobeyed the governor's orders. Several Egyptian and Sudanese officers deserted, often accompanied by their men. They started new carriers as bandit chiefs in and around Makraka or joined the Mahdi (Emin 1922, vol. 3, Gray 1961, Mounteney-Jephson 1890, Headley and Johnson 1890). They were replaced by the lower ranks and by soldiers recruited from the local population (Hansen 1991a, 318–42). This implies that the number of native Arabic speakers decreased in contrast to the number of non-native speakers. The second battalion, which was in charge of the southern territories, consisted of approximately 650 armed men. They remained loyal at first sight (Headley and Johnson 1890). Emin was, however, not very enthusiastic about them either, since most of the 56 Egyptian officers and clerks in the Province had criminal records. While the troops in the north were reduced, Emin himself and most of the men retreated to Lake Albert, where they lived in isolation for several years (Emin 1919, Mounteney-Jephson 1890).

Eventually, the British-American explorer Henry Morton Stanley came with an expedition to escort Emin to the coast. They met on Lake Albert on 29 April 1888. While Stanley went to collect some of his men who had been trailing behind, A.J. Mounteney-Jephson, one of Stanley's officers was left with Emin. Emin's men, however, were not at all eager to leave with him, since, for many of them, that would mean leaving their homelands. Moreover, many of the Egyptians were former criminals or former members of the ʿUrābī-revolt in the early 1880s and so had no desire to return to Egypt.[22] Moreover, the men feared that they would have to leave their wives, children, and slaves behind. Thus, a mutiny broke out under the command of a Sudanese officer, Faḍl al-Maulā Muḥammad. Mounteney-Jephson and Emin were held prisoner in Dufile. In the meantime, the Mahdists made a second approach and managed to capture ar-Rajjāf, but tough resistance from Faḍl al-Maulā and his troops kept them from seizing Dufile. In the meantime, Emin and Mounteney-Jephson had been released and hurried southwards to meet Stanley at Lake Albert (Emin 1922, vol. 4, Holt 1958, Mounteney-Jephson 1890, Slatin 1896).

Eventually, Emin joined Stanley with a group of 570 people and went to Zanzibar on April 10 1889 (Emin 1922, vol. 4). The group of mutineers remained in Dufile under the command of Faḍl al-Maulā. Although they had become loyal to Emin again and wished to join him, another group of people led by Selīm Bey, one of Emin's officers, had been left behind. They had mainly been delayed due to the large number of women, children and slaves, who travelled very slowly. After they heard that Emin had already left, many rejoined Faḍl al-Maulā's troops. The remaining group under the command of Selīm Bey settled down in Kavalli, at the southwestern corner of Lake Albert, and is said to have consisted of 300 women and children and of 90 men, 50 of whom were killed soon after by the 'natives' (Lugard 1968, 203). The disagreements and conflicts among Faḍl al-Maulā's men forced several groups to leave and find their own livelihood in the province (Slatin 1896). Others, a force of about 800 well-armed men with about 10,000 followers, are said to have left Faḍl al-Maulā to join Selīm Bey. On their way, many people of the Lendu and Lur tribes entered the group, "some as slaves, but the majority as freemen, though servants" (Lugard

---

[22] The militant nationalist ʿUrābists, called after their leader, ʿUrābī Pasha, revolted against foreign interference in Egypt. Their actions came to an abrupt end in September 1882, when Great Britain succeeded in occupying Egypt.

1968, 205). They eventually arrived in Kavalli in April 1891, just before Capt. Lugard, who represented the Imperial British East Africa Company, found them there. Lugard (1968, 210) describes the scene as follows:

> There was great joy and kissing of my hand (which they touch with their foreheads), and handshaking with Shukri and my Sudanese. Every one talked at the same time, and congratulated each other, and every one temporarily became a fool, and smiled extremely, and talked incessantly, as is right and proper on such an occasion.

Lugard had been looking for cheap replacements for his more expensive Swahili and Sudanese troops and for extra manpower to hold the British territories of Uganda and Unyoro. Therefore, he was very eager to convince Selīm Bey of the close alliance of the British with the Khedive, to whom Selīm had always remained loyal, and of their enlistment as irregular troops under Lugard's command. Selīm accepted, and conditions were agreed upon. In October 1891, the group left Kavalli. Lugard (1968, 230) talks of 4,000 people, while Hansen (1991a, 322) says the group consisted of about 9,000 people, of whom some 900 were armed men. Lugard (1968, 217) says of them, that:

> The original soldiers had for the most part assumed the titles of ranks much superior to those which they held under the Egyptian Government. The non-commissioned officers had become commissioned officers, the privates were all non-commissioned officers, and such few private soldiers as still deigned to hold that lowest rank were "new askars" recently enlisted.

Initially, they were stationed in Western Uganda, but they moved later to Buganda territory.[23] In 1901, the King's African Rifles were formed, and the Sudanese or Nubian soldiers were incorporated into

---

[23] In the meantime, in 1892, Faḍl al-Maulā was approached by an expedition from Congo Free State and accepted their proposal. "The former Egyptian employees and troops entered the service of the Congo Free State and undertook to hold their posts in its name, flying its flag and obeying its laws. Faḍl al-Maulā received the title of governor of Equatoria (*mudīr Khaṭṭ al-Istiwā'*)." (Holt 1958, 200) The Mahdists under ʿArabī Dafaʿallāh, however, turned again to the area south of ar-Rajjāf in 1893. In January 1894, Faḍl al-Maulā and most of his men were killed near Wadelai, while the women and children were taken prisoner by the Mahdists (Holt 1958, Slatin 1896).

them as regular forces, thus becoming part of the 4th (Uganda) Battalion (Hansen 1991a, 318–42). Part of them were sent to Nairobi, where they settled in 1902. The other part remained in Uganda, where in 1906, the military headquarters were organized in Bombo, about 30 kilometres north of Kampala. They became the ancestors of the present-day Nubi.

1.1.3. *The Nubi in the Twentieth Century*

In the first two decades of the twentieth century, the Nubi were active in the military forces in British East Africa, and as 'immigrant mercenaries' accordingly received certain facilities from the Protectorate Government. It was only after World War I that a small part of the Nubian community was demilitarized for the first time and that the question of the status of the Nubi people was raised. However, the privileges of the Nubi, who were still viewed as foreign mercenaries, were retained. They were allowed to live in their own settlements, the so-called *mulkis*, and were exempted from ordinary tribal obligations. However, the question became more pressing in the 1930s when the links with the armed forces had become weaker, and only about a sixth of the armed forces consisted of Nubi. Moreover, in 1936, the military headquarters were moved away from Bombo. It was suggested that the Nubi would refrain from their extra-tribal status and would come under the jurisdiction of the Buganda Government. The Nubi, however, with their overwhelming feeling of distinctiveness from the Baganda, wished to retain their status as immigrants and subjects of the colonial administration and did not want to deal with the Buganda Government. Their claims were not accepted: the Nubi had to choose either to become Buganda subjects or to leave for the West Nile province.

The Nubi survived either as small merchants or as unskilled labourers. Their ties with the military loosened. They were reluctant to attend the missionary schools, being afraid that the Christian religion would be forced upon them. The result was that most of the Nubi received no or very little education. As a consequence, they were not accepted in high functions, the army, or politics. In the first decades of the twentieth century, many people originating from the local tribes of present-day Uganda had joined the Nubians, attracted by their special status and refined culture. Since they had

adopted the language, religion, and customs, the process of Sudanization
or Nubianization that had started in the Sudan, had continued.
However, by 1930, the Nubi community had lost its attraction to
outsiders. It had become a stable community, sticking to Islam, having their own language, and maintaining their own cultural elements.
However, being quite pragmatic and understanding that without
intercourse with their non-Nubi neighbours, life would be extremely
difficult, they had learned to be flexible and had learned the others'
languages and customs and used them when necessary.

    When Idi Amin came to power in 1971—although in general his
regime was characterized by brutality—he brought a positive change
in the situation of the Nubi. Being a Kakwa from the West Nile
Province, he knew many Nubi people and had some knowledge of
their language. He had not forgotten their value in the military and
sought means to attract them. Since the new regime was a military
one, the Nubi received the opportunity to enter politics and commerce, which they eagerly accepted. Uganda saw another wave of
Nubianization, stimulated by Amin.

> Amin deliberately used an expanded concept of the Nubian. He gave
> clear priority to the Muslim criterion while reducing the significance
> of traditional affiliation with the original immigrant group. This means
> that it is difficult to assess qualitatively the real Nubian impact on and
> advantages gained from the Amin regime (Hansen 1991a, 339).

The days of renewed glory ended in 1979 when Amin went into
exile. The Nubi could not maintain their positions, and many fled
to Sudan, Kenya, or present-day Congo. Only after Museveni had
gained power in 1986 did the Nubi dare to come back, often finding
that their belongings had been confiscated.

    Over the past fifteen years, the Nubi have been struggling to find
a livelihood. Being excluded from the military, they mainly turned
to small-scale trading or skilled or semi-skilled labour. While still in
exile in southern Sudan, many boys were selected by the United
Nations to study in Kharṭūm. They returned in the early nineties
and are now active as Muslim teachers or as social workers. Nubi
are despised by the Ugandese because of their cooperation with the
Amin regime, so many Nubi claim to be of other than Nubi descent.
However, the refined Nubi culture and customs still attract people
from other tribes, especially outside Buganda, the territory of Uganda's
largest tribe. In Buganda, more and more girls are marrying out-

side the Nubi group and partially give up their affinities with the
Nubi language and culture.[24]

1.1.4. *Conclusion*

Before 1820, travellers were using routes through the Sudan in all
directions for commercial purposes and pilgrimages. After 1820, intertribal contacts increased in Egypt in Muḥammad ʿAlī's military training camps and in the eastern Bilād as-Sūdān through an increase
in trading activities and through an extension of military stations in
the newly annexed areas: the White Nile Basin, the Baḥr al-Ghazāl,
and the Equatorial Province. The military forces were reinforced by
black Sudanese men directly by forced recruitment or more indirectly by the purchase of slaves from merchants in southern Sudan.
In the trading camps themselves, black slaves, both male and female,
were kept for domestic purposes and to assist the ʿasākir to defend
the zarība. Soon after, however, inhabitants from indigenous tribes
entered the camps deliberately, attracted by the potential advantages
of camp life. From figures of around 1874 and 1882, we learn that,
in the trading camps or zarība and in the military camps, a dominant military and/or economic minority of native or near-native
speakers of Arabic were facing a vast majority of indigenous people,
the latter being in close contact with the first through different functions—dragomen, slave soldiers, domestic slaves—and through intermarriage. It seems that a semi-Arab population came into existence
whose members were distanced from their tribal origins by language
(a simplified Arabic), religion (Islam), and customs. They could, however, not obtain the same levels as the Arabic-speaking population
as much as they may have wished to. The minority groups of Arabs
and Danāqla, the arabized inhabitants of Dunqula, may have continued the Arabic habit of looking down on black people (see below:
1.2.2.1), maintaining their distance from the indigenous population
even when the value of these people had become evident.

When Emin and his troops became isolated in the Lake Albert
area in 1885, forced by the pressure of the Mahdists, many Arabs

---

[24] Sources: Hansen (1991a and b), Mazrui (1977, 21–38), Nasseem and Marjan
(1992, 196–214), Johnson (1988, 142–56).

of his officer corps joined the ranks of the Mahdists. They were
replaced by former slave soldiers. At the same time, Emin's troops
faced an influx of local people: men, women, and children. A process
of gradual reduction of the number of Arabic speakers in comparison with an increasing amount of local Sudanese people, was thus
taking place. A climax was reached after Emin, and with him many
of his Egyptian and Kharṭūm officers and clerks, left for the coast
in 1889, leaving the groups of Selīm Bey and Faḍl al-Maulā behind.
They were subsequently joined by a large group of mainly Lendu
and Lur people. The number of near native speakers of Arabic, however small, was never reduced to zero. The remaining groups lived
in solitude for about three years until they were met and enlisted
by Capt. Lugard, who representated the British East African Company.
It is from this group of 'Sudanese', approximately 900 armed men
and 8,000 to 9,000 followers, that the present-day Nubi derive.

At the time, these people were not referred to as Nubi. Lugard
nowhere talks about Nubians or Nubi. He refers to the group led
by Selīm Bey as Sudanese. Meldon, however, says that "the Sudanese
are sometimes spoken of as Nubis" (Meldon 1907, 139).[25] According
to Hansen (1991a, 318–42), it was only after World War I that these
people began to be addressed as Nubians on a more regular basis.
Kokole (1985, 420) tells us about his Kakwa father, who spoke Nubi
as a second language and who called it 'Arabic' without exception.
This brings us to the etymology of the term 'Nubi', for a people
and a language.[26] The hypotheses are many. Heine (1982) and
Prokosch (1981) claim that the name derives from the Nūba people
since they represented quite a large portion of the first recruits in
the Turco-Egyptian army. According to Trimingham (1964), however, the word Nūba, originally referring to the inhabitants of the
Nūba Mountains in Kordofān, was used to refer to the Sudanese in
general. Soghayroun (1981), on the other hand, says that Nubian

---

[25] According to Emin, his troops were called 'Turks' (Emin 1919, 28), while he
himself was referred to as 'Turk kebir' (big Turk) (Emin 1919, 242). Probably,
'Turks' was used to designate the non-Arabic Sudanese 'black' people associated
with the military (Lugard 1968, 436, Tosco and Owens 1993, 183).

[26] The Bantu prefix *ki-* is sometimes attached to the name of the language: kiNubi
(see also Kaye 1991, 4–16). I assume it is rather a Kenyan habit. In Kenya, more
languages, like kiKuyu, kiSwahili, etc. are specified by the *ki-* prefix, whereas in
Uganda this is less frequent.

was the more common term in Egypt for black Sudanese troops, and Kaye (1991, 4–16) suggests a mixture of these elements. Kokole's explanation is less likely. He assumes that the Nubi language is related to the colloquial Arabic of southern Sudan or Junubi (from Arabic *janūb* 'south'), from which the name Nubi would be derived (Kokole 1986, 420).

According to Roth-Laly (1972, 501), who studied the works of Carbou (1913, on the Arabic of Wadaï and Eastern Chad), Trenga (1947, on the Bura-mabang of Wadaï), and Lethem (1920, on the Arabic Shuwa dialect of Bornū, Nigeria, and the Lake Chad area), the word *nubāī* is to be translated as 'nègre', 'noir' (from Trenga), and 'negro', 'also used of non-Arab Muslims; and of a particular race in Kordofãn' (from Lethem), and finally as 'qui n'est pas arabe et qui n' est pas fétichiste' (from Carbou). The latter implies that *nubāī* was used for non-Arab Muslims, a status that, of course, applied to the Islamicized black population of the army and trading camps. Moreover, the term Nubian must have been in use as well, at least among Europeans, to refer to the Nubian *jallāba* and soldiers in the camps, who were Nile Nubians consisting of Danāqla, Mahas, and Kenzi. Herzog (1957) suggests that Schweinfurth (1922) used the word for others and not merely for the pure Nile Nubians. Considering the above, I assume that the whole group of non-Arab Muslims and their language came to be designated by the name 'Nubi' through the association of the word for black non-Arab Muslims with the Nubian/Danāqla officer corps and soldiery, whose positions they gradually came to occupy in the administration and military forces of the Equatorial Province.

For the pidginized variety in southern Sudan, the name Bimbashi-Arabic or Mongalla-Arabic may have been used (Tucker 1934, 28–36). In the military camps in the southern Sudan, the officer corps had Turkish titles, *bimbashi* referring to the rank of major. Mongalla, on the other hand, is a district a bit to the northwest of Juba in southern Sudan (see also Prokosch 1986). However, in none of the diaries of travellers or governors in the southern Sudan did I find these terms being used for the pidgin/creole (p/c) Arabic.

1.2. *Linguistic Background*

It is believed by some authors (Owens 1996, 125–72, Versteegh
1984), both on linguistic and socio-historical grounds, that present-
day Nubi is an Arabic creole language that developed from a pidginized
Arabic. I tend to accept their opinion, although I'd rather leave it
to creole specialists to decide on this matter. However, exploring the
development of Nubi against theories of pidgin and creole linguistics may add to its understanding. Since creolistis themselves have
not yet reached a final agreement on how to define pidgins and creoles, to avoid misunderstandings it is absolutely necessary to give
some brief definitions of pidgins and creoles and their features.

1.2.1. *Pidginization and Creolization*

Nubi is generally considered to be a creole language, having originated from an Arabic pidgin spoken in the southern Sudan and
northern Uganda. There is much disagreement about how pidgins
and creoles should be defined.[27] For my present purpose, the following definition, which compiles elements extracted from the relevant literature, will do.

Pidgins typically come into being in multilingual groups, when no
common language is present to satisfy the need for communication.
None of the native languages dominates in prestige or number of
its speakers. Therefore, the members of the multilingual community
seek recourse in another prestigious language. Pidgins are only spoken in contact situations, such as trade, and are therefore function-
ally restricted. Moreover, their structure and vocabulary are restricted
in comparison with the target language (lexifier or superstrate language). The structure of pidgins may go from very rudimentary and
variable to stable and expanded. Heine (1982, 17) summarizes the
features of the process by which pidgins arise, as follows:

A   Explicit linguistic transmission tends to become more implicit.
B   Linguistic items and rules which are dispensible from a com-
    municative point of view tend to be eliminated.

---

[27] Sources: Arends, Muysken and Smith (1995), Bickerton (1975, 1977, 1981),
Boretzky (1983), Crowley (1992), Hancock (1979), Heine (1982), Holm (1988),
Mühlhäusler (1986), Todd (1974).

C   Inflectional-agglutinating structures are replaced by analytic-iso-
    lating structures.
D   If there are linguistic categories involving an unmarked-marked op-
    position then the marked tends to be suppressed and the unmarked
    used for both.
E   Context-sensitive rules . . . tend to be replaced by context-free
    rules.

Pidgin languages are learned by their speakers as a second language.
A pidgin language may develop into a creole when it is nativized,
instantaneously or gradually, when children born in mixed marriages
are confronted with the pidgin input and learn it as their mother
tongue. Unlike the pidginization process, which is marked by reduction of vocabulary and simplification of grammar, the creolization
process is characterized by expansion and elaboration, both lexically
and structurally, resulting in a fully fledged language that meets the
communication needs of mother-tongue speakers. If, in later developments, the structure of the lexifier language affects the creole language, we speak of decreolization.

1.2.2. *The Development of the Arabic Pidgin/Creole from a Socio-linguistic Viewpoint*

1.2.2.1. *The Arabic Pidgin/Creole Language in the Nineteenth Century*
Even before the conquest of the Sudan, Arabic had become established as a trade language. Owens (1985a, 229–71) hypothesizes that
already in the early centuries of Islam a pidgin Arabic came into
existence.[28] From the late seventh century onwards, Arab groups
migrated in several waves into eastern Sudanese Africa, going as far
as Lake Chad and beyond and taking with them their language and
culture. This resulted in a slow but continuous process of Arabicization
and Islamization through intermarriage, close contacts, and interre-
lationships (Braukämper 1993, 13–46). By the fourteenth century,
the Christian Nubian states had evolved into Muslim states. The status of Arabic as the language of Islam gained importance, and Arabic

---

[28] Thomason and Elgibali (1986, 317–49) analysed a small excerpt, which was
possibly a form of pidginized Arabic from the mid-eleventh century and which they
called Maridi Arabic. They maintained that the town of Maridi is to be situated
in the western Sahara, in present-day central Mauritania.

then became the official language (Rouchdy 1991). Arabic became
the second language for most Nile Nubians (Adams 1977). It is, however, not possible to verify how well they spoke Arabic (see also
Owens 1996, 125–72). By the seventeenth century, long distance
trade between Egypt, North Africa, and the states of the Sudan had
become common. Arabic made headway as a commercial language
and by 1850 had become fully established (Hill 1959). It could be
expected, however, that in the contact between speakers of Arabic
and the indigenous population simplified registers of Arabic had
arisen (see also Owens 1996, 125–72).

Owens (1996, 125–72) suggests that this Arabic trade language
may have influenced the formation of pidgin and creole varieties
spoken in the southern Sudan although there is no direct evidence
for this. Neither is there any direct evidence for the use of a pidgin Arabic in the training camps of the Niẓām al-jadīd in Aswān in
1821 and just beyond. Hill (1959) mentions that commands were
given in Turkish until 1863. We do not know, however, about the
language of other instructions. It is, however, likely that a kind of
Arabic, based on the pre-1820 Arabic trade language, was common
among the recruits who originated from different tribes. Only Thorburn
(1924, 314) suggests something of the kind when he says that the
Shilluk, Dinka, and Nūba recruits learned a 'pidgeon' Arabic, when
enlisting. We do know for certain that a simplified form of Arabic
was common in the military camps and in the *zarība* in Equatoria
and the Baḥr al-Ghazāl after 1869 (see below). This pidgin Arabic
must have reached the area through the movements of the Egyptian
military and/or more directly through the traders, who used it as
commercial language and for communication with their southern
Sudanese native inferiors.

We have seen above (1.1.2.2.) that the trading camps comprised an
amalgam of many different groups of people. Figures for the Khartūm
zarības in the Baḥr al-Ghazāl Province at around 1874 were given
in tables 1 and 2. From a thorough analysis by Owens we learn that:

> Of the ca. 250,000 inhabitants of Bahr el-Ghazal in 1870, 60,000, or
> about one quarter belonged to the trading camps. Of those in the
> camps, only 9,000–14,000 would have been native or near-native Arabic
> speakers (Owens 1996, 139).[29]

---

[29] Owens (1996) expected a subsequent decrease of the Arabic-speaking popula-

Arabic speakers were mainly found among the *jallāba* and *'asākir*. There were Arabic-speaking Shā'iqīya and Bedouins among the *'asākir*. The *jallāba* originated from Egypt and from all over the northern and central part of what is nowadays the state of Sudan. They were mainly Arabic-speaking. The Danāqla, found both among the *jallāba* and the *'asākir*, are supposed to have spoken at least some Arabic. How good their Arabic was, however, is quite uncertain. The other part of the camp population consisted mainly of black slaves of southern Sudanese origin, who were drawn to the attractive camp life. We may assume that processes like those in the *zarība* took place in the military camps. Among the regular troops were Egyptians and Sudanese (northern Sudanese Arabic speakers and black soldiers who had been recruited shortly after the occupation from among the Nūba, Shilluk, and Dinka (see 1.1.2.1.). Besides the irregular troops, among whom there were mainly Danāqla and Shā'iqīya, there were interpreters who were able to translate between the local languages and Arabic, and black soldiers, recruited more recently from among the southern tribes. After the time of az-Zubair from 1873 onwards, many trading camps took up government functions. Trading and military camps gradually evolved towards one another.

Camp life thus was prestigious and attractive for the local population. The dominant group in the camps were the native and near-native Arabic-speaking soldiers and traders. Hill (1959, 140) writes about language use in Equatoria Province and Baḥr al-Ghazāl after 1874:

> In spite of the many languages spoken in these two provinces, the government admitted no complications on that score. Among themselves the officers spoke Arabic, the language of administration. In their business with the natives they used a simplified, pidgin Arabic which became the *lingua franca* of the Southern Sudan. Native languages were officially ignored, though Emin in his spare time made careful studies of several.

If Hill is correct, the southern Sudanese variety of Arabic developed through foreigner talk of the native and near-native Arabic speakers with the southern Sudanese population: this foreigner talk served as the input for processes of imperfect language learning on the part

---

tion through birth within the camps and through the government policy of 1878, which led to an increase of local southern people in the camps, while northern traders were barred.

of the Sudanese non-Arabic speakers. We understand the same from
Thorburn, who speaks of a 'pidgeon' language (1924, 314). Considering
the way medieval Muslim geographers looked upon the black population or Zanj, we can assume that the Arab Muslims could hardly
imagine them ever becoming full Muslims or as living at the same
level as they did. Moreover, it was generally considered that these
people, coming as they did from these backward environments, could
not be taught the true faith and culture. Therefore, it is not difficult
to imagine that the Arab officers, soldiers, and merchants in the military and trading camps would use a simplified form of Arabic when
communicating with the native slaves. They were simply considered
to be deprived of the necessary intelligence to understand the Arabic
language properly, let alone to learn to speak it. However, since they
lived in the same environment, the black Sudanese were exposed to
native Arabic speech, which they may have attempted to speak. They
must have heard native Arabs converse, and as such they may have
picked up some notions. However, restricted access to Arabic and
processes of imperfect language learning must have hindered the
learning process.

The black population consisted of several groups. Besides the male
slave-soldiers and domestic slaves, there were the women folk and
the dragomen. Local interpreters were found both inside and outside the camps. Outside the camps, some men had managed to pick
up some Arabic.

> All of them were the indispensable intermediaries between African
> tribal communities and the Arab intruders with whom it was politic
> to form a loose, and if possible distant, alliance against rival tribes
> (Gray 1961, 100–01).

Gray refers to Gordon who seems to have found a village where
many villagers had some knowledge of Arabic (Gray 1961). Emin
(1919) tells of the son of a Schuli chief who was half 'civilized' and
spoke Arabic very well. A little further, he describes Aguok, a Schuli
chief, who dressed and behaved like a Dunqulāwī. Gray mentions
Zemio, an arabicized Zande chief. Gray (1961) adds that in the
camps themselves there were many native young men and women
who had learnt Arabic and had become very influential in contacts
between the southern Sudanese tribes and the Egyptian administrators. They had often outgrown their tribal backgrounds and must
therefore be distinguished from the *targāma*. Particularly in Emin's

diaries, we see how important these *targāma* had become in his contacts with the tribal chiefs (Emin 1919, 1922, vols. 3 and 4). The *targāma*, who initially must have acted merely as interpreters, could obtain high positions and constituted quite a large group in the camps. Note the following numbers from table 5:

Table 5. Population Amadi district station, September 1881

Population groups	Figures
Resident Danāqla	96
Employed Danāqla	40
Dragomen from among the Djur, Moru, Agar, Niamniam, Mangbattu, Bongo	319
Men, accompanied by women and children, who amount to approximately five times this figure.	455

Source: Emin 1919, 254–55

The dragomen here amounted to about 2.5 times as many as the Danāqla. Emin gives more figures for the population of a *zarība* in the Rohl district (table 6). Of the 300 men with higher positions in the *zarība*, 15% were dragomen.

Table 6. Population of a Rohl district *zarība*, October 1881

	Figures	Population groups	Figures
Residents	121	Traders	7
		Unemployed	57
		Farmers	57
Dragomen	73	Niamniam	30
		Jur	14
		Agar	10
		Bongo	19
Itinerant *jallāba* from the Bahr al-Ghazāl and Khartūm	appr. 100		
Slaves	appr. 1,200		
Total	appr. 1,500		

Source: Emin 1919, 292

Besides the interpreters, other groups in the *zarība* also came into contact with Arabic. Many Arabic-speaking *jallāba* and *ʿasākir* married

local women and often more than one, if we may believe Emin
(1922, 3:70) who complains that his men had too many wives.
Marriage thus also exposed the local women at least to pidginArabic.
That learning Arabic did not always happen rapidly, we hear again
from Emin (1922, 3:234), who grumbles about one of the local
women who had been with them for more than two years but still
only spoke a few words of Arabic. He also tells about the misunderstandings that occurred because of the 'broken negro-Arabic'
(Emin 1919, 242). We may assume that the native language was still
used for quite some time in the native households or that both the
native language and the pidgin Arabic were spoken. Children raised
in these families must have been affected by the multilingual situation, and may have learned the pidgin Arabic alongside the native
language of the mother or maybe as their mother tongue. Initial
creolization of the Arabic pidgin may thus have taken place (see
below). Owens (1996, 145) hypothesizes that the Arabic pidgin evolved
into an 'expression of social class' for its speakers. The native people living in the camps were in between their superiors of Nubian
and Arabic origin and the group of natives, whom they had left
behind in their villages. They did not belong to either group and
so formed a new class, the "semi-native semi-arab by contact population of lads and women" Gordon talked about (Gray 1961, 113).
Besides the language, religion proved to be another feature of this
marginal social entity. When entering the camps, the normal procedure for the local people was conversion to Islam.[30]

Owens (1996, 125–72) suggests, probably correctly, that the formative period of the ancestor of present-day Nubi began at around
1854, when, through the presence of the Egyptian army, the area
had become safe enough for the traders to expand their activities.
However, the few references in the literature only allude to a pidgin variety of Arabic in the times of Baker, Gordon, and Emin (i.e.
not earlier than 1869). Hill (1959), for instance, refers to the simplified
way of talking of the officers when approaching local people at the
time of Emin. Meldon (1907, 129) talks about the Nubi soldiers in
Uganda and their language, which was being corrupted by many
Bari, Lur, Lendu and Swahili words but which had supposedly been

---

[30] Outside the camp as well, the Islamic faith found its way. Emin (1919, 258)
talks about Gambari, a Mangbattu-chief who prayed as do Muslims.

much purer at the time of Emin, "though even then it was probably a patois of felaheen-Arabic, and must have been much corrupted during the decade of years when Emin governed the Nile Province." Crabtree (1913, 154–55) discusses "a modified form of Arabic known as Nubian". Its speakers were the soldiers of Baker, Gordon, and Emin, or their followers.[31] The lack of allusions to language use in previous times may be due to the fact that only these three administrators kept diaries. For the preceding period we can only guess.

Most likely, the initiative in communication came from the officer corps and traders who addressed their subordinates, slaves, and local wives by means of a simple, broken Arabic, which may have been similar to the pre-1820 trade language. Since no other means of communication were available in the interethnic communities of the military and trading camps and owing to its high prestige as the language of the superiors and the language of the newly acquired religion, the p/c Arabic soon gained ground as an important means of communication. Owens (1996, 125–72) even suggests that it became a symbol for the newly formed class in between the villagers and the camp superiors.

1.2.2.2. *At the Turn of the Century*
Owens (1996, 125–72) is probably correct in stating that by 1888, the year Stanley met Emin at the shores of Lake Albert, the p/c Arabic had reached the stabilization phase, and that some initial, although limited creolization had taken place. His conclusion is based on a comparison between Nubi and Juba Arabic.[32] Juba Arabic is a pidginized variety (which recently has been creolized as well), spoken in the southern part of the present state of Sudan. The pidginized variety that evolved into present-day Juba Arabic must have been very similar to the pidgin ancestor of Nubi. The differences between Nubi and Juba Arabic are minimal, taking the respective substrate and adstrate influences into account and the fact that Nubi was

---

[31] Crabtree (1913, 152–66) suggested that it was still in use all along the Nile Valley as far as Cairo at the time of his writing, 1913, although it was supposedly unintelligible to speakers of the Arabic dialect of Egypt. I understand the same from Thorburn (1924, 314–21). Thorburn gives several examples of songs representing post-Dervish times (the Mahdists). The language of the songs contains both dialect elements and elements of an Arabic pidgin that resembles Nubi and Juba Arabic.

[32] For a comparative analysis of Juba Arabic and Nubi, see chapter 7, Miller (1994, 225–46), and Owens (1996, 125–72).

creolized whereas Juba remained a pidgin until only recently. However, unlike the ancestors of the present-day Nubi people who withdrew to the south, the Juba Arabic speakers remained in southern Sudan. The similarities between Juba Arabic and Nubi can only be explained, if, at the time of their separation, they had reached a more or less stable stage. The groups of Selīm Bey and Faḍl al-Maulā were relatively small: 40 armed men and 300 followers and 800 armed men with 10,000 followers respectively. They were, however, joined at around 1890 by a large number of people from mainly the Lendu and Lur tribes (see 1.1.2.4. and 1.1.3.). The pidgin Arabic managed to survive this huge non-Arab influx with minimum change, which supports the argument that the p/c Arabic had developed into a more or less stable language by 1888. On the other hand, scholars like Kaye and Tosco (1993, 301) argue that:

> the language they [the Sudanese in the Ugandan military camps] brought with them from southern Sudan was not yet stabilized at that period [1891–], and that Arabic influence (from different superstratal dialects) was still exerting pressure on the developing pidgin. This was surely the case of those Sudanese soldiers and families who were living in the Sudan prior to their departure for Uganda, and, who in all likelihood, had come into contact with speakers of many different Arabic dialects.

Kaye and Tosco come to this conclusion after having analysed an account of the p/c Arabic in Uganda, which was written in Bombo in Buganda-area, the most important settlement of the Nubi troops in Uganda, in 1908 by a Major Jenkins. In addition to a few pages on grammatical features, Jenkins compiled an English-pidgin Arabic dictionary, including some pages with short sentences. Surprisingly enough, according to Kaye and Tosco, the material contains both Arabic dialect and pidgin vocabulary and grammatical items:

> we nevertheless think that two linguistic layers are found in Jenkins's book, and must be kept, wherever possible, strictly separated. They are: (1) a basilectal variety, most likely a pidgin, which we label "Ugandan Pidgin Arabic (UPA); (2) a more acrolectal variety, "Ugandan Dialectal Arabic" (UDA), probably not strictly a pidgin, although it contained some "reduced" features characteristic of a pre-pidgin continuum where languages and dialects are in contact (Kaye and Tosco 1993, 273).

The differences lie in the vocabulary and phonology (such as gemination and vowel length) but are mainly found in "the presence in

UDA of Arabic derivational and inflectional morphology, and also
a few categories absent in UPA, such as the article and the com-
plementizers" (Kaye and Tosco 1993, 273). Kaye and Tosco (1993,
269–306) consider 10% to 20% of the material in Jenkins's vocabulary to be of dialect origin. They do not give any estimates for the
pidgin Arabic, which must be less than the remaining 80% to 90%,
since the source forms of many items remain obscure. The above
implies that colloquial Arabic elements would still have been present
even after 1900. Kaye and Tosco (1993, 269–306) conclude that
these elements must have continued to influence the p/c Arabic spoken in Bombo and probably in other military settlements. Owens
(1993, 125–72), however, refutes this hypothesis by arguing that one
linguistic layer may have existed next to the other without exerting
much influence if any at all.[33] If Owens' hypothesis (Owens 1996,
125–72) of p/c Arabic evolving into a distinctive marker of the social
layer of the speakers is correct, he is right in disregarding Jenkins'
material. He adds that the nature of the relations between the social
layers and the number of speakers of the socially dominant group
also need attention.

For an evaluation of these social relations, it is necessary to revert
to the time of Emin. At around 1888, although many Egyptian and
Sudanese officers had joined the Mahdists, others remained loyal to
Emin (Gray 1961). In his and Mounteney-Jephson's diary, we find
several references to the presence of native Egyptians, Danāqla, and

---

[33] Owens (1993, 11) criticizes Kaye and Tosco:

As Kaye and Tosco point out and illustrate, however, Jenkins is not a very
reliable document linguistically. Moreover, there are further considerations. . . .

(1) Jenkins' own background. From remarks in the preface, he appears to
have a knowledge of classical Arabic ('well known books on Arabic'). It could
have been Jenkins himself, as well as his informants, who standardized the
description in places.

(2) The presence of acrolectal speakers does not guarantee that their variety will be automatically transmitted. The nature of the social relations between
the acrolectal and basilectal is also important, as well as the number of speakers of the acrolectal variety, two points requiring more careful attention.

(3) There is some evidence in Jenkins' data that the acrolectal model did
not gain widespread acceptance among the Nubi. It is notable that in Kaye
and Tosco's list of words with the Egyptian (acrolectal) reflex *g* of the sound
'jim' . . . only 4 of 19 survive in modern day Nubi. Much of Jenkins' material
could thus represent a sociolectally restricted variety which co-existed with other
varieties, one which could have been the stabilized variety postulated by Owens.

Khartūm people (Emin 1922, vol. 3 and 4, Mounteney-Jephson 1890).[34]
Emin (1922, 4: 142) speaks of Sheikh Murjān, a black Sudanese
raised in Egypt who performed the call for prayers. These were particularly the people who wished to join Emin on his way to Zanzibar
and then to Egypt. However, not all of them, especially those joining Selīm Bey, may have actually managed to leave Uganda, which
implies that at least a few native speakers of colloquial Arabic remained
with Selīm Bey or left with Faḍl al-Maulā (Holt 1958). Lugard (1968)
found a few pure Egyptians among Selīm's officers and clerks in
1891. Figures are given nowhere, but we can imagine that they were
very few in number.[35] Many of the original officers had been killed
and had been replaced by those previously holding lower ranks (see
1.1.2.4. and 1.1.3). We may thus assume that the few remaining
Egyptian and Sudanese Arabs and Danāqla held positions at the top
of the military hierarchy, thus constituting a small elite group. We
know very little about how they treated men of inferior ranks or
how the lower ranks treated them. Lugard (1968) mentions, however, that superior and other ranks were distinguished by dress: the

---

[34] Proof of Emin's knowledge and use of Arabic is given as well (Emin 1922,
vol. 4, 111–12, 130–31).
[35] Selīm's Sudanese were reinforced by those who had joined Lugard from the
coast. Among them were men like Shukri Aga, who had left with Emin for Zanzibar
but who thereafter had been engaged by Lugard. Lugard (1968) also calls them
'Sudanese': "I had many men with me who had been through the 'Emin Relief
Expedition' . . ." (Lugard 1968, 200). Nothing is said about their homeland or language, but among them may have been native Arabs, since those constituted the
bulk of men who had left. Also, there were the Sudanese soldiers who had come
via Egypt to Zanzibar. Of Lugard's second-in-command Captain Williams it is said
that: "He spoke Turkish and French, and had acquired a colloquial knowledge of
Arabic. Having enlisted the Sudanese in Egypt for the Imperial British East African
Company, he naturally looked on them as his special charge . . ." (Lugard 1968,
61). Furley (1959, 311–28) adds that four officers, speakers of Arabic, were appointed
to command the Sudanese. However, the language of the Sudanese was probably
not an Arabic dialect, but a p/c Arabic that they had learned when they were
recruited (see also Thorburn 1924, 314–21). We know, however, nothing of the
Arabic of Williams and the four officers. Was it a colloquial type of Arabic or the
pidginized variety? Or maybe, they had knowledge of both and used the pidginized
variety in addressing the 'Sudanese'.
   For April 1891, Lugard (1968, 114) gives the following figures: "With the new
arrivals our force numbered some 150 Sudanese, 160 Zanzibari Levy, and 300
porters, . . .". It is possible that at least some of these Sudanese remained in Uganda
to join Selīm's Sudanese troops, and it is possible that among them were native
Arabic speakers. However, their numbers were probably not large, hence their
influence must have been minimal.

highest ranks were dressed in cotton material, whereas the others covered themselves with animal hides. In the following quotation from Meldon (1907, 142), we sense the same discriminatory mentality that may have characterized the native Arabs and true Muslims towards the 'Sudanese' and Muslims-in-name.

> They profess to be Muhammadans, but in no way do they practise the religion; only three of the Native Officers and here and there a private or N.C.O., can read and write a little. Many of them have learnt the first chapter of the Koran (Surat-el-Fātihat or el-Fatha) and other well-known verses by heart, but they do not keep the Ramazan, nor do they by any means confine themselves to the use of water as a beverage.

We may assume that a separation was maintained between the higher and the lower ranks and that contacts between them were infrequent. Moreover, even if the few remaining Arab superior officers still spoke a colloquial Arabic among themselves, they probably used the p/c Arabic when communicating with their non-Arab wives, soldiers, and slaves.[36] It is not unlikely that Jenkins, who himself held the rank of major, turned wholly or partially to those to whom he felt affiliated through rank so that he would have received a biased picture of the p/c Arabic. Moreover, it is extremely difficult for someone who is not familiar with a language to recognize different lects and to describe them adequately.

Around 1900, the number of native speakers of Arabic was very small, and they probably remained separate from the p/c Arabic speakers. Therefore, even if, theoretically, the presence of native speakers of Arabic meant some continuing influence, in reality, most likely, they did not affect the speakers of p/c Arabic, as they lacked the opportunity. These two groups of speakers probably lived separately, and the number of native speakers had been reduced considerably. Jenkins' book can thus be considered proof that native Arabic was still in use. However, it does not show whether this native Arabic had any influence on the p/c Arabic.

Another account was written in 1907 by Meldon. Like Jenkins, he had a function in the army, and like Jenkins, was not a linguist, although he may have had some knowledge of Arabic. Unlike Jenkins,

---

[36] See also Kaye and Tosco (1993, 269–306).

Meldon's article only gives linguistic information indirectly. The article consists mainly of historical and anthropological notes on the 'Sudanese' in the Ugandan military camps, which are, however, interspersed with 'Sudanese' words and short sentences.

Vocabulary: Pure pidgin words, like *tenu* "wait" (132) co-occur with colloquial Arabic elements, such as *shok* "thorn bushes" (132), *gild* "skin", "leather" (137), and classical Arabic elements, like *rajul* "man" (131). Other vocabulary items are of non-Arabic Sudanese origin, like the Nubian word *angarib* "camp bed" (131), and the Mundu (?) word *rambangili* "burial" (131).

Phonology: Meldon's transcription is not consistent, which makes it difficult to give a correct interpretation, e.g. *tabakh* "plate" (142) (in Egyptian Arabic *ṭabaqa* "cover", "lid", in Sudanese Arabic *ṭabag* "lid", "tray") is in present-day Nubi *'tabaga* "plate", "tray", which exhibits a regular development: $q > g$. There is no reason to assume an intermediary stage with a velar fricative. Meldon's *kh* thus stands either for q or for g, or for a word-final allophone: aspirated k? In *yarkhu* "they soften" (137) *kh* probably stands for the velar fricative [x], since the verb is derived from the colloquial (Egyptian and Sudanese) root *r-kh-y*. Meldon thus used *kh* for the velar fricative as well as for q or g. *sagh* (142) "iron slab used as a frying pan" may have been derived from Egyptian *ṣāg* "iron sheet", "baking tin". Meldon thus writes *gh* for plain g, while in *gotta* "food cover" (142) (in Nubi *'kuta*), g also stands for plain g. The colloquial (Egyptian and Sudanese) Arabic source form is probably $\bar{g}$ [ɣ]-*ṭ-w*. Did Meldon wish to differentiate $g < \bar{g}$ [ɣ] from $g < g$, based on his knowledge of Classical Arabic, or did he only distinguish between word-initial and word-final g, which may have different pronunciations?

Meldon writes about the *rahad* "leather loin cloth for girls" (136) from Sudanese Arabic *rahaṭ* with the same meaning. Instead of taking *ṭ* to have developed into *d*, which is quite an uncommon change, we would rather suggest that Meldon, assuming devoicing of a final consonant, interpreted or mis-interpreted *ṭ* (or *t*) as a *d*. On p. 139, children born in the Uganda Protectorate of parents of different tribes, are called *mowalat*, which must have come from Arabic *muwallad*, and which in present-day Nubi is still heard as *mo'weledu*. Note again the final dental consonants. The present-day Nubi form is similar to the original Arabic form. The final voiceless dental consonant in Meldon's article is in this case probably a reflection of what he heard. Meldon also writes about the *leb* "dance" (128). In present-day Nubi it is *'lib*, and it obviously comes from Arabic *li'b* "play", "game". Has there been an intermediate stage with *i* > *e*? *e* then could have become *i* again through (early) decreolization. It could, however, just as well have been a writing mistake or an incorrect interpretation on Meldon's part. *sh* in *farash* (132) from Arabic *faraj* "freedom from grief or sorrow" (*farag* in EA) is again an example of final devoicing.

Meldon's words contain typical pidgin elements, such as Ø < ʿ as in *azib* (135) from EA/SA *ʿazab* "unmarried", "single", *ajin* "dough" (139) from EA/SA *ʿajīn* "dough", *h* < *ḥ* as in *hizam* "cloth" (131) from EA/SA *ḥizām* "belt", "girdle", *hakim* "doctor" from EA/SA *ḥakīm* "physician", *t* < *ṭ* in *tabakh* "plate" from EA/SA *ṭabaq* "cover", "lid". The addition of final *-h* in the spelling of *maryah* "woman" (130) and *surah* "umbilical cord" (131) both derived from feminine Arabic words, suggests that Meldon was not unfamiliar with Arabic. The singular form of *el shayebeen* "elders" (128) is, according to Meldon, *shaybah* (128, n. 1), instead of the more usual *shāyib* "old man". Meldon again shows a tendency towards Classical Arabic, as shown by the retention of the diphtong *ai*.

Morphology: The use of the definite article is the most conspicuous classicizing feature. For instance in *Shaitan fi 'l ras* "a devil in his head" (127), *El Shayebeen* "elders" (128), *tenu fil farash*, which Meldon translates as "seven days' mourning" (132), *el gild* here "goat leather" (137), *el rahad* "skirt of goat leather worn by unmarried girls" (136–137), *el ajin* "mixture of flour and water" (139). *yarkhu el gild* is translated by Meldon as "the softening of the goat leather by rubbing" (137). The verb *yarkhu* is obviously a colloquial imperfective third person plural from a stem with weak consonant III from the verb *raxa* "loosen" (Worsley 1925). The expression *Nas alhaguni rajul betai maut*, translated by Meldon as "Help me! My man is dead" (131), literally to be translated as "people, help me, my husband is dead", could be interpreted as a foreigner-talk utterance. *alhagu* is an Arabic plural imperative form to which the first person pronominal object suffix *-ni* is attached. The verb is SA *liḥig (a)* "reach", "overtake". The first word of the second part of the sentence *rajul* "man" is a plain Classical Arabic word. The analytic genitive is expressed by means of the Egyptian/Sudanese *betai* "of me". *maut* is a Classical Arabic form of the verbal noun from the verb *māta* "die", which serves here as a verb. This sentence is thus a mixture of mainly Sudanese and Classical Arabic elements, and contains a grammatical mistake,

namely the use of a verbal noun for a verb. The latter cannot be
linked to pidgin influence, since in Nubi the verb is *'mutu* "die". The
sentence also lacks the Arabic particle *yā*, which links it to the Arabic
p/cs.

The above could mean several things. Either, as Kaye and Tosco
(1993, 269–306) suggest, the p/c Arabic had not yet evolved into a
stable pidgin at around 1900 and still contained elements from Arabic
dialect(s). Or an utterance like *nas alhaguni* . . . was introduced as a
fixed expression into the p/c Arabic.[37] However, since this cannot
explain the other vocabulary items, it is more likely that Meldon
himself or his informant(s) had some knowledge of colloquial and
even of Classical Arabic. Native speakers of Arabic were still present at the time. Meldon (1907, 123–46) mentions one of them,
Bimbashi Rehan Effendi Raschid, who was of Tunisian origin but
who grew up in Egypt. It is possible that Meldon employed one or
more of them as informants/assistants, which could explain the large
number of colloquial words in the article. The presence of Classical
Arabic elements in addition to colloquial Arabic may be explained
by an attempt by Meldon himself or his informant(s) to give the
'correct' Arabic forms instead of the language as it was used in reality, although their knowledge of Classical and/or colloquial Arabic
was not perfect. Some of the words and elements used can only be
explained as hypercorrections, which leads us to the same conclusion, namely that Meldon described an ideal language instead of the
'corrupted' and, therefore, inferior language. Moreover, Meldon's
transcription is not consistent and so in some ways useless. This article can therefore not serve as evidence of the development of the
p/c Arabic or for evaluating the influence of Arabic colloquial(s) on
the p/c Arabic.

Above I have given arguments to support Owens' hypothesis that,
by 1888, the p/c Arabic had evolved into a stable pidgin. Owens
(1996, 125–72) suggests that creolization had also taken place by that
time. I do not believe the pidgin variety had been creolized already
on a large scale by the time Emin and his troops arrived at the
shores of Lake Albert. However, creolization must have taken place
soon after. As mentioned above (1.1.3.), part of the Nubi found by
Lugard had settled in Nairobi by 1902. Their creolized language is

---

[37] I have never heard it being used in present-day Nubi.

virtually the same as the Nubi language in Uganda, except for some details, which could be attributed to substrate influence (see chapter 7). Therefore, creolization processes must have resulted in a more or less stable language prior to the split of the two groups, so that further developments on an independent basis did not result in much differentiation.

Was there any creolization before 1888? At first sight, considering Juba Arabic, it could be concluded that it had not yet occurred. Juba Arabic was creolized only recently. It remained a pidgin during the first half of the century, and it was still in a pidgin phase at the end of the 19th century when the ancestors of the Nubi people left the southern Sudan. By that time, a stable pidgin may well have developed, which was creolized later on in Uganda, while no creolization occurred in southern Sudan. Another possibility is that the ancestors of the speakers of Juba Arabic were not members of the camp population who stayed behind when Emin withdrew to the Lake Albert area but that they were local villagers who had never entered camp life but who had acquired some knowledge of the pidgin Arabic through extensive contacts with the camps. If so, we should differentiate between the pidgin Arabic speakers in the camps and those outside the camps. Whereas camp-born children may have nativized the pidgin variety at a certain stage, it is not very likely that village-born children did so, since normally both parents in the village shared their tribal background and language and since the pidgin Arabic was most likely no more than a second language in the village used for out-group communication. In the camps, the pidgin Arabic may have become a first language owing to its prestige and to the fact that it was indispensable, being the only means of communication in the interethnic community.[38] At least, some newborn children may have acquired the p/c Arabic and spoken it as their mother tongue, so that creolization may have taken place at least on a limited scale.

In the camps, besides children who were born in mixed marriages, there must have been children of couples from the same tribe since it is hard to imagine that all marriages involved different ethnic

---

[38] The mother tongue is the language first acquired by a child. The first language is the language preferred in a multilingual situation. These languages, therefore, are not always the same.

groups. Therefore, the question arises as to whether the scale on which this process happened was large enough to speak of general creolization of the pidgin Arabic. Above (1.1.2.2. and 1.1.2.3.), we have seen that people of the local tribes, looking for a better way to earn their livelihood, continued to enter the trading and military camps. This involved a constant input of village-born children, so that it is doubtful that the number of camp-born children was high enough to outnumber the village-born children. Arends and Bruyn (1995, 111–20) suggest that creolization cannot take place until the locally born children outnumber the village-born children. According to them, creolization may extend over several generations. If we now turn to our group of 'Sudanese' in Kavalli, we see that, between the years 1889 and 1891, the original group of 'Sudanese' was reinforced by a large group of local people, mainly of the Lendu and Lur tribes (Lugard 1968). We have figures for the groups of 'Sudanese': approximately 350 with Selīm Bey and about 10,800 who had left with Faḍl al-Maulā. For the Lendu and Lur, unfortunately, there are no figures.

I conclude that the number of native speakers of Arabic must have been minimal, that extensive mutual contact between the native speakers and the pidgin speakers was probably not the case, and that creolization must have taken place by the end of the 19th century because only then had the proportion of 'Sudanese' born children become high enough for the Arabic p/c to make headway as a stable creole. By 1902, when the 'Sudanese' troops were separated geographically, the creolization process must have reached a more or less stable phase, so that, in spite of the large distance, both developments continued along the same lines, thereby resulting in two very similar varieties (Ugandan and Kenyan Nubi).

1.2.2.3. *In the Twentieth Century*
Selīm's troops became separated during Lugard's trip to the south. Several garrisons were left behind in the area west of the Nile, the present-day Ugandan West Nile Province, and in the Kingdom of Bunyoro, in the west of present-day Uganda. The remainder joined Lugard to settle in the Buganda Kingdom, extending north and west of Lake Victoria, and especially at the military headquarters in Bombo, while some of the troops went on to Nairobi, where they settled in 1902. The present-day Nubi language of the north of Uganda and that of Kenya are more alike than the Nubi language

of the northern and southern part of present-day Uganda. This must be related to substrate and adstrate elements influencing the otherwise stable creole language. Of course, through intermarriage and intensive contacts between the Nubi speakers of all the different areas, the differences between all three regional varieties have been levelled. After 1979, for instance, many Ugandan Nubi fled to Kenya. In the north and in Kenya, Swahili had long been the language of intertribal communication, whereas in southern Uganda, the Bantu language Luganda is the main, and for many the only, language. Both languages have left their mark on the Nubi language of the respective areas. Others, also from the Buganda area, sought refuge in southern Sudan. After their return to Uganda, many chose to reside in the northern or central part of the country instead of going back to their previous villages.

The Nubi have been living scattered over the country since their ties with the military forces were weakened and especially after their return from 1986 onwards after the civil war. They always constituted minorities surrounded by larger tribal populations, and were, therefore, forced to learn other languages than their own in order to communicate outside their own small group. Their language repertoire may contain as many as eight other languages. Heine (1982, 15) suggests that "Nubi people probably constitute the most multilingual group of East Africa" (see also 7.1.1.1.).

In the northern part of Uganda, Nubi has become an important language for out-group communication besides Swahili. The process is probably being reinforced by the high influx of Juba Arabic-speaking refugees from southern Sudan.

1.3. *Conclusion*

Native and near-native Arabs penetrated into the southern Sudan through military operations and trading activities in which black Sudanese were involved either having been taken as slaves or having deliberately entered the military and trading camps. At around 1885, both activities came to an abrupt end through the Mahdist revolt. Emin Pasha, at the time governor of Equatoria Province, withdrew to the Lake Albert area in present-day Uganda with his mixed Arab and black Sudanese troops. After a three-year period of seclusion, Stanley came to their rescue. Selīm Bey and Faḍl

al-Maulā did not join Emin and Stanley on their journey to the
coast. They remained with approximately 900 armed men and 10,300
followers and were joined by many native Lendu and Lur. The
group was met in 1891 by Capt. Lugard, representative of the
Imperial British East Africa Company, and later incorporated into
the King's African Rifles. The group was divided into garrisons, and
scattered all over present-day Uganda and Nairobi. The downfall of
the Ugandan Nubi came soon after. Idi Amin, however, brought
them a period of revival, which came to an end in 1979, when Amin
fled and the Nubi were forced to seek exile in the surrounding countries. From 1986 onwards, under Museveni, the Nubi gradually began
to return and are resettling all over Uganda.

While outlining the development of p/c Arabic against its historical background, I have assumed that the Arabic lingua franca used
mainly for commercial purposes in the Sudan before 1820 found its
way initially to the training camps in and around Aswān and later
on in the southern Sudan through southward movements of the military and through the activities of merchants in the White Nile Valley,
Equatoria, and the Baḥr al-Ghazāl. The high-status Arabic-speaking
officers and traders probably used a simplified Arabic when communicating with their southern Sudanese subordinates. The black
slaves were thus addressed directly with a foreigner-talk variety of
Arabic. Through contacts with the Arabic-speaking population, they
must have picked up some knowledge of Arabic native speech as
well although they were impeded by limited access to Arabic and
by processes of imperfect language learning. The pidgin Arabic may
have become a symbol of group membership for its speakers,
differentiating them from their own tribal background and from their
Arabic-speaking superiors. By 1888, when Emin and his troops were
met by Stanley at the shores of Lake Albert, the pidgin Arabic probably had already evolved into a stable pidgin. It was then confronted
with a huge input from speakers of local languages from the Lake
Albert area, especially Lur and Lendu. It must still have taken many
years before the group of newborn children in the group was large
enough to bring about structural nativization/creolization of the language. However, by the time the groups were separated and the
Nubi settlement in Nairobi was set up in 1902, creolization must
have taken place on a large enough scale to explain the lack of
major structural differences between the regional varieties, which
were only affected marginally by substrate and adstrate influences.

The extensive contacts between the Nubi people who nowadays live scattered in the larger towns of Kenya and Uganda, especially after 1979, when many Nubi went into exile, affected the Nubi regional varieties, and reduced their differences.

The Nubi people are very much aware and proud of their descent and of the Arabic origin of their language. In the past few decades, Nubi young men had the opportunity to acquire a proper knowledge of Arabic. During the years of Amin's government, many Ugandan Nubi, mainly men, studied in Arab countries. Through a programme sponsored by the United Nations, many young Ugandan Nubi were able to study at the Islamic University in Khartūm. Therefore, among male thirty- or forty-year-old Ugandan Nubi, the knowledge of Arabic is considerable. These young men keep a rather strict division between their mother tongue, Nubi, and Arabic. The older generation of Sheikhs, on the contrary, who know some Arabic through Qur'ānic teaching, like to add Arabic words and non-p/c phonemes, such as the emphatic sounds, and velar and pharyngeal fricatives to their speech. However, this process cannot be called decreolization, since knowledge of Arabic is limited to a few individuals. Moreover, the younger men tend to speak Arabic only within the group of ex-Islamic University students.

CHAPTER TWO

PHONOLOGY

The Nubi phonemic inventory consists of twenty one core consonants and nine consonants with marginal status. The situation of the
vowels is less clear. Stress is lexically and grammatically distinctive,
as is tone in limited cases. Phonological processes, such as elision
and assimilation, may affect vocalic and consonantal quality. In Nubi,
such processes have a profound impact, so that a considerable
difference between lento and allegro forms exists. In the examples
that will be given in th is and in the following chapters, I will use
a broad allophonic transcription.[1]

2.1. *Phonological Segments*

2.1.1. *Consonants and Semi-vowels*

2.1.1.1. *Phonemes*

The Nubi consonants are listed in table 7:

Table 7. Nubi consonant inventory

	Bilabial	Labio-dental	Dental	Alveolar	Post-alveolar	Palatal	Velar	Uvular	Pharyn-geal	Glot-tal
Plosive	p b			t d			k g	(q)		(ʔ)
nasal	m	(ɱ)		n		ɲ	(ŋ)			
Trill				r						
Flap				(ɾ)						
Fricative		f v	(θ)(ð)	s z	ʃ		(x)		(ħ)	h
Affricate					tʃ dʒ					
Approx	w					j				
Lateral Approx				l						

[ʃ] = *sh*; [tʃ] = *ch*; [dʒ] = *j*; [ŋ] = *ny*; [w] = *w* or *u*; [j] = *y* or *i*; [θ] = *th*; [ð] = *dh*; [x] = *kh*,
[ħ] = *ḥ*[2]

---

[1] This implies that the ideal Nubi, according to its speakers, may deviate from

On the chart, the consonants in parentheses have marginal status and occur in Arabic and English loanwords or as the result of phonological processes. Nasal compounds may occur in loanwords from Bantu languages as in (1):

(1) *mb* in *mbe'renge* "pop corn" < Luganda `mberênge* "dried head of maize"
nj in `gonja* < Luganda *gònjâ* "large sweet banana"

2.1.1.2. *Consonant Opposition Pairs*

(2)
b–p	`basi* "well", "OK"	–	`pasi* "iron box"
b–m	`bal* "attention"	–	`mal* "wealth"
b–w	`baga* "even"	–	`waga* "fall"
b–f	*bi* FUT	–	*fi* "in"
b–v	`libu* "game"	–	`livu* "leave"
b–t	`bal* "attention"	–	`tal* "come! (IMPER)"
b–d	`abula* "swallow"	–	`adulu* "prepare"
p–f	`lipa* "pay"	–	`lifa* "washing cloth"
p–t	`pima* "measure"	–	`tim* "be enough"
m–n	`ma* NEG	–	`na* "there"
m–w	`masa* "rub"	–	`wasa* "leave"
n–d	`nar* "fire"	–	`dar* "back"
n–l	*gi'ben* "PROG-look like"	–	*gi'bel* "before"
w–y	*wa'la* "or"	–	*ya'la* "children"
w–Ø	`wasa* "leave"	–	`asa* "now"
w–v	`womba* "ask (from God)"	–	`vumbi* "dust"
f–v	`lifu* "dizzy s.o."	–	`livu* "leave"
f–t	`fu* EXIS	–	`tu* "only"
f–s	`faga* "split"	–	`saga* "lightening"
f–z	`furu* "boil s.th."	–	`zuru* "visit each other"

the way the language is transcribed here. For instance, through processes of vowel assimilation, `ina* PRON 1PL may be expressed `ino*, which will be the form mentioned. I also illustrate this with the syllable structure. Nubi shows a tendency towards open syllables. A Nubi speaker would pronounce the word for "early" in slow speech as `bediri*. However, in allegro speech, the speed of which approximates that of Spanish, the word is heard as `bedri*, and this is how I shall write it.

[2] With transcriptions such as *dh, th, kh*, I follow Nubi orthography (in the few instances it is written), which in turn follows Swahili orthography. In doing this, I realize that I deviate from the usual transcription of Arabic phonemes, where one phoneme represents one grapheme, as well as from IPA conventions.

f–sh	*fulu* "groundnut(s)"	–	*shulu* "take s.th."
v–z	*wivu* "jealousy"	–	*izu* "shake"
t–d	*toru* "wake up"	–	*doru* "wander about"
t–s	*ta'ban* "feel bad"	–	*sa'ban* "be satisfied"
t–sh	*tor* "bull"	–	*shor* "advice"
t–ch	*tai* "my", "mine"	–	*chai* "tea"
d–l	*de* "the (DEF)"	–	*le* "why"
d–z	*duru* "harm s.o."	–	*zuru* "visit each other"
d–j	*du'ban* "fly"	–	*ju'ban* "dirt"
r–l	*kisi'ran* "misfortune"	–	*kisi'lan* "laziness"
s–z	*sidu* "close"	–	*zidu* "add"
s–sh	*sukur* "snore"	–	*shukuru* "thank"
s–ch	*sama* "forgive"	–	*chama* "organisation"
ch–sh	*chama* "organisation"	–	*shamba* "field"
ch–j	*cha'ran* "sewing machine"	–	*ja'rara* "button"
ch–k	*cha'ran* "sewing machine"	–	*ka'ran* "secretary"
g–j	*gidu* "weave", "come straight"	–	*jidu* "add"
g–h	*gari* "car", "bicycle"	–	*hari* "hot"
k–g	*kara* "faeces"	–	*gara* "pumpkin"
k–y	*ka'la* COMPL	–	*ya'la* "children"
k–h	*kadi* "Muslim judge"	–	*hadi* "limit"
y–Ø	*yalla* "OK"	–	*alla* "God"
y–h	*yal* "children"	–	*hal* "condition"

2.1.1.3. *Phonemic and Sub-phonemic Variation*

There are a considerable number of words with variant pronunciations in Nubi. However, variation is restricted to certain words. In chapter 7, I will show that the following types of phonemic and subphonemic variation are etymological in nature because more than one source dialect was probably involved in the developmental process of Nubi or because they are probably linked to substrate/adstrate influences.

Phonemic variation:

d–z: Variation between these phonemes is limited to the word *'dahab/'zahab* "gold". *'dahab* is more common than *'zahab*.

s–sh: In many words, *s* varies with *sh*, for instance *'asrubu/'ashrubu* "drink", the latter being particularly common in the speech of older speakers. In many words, however, *sh* is never replaced by *s* as in *'shida* "problem". Conversely, many words are expressed only with *s*, for example, *'sana* "year", while *'shana** is not acceptable. However, some people, especially older inhabitants from Entebbe, may apply a kind of 'hypercorrection' when talking, for example, about a *'shabal 'bele* "inhabitant", "resident", which in Nubi is normally referred to as *'sabal 'bele*, or *Ishi'lam*, referring to the Islamic religion, for which the more usual expression is *Is'lam* in Arabic and Nubi. In Kigumba (central Uganda) and less frequently in the south, the sibilant in words with a *sh* origin is pronounced somewhere between *s* and *sh*, resulting in an apical, weakened, sissing *s*.

j–g: In certain Nubi words, *j* and *g* are variably used, sometimes even by one and the same speaker. These are *'jili/ 'gili* "skin", "body", *'lajer/ 'lager* "stone", and *'jins/ 'gins* "type", "sort", *'ragi/ 'rajil* "man". The *j*-forms are used by people who took refuge in southern Sudan during the civil war.

z–j: *j* is often used as a variant of *z*. In the speech of northern and older speakers, *z* is more frequent than in the speech of younger speakers and speakers from the south. There may be variation in the speech of one and the same speaker, even for the same word. One of the most common examples is *a'zol* "person", "man", which in the Buganda area generally becomes *a'jol*. However, not all words are susceptible to variation. For instance, *'jeba* "pocket" will never be *'zeba**, and *zi'na* "adultery" will never be *ji'na**.

n–ny–l: In the north, a formal distinction is made between *'legetu/ 'negetu* (1) "pick", "select", (2) "gather", "collect", and *'nigitu* "get ripe", while in the south this distinction has been neutralized. *'Nigitu* and *'negetu* are used for all three meanings, while *'legetu* has disappeared from the southern vocabulary. Similarly, in southern Uganda, *'nenzil* and *'nyenzil* "descend" are used, while in the north both forms co-exist with *'lenzil* and *'lengil*.[3]

l–r: In the southern variety of Nubi spoken in the Buganda area, the distribution of *l* and *r* is partially neutralized. *l* and *r* may be

---

[3] More variant forms occur for this word, namely *'nyenzil, 'nyenjil, 'nyengil, 'lengil* "descend". In one instance, *'lengil* was translated as "offload".

variably used, e.g., *'fadur* instead of the form *'fadul* "remain", or the Luganda word for "village" *ekyalo* ['tʃaːlo], which may be articulated in Nubi as *'charo*.

p–f: The pair *'pasa/'fasa* "break wind noiselessly" is distributed regionally. In the southern part of Uganda, *'pasa* is the normal form, while in the north *'fasa* is used next to *'pasa*. *'afoyo* "rabbit" is used countrywide, while the use of *'apoyo* is limited to the north.

k–g: *g* and *k* are interchangeable in a few words as in *gur'baba/ kur'baba* "women's undergarment", *gala'moyo/kala'moyo* "goat", *'goful* "lock" (V)/*'kuful* "lock" (N), in UN *ma'kas* and KN *ma'gas* "scissors", etc.

w–j -Ø: *'wegifu, 'yegifu,* and *'egifu* (1) "stop", "come to a halt", (2) "to stop s.th." are in free variation.

Subphonemic variation:

r–ɽ: Intervocalic *r* may be realized as retroflex [ɽ], for instance in *be'riya* "be at a distance", "be innocent". According to Heine (1982), retroflex [ɽ] is the usual realization of *r* in Kenyan Nubi.

t–tʰ; d–dʰ; g–gʰ: Plosives, and especially *t, d,* and *g,* may be articulated with a slight aspiration when preceding non-round vowels as in *'tim* "be enough", *a'dan* "ear(s)", and *'gasi* "difficult".

k–q; t–th; d–dh: *q* may be used in Islamic expressions or by speakers who have some knowledge of Arabic, e.g. *da'qiqa* "minute" while *k* is normally used. Similarly, *th* [θ] and *dh* [ð] may be used in religious contexts or by educated Arabic speakers. *t* and *d* are the more usual equivalents, e.g. *ke'thir* next to *ke'tir* "many" and *'dhahab* next to *'dahab* "gold".

ḥ–kh–h: The same applies to *ḥ* and *kh* [x], which are the learned variants of *h*. However, they are seldom distributed consistently. For instance, a given speaker may use *'bahar, 'baḥar,* and *'bakhar* "sea", "lake" from EA/SA *baḥr* interchangeably.

2.1.2. *Vowels*

2.1.2.1. *Phonemes*

Nubi has five vowel phonemes. Vowel length is not distinctive:

	i		*u*	
	e		*o*	
		a		

Allophonic variants of the vowels are: *a* [a; aː; ɐ; ɐː; α; αː]

$\quad\quad\quad\quad\quad\quad\quad\quad\quad\quad\quad\quad\quad\quad\quad$ *e* [e; eː; ɛ; ɛː; æ; æː; ə; ɜ]

$\quad\quad\quad\quad\quad\quad\quad\quad\quad\quad\quad\quad\quad\quad\quad$ *i* [i; iː; ɜ]

$\quad\quad\quad\quad\quad\quad\quad\quad\quad\quad\quad\quad\quad\quad\quad$ *o* [o; oː; ɔ; ɔː]

$\quad\quad\quad\quad\quad\quad\quad\quad\quad\quad\quad\quad\quad\quad\quad$ *u* [u; uː; ɜ]

Vocalic quantity is not distinctive in Nubi, neither lexically nor grammatically. Heine and Owens, however, mention at least one minimal pair for Kenyan Nubi: *ʹbara* "outside(ADV)"—*ʹbaara* "the outside(N)" (Heine 1982, 25), *ʹsara* "herd cattle"—*ʹsaara* "bewitch" (Owens 1985a, 234). In Ugandan Nubi, this distinction is not made, neither for the above words nor for others.[4] There is, however, a general tendency for vowels to be realized as long in stressed syllables, while short vowels tend to occur in unstressed syllables, for instance in *ʹbasala* [ˈbɑˑsala] "onion(s)" and *biʹniya* [biˈniːja] "girl", "daughter" (see also 2.1.4).

a is usually realized as [a], e.g. in *ʹaju* [ˈaːdʒu] "want", or slightly higher, tending towards [æ] in the vicinity of *n*, e.g. in *ʹana* "I" [ˈaˑna] or [ˈæˑnæ]. After the bilabials [b], [p], [m], and [w], *a* is pronounced as [α], for instance in *baʹna* [bɑˈnaˑ] "girls", *ʹlipa* [ˈliˑpα] "pay", *ma* [mα] "with", *nuswaʹna* [nuswαˈnaˑ] "women", *masʹwal* [mαsˈwɑːl] "question".

The pronunciation of *e* depends much on the quality of the vowel in the source form. The following overview applies in general:

e is [ɛ] in some <u>unstressed</u> syllables, whether <u>open or closed</u>, for instance in *ʹmile* [ˈmiːlɛ] "salt",

$\quad$ *keʹbir* [kɛˈbiːr] "big", *ʹseregu* [ˈsɛˑrɛgu] "steal", *ʹlager* [ˈlaˑgɛr] "stone", *ferteʹku* [fɛrtɛˈku] "be split up";

$\quad$ in <u>prefinal stressed open</u> syllables <u>before non-closed vowels</u> as in in *ʹbele* [ˈbɛːlɛ]

---

[4] In Ugandan Nubi, no distinction is made between *ʹbara* "outside" and *ʹbara* "the outside". In Ugandan Nubi "bewitch" is *sa'ara*, *sa'hara* or *sa"ara*, consisting of three syllables of which the second is the vowel -*a*-. It is thus different from bisyllabic *ʹsara* "herd cattle". In UN, *ʹke* [ˈkɛ] SUBJ is, however, distinguished from *ʹke* [ˈkeˑ] "thread". However, both words are not only distinguished in vowel length but also in vowel quality. This is the only instance of an /e/—/ɛ/ opposition.

"country", *jere* ['dʒɛːrɛ] "run";
in <u>non-final stressed closed</u> syllables as in *debba* ['dɛbbɑ] "snake",
dengir
['dɛŋgir] "bend down", *ferteku* ['fɛrtɛku] "split up".

e is [e] in <u>prefinal stressed open</u> syllables <u>before closed vowels</u> as in
ebu ['eˑbu] "shame",

>   *geru* ['geːru] "change";
>   in <u>final stressed</u> syllables such as in *be* ['beˑ] "house", *gen* ['geˑn]
>   "stay", *gi'bel* [gi'beːl]
>   "before", and *ti'nen* [ti'neːn] "two". An exception is the determiner
>   *de* ['dɛˑ].

e may be realized as a schwa [ə] in some <u>unstressed</u> syllables as in
leben ['lɛbən] "milk",

>   *le'bis* [lə'biːs] "dress", *keregi* ['kɛˑrəgi] "drawn", *seke'-seke* ['sɛkə͵sɛkə]
>   "drizzle".

e may be articulated more backwards as [ɜ] when preceded by *w* as
in *we'ri* [wɜ'riˑ] "show"

or *we'le* [wɜ'lɛˑ] "boys".

i is usually realized as the high front vowel [i], e.g. *tim* ['tiˑm] "be
enough". In unstressed short syllables it may be centralized as [ə]
as in *bediri* ['bɛdəriˑ] "early".

o is [ɔ] in <u>unstressed syllables</u> as in. *abo'bo* [abɔ'boˑ] "mute", *son'du*
[sɔ'n'duˑ] "suitcase";

in <u>non-final stressed</u> syllables before non-close vowels or before *y*,
e.g. *okti* ['ɔkti]

>   "sister", *sokol* ['sɔkɔl] "thing", *fotom* ['fɔˑtɔm] "wean", *moyo* ['moˑjɔ] "water".

o is [o] in <u>non-final stressed</u> syllables <u>before close vowels</u> as in *doru*
['doːru]

>   "wander about";
>   in <u>final stressed</u> syllables, e.g. *tob* ['toˑp] "large scarf", *abo'bo*
>   [abɔ'boˑ] "mute".

u is mainly realized as a back closed vowel [u] as in *hum* ['huˑm]

"swim", *ʾkasulu* ['kaːsulu] "wash", *ʾitokum* ['iˑtɔkum] "you (PL)". In
<u>unstressed</u> syllables, *u* is sometimes realized as [ə] as in *ʾamsuku*
['aːmsəku] "take".

2.1.2.2. *Insertion of Glide or Glottal Onset between Vowels*

Two adjacent vowels can be separated by a glide or a glottal stop
(for an alternative solution see 2.2.1.2). The glide *w* is normally
inserted between *u* and *o/a*, e.g. *ʾjua* ['dʒuˈwɑ] "house", *ʾuo* ['uˈwɔ]
"he", "she", "it", and *tawuʾrati* "Torah", while *y* is used to separate
i from *o* and *a* as in *ʾbio* ['biˑjɔ] "buy", *biaʾshara* [biˑjaˈʃaːra] "business", and *aʾyin* "seeing". In learned variants, the glottal stop may
be inserted between two vowels of the same quality and is always
optional as in *ʾbaʾad* "after", *maʾaʾruf* "well-known", *taʾaʾlim* "tuition".
These lexical items are also realized as *ʾba-ad/ ʾbad, ma-aʾruf/ maʾruf,*
and *ta-aʾlim/ taʾlim* respectively, resulting from an evolution *aʾa >
a-a > a*. With verbs, the glottal onset may be inserted between the
vowel of the verbal markers *gi-* or *bi-* and the initial vowel of the
verb, e.g. *gi-ʾisabu* "be counting", *gi-ʾuza* or *gu-ʾuza* "be selling",
gi-ʾataku or *ga-ʾataku* "be laughing".[5] Also word-initial vowels may
optionally have a glottal onset as in *ʾʾina* "we".

2.1.2.3. *Vowel Opposition Pairs*

(3)	a–i	*ʾtam* "be nauseous"	—	*ʾtim* "be enough"
	a–e	*ʾlala* "saucepan"	—	*ʾlela* "night"
	a–o	*ʾbara* "outside"	—	*ʾbora* "cat"
	a–u	*ʾrada* "breastfeed"	—	*ʾrudu* "agree"
	e [e]–e [ɛ]	*ʾke* "thread"	—	*ʾkɛ* SUBJ (only instance)
	e–i	*ʾden* "debt"	—	*ʾdin* "religion"
	e–o	*ʾteri* "bird"	—	*ʾtoru* "wake up"
	e–u	*ʾseder* "tree"	—	*ʾsudur* "breast"
	i–o	*ʾfi* "there is", "there are"	—	*ʾfo* "up", "on top"
	i–u	*ʾbikra* "virgin"	—	*ʾbukra* "tomorrow"
	o–u	*ʾtobu* "large scarf"	—	*ʾtubu* "spit"

---

[5] If the glottal onset is not inserted, the vowel of the prefix is deleted in front
of a verb vowel, thus becoming, for instance, *ʾg(i)-ataku* "be laughing" (see also
2.2.1.1). The vowel of the prefix is not elided if preceding the verb *aʾyan* "be sick",
and verbs of Swahili origin like *ʾuza* "sell" and *ʾisabu* "count".

2.1.3. *Syllable Types*

There is a tendency towards a CV structure. However, syllables of
the following types may occur in Nubi:

V	*ju-a* "house", *ju-'a* "houses"
VC	*'am-suku* "grab", "take"
C	*m-'ze* "old man", *kele-'m* "it was said"
CV	*'ka-su-ru* "build"
CVC	*li-'fil* "elephant"
CVCC	*'bint* "girl"
CCVC	*'sten* "wait for"

The last two types of syllables are far less common than the others.
Disyllabic and trisyllabic words are more frequent than monosyllables. Words with more than three syllables occur infrequently. The
following Ugandan Nubi consonant clusters may occur within the
syllable:

(4)	bw	*'bwangiri* "cheek"		mp	in English loans, e.g. *'camp*
	kw	*'kweis* "good"		nt	*'bint* "girl"
	gw	*'gwam* "quick"		nk [ŋk]	in English loans, e.g. *'bank*
	sk	*'skul* "school"		kt	*'okt* "sister"
	st	*'stan* "thirsty"		rt	in English loans, e.g. *'court*
				[jt]	*'zeit* ['zɛ'jt] "cooking oil"
				[js]	*'kweis* ['kwɛːjs] "good"
				ms	*'sems* "sun"
				ns	*'gins* "type", "like"
				fs	*'nafs* "soul"
				[jl]	*'leil* ['leːjl] "night"
				wm]	*'youm* ['joːwm] "day"

All consonants may occur in the word-initial position. The consonants *t, d, k, g, ny, v, z, ch, j,* and *h* do not normally occur in word-
final position in Nubi. The only exceptions are the verb *'adaku* "brush"
which often appears without final vowel *-u* in the expression *'adak
su'nun* "brush teeth", *ta'rik* "date" in variation with *ta'riki*, the nouns
'bit and *'bint* both meaning "girl", *'lak* "hundred thousand", the adjective *je'did* "new" in variation with *je'didi*, and the preposition *'bada*
"after" in expressions like *'bad su'nu?* "what now?" and *'bad 'bukra*
"day after tomorrow".

2.1.4. *Stress, Pitch, and Tone*

Stress is confined to one of the last three syllables in the word.
Exceptions are the verbs *'agurusu* "pinch" and *'agilibu* "change", where
the stress falls on the first of a four-syllable word. As mentioned in
2.1.2.1, there is a relation between stress and vowel length in Nubi.
Vowels in stressed syllables are mainly articulated long, whereas vowels in unstressed syllables are generally short. Stress is also marked
by loudness and by high pitch.[6] Word stress in Nubi depends much
on the stress patterns in the source languages of the Nubi words. In
words derived from Swahili, the stress is placed on the penultimate
syllable as is the case in Swahili, e.g. *kari'bisha* "welcome". For words
taken from other languages, like Luganda, e.g. *ma'wulire* "newspa-
per" from *ama'wulire* "news" (Chesswas 1954, 39), the stress pattern
of the source language is maintained as well.[7] Only exceptionally
borrowings underwent a stress shift, e.g. English *'cholera* becomes
ko'lera in Nubi. The great majority of the vocabulary originally derives
from the Arabic lexifier language. Although the words may have
undergone phonemic changes, stress is usually retained. This can be
illustrated by Nubi *ge'ri* "near(by)" which is most likely derived from
SA *ga'rib*. For some words, variants with different stress patterns may
co-occur, without a change of meaning.

(5) *'masgit – mas'giti* "mosque"
    'madrasa – mad'rasa "Qur'anschool"
    'zaman – za'man "time", "old days"
    'mahal – ma'hal "place"
    'fitna – fi'tina "mischief"
    'dirisa – di'risa "window"
    'fahamu – fa'hamu "understand"

In a few cases, stress is lexically distinctive as in (6). The first seven
pairs contrast stressed words with function words without stress.

---

[6] Heine (1982, 27) considers high tone to be the decisive factor for Kenyan Nubi:
"In addition to the two tonemes there is a stress unit. It is, however, not marked
here since its occurrence is predictable: stress is placed on the first high tone of a
word. Thus there is only one stress unit per word." However, Heine himself, partly
questions his tonological approach.
[7] In Luganda, the stress falls on the first syllable of the stem (Ashton 1954).

(6) 'na   "there"   – na   "to", "for"
     'ja   "come"   – ja   "as", "like"
     'ta   "light"   – ta   "of (GEN)"
     'to   "of him", "his"   – to   "of (GEN)"
     'ma   NEG   – ma   "with (PREP)", "and (COM)"
     'kan   "be (ANT)"   – kan   "if"
     'le?   "why?"   – le   "to (PREP)"
     'saba "seven"   – sa'ba "tomorrow"[8]
     'kede EMPH   – ke'de SUBJ
     'zina "adornment", "decoration" – zi'na "adultery", "sin"

Stress is associated with grammatical meaning in some domains of grammar. Linked to vowel length and pitch, it distinguishes the predicatively used singular demonstrative from the one in attributive position: 'wede DEM (PRED) >< we'de DEM (ATTR) (see 3.3.1.2). In plural formation as well, stress is shifted to the final syllable, for instance in: 'jua "house (SING)" >< ju'a "house (PL)", 'bagara "cow (SING)" >< baga'ra "cow (PL)". Stress shift in verbs can be seen in table 8, where bold H/L indicate stressed syllables. The bare verb form usually has the stress on the first syllable, with the exception of verbs in (d), (e), and (f). To form a gerund, the stress is shifted to the penultimate syllable, while the passive has the stress on the last syllable. However, tonal contrasts are involved as well as in table 8, where H stands for high tone and L for low tone. Italics indicate stress:

Table 8. Stress and tone in verbs
(bare verb, gerund, infinitive, and passive)

	trisyllabic	disyllabic	monosyllabic
	(a) 'kasulu "wash"	(b) 'fata "open"	(c) 'so "do"
bare verb	*H* L L	*H* L	*L*
gerund	L *H* L	*H* L	*L*
infinitive	*H* H L	*H* H	*H*
passive	L L *H*	L *H*	*H*

---

[8] However, in the expression 'ita 'saba ke'fin? "How are you this morning?", the stress falls on the first syllable, unlike in sa'ba "morning" where the stress is placed on the final syllable.

Table 8. (*cont.*)

	trisyllabic	disyllabic	monosyllabic
	(d) *ni'situ* "forget"	(e) *we'di* "give"	
bare verb	L *H* L	L *H*	
gerund	L *H* L	L *H*	
infinitive	H *H* L	H *H*	
passive	L L *H*	L *H*	
	(f) *fata'ran* "be tired"		
bare verb	L L *H*		
gerund	L L *H*		
infinitive	H H *H*		
passive	L L *H*		

Note, first, that the stress of the passive verb form seems heavier than that of the other verb forms, so that a difference may be heard between the bare verb and the gerund and the passive, e.g., in *we'di* "give" (e) and *fata'ran* "be tired" (f). Second, when the passive verb is preceded by the progressive marker *gi-* or the future marker *bi-*, the pitch—but not the stress—on these markers is slightly higher than it would be on the active verb (see also Owens 1977, 197, n. 2 and 4.3.1) as in (7):

(7) A'dan   'tena   we'de,   'fogo 'ma   'bab
    ear(s)   PRON POSS 1PL   DEM PROX   in it NEG   door
    al   *gí-*   *ka'ti*   je   'de.
    REL   PROG-   cover-PASS   like   DEM PROX
    "This ear/these ears of ours, there is no door in it which can be closed like this."

Third, in monosyllabic verbs, pitch behaves independently of stress in marking verbal forms. The bare form and the gerund have low tone, but the passive and infinitive have high tone, e.g., *'so* "do": bare form and gerund: L; passive, infinitive: H. Moreover, the high tone of the passive is in fact higher than that of the infinitive. Fourth, although for verbs stress on the infinitive is generally in the same location as in the bare form, high tone appears before and after the stressed syllable in the infinitive but not in the bare form.[9]

---

[9] Tone in verbs is currently the subject of further research.

2.2. *Phonological Processes*

The application of the following rules varies from speaker to speaker. Even within one speaker's speech, considerable variation may occur. It seems, however, that speakers from the northern part of Uganda apply less variation, while variation is more acceptable in the southern variety of Nubi. I will discuss v elision first and go on to assimilation and some marginal phenomena, such as the addition of a final vowel, consonant deletion, and gemination/degemination.

2.2.1. *Vowel Elision*

2.2.1.1. *Vowel Elision before Consonants*

Vowels are sometimes elided in allegro forms after and before all types of consonants but most commonly between two consonants of the same place of articulation.

* Vowel elision within a word (syncope) generally occurs with unstressed vowels. These vowels are often the result of diachronic processes of vowel epenthesis conducted in order to obtain open syllables (see 7.2.1.2). The CV structure is retained in citation forms as in (8):

(8) *'gezima* ~ *'gezma* "shoe"
    'asurubu ~ *'asrubu* "drink"

In the following words, the stressed vowels seem to have been lost. This feature, however, assumes an intermediate stage in which the stress was shifted, thereby causing the formerly stressed vowel to become unstressed as in (9). Vowel elision is thus applied to an unstressed vowel. The intermediate stage is, however, often absent in present-day Nubi.

(9) *me'dida* > *'medda* (via *'medida**) "porridge"
    ka'bila > *'kabla* (via *'kabila*) "tribe", "type"
    'itokum > *'tokum* (via *i'tokum*) "you (PL)"
    gu-'rua > *'gurwa* (via *'gu- rua**) "be going"

* Nubi words tend to end in a vowel. In allegro forms, however, this vowel is often deleted (apocope). There are three exceptions: First, vowels following the consonants *k*, *g*, *d*, *t*, *ch*, *j*, *z*, *v*, *ny*, and *h*, which never occur in word-final position in Nubi, are always retained (see 2.1.3). Second, vowels in pre-pausal position tend to be retained as well, especially when the word would otherwise be monosyllabic as in (10). Round brackets indicate deleted vowels in the examples.

(10) ... a'nas 'kul(u) 'ralu   min   *tabu.* ... 'umon   *kulu.*
        people all   move-Ø from problem(s) PRON 3PL   all
     "... all the people move because of problems. ... they all."

Third, monosyllables are avoided, especially if the second consonant is *r*. In those cases, there is a tendency towards the presence of a final vowel. Consider (11):

(11) '(I)na   ka'las   *'geru*   'mara ta'lata.
     PRON 1PL COMPL   change-Ø times NUM
     "We had already changed three times."

Otherwise, as mentioned above, in allegro forms a vowel may be deleted, especially between homorganic consonants. As a result, the number of syllables in the word may be reduced. Deleted vowels are marked by round brackets as in (12):

(12) 'Umon   *'badul(u)*   le'bis   'tena.
     PRON 3PL   change-Ø   traditional dress   PRON POSS 1PL
     "They changed our traditional dress."

(13) 'Ya   *'uo*   *'asur-'asur(u)*   *nyere'ku'de.*
     CONJ   PRON 3SING   massage-REDUP-Ø   child DEF
     "Thus she massaged the child."

Word final *-u* tends to be absorbed by a following *w* as in (14) and (15):

(14) *f(u) 'wen? > f 'wen?*[10] "where?"

(15) Yo'wele 'de   *'kalas(u)*   wa'nasa   'to.
     boy   DEF finish-Ø converse-GER PRON POSS 3SING
     "The boy finished his conversation."

The above examples are tendencies rather than rules. It is thus possible that a word-final vowel is elided, even if the result is a monosyllabic word as in (16):

---

[10] The resulting *f-wen?* "where?" has come to be considered one word.

(16) . . .   ʿan(a)   ʿsebu   reʾport   fi   ʿheadquarter.
             PRON 1SING   leave-Ø   report   in   headquarter(s)
     ". . . I left the report in the headquarters."

Similarly, vowels between homorganic consonants are sometimes
retained as in (17):

(17) ajaʾma ʿtena   ʿnaʾde   ><   ʿwakti ʿten(a)   ʿnaʾde
     people PRON POSS 1PL   DEM DIS   time   PRON POSS 1PL   DEM DIS
     "those people of us"   "that time of us"

The second form (ʿten(a) ʿnaʾde) is the more common one. Notice also
that the vowel *i* of ʿwakti is not elided even if it stands between two
t's. It is also possible that a vowel in pre-pausal position is elided,
unlike the more general tendency of vowel retention in that position
as in (18):

(18) ʿAna   gi-   ʿdoru fi ʿbasi ʿin,   fi ʿsika   ʿin.   (>< ʿini)
     PRON 1SING PROG- travel in bus here in street(s)here
     "I was travelling in the bus here, in the streets here."[11]

Vowel elision in stressed syllables occurs frequently in allegro forms
of words, particularly of question words and of passive verbs whose
last consonant is *m, n, l, f,* or *b* (and seldom *s*) as in (19) and (20).
The following vowel, which has high pitch (since stressed), is dropped.
The consonant may be slightly lengthened. Anticipatory high pitch
is heard in the preceding vowel. Elision of stressed vowels occurs
also in pre-pausal position.

(19) *suʾn(u)?* > *suʾn?* "what?"
     keleʾm(u) ʿnana > *keleʾm ʿnana* "it was said to me"
     rasuʾl(u) > *rasuʾl* "be sent"

(20) *Gi-*   *rakaʾb(u)*   ʿneta   ʿakili.
     PROG-   cook-PASS   for + PRON 2SING   food
     "Food is being cooked for you."

*Deletion of word-initial vowels (aphaeresis) occurs mainly when the
final consonant of the preceding word and the consonant following
the vowel have the same articulation place. Nasal consonants are more

---

[11] The examples are taken out of their context, but I will still adhere to the con-
textual translations. Since one form may have more than one meaning in Nubi,
the English translation may differ from a morph-by-morph translation.

likely to trigger vowel elision than do other consonants. Elision of word-initial vowels may occur in sentence-initial position as well. In general, as a consequence of aphaeresis, the number of syllables in the word is reduced, and changes in the stress pattern may occur as in (21):

(21) *min ('i)na > min 'na* "from us"
      (a)m'bari > 'mbari "yesterday"
      (a)nka'buti > nka'buti "spider"

In a few instances, both the final vowel of the preceding syllable and the first vowel of the following syllable are elided. Again; this seems to occur most often when the consonants occurring before and after the omitted vowels are realized at the same articulation place, especially with nasal consonants. Accordingly, degemination of consonants, may, but does not necessarily, take place as in (22):

(22) *'umon 'lim(u) ('u)mon > 'umoñlim-'mon > 'umon 'li'mon* "they came together"
      je'n(u)~ina > je'n-'na > je'nna "we were shaved"

2.2.1.2. *Vowel Elision before Other Vowels*

In allegro forms, vowels, especially unstressed ones, are sometimes elided before other vowels (fusion, cf. Crystal 1992). In some vowel combinations, both vowels are absorbed and emerge as a new single vowel. This may occur across word boundaries, leading to new syllabic structures. As a result, the stress pattern may change.

Before *a* and *e*, the preceding vowel is elided. No vowel shift takes place as in (23):

(23) *'al(i) a'sasi* "which is beautiful"
      a'b(u) 'ena 'to "whose eyes"
      'ita gi- 'ataku 'ana > 'ita ˌg(i)- atak(u) 'ana "you (SING) are laughing at me"
      'uo 'aju 'ana > uw(o) ˌaj(u) 'ana "he likes me"[12]

Before *i* the vowels *i* and *u* are dropped as in (24):

(24) *'an(a) 'amsuk(u) 'ita* "I caught you"
      'ana we'r(i) 'ita "I showed you"

a, o, and *e* are fused with a following *i* and emerge as a new vowel *e* as in (25):

---

[12] See also Owens (1996, 125–72).

(25) *'n(a) ana 'ini > n(a) an(a) 'eni* "to me here"
    je 'ina > 'j(e) ena "like us"
    'ana li'go 'ita > 'ana li'g(o) 'eta "I met you"

There is considerable variation before *u. u* and *i* are dropped before
u as in (26):

(26) *fi 'ustu/ fu 'ustu > f(i) 'ustu / f(u) 'ustu* "in between"

o before *u* is retained. *u*, however, changes into the semi-vowel *w*
before a vowel as in (27):

(27) *'ragi 'so 'uo > 'ragi 'sowo* "a man did it"

No instances of *o* before *uC* were found. *a* and *e* are sometimes elided
before *u*, or they are fused to become the vowel *o* or the diphthong
ou as in (28):

(28) *ke'de 'uo > ke'd(e) owo / ke'd(e) uo* "so that he"
ja 'umon   > 'j(a) omon / 'j(a) oumon "like them"

In the few instances of word-initial *o* occurrence, no elision or fusion
of this kind seems to take place. In *fi'jo* "inside", a variant of *fi 'jua*,
the vowels *u* and *a* merge into *o*. The same applies to *'rua* "go", which
is often pronounced *'ro*. There is no real difference in the frequency
and quality of vowel elision and/or fusion between the north and the
south of Uganda. It is quite a common phenomenon in both areas.

2.2.2. *Assimilation*

Assimilation rules apply in rapid casual speech. The application of
some or all of the following phonological rules differs very much
from area to area and from speaker to speaker. They are, however,
especially common in Buganda territory (southern Uganda).

2.2.2.1. *Vowel Assimilation*

Usually, front vowels do not co-occur with back vowels morpheme
internally[13] (vowel harmony). The final vowel, however, is exempted

---

[13] The vowel *i* of verbal prefixes *gi-, bi-* often assimilates to *u* before verbs containing *u. gi-* and *bi-* are, however, acceptable forms as in *gi- 'sulu* "be taking", *bi-
'num* "will sleep", etc.

from this general tendency. The low vowel *a* may co-occur with both groups of vowels (see also Owens 1996, 125–72) as in (29):

(29) *anka'buti* "spider"
    'beredu "bath"

In contemporary Nubi, regressive vowel assimilation is a common phenomenon (see also Owens 1996, 125–72) and occurs more frequently in the speech of southern Ugandans and young speakers. A back vowel may cause a preceding vowel to become *o* or *u* as in (30):

(30) *'silu > 'sulu* "take"
    li'go > lo'go "receive"
    ja'nub > jo'nub "south"

On the other hand, *a* may change into a front vowel, influenced by a following front vowel.

(31) *man'dil > men'dil* "handkerchief"[14]
    'agif > 'egif "stop", "come to a halt"

In one instance , namely *bi'mara > bu'mara* "very much", *i* becomes *u* in the vicinity of labial consonants. Also the consonants *r* and *l* may affect an adjacent open vowel *a*, both stressed and unstressed, and cause its change into *e* as in (32):

(32) *tara'biya > tere'biya* "custom(s)"
    bia' shara > bia'shera "business"
    da'lil > de'lil "deprivation"

Vowel assimilation processes optionally take place across morpheme boundaries. Both forms (the assimilated and non-assimilated forms) may co-occur, even intrapersonally. Short unstressed *a* may change into *o* when preceding back vowels and/or in front of labial consonants as in (33):

(33) *ta 'Nubi > to 'Nubi* "of the Nubi"
    ma su'nu? > mo su'nu? "with what?"
    ma ma'isha > mo ma'isha "with the life"
    ita we'ri > 'ito we'ri "you showed"
    ma 'kweis > mo 'kweis "properly"

---

[14] One instance of progressive vowel assimilation is *ti'nin*, derived from *ti'nen* "two".

Short unstressed *a* may become *e* when preceding front vowels and/or the semi-vowel *y* as in (34):

(34) *ma 'gelba 'taki > me 'gelba 'taki* "with your heart"
       'ita bi-'geni > 'ite bi-'geni "you will stay"
       ma ya'la 'de > me ya'la 'de "with the children"
       ma yo'wele > me yo'wele "with the boy"
       ta 'youm ti'nen, ta'lata > te 'youm ti'nen, ta'lata "of two, three days"

Adjacent *l*, and less frequently *r*, may also provoke a shift of *a* into *e* as in (35):

(35) *'bila 'tabu > 'bile 'tabu* "without problem(s)"
       'ita lo'go > 'ite lo'go "you received"
       ma lu'far > me lu'far "with a rat"
       'ina 'rua > 'ine 'rua "we went"

Stressed *a* changes into *e*, mainly before a fronted high vowel as in (36).[15] This happens less frequently than with unstressed *a*.

(36) *'uo ja 'kelem > 'uo je 'kelem* "he happened to say"
       'uo 'ma 'endis > 'uo 'me 'endis "he does not have"
       'itokum ja 'ini > 'itokum je 'ini "you(PL) came here"

In the last two examples, the stressed vowel of the word is not contracted with the first vowel of the following word, as would be the case with unstressed vowels (see 2.2.1.2). A vowel shift from stressed *a* to *o* does occasionally occur, mainly before C + back vowel, or before *w* as in (37):

(37) *bi-ja 'kun > bi-jo 'kun* "will become"
       'ana ja 'rua jowzu > 'ana jo 'ro jowzu "I came to marry",
       'ina ja 'wasa > 'ina jo 'wasa "we left"

i is more likely to be affected by rules of vowel harmony in the speech of Nubi speakers from Bombo than that of speakers from the north, both from Arua and Gulu. Vowel harmony may affect stressed *i* as well. This, however, occurs less frequently. *i* optionally changes into *u* when preceding *u*, *o*, or the semi-vowel *w* as in (38):

---

[15] The form *je-ja*, the reduplicated form of *ja* "come", although frequently occurring, is rather exceptional, since *a* changes into *e* before *a*.

(38) *fi 'dul 'to > fu 'dul 'to* "in its shade"
    gi- lo'go > gu- lo'go "be finding"
    gi- 'weledu > gu- 'weledu "be giving birth"

The vowel of the preposition *fi* or the existential marker *ꞔi* often shifts to *u*. This happens especially in the vicinitiy of *f, b, w,* or *m* as in (39):

(39) *fi 'bele > fu 'bele* "in the country"
    fi we'ledu > fu we'ledu "at birth"
    ꞔi min 'umon dakta'ra > ꞔu min 'umon dakta'ra "among them, there are doctors"
    ꞔi a'nas > ꞔu a'nas "there are people"

In the last example, the change from *i* to *u* is probably due to influences of initial *f* itself. *u* preceding the palatal semi-vowel *y* may change into *i* (see also Heine 1982) as in (40):

(40) *su'nu 'ya > su'ni 'ya* "what is it that"
    katu'lu yo'wele 'de > kati'li yo'wele 'de "the boy was killed"

In other words, back vowels and/or labials may trigger the realization of *a* and *i* as *o* and *u* respectively, while *a* and *u* may become fronted when followed by a front vowel or the glide *y*. The alveolars *l* and *r* may trigger a change from *a* into *e*.

Unstressed *i* and *u* may be realized as a centralized vowel as in (41):

(41) *fi 'sokol* > [fə 'sɔkɔl] "in something"
    'amsuku > ['aː msəku] "grab", "catch"

Exceptionally, *u* or *i* are influenced by a following *a* and become *a* as in (42):

(42) *'ina na'di a'nas > 'ina na'da a'nas* "we called the people"
    gi- je'nu a'ku > gi-je'na a'ku "a brother is being shaved"[16]

---

[16] There are, however, instances that cannot be explained by the above-mentioned rules of regressive vowel assimilation. They were mainly recorded from speakers of southern Nubi. Among them are:
    'dula ma 'dula > 'dula me 'dula "side by side",
    'uo ꞔa 'kelem > 'uo ꞔo 'kelem "he came to tell"
    'ita gi-'tub > 'ito gi-'tub "you are spitting"
    ꞔi ti'nen > ꞔu ti'nen "there are two"

2.2.2.2. *Assimilation of Voice*

Devoicing: In Nubi, voiced consonants are generally devoiced in the pre-pausal position and before voiceless consonants, whether word internally or across word boundaries:

(43) [dʒ] > [tʃ]: *'haj* > ['hatʃ] "pilgrimage"
[b] > [p]: *kalabtu* > ['ka'laptu] "mix"
[d] > [t]: *'bada su'nu* > *'bad su'nu* > ['bɑ't su'nu] "and what else"
[z] > [s]: *'kazi 'tai* > *'kaz 'tai* > ['ka's 'tai] "my work"
[g] > [k]: *'fogo ka'lam* > *'fog ka'lam* > ['fo'k ka'laːm] "in it is a problem"

When the last consonant of the preceding syllable and the first consonant of the following syllable have become identical after devoicing, they may, but not necessarily, be degeminated (see also 2.2.3.3) as in (44):

(44) *'fogo ka'lam* > ['fo'k ka'laːm] > ['fo'ka'laːm] "in it is a problem"

Before voiceless consonants *l* is devoiced as in (45):

(45) *'bil ta ba'lala* > ['biːl̥ ta bɑ'la'la] "the wetting of the thread"

Voicing: Voiceless consonants may become voiced if followed by a voiced plosive:

(46) [f] > [v]: *'katif 'buku* > [ka'tiv 'bu'ku] "write a book"
[ʃ] > [ʒ]: *gu'rush 'de* > [gu'ru'ʒ 'dɛ] "the money"

2.2.2.3. *Assimilation of Place*

Assimilation of nasal consonants: Nubi nasal consonants tend to change place under the influence of the articulation place of the following consonant, whether word internally or across word boundaries as in (47):

(47) [m] > [n] before [n]: *kele'm 'neita* > [kɛlɛ'n 'ne'ta] "you were told"
[m],[n] > labiodental nasal [ɱ] before [f], [v]: *'memvu* ['mɛːɱvu] "small sweet banana"
[m],[n] > velar nasal [ŋ] before [k], [g]: *'mimkin* > ['miŋkin] "possible"
'jengis ['ɟɛŋgis] "like"
'umon gi-'ja > ['u'mɔŋ gi'ɟa'] "they are coming"

[m],[n] > [ŋ] before [j]: *itokum ʼya* > [ʼiˑtɔkuˌŋaˑ] "you (PL) are the ones who. . . ."

ʼ*umon ʼya* > [ʼuˑmɔˌŋaˑ] "they are the ones who . . ."

[m] followed by a vowel may be articulated as [n]: ʼ*itokum ʼain* > [ʼiˑtɔkun ʼajn] "you (PL) saw"

Palatalization: *k, d, h, and l* may be realized as *y* in the vicinity of front vowels. The transformation of *k* and *d* into *y* is quite widespread as in (48):

(48) *laʼkin* > *laʼyin* "but"
keʼd(e) ʼana > *keʼy- ana* "so that I"
kalʼti > *kayʼti* "maternal uncle"
ʼ*fahim* > ʼ*fayim* "understand"

2.2.3. *Other*

2.2.3.1. *Addition of a Final Vowel*

To avoid closed syllables, and particularly to avoid monosyllabic words, final vowel addition is used. It is quite common in the prepausal position but may also be found sentence internally. The alveolar *r*, in particular, seems to attract the addition of a vowel. If the word-final consonant is alveolar and/or the preceding vowel is a front vowel, then the attached vowel is *i* as in (49):

(49) *keʼbir* > *keʼbiri* "big"
aʼnas > *aʼnasi* "people"
ʼ*gen* > ʼ*geni* "stay", "remain"

However, if the word-final consonant is non-alveolar and/or the preceding vowel is a back vowel, then the added vowel is *u* as in (50):

(50) ʼ*num* > ʼ*numu* "sleep"
aʼjol > *aʼjolu* "person"
ʼ*Nasur* > *Nasuru* (NPROP)

Rarely, *a* is attached as in ʼ*nyakam* > ʼ*nyakama* "confiscate". Final vowel attachment occurs more often in the southern variety of Ugandan Nubi than in the north and in Kenya.

2.2.3.2. *Consonant Deletion*

Consonant elision does not occur frequently. It may, however, take place between two vowels, especially if they have the same tongue height. Accordingly, the two adjacent vowels may fuse and become one vowel as in (51):

(51) *la'kata* > *'lata* "(fire)wood"
     'bahati > *'bati* "luck"
     'itokum > *i'tom* (via *i'tokum)* "you(PL)"
     'mara 'wai > *ma'rai* "at once"

Glide loss from the coda may take place in allegro forms as in (52):

(52) *'youm* > *'yom* "day"
     'leil > *'lel* "night"
     ba'rau > *ba'ra* "alone"

When intervocalic *n* is elided, the preceding vowel tends to be nasalized as in (53):

(53) *'umon 'aju* > [ˈuˑmoˑʷ ˈaˑdʒu] "they want"

Also as a result of vowel elision, a preceding consonant may be dropped, causing the loss of one or more complete syllables as in (54):

(54) *'bat(na) 'taki* > *'bat- 'taki* "your belly"
     'gil(du) 'tai > *'gil- 'tai* "my body"
     'mar(ya) ba'ba > *'mar- ba'ba* > *mar'ba* "wife of father", "stepmother"

2.2.3.3. *Gemination/Degemination*

Geminates are not very common in Nubi. *'tenna* (an allomorphic variant of *'tena* "our"), *'Allah* "God", and *'yalla* "well", "OK" are the only instances I am aware of. However, consonants can become geminated after processes of vowel deletion (see 2.2.1.1) and/ or consonant assimilation (see 2.2.2.2). Word internally, geminated consonants are usually articulated by retaining the air slightly longer before releasing it as in (55):

(55) *'tenna* [ˈtɛnna] "of us", "ours"
     me'dida > *'medda* [ˈmɛdda] "porridge"

Geminated forms that have come into existence through vowel elision may be retained. The first consonant is usually articulated with a slight pause, contrary to word internal gemination where the consonant is lengthened. The syllable structure is thus retained. The doubled consonant, however, may be degeminated and often is in allegro forms as in (56):

(56) *'danab̃bagara* > ['danab'bɑgara] > ['dana'bɑgara] "a cow's tail"
      'ina 'gurw(a) 'wara > ['i·na ˌgu·rw'wɑ·ra] > ['i·na ˌgu·r'wɑ·ra] "we are going after . . ."

2.3. *Conclusion*

The above survey of the Nubi phoneme inventory will be compared with the sound systems of Arabic dialects, African languages, Juba Arabic, and Turku in the last chapter. As may be expected, the Nubi sound system resembles Juba Arabic and Turku but is reduced in comparison to Arabic in that it lacks, among other things, emphatic and pharyngeal sounds. Sounds, like *p* and *v* occur in loanwords from African languages. There is quite a bit of phonemic variation for both consonants and vowels. For consonants, the variation is partly due to phonological processes such as assimilation of voice and place, palatalization, and gemination/degemination. The origin of phonemic variation is to be traced partly to different source forms, such as *g* and *j*, or to substrate/adstrate influences, which is the case, for instance, for the variation between *z* and *j*, and *sh* and *s*, and which is therefore linked to regional varieties. These two types of consonant variation, however, pertain only to a limited range of phonemes. Vowel variation, on the other hand, occurs much more frequently in Nubi. The vocalic and consonantal contexts are mainly responsible for the variation. As such, unstressed vowels in particular are influenced and agree in certain features, thus creating allophonic variants.

Concerning stress, on the one hand, there may be some free variation, limited to a few words, that should be linked to variation of the stress patterns in the source forms (see chapter 7). On the other hand, stress, which usually co-occurs with vowel length and high pitch, is distinctive lexically for a few words only. Grammatically, stress is crucial in the formation of plural forms on *-'a*, for differentiating

between the singular proximal attributive and predicative demonstratives, and for distinguishing between the zero form of the verb,
the passive and the gerund. Tone is found to be relevant only in the
formation of the infinitive form, and the passive of monosyllabic verbs.

    Nubi speakers tend to talk at high speed, which causes allegro
forms to differ from lento forms to quite some extent. As such, the
general tendency towards a CV structure may be obscured. It is also
then that the phonological processes discussed above may result in
considerable variation, even within the sound system of one single
speaker.

CHAPTER THREE

THE NOUN PHRASE

Nubi distinguishes number but not gender. This applies to nouns, pronouns, demonstratives, and adjectives. Plural marking is compulsory only in the pronominal and demonstrative systems. The indefinite article *'wai*, the definite article *'de*, and zero-marked nouns complement each other in a rather complex system. The demonstratives may be used both anaphorically and deictically and may denote temporal and spatial deixis. Nubi expresses possession in an anlytic construction.

3.1. *Pronouns*

The Nubi prononominal system is composed of two numbers and three persons and no distinction is made for gender. The independent pronouns are listed in table 9. Possible variants are given between brackets.

Table 9. Independent personal pronouns in Nubi

Person	Singular	Plural
First	*'ana ('an)* "I"	*'ina*[a] "we"
Second	*'ita ('ta)* "you"	*'itokum ('itakum,*[b] *'tokum, 'tom)* "you (PL)"
Third	*'uo ('owo)* "he", "she", "it"	*'umon ('omon)* "they"

a. Occasionally, the first person plural pronoun is *'nina*. It is mainly used by older people.
b. The pronoun *'itakum*, which is the normal form in Kenyan Nubi, is probably the older one. Through regressive vowel assimilation *-a-* must have been evolved into the back vowel *-o-*. This has become the more common form in Ugandan Nubi.

The possessive pronouns and adjectives are given in table 10.

Table 10. Possessive pronouns and adjectives in Nubi

Person	Singular	Plural
First	*'tai / ta'yi* "my"; "mine"	*'tena* "our"; "ours"
Second	*'taki*[a] "your"; "yours"	*'takum / 'tokum* "your (PL)"; "yours (PL)"
Third	*'to* "his", "her","its"; "his", "hers"	*'toumon* "their"; "theirs"

a. I noted one instance of an expression of possession on *-ak*, namely *'dom-ak* "your blood".

Nubi does not have a set of pronominal suffixes (verbal, prepositional) but uses the independent pronoun. The vowel of the prepositions *na* "to", "towards", "for" and *ma* "with" is fused with the vowel of the pronoun (see also 2.2.1.2) as in table 11.

Table 11. The prepositions *na* "to" and *ma* "with" + following pronouns

na "to"	Singular		Plural	
	Lento forms	Allegro forms	Lento forms	Allegro forms
First	*na- 'ana* −	*'nana* "to me"	*na- 'ina* −	*'nena* "to us"
Second	*na- 'ita* −	*'neta*[a] "to you"	*na- 'itokum* −	*'netokum* "to you (PL)"
Third	*na- 'uo* −	*'nouo* "to him/her/it"	*na- 'umon* −	*'noumon* "to them"

ma "with"				
First	*ma- 'ana* −	*'mana* "with me"	*ma- 'ina* −	*'mena* "with us"
Second	*ma- 'ita* −	*'meta* "with you"	*ma- 'itokum* −	*'metokum* "with you (PL)"
Third	*ma- 'uo* −	*'mouo*[b] "with him/her/it"	*ma- 'umon* −	*'moumon*

a. Several speakers, mainly older Nubi, used *'neki* "to you", from *na-ki*, analogously to *ta-ki* "of you".
I also heard one instance of *'nei* "to me" (< *na- yi*, analogously to *ta-yi / tai* "of me", "mine"). Similar to *'neki*, there exists *'meki* "with you".

b. Inanimate nouns, whether singular or plural, are not necessarily referred to pronominally. In combination with the preposition *ma* "with", inanimate, and occasionally also animate, pronominal referents may become *'ma, 'mo* or *'me* "with it", "with them".

Personal pronouns can have the function of subject, object, indirect object, and prepositional object as in (57) and (58):

(57) Nyere'ku   ta   aw'lan,   'ana   'weledu   nyere'ku   yo'wele.
     child   GEN   first   PRON 1SING   bear-Ø   child   boy
     'Asma   'to   A.   'Ana   'weled(u)[1]   'uo
     name   PRON POSS 3SING   NPROP PRON 1SING   bear-Ø   PRON 3SING
     'wakt(i)   al(i)   'an(a)   'weled(u)   'uo,   'ana   'weled(u)
     time   REL   PRON 1SING   bear-Ø   PRON 3SING   PRON 1SING   bear-Ø
     'uo,   lo'go   'kan   'ana   'fi   'kweis.   'Kena[2]
     PRON 3SING   while   ANT   PRON 1SING   EXIS   fine   SUBJ + PRON 1PL
     'kelem: 'uo   li'go   'raha.   'Uo   li'go   'raha,
     say-Ø   PRON 3SING   receive-Ø   comfort   PRON 3SING   receive-Ø   comfort
     Ø   'g(i)-   asrub   'leben.   Gu'mas   al   'kweis   'kan   'fi   je'de,
     Ø   PROG- drink   milk   clothes   REL   good   ANT   EXIS   EMPH
     'ana   gi-   'bio   'nouo.
     PRON 1SING   PROG buy   for + PRON 3SING
     "The first child, I gave birth to a baby boy. His name is A. I bore him, the time
     that I bore him, I bore him when I was in good condition. Let us say that he
     found comfort. He found comfort, drank milk. Good clothes were here, I bought
     them for him."[3]

(58) 'Hasan   ka'las   'gen   'moumon   'youm to'wil.   'Umon   'kelem:
     NPROP COMPL   stay-Ø   with+PRON 3PL   day(s) long   PRON 3PL   say-Ø
     'Hasan,   'ita   'de   a'zol   'tena   ka'lasi.
     NPROP PRON2SING   DEF   person   PRON POSS 1PL   COMPL
     'Ina   bi-   'seb(u)   'ita   'maf.   'Be   'takum   'fwen?
     PRON1PL   FUT-   leave   PRON2SING   NEG   house   PRON POSS 2PL   Q-word
     'Uo   kelem: 'Be   'tena   'fi   'na,   fi   Bag'dad.
     PRON 3SING   say-Ø   house   PRON POSS 1PL   EXIS   there   in   NPROP
     "Hasan had already stayed many days with them. They said: "Hasan, you are already our
     person. We will not leave you. Where is your(PL) house?" He said: "Our house is there, in
     Bagdad."

Reflexive and reciprocal pronouns: There are no specific pronouns expressing reflexivity. Reflexive pronouns are the same as the personal pronouns and follow the verb as in (59):

---

[1] The high speed of the utterances results in the deletion of sounds, vowel assimilation and other phonological processes. I have tried to approach the spoken language as much as possible. This implies that the assimilated and not the basic sound is written. Deleted sounds are given between round brackets.

[2] The subjunctive marker 'ke may also be fused with the pronoun:
    'ke + 'ana — 'kana   'ke + 'ina — 'kena
    'ke + 'ita — 'keta   'ke + 'itokum — 'ketokum
    'ke + 'uo — 'kouo   'ke + 'umon — 'komon

[3] The examples are taken out of their context. Therefore, it is possible that information, especially on tense and aspect, that is indicated in the texts, is not found in the examples. In the translation, I will, however, adhere to the original situation, even if that involves discrepancies between the parsed and the English data.

(59) ʻIt(a)   ʻasas(u)   ʻita.
     PRON 2SING   make beautiful-Ø   PRON 2SING
     "You made yourself beautiful."

The reciprocal pronoun is *badu, ba'dum* "each other", optionally followed by the preposition *ma* "with" and personal pronoun. *ba'dum*
may also mean "together".[4]

(60) . . .   ʻumon   ʻaju   *badu*   ʻmena.
              PRON 3PL   like-Ø   RECIP   with + PRON 1PL
     ". . . they like us / we like each other."

(61) . . .   nyere'ka   ʻtena   ke'd(e)   ʻaruf   *ba'dum.*
              child-PL   PRON POSS 1PL   SUBJ   know-Ø RECIP
     ". . . our children should know each other."

Stressed devices: In Nubi, in addition to the usual pronominal system, there are stressed anaphoric devices that virtually always refer
to human beings.[5] The reflexive pronoun itself can add some emphasis. For instance, in (62), the speaker uses the reflexive pronoun to
stress that the girls wash 'themselves', whereas the more common
expression does not include a reflexive pronoun as in (63).

(62) ʻUmon   gi-   ʻbered(u)   *ʻumon*   a'sas, . . .
     PRON 3PL   PROG- wash   PRON 3PL   beautiful
     "They wash themselves [to become] beautiful, . . ."

(63) ʻUo   ʻro   ʻberedu.
     PRON 3SING   go-Ø   wash-Ø
     "He went to wash (himself).'

---

[4] The reciprocal marker *badu* or *ba'dum* "each other" is also used in sentences
like the following to emphasize the involvement of the agent on the patient:
     . . .   ʻumon   gi-   li'go   *badu*   *ma*   ʻyal   we'le . . .
             PRON 3PL   PROG-meet   RECIP   with   child-PL   boy-PL
     "They are meeting [with] the boys [together]."

     ʻIna   ʻseb   *badu*   ʻmouo.
     PRON 1PL   leave-Ø   RECIP   with + PRON 3SING
     "We left [with] her [each other]."
[5] Seldom, a non-human NP is modified by *bi'zatu*:
     ʻAse,   ʻsa   ʻde   *bi'zatu*   ʻkan   ʻuo   ʻrua.
     now   hour   DEM PROX   EMPH   ANT   PRON 3SING   go-Ø
     "Now, this very moment, he had gone."

Other stressed devices actually consist of the pronoun or noun phrase followed by a reflexive emphatic marker. This marker is either the possessive pronoun (64), *a'gi* + possessive pronoun (65), *bi'nafsi*[6] (66), *bi'zatu* (67), or *'sidu* (68), or a combination as in (69). They typically refer to highly pragmatic referential NPs.[7]

(64) La'kin *'ina* *'tena* ka'man 'arufu 'ma.
       but   PRON 1PL   PRON POSS 1PL   EMPH know-Ø NEG
       "But we ourselves do not know."

(65) 'Dukur a'nas ta ja'man 'de *a'gi 'toumon* 'kan ke'fin 'ya?
       then   people GEN old days DEF self PRON POSS 3PLbe-ANThow EMPH
       "Then, how were the people of the old days themselves?"

(66) 'Lad(i) 'ase'de, kan   'ana   *bi'nafsi* 'de, kan 'rua fi 'Arua,
       until   now   if   PRON 1SING self   DEF if   go-Ø to NPROP
       ana   'g(i)-   asma hu'ruma, ...
       PRON 1SING PROG- feel   sympathy
       "Until now, when I myself, when I go to Arua, I find sympathy, . . ."

(67) Ta   'ase'de 'ita   kan   'gu-   rwa 'hukum   nyere'ku ta
       GEN   now   PRON 2SING if   PROG- go   command-Ø child   GEN
       a'ku, a'ku   'de *bi'zatu* je'de gi-   'ja 'neta   'hari.
       relative relative DEF   self   EMPH PROG- come to + PRON 2SING hot/angry
       "For now, if you command the child of a relative, the relative himself will come angry to you."

(68) 'Ana   'tai   bi-   'jowz(u) 'uo,   sul'tan *'sidu*.
       PRON 1SING PRON POSS 1SING FUT- marry PRON 3SING sultan   self
       "I, myself, will marry him, the sultan himself."

---

[6] *Bi'nafsi* is also used in the following sense:
After two weeks,   ma'ma 'tai   te   *bi'nafsi* a'yan.
After two weeks   mother PRON POSS 1SING GEN   self   ill
"After two weeks, my own mother became ill."

[7] *A'gi* + PRON POSS in some contexts has the meaning of "alone". In those cases, high pragmatic referentiality is not a prerequisite for its use.
'Uo   gu-   'hukum, 'uo   *a'gi 'to*,
PRON 3SING PROG- reign   PRON 3SING   alone PRON POSS 3SING
'uo   ba'rau   ....
PRON 3SING alone
"He reigns alone, he alone . . ."

'Ana   'me   'endi ma'ma, 'ana   'me   'endi   ba'ba.
PRON 1SING NEG   have-Ø mother PRON 1SING NEG   have-Ø   father
'Bes,   'ana   *a'gi*   'tai   je'de.
just   PRON 1SING alone   PRON POSS 1SING   EMPH
"I do not have a mother, I do not have a father. I am just alone."

(69) 'Fatna   *bi'zatu*   *a'gi*   *'to*   'na, ...
     NPROP   self   self   PRON POSS 3SING   there
     "Fatna herself there . . ."

A'gi + PRON POSS, and *bi'nafs(i)* are restricted to people from the
north and old people. In general, the modifier immediately follows
the NP. Occasionally, however, another word or phrase may come
between the modifier and the NP as in (70):

(70) *'An*   'gu-   rwa   'rasul   *'tai*
     PRON 1SING   PROG-   go   reach   PRON POSS 1SING
     fi   'sana   ta   ar'bein.
     in   year   GEN   NUM
     "I myself am going to reach the year/age of forty."

Pragmatic use of personal pronouns: When expressing that a single
person joins another person or persons in an action, the agent is
optionally marked by a plural.[8] Thus the pronominal subject includes
the person who joins and the one who is joined. The latter is expressed
by means of the comitative marker *ma* "with" as in (71) and (72):

(71) Nyere'ku 'de   'kelem: Ma'ma *'ina*   'rua 'meki   'sawa.
     child   DEF   say-Ø mother PRON 1PL   go-Ø with + PRON 2SING   together
     "The child said: Mama, I go with you together."

(72) *'Umon*   'gai   ma   'marya   'to   'de.
     PRON 3PL   stay-Ø   with   wife   PRON POSS 3SING   DEF
     "He stayed with his wife."

Inanimate NPs are often not referred to by a pronoun when the
context is such that it is likely that the addressee will understand.
Although inanimates in particular are suppressed in object position
or after a preposition are suppressed, the same may happen to inanimates in subject position.

(73) 'Itokum   bi-   'sten   helicopter. Bi-   'tala   min   En'tebbe.
     PRON 2PL   FUT-   wait for   helicopter FUT-   leave   from   NPROP
     "You(PL) will be waiting for the helicopter. It (the helicopter) will leave from
     Entebbe."

---

[8] Singular expression of the agent in subject position is as well possible:
    . . . *'ana*   'gu-   rwa   'metokum   'sawa.
         PRON 1SING   PROG- go   with + PRON 2PL   together
    ". . . I am going with you (PL) together."

Occasionally, animate NPs are also not expressed overtly as in (74):

(74) 'Umon   'fi   fi   'sida,   gi-   'lim   ba'dum.
     PRON 3PL   EXIS   in   problem(s)   PROG-   gather   RECIP
     "They are in trouble, they are gathering (together)."

3.2. *Nouns*

3.2.1. *Number*

Form: There are many different ways to form plurals in Nubi:
  * stress shift: the stress is shifted towards the last syllable from whichever syllable it was on. As a consequence of the heavy stress, the pitch on the last syllable becomes high, as in (75): [9]

(75) *gi'dida* "chicken"—*gidi'da*
     si'adum "owner"—*sia'dum*
     (yo)'wele "boy"—*(yo)we'le*[10]
     'bele "country"—*be'le*

  * suppletion:

(76) *marya* "woman", "wife"—*nus'wan*
     a'ku "brother", "friend"—*ak'wana*
     nyere'ku "child"—*'yal/ya'la*
     a'jol "person"—*a'nas/aja'ma*[11]

  * ablaut:

(77) *ke'bir* "director"—*ku'bar*

  * suffixation: the word stress is shifted towards the suffix:

—*'(y)a:*

---

[9] Words like *kal'ti* "maternal uncle", *ji'di* "grandfather" already have the stress on the last syllable, and do not change to form a plural.

[10] The prefix *yo-* is probably derived from the Arabic vocative particle *'ya*, which combines with *'walad* "boy" as *'ya 'walad*, and through phonological changes has become *yo'wele*. In the singular, *yo'wele* is mainly used, while in the plural the most common form is *we'le*.

[11] *Aja'ma* is essentially a vocative form, used to address a group of people: *'ya aja'ma*. The use of *a'nas* is in this context incorrect: **'ya a'nas*.

(78) *ma'lim* "teacher"—*mali'ma*
      'Nubi NPROP—*Nubi'ya*
      lu'far "mouse"—*lufa'ra*
      'seder "tree"—*sede'ra*
      gala'moyo "goat"—*galamo'ya*

      —*'iya:*

(79) *'asker* "soldier"—*aske'riya*
      mo'bus "prisoner"—*mobu'siya*

      —*'in:*

(80) *'tajir* "rich person"—*taji'rin*
      'sokol "thing"—*soko'lin*

suffixation of -*'an*; the final vowel of the singular noun is replaced by the suffix:

(81) *'ter* "bird"—*te'ran*
      nyere'ku "child"—*nyere'kan*

      —*'na:* rather exceptional:

(82) *'sokol* "thing"—*sokol'na*

      —*'ka:* rather exceptional

(83) *nyere'ku* "child"—*nyereku'ka*[12]

      —*'u:* rather exceptional

(84) *'bab* "door"—*ba'bu*

* replacement of the Bantu prefix *m(u)-* by *wa-*:

(85) *mu'ze* "old man"—*wa'ze* < SWAH *m-zee*—*wa-zee* "old man"
      muzu'ku "grandchild" – *wazu'ku* < SWAH *m-jukuu*—*wa-jukuu* "grandchild"
      M'zungu "European"—*Wa'zungu* < SWAH *m-zungu*—*wa-zungu* "European"

* use of a second plural marker. These plural forms always co-occur with a more regularly formed plural as in (86):

---

[12] May also appear as *nyere'ka*. *Nyereku'ka* should be linked to JA *nyerkukât*, the regular plural on -*ât* of JA *nyer'kuk*.

(86) *'marya* "women", "wife"—*nus'wan / nuswa'na*
  ke'bir "director"—*ku'bar / kuba'rin / kubari'na*
  mu'ze "old man"—*wa'ze / wa'zeya / waze'ya*
  nyere'ku "child"—*'yal / ya'la*

Many words have more than one plural form as in (87):

(87) *nyere'ku* "child"—*nyereku'ka / nyere'ka / 'yal / ya'la*
  Is'lam "Muslim"—*Isla'ma / Isla'miya*
  a'jusi "old person"—*aju'sin / ajusi'ya*
  mas'kin "poor person"—*maski'nin / masa'kin*
  sa'bi "friend"—*sab(i)'yan / sabi'ya/ suhu'ban*

Occasionally, borrowings from English, Luganda, etc. follow the Nubi pattern of plural formation:

(88) *jerryca'na ta'lata*—"three jerrycans"
  'buku "book"—*bu'ka*

Use: Nubi does not obligatorily mark number in the noun itself. This implies that a plural form is not always used in daily speech even if it exists in Nubi. The question is, then, in which cases is plurality marked overtly in the noun and in which cases it is not. Nouns applying to more than one human being expressing gender, kinship, or other group relations usually use their plural forms. Nouns denoting human beings not in their relation to kin but as executors or performers of a task or job, often, but not obligatorily use a plural form when denoting multiplicity. Animate nouns are optionally marked for number in the noun. It appears, however, that there is a certain gradation. *'bagara, gala'moyo* and *gi'dida*, translated as "cow", "goat" and "chicken" respectively, are more likely to be marked than other animals, since these types of animals, especially cows, are commonly kept by Nubi people. The Nubi thus give grammatical expression to the special position of domestic animals. This is a cultural phenomenon that the Nubi share with their Nilotic neighbours (see Spagnolo 1933, Nebel 1948). Non-domestic animals and inanimates are infrequently marked for number in the noun. Exceptions are words associated with the house and housekeeping, e.g. *'jua* "house"—*ju'a* "houses", *'san* "dish"—*sa'na* "dishes", and the frequently occurring and widely distributed *ka'lam* "thing", "problem", "matter"—*kala'ma* and *'sokol* "thing"—*soko'lin / sokol'na*. No plural form exists for many inanimates, e.g. *'sana* "year(s)", while for others a plural may be given in quotation forms but is not or hardly ever used in free speech, e.g. *ka'bila* "tribe", whose plural is given in lexical lists as *kabi'la*, while in the text material it generally appears as *ka'bila* whether used for one or for more tribes. Thus, the lower the noun is situated on the list, the less likely it is to be marked overtly on the noun for plurality:

human beings: kin, tribe and/or gender terms
human beings in reference to their activities
domestic animals
non-domestic animals
inanimates, associated with the house and housekeeping/
ka'lam, 'sokol "thing"
other inanimates

Paraphrasing of plural/quantifiers: If plurality is not marked in the noun, it is inferred from the context (89), or expressed periphrastically by means of separate quantifiers, such as *mi'lan, 'zaidi, ke'tir* "many" (90), by means of numerals (91), and/or via the use of plural demonstratives (92):

(89) La'kini fi   Za'ire   'na, ...   'ita   'g(i)-   ain(u)
     but   in   NPROP   there   PRON 2SING PROG- see
     a'nas   gi-   'num   fu   *'jua*   'gesi.
     people   PROG-   sleep   in   house grass
     "But over there in Zaire, ... you saw the people sleeping in grass thatched huts."

(90) 'Ana   'feker   *ka'lam*   *ke'tir*   'maf   ....
     PRON 1SING   think-Ø   thing   many   EXIS NEG
     "I think there are not many things. ..."

(91) Abu'gada min   'jua   'moyo 'na   gu-   'weledu *ma'yai 'ladi si'tin*.
     turtle   PREP inside water there PROG- bear   egg(s) until NUM
     "The turtle over there in the water even bears sixty eggs."

(92) fi   *ma'hal*   'umon   *'dol'de*
     in   place(s)   PRON 3PL   DEM PROX PL
     "in these places"

Count nouns vs. mass nouns: Whereas count nouns refer to items that can be counted, mass nouns denote substances like water, air, wood, or groups of people, etc. In Nubi, mass nouns either take the form of a singular, e.g., *'chai* "tea", *Ingi'lis* "the English (PL)" or of a plural, e.g. *ma'tunda* "passion fruit", *'maua* "flora".

(93) ... uo   'sul   'nouo   *lese'ri, m'kate, 'samaga,....*
     PRON 3SING take-Ø for +PRON 3SING maize bread fish
     "... he takes for him maize, bread, fish, ..."

The different entities are expressed by means of a numeral (94), words like *kilo, litre*, the units of weight and volume respectively, followed by a numeral (95), or by plural marking on the noun (96):

(94) *mu'la   'saba*
     sauce   NUM
     "seven plates of sauce"

(95) ... nyere'ku   'tai   'gu-   rwa 'jowju   'bes 'ya
         child   PRON POSS 1SING PROG- go   marry-Ø only FOC
     ma *'lam,   'kilo   ti'nin!!?*
     with meat   kilo   NUM
     "... is my child going to get married with only two kilos of meat!!?"

(96) 'Ita   gi-   re'ceive *sama'ga.*
     PRON 2SING   PROG- receive fish-PL
     "You are receiving fishes."

Mass nouns take singular modifiers (see also Owens 1977) as in (97):

(97) *'moyo   was'kan*
     water   dirty-SING
     "dirty water"

The collective marker *'nas*: *'nas* conveys the idea of "and company", "and the like". It means that there is a group of people, animals, things, abstract notions, such as infinitives, among which the one expressed is salient, such as *'nas 'abba 'tena* "our grandmother and relatives". The marker *'nas* is mainly followed by a singular noun as in (98) and (99):

(98) *'nas   'ásrúbu   'de   'kul*
     COLL   drink-INF   DEF   all
     "all the drinking"

(99) 'Ita   'masa *'nas   'dikin.*
     PRON 2SING rub-Ø COLL oil

'It(a)   'adul   'nas   'su   'ras   'taki.
PRON 2SING prepare-Ø   COLL hair head PRON POSS 2SING
"You rub oil, you prepare your hair."

'Nas may also stress that the noun refers to a mass or a plural. In the latter case, the noun is often marked for plurality as in (100):

(100) 'nas godu'ru "pigs"
       'nas sede'ra "trees"
       'nas Kha'mis "group of people with the name Khamis"

Collective nouns marked by 'nas are considered grammatically to be plural as in (101) and (102).

(101) 'nas   'yembe   'dol'de
       COLL   mango(s)   DEM PROX PL
       "these mangos"

(102) 'nas   'akil   ta'nin   'dol'de
       COLL   food   other-PL   DEM PROX PL
       "these other foodstuffs"

Reduplication of nouns is not very common in Nubi. The meaning of reduplicated forms is different from that of single forms in several respects. Reduplication may convey that items are scattered, dispersed, should be situated on all sides, in all directions; that items are subjected to intensive activity; that there is a multiplicity of items; that there is a great variety of items; or that something is on the verge of becoming something else as in (103), (104), and (105):

(103) 'Moyo 'de, gi-   ge'r(u)   'uo,   gi-   'kun 'dom-'dom.
       water DEF PROG- change-PASS PRON 3SING PROG- be blood-REDUP
       "The water, it was changed, it became blood."

(104) repair-repair   'dol'de
       repair(s)-REDUPDEM PROX PL
       "these repairs"

(105) 'Ina   . . . 'tunda so'bun, 'tunda maran'gwa, 'tunda 'sim-'sim, 'tunda
       PRON 1PL   sell-Ø soap   sell-Ø bean-PL   sell-Ø sesame   sell-Ø
       'fulu,   'tunda soko'lin-soko'lin
       peanuts sell-Ø things-REDUP
       "We . . . sold soap, (we) sold beans, (we) sold sesame, (we) sold peanuts, (we) sold many different things."

3.2.2. *Gender*

Gender marking as such does not occur in Nubi, but persons and domestic animals have separate names for masculine and feminine.

(106) *bi'niya* "girl"—*yo'wele* "boy"
       'marya "woman"—*'ragi* "men"
       a'buba "grandmother"—*ji'di* "grandfather"
       'bagara "cow"—*'toru* "bull"
       gala'moyo "goat"—*'tesi* "he-goat"
       gi'dida "chicken"—*'di* "cock"

Feminine and masculine members of a pair may also be indicated by juxtaposing *'marya* or *bi'niya* and *'ragi* or *yo'wele* respectively as in (107):

(107) *nyere'ku bi'niya* "(baby) girl"—*nyere'ku yo'wele* "(baby) boy"
       a'ku bi'niya "sister"—*a'ku yo'wele* "brother"
       ko'ru 'marya "ewe"—*ko'ru 'ragi* "ram"

3.3. *Modifiers*

3.3.1. *Determiners*

3.3.1.1. *Articles*

In Nubi, we find the articles *'wai* and *'de*, which I will call the indefinite (INDEF) and the definite (DEF) article respectively. Apart from both articles, we find the bare form of the noun, which appears without any marker. I will look at the distribution of the articles and the bare form using Givón's (1984) and Bickerton's (1981) discussion of article use in creole languages as a starting point. Bickerton and Givón claim that the use of articles can be generalized to all creole languages. They postulate two articles, a definite and an indefinite one, which are in opposition to zero-marking, thus the bare noun. Bickerton thus proposes the following division, based on the oppositions: specific (SPEC) versus non-specific (NON-SPEC), and presupposed (PRESUPP) versus non-presupposed (NON-PRE-SUPP) as in table 12.

Table 12. Bickerton's three-way division of article use in creole languages

	PRESUPP	NON-PRESUPP
SPEC	Definite article	Indefinite article
NON-SPEC	Bare noun (Ø)	

Source: Bickerton 1981

'Specificity' refers to images of particular entities on particular occasions, and can be linked to 'percepts', whereas 'non-specificity' can be connected with 'concepts' or images of classes of entities. 'Presupposed' information is supposedly shared by both speaker and listener. For 'non-presupposed' information Bickerton also uses the term 'asserted' (Bickerton 1981). Specific referents are marked by the definite article if they are assumed to be known by the listener. On the other hand, if specific referents are mentioned for the first time in the conversation, and therefore were previously unknown to the hearer, they are marked by the indefinite article. All other NPs are not marked, neither with an article, nor with any other marker. To these belong generic NPs (NON-SPEC + NON-PRESUPP), ". . . NPs within the scope of negation -i.e. clearly nonspecific NPs- and cases where, while a specific referent may exist, the exact identity of that referent is either unknown to the speaker or irrelevant to the point at issue." (Bickerton 1981, 23). A problem with Bickerton's notion of specificity is that it is mostly impossible to establish whether a NP is SPEC or NON-SPEC by any other means than the presence or the absence of an article (see also Bruyn 1995b).

Like Bickerton, Givón (1984) considers a three-way division to be prototypical for the determining system in all creole languages. Givón's system corresponds to the one postulated by Bickerton, although Givón uses another terminology: referential (REF) versus non-referential (NON-REF), and definite (DEF) versus indefinite (INDEF). Givón distinguishes between referential, indefinite-referential, and non-referential.

Table 13. Givón's three-way division of article use in creole languages

	DEF	INDEF
REF	Definite article	Indefinite article
NON-REF	Bare noun (Ø)	

Source: Givón 1984

Definiteness according to Givón (1990, 899) pertains to NPs which are:

"(a) talked about in the preceding discourse; or
(b) assumed by the speaker as identifiable to the hearer."

Usually in the literature, 'referentiality' is used in the sense of 'semantic referentiality', in other words referring to a factive real world (related to past, present, and affirmative). Givón (1984) argues that it is rather 'pragmatic referentiality' that plays a determining role in the choice of article in a language. 'Pragmatic referentiality' refers to the communicative importance of nouns in discourse, which is usually reflected by frequent recurrence.[13] Considering pragmatic reference, Givón distinguishes between topic continuity, which touches upon pre-existing allusions to an already mentioned topic (REF DEF), and topic persistence, which is related to new information, presumably unknown to the hearer, that will be referred to in the subsequent discourse (REF INDEF). Pragmatically non-referential nouns, or, more specifically, nouns that will not receive any reference in subsequent discourse, appear in their bare form.

   Givón (1984) and Bickerton (1981) both claim that the pattern they present is valid for all creole languages. On the assumption that Nubi is a creole language, we may ask whether the pattern can be generalized to Ugandan Nubi as well. In table 14, the Nubi articles are arranged similar to Givón's pattern:

Table 14. Three-way division of article use in Nubi

	DEF	INDEF
REF	*de*	*wai*
NON-REF	Bare noun (Ø)	

---

[13] According to Givón 1984), semantically non-referential nouns in creoles and in many other languages, are only marked by an indefinite article, derived from the number 'one' (Nubi *wai*), when they are pragmatically referential. Semantically referential nouns which are communicatively unimportant, and do not receive subsequent reference in the discourse, could be called 'pragmatically non-referential'. These are left unmarked and are expressed as bare nouns.

'Dukur   'umon   'amsuku 'sika.
Thus   PRON 3PL   grab-Ø   road-Ø.
"Thus they took the road/left."

While at first sight the Nubi article system fits into the general pattern of Givón and Bickerton, a second, closer look reveals several differences, the most conspicuous being that the bare form can replace both the definite and indefinite article in various contexts. Givón defines his terminology in a more specific way, which leaves less chance for misunderstandings. Therefore, I will use the terms REF vs. NON-REF and DEF vs. INDEF.

3.3.1.1.1. The Indefinite Article 'wai

Form: In Nubi as in many creole and other languages, the indefinite article 'wai (INDEF) is derived from the numeral 'one', which in Nubi is the homophonous 'wai (see Givón 1984).[14] Its position in the NP is directly after the noun, before optional adjectives, the second part of a genitive construction, etc. as in (108) and (109):

(108) 'Wede   'baga   'fogur   'wai   ba'tal 'ya'de.
      DEM PROX   EMPH   shame   INDEF   bad   PRES PROX
      "This is quite a shame here."

(109) . . .   'kun   ka'lam   'wai   ta   'gudra.
                 be-Ø   problem   INDEF   GEN   strength
      ". . .   it is a tough problem."

Conversely, semantically non-referential NPs may be marked by the article 'wai on the condition that their referential identity is of importance in the subsequent discourse.

'Ma   gi-   si'bu   a'k(u)   'wai
NEG   PROG-   leave-PASS   friend   INDEF
ke'd(e)   uw(o)   'mutu   'uo   ba'rau.
SUBJ   PRON 3SING   die-Ø   PRON 3SING alone
"A brother was not left behind to die alone."

Givón (1984, 427) thus concludes that semantic non-referentiality is ". . . a special, more marked case of the more general feature of pragmatic non-referentiality".

[14] 'wai may also be used as a kind of emphasizer, underlining a noticeable characteristic of the noun, which is sometimes expressed by a following adjective. In the following example, the speaker wants to express that Zaire is not just an ordinary country, but that it is extremely strange. He draws attention to his statement by means of 'wai.

Fi Za'ire   'de,   'bele   'nade   'de   'bele   'wai   ma'tata.
in Zaire   DEF   country   DEM   DIS   country EMPH   strange
"Zaire, that country is one strange country."

'Ana   'gum,   'rusu   bi'niya 'de   'kof 'wai.
PRON 1SING get up-Ø   throw-Ø girl   DEF   slap EMPH
"I gave the girl one slap [not to be easily forgotten]."

Use: As mentioned above, the indefinite article *'wai* is typically used in creole languages to mark the indefinite referential NP. From Givón's discussion on semantic and pragmatic referentiality it follows that it is the pragmatic rather than the semantic referentiality, i.e. the thematic importance of the NP, that determines whether the NP is marked by the indefinite article. The above may be illustrated for Nubi with some examples of non-factive or irrealis contexts where the semantically non-referential NP that has high thematic value is marked by *'wai*.[15] In Bickerton's terminology this is called non-pre-supposed specificity, which deals with the introduction of thematically important topics that were presumably unknown to the addressee:

* in the scope of non-implicative verbs (see n. 15) as in (110) and (111):

(110) ...   'uw(o)   'aju   'so   'hafla   'wai   'sia. ...
              PRON 3SING   want-Ø   do-Ø   party   INDE   bit
        'Bas, 'uo   tayi'risha   'hafla   'de.
        Well, PRON 3SING   prepare-Ø   party   DEF
        "...he wanted to give a small party.... Well, he prepared the party."

(111) 'In(a)   'aju   'ketakum ...   'gusu   'nena
       PRON 1PL   want-Ø SUBJ+PRON 2PL   look for-Ø   for+PRON 1PL
       'madam 'wai   ke'de   'ro   'alim(u)   'ina.
       madam INDEF SUBJ   go-Ø   teach-Ø   PRON 1PL
       "We want you to look for a woman for us to (to go and) teach us."

* future tense:

(112) 'Kila ba'kan ... , kan 'ita   'b(i)-   ajira   'fogo   'akil,
       every place   if   PRON 2SING FUT-   plant   on (it) food-Ø
       'fi   'youm 'wai   al   'akil   'wede'de   bi-   'raba, ...
       EXIS day INDEF REL food   DEM PROX   FUT-   grow
       "Everywhere ..., if you will plant food (seeds) on it, there will be a day when this food will grow, ..."

---

[15] Non-factive or irrealis contexts include: the scope of negation, the scope of non-implicative verbs, such as the non-implicative modality verbs 'look for', 'want', 'dream', 'imagine', and the non-implicative manipulation verbs 'tell (to do something)', 'make', 'force (to do something)', the scope of non-factive verbs such as 'think', imperative and interrogative speech acts, future or habitual tense, the scope of modal operators, both verbs, such as 'can', 'may', 'must', 'should', 'might', 'would' and adverbs, such as 'maybe', 'possibly', 'surely', 'likely', and 'supposedly', and the scope of conditional clauses with 'like' (Bruyn 1995b, Givón 1984).

(113) 'Bes   ba'ba   'wai   'b(i)- ain
       well   father   INDEF FUT- see
       nyere'ku 'to   'tim   ka'las, 'aju   'marya.
       child   PRON POSS 3SING be enough-Ø COMPL want-Ø wife
       "A father will see that his child is old enough already, (that he) wants a wife."

* in the scope of conditional clauses:

(114) 'Ase, a'jol   'wai   kan 'ja   'na, 'uo   bi-   'kelem 'gal: . . .
       now person INDEF if   come-Ø there PRON 3SING FUT- say   that
       "Now, if someone comes there, he will say that: . . ."

Once the thematically important topic has been introduced, its recurrence is expressed by the definite article 'de, with anaphoric expression, incorporated in a verb or preposition, with an adverb, in an
adverbial clause, etc. as in (115):

(115) 'Youm ju'ma'wai, mas'kin   'wai   'ro   'ja.
       Friday INDEF poor man   INDEF go-Ø   come-Ø
       Kan mas'kin   'de 'ja . . . 'bas, 'uo   'rasul fi 'be.
       if   poor man DEF come-Ø well   PRON 3SING arrive-Ø at house
       "On a Friday, a poor man came. When the poor man came . . . well, he
       arrived at the house."

In the above example, the NP, which is both semantically and pragmatically referential, is initially introduced by the use of 'wai. Then,
the 'poor' man is referred to by means of an NP marked by the
definite article 'de, and subsequently by means of the anaphoric pronoun 'uo (3SING). In (116), the 'nursery school', at its first mention,
is marked by the indefinite article. In the next two sentences, it is
incorporated in the passive verb and subsequently in the preposition
'fogo and repeated by the adverb 'na "there":

(116) 'Dukuru,   'wakati 'na'de 'kan   'fi   nursery school 'wai   'fi,
       then time   DEM DIS   ANT EXIS nursery school INDEF EXIS
       abi'n(u)   'jamb 'ina   'na   je'de.
       build-PASS-Ø beside PRON 1PL   there EMPH
       'Yo   'uo   'gu- rwa 'fogo 'na.
       CONJ PRON 3SING PROG- go   in (it) there
       "Then at that time there was a nursery school here, it was built next to us
       there. Thus he was going there."

In general, the indefinite article fits nicely into the patterns introduced by Givón and Bickerton. However, it is not exceptional to
find pragmatically referential NPs without an article as in (117). This
will be discussed below (3.3.1.1.3).

(117) I'tom   'wonus   'fogo   a'jol
      PRON 2PL   talk-Ø   about   person
      lo'go   'owo   'fi   'jamb   'itokum   'in.
      while   PRON 3SING EXIS   beside   PRON 2PL   here
      "You(PL) talk about someone while he is here beside you(PL)."

3.3.1.1.2. The Definite Article 'de

The article 'de is the definite marker for singular and plural definite nouns. The definite article predominantly takes the final position in the noun phrase. It closes the entire NP and is not necessarily found in close position to the noun it marks. Which noun is marked should, therefore, be inferred from the context.

* marking the first part of a genitive construction:

(118) 'Kan   'ina   'wuza gu'niya 'gwanda 'tena   'de.
      ANT PRON 1PL sell-Ø bag(s) cassava PRON POSS 1PL DEF
      "We sold our cassava-bags."

* marking the second part in a genitive construction:

(119) ku'ra   ta   'ragi   'de
      leg(s)   GEN   man   DEF
      "the legs of the man"

* marking the head noun of a relative clause:

(120) A'nas   al(i)   gi-   'rakab 'de,   gi-   'rakab 'saki.
      people REL   PROG-   cook   DEF   PROG-   cook   for free
      "The people who are cooking, are cooking for free."

Theoretically, when an NP is or has become part of culturally shared knowledge (belonging to the permanent file or to absolute deictic availability) or of textually shared knowledge, the speaker may assume that the NP is known to the hearer and thus may code the NP as definite. However, trom the texts it appears that NPs conveying information common to both speaker and hearer, whether culturally based or emerging from the previous discourse, are often not marked by the definite article. Therefore, it is essential to explain the notion of 'definiteness' and the environments in which the definite article is supposed to appear. To the permanent file belong proper names and referentially unique physical or cultural entities, such as 'the sun', 'the earth', etc. which are uniquely identifiable to all members of all human cultures. Similarly, geographic and other entities may be recognizable to all members of a limited group, such as 'the sea' is the North Sea to all Belgian and Dutch people. A referent that belongs to the permanent file is culturally shared by all members of a group. A speaker addressing a member of the group may assume that the addressee can allocate unique identity to the referent and consequently can assign definiteness to it, even if the referent has not been mentioned in previous discourse as in (121):

(121) 'Besi, ka'lam   *'dunia 'de*   'endisi a'bidu   'to
    well   because world DEF have-Ø begin-GER PRON POSS 3SING
    ma   ka'las   'to.
    with   finish-GER   PRON POSS 3SING
    "Well, because the world has its beginning and its end."

Similarly, the participants in the communication 'I' and 'you' and entities that can be uniquely associated with them, such as 'my head', are assumed to be identifiable by both, which is what Givón (1984, 400) calls 'absolute deictic availability'. The addressee in (122) understands that the speaker is talking about his wives and not about someone else's.

(122) 'K(e)   ana   'gata   'agil   na *nus'wan 'de.*
    SUBJ   PRON 1SING cut-Ø intelligence for wife-PL DEF
    "Let me deceive (my)/the wives."

We have already seen that one of the characteristics of pragmatic salience is frequent recurrence in discourse. A pragmatic referential NP at its initial introduction is often marked by the indefinite article. In subsequent discourse, it can be referred to by means of an anaphoric pronoun, incorporated in a verb or preposition, with and adverb, in an adverbial clause, etc., or marked by the definite article. Thus, once a referent has been introduced in discourse, it can be assumed that the hearer can identify the referent, which is the prerequisite for marking by the definite article.

(123) Fi   za'man, 'fi   *'ragi 'wai* 'kan   'tajiri 'sei'sei 'de. *'Ragi 'de*
    in   old time EXIS man   INDEF be-ANT   rich   very   EMPH man DEF
    'tajir, 'tajir, 'tajir ta   'fo   'zaidi. 'Bas, 'youm 'wai,
    rich   rich   rich   GEN highness very much well day   INDEF
    'uo   'ja   lo'go bi'niya wai   ka'man a'sas.
    PRON 3 SING come-Ø meet-Ø girl   INDEF EMPH beautiful.
    "Once upon a time, there was a man who was very, very rich. The man was rich, rich, rich to a very high degree. Well, one day, he met a very beautiful girl."

Moreover, referents that are closely associated with NPs already mentioned in the discourse, such as 'part of wholes', kinship relations, body parts, etc., are supposed to be common knowledge. Relying on the permanent file and previous discourse, a hearer is assumed to be able to understand and recognize the information as uttered by the speaker. Therefore, the referent may be coded with the definite article.

(124) 'Uo   'jo   'weledu*nyere'ka   'to   'de   ta'lata.
      PRON 3SING come-Ø bear-Ø child-PL PRON POSS 3SING DEF NUM
      "She bore her three children."

However, it seems that elements belonging to culturally and textually shared knowledge, as discussed above, do not obligatorily require an overt use of the definite marker in Nubi. Rather, it seems that definite marking is sometimes regarded as unnecessary or superfluous precisely because of the high thematic centrality of the element in question, which may be inferred from the pragmatic salience (frequent recurrence) of the element, the permanent file it belongs to, or the relationship between the element and another referent, which is uniquely identifiable as in (125) and (126):

(125) 'Wakti, 'kil(a) a'jol   gu-   'doru ma   *'gelba 'to*   fi 'ida.
      time   every person PROG- walk with heart PRON POSS 3SING in arm
      "At [that] time, everybody was walking around with his heart under his arm/ everybody was very scared."

(126) 'Uw(o)   'awun(u) 'ita   min   'hari ta   'shems.
      PRON 3SING help-Ø   PRON 2SING from   heat GEN   sun
      "He helped you to avoid the heat of the sun."

In (127), *bi'niya 'de* is marked by the definite article, since it is pragmatically referential, ('the girl' is actually one of the main actors in the narrative), but she is suddenly referred to with the bare form *bi'niya*. 'The girl' as a definite and referential participant has been confirmed several times, so the speaker assumes that by now the hearer should be able to identify 'this specific girl', even without any overt marking. Consider also (128):

(127) 'Bas, 'uo   'jowzu *bi'niya* 'de. Ba'kan 'uo   'jowzu *bi'niya 'de*
      well   PRON 3SING marry-Ø girl   DEF   when   PRON 3SING marry-Ø girl   DEF
      'y(a) ow(o)   'so   'jowzu   ke'bir 'zaidi.
      FOC   PRON3SING do-Ø   wedding-Ø   big   very
      Gedi'm(u)   *bi'niya* fi   'be.
      escort-PASS-Ø   girl-Ø   in   house
      "Well, he married the girl. When he married the girl, he organized a very big wedding. The girl was   escorted to [their] house."

(128) Ya'la   'dol'de   'amsuku   'sika. . . .   *Nyere'ku*   *ta*   *aw'lan* . . .
      children DEM PROX PL   take-Ø   road(s)   child   GEN   first
      Wu   *nyere'ku*   *ta*   *ti'nin*, ka'lam 'umon   'aju . . . nyere'ku sa'kar
      and   child-Ø   GEN   second because PRON 3PL want-Ø child   small
      'na'de   'ma.   'Kila   'youm   *gata 'leben*,
      DEM DIS   NEG   every   day   youngest child
      "These children took [their] way/ left . . . . The first child. . . . And the second
      child, because they did not like that small child. Every day, the youngest child, . . ."

In previous discourse, the 'three children' were mentioned several
times. No definite article appears either with the first child or with
the second, the relationship of the children being clear since from
the previous discourse. In the Nubi community, the 'youngest' or
'last-born' child is referred to as *gata 'leben* "cutter of the milk", since
it was the last one to drink its mother's breast milk, and, after wean-
ing, may be said to cut off its mother's milk. It seems that, since
the reference is common knowledge among the Nubi, the absence
of the definite article with *gata 'leben* is intelligible. (129) is similar
to (128). The children have been discussed, as well as their father.
When 'the old man' is introduced, the association father-old man is
comprehensible. There is no need for *mu'ze* to be marked by the
definite article.

(129) 'Bas,   *mu'ze*   'kelem: 'Ase'de, ya'la   'tai . . .
      well   old man   say-Ø   now   children PRON POSS 1SING
      "Well, the old man said: 'Now, my children . . .'."

Traditionally, Nubi and Africans in general own a plot where they
cultivate some fruit and vegetables. It can thus be inferred that the
bare form *'samba* "field" is comprehensible to all the participants in
the conversation. A marker would only give redundant information
as in (130). The same applies to *'be* 'house', 'home', which seldom
occurs with a marker as in (131):

(130) . . ., 'ina   'ja   'amrugu   'gwanda 'tena   fi   *'samba*.
            PRON 1PL   come-Ø   remove-Ø   cassava PRON POSS 1PL from   field
      ". . ., we took away our cassava from the field."

(131) 'Marya 'de . . . bi-   gen   'moumon   fi   *'be*   'in.
      wife   DEF   FUT-   stay   with + PRON 3PL in   house   here
      "My wife will stay with them here at home."

Proper names, whether names of persons, tribes, places, etc., belong
to the permanent file since unique reference can be assigned to them.
They may occur without any marking as in (132):

(132) 'Ya   *Nubi*   gi-   'kelem 'gal: . . .
      CONJ   NPROP   PROG- say   that
      "Thus the Nubi say that: . . ."

Two contradictory devices determining the use of the article *'de* have
emerged in Nubi. In the first one, definite and referential NPs are
marked by the definite article, whereas non-referential NPs appear
in their bare form. This corresponds to the general trend in creole
languages as claimed by Givón (1984) and Bickerton (1981). In the
second device, however, it is possible for definite, referential NPs to
appear without any overt marking, precisely because of their thematic centrality.[16]

3.3.1.1.3. Bare Nouns

As we have seen in the introduction, Givón (1984) proposed a three-
way division between DEF NPs, INDEF REF NPs, and NON-REF
NPs, which are marked by the definite article, the indefinite article,
and a bare noun respectively. From Givón's considerations and from
our analysis of the indefinite article, it can be inferred that pragmatic referentiality is a scaled phenomenon and that referential and
non-referential should not be viewed as two opposing poles but rather
as elements on a continuum. Therefore, the group of non-referential NPs includes those NPs that the speaker judges as having no or
little thematic importance as in (133) and (134):

(133) 'Fara   'de,   'mana   'to   je   *'hafla   ke'bir.*
      feast   DEF   meaning   PRON POSS 3SING like   party   big
      "The feast, its meaning is that it is like a big party."

---

[16] In a limited number of instances, the definite article occurs in contexts (a)
where a bare noun would be expected since new non-recurrent information is introduced or (b) where the indefinite article would be more appropriate since new recurrent information is given. Both 'chicken' and 'sesame' are commonly used ingredients
for meals in general and for special meals, such as festivities, in particular. Therefore,
it is possible that both items should be regarded as belonging to the culturally
shared knowledge of the Nubi, or even the group of East Africans, which explains
the use of the definite article.
(a) Gi-   raka'bu   *gi'dida*   'de,   . . .
    PROG-   cook-PASS   chicken(s)   DEF
    "The chickens are prepared."
(b) *'Sim-'sim*   *'de*   b(i)-   a'j(u)   aguru's(u)   'uw.
    Sesame   DEF   FUT- need-PASS   nibble-PASS   PRON 3SING
    "The sesame will be needed to be nibbled."

(134) 'Kila a'zol   ke'd(e) 'amsuku *'sika.*
    every person SUBJ take-Ø   road
    "Let everybody take the road/ leave."

According to Mufwene (1981, 221–38, 1986c, 33–60) (see also Bruyn 1995b), the distinction individuation vs. non-individuation may play a role in the article use. The notion of individuation or non-individuation corresponds to the distinction count vs. mass. Non-individuation should be regarded as a lexical feature, but individuation is related to the use of a noun in a certain context and not to the noun itself. Therefore, individuation should not be perceived as a clearly distinguished feature, but should be seen on a scale going from INDIV SING to INDIV PL to NON INDIV. Languages then vary with respect to the morpho-syntactic marking of the different steps of the scale (see Bruyn 1995b). Only individuated NPs take articles and plural marking as in (135):

(135) 'Ya 'jó   wele'du   ya'la   'de 'in, . . .
    CONJ come-PASS-Ø bear-PASS-Ø child-PL DEF here
    "Thus the children were born here, ..."

Non-individuated NPs do not as in (136), (137), and (138):

(136) 'An(a)   'arij(a) 'abidu 'kidima ta tu'jar ta 'túndá tolo'bun,
    PRON 1SING return-Ø begin-Ø work GEN salesman GEN sell-INF (red) millet
    'túndá ga'ya, 'túndá 'sim-'sim, . . .
    sell-INF millet sell-INF sesame
    "I began again the work of salesman of selling (red) millet, selling millet, selling sesame, . . ."

(137 *Lo'bu*   'g(i)-   afuku.
    wind   PROG- blow
    "(The) wind is blowing."

(138) 'Umon   . . . gi-   'jib *'sela* *'toumon.*
    PRON 3PL   PROG- bring goods PRON POSS 3PL
    'Umon   kan 'jib *'sela,* 'yala   . . . .
    PRON 3PL   if   bring-Ø goods well
    'Sela   *'de* gi-   ji'bu   ka'man mo lun'gara.
    goods   DEF PROG- bring-PASS   also with drum(s)
    "They . . . are bringing their goods. If they bring goods, well. . . . The goods are brought as well with drum-beating."

In (138), in the first sentence, the goods to be brought in for the dowry by the bridegroom's family are introduced as 'their goods'. In the second sentence, a remark about 'goods' in general at 'wed-

dings' in general is expressed. 'Sela is plural and refers to a type
rather than to a specific entity and thus appears without any
definite/indefinite marking. In the third sentence, the NP is marked
by the definite article 'de, which may be explained by its reference
to the 'goods' brought in by the family thus a specific entity. It is
thus possible that Nubi pragmatically referential NPs occur without
the indefinite article when the NP scores high on the scale of non-
individuation as in (139) and (140):

(139) 'Fi   'mali   a'li   'tai.
      EXIS   wealth   REL   PRON POSS 1SING
      "There is wealth which is mine."

(140) Fi Za'ire   'na   'kan   'kidima al   'ino   gu-   'so, . . .
      in NPROP   there   ANT   work   REL   PRON 1PL   PROG-   do
      'ino   gu-   'tunda fu   'su.
      PRON 1PL   PROG- sell   in   market
      "In Zaire there, the work which we were doing, was . . ., we were
      selling on the market."

Let us now look again at (117). This sentence is taken from an explanation of a Nubi proverb, in which a'jol "person" does not especially
refer to an individual. The speaker could just as well have used a'nas
"people". Because of the general aspect of the explanation of a proverb,
which actually deals with a fictive situation, the sense of non-individuation
may have prevailed over the aspect of pragmatic referentiality.

Above it is noted that, in certain contexts such as non-individuated ones, the bare form may occur instead of the indefinite article
'wai (see (117), (139), and (140)). Just as the bare form can replace
the indefinite article, it can take the place of the definite article. The
bare form may also occur in contexts where at first sight, according
to the definitions of referentiality and definiteness, we would expect
the NP to be marked by the definite article. We have seen above
that definiteness stands for common knowledge, or at least presumably common knowledge, for both speaker and hearer by its previous occurrence in the conversation, by its deictic availability to the
elements in the conversation, or by its belonging to the permanent
file. If the speaker assumes that the item he wishes to mention in
discourse is known to the hearer because of one of these reasons,
he may use the definite article. It seems, however, that some mutual
information is regarded as basic to such an extent so that no marking
is required as in (141):

(141) 'Ró   cha'p(a)   ana   la'saya fi   ka'liya.
      go-PASS-Ø   beat-PASS-Ø   PRON 1SING   stick   on   buttocks.
      "I was beaten with a stick on the (my) buttocks."

Thus, the use of the bare noun in Nubi differs somewhat from the
uses claimed by Bickerton (1981) and Givón (1984), who argue that
the bare noun in creole languages is marked by a zero article, which
is opposed to the definite and indefinite articles. Bruyn (1995b), however, contends that the bare noun in Sranan should not be understood as a unified category marking non-referentiality, non-specificity
or non-individuation but rather as neutral with respect to these
notions. She derives this neutrality from the failure of bare forms in
Sranan to appear not only in cases where zero-marking is expected
to occur but also in contexts where the appearance of the indefinite
or definite article is anticipated. Bruyn infers this from the fact that
neither the indefinite article *wan* in Sranan, derived from the English
numeral 'one', nor the definite article *da*, which derives from the
Sranan demonstrative *dati*, in turn derived from the English demonstrative 'that', have already been established entirely as determiners.
Rather, these developments are not yet completed, according to
Bruyn, which may account for their variable usage in Sranan. Since
the bare noun in Nubi can be used as an alternative for both the
indefinite and the definite article, Bruyn's theory on the neutrality
of the bare noun in Sranan may be generalized to Nubi as well.

3.3.1.2. *Demonstratives*
The variable usage of bare forms and indefinite and definite articles
in Nubi shows that the Nubi article system has not yet become fixed.
There are two points here that are relevant to the discussion on
demonstratives. First, *'de* has not yet been established fully as a definite
article since it may be replaced by the bare noun. Second, *'de* functions also as a demonstrative, although infrequently. It is very likely
that the definite article *'de* developed diachronically from a demonstrative (see also 7.4.3.1). However, although *'de*'s main function gradually shifts from demonstrative to definite article, its deictic meaning,
denoting proximity, has not disappeared completely, as is illustrated
in (142):[17]

---

[17] Owens (1977) mentions both *'de* and *'uwede* as proximal demonstratives in
Kenyan Nubi. He adds that *'de* is sometimes also used for plural.

(142) 'Ter   'de   kan   'b(i)-   arija   'ja   'gai
      bird   DEF   if   FUT-   return   come-Ø   sit-Ø
      fi   'ras   ta   nyere'ku   'de,   . . .
      in   head   GEN   child   DEM PROX
      "If the bird will come back and sit on the head of this child, ..."

Since 'de has gradually lost its deictic value while taking on the function of definite article, alternative demonstratives have become necessary in Nubi. A new demonstrative system thus emerges.

Form: The core element of the Nubi demonstrative is 'de. The plural is marked by 'dol. The distal aspect is marked by the addition of the adverb 'na "there". Only the singular proximal demonstrative makes a division between attributive or predicative use (see table 15):

Table 15. Demonstratives in Nubi

	PROX	DIS
SING	('u)we'de (ATTR)/(u)'wede (PRED)	'na'de
PL	'dol'de	'na'de, 'na 'dol'de

The singular proximal demonstrative is the pair 'uwe'de (for attributive demonstratives) and u'wede (for stand-alone constituents), or it is 'de for both:

(143) 'An(a)   'alim   ru'tan   'de   ma   'álim.
      PRON 1SING   learn-Ø   language   DEM PROX   with   learn-INF
      "I learned this language with learning."
(144) 'De   'ya   ka'lam   . . .
      DEM PROX   FOC   matter
      "This is the matter . . ."

'Uwe'de and u'wede are composed of the third person pronoun 'uo followed by 'de. 'Uo 'de is interpreted as one form and has undergone minor phonological changes (fronting of the back vowel /o/) to become realized as 'uwe'de.

(145) 'rag(i) 'uwe'de "this man"
      ba'kan 'uwe'de "this place"

The independent demonstrative has undergone a shift of stress to the penultimate syllable to become *u'wede*, as in (146):[18]

(146) *U'wede*   'ya   'ase'de   'taki.
      DEM PROX   FOC   now   PRON POSS 2SING
      "This is now yours."

In allegro forms, the first vowel *u-* tends to be dropped. Consequently, the attributive and the independent demonstrative are realized as *we'de* and *'wede* respectively.[19]

(147) ka'lam *we'de* "this problem"

(148) *'Wede*   'ya   'dabara?
      DEM PROX   FOC   wound
      "Is this a wound?"

The plural proximal demonstrative is *'dol'de*. *'Dol* is the marker of plurality, while *'de* has deictic value.

(149) *'dol'de*   a'nas   al   'endi   'ilim
      DEM PROX PL   people   REL   have-Ø   knowledge
      "these are people who have knowledge"

(150) ya'la   ti'nin   *'dol'de*
      children   NUM   DEM PROX PL
      "these two children"

The distal demonstrative consists of the deictic adverb *'na* "there" + *'de*. The plural form *'na 'dol'de*, containing the marker for plurality *'dol*, does not occur frequently, although several Nubi informants said that it is the correct plural form. Most commonly, *'na'de* stands for both the singular and plural distal demonstrative.

---

[18] In two instances uttered by the same speaker, *u'wede* occurred attributively: *mistake u'wede* "this mistake" and *min 'youm u'wede* "from this day".

[19] Occasionally, *we'de* is used in the southern variety of Ugandan Nubi as a stand-alone constituent. It hardly ever occurs in the North.
    'K(e)   'an   'amrugu   'fogo   *we'de*
    SUBJ   PRON 1SING   remove-Ø   from it   DEM PROX
    "Let me remove this from it."
On the other hand, *'wede* occurs as an attributive demonstrative in a very limited number of instances in the northern part of the country.
    min   'youm   *'wede*
    PREP   day   DEM PROX
    "from this day"

(151) *'Na'de*   'mutu   'bedir   'de .
      DEM DIS   die-Ø   early   EMPH
      "That one died early."

(152) Wu *'yal*   *'toumon*   *'na'de*   'kul 'dom ta   Su'dan.
      and child-PLPRON POSS 3PL DEM DIS PL all blood GEN NPROP
      "And those children of them are all Sudanese blood/have all Sudanese
      blood."

(153) 'bele   ta   'Arab   wa'din   *'na 'dol'de*
      country(ies)   GEN   Arabic   others   DEM DIS PL
      "those other Arabic countries"

The particle *'de*, which has the same form as the demonstrative and
the definite article *'de*, is optionally attached to the demonstrative
pronoun, to convey a certain emphasis. I will call it an emphasizer
(EMPH). With singular proximal demonstratives, it is added to the
reduced form *we'de/ 'wede*. Both the attributive and the independent
demonstratives become realized as *(u)'wede'de*. This implies that the
syllable preceding the penultimate syllable and the last syllable of
the attributive demonstrative receive the stress at the expense of the
first and the penultimate syllables. The emphasizer *'de* may also be
joined to the plural proximal demonstrative and the distal demonstrative as in (154), (155), and (156):

(154) bi'niya *'wede'de* "this girl"
      ma'hal *u'wede'de* "this place"
      soko'lin *'dolde'de* "these things"
      ak'wana *'nade'de* "those friends"

(155) 'Ino   'ke   'jowju   'nouo   *'wede'de.*
      PRON 1PL   SUBJ   marry   to + PRON 3SING DEM PROX
      "Let us marry this (girl) to him."

(156) *'Nade'de*   'raha.
      DEM DIS   peace
      "That is peace."

The addition of emphasizing *'de* occurs more frequently in the northern variety of Ugandan Nubi than in the southern variety. The insertion of the emphasizer *'de* is optional, but often its occurrence increases
as the demonstrative recurs more often in a sentence or group of
sentences as in (157):

(157) ... 'itokum   'b(i)-   arija   'kun   mo   fu'rai   al   kan
          PRON 2PL   FUT-   return   be-Ø   with   happiness   REL   if
      ji'b(u)   akili   ma   la'siya   'de   'mara 'wai
      bring-PASS-Ø   food   for   afternoon DEM PROX   at once
      ma   fi 'lel   'wede'de.
      for night   DEM PROX
      ... a'nas   'gu-   rwa   fi   'amsuk(u)   'akili
          people   PROG- go   in   take-GER   food
      ma   fi 'lel   we'de   min   ji'yan.
      for night   DEM PROX from   hunger
      "You (PL) will again be happy if food is brought for this afternoon, [and]
      at once for tonight. ... people are going to take food for tonight from hunger."

A personal pronoun is optionally added to demonstratives: 'uo for
singular demonstratives, and 'umon for plural ones. The personal pronoun is used for both animate and inanimate NPs. The singular
form occurs infrequently.

(158) Wu   'asker   'uo we'de,   'uo   'ya   ....
      and   guard   DEM PROX   PRON 3SING   FOC
      "And this guard, he was the one who ...."

(159) ba'kan 'uo 'na'de   "that place"

Northern Nubi speakers always attach the plural personal pronoun
to the proximal demonstrative 'dol'de, but only a few tokens of 'umon
'dol'de were recorded in the southern variety. On the other hand, 'uo
'na'de and 'umon 'na'de are hardly ever used by speakers of the northern variety. However, they occur among the utterances of speakers
from Bombo and Entebbe, among whom several resided for some
time in South Sudan and in Kenya. It would be interesting to find
out whether these forms are current in the two areas mentioned.

   Finally, the notion of proximity, whether in time (160) or place (161),
may be emphasized by means of the adverb 'in "here". This occurs
far more frequently in the northern part of Uganda than in the south.

(160) 'Kila 'youm min   'bedir   'na'de, ... soko'lin 'dol'de   'fi,
      every day   from previous times DEM DIS things DEM PROX PL EXIS
      la'kin yeu'min'de   do'lin'de   'maf.
      but   nowadays   DEM PROX PL EXIS NEG
      "In those previous times, these things were always there, but nowadays these/
      they are not."

(161) ... a'nas   al   gi-   sponsor kala'ma   'tena
           people   REL   PROG-   sponsor thing-PL   PRON POSS 1PL
      ma 'nas   activities   'tena   *do'lin'de,*
      and COLL   activities   PRON POSS 1PL   DEM PROX PL
      wa'din   'fi   fi   Sau'dia, wa'din   'fi   fi   'Qatar, ...
      other-PL   EXIS   in   NPROP   other-PL EXIS   in   NPROP
      "... the people who sponsor our things and these activities of ours, some
      are in Saudi Arabia, others are in Qatar, ..."

Use: The demonstrative pronouns may occur both attributively or as stand-alone constituents. The demonstrative attributive adjective stands postnominally and generally closes the noun phrase. Several demonstratives or a definite article and a demonstrative may co-occur in one NP.

(162) ya'la   lu'far *'dol'de*   du'ga,   du'ga,   du'ga   *'dol'de*
      children mice   DEM PROX PL   small-PL small-PL small-PL DEM PROXPL
      "these small, small, small baby mice"

(163) Gi-   rasu'lu   ma   ma'ma   *'de*   *'na'de.*
      PROG-   arrive-PASS   with   mother   DEF   DEM DIS
      "They arrived with that mother."

All Nubi demonstratives can be used both deictically and anaphorically.[20] Demonstratives may express spatial and temporal deixis. Both types of deixis refer to the position of the speaker in his/her spatio-temporal context. The speaker points (with a gesture of his hand or any other body part) at a referent, whether a time referent or a referent that is locally immediately available.

(164) 'Bambara 'toumon   'de fi 'sikil   'bambara *we'de.*
      stool   PRON POSS 3PL DEF in manner stool DEM PROX
      "Their stool is like this stool."

(165) 'In(a)   'agder 'gusu   nyere'ku
      PRON 1PL can-Ø look for-Ø child
      te   ji'ran   'tena   al   'fi   min 'fo *'na'de.*
      GEN   neighbour PRON POSS 1PL REL EXIS from up DEM DIS
      "We can look for the child of that neighbour of ours who is from up (there)."

The attributive demonstrative plural *'umon 'dol'de* emphasizes the plurality of the noun, whether animate or inanimate. Note that inanimate

---

[20] Demonstrative adverbs and sentential particles should be excluded from this generalization.

nouns in Nubi usually get zero-reference, which gives a rather exceptional status to NPs like those in (166) and (167):

(166) fi   kala'ma   je   *'umon 'dol'de*
      in   thing-PL   like   DEM PROX PL
      "in things like these"

(167) ma'hal   *'umon 'dol'de*
      place(s)   DEM   PROX   PL
      "these places"

(168) . . . ke'd(e)   *umon 'na'de*   'liju   'motoka   'de
         SUBJ   DEM DIS PL   push-Ø   car(s)   DEF
      ". . . let those/them push the cars."

'Umon 'dol'de occurs nowhere in the subject position. Instead, the noun phrase in question is topicalized while it is referred to in the main clause by a personal pronoun or with zero anaphora as in (169):

(169) A'nas   *'umon 'dol'de,*   'umon   li'go   govern'menti 'tan.
      people   DEM PROX PL   PRON 3PL   find-Ø   government   other
      "These people, they found another government."

Semantics: Demonstrative pronouns, whether adjectives or stand-alone elements, can be used anaphorically, which means that they are applied to keep the hearer's attention focused on a previously mentioned item, unlike the deictic application of demonstratives by which means the speaker attempts to re-orient the hearer's attention towards a new referent. However, the meaning of demonstratives used as anaphoric pronouns approaches closely the meaning of the definite article. Conversely, *'de*, although its basic use in present-day Nubi is that of the definite article, may still occur with demonstrative meaning. The definite article marks NPs belonging to the deictically available context, culturally shared knowledge, and the preceding discourse (see 3.3.1.1.2). Both the anaphorically used demonstratives and the definite articles refer to items that are pragmatically salient in discourse. Anaphoric demonstratives, however, diverge from definite articles in that they can only refer to items that were focused on in previous discourse, while definite articles can also be used with newly introduced referents that are known to both speaker and hearer because they belong to a common culture or to the common speech situation (see also Croft 1990). Moreover, anaphoric demonstratives emphasize the pragmatic importance of the referent for the subsequent discourse, unlike the article which marks less important items (see also Givón 1990). In (170), the pragmatic salience of *ǰua/'be* "house" is gradually advanced. The indefinite article *'wai* represents the new information, which is confirmed by means of the definite article *'de*. Subsequently, the demonstrative *'na'de* stresses its increasing importance in the ongoing discourse.

(170) 'It(a)   'ain   du'kan gi-   'tala fi   'ras 'ǰua 'wai, ...
        PRON 2SING see-Ø smoke PROG- leave in   head house INDEF
        'It(a)   'ain   du'kan gi-   'tala fi   'rasu 'ǰua 'de. ...
        PRON 2SING see-Ø smoke PROG- leave in   head house DEF
        'Ita   'gal: " 'ma!" Ke'd(e) 'uo   'rua fi   'be *'na'de.*
        PRON 2SING say-Ø no   SUBJ   PRON 3SING go-Ø in   house DEM DIS
        "You see smoke coming out of the roof of a house, ... You see smoke coming out of the roof of the house. . . . You say: "No!". He should go to that/the house."

The anaphoric demonstrative thus strongly retains the focus on a previously mentioned item. This implies that the deictic context of the anaphoric demonstrative is found in the text itself. The spatial and/or temporal characteristics of the referent are emphasized in relation to the spatio-temporal framework of the text by means of the demonstrative. The deictic and anaphoric demonstrative should, therefore, not be opposed to each other. The values of the Nubi anaphoric demonstrative should be seen on a gliding scale, from high to low deictic value (see also Ehlich 1982). For the latter, the deictic value has almost entirely been neutralized, which, however, does not diminish the referential function of the anaphoric demonstrative. In these cases, the meaning of the Nubi demonstrative approaches the meaning of the Nubi definite article, and can be translated as such.

(171) ... 'ita   'ya   gi-   'ja   ma   la'kata bu'kuru,
               PRON 2SING FOC   PROG- come with wood incense
        'ita   'ya   gi-   'gata 'na, 'yala, 'lata du'kan *we'de.*
        PRON 2SING FOC PROG- cut   there well wood smoke DEM PROX
        'Ya   'lata du'kan 'de   gi-   'faga-fa'ga   'na, ...
        CONJ   wood smoke DEF   PROG- split-REDUP-PASS there
        ". . . it is you who is coming with aromatic wood, it is you who is cutting it there, well, the/this aromatic wood. Thus the aromatic wood is cut into small splinters there, ..."

(172) Wu   ta   ti'nen 'de   ka'man   fu   'ras   ta   ke'ni
      and   GEN   NUM   DEF   also   in   head   GEN   co-wife
      ma   nyere'ka   ta   'ragi   'to.
      with   child-PL   GEN   husband PRON POSS 3SING
      Ka'man 'ragi   'nade'de,   . . .
      also   husband DEM DIS
      "And the second [story] is also on a co-wife and the children of her husband.
      Also the husband, ..."

Not only the distal demonstrative but also the proximal demonstrative is used in this sense. This contradicts the assumption of Harris
(1980: 78) that it is the remote member within a demonstrative system that serves as the unmarked form and thus as the marker for
definiteness.[21] In present-day Nubi, it seems that both the distal and
proximal demonstratives may be stripped of their deictic value and
function as definite articles.

(173) 'Sente gi-   ku'bu   ba'kan 'de   'te   te   ben'dera.
      money PROG-throw-PASS place DEM PROX   under GEN   flag
      'Mirsidi   'ya   gi-   'sulu 'sente we'de.   'Uo   gi-   'sul
      spiritual guide FOC PROG- take money DEM PROX   PRON 3SING PROG- take
      'to.   'Uo   gu-   'kutu fi   'jeba.
      PRON POSS 3 SING PRON 3SING PROG-put   in   pocket
      "Money is thrown here under the flag. It is the spiritual guide who takes the/this
      money. He takes his [share].   He puts it in [his] pocket."

The Nubi demonstrative system also does not support Harris's (1980)
claim that the remote demonstrative, the anaphoric pronoun, the
third person pronoun; and the definite article are linked to one
another since both the Nubi proximal and distal demonstratives can
be used as pronouns.[22]

(174) Fi   'ja   'toumon,   'umon   'ja
      in   come-GER   PRON POSS 3PL   PRON 3PL   come-Ø
      ma   'nas   'Salim 'Bey- 'wede   'ya   'kan   ke'bir 'toumon   . . . .
      with   COLL Salim Bey DEM PROX   FOC   ANT   leader PRON POSS 3PL
      "In their coming, they came with Salim Bey and his men—he was their leader. . . ."

---

[21] See also Givón (1984) who comes to the same conclusion through a different
reasoning. In his theory, it is the deictic meaning of the demonstratives that leads
to the relation between the proximal and distal demonstratives and the indefinite
and definite articles respectively.
[22] A special use of the proximal and distal demonstratives as pronouns is their
use as 'the one' and 'the other'.

Nubi may thus use the proximal demonstrative as a device to bring the speech situation and the text closer to each other with respect to time or place. The speaker in a sense cuts the narrated event out of its original spatio-temporal context and, by means of the proximal demonstrative, brings it right in front of the hearer so that the event described becomes more vivid for the latter. Frequently, the use of the proximal demonstrative in this sense goes together with the use of the progressive marker *gi-*, which denotes duration, habit or repetition as in (175):

(175) 'Ase, 'Nubi 'namba ti'nin, ba'kan 'umon   gi-   'ja,   'fi   a'nas   al
      now Nubi number NUM   when PRON 3PL   PROG- come EXIS people REL
      'umon   gi-   lo'go, 'umon   gu-   'sul   je   la'bi
      PRON 3PL PROG- find   PRON 3PL   PROG-take   like   servant-PL
      'toumon.   ...   'Ya   'umon   'ja   mo   a'nas 'umon 'dol'de.
      PRON POSS 3PL CONJ PRON 3PL   come-Ø with   people DEM PROX PL
      "Now, the Nubi of the second type, when they came, there were people whom they found, they took them as their servants. . . . . Thus they came with these people."

3.3.1.3. *Non-referring 'any'*

'Any' is expressed with *'ayi/ 'aya, 'sambala* or more commonly with Swahili *yo'yote*, e.g. *'aya 'zaman* "any time", *ru'jal 'sambala* "any men", *'sa yo'yote'* "any time". Note that *'aya* precedes the noun, while *'sambala* and *yo'yote* follow it.

3.3.2. *Adjectives and Adjective Phrases*

Adjectives specify some property of the head noun of the phrase. Adjectives may have a predicating or a modifying function when part of the noun phrase. Many are also used adverbially as in (176):

(176) 'Ina   gi-   'ish   'moumon   'kweis.
      PRON 1PL PROG- live   with + PRON 3PL   good-ADV
      Ka'man 'umon   'aju   'badu 'mena   ma 'namna 'kweis
      also   PRON 3PL like-Ø RECIP with + PRON 1PL with way good-ADJ
      "We are living well with them. Also we like each other in a good way."

A'nas   'g(i)-   akulu   'diet   to   ba'rau-ba'rau.   *Wede*   'jibu
people   PROG-eat diet   GEN   difference-REDUP   DEM PROX bring-Ø
ko'rofo. *Na'de*   'jibu   maran'ga.   *Na'de*   'jibu   su'nu?
leave(s) DEM DIS   bring bean(s)   DEM DIS bring-Ø   what?
"The people were eating different diets. This one brought leaves. That one/ the other one brought beans.
What did that one/the other one bring?"

All Nubi adjectives can appear as nouns as in (177):

(177) mo 'kweis "with goodness"

3.3.2.1. *Gender and Number*
Form: Nubi adjectives are not marked for gender, but they may be
marked for number in the following ways:

* suppletion:

(178) sa'kar "small"—du'ga/ duga'ga

* ablaut:

(179) ke'bir "big"—ku'bar
      to'wil "long"—tu'wal

* addition of a suffix. The word stress is shifted towards the suffix:

—'in:

(180) a'sas "beautiful"—asa'sin
      je'did "new"—jedi'din

—'ya:

(181) a'jusi "old"—ajusi'ya

—'iya:

(182) fi'lan "certain"—fila'niya

* with a combination of two of the above-mentioned ways:

(183) ke'bir "big"—kuba'rin
      sa'kar "small"—duga'gin

Some adjectives may be marked for plurality in more than one way
as in (184):

(184) sa'kar "small—saka'rin/ du'ga/ duga'ga/ duga'gin
      mis'kin "poor"—miski'nin/ masa'kin

Other adjectives, such as 'muru "bitter", 'aswe "black", have no overt
plural form.

   Use: Adjectives optionally receive plural marking, whether in predicate or modifying position. Adjectives expressing properties of

human beings/animates are more frequently marked for number than others.

(185) a'nas   al   awi'rin
      people   REL   stupid-PL
      "people who are stupid"

(186) 'Ina,   ka'lam   'kan   du'ga . . . .
      PRON 1PL   because   be-ANT   small-PL
      "We, because we were small, ..."

(187) 'sin   'to   kubar'in 'na'de
      tooth-PL   PRON POSS 3SING   big-PL   DEM DIS PL
      "those big teeth of him"

3.3.2.2. *Restrictive and Non-restrictive Adjectives*

Nubi adjectives often modify the noun in a kind of relative clause construction. Thus besides *'ragi ke'bir*, we often find *'ragi al ke'bir*, where the noun *'ragi* "man" and the adjective *ke'bir* "big" are linked with a relative marker which can be *'ali, a'li, al, 'abu, a'bu,* or *ab* (see 3.3.7. below). The distinction between both phrases (*'ragi ke'bir* and *'ragi al ke'bir*) is related to the distinction between non-restrictive and restrictive modifiers respectively. Givón (1990, 473) explains this distinction as follows:

> Restrictive modifiers *restrict the domain* of the noun in terms of specific identification. They thus have the potential of being contrastive. Non-restrictive modifiers, on the other hand, tend to supply information that is *habitually known* as part of the normal characterization of the individual in question. They thus have the potential of forming a compound lexical noun together with their head noun.

Thus consider (188) and (189):

(188) 'Ana   ka'man   'fu   *a'jol*   *ke'bir*.
      PRON 1SING   EMPH   EXIS   person   old
      "I am an old man."

(189) 'Mana   'to,   *a'nas   ab   ku'bar,*   'umon   'shinda.
      meaning PRON POSS 3SING   people REL old-PL   PRON 3PL   win-Ø
      "Its meaning is (that) people who are old/old people, they win."

In (188), *ke'bir* refers to an habitual, generic quality of the speaker. In (189), the quality of 'being old' is used contrastively, to differentiate the group of people who exhibit this quality from those who do not. An NP marked by a restrictive adjective often refers to a generic nominal, e.g., a good man/good men, which is different from a generic quality of a nominal, e.g., the man whose habit it is to be good. In those cases, it is not marked by an article or demonstrative. It appears, however, that once specific identification has been marked by means of the relative marker, it is no longer compulsory. Consider (190):

(190) ... 'ya   *a'jol*   *ab*   *sa'kar*   ke'de 'ma   'alis(i)   *a'jol*   *ab*   *ke'bir.*
     CONJ person GEN young   SUBJ NEG   insult-Ø person GEN old
     'Fi   kala'ma   al   *a'jol   ke'bir* 'arufu, a'li   *a'jol*   *sa'kar* 'arufu 'ma.
     EXIS thing-PL   REL person old   know-Ø REL   person young know-Ø NEG
     ". . . thus a young person should not insult an old person. There are things which an old person knows, (and) which a young person does not know."

The head noun of the restrictive relative clause can be deleted. In those cases, either the head noun stands for a person (191) or it alludes to a referent mentioned in the ongoing discourse (192):

(191) Ab   a''wiri   b(i)-   ali'mu.
     REL   stupid   FUT-   teach-PASS-Ø
     "The stupid one will be taught."

(192) Al   duga'gin   'de   mi'lan   bi'mara.
     REL   small-PL   DEF   many   very
     "The small ones were many./ There were many small ones. (boats)"

There are adjectives in Nubi that hardly ever occur non-restrictively when in modifying position. It seems that the properties they refer to are so extreme, generally in a bad sense, that they can only be mentioned as opposed to the normal qualities, which are supposedly good.

(193) *kisi'lan* "lazy"
     kara'ban "ugly"
     siji'man "ugly"
     ha'gar "mean"
     a'wir "stupid"

Therefore, this class of adjectives mainly occurs with marking by the relative particle:

(194) *'marya al kara'ban* "a woman who is ugly", "an ugly woman"
     a'jol ab ha'gar "a person who is mean", "a mean person"
     a'jol ab a'wiri "a person who is stupid", "a stupid person"

In predicate position, however, the adjective is not preceded by the relative particle:

(195) Bi'niya   'de   *kisi'lan,*   bi'niya   'de   *ha'gari.*
      girl   DEF   lazy   girl   DEF   mean
      "The girl is lazy, the girl is mean."

3.3.2.3. *Verbal Adjectives*

Certain concepts in Nubi, especially those concerning human mental and physical characteristics, are lexicalized as verbs. They refer to non-permanent qualities. When used as a predicate, they may take on verbal morphology and thus resemble stative verbs. These are:

(196) *ja'lan* "(be) angry"
      fu'rai "(be) happy"
      a'yan "(be) sick"
      sa'ban "(be) satisfied"
      hara'gan "(be) sweaty", "sweat"
      ta'ban "(be) unwell", "(be) annoyed"
      fata'ran "(be) tired"
      'abis "(be) dry"
      'zalim "(be) unfair"
      'bari "(be) cold"
      'hari "(be) warm"
      'seme "(be) good"
      'hilu "(be) sweet"

When marked by progressive *gi-* (see 4.2.1.1), the verbal adjective takes the meaning of an inchoative: "becoming tired, sweaty, sick, etc" as in (197):

(197) Ak'wana   wa'din   'de   'dukur   gi-   ja'lan.
      relative-PL other-PL   DEF   then   PROG-   be angry
      "The other relatives then are becoming angry."

Without any marking, the verbal adjective denotes a state as in (198):

(198) Kan   'ita   'seb   bu'ja   'de   'abis, ...
      if   PRON 2SING   leave-Ø   saliva   DEF   be dry-Ø
      "If you leave the saliva (to be) dry, . . ."

These adjectives, in their bare form, can also take plural marking as in (199). Plural marking is a characteristic of nouns and adjectives. Therefore, these adjectives cannot be considered true verbs.

(199) 'Umon,   a'nas   al   'zalim   ka'man . . .
      PRON 3PL   people   REL   be unfair-Ø   also
      'Umon   'kulu   *zali'min.*
      PRON 3PL   all   unfair-PL
      "They, the people who are also unfair. . . . They are all unfair."

These adjectives, when in modifying position, are mainly used in a
relative phrase with the marker *a'li/ al/ a'bu/ ab*. In predicate position, however, they appear as such.

(200) 'Uo   'sulu   m'kate 'to   al   'abis-'abis
      PRON 3SING   take-Ø bread   PRON POSS 3SING   REL   be dry-REDUP-Ø
      "He took his bread which was dry."

(201) a'zol   ab   ta'ban
      person   REL   annoyed
      "someone who is annoyed"

3.3.2.4. *Comparison*

Equality is expressed by means of the prepositions *ja/je* "like" or
'sawa(-'sawa) ma "the same as", as in (202) and (203):[23]

(202) 'Lon 'to   'mus   gi-   'ben *je* 'lon 'taki.
      face PRON POSS 3SING EMPH PROG- look like face PRON POSS 2SING
      "His face looks like your face, isn't it?!'

(203) A'jol   ta   'sana   kam'sin, 'uo   'ma   *'sawa*
      person   GEN   year(s)   NUM   PRON 3SING   NEG   same
      ma   a'jol   ta   'sana   taman'tashar.
      with   person   GEN   year(s)   NUM
      "Someone of fifty years, he is not like someone of eighteen years."

The English adjective 'same' is translated in Nubi by *'wai-'wai, 'sawa-
'sawa*, or *'wai 'sawa*.

(204) Fa'rash   'de   'bes   gu-   we'ri   ba'kan   'wai-'wai   'de.
      horse   DEF   EMPH   PROG- show   place   same   DEF
      "The horse is showing the same place."

There are no morphological comparatives or superlatives in Nubi
except for *a'ker* "better" and *'aksen* "better", which are both supple-

---

[23] Single *'sawa* means "together".

tive comparative forms for ʼkweis "good". The standard or item with which the subject of the clause is compared is introduced by the preposition min:

(205) ʼUo   ʼaksen   min   aʼjol   ta   saʼtara.
      PRON 3SING   better   than   person   GEN   dominance
      "He is better than a person of dominance/a dominant person."

Aʼker keʼde is often used in an impersonal clause 'it is better that . . .'

(206) Aʼker   keʼd(e)   ʼuo   ʼmutu   ʼna
      it is better SUBJ   PRON 3SING   die-Ø   there
      min   ʼuo   ʼja   ʼkelem. . . .
      than   PRON 3SING   come-Ø   say-Ø
      "It is better that he dies there than that he comes to say . . ."

Comparison is expressed mainly by means of the preposition ʼfutu derived from the verb ʼfutu "pass' (207) and infrequently by means of the preposition min (208). The quality that is compared may be expressed by an adjective/verbal adjective, quantifier, or noun and is often followed by a non-numeral quantifier, or an adverb of degree.

(207) ʼBei   ta   leseʼri ʼhari ʼfutu   ʼbei   ta   ʼgwanda.
      price GEN   maize high   in comparison with   price GEN   cassava
      "The price of maize is high in comparison with the price of cassava."

(208) ʼIna   ʼfi   fi   ʼraha   ʼsia   min
      PRON 1PL   EXIS   in   comfort   bit   in comparison with
      al   ʼkan   ta   ʼwara   ʼna.
      REL   be-ANT   GEN   back   there
      "We are (living) a little bit comfortably in comparison with what was there in the past."

One alternative is a clause with the verb ʼfutu/ʼs(h)inda "surpass": 'X (sur)passes Y, regarding quality Z'. Consider (209) in which a chicken boasts to an elephant about her ability to eat a lot.

(209) . . . Kan   fi   ʼsafa ta   ʼakili, ʼana   ʼg(i)-   akulu ʼakili
                if   in   side GEN   food   PRON 1SING PROG-   eat   food
      al   gi-   ʼfutu   ʼtaki.
      REL   PROG-   surpass PRON POSS 2SING
      "If concerning food, I am eating [an amount of] food which sur passes yours."

(210) . . . 'umon   'arufu   Li'fili   bi-   'sinda   Gi'dida   fu   'ákúlu.
       PRON 3PL   know-Ø   Elephant   FUT-   surpass   Chicken   in   eat-INF
       ". . . they knew that Elephant would surpass Chicken in eating."

Another alternative is the very simple construction: 'this thing is big, and that one is not big/is small'. Consider (211), where the speaker introduces two brothers:

(211) 'Wai   'ya   ke'bir,   'tan   'ya   sa'kar.
       NUM   FOC   big   other   FOC   small
       "One is big, the other one is small."

Qualities are emphasized in relative clauses. A subgroup exhibiting this quality may be selected from the rest of the group, which does not. In (212), the two elder ones among three children are singled out:

(212) nyere'ka   al   kuba'rin   'de
       child-PL   REL   big-PL   DEF
       "the children that are big"

As with the comparative, the superlative is not expressed in the adjective itself but is realized with the aid of adverbs of degree following the adjective as in (213) and (214):

(213) 'bele   ke'bir   'sei-'sei   'de
       country   big   very   EMPH
       "a very big country"

(214) Ma'ish   ta   'Bombo   'kan   ba'tal   'zaidi.
       life   GEN   NPROP   be-ANT   bad   very
       "Life in Bombo was very bad."

A relative phrase may also express the meaning of a superlative as in (215):

(215) 'Ana   je   ab   ke'biri . . .
       PRON 1SING   like   REL   big
       "I as the biggest one . . ."

Another possibility resembles the Shukriyya Arabic superlative *akbar wâḥid* (Reichmuth 1983, 173).

(216) fu 'ustu   ak'wana   taki   'de   al   ke'bir 'wai   'de
       in middle   relative-PL   PRON POSS 2SING   DEF   REL   old   NUM   DEF
       "the eldest one among your relatives"

One of the meanings expressed by the reduplication of adjectives is
that of the superiority of its quality as in (217):

(217) 'Sika   'de   'kan   ba'tal-ba'tal.
      Road(s)   DEF   be-ANT   bad-REDUP
      "The roads were very bad."

Repetition also conveys the idea of intensity.

(218) La'ta   'ja   'hari,   'hari,   'hari   na   'Hasan.
      weather   come-Ø   hot   hot   hot   for   Hasan
      "It became very, very hot for Hasan."

3.3.3. *Possessive Phrases*

Form: Possession in Nubi is expressed by means of an analytic construction that binds the possessee to the possessor by means of the
genitive marker *ta*: POSSESSEE *ta* POSSESSOR, e.g. *'kalwa ta 'sheik
Musa* "the religious school of Sheikh Musa". Another possibility is
to juxtapose possessee and possessor, e.g. *ba'kan be'redu* "place used
for bathing", "bathroom". Both constructions will be discussed below.
Several sequences of possessive constructions may occur as in (219):

(219) ta'biya   ta   'nas   ta   'be   'toumon
      habit(s)   GEN   people   GEN   house   PRON POSS 3PL
      "the habits of the people of their house"

Consider a complex construction as in (220):

(220) sa'na   'tena   te   'ida
      craft(s)   PRON POSS 1PL   GEN   hand(s)
      "our handcrafts"

Both *'tena* "our" and *te 'ida* "of the hands" refer to *sa'na* "crafts",
resulting in "our crafts" and "crafts of the hands", and combined
"our handcrafts". The first or possessee part of the construction may
be dropped if the deleted item has been mentioned in the previous
discourse as in (221):

(221) . . . 'ke   it(a)   'asma   *ta*   ba'ba   *'de*!
             SUBJ   PRON 2SING   hear-Ø   GEN   father   DEF
      ". . . you should hear the [matter] of the father!"

N N constructions vs. N *ta* N constructions: The factor that distinguishes noun-noun constructions and *ta*-marked constructions is not
always apparent. In general, it can be said that the *ta*-marked construction marks alienable constructions, whereas noun-noun constructions express inalienable constructions. Alienable possession is
associated with terminable possession, whereas inalienable possession
cannot be terminated. Inalienable possession in Nubi applies to kinship terms (222), body parts (223), some other part-whole relations
(224), and goal.[24]

(222) *'marya ba'ba* "wife of father", "stepmother"
       a'ku ba'ba "brother/sister of father", "paternal uncle/aunt"[25]

(223) *'su 'ras* "hair of the head"
       'batna 'ida "inside of the hand", "palm of the hand"
       'kab ku'ra "heel of the foot", "heel"

(224) *'ras 'jua* "head of the house", "roof"
       'gar 'kuta "central part of a tray"

Many material items are produced or used for one single goal, e.g.,
'guruma 'moyo is a pot or jar for storing water as opposed to *'guruma
'maua*, which is for holding plants. Their shapes differ, and they are
used for only the one purpose. Their relationship with this purpose
is regarded as interminable. However, the distinction terminable/inter-
minable does not hold for all possessive constructions. For instance,
an item cannot change its material. Yet within this type of possessive construction the possession constructions are marked by *ta* as in
(225):

(225) *ku'baya ta 'plastic* "cup made of plastic", "plastic cup"
      'jua ta 'gesi "a hut made of grass"

---

[24] Possessive constructions in which *a'ku* "relative", *nyere'ku* "child", and animals
are the possessed items and *yo'wele* "boy", *bi'niya* "girl", *'marya* "woman", and *'ragi*
"man" are the possessors, obligatorily occur with the genitive marker which distinguishes them from NPs such as *nyere'ku bi'niya* "girl", *'bagara 'ragi* "bull", in which
the second word serves as a gender marker.

[25] An expression such as *ma'ma 'Jenna* has two meanings. In Bombo as in Swahili,
ma'ma 'Jenna stands for "the mother of Jenna". In other parts of the country,
however, when using *ma'ma 'Jenna*, Nubi are talking about a woman whose name
is "Jenna".

Terminable possessive relationships, such as typical owner-possessed relations (226), class (227), time (228), and location (229), are always expressed by means of the possessee *ta* possessor-construction.

(226) *jua te ji'ran* "the house of the neighbour"
'shamba ta aja'ma 'de "the field of the people"

(227) *ga'raya ta 'din* "studies of the religion", "religious studies"
'kazi ta 'shamba "the work of the field"

(228) *'zaman ta 'ase'de* "period of now", "nowadays"
'sa ta do'luka "the time of the dance"

(229) *'masgit ta 'Lira* "the mosque of Lira"
'sika ta Kampala "the roads of Kampala"

However, the opposition definite-indefinite may intervene in possessive constructions, which apply to goal, part-whole relations, and locations where actions, expressed by means of a gerund, are usually taking place. Definiteness applies to items that have been introduced in previous discourse, which are deictically available or generally known to the hearer because they belong to the permanent file (see also 3.3.1.1). Alienable constructions that are indefinite, i.e., that have not yet been entered in the active discourse file, may be expressed without the genitive marker, whereas the *ta*-marked alienable construction refers to definite NPs. *ta* therefore acts more or less as a definite particle (see also Owens 1977). It differs, however, from the definite article, where the notion of pragmatic salience is also taken into account. Consider (230), where the initially mentioned *ba'kan jowju* refers to the location of a wedding ceremony, which is referred to in subsequent discourse: *'ba'kan ta 'jowju 'na'de* with the genitive marker and an anaphorically used demonstrative.

(230) ... 'itokum 'ja ma ma'lim 'takum,
PRON 2PL come-Ø with preacher PRON POSS 2PL
ma a'nas 'takum al 'itokum na'di
with people PRON POSS 2PL REL PRON 2PL invite-Ø
fi *ba'kan jowju.* ... 'Ke 'ina 'kelem
in place wedding SUBJ PRON 1PL say-Ø
kan i'tom gi- 'fi ... fi *ba'kan ta jowju 'na'de,* ....
SUBJ PRON2PL PROG- EXIS in place GEN wedding DEM DIS
"... you (PL) came with your preacher, with your people whom you invited to the wedding place.... Let us say that if you (PL) were there ... in that wedding place, ..."

In (231), *ǰeriba ʾbagara* and *ǰeriba ta ʾbagara* both occur, expressing "cattle pens" in general, and the definite "cattle pen" (which you have made) respectively.

(231) *J̌eriba*   *ʾbagara,*   ʾde   ʾya   baʾkan al   gu-   kuʾtu   ʾfogo ʾbagara.
      pen   cow(s)   DEF   FOC   place   REL   PROG-   put-PASS in it cow(s)
      Kan   ʾbagara   ʾfi   miʾlan   ʾneta,
      if   cow(s)   EXIS   many   for + PRON 2SING
      ʾit(a)   ʾadul   baʾkan je   ʾde,
      PRON 2SING   prepare-Ø   place   like   DEM PROX
      ʾita   ʾkut(u) ʾumon   fiʾjo   jeʾriba, *ǰeriba*[26]   ta   *ʾbagara.*
      PRON 2SING   put-Ø   PRON 3PL inside pen   pen   GEN   cow(s)
      "A cattle pen, this is a place in which cows are put. If you have a lot of cows, you prepare a place like this, you put them inside the pen, the pen for cattle."

Rarely, a similar distinction is manifested with body parts and other part-whole relations as in (232):

(232) *ʾZuburu*   *huʾmar*   fiʾjo . ʾsidu.   ʾMana   ʾto
      penis   donkey   inside   owner   meaning PRON POSS 3SING
      ʾzubur   *to*   *huʾmar* ʾfi   keʾbir, aʾkin. . . .
      penis   GEN   donkey   EXIS   big   but
      "A donkey penis is inside [its] owner. The meaning of it is [that] the penis of a donkey is there [being] big, but . . .".

Agents and patients of gerund forms are expressed in alienable-like possessive constructions with the genitive particle as in (233), while the patient of infinitives is related to the infinitive in a construction consisting of N N (Patient), i.e., an inalienable-like construction as in (234) (see 4.3.3).

(233) *weʾledu*   *ta*   *aʾnas*   *ʾnaʾde*
      give birth-GER   GEN   people   DEM DIS PL
      "the bearing of/by those people"

(234) ʾUo   ʾaba   ʾgum   fi   *ʾsídú*   *ʾbab.*
      PRON 3SING   refuse-Ø   get up-Ø   in   close-INF door
      "She refused to get up to close the door."

Compounds: Ownership in the strict sense of the word, which means terminable ownership, is always expressed by means of the genitive marker. *ʾSidu ʾbe* "owner of the house" and *ʾsidu ʾkuris* "owner of the

---

[26] *J̌eʾriba* and *ǰeriba* "(cattle) pen" co-occur in Nubi (see also 2.1.4.).

chair" seem to be counterexamples, apparently indicating the class
of landlords or owners of houses. However, the meaning of the total
construction is different from what both parts would suggest. *'sidu
'be* refers to "the one who has the authority in the household".
Similarly, *'sidu 'kuris*, without *ta*, does not apply to "owners of chairs"
but takes the meaning of "chairman" who presides over a meeting.
'Sidu 'be and *'sidu 'kuris* belong to a category of inalienable possessive constructions, or noun modifier constructions, which have yielded
compounds.

True compounds are not very common in Nubi. It is also difficult
to establish whether the noun-modifier construction should still be
considered an inalienable possessive construction or whether it has
evolved into a compound. An effective criterion could be a change
of meaning such that the meaning of the noun modifier construction can no longer be derived directly from the fusion of the meanings of the separate entities of the construction. *ku'baya 'chai* could
still be considered an inalienable possessive construction, since it is
"a cup meant for drinking tea", thus "a teacup". *'Lam 'gaba* "wild
animals" would rather be listed among the compounds, since the lit-
eral translation "meat of the forest" does not explain the meaning
of "animals of the forest" or "wild animals" as opposed to domestic animals. Some other compounds of this type occurring in the
text material are given in (235):[27]

(235) *gata 'leben* "person who cuts off the milk" > "youngest child", "last born"
       marai 'ena "mirror for the eyes" > "glasses"
       'moyo 'ena "water in the eye" > "tear"
       mu'kosa ka'bila "person who has no tribe" > "immigrant"
       'gifir li'san "dirt on the tongue" > "bad language"
       'kasma 'bab "mouth of the door" > "doorstep"
       'kasur 'be "breaking house" > "compensation", "fine for committing adultery"
       'lata 'saba "dawn of the morning" > "early morning"
       'gahar 'dum "cave of blood" > "gum"
       'labil la'ta "rope on the floor" > "snake"
       mar'ba < *'marya ba'ba* "wife of the father" > "stepmother"
       'akir 'zaman "end of the times" > "end of the world"[28]
       su'nun li'fil "teeth of an elephant" > "tusk"
       'marya 'ragi "woman of a man", "married wife" > "housewife"

---

[27] Compounds are quite common in proverbs and in proverbial expressions. For
instance, *'dom boro'gu* "blood of the bedbug" refers to the English 'black sheep': a
bad or worthless member of a group, whose blood smells.
[28] *'Akir ta 'zaman* means "end of a (specific) period".

'*jua 'gesi* "hut with grass-thatched roof" > "grass-thatched hut"[29]
'*jua 'bati* "house with iron roof"
a'yan 'shar "disease of the month" > "menstruation"
ji'an 'be "hunger for home" > "homesickness" (N), "homesick" (ADJ)[30]
sa'ba du'wan "tomorrow in jail" > "someone who is always in jail"[31]

Another criterion applicable for Nubi is that certain formerly inalienable noun-noun constructions are used so often that they have become fixed in their specific meaning. As such, they can often be opposed to their *ta*-marked equivalents whose meaning differs as in (236):

(236) *ba'kan 'mutu* "place where someone died recently" ><
           ba'kan ta 'mutu "place where people are executed"
    ba'kan be'redu "place meant for bathing", "bathroom" ><
           ba'kan ta be'redu "place which is occasionally used for bathing"
    mu'la 'samaga "sauce which main ingredient is fish", "fish sauce" ><
           mu'la ta 'samaga "sauce/food for feeding the fish"
    'dar 'jua "back of the house", "any space at the back of the house" ><
           'dar ta 'jua "the back wall of the house"

The above indicates that some possessive constructions remain unexplained. In (237), there is no reason why 'sleeves of a shirt' would be treated differently from 'trouser legs'.

(237) . . . 'ita   gi-   'somuru   *'ida*   *ge'mis*   'taki
          PRON 2SING PROG- roll up   arm(s)   shirt   PRON POSS 2 SING
     au   *ku'ra*   *ta*   *lu'bas*   'taki.
     or   leg(s)   GEN   trouser   PRON POSS 2SING
     ". . . you are rolling up the sleeves of your shirt/your sleeves or the legs of your trousers/ your trouser legs."

I did not find many instances of plural compounds. Number is mainly indicated by external means, such as quantifiers and/or modifiers or is understood from the context as in (238):

(238) . . . la'kin   'zaidi   *mu'kosa ka'bila*   'ya   'fi   'na.
          but   often   immigrant   FOC   EXIS   there
     ". . . but   often immigrants are there."

---

[29] '*Jua ta 'gesi* is either "a hut which is entirely made of grass", or "a hut which is meant to store grass".

[30] I know of only two other instances of adjectival compounds, namely:
ke'tir 'mesiya (ADJ + V) "being a lot more than enough" ~ "lavish (ADJ)"
'stan 'chai (ADJ + N) "thirsty for tea (ADJ)"

[31] This compound is exceptional since it is composed of an ADV + N, yielding a noun.

Note, however, (239):

(239) *ŋua 'bati* "house with iron roof"—*ju'a 'bati*
      'lam 'gaba "wild animal"—*'lam ga'ba*

In *ju'a 'bati* number is marked in the head of the compound noun.
'lam 'gaba, however, is regarded as one noun. Consequently, its plural
is marked, quite regularly, in the final syllable: *'lam ga'ba*.

   Modification: Some problems regarding interpretation may occur
when the parts of the possessive construction are modified. In inalienable possessive constructions, the modifier comes in last position and
usually refers to the head noun, which occupies the left position as
in (240), (241), and (242):

(240) ba'kan   'num   'taki
      place   sleep-GER   PRON POSS 2SING
      "your bedroom"

(241) ku'baya 'chai   al   'endi   'tamaga
      cup   'tea   REL   have-Ø   mark
      "a tea cup which has a mark"

(242) 'ŋua   'sokol   'gaba   'dol'de
      house(s)   thing(s)   forest(s)   DEM PROX-PL
      "these houses of the things/animals of the forest", "these animal holes"

In alienable possessive constructions, the pronominal possessor follows
the possessee (or head noun) when modifying the possessee as in
(243), and the possessor (or modifier noun) when modifying the possessor as in (244):

(243) ta'biya   'tena   ta   'Nubi
      custom(s)   PRON POSS 1PL   GEN   NPROP
      "our customs of the Nubi"

(244) fi   'dar   ta   ba'ba   'tai
      on   back   GEN   father   PRON POSS 1SING
      "on my father's back"

If the modifier in an alienable construction is other than a pronominal possessor (an adjective, relative clause, determiner), it comes in
final position whether it modifies the possessee (or head noun) or
the possessor (or modifying noun). It should be inferred from the
context which of the nouns is modified. In (245), the relative clause

is related to the possessor noun, whereas in (246) it modifies the possessee or head noun.[32]

(245) ya'la   to   u'ziri   al   'ase   fi
      child-PL   GEN   minister   REL   now   EXIS
      "the children of the minister who is now here/in charge"

(246) 'kidima 'tai   ta   'be   'in
      work   PRON POSS 1SING GEN   house   here
      al   kila   'youm   'ita   gi-   'so   'de
      REL   every day   PRON 2SING PROG- do   DEF
      "my work of the house here, which you are doing every day"

In (247), the demonstrative must be determining wa'kati "period", "time", and not sha'ria "law", since 'that law of time' is meaningless.

(247) sha'ria   ta   wa'kati   'na'de
      law   GEN   time   DEM DIS
      "the law of that time"

In (248), the demonstrative could be determining both the head noun and the modifying noun. However, the non-numeral quantifier 'kul closes the phrase. It can be assumed that both modifiers refer to the same noun (although in theory it would be possible for the demonstrative 'na'de to determine 'shamba "field" and 'kul "all" to modify a'nas "people" (see also Owens 1977). From the context, it is clear that the speaker talks about many people from one field and not about people from many fields. Therefore, doubtlessly 'kul refers to a'nas and most likely 'na'de as well.

(248) a'nas   ta   'shamba   'na'de   'kul
      people   GEN   field   DEM DIS PL   all
      "all those people from the field"

In (249), the demonstrative could determine both asker'ya "soldiers" and 'shamba "field". Neither the context nor the word order disambiguates this.

---

[32] In the following clause, however, it is not clear whether it is the head or the modifying noun to which the subordinate clause adds information: is it "the manner which he is with", or "the knowledge he is with"?
    'namna   ta   'ilim   al   'uo   fi   'mo
    manner   GEN   knowledge   REL   PRON 3SING   EXIS   with it
    "the manner of knowledge which he is with"

(249) asker'ya   ta   'shamba   'na'de
      soldier-PL   GEN   field   DEM DIS SING/ PL
      "those soldiers of the field" or "the soldiers of that field"

From the context and from the meaning of the phrase in (250), it can be deduced that the demonstrative 'na'de and the definite article 'de determine the last noun in the sequence.

(250) ta'biya   te   nyere'ku bi'niya ta   a'ku   'na'de
      habit(s) GEN   child   girl   GEN   brother   DEM DIS (SING/PL)

In theory, this phrase could be translated as follows:

> "those habits of the daughter of a (???) brother"
> "the habits of that daugher of a (???) brother"
> "the habits of the daughter of that brother".

Only the third possibility sounds reasonable, since without any determination, it would remain obscure which brother is involved. In (251), the adjective sa'kar "small" modifies the head noun, even though the head noun and the genitive particle + the modifying noun are separated by the emphasizer je'de.

(251) 'jina   ku'baya   je'de   ta   za'habu   sa'kar
      smallness   cup   EMPH   GEN   gold   small
      "a small cup (filled) with gold"

3.3.4. Diminution and Augmentation

In Nubi, unusual sizes of nouns, such as large quantities or small size, are indicated by means of nouns placed in front of the noun in inalienable-like expressions. By placing jina in front of the noun, diminution is expressed as in (252).[33] The noun is often followed by an adjective conveying small size as in (253):

(252) jina   'meli
      smallness   boat
      "a small boat"

(253) jina   'lager   sa'kar
      smallness   stone   small
      "a small stone"

---

[33] 'Jina also means "child", "offspring" as in jina zi'na "child of sin", "a bastard

The non-numeral quantifier ʿsia may also convey the idea of diminution as in (254) and (255):

(254) ʿija   ʿwai   ʿsia
      fairy tale   INDEF   a bit
      "a short fairy tale"

(255) ǰin(a)   a'dis   ʿtai   ʿsia
      smallness   story   PRON POSS 1SING   a bit
      "my small story"

With plural nouns, ʿyal "children" may be used to indicate small
size, with or without the addition of du'ga/duga'gin "small (PL)" as
in (256) and (257):

(256) ʿyal   ʿgara   ʿdol'de
      child-PL   pumpkin(s)   DEM PROX PL
      "these small pumpkins"

(257) ʿyal   ʿdim   duga'gin   ʿde
      child-PL   light(s)   small-PL   DEF
      "the small lights"

ʿDaya/ʿdayama is used to express the hugeness, vastness, or enormity
of something. It is placed in front of the noun, which is often followed by an adjective expressing largeness or length as in (258) and
(259):

(258) ʿdaya   ʿluguma   ke'bir
      enormity   dough paste   big
      "a large dough paste"

(259) ʿNas   ba'ba ʿde,   ʿitokum   ʿwala   ʿdayama   ʿnari ʿde.
      COLL   father DEF   PRON 2PL light-Ø   enormity fire DEF
      "The father and relatives, you (PL) are lighting the huge fire."

Largeness and large quantities are expressed by means of ʿdinya.
Unlike ʿdaya and ǰina, ʿdinya + N is infrequently followed by an adjective conveying the same quality.

---

child", ǰina mes'kin "child of a poor man". It is very likely that ǰina "smallness" is
derived from ǰina "child".

(260) *'dinya 'sana* "many years"
'dinya ki'lele "much noise"

One instance was found with *to'wil* "long", "length", expressing length (of time),

(261) *to'wil 'bala* "long attention"

and one instance with *'tor*, apparently expressing largeness. *'Tor* usually means "bull", a large animal, which may have led to its use in this context.

(262) *'tor* 'lager *ke'bir*
bigness stone big
"a big stone"

The adjectives following the noun, which actually convey the same meaning as the diminutive/augmentative noun in front of the noun, may add to the quality or quantity expressed. Augmentation and diminuation may also be indicated by means of non-numeral quantifiers.

3.3.5. *Non-numeral Quantifiers*

In Nubi, the class of non-numeral quantifiers is small and includes:

(263) *mi'lan* "many", "a lot of"
ke'tir "many", "a lot of"
'sia[34] "few", "some"
'kulu[35] "all of"
'kila "every"

Mi'lan often occurs, unlike *ke'tir* which is not commonly used. *Mi'lan, ke'tir, 'sia, and 'kulu* belong morphologically and syntactically to the class of adjectives, which implies that they can be used in the

---

[34] *'Sia* is often used as an adverb: 'An(a) 'agara 'sia.
PRON 1SING study-Ø a little bit
"I studied a little bit".
[35] *'Kulu* also means "whole", such as in: fi Afri'k(a) 'en 'kulu
in NPROP here whole
"in the whole of Africa here"

attributive and the predicative position. *Kila* "every" is only used attributively and precedes the noun. Except for *kulu* "all", all quantifiers typically modify indefinite, often non-referential nouns as in (264), (265), and (266):

(264) 'Sana   'de   *mi'lan*   'zaidi.
      year(s)   DEF   many   very
      "The years are very many."

(265) ka'lam   'toumon   *kul*[36]
      thing   PRON POSS 3PL   all
      "all their things"

(266) *kila 'sana* "every year"

Kul and *'sia* often occur reduplicated as in (267):

(267) *Nubi 'kulu-'kulu* "all the Nubi"
      ta'biya 'sia-'sia "few habits"

Kila is often found in combination with *kulu* as in (268):

(268) *kila*   'bab   'dol'de   *kulu*
      every   door   DEM PROX PL   all
      "all these doors"

Infrequently, the Nubi non-numeral quantifier is used in a partitive construction followed by the genitive particle + noun as in (269):

(269) *mi'lan*   *ta*   *a'nas*
      many   GEN   people
      "many of the people

3.3.6. *Numerals*

Cardinals: The Nubi numeral system is a decimal one. Cardinals are given in (270):

---

[36] Exceptionally, *kulu* is placed in front of the noun it modifies, *kulu 'youm* "all the days". This resembles its position in Arabic.

(270) *'wai* "one"[37]   *i'dashar* "eleven"   *tele'tin* "thirty"
      ti'nin/ ti'nen "two"   *it'nashar* "twelve"   *ar'bein/ arbe'yin* "forty"
      ta'lata "three"   *tala'tashar* "thirteen"   *kam'sin* "fifty"
      'arba/ 'aruba "four"   *arba'tashar* "fourteen"   *si'tin* "sixty"
      'kamsa "five"   *kam(i)s'tashar* "fifteen" *se'bein/ sebe'yin* "seventy"
      'sita "six"   *si'tashar* "sixteen"   *tama'nin/ tema'nin* "eighty"
      'saba "seven"   *saba'tashar* "seventeen"   *ti'sein/ tise'yin* "ninety"
      ta'maniya "eight"   *taman'tashar* "eighteen"   *'mia* "hundred"
      'tisa "nine"   *tisa'tashar* "nineteen"
      'ashara "ten"   *ishi'rin* "twenty"

After twenty, the cardinal numerals are composed of the numeral followed by the tens and optionally linked by *u, wu,* or *wa* "and", whose vowel is fused with the vowel of *ishi'rin* "twenty" and *ar'bein* "forty". An exception is *'wai* "one", which is realized as *'waid*. It is joined with *ishi'rin* by *u*, which is generally assimilated to *i*.

(271) *'waid (i) ishi'rin* "twenty one"   *'waid i tele'tin* "thirty one"
      ti'nin w(u) ishi'rin "twenty two"   *ti'nin w(u) tele'tin* "thirty two"
      ta'lata w(u) ishi'rin "twenty three" *ta'lata w(u) ar'bein* "forty three"
      'arba w(u) ishi'rin "twenty four"   *'arba w(u) kam'sin* "fifty four"
      'kamsa w(u) ishi'rin "twenty five"   *'kamsa w(u) si'tin* "sixty five"
      'sita w(u) ishi'rin "twenty six"   *'sita w(u) se'bein* "seventy six"
      'saba w(u) ishi'rin "twenty seven"   *'saba w(u) tama'nin* "eighty seven"
      ta'maniya w(u) ishi'rin "twenty eight" *ta'maniya w(u) ti'sein* "ninety eight"
      'tisa w(u) ishi'rin "twenty nine"   *'tisa w(u) ti'sein* "ninety nine"

Hundreds and tens may also be linked by *u, wu,* or *wa* as in (272):

(272) *'mia* "hundred"   *'mia u ishi'rin* "hundred and twenty"
      mi'ten "two hundred"   *'kamsa 'mia wu 'sita se'bein* "five hundred and seventy six"
      'arba 'mia "four hundred"
      etc.

The order of numerals when counting the thousands is *'elf* "thousand" + NUM, and is therefore different from the hundreds where the numeral precedes *'mia* "hundred" as in (273):

---

[37] *'Wai* "one" also occurs as an adverb, meaning "together", or in adverbial phrases, such as *'mara 'wai* "at once", "all of a sudden".
    'Umon   gu-   'robutu ka'lam   'toumon   *wai*   me Ingi'lis.
    PRON 3PL PROG- tie   problem PRON POSS 3PL together with NPROP
    "They are tying their problem together with [that of] the English."

(273) *'elf 'wai* "one thousand"
'elf ti'nin "two thousand"
'elf ta'lata "three thousand"
'elf 'arba 'kamsa 'mia 'sita wu ti'sein "four thousand five hundred and ninety six"

The Nubi numeral follows the noun it modifies.[38] Nubi numerals do not agree with their head nouns. Similarly, Nubi head nouns do not compulsory agree with numerals. If a numeral modifies the head noun, the head noun optionally occurs with plural marking as in (274):

(274) *ku'baya ti'nin* "two cups"
'yal ba'na ta'lata "three girls"

Ordinals: Ordinals are formed by the head noun followed by the numeral and linked by the genitive particle *ta*: N *ta* NUM. This resembles an alienable possessive construction. The ordinal 'first' is expressed either by *aw'lan* or by *'wai*, the Nubi cardinal number 'one'.

(275) *ta aw'lan, ta 'wai* "first"
ta ti'nin "second"
ta ta'lata "third"
etc.

(276) 'Asker   *ta*   *'arba*   'futu.   *Ta*   *'kamsa*   gi-   'ja.
soldier   GEN   four   pass-Ø   GEN   five   PROG- come
"The fourth soldier passes. The fifth one is coming."

Time: Years are produced in English or in Nubi. When produced in Nubi, *'elf 'wai 'tisa 'mia* "nineteen hundred" is mainly deleted when speaking about the 20th century. The year follows *'sana* "year" in an alienable-like construction containing the genitive exponent *ta* as in (277). It may also appear alone as in (278):

(277) fi   *'sana*   *ta*   *'arba ar'bein*
PREP   year   GEN   four forty
"in the year forty four"

(278) 'Ana   'ja   'tala   fi   *'tisa*   *wu*   *ar'bein.*
PRON 1SING   come-Ø   leave-Ø   in   nine   and   forty
"I left in forty nine".

---

[38] One elder speaker from the North placed *'wai* (and *'wakhid* from Arabic *wāḥid*) "one" in front of its head noun: *'wai a'zol* "one person"
'wakhid 'zol "one person"

The months (*'shar, 'sar*) of the solar year, which is the official system in Uganda, are expressed with ordinal numerals.[39]

(279) *'shar ta 'wai* "the first month", "January"
　　　 'shar ta ti'nin "the second month", "February"
　　　 'shar ta ta'lata "the third month", "March"
　　　 etc.

However, since all Nubi are Muslims, the months of the Islamic year are important in daily life. The Nubi names for the Islamic months are derived from the Arabic names and may be preceded by *'shar* "month" as in (280):

(280) *('shar) Rama'dan* "the month of Ramaḍân"

Ta'rik "date" is used to express dates. It precedes the cardinal numeral and usually follows the indication of the month as in (281):

(281) fi　　　'shar　　　te　　　　i'dashar,　　　*ta'rik*　　*arba'tashar*
　　　 in　　　 month　　 GEN　　　eleven　　　　date　　　fourteen
　　　 "on the fourteenth of November"

The days of the week are adopted from Arabic.

(282) *'youm la'ha* "Sunday"
　　　 'youm le ti'nin "Monday"
　　　 'youm tala'ta "Tuesday"
　　　 'youm lar'ba "Wednesday"
　　　 'youm ka'mis "Thursday"
　　　 'youm ju'ma "Friday"
　　　 'youm 'sebi "Saturday"

Time indications follow the Bantu system, which means that the day is divided in two parts, the night and the day. The day starts at six o'clock in the morning according to Western reckoning. This is approximately the time the sun raises and is for the Nubi and others *'sa it'nashar ta min 'subu* "hour twelve". Similarly, the night starts six hours before our time reckoning, when the sun is about to set,

---

[39] The English names of the months are used as an alternative: *'Januar, 'Februar, 'March, 'April, 'May, 'June, July, 'August, Sep'temba/ Sep'tember, Oc'toba/ Oc'tober, No'vemba/No'vember, De'cemba/ De'cember.* The forms in *-a* of the last four months resemble the Swahili months (see Ashton 1947, 321).

e.g. *'sa 'kamsa* "hour five". For reasons of clarity, time adverbs, given
in (283), referring to different parts of the day and night and resembling the time adverbs in Arabic, may accompany the Nubi time
indications in an alienable like-construction with the genitive marker
ta followed by the adverbs of time as in (284):

(283) *min 'sub(u)* "morning"
        'kabla 'zuhur "before noon"
        'bada 'zuhur "afternoon"
        la'siya "late afternoon", "(early) evening"
        fi'lel "night"

(284) min   'sa   'wai   ta   la'siya   'ladi 'sa   ta'lata ta   min 'sub
       from   hour one   GEN evening   until hour three   GEN   morning.
       "from seven o'clock in the evening until nine o'clock in the morning"

Thus, a complete time and date may be indicated as in (285):

(285) 'Ana   'jowzu   'Hawa fi   'sana   ta   waid   i   tama'nin
       PRON 1SING marry-Ø   NPROP in   year   GEN one   and   eighty
       fi   'sar   ta   'saba,   ta'rik tala'tashar fi   'youm   'sebi.
       in   month GEN   seven   date   thirteen   in   Saturday
       Fi   'sa   'arba   'ya   'ana   'so   ni'ka   fi   Bi'yago.
       in   hour   four   FOC   PRON 1SING   do-Ø wedding in   NPROP
       "I married Hawa in the year of eigthy one in July, the thirteenth, on (a) Saturday.
       At ten o'clock it was that I did the wedding at Biyago."

3.3.7. *Relative Clauses*

Nubi relative clauses consist of the relative marker, which can be
'ali, a'li, al, 'abu, a'bu, or *ab,* and the subordinate clause. Usually, relative clauses are placed directly after their head noun. Sometimes
the subordinate clause and the head noun are separated by a word
or phrase as in (286):

(286) Kala'ma   'tai   mi'lan al   'an(a)   'aju.
       thing-PL   PRON POSS 1SING   many   REL PRON 1SING   want-Ø
       "My things are many which I want"

Restrictive vs. non-restrictive relative clauses: Above (3.3.2.2), we
have seen that a phrase like *'ragi al ke'bir'* differs from *'ragi ke'bir'* in
that the relative pronoun marks the quality 'bigness' as outstanding
and thus as the quality which exemplifies the man and which distinguishes him from others who do not display this characteristic.
Nubi also distinguishes morphologically between non-restrictive rel-

ative clauses and restrictive relative clauses. A restrictive relative clause adds information to the noun that is essential for its understanding and thus distinguishes the noun from any other noun. The head noun may be definite or indefinite. A non-restrictive relative clause on the other hand, adds inessential information, which is not distinctive but may have some value for the hearer. The head noun is referentially unique, which implies that it belongs to the culturally or textually shared information, or that it is deictically available. In Nubi, items belonging to the culturally- or textually information are optionally determined by a definite article. Deictic availability is expressed with the deictic first and second personal and deictic demonstratives, and in uniquely identifying possessive constructions, such as kin terms, body parts, and parts of wholes. Very often, non-restrictive relative clauses (head + relative modifier) are modified by the definite article, or a demonstrative as in (287), (288), (289), and (290):

(287) *fu workshop 'tena   al 'ina   'g(i)- alim 'fogo 'de.*
      in workshop PRON POSS 1PL REL PRON 1PL PROG- learn in it DEF
      "in our workshop, in which we are learning"

(288) *'ahadi   'na'de   al   ku'tu   'nena   'na'de*
      agreement   DEM DIS   REL put-PASS-Ø for + PRON 1PL DEM DIS
      "that agreement, which was made for us"

(289) . . .   *'uo   'dakal   fi   'be.*
               PRON 3SING   enter-Ø   in   house
      'Be   al   'uo   'dakal   'fogo   'de   . . .
      house REL PRON 3SING   enter-Ø   in it   DEF
      ". . . he entered the house. The house, which he entered (in it), . . ."

(290) *'Ana   al   gu-   'wonus   we'de,* . . .
      PRON 1SING REL   PROG-   talk   DEM PROX
      "I, (this one) who is talking, . . ."

The definite article *'de* in the non-restrictive relative clause in (291) modifies *ka'lam* "thing" instead of determining the relative clause. It seems then that if two elements (definite article and/or demonstrative) co-occur, the one determining the relative clause is dropped. The slot is filled by an article or demonstrative. The addition of another element would only cause confusion.

(291) M'ze   'tai   'na'de
      old man PRON POSS 1SING   DEM DIS
      al   we'ri   'nana   ka'lam   'de,   . . .
      REL   show-Ø to + PRON 1SING   thing   DEF
      "That old man of mine, who showed me the thing,. . . ."

Restrictive relative clauses are normally not marked by a determining element.[40] Consider (292) and (293):

(292) 'San(a)   al   ma'ma   'mutu   'fogo,   'an(a)   'arufu   'ma.
      year   REL   mother   die-Ø   in it   PRON 1SING   know-Ø   NEG
      "The year that my mother died (in it), I do not know [it]."

(293) 'Ita   bi-   'sibu   'sika   ta   ba'ba   'taki
      PRON 2SING   FUT-   leave   way(s)   GEN   father   PRON POSS 2SING
      ab   'uo   'rasul(u)   'ita   'fogo.
      REL   PRON 3SING   send-Ø   PRON 2SING   in it
      "You will leave the ways of your father on which he sent you/You will
      abandon the ways of your father, which he aimed at for you."

Marking of the restrictive relative clauses, however, occurs optionally when the referent is important for the subsequent discourse, thus when it is pragmatically referential, as in (294) and (295):[41]

(294) ka'lam   al   'it(a)   'aju   'na'de . . .
      thing   REL   PRON 2SING   want-Ø   DEM DIS
      "that thing that you want"

---

[40] Relative clauses may follow gerunds. The information thus conveyed may be crucial as is the case with (a) (with the English), or it may be redundant as is the case in (b). In (a), the relative clause can be considered restrictive, so it does not require determination of the relative clause by a determiner. The relative clause in (b) should, however, be regarded as non-restrictive and is marked by the demonstrative 'na'de.
(a) . . .   'ja   to   'Nubi
             come-GER   GEN   Nubi-PL
      al   'umon   'je   'ini   me   Ingi'lish
      REL   PRON 3PL   come-Ø   here   with   NPROP
      ". . . the coming of the Nubi that they came [with] here together with the English."
(b) Da'kal   al   'uo   'ro   'dakal   'na'de   . . .
    enter-GER   REL   PRON 3SING   go-Ø   enter-Ø   DEM DIS
      "That entrance, which he went and entered [with], . . .",/ "That occasion on which he entered. . . ."
[41] In the following restrictive clause, the demonstrative 'nade'de modifies the proper noun Zaire and not the head noun of the relative clause.
      A'nas ab 'an   'rua 'mo   fi Za'ire 'nade'de,
      people REL PRON 1SING   go-Ø with + PRON 3SING in NPROP DEM DIS
      'umon   'kan   family ta   'awa   'tai.
      PRON 3PL   be-ANT   family GEN   aunt   PRON POSS 1SING
      "The people whom I went with to (that) Zaire, they were the family of my aunt."

(295) *Ab*   '*ito*   '*gu-*   *rwa*   '*gusu*   '*nouo*   '*de,*
      REL PRON 2SING   PROG- go   seek-Ø for + PRON 3SING DEF
      '*uo*   '*gu-*   *rw(a)*   '*aju*   '*ma.*
      PRON 3SING PROG- go   want-Ø NEG
      "The one [girl] you are going to seek for him, he is not going to want her."

Reference in the relative clause: In Nubi relative clauses, reference
in the subordinate clause is effected by means of a resumptive pronoun or *fogo* "in it" or else it is not referred to. If the head noun
or its co-referent takes the subject position in the subordinate clause,
nominal or pronominal reference is concealed as in (296):

(296) '*Uw(o)*   '*endi*   '*hikma,*   *a'jol*   *ab*   '*endis*   '*sana*   *mi'lan.*
      PRON 3SING have-Ø wisdom person REL have-Ø year(s) many
      "He has wisdom, someone who has many years/ who is old."

It is, however, optionally marked if the verb is passive. For instance,
in (297) the object position is marked, while it is not marked in
(298):

(297) *kala'ma*   *al*   *gu-*   *wonu's(u)*   *uo*
      thing-PL   REL   PROG- talk-PASS   PRON 3SING
      "the things that are being talked about (them)"

(298) '*Fi*   *nus'wan*   *ab*   *gi-*   *jow'zu*   *fi*   *sabab*   *fila'niya.*
      EXIS woman-PL REL   PROG- marry-PASS in   reason(s) certain-PL
      "There are women who are being married for certain reasons."

The object position in the subordinate clause is generally not marked
overtly as in (299):

(299) *me*   '*namn(a)*   *ab*   *it(a)*   '*ain*
      with   way   REL   PRON 2SING see-Ø
      "with the way you see (it)"

When the head noun is referred to in the relative clause by means
of a prepositional or possessive phrase, a resumptive pronoun is compulsory as in (300) and (301):

(300) . . . '*ina*   '*kan*   '*indu*   '*nas*   *ma'ma*   *fi*   '*jua*   '*motoka* '*de*
      PRON 1PL ANT   have   COLL woman in inside car   DEF
      al   '*ina*   *gi-*   '*ja*   '*moumon.*
      REL PRON 1PL PROG- come with + PRON 3PL
      ". . . we had women, whom we came with (them), inside the car."

(301) '*marya*   *ab*   '*ragi*   '*to*   '*mutu*
      woman REL   husband PRON POSS 3SING die-Ø
      "the woman whose husband died"

If the adverbial phrase expressed in the subordinate clause is one of manner, reference is indicated by *fogo* "in it" as in (302):

(302) ta'biya   a'l(i)   'ina   'raba   fogo
      custom(s)   REL   PRON 1PL   grow up-Ø   in it
      "the customs that we grew up in [them]"/ "the customs that we grew up with"

The locative is generally marked by *fogo* "in it" in the subordinate clause as in (303), as are adverbial phrases denoting purpose as in (304):

(303) ma'hal   al   nyere'ku   'de   ku'tu   fogo
      place   REL   child   DEF   put-PASS-Ø   in it
      "the place where the child was put in"

(304) ...   'sokol 'tai   'de   ...   'Ita   'ro   'bio
            thing PRON POSS 1SING   DEF   PRON 2SING go-Ø   buy-Ø
      'sokol   al   ba'ba   'taki   'rasul   'ita   fogo   'de.
      thing   REL   father   PRON POSS 2SING   send-Ø PRON 2SING   in it   DEF
      "... my thing.... You went to buy the thing which your father sent you for."

Time is either marked by *fogo* "in it" (305) or with zero pronominalization (306):

(305) 'sa   a'l(i)   'ina   gi-   'rasul   fogo, ...
      hour   REL   PRON 1PL   PROG-   arrive   in it
      "the time when we are arriving (in it), ..."

(306) 'sa   al   'ita   ja, ...
      hour   REL   PRON 2SING   come-Ø
      "the time when you came, ..."

Thus the coreferent of relative clauses related to place, time, manner, and purpose is indicated by *fogo*, either compulsorily (place, purpose) or optionally (time, manner).

Reference to the head noun is often absent in the subordinate clause in constructions like the following where the subordinate clause consists of a subjunctive clause. *al ke'de* acts more or less like a conjunction 'so that'. However, the notion of relativization remains present as in (307):

(307) 'Ya   bi'niy(a)   'abidu   'wonusu   ma   'luga
      CONJ   girl   begin-Ø   talk-Ø   with   language
      al   ke'de   'ragi   'd(e)   'aruf(u)   'asma   'ma.
      REL   SUBJ   man   DEF   know-Ø   understand-Ø   NEG

"Thus the girl began to talk in a language (which was such) so that the man could not understand."

Asyndetic relative clauses: In case of an indefinite antecedent, the relative marker may be omitted. The two propositions then occur juxtaposed and may or may not be linked by a resumptive pronoun or *fogo* as in (308) and (309):

(308) Ka'rib-   'tokum   *'chai*   *'ana*   *'rakabu.*
       be welcome-Ø ADR-PL   tea   PRON 1SING cook-Ø
       "Be(PL) welcome for tea [which] I prepared."

(309) A'jol   'ainu   *'sokol*   *'gelba* *'to*   *'dugu*   *fogo.*
       person see-Ø   thing   heart PRON POSS 3SING beat-Ø in it
       "Someone sees something [that] his heart beats for / [that] his heart desires."

Embedding: Several relative clauses may occur in one sentence, either in complex multiple embeddings, where two or more relative clauses each modify a distinct head noun (310), or conjoined, all relative clauses referring to the same head noun (311):

(310) *Wa'din*   *al*   *'endisi* *'gelba* *al*   *ne'siya*   *'gal:* . . .
       others   REL   have-Ø heart   REL   good   say-Ø
       "Others who have a heart that is good, say: . . ."

(311) fi   'dar   'gala   'wai   'na'de   al   ke'bir 'de,
       in   back   hill   NUM DEM DIS SING REL big   DEF
       al   gi-   na'di   N'samishi.
       REL   PROG- call-PASS   NPROP
       "at the back of that one hill, which is big, which is called Nsamishi."

The relative pronoun may occur in a possessive-like construction. The possessee or head noun is separated from the genitive particle *ta* and the possessor or modifier by the relative pronoun. The whole phrase conveys the meaning of being part of the total class of possessors or modifiers as in (312) and (313):

(312) *'sokol*   *ab*   *ta*   *a'dil*
       thing   REL   GEN   justice
       "something which takes part in justice"

(313) Ka'man 'umon   'ya   a'nas   al   to   'Nubi.
       also   PRON 3PL FOC   people   REL   GEN   NPROP
       "Also they are the people who are from among the Nubi (peoples)."

Headless relative clauses: A relative clause may be headless when it modifies a pronoun (i.e. a person) or when it refers to an item that is known to the hearer because it has been mentioned in previous discourse as in (314) and (315):

(314) *Al*   *ja*   *'moumon*   'ya   'dukuru
      REL   come-Ø   with + PRON 3PL   CONJ   then
      'já   amru'g(u)   'umon   fi'lel.
      come-PASS-Ø   remove-PASS-Ø   PRON   3PL   at night
      "Those who came with them were removed at night."

(315) 'Fi   'yal   we'le   ti'nen. . . .   Yo'wele 'wai   'de   ke'bir,
      EXIS   child-PL boy-PL NUM   boy   NUM   DEF   big
      'wai   'de   sa'kar.   . . .   *Ab*   *ke'bir*   *'de*   'kelem: . . .
      NUM   DEF   small   REL   big   DEF   say-Ø
      "There were two boys. . . .The one boy was the big one, the one was small. . . . [The one] who was big/ the big one said: . . . ."

Also time may be indicated by a headless relative clauses. The head, which is *'wakti* "time", *'sa* "hour", etc. is omitted.

(316) *Al*   *'umon*   *'gen*   *ba'kan* *'de*,   aja'ma te   min   'na
      REL   PRON 3PL   stay   place   DEF   people GEN   from   there
      gi-   'jibu   'noumon   'memvu.
      PROG- bring   for + PRON 3PL bananas
      "[The time that /when] they stayed there, the people from around there were bringing them bananas."

In some cases, *'ab* should be interpreted as 'possessor of a particular characteristic' when followed by a noun expressing a quality. These quasi-adjectives are infrequently placed after a head noun. In general, however, they are used as such. *Ab* + N is only partly productive in Nubi. Most forms of this type of compound are derived directly from Arabic source forms. I assume that the forms in (317) are among the few Nubi innovations.

(317) *ab 'guwa* "possessor of power", "someone who is powerful"
      ab lan'gaba "possessor of a mentality of walking around idly", "an idler"

3.4. *Constituent Order and Agreement within NP*

3.4.1. *Constituent Order within NP*

Postmodification: The head noun comes first immediately followed by either the indefinite article ʻ*wai* (318) or a pronominal possessor (319). The next position is occupied by the adjective (318) and/or the numeral (319). The latter two may exchange positions (311). The relative clause follows next (321). The definite article or a demonstrative, if present, comes in final position. It may, however, be followed by ʻ*kul* "all" (322):

(318) ʻmarya   ʻwai   ʻkweisi
      woman   INDEF   good
      "a good woman"

(319) waʼze   ʻtaki   tiʼnin
      parent-PL PRON POSS 2SING   NUM
      "your two parents"

(319) aʼku   ʻto   ʻwai   keʼbir ʻde
      brother   PRON POSS 3SING   NUM   big   DEF
      "his one eldest brother"

(320) ʻkeya   keʼbir   al   ʼjibu   Nubiʼya   min   Suʼdan
      army   big   REL   bring-Ø   NPROP   from NPROP
      "the big army that brought the Nubi from Sudan"

(321) kaʼbila   waʼdin-waʼdin   ʻdolʼde   ʻkulu
      tribe   other-PL-REDUP   DEM PROX PL   all
      "all these other tribes"

Premodification: ʻ*Kila* "every", ʻ*aya* "any", the collective marker ʻ*nas* and the markers for diminution and augmentation immediately precede the head noun as in (323) and (324):

(323) ʻkas   ʻto   te   ʻkila   ʻyoum
      work   PRON POSS 3SING   GEN   every   day
      "his work of every day"

(324) ʻnas   bagaʼra ta   baʼba
      COLL   cow-PL   GEN   father
      "father's cows"

Constituent order in possessive phrases: See 3.3.3.

Unusual word orders: Occasionally, the noun phrase is split up by short adverbs or interjections as in (325) and (326):

(325) 'Uo   'weledu ya'la   'na   ta'lata.
      PRON 3SING   bear-Ø   child-PL   there NUM
      "She bore three children (there)"

(326) 'Jina   'jua   'bes   'to   'fi   sa'kar je'de.
      smallness house   just   PRON POSS 3SING EXIS   small EMPH
      "His small house exists (just) small."

Coordination within the NP: See 6.6.1.

3.4.2. *Agreement within the NP*

As mentioned in 3.2.1 and 3.3.2.1, human beings, domestic animals, and household utensils are more likely to attract number agreement than non-domesticated animals and other things. Nevertheless, agreement is optional and may occur as in (327) and (328):

(327) 'wele   wa'din   'dol'de
      boy-PL   other-PL   DEM PROX PL
      "these other boys"

(328) kala'ma   ta'nin
      thing-PL   other-PL
      "other things"

And contrary to Owens' findings (1977) on Kenyan Nubi, agreement may be lacking as in (329) and (330):

(329) a'nas   'tan
      people-PL other-SING
      "other people"

(330) kala'ma   we'de
      thing-PL   DEM PROX SING
      "these things"

A noun may remain singular when, from the context or by any other device, such as a plural demonstrative or a non-numeral or numeral quantifier, it is clear that a plural form is denoted.

3.5. *Conclusion*

Nubi pronouns are part of quite a fixed set and indicate number but not gender. This corresponds to most creoles (Holm 1988). Reflexives are generally expressed by the pronoun and follow the verb. Variation only occurs within the group of emphatic reflexive pronouns. Most of them, except for *a'gi*+ PRON POSS have equivalents in many creole languages (Muysken and Smith 1995, 271–88).[42] It seems that *a'gi* followed by the possessive pronoun and *bi'nafsi* are gradually being replaced by the other forms since their use is restricted to northern areas and some old speakers.

Whereas nouns in most pidgin/creole languages are not inflected for number (see Holm 1988), plural marking exists in Nubi and is optionally applied. According to Owens (1977), agreement is even common in Kenyan Nubi. Nhial (1975, 81–93), however, denies that there is any agreement between noun and adjective. In fact, he even claims that, except for a few words, there are no plural forms of nouns and adjectives. Plurals of nouns and adjectives definitely exist in Nubi, although they are more frequent in lexical listing than in free speech. Plural formation also pertains more frequently to words referring to human beings and animates than to the other word classes. Holm (1988) and Bruyn (1995a, 259–70) mention a free morpheme that acts as a pluralizer and that is homophonous with PRON 3PL for the Atlantic and other creoles. In Nubi, no such marker occurs. Number may, however, be indicated by means of numeral and non-numeral quantifiers.

Creole definite articles—and the Nubi definite article shares this feature—are generally not derived from the definite article in the source languages but are based on demonstratives or other particles. However, while in most creole and other languages, the definite article derives from a distal demonstrative (Givón 1984, Bruyn 1995a, 259–70, Holm 1991), in Nubi it developed from the proximal

---

[42] UN *'agi ta* is probably a reflex of Sudanese Arabic *ḥagg*, which, on the one hand, is a particle expressing possession as in *el bêt da ḥaggî* "this house belongs to me", *da ḥagg minu?* / *ḥagg yâtu?* "whose is this?, while, on the other hand, it is an adjective or noun expressing truth or reality (see Roth 1969a, 121) and functioning as a kind of confirmation of the previous phrase.

emonstrative. The distribution of the articles (definite, indefinite) as opposed to the bare noun corresponds roughly to the use of the article that Bickerton (1981) and Givón (1984) sketch for creole languages, namely definite referential and indefinite referential NPs are marked by the definite and the indefinite article, respectively, whereas non-referential NPs receive zero marking (bare noun). However, the use of the Nubi bare noun is not restricted to the category of non-referential NPs. It may also occur instead of the definite article in cases of high thematic centrality of the NP and instead of the indefinite article when the NP scores high considering non-individuation.

De, whose main use is that of definite article, may also act as a demonstrative. On the other hand, demonstratives may function anaphorically besides coding temporal and spatial deixis. The deictic adverb denoting proximity, which is added to the proximal, plural demonstrative is associated with a sense of nearness, a feature that occurs in many pidgins and creoles as well (Holm 1988).

Alienable possessive relations are generally expressed by means of the genitive marker *ta* linking possessee and possessor, whereas inalienable possessive relations do not. Both types maintain the order possessee possessor, and both types have equivalents in many creole languages (Holm 1988, Bruyn 1995a, 259–70). Some inalienable possessive constructions have evolved into compounds and have become fixed semantically. Alienable possessive constructions refer to terminable possession, which applies to owner-possessed relations, class, time, location, and also material. Inalienable possessive constructions are associated with interminable relations and apply to kin terms, body parts, other part-whole relations, and goals. For some possessive constructions, such as goals, some part-whole relations, and locations where a certain action (in gerund) takes place, there is variation that most likely correlates with the degree of definiteness.

Non-restrictive relative clauses are often marked by a determiner while restrictive relative clauses are not. However, high pragmatic referentiality seems to interfere in such a way that restrictive relative clauses of topical persistent NPs are optionally marked by a determiner. Optional coding of pragmatically salient NPs marked by a restrictive relative clause may thus be a feature of an evolution that involves the definite article or anaphorically used demonstrative to emphasize pragmatic referentiality more than 'definiteness', i.e., identifiability to the hearer.

The last chapter will treat the above mentioned nominal, adjec-tival and other forms and their distribution and features from a diachronic perspective and relate them to the Arabic dialects of the Sudan, to the Arabic pidgins Juba Arabic and Turku, and to the substrate and adstrate languages.

CHAPTER FOUR

THE VERB PHRASE

In prototypical creoles, the verbal system is based on characteristic semantic distinctions. Nubi, at first sight, seems to fit into this pattern. A second look, however, teaches us that there is a wide variation of forms that express sometimes only slight semantic nuances. On the other hand, there may be quite some overlap, different forms pointing to the same meaning.

4.1. *Final -u: Verbal Particle or Transitivity Marker?*

Most Nubi verbs end in a vowel, whether *-i, -e, -a, -o,* or *-u,* a feature that corresponds to the Nubi tendency towards CV syllables. In Ugandan Nubi, about 57% of the verbs end in the vowel *-u.*[1] For Kenyan Nubi, Owens (1985a, 229–71) gives a figure of approximately 45% for the verbs that occur with final *-u.* This percentage is too high to be coincidental. Moreover, in some instances verbs are found with the *-u* ending, while in other cases they occur without it, e.g. *'awunu* or *'awun* "help", "assist". In this connection I would like to point out that verbs ending in *-i, -e, -a, -o* hardly ever drop the final vowel, so that the variation of *-u* requires an explanation. It has been suggested that *-u* is a verbal particle (Owens 1985a, 229–71) or alternatively that it is a transitivity marker (Versteegh 1984). I will discuss this problem from a synchronic perspective and from a diachonic perspective (7.5.1).

According to Owens, *-u* is predominantly present in verbs, as compared to other vowels and as opposed to nouns and adjectives, which mainly end in a final consonant and less frequently in the vowel *-i.*

---

[1] The Nubi lexicon includes a lot of Swahili verbs, which mostly end in *-a.* For the above-mentioned percentage, only those Swahili verbs were counted that are used in Nubi but do not have a Nubi synonym. Other Swahili verbs, which can be used in addition to a Nubi equivalent, were not added to the count.

To some extent, then, -i would have become identified as the vowel
of nominals and -u the vowel of verbs, with C-final forms being neutral between the two. (Owens 1985a, 258).

However, in the Ugandan Nubi material final -*i* being part of
the root, whether nominal or verbal, is rather uncommon. More
frequently, -*i* is attached as a binding vowel to a consonant final
root, whether verbal or nominal (see also Owens 1985a, 229–71). If
the final consonant is an alveolar and/or if it is preceded by a front
vowel, paragogic -*i* may occur, e.g. *'kuris(i)* "chair", *'feker(i)* "think",
'visit(i) "visit". Similarly, in certain cases -*u* should be analysed as a
paragogic vowel if attached to nominals and verbs ending in a non-
alveolar consonant and/or after a back vowel, e.g. *'tab(u)* "problem",
'num(u) "sleep" (see 2.2.3.1). -*i* and -*u* as binding vowels after nominals and verbs occur far less frequently in the variety of Nubi spoken in northern Uganda. Owens himself mentions that -*i* occurs
more frequently in the Ugandan variety than in Kenyan Nubi.[2] In
view of this, Owens' suggestion of identifying -*i* as the marking vowel
for nominals may be too strong. More likely, final -*i* should be treated
as a paragogic vowel both for verbs and nominals whose specific
quality (high front) depends on the vowel and/or the final consonant of the root it is attached to.[3] Although Owens does not completely ignore the variable occurrence of -*u* in texts—he refers to
Heine who says that vowels may be deleted when occurring between
two consonants, especially when these vowels are not stressed and
in fast speech (Heine 1982)—he does not seek a pattern in the usage
of -*u*.[4]

Regarding this variation, it has been suggested (Versteegh 1984)
that -*u* should be regarded as a marker of transitivity rather than as
a verbal marker. The correlation between the occurrence of -*u* and

---

[2] As far as I know, Owens' material does not include the Nubi variety of northern Uganda.

[3] Parallels are found in Swahili. Tucker (1947, 214–32), in investigating the
Swahili verb, argues that the imperative state of the Arabic verb is the basis of the
Swahili verb form through metathesis of the first vowel and consonant. However,
the quality of the vowel suffixed to the verb stem is linked to the vowels of the
verb stem itself (if fronted, it becomes -*i*; if a back vowel, it will be -*u*), and to the
quality of the final consonant (if labial, the final vowel is -*u*).

[4] Tosco (1995, 455, n. 1) mentions that verb final -*u* is often deleted, especially
before a vowel or glide.

the inherent transitive meaning of a verb is indeed undeniable in Heine's lexical list and in the information I elicited from native speakers (see also table 18, in which Nubi transitive/intransitive verbs are listed). Nubi speakers give different citation forms for the same verb stem, depending on whether it is used in its transitive or in its intransitive sense as in (331) and (332).

(331) *'num* "sleep"
       'gum "get up"
       'hum "swim"

(332) *'kasuru* "break s.th."   >< *'kasur* "break"
       'karabu "spoil s.th."   >< *'karab* "spoil", "be spoilt"
       'woduru "loose s.th."   >< *'wodur* "be lost"
       etc.[5]

I will investigate whether the occurrence of *-u* also correlates with high transitivity at the clause level. Hopper and Thompson (1980, 251–99) regard transitivity as a global property of a clause that includes many separate components.[6] Each component or transitivity parameter contributes to the effective transfer of an action from

---

[5] The verbs *'abidu* "begin", "begin s.th.", *'ataku* "laugh", "ridicule s.o.", *'beredu* "take a bath", "wash s.o.", *'ferteku* "be separated", "separate s.th.", *'furu* "boil", "boil s.th.", *'futu* "pass by", "pass s.th.", *'geru* "change", "change s.th.", *'haragu* "burn", "burn s.th.", *'lesegu* "be sticky", "stick s.th.", *'nigitu* "get ripe", "pick s.th.", *'rudu* "agree", "accept s.th.", *'setetu* "be scattered", "scatter s.th.", *'zidu* "increase", "increase s.th." are both transitive and intransitive and have a fixed form, owing to phonological constraints (see 2.2.1.1). Similarly, the verbs *'agider* "be able to", *'feker* "think s.th.", *lebis* "get dressed", "dress s.o.", *'gisir* "loose skin", "peel s.th.", *fata'ran* "be tired", "tire s.o.", *sa'ban* "be satisfied", "satisfy s.o.", *ta'ban* "be worried", "worry s.o.", and *was'kan* "be dirty", "make s.th. dirty" have a C-final ending, although a paragogic vowel *-i* may be added in allegro forms.

[6] Hopper and Thompson (1980, 252) present the following parameters:

	HIGH	LOW
A. PARTICIPANTS	2 or more participants, A and O	1 participant
B. KINESIS	action	non-action
C. ASPECT	telic	atelic
D. PUNCTUALITY	punctual	non-punctual
E. VOLITIONALITY	volitional	non-volitional
F. AFFIRMATION	affirmative	negative
G. MODE	realis	irrealis
H. AGENCY	A high in potency	A low in potency
I. AFFECTEDNESS OF O	O totally affected	O not affected
J. INDIVIDUATION OF O	O highly individuated	O non-individuated.

one participant to the other, and transitivity must be understood as a manifestation on a gliding scale or continuum, rather than as a fixed reference point. The transitivity notion is expressed grammatically in its entirety, rather than one single aspect. In Ugandan Nubi, a correlation between the occurrence or non-occurrence of -*u* and the transitivity of the clause seems to exist, where transitivity is interpreted as the effective transfer of an action from an agent to a patient. Thus, the number of participants involved in the verbal action can be considered one of the most if not the most decisive factor causing the occurrence of the verbal vowel -*u*. In a significant number of cases in the text material from Ugandan Nubi, verbs with only one participant occur without the suffix -*u* as in (333):

(333) 'Uo   '*meles*   fu   'lufra 'de.
      PRON 3SING   slip-Ø   in   hole   DEF
      "He slipped into the hole."

(334) 'Ita   'ma   'aju   'sokol 'taki   'de
      PRON 2SING   NEG   want-Ø   thing   PRON POSS 2SING   DEF
      ke'de   '*karab*.
      SUBJ   be spoilt-Ø
      "You do not want the thing of you to get spoilt."

Inherently transitive verbs that do not take a second participant in the clause occur more often without -*u* than with it as in (335):

(335) 'Ya   nyere'ku   'de   '*g(i)*- *akul*.
      CONJ   child   DEF   PROG-   eat
      "Thus the child was eating."

The converse situation, however, where two or more participants are available, is less evident. It is not the mere presence of an agent and an object that is relevant but also the strength of the features that are related to them like the potency of the agent, affectedness, and the individuation of the object. Individuation of the object indicates the degree to which the object is distinguished from the agent and from its own background. This notion itself includes several features, as shown in table 16:

The merger of these different parameters—each varying on a gliding scale—defines the position of the entire clause on the transitivity scale, ranging from more to less transitive.

Table 16. Features of (non-) individuation of the object

Individuated	Non-individuated
Proper	Common
Human, animate	Inanimate
Concrete	Abstract
Singular	Plural
Count	Mass
Referential, definite	Non-referential

Source: Hopper and Thompson (1980, 253)

According to Hopper and Thompson (1980, 251–99) the transfer of an action to an individuated patient is effected more successfully than to a non-individuated patient.

Since so many features are involved, an object cannot simply be categorized as individuated or not but must be evaluated according to its position on a gliding scale. The Nubi material conforms to the above, since non-individuated or only slightly individuated objects are mainly found with verbs to which -*u* is not attached as in (336):

(336) *rakab 'chai* "cook tea"   common, inanimate, mass, non-referential
      'kasul sa'na "do the dishes"   common, inanimate, mass, non-referential
      'selim 'badu "greet each other"   common, plural, non-referential
      'kasur la'kata "chop wood"   common, inanimate, mass, non-referential
      'akul ka'sara "eat at a loss", "eat for free"   abstract, non-referential.

On the contrary, individuated objects, rating higher on the gliding scale because of the features 'referential' or 'human, animate' seem to co-occur with verbs ending in -*u* as in (337), (338), (339), and (340):

(337) 'Rabana   *jibu*   *fruits*   *ta*   *'yembe.*   referential
      God   bring-Ø   fruits   GEN   mango
      "God brought the fruits of the mango."

(338) 'Ita   *'kubu*   *la'kata*   *'de.*   definite
      PRON 2SING   throw-Ø   wood   DEF
      "You threw the wood."

(339) 'Itokum   *'sulu*   *nyere'ku*   *'de.*   human, definite
      PRON 2PL   take-Ø   child   DEF
      "You took the child."

(340) Su'nun li'fil   'ma   *gi-*   *'gelibu 'sidu.*   animate, referential
      tusk(s) elephant NEG   PROG-   trouble owner:
      "The tusks of an elephant do not trouble the owner."

When the object is topicalized or has been mentioned in a previous sentence, the same applies. The more individuated, the higher the chance that the verb occurs with the verbal vowel -u. In (341), the object, even if inanimate, is referential, definite, and concrete. The verb occurs with -u.

(341) Ko'rofo   'libya   'de   'aswe   je'de   'ya   'itokum   'g(i)-   asrubu.
      leaves   peas   DEF   black   EMPH   FOC   PRON 2PL   PROG-   drink
      "It is [the sauce of] the very black leaves of the cowpea which you are drinking."

For the above-mentioned features (two or more participants, the individuation of the patient), a correlation could be ascertained with the occurrence or non-occurrence of -u. These features are particularly relevant for the essence of transitivity: one participant acts effectively upon another. From this, it follows that stative verbs, even if occurring with a second participant, can be considered rather low in transitivity. Such clauses can be encoded as intransitive in Nubi. For instance, 'like someone' may be expressed as 'be pleasant to someone'. A clause with two participants whose second participant is not very much affected as the result of a voluntary action by the first participant can then be encoded as a single participant clause with an intransitive verb (see also Hopper and Thompson 1980, 251–99) as in (342):

(342) . . .   ka'man   je   'nana   'hilu.
              EMPH   become-Ø   to + PRON 1SING   nice
      ". . . it became nice to me / I began to like it."

From the Ugandan Nubi text material, it appears that Nubi stative and involuntary verbs, even with two participants present, tend to occur without the final vowel -u as in (343) and (344):

(343) 'Uw(o)   'aruf   te'gil   al   'fi   fi   'batna   'jua.
      PRON 3SING   know-Ø   hardship(s)   REL   EXIS   in   inside   house
      "She knows the hardships that are inside the house."

(344) 'An   je'de   'ain   ka'las   nyere'ku   'tai,
      PRON 1SING   EMPH   see-Ø COMPL   child   PRON POSS 1SING
      bi'niya   'de   'tim   'marya.
      girl   DEF   be enough-Ø   woman
      "I see that my child, the girl, has already become a woman."

Since transitivity should be regarded as a continuum and therefore cannot be explained in terms of an absolute transitive/intransitive

division, the consequence for the verbal vowel *-u* is that its occurrence or non-occurrence cannot be described in one simple rule.
Even so, there are clauses where the attachment of *-u* to the verb
cannot be justified by the transitivity of the clause, since the properties of transitivity in the clause are very low as in (345) and (346):

(345) Mali'ma   'de   'g(i)-   aruf,   ma   'umon   *gi-*   *'doru.*
      teacher-PL   DEF   PROG- know   and PRON 3PL PROG- wander about
      "The teachers know, and they are wandering about."

(346) Ba'na 'de   *'ataku*   'sei-'sei.
      girl-PL DEF laugh-Ø very much-REDUP
      "The girls laughed a lot."

Similarly, there are examples of verbs occurring without *-u* where
final *-u* would be expected on the basis of the transitivity of the
clause as in (347) and (348):

(347) 'Uo   *jib*   *bi'niya* 'de   fi   'batna   'be   'in.
      PRON 3SING bring-Ø girl   'DEF   in   belly   home   here
      "He brought the girl into our home here."

(348) . . . 'ina   *gi-*   'sul   *ya'la* *de.*
            PRON1PL   PROG- take   child-PL DEF
      ". . . we are taking the children."

It appears that in such cases phonological conditions are to be taken
into account as well (see especially 2.2.1 and 2.2.3.1). Since these
phonological rules have an impact regardless of the transitivity of
the clause, they could conceivably be assumed to weaken the arguments that verbal *-u* correlates with high transitivity. However, these
phonological rules are general and apply to all grammatical categories. Therefore, they should be treated as an explanation for the
unexpected absence of *-u* in verbs rather than as an argument under-
mining the evaluation of *-u* as a transitivity marker.

   I have contrasted the analysis of *-u* as a verbal marker with the
theory of *-u* as a transitive marker. Owens took the high correlation
of the occurrence of *-u* with verbs as evidence for considering *-u* to
be a verbal marker as opposed to the vowel *-i*, which he related to
Nubi nouns. He believes that the verb form to which *-u* is suffixed
is the base form from which, in rapid speech, *-u* can be omitted. It
is true that *-u* is found relatively more often with verbs than with
nouns and similarly that the final *-i* occurs more frequently with
nouns than with verbs.

I would rather agree with Versteegh (1984), who considers *-u* to mark transitivity. Transitivity can be defined as an effective transfer of an action from an agent to a patient. This implies that there is more than one participant (an active agent and at least one patient) available and that the action is transferred by a kinetic/volitional verb to an individuated object that is involved in receiving the action. Transitivity should therefore be considered a continuum, going from lower to higher transitivity. Evidence for Versteegh's approach was obtained from the Ugandan Nubi material. Citation verb forms in lexical lists and elicitation exhibit a variable form. Transitive verbs tend to occur with the vowel *-u*, while verbs with only one partici-pant tend to appear without it. Moreover, a study of the Ugandan Nubi text material shows that there is a relation between the occur-rence of the *-u* ending and the notion of transitivity. In clauses that are higher on the scale of transitivity, the verb tends to occur with the vowel *-u*, while in clauses that are low in transitivity, the verb is more likely to occur without *-u*. In discourse, however, the rela-tion between transitivity and occurrence of *-u* may be obscured by phonological processes.

In the case of some other pidgin languages, a similar assumption is based on clear evidence. In New Guinea Pidgin, for example, in the stabilizing phase, the transitive marker *-im* is used in the for-mation of transitive verbs from nouns and intransitive verbs. Attached to intransitive verbs, adjectives, and even to transitive verbs, it adds a transitive or a causative meaning. Mühlhäusler (1979, 374) states that:

> The number of genuine transitive bases in NGP is relatively small and many of the forms traditionally listed as transitive verbs by virtue of the fact that they are never found without -im are transitive verbals derived from noun bases or causative verbals derived from adjective or intransitive verb bases.

The hypothesis of the transitive function of *-u* does not contradict the high frequency, mentioned by Owens (1985a, 229–71), of the occurrence of *-u* in verbs, but it does specify its meaning.

4.2. *TMA-marking*

The core element of the Nubi verbal system is the unmarked verb form, to which I also refer as 'bare' or 'simple verb form'. Verbs are not inflected morphologically, except for the passive and gerundival verb forms. TMA is marked by markers and/or auxiliaries or may be left unexpressed if time references are indicated by lexical means such as adverbs and adverbial phrases or by the context or situation.

4.2.1. *TA-marking*

4.2.1.1. *The Simple Verb Form (Ø) and the Progressive Marker gi-*
In the following sections, the functions of the unmarked verb form and the progressive marker *gi-* will be discussed. Common to both is that they are neutral with regard to tense. The unmarked or simple verb form typically expresses punctual aspect, while the progressive marker *gi-* denotes the non-punctual aspect. Stative verbs will be discussed as a special group whose use of both aspect markers (Ø and *gi-*) differs from non-stative verbs. Moreover, the unmarked verb form is in some cases neutral as regards aspect and/or tense. The *gi-* marked verb may be neutral with respect to tense, but not to aspect. In those cases, the hearer is informed about tense and aspect by marking in other verbs, adverbs, and/or the context.

Stative versus non-stative verbs: Nubi distinguishes between stative and non-stative or dynamic verbs. Stative verbs semantically denote a state and so do not involve a dynamic process ultimately leading to change (see also Bickerton 1975). Stative verbs include:

* verbs expressing feeling and emotions (see also Owens 1977, 109) as in (349):

(349) *'asma* "feel"
       'aju "wish", "want", "like", "need"
       'hibu "love", "like"
       'kariha "hate"
       fu'rai "be happy"
       ja'lan "be happy"
       etc.

* verbs reflecting a mental activity (see also Owens 1977, 109) such as:

(350) *'rudu* "agree", "accept", "allow"
       'aba "refuse", "deny"
       'ainu "understand", "feel", "mean"
       'kelemu "mean"

'sulu "consider"
'fahamu "understand"
'feker "think"
'arufu "know"
'alimu "be used to"
'aminu "believe", "trust"
tuma'ini/ tege'mea "rely on", "expect", "trust"
ni'situ "forget"
'sama "forgive"
siki'tika "regret", "feel sorry"
kum'buka "remember"
etc.

* verbs semantically pertaining to state:

(351) *'gen* "stay", "sit", "reside", "remain"
 'gai "stay", "sit", 'reside", "remain"[7]
 'fi EXIS
 'fadul "remain"
 'ben "look like", "seem"
 'tim "be enough", "be sufficient", "be present", "be completed"
 'tosha "be enough", "be sufficient"
 'weza "be able to"
 'agider "be able to"
 etc.

* verbs of (non-)possession such as:

(352) *'endi(s)(i)* "have"
 'kosa "lack", "be lacking"
 etc.

Non-stative verbs express a dynamic event and include all other verbs.

The bare verb form versus the *gi-* marked verb: The unmarked verb form of non-stative verbs marks punctual aspect and realis and thus essentially refers to past events. It often occurs in narratives referring to in-sequence events.

---

[7] *'Gen* and *'gai* are absolute synonyms. Their distribution depends on the region. *'Gen* is mainly used in the northern part of Uganda, while *'gai* is the form used by southern Nubi speakers. If there are exceptions, they are mainly among northern speakers who may use *'gai* besides *'gen*, or as an alternative of *'gen*.

(353) 'Ina   'weledu,   'ina   'sul   ya'la,
      PRON 1PL   give birth-Ø   PRON 1PL   take-Ø   child-PL
      'ino   we'di   fi   'school.
      PRON 1PL   bring-Ø   to   school
      "We gave birth, we took the children, we brought [them] to school."

(354) 'Ita   'kalas   ku'ruju,   'ita   'nedif(u) 'ita,
      PRON 2SING   finish-Ø   work the field-GER   PRON 2SING   clean-Ø   PRON 2SING
      'ita   'ja.
      PRON 2SING   come-Ø
      "You finished working the field, you cleaned yourself, you came."

The progressive marker indicates the non-punctual aspect. The situation is taken as an ongoing process and is viewed from within. Essentially, it refers to present time. Subtypes of the non-punctual aspect, marked by Nubi *gi-*, are:

* continuation of actions/events, expressing duration and non-punctuality as in (355):

(355) 'Mutu   ke'tiri   'fara.   'Wede   wa'nasa
      die-GER   many   party   DEM PROX   talk-GER
      ta   wa'ze   za'man   al   gu-   we'di   'guwa   'noumon.
      GEN old person-PL old days REL   PROG-   give   strength   to + PRON 3PL
      "Dying with many is a party. This is talking/an expression of the old people in the old days, which gave them strength."

* iterativity as in (356):

(356) A'ta   at 'times   kan   'ana   gu-   'wonus, ...
      no   at times   if   PRON 1SING   PROG-   talk
      "No, at times when I am talking, . . . "

* the habitual aspect gives a rather general statement about events occurring from time to time as in (357). Habitual and generic aspect are closely related and will not be treated separately here.

(357) . . . 'ija   . . .   Kan 'ita   'gu-   rw(a) 'abidu   je'de,
            fairy tail   if   PRON 2SING PROG- go   begin-Ø   EMPH
      'ita   gi-   kelem 'gal: 'ijama'jako.
      PRON 2SING   PROG- say   that   ijamajako
      'Dukuru 'ita   'g(i)-   abidu.
      then   PRON2SING PROG- begin
      ". . . a fairy tail . . . When you are going to begin [it], you say that: ijamajako. Then you begin."

Whereas the unmarked verb form in narratives relates to the back-
bone of the story or the foregrounded information, verbs with the
progressive marker give additional information, referring to the back-
grounded portion of a text as in (358):

(358) 'Ya   'ini   sul'tan,   'sa   al   'ita   'rua,
      CONJ   here   sultan   moment REL   PRON 2SING   go-Ø
      'ite   'sebu   kala'ma   ta   'be   'de   ka'waida
      PRON 2SING leave-Ø thing-PL   GEN   house   DEF   like usual
      ja   'kila   'youm   'ana   gu-   'so   'de.
      like   every   day   PRON 1SING PROG- do   DEF
      "Thus here, sultan, the moment you went, you left the matters of the house
      as usual, like I am doing [them] daily."

Both the bare form marking punctuality and the verb with the *gi-*
prefix may express a subjunctive, a condition, an imperative, or the
complement of a main verb. The bare form is used when completion of the action or event is suggested, and the *gi-* marker is used
to convey duration or repetition of the action (see below).

Stative verbs, which are found at the extreme end of the punc-
tual/non-punctual axis, do not normally take the progressive marker.
For most verbs, the unmarked form of the stative verb indicates a
state that was initiated some time previously and that continues and
will continue up to an unmarked future. For instance, the verb
kum'buka "remember" refers to an act of remembering which took
place in the recent past. Consequently, the agent still remembers
and will continue to remember. Consider also (359):

(359) 'Uw(o)   'aju   'keta   'wonus'fogo nyere'ku
      PRON 3SING   want-Ø   SUBJ + PRON 2SING talk-Ø on   child
      'to   'ma.   'It(a)   'ain   'sa   al   'ase'de 'ya'de.
      PRON POSS 3SING NEG   PRON 2SING see-Ø time REL now PRES PROX
      "She does not want you to talk about her child. You see that current times are as
      such."

Stative verbs may, however, take the *gi*-marker in three cases. First,
the progressive marker can precede stative verbs and express that
the state has only come into being at the very moment of speaking
or that the action resulting in a state is only taking place now. It
thus involves inchoative meaning as in (360):

(360) Fi   'mwisho wa'ze   'bes   gu-   'rudu   'so   'jowzu   'de.
      in   end   parent-PL simply PROG- agree   do-Ø wedding DEF
      "In the end, the parents simply agree to do the wedding."

It is often preceded by the auxiliary *ja* "come" which also marks inchoativeness (see below):

(361) 'Ana   *je-'ja*   *gi-*   *ni'situ* 'tan   ka'man.
      PRON 1SING   come-REDUP-Ø PROG- forget other(s) also
      "I also began to forget others."

The same applies to the group of Nubi adjectives that are lexicalized as verbs. These refer to non-permanent qualities, such as human mental and physical characteristics (see also 3.3.2.3). Left unmarked, this type of adjectives expresses a state as in (362):

(362) Ka'lam   'taki   'de   *'hilu*   'nana   'ma.
      problem   PRON POSS 2SING DEF   sweet   to + PRON 1SING   NEG
      "Your problem is not sweet/pleasant to me."

When marked by the progressive prefix, however, a process is indicated that refers to the inception of the state, to its creation (see also Bickerton 1975) as in (363):

(363) 'Sa   ab   'guna   'de   *gi-*   *'hilu*   'nana, . . .
      moment   REL   song   DEF PROG- be sweet   to + PRON 1SING
      "The moment the song becomes sweet to me, . . ."

Second, habitually recurring states are often, but not obligatorily, marked by preverbal *gi-*. Adverbs, like *'kila 'youm* "everyday", "always", *'zaidi* "often", may co-occur with *gi-* marking as in (364) and (365):

(364) 'Gal: 'ahah, 'gari   'taki,   kan a'nas *'g(i)-*   *aj(u)*   *'alim(u)*,
      that INT   bicycle PRON POSS 2SING if people PROG-   want   learn-Ø
      'ita   *'g(i)-*   *aba*   na   a'nas 'gal   ka'lam su'nu?
      PRON 2SING PROG- refuse to   people that(EMPH) why?
      "That: ahah, your bicycle, if/every time people want to learn [to drive] it, why do you refuse the people?"

(365) Nyere'ku kan 'ita   *'g(i)-*   *alim(u)*, 'aju 'dugu   *gi-*   *'fi*   'sia.
      child   if   PRON 2SING PROG- teach   need-Ø beat-GER PROG- EXIS bit
      "If you teach a child, there should be a bit of beating."

Third, some speakers apparently treat the verbs *'gen* and *'gai* "stay", "sit", "live", "remain", and *'ben* "look like", "resemble", grammatically as non-stative verbs, which means that in their speech these verbs mainly occur with the progressive marker *gi-* even when not conveying habitual or inchoative meaning. Several of these speakers have stayed for a longer or shorter time in southern Sudan and may

thus have been influenced by Juba Arabic, where, according to
Mahmud (1979), the marker *gi-* and verbs like "stay", "stay silent",
"live" regularly co-occur. Although other verbs are affected as well—
albeit rather infrequently and irregularly, for instance *'arufu* in (368)—
the main verbs that take the progressive marker are *'gen, 'gai* "sit",
"remain", and *'ben* "seem", "look like" as in (366) and (367):

(366) La'kin 'nas   ma'ma 'tena   gi-   'gai   bo'yi min   'na.
      but   COLL mother PRON POSS 1PL PROG- stay   far   from   there
      "But my mother and her family stay far from there."

(367) Gi-   'ben   'j(e) ina   'ya   'katul(u)
      PROG- seem like   PRON 1PL   FOC   kill-Ø
      nyere'ku   'toumon   'de.
      Child   PRON POSS 3PL   DEF
      "It looks as if we are the ones who killed their child."

(368) nyere'ku   . . . ke'd(e) uo   'alim   ta'biya ta   'gai
      child   SUBJ PRON 3SING learn-Ø habit   GEN   stay-GER
      ma   a'nas 'kweis, ke'd(e) uo   'g(i)- aruf   'selem difa'na . . .
      COM people well   SUBJ PRON 3SING PROG- know greet-Ø guest-PL
      "a child . . . it should learn the habit to stay well with people, it should know
      [how] to greet guests. . . ."

Summarizing the above, the unmarked simple verb form can be
linked to the punctual aspect, whereas the progressive marker *gi-* is
the marker for the non-punctual aspect. As long as no other time
marking is available, the bare form of non-stative verbs refers to the
past while the non-stative verb preceded by the *gi-* marker refers to
a present event. Stative verbs do not normally take the progressive
marker except when indicating the inchoative of stative verbs and
verbal adjectives when denoting the habitual or generic aspect and
with the verbs *'gen, 'gai* "sit", "stay", and *'ben* "look like", "seem" in
the speech of a limited group.

However, besides its use expressing punctual aspect, the simple
verb form can be used in all other contexts and may therefore refer
to all other aspects and tenses, like the durative, habitual, iterative,
past, present, and future. The context, other marked verbs, and/or
adverbs give information about the time and aspectual framework
in which the action or situation expressed by the unmarked verb
form is situated:

* future as in (369):

(369) 'Itokum   bi-   'arija,   .
      PRON 2PL   FUT-   return
      'itokum   'rua   'gai   fi   'be   'takum
      PRON 2PL   go-Ø   stay-Ø   in   house   PRON POSS 2PL
      "You(PL) will come back, you will go to stay at your(PL) place."

* durative:

(370) 'Dinya   ki'lele 'de   'kul, 'ita   'gus   'wélédu?!!
      enormity noise DEM PROX all   PRON 2SING look for-Ø   bear-INF
      "All this noise, you are attempting to give birth/ you are mating?!!"

* habitual as in (371):

(371) Yo'wele,'kila min 'sub,   'uo   kub   'moyo 'te   te   'maua.
      boy   every in morning PRON 3SING pour-Ø water under GEN flowers
      "The boy, every morning, he pours water under the flowers."

The progressive marker *gi-* is equally neutral as regards tense. It is,
however, not neutral with respect to aspect. Events expressed by
non-stative verbs with the progressive marker *gi-* can be situated in
past, present, or future as long as the tense is marked by other means
such as adverbs, tense marking on other verbs, or the context:

* the progressive marker in the past: In (372), tense is marked
in the introductory sentence and again in the second sentence,
both times by *'kan*. *'Kan* is, however, not repeated in the following
sentences.

(372) 'Ana,   fi   wa'kati al   'kan   'ana   fi   gi-   'raba,
      PRON 1SING in   time   REL ANT   PRON 1SING   EXIS PROG- grow up
      ma'ma 'tai   'me   'endi   'hukum   'fog(o) 'ana.
      mother PRON POSS 1SING NEG have-Ø authority   on   PRON 1SING
      'Kan   ma'ma 'de,   ma'ma 'wai,   ji'ran   'bes   je'de   'ya
      ANT   mother DEF   mother INDEF neighbour EMPH EMPH FOC
      gu-   'hukum(u)   'ita   fi   'batna 'be   'takum.
      PROG- have authority over   PRON 2SING on   inside house   PRON POSS 2PL
      Gi-   'ben   je   'uo   'ya   ma'ma 'taki.
      PROG- look   like PRON 3SING   FOC   mother PRON POSS 2SING
      "I, at the time when I was growing up, my mother did not have authority over me.
      It was the mother, a mother, the neighbour who had authority over you inside your
      (PL) house. It looked as if she were your mother."

* the progressive marker in the future:

(373) 'Itokum   bi-   'arija   'gai   fi   line,
      PRON 2PL FUT-   return   stay   in   line
      'itokum   *gi-*   *'juru*   'youm.
      PRON 2PL PROG-   pull   day(s)
      "You (PL) will stay together again, you will pull/increase the days."

Essentially, the simple verb form and the *gi-* marker refer to punctual and non-punctual aspects respectively. Moreover, the simple verb form can express any tense or aspect, including continuation and repetition, if they are marked by other means, such as adverbs, adverbial phrases, and the context. The progressive marker is neutral with respect to time and always denotes non-punctuality.

4.2.1.2. *The Future Marker bi-*
The verbal prefix *bi-* marks unrealized future events and is commonly found in conditional sentences. Besides marking future events, it can also mark habitual actions irrespective of time. We will first take a look at the use of *bi-* to mark future events. Rather than expressing strict futurity, the prefix *bi-* adds a modal meaning signifying volition or strong expectation of future events. No clear time indication is given as is illustrated in (374) and (375):

(374) 'Ina   'bes   gi-   'doru,   ...,   ba'kan   al   ya'tu?
      PRON 1PL   just   PROG-   wanderaround   place   REL   what?
      'Ana   *bi-*   *lo'go*   'fogo   'be.
      PRON 1SING FUT-   find   in it   home
      "We are just wandering around,..., [to] which place? I will find a home in it."

(375) 'Kweis,   'ana   ka'man   *bi-*   *'wonusu*   'sia ....
      good   PRON 1SING   also   FUT-   talk   a little bit
      "Good, I will also talk a little bit...."

The above sentences are examples of the absolute future, i.e., future events as seen from the present moment. Relative future events, those seen from a reference point in the past, are also expressed with the future marker *bi-* as is illustrated in (376):

(376) DMO, medical districti ta   'Toro we'di 'nena   'sente 'sia
      DMO medical district GEN Toro give-Ø to + PRON 1PL money bit
      al   *'b(i)-*   *awun(u)* 'ina   fu   'akil   'tena.
      REL FUT-   help   PRON 1PL in   food   PRON POSS 1PL
      "The DMO, the medical district of Toro gave us a little money which would help us for [buying] our food."

The future marker *bi-* may also express a present or future possibility or potentiality. When occurring with the negative marker *'ma*, it may indicate non-possibility or non-potentiality as in (377) and (378):

(377) A'jol   ab   a'wiri   *bi-*   *ali'm(u)*   uo   ke'fin?
      person   REL   stupid   FUT- train-PASS   PRON 3SING   how?
      "How can a stupid person be trained?"

(378) 'Bele   *bi-*   *'raba*   *'ma*   u   'Nubi   *bi-*   *'raba*   *'ma*!
      country FUT- develop NEG   CONJ   Nubi   FUT- develop NEG
      "The country won't develop and the Nubi won't develop!"

The future marker *bi-* is common in conditional clauses as in (379) and (380):

(379) Kan   'sa   'to   'lisa, . . .,
      if   time   PRON POSS 3SING   still
      'ite   *bu-*   *'endi*   'kutu   'nouo   'moyo.
      PRON 2SING   FUT- have   put-Ø   for + PRON 3SING   water
      "If his time is still [continuing], you will have to put water for him."

(380) Ma'isha   'de   'ya   kan bi-   'gai   jo   wede'de,
      life   DEM PROX   FOC   if   FUT- stay   like   DEM PROX
      bu-   *'kun*   *ke'fini?*
      FUT- be   how?
      "If this life will stay like this, how will it be?"

Besides future marking, *bi-* may as well indicate an habitual action or event irrespective of time as in (381) and (382). In this respect, it is interchangeable with the marker *gi-*. Below, I attribute this interchangeability to an ongoing process in which *bi-* is gradually being replaced by *gi-* in marking the habitual.

(381) Ya'la   ta   'ina   te   you'min'de, ta'fauti   'fi   'fogo.
      child-PL   GEN   here   GEN nowadays   difference(s)   EXIS   in it
      Ka'lam 'uo   *'b(i)-*   *aj(u)*   'ainu   ma'ma 'taki   'ma.
      because PRON 3SING FUT- want   consider-Ø   mother PRON POSS 2SING NEG
      "The children of here and of current times are different. Because he/they do not
      want to consider your mother."

(382) La'kini 'ma   'ya   je   ta   'ase'de.   'Sente   'ma'fi.
      but   NEG   FOC   like   GEN   now   money   EXIS NEG
      Gi-   'só   'saki.   'Itokum   *bi-*   *'zikiri*
      PROG- do-PASS   for free PRON 2PL   PROG- recite (for)
      a'nas   ta   ra'kabu,   . . .
      people GEN   cook-GER
      "But it is not like (of) now. There is no money. It is done for free. You(PL)
      ecite for the cooks, ..."

Let us consider the use of *bi-* and/or *gi-* in marking habituality in Nubi. For Kenyan Nubi, neither Heine (1982) nor Owens (1977) mention the use of *bi-* to mark the habitual. However, if we take a look at Heine's text on wedding customs (Heine 1982, 53–55), it seems that as in Ugandan Nubi, both *bi-* and *gi-* are used to indicate the habitual. The text material is, however, not extensive enough to see whether there are any developments. In Ugandan Nubi, *bi-* marks the future and the habitual whereas *gi-* is obviously a marker of non-punctuality, including among its functions the marking of duration and iterativity/habituality. In one text portion and even in one sentence, speakers, whether from the north or the south, whether old or young, may use both *gi-* and *bi-* to express habituality. Generally, *gi-* marks the habitual more frequently than *bi-*, as is the case in the Kenyan Nubi text on wedding customs (twenty one times *gi-* compared to eigth times *bi-*). Moreover, in Heine's texts, *gi-* is used instead of *bi-*, with the stative verbs *'gen* "sit", "stay", *'gai* "sit", "remain", and *'ben* "look like", and with all other stative verbs to mark habituality. Generally in Nubi, a distinction is made for stative vs. non-stative verbs. On the other hand, some stative verbs, the most outstanding being *'gen* and *'gai*, may appear with the marker *gi-*. Moreover, in general, stative verbs use the progressive marker *gi-* to denote habituality or inchoativeness. This implies that a process in which the stative/non-stative distinction is gradually smoothened seems to be taking place, both in Ugandan and in Kenyan Nubi. However, *gi-* rather than *bi-* marks stative verbs. Therefore, I have the impression that an evolution is taking place in which *gi-* is gradually taking over the function of *bi-* in expressing habituality. Since *gi-* and *bi-* are used in Nubi to refer to habitual events and because at the same time the bare verb form is neutral as regards aspect and time on condition that tense and aspect are clearly set in the text, the simple verb form and the *bi-* and *gi-* markers may co-occur in one text portion to express habituality as in (383):

(383) *Gi-*   *ji'bu*   'waraga.   'Waraga, 'ragi 'de   *bi-*   'katif
　　　 PROG- bring-PASS letter　　　 letter   man   DEF   FUT-   write
　　　 'waraga.　　　　 *Uo*　　　 'rasul.
　　　 letter　　　　　　 PRON 3SING send-Ø
　　　 "[Usually], a letter is brought. A letter, the man writes a letter. He sends [it]. (wedding custom)"

*Bi-gi-*V: Although only attested in a few instances, *bi-* and *gi-* may co-occur in Nubi in the order *bi-gi-*V to mark a future progressive.

Its users are mainly from the southern part of Uganda. In this combination, *bi-* mainly marks futurity, whereas *gi-* marks the non-punctual.

(384) Ka'man mo du'a al wa'ze 'de *bu- gu- 'womba*
EMPH with plea REL parent(s) DEF FUT- PROG- ask
'nouo, 'ya *bu- 'kun* 'nouo ja 'heiri.
for + PRON 3SING CONJ FUT- be for + PRON 3SING like good thing
"With the plea to God which the parents will be asking for him, it will be for him like a good thing."

However, in two instances (out of eigth) uttered by the same speaker, *bi-* does not refer to a future but seems to confirm the habitual aspect already conveyed by the marker *gi-*:

(385) 'Bes 'libu *gu- 'nutu-nu'tu.* 'Bes *gi-* 'ben
EMPH dance PROG- jump-REDUP-PASS EMPH PROG- seem
ka'lam ta fu'rai 'tu na a'nas al *bi- 'g(i)- ainu.*
thing GEN fun EMPH to people REL FUT- PROG- watch
"The dance is being jumped. It seems to be a funny thing to the people who are watching."

(386) Ka'man 'yo 'uo *gu- 'sulu,* 'uo *bi- 'gu- rwa,*
also CONJ PRON 3SING PROG- take PRON 3SING FUT- PROG-go
'uo *gi- 'raba* me ta'biya we'de.
PRON 3SING PROG- grow up with custom DEM PROX
"Thus he also takes [it], he goes [with it], he grows up with this custom."

4.2.1.3. *The Anterior Marker 'kan*

Nubi *'kan* is the past tense of the verb 'be'.[8] It also marks anteriority. *'Kan* indicates that the event or state, expressed by the verb, took place before the time in focus, and is not in existence anymore. The anterior marker may thus mark a past-before-past as in (387) and (388):

(387) Ka'lam al gi'bel *'kan rasu'l(u)* 'nana,
thing REL before ANT send-PASS-Ø to + PRON 1SING
'ana 'so ka'la.
PRON 1SING do-Ø COMPL
"The thing which was sent to me before, I have done [it]."

(388) 'It(a) 'arija 'adul(u) ba'kan 'de
PRON 2SING return-Ø repair-Ø place DEF
ja ba'kan al *'kan afu'ta* 'ma.
like place REL ANT dig-PASS-Ø NEG
"You repaired the place again like a place which had not been dug."

---

[8] Anterior *'kan* differs from conditional *kan* in Nubi in that the first one is stressed, and accordingly has high pitch, while conditional *kan* does not.

With stative verbs, the anterior marker may denote a remote past
state as in (389):

(389) ʼKan   fi   ʻragi   ʻwai   fi   Riya'ga   ʻna.
      ANT   EXIS   man   INDEF   in   Riyaga   there.
      "There was a man in Riyaga there."

or it expresses a past-before-past as in (390):

(390) ʻKabla   ʻita   ʻsulu   ʻbadu   ma   ʻsheik,
      before   PRON 2SING   take   RECIP   with   sheikh
      ʼkan   ʻita   fi   fi   ba'kan   ya'tu?
      ANT   PRON 2SING   EXIS   in   place   what?
      "Before you lived together with the sheikh, at which place had you
      been?"

However, ʼkan followed by a non-stative verb may denote perfective
aspect. In this context, it may co-occur with the completive marker
ka'las (see also below) as in (391) and (392):

(391) ʻNa're,   ʻlam   ʻgaba   ʼkan   ʻakul(u)   nyere'ku   ʼtai.
      today   meat   forest   ANT   eat-Ø   child   PRON POSS 1SING
      "Today, a wild animal has eaten my child. (and now my child is
      gone)."

(392) ʻWede   ʼkan   ʻina   ʻwonus   ʻfogo   ka'las.
      DEM PROX   ANT   PRON 1PL   talk-Ø   on it   COMPL
      "This, we have talked about it already. [and now we know it]"

The marker ʼkan may come between the subject and the main verb.
More often, however, it precedes the subject as in (393):

(393) ʻTaki,   ʼkan   ʻita   ʻfeker   ya'tu?
      PRON POSS 2SING   ANT   PRON 2SING   think-Ø   what?
      "Yours, what did you think of?"

In several clauses, given the context and its temporal structure, the
function of the marker ʼkan cannot be one of marking anteriority.
Consider (394), where the distribution of money occurred before
'going and doing' something with it. Yet the marker ʼkan stands with
the second consecutive verb. It seems that, rather than simply asking what the son did with the money, the question is what he could
have done with it. In other words, a certain vagueness and contingency is conveyed and, in conditional clauses, conditionality. It thus

appears that in this and other related sentences, *ʻkan*, rather than being a marker of anteriority, is a marker of modality.

(394) ʻSente ta   baʼba ʼtena,   al   weʼdi   ʼnena,
       money GEN   father PRON POSS 1PL   REL   give-PASS-Ø   to + PRON 1PL
       ʻuo   *ʻkan*   ʻro   ʻso   ʼmo   su'nu?
       PRON 3SING ANT   go-Ø   do-Ø   with+ PRON 3SING   what?
       "The money of our father, which was given to us, what could he have gone to
       do with it?"

The anterior marker *ʻkan*, marking modality, occurs most frequently with stative verbs. *ʻKan* followed by the verb *ʻaju* "want", "like" is very common among Nubi speakers, and conveys a polite request or a modest wish as in (395) and (396):

(395) ʻSokol   ab   *ʻkan*   ʻit(a)   ʻaju,   ʼbes ʻkelem   ʼnana.
       thing   REL ANT   PRON 2SING   want-Ø just tell-IMPER   to + PRON 1SING
       "Anything that you would like, just tell me."

(396) Aʼsa,   *ʻkan*   ʻin(a)   ʻaba   ʼma.
       now   ANT PRON 1PL   refuse-Ø   NEG
       "Now, we would not refuse/we cannot refuse."

I found only a few instances of *ʻkan*, marking modality, being used with non-stative verbs as in (394) and (397):

(397) Aʼta,   *ʻkan*   ʻino   ʻso   saʼfari. ʻIn(a)   ʻaju   ʻro
       no   ANT PRON 1PL   do-Ø   trip   PRON 1PL   want-Ø   go-Ø
       ʼmou(o)   ʻsawa.   ʼJa   ʻkun   ʼbakti baʼtali.
       with + PRON 3SING   together   come-Ø be-Ø   luck   bad
       ʻUo   ʼjo   ʼmutu   ʼgaflan.
       PRON 3SING come-Ø die-Ø   suddenly
       "No, we would make a trip. We wanted to go together with him. Bad luck came.
       He died suddenly."

Combinations of the core markers *gi-*, *bi-*, and *ʻkan*: *ʻKan* may be combined with the marker *gi-* to express a past progressive and with the marker *bi-* to express counterfactuality. In theory, it can co-occur with both markers *gi-* and *bi-* to express a non-punctual counterfactual. However, in practice, this combination occurs only seldom.

ʻKan gi- V: The combination of the anterior marker and the progressive marker denotes non-punctual states or events that have come to an end before the time of speaking.

(398)
```
Gu'mas 'to              al    'kan    'uo           gu-    'so
cloth  PRON POSS 3SING  REL   ANT     PRON 3SING    PROG-  do
te     'sélís(i)        a'nas    'de,  'uw(o)         'amrug(u),
GEN    preach-INF       people   DEF   PRON 3SING     take off-Ø
'uo          'kutu    'na.
PRON 3SING   put-Ø    there
```
"His cloth which he was using for preaching to the people, he took it off, he put it there."

If time reference is indicated by other means, non-punctuality in the past can be expressed by simply using the progressive marker (cf. above 4.2.1.1). In (399) the past time is initially referred to by means of an adverb. In the next sentence, however, the anterior marker is used.

(399)
```
Za'mani,      'ana         gi-     'gen   fi    En'teb(be). 'Ase,  'gen
in the past   PRON 1SING   PROG-   stay   in    NPROP       now    stay-GER
al    'ana         'gen   fi    En'tebbe     'na'de,
REL   PRON 1SING   stay-Ø in    NPROP DEM    DIS
je     'ragi      'tai              al    'kan    'jowj(u)    'ana         ta
like   husband    PRON POSS 1SING  REL   ANT     marry-Ø     PRON 1SING   GEN
aw'lani 'umon       'kan   gu-    'so      'kidima ta     aja'ma ta     'moyo.
NUM     PRON 3PL    ANT    PROG-  do       work    GEN    people GEN    water
```
"In the past, I stayed in Entebbe. Now, that staying which I stayed in Entebbe, like my husband who had married me first, they were doing the work of fishermen."

'Kan bi- V: The combination of the anterior marker *'kan* and the future marker *bi-* may denote a perfect action in a future as seen from a time in focus as in (400):

(400)
```
'Sa       al    'kan    'uo          bi-    'ja   fogo,
moment    REL   ANT     PRON 3SING   FUT-   come  in it
'uo          gi-     'ja-'ja           'gai    fi    'ras ta     a'jol al....
PRON 3SING   PROG-   come-REDUP        sit-Ø   in    head GEN    person REL
```
"The moment that it will have come, it comes and sits on the head of the person who . . ."

The combination of the marker *'kan* and the future marker, however, mainly expresses counterfactuality. The agent had a strong intention to conduct an action or there was a strong expectation for an event to occur, but the action or the event did not take place:

(401)
```
'Dukur    ka'lam    'to                       'de    gi-     'ja        ke'fifu
then       problem   PRON POSS 3SING DEF      DEF    PROG-   become    light
min        'kan      bu-     'kuwa   te'gili.
instead    ANT       FUT-    be      tough
```
"Then his problem becomes light instead that it would have been tough."

(402) 'Moyo   al   ka'las   ke'bir 'ya   'kan   al   'uo   'b(i)- agider
      water   REL   EMPH   big   CONJ ANT   REL   PRON 3SING   FUT-   be able
      'adi   'ma   'de,   'yal(a) a'nasi 'de   'gata 'mo   'seri. . . .
      cross-Ø NEG   DEF   well   people DEF   cut-Ø with+ PRON 3SING   shore
      "The water which was very big, thus which he would not have been able to
      cross, well the people crossed it with him."

Kan bi-V frequently occurs in the main clause of conditional clauses
and expresses an hypothesis or counterfactuality as in (403):

(403) Kan 'kan   'it(a)   'arufu   a'nas   'to,
      if   ANT   PRON 2SING   know-Ø   people PRON POSS 3SING
      'kan 'ina   'b(i)-   aburu   'so   su'nu?
      ANT PRON 1PL   FUT-   try   do-Ø   what?
      "If you had known his people, what could we have tried to do?"

The same meaning of contingency, vagueness, conditionality, and/or
counterfactuality may also be expressed by means of modal *'kan* +
verb (see above). However, the latter combination only occurs in the
northern part of Uganda, and its use is restricted to older people,
whereas modal *'kan bi-* V is common in the south and among younger
speakers of Nubi. This may be an indication for the gradual loss of
the modal *'kan* V-construction in favour of *'kan bi-* V. Modal *'kan* +
bi-V may also convey strong obligation as in (404):

(404) *'Kan* 'ita   *bi-*   'kelem   'nena.
      ANT PRON 2SING   FUT- tell   to + PRON 1PL
      "You should have told us!"

'Kan bi- gi- V: Although considered to be correct by my informants,
this combination does not occur in the text material. From elicitation, I give the following (context neutral) example with *'kan* expressing an unrealized event in the past of habitual nature.

(405) Kan 'kan   'ana   'endi   'gudra   mi'lan,
      if   ANT   PRON 1SING   have-Ø   energy   much
      'kan 'ana   *bi-*   *gi-*   'kasul   'kila   'youm.
      ANT PRON 1SING   FUT- PROG- wash   every   day
      "If I had had a lot of energy, I would have been washing daily."

4.2.1.4. *Auxiliaries and Other Markers*
Besides the core verbal markers of Nubi discussed above, Nubi uses
the non-core verbal markers *ka'las* and *'lisa* for completion and non-
completion, respectively, and the auxiliaries *'rua* "go", *'ja* "come",

'gum "get up", 'arija "return" and 'gen/'gai "sit", "stay" and the existential marker fi. These verbs may occur as free verbs. However, they can also be considered auxiliaries since their original meanings have been lost and later reinterpreted and grammaticalized as markers of intention, future, inception, duration, iterativity, etc. The above verbs have all undergone semantic depletion and as such have been reanalysed as auxiliaries. In every single instance, however, the rate of depletion varies. Even if gi- 'rua V particularly marks an immediate future, the idea of motion towards may still be relevant. Similar considerations apply to the other auxiliary verbs. For instance, in (406), the verb construction gi- ja 'masi refers especially to the beginning of the action of walking that is repeated daily from today onwards untill the day the other man comes back. The verb ja thus marks the inception of the action. Yet the verb 'masi "walk" implies motion, and from the context we know that it is a motion towards the speaker, which is implicit in the verb ja "come".

(406) 'Ase   ba'ba   gi-   ja   'masi   min   fi   ta'riki we'de ...
      now   fatherX   PROG-   come   walk-Ø   form   in   date   DEM PROX
      'ladi fi   ta'rik   al   ba'ba   'de   'b(i)- arija   'fogo.
      until in   date   REL   father Y DEF   FUT-   return   in it
      "Now, the father X starts walking from this date ... until the date when
      father Y will return."

In other instances, however, the original meaning of the auxiliary verb has been totally lost as in most of the above mentioned sentences.

4.2.1.4.1. The Auxiliary 'rua

'Rua V marking intention: The auxiliary 'rua takes a simple verb. No instances were found of 'rua gi-V. It does not occur frequently and seems to indicate a movement on the part of the agent that is more or less strongly intended and does not accidentally come about as in (407):

(407) 'Umon   'ro   'agif   'in   'ladi   'na're.
      PRON 3PL   go-Ø   stop-Ø   here   until   today
      "They stopped here until today."

Gi- 'rua V marking an immediate future: The progressive marker gi-followed by 'rua V, generally realized as 'gurwa V, expresses that the event referred to by the main verb is expected to take place at any moment. Gi- 'rua V thus differs from bi-V in that the former denotes

an imminent future while the latter refers to a general future. Both
transmit the idea of strong intention and/or definiteness, *gi- 'rua* V
because of the immediacy of the event and *bi-* V because of the
strong volition on the part of the subject (see also Owens 1977).

(408) 'Ase'de ka'las   'ja   la'siya. 'Gu-   rwa 'ja   'sa   ta   'num.
       now   COMPL come-Ø evening PROG- go come-Ø hour GEN sleep-GER
       "Now, it has already become evening. It is going to become the time of sleeping."

(409) Mo'hammed   gi-   'gai-'gai   'bara
       NPROP   PROG-   stay-REDUP   outside
       'ladi gu-   ru'a   ji'b(u)   uo   ma   'jibu.
       until PROG- go-PASS   bring-PASS-Ø   PRON 3SING with bring-GER
       "Mohammed stays outside until he is going to be brought (with bringing)."

'Kan 'gurwa V: It refers either to a future event of which the speaker
is certain that it is not going to be realized as in (410), or to an
unrealized event that was going to take place in the past as in (411)
(cf. *'kan bi-* V).

(410) 'Sa   'na'de   kan 'kan gu-   ru'wa   raka'b(u)   akili 'ma,
       moment DEM DIS   if   ANT PROG- go-PASS cook-PASS-Ø food   NEG
       'uo   'ja   ma   'samaga. . . . .
       PRON 3SING   come-Ø with fish
       'Akil   'to   'de   'ya   gu-   su'lu.
       food   PRON POSS 3SING DEF FOC   PROG- take-PASS
       "If food will not have been prepared by that moment, he comes with fish, ...
       His food is being taken."

(411) 'Bas,   'ana   gi-   'dakal 'motoka. Gu-   'gum.   'Kan 'an
       well   PRON 1SING PROG- enter   car   PROG- get off ANT PRON 1SING
       'gu-   rwa 'fadul   fu   ba'kan   'na'de.
       PROG-go   remain-Ø   in   place   DEM DIS
       "Well, I was going in the car. It was setting off. I was going to be left in that
       place."

'Gurwa V *bi-*V: In my recordings, I found one instance of *'gurwa* V
followed by the marker *bi-* + verb. It seems to mark an habitual.
According to my main informant, this is not a correct form.

(412) A'zol   'gu-   rwa   bi-   'dakal fi   'din   te   Is'lam je'didi,
       person PROG- go   FUT- enter   in   religion GEN   Islam   newly
       kan   'ita   bi-   'jib   sha'hada   'mafi,
       if   PRON 2SING FUT- bring   testimony   NEG
       Is'lam 'taki   'de   'gi-   'tim   'mafi . . . .
       Islam   PRON POSS 2SING DEF PROG- be sufficient   NEG
       "Someone who is going to convert newly to the religion of Islam, if you do not
       bring [your] testimony, your Islam is not sufficient. . . ."

Gi- ʿrua gi-V marking gradualness: Contrary to *ʿgurwa* V, *ʿgurwa gi*-V may refer to a present as well as a future time. More important than the temporal reference is the indication of the gradual nature of the event or state. The idea is conveyed that either the continuous process is developing step by step or that the iterative action is repeated incessantly as in (413) and (414):

(413) Ru'tan   ʿgu-   rwa   gi-   ʿso   su'nu?   Gu-   ʿwodur   ma'rai.
      language   PROG-   go   PROG-   do   what?   PROG- disappear at once
      ʿAna   gu-   ʿwonus(u)   ru'tan   Mu'ganda ʿfogo, ...
      PRON 1SING   PROG-   talk   language   NPROP   in it
      "What is the [Nubi] language doing gradually? It is disappearing altogether. I am talking the Luganda language in it,. . . ."

(414) Ju'a   to   'nus   'umon   al   'umon   'sebu   'na'de,
      house-PL   GEN   among   PRON 3PL   REL   PRON 3PL   leave-Ø DEM DIS
      'kulu gu-   ru'o   gi-   hara'gu,   gi-   hara'gu.
      all   PROG-   go-PASS   PROG-burn-PASS   PROG-burn-PASS
      "Those houses from among those which they left, are all being burnt down one by one."

Bi- ʿrua V marking an uncertain future: *Bi- ʿrua* V or *ʿburwa* V refers to a very vague, remote, uncertain future as in (415) and (416):

(415) . . .   kan   sa'ba . . .   ʿita   ja   a'yan, mu'nu   ʿya
              if   tomorrow   PRON 2SING   become-Ø ill   who   FOC
      bi-   ʿjo   ʿgum,   ʿbu-   rwa   ʿso   'badul   ʿita   na?
      FUT-   come   get up-Ø FUT-   go   do-Ø   instead of   PRON 2SING   there
      ". . . if tomorrow . . . you will become ill, who is it who will get up, [who] will do [it] instead of you there?"

(416) ʿRabana   ʿbu-   rw(a)   ʿasad(u)   ʿita   fi   ʿrizigi
      God   FUT-   go   question-Ø   PRON 2SING   in   wealth
      al   ʿita   gi-   lo'go.
      REL   PRON 2SING   PROG-   receive
      "God will question you about the wealth that you are receiving."

4.2.1.4.2. The Auxiliary ʿja

Ja V marking inchoativeness: The auxiliary *ʿja* frequently denotes inchoativeness.

417) ʿYa   ʿragi   ʿto   ʿjo   ʿrua   fi ʿkátúl   'lam   ʿgaba.
     CONJ   husband   PRON POSS 3SING   come-Ø go-Ø   in kill-INF meat   forest
     "Thus her husband left to kill wild animals/hunting."

It is often reduplicated but without a change of meaning as in (418):

(418) . . .   kan   'kan   ma'ma   'de,
               if   be-ANT mother   DEF
        school fees 'je-'já   ga'ta   'ma.
        school fees come-REDUP-PASS-Ø   cut-PASS-Ø   NEG
        ". . ., if the mother had been there, the school fees would not have been cut."

The auxiliary *ja*, expressing inchoativeness, often co-occurs with the
verb *'abidu* "begin":

(419) 'Ya   min   'na   'ina   'ja   'abidu   'arij(a)-'arija
      CONJ   from   there   PRON 1PL come-Ø   begin-Ø   return-REDUP-Ø
      fi   ga'raya.
      in   study-GER
      "Thus from there we began to return to studying/we began to study again."

The auxiliary *ja* with a *gi*-prefix may, like the bare form *ja*, denote
inchoativeness in the past, present, or future in verbal and nominal
sentences. *Gi-* adds the notion of non-punctuality as in (420):

(420) 'Ase'de,   fi   'sana   ta   'tisa wu se'bein
      now   in   year   GEN   NUM
      'ya   'ina   gi-   'ja   'jere   'wen?   Fi   Su'dan.
      FOC   PRON 1PL   PROG- come   run-Ø   where?   in   NPROP
      "Now, in the year seventy nine it was that we were setting off to run off where?
      To Sudan."

Gi- ja V may also refer to the inception of any action that is part
of a series of iterative and/or habitual actions as in (421):

(421) Ba'kan   'na'de   'fogo   'ges   to'wil . . .
      place   DEM DIS   in it   grass long
      'An(a)   'aju   keta   gi-   'ja   'rua   fogo 'ma.
      PRON 1SING   want-Ø SUBJ + PRON 2SING PROG- come go-Ø   in it NEG
      "That place, there is long grass in it. . . . I don't want you to go repeatedly
      into it."

With the future prefix *bi-*, *ja* marks a future inceptive as in (422):

(422) 'Nuru   'g(i)-   abidu   'ben
      light   PROG-   begin   look like-Ø
      je   'semsi   ka'la   ge'ri   bi-   'ja   'tala.
      like   sun   COMPL   nearly   FUT-   come   come out-Ø
      "The light begins to look as if the sun nearly will already rise/as if the sun
      is already about to rise."

The auxiliary *ja* can be marked by the marker *'kan*. As such, it
expresses a perfect state that is the result of a change of situation
as in (423):

(423) 'Bada 'leavu, gi- ji'b(u) umon
      after   leave   PROG- bring-PASS PRON 3PL
      'ladi 'namna 'toumon 'kan 'jo 'wegif.
      until/unless way PRON POSS 3PL ANT come-Ø stop-Ø
      "After leave, they are brought unless their way/trip has come to stop."

In the above sentences, the main verb occurred in its bare form. Less frequently, *ja* (or *gi- ja*) is followed by a verb with the progressive marker *gi-*. It refers to the inception of an action that takes place continuously or iteratively as in (424):

(424) 'Ana je-ja gi- ni'situ 'tan ka'man.
      PRON 1SING come-REDUP-Ø PROG- forget other EMPH
      "I began to forget others."

Gi-ja V marking a future: *Gi- ja* V refers to a future. Time reference is vaguer than with *gi- 'rua* V. A less strong intention is involved as in (425):

(425) *Gi- ja 'waja 'zaidi kan 'itokum 'fiku.*
      PROG-come hurt-Ø a lot when PRON 2PL untie-Ø
      "It will hurt a lot when you(PL) untie [it]."

Bi-ja V marking a remote future: The combination of the future marker and the verb *ja* "come" followed by the main verb expresses confidence that a future event will happen on the basis of what is taking place now or on what is expected to take place in the future. However, since we are relying on other unrealized events, we cannot be too certain that the event will really take place.

(426) Kele'm(u) 'keta gi- 'gen 'in.
      tell-PASS-Ø SUBJ + PRON 2SING PROG- stay here
      'Yeta bi- ja 'gen ma 'sudur.
      CONJ + PRON 2SING FUT- come stay-Ø with breast(s)
      "It is told that you should stay here. Then you will be with/have breasts."

The future marker *bi- ja* V closely resembles the future inchoative *bi- ja* V. Both, indeed, refer to a future event or a future change of state. Inchoative *bi- ja* V, however, expresses a change of situation, while future *bi- ja* V emphasizes in particular that the event cannot take place without another action/event occurring first.

As seen above, Nubi has several means to mark a future event/state, which, however, all express subtle differences relating to intention and remoteness in the future. They are summarized in table 17:

Table 17. Future expressions

Speakers' certainty	Strong	→	→		→	→Less strong
Immediate future	'gurwa V					
Indefinite future	bi- V		gi- 'ja V			
Remote future					bi- 'ja V	'burwa V

4.2.1.4.3. The Auxiliary 'gum

The verb *'gum* means "get up", "wake up", "stand". *'Gum (gi-)* V may, however, function as an auxiliary marking inchoativeness as in (427) and (428). It occurs less frequently than *'ja (gi-)* V.

(427) 'Ya   ma'ma 'baga *'gum*   gi-   *'kore.*
      CONJ   mother even   get up-Ø PROG-   cry
      "Thus even mother began to cry."

(428) 'Sa   al   'ina   *'gum*   *'jere*   fi Su'dan, . . .
      hour   REL   PRON 1PL get up-Ø   run-Ø   in NPROP
      "The moment that we started running off to Sudan, . . ."

4.2.1.4.4. The Auxiliary 'arija

The zero-marked form of the verb *'arija* "come back", "return" can be reanalysed as an auxiliary used to mark repetition. In (429), we see that the repeated actions may be conducted by different agents. The adverb *'mara 'tan* "another time", "again", optionally emphasizes the meaning of *'arija* as in (430):

(429) 'Lam 'gaba   'tan *'arija*   *'ja.*   *Ari'ja*   asa'd(u)   uo.
      meat forest other return-Ø come-Ø return-PASS-Ø ask-PASS-Ø PRON 3SING
      'Uw(o)   *'arija* *'kelem:* . . .
      PRON 3SING return-Ø say-Ø
      "Another wild animal came. It was again/also asked. It again/also said . . ."

(430) 'It(a)   *'arija* *'ja* *'gai* fi 'ras ta   Mo'hamed 'mara 'tan.
      PRON 2SING return-Ø come-Ø sit-Ø on head GEN NPROP   time   other
      "You came again to sit on Mohamed's head."

When the main verb is marked by the progressive marker *gi-*, the construction expresses that the event/action is repeated continuously as in (431).

(431) . . .   wu   ka'man 'uw(o)   'arija gi-   'sulu   'wai-'wai
              and   EMPH   PRON 3SING return PROG take   NUM-REDUP
      'ladi al   'ase'de   'fadulu.
      until REL   now   remain-Ø
      ". . . and he keeps on taking one by one until/leaving [those] who remain
      [by] now."

The auxiliary *'arija* may also convey that something is restored to its
original condition.

(432) 'It(a)   'arija   'adul(u)   ba'kan 'de
      PRON 2SING   return-Ø   repair-Ø   place   DEF
      ja   ba'kan al   'kan afu'ta   'ma.
      like   place   REL   ANT   dig-PASS-Ø   NEG
      "You repaired the place again like a place which had not been dug."

4.2.1.4.5. The Auxiliaries 'gen/ 'gai

The auxiliaries *'gen/'gai* "sit", "remain", are mainly followed by *gi-*
verbs. *'Gen/'gai gi-*V typically marks duration of an action or state
as in (433):

(433) 'Ase   ka'man 'ter   'gen   gi-   'guna   je'de.
      now   EMPH   bird   stay-Ø PROG-   sing   EMPH
      "Now, the bird keeps singing."

The auxiliary can be marked by any of the core markers as in (434)
and (435):

(434) 'Kan 'ita   'feker   mu'nu
      ANT   PRON 2SING   think-Ø   who
      'ya   *bi-*   'gen   gu-   'so   'nouo?
      FOC   FUT-   stay   PROG-   do for + PRON 3SING
      "Who do you think it is who will go on doing [it] for him?"

(435) . . . 'ya   'sokol 'de   gi-   'ja   'kila   fi'lel-fi'lel,
            CONJ   thing DEF   PROG-   come   every   night-REDUP
      . . . *gi-*   'gai   gi-   'izab(u) bi'niya 'de,   . . .
            PROG- stay   PROG-   punish   girl   DEF
      ". . . thus the thing comes every night,. . .it keeps punishing the girl
      again and again, . . ."

4.2.1.4.6. The Auxiliary 'fi

The auxiliary *fi* is generally followed by a verb marked by the progressive marker *gi-*. Although *fi (gi-)* V refers to a temporary state
as does *'gai/'gen gi-* V, the period under consideration is generally
longer as in (436):

(436) 'Umon   'endi   'jua   'toumon   fi   gi-   pangi'sa.
      PRON 3PL have-Ø house PRON POSS 3PL EXIS PROG- rent out-PASS
      "They have their house being rented out."

4.2.1.4.7. The Non-core Marker ka'las

The marker for completion *ka'las* is frequently reduced to *ka'la* or
enlarged through the addition of word-final *-i* becoming *ka'lasi*.[9] In
particular, *ka'la(s)(i)* signals completion of the action or event and
should be translated as "already". In some contexts, it closely
approaches the perfective aspect in that it may describe a currently
relevant state resulting from the situation expressed by the verb.
Ka'las may occupy any position in the clause.

(437) Fi   'bele   wa'din   'de   'kulu,
      in   district(s)   other-PL   DEF   all
      fa'ta   'kazi   ka'las   na   a'nas.
      open-PASS-Ø   work   COMPL   to   people
      "In all the other districts, the work has already been opened to the
      people."

(438) Kan   'ina   'ro   fi   'ámsúku   du'ban, . . .
      if   PRON 1PL   go-Ø   in   catch-INF   white ant(s)
      'yala,   'in(a)   'amsuku   du'ban   ka'la,
      well   PRON 1PL   catch-Ø   white ant(s)   COMPL
      'dukuru 'yena   bi-   'je   'gen   'seme.
      then   CONJ + PRON 1PL FUT- come stay-Ø fine
      "If we go to catch white ants, once we have caught the white ants, then
      we will live fine."

The completion of the action is referred to a past time by means
of the anterior marker *'kan*.

(439) 'Fi   yowe'le fi 'wakti al   ka'las   'kan   'ana   lo'go 'kazi
      EXIS   boy   in time   REL COMPL   ANT   PRON 1SING find-Ø work
      'mara ti'nin, ...
      time   two
      "There was a boy/son at the time that I had found two jobs, . . ."

With *gi-* marked verbs, and stative verbs, *ka'las* emphasizes the current relevance of states or processes as in (440) and (441):[10]

---

[9] Besides functioning as a verbal marker, *ka'las* is sometimes interpreted as an
emphasizer (see below).
[10] An idiomatic expression in Nubi to announce that one is leaving is:

(440) 'Namn(a) al   *ka'las*   'uw(o)   *aruf*   abu'su   'nouo
       way   REL   COMPL   PRON 3SING know-Ø forbid-PASS-Ø for + PRON 3SING
       'bab   ta   'saba   'de, ...
       door   GEN   seven   DEF
       "The way he now knows that the seventh door is forbidden for him, . . ."

(441) 'Ita   'dakal   fi   'jua   'bes   ma   bi'ses
       PRON 2SING enter-Ø   n   house   just   with   slowness
       ja 'num   *ka'la*   *gi-*   'seregu ba'na   'de.
       as sleep-GER   COMPL   PROG-   steal   girl-PL DEF
       "You entered the house just slowly as the sleep was taking the girls."

When the main verb is marked by the future/irrealis marker *bi-*,
ka'las signals that the action eventually occurs after some discussion
or after a long period of non-action as in (442):

(442) 'Rabana   'jib   'nouo   bi'nadum
       God   bring-Ø to + PRON 3SING   human being
       al   *ka'las*   *'b(i)*   *awun(u)*   'uo.
       REL   COMPL   FUT-   help   PRON 3SING
       "God brought him a human being who will help him eventually."

In combination with the negative marker *ka'las* means "not anymore", "no longer" as in (443):

(443) *Ka'las*   'tokum   'selim   'badu   'ma.
       COMPL   PRON 2PL   greet-Ø   RECIP   NEG
       "You(PL) do not anymore greet each other."

Ka'las in combination with *kan* "if" and *ba'kan/kan* "when" can be
interpreted as "after", "once".

(444) *Kan*   *ka'las*   ma'lim   'adibu   nyere'ku   de   fi   ma'kosa
       when   COMPL   teacher   punish-Ø   child   DEF   in   mistake(s)
       al   'uo   'so,   'uo   'dugu   nyere'ku   'de,
       REL   PRON 3SING   do-Ø   PRON 3SING beat-Ø child   DEF
       nyere'ku   *gi-*   'jere   'neta.
       child   PROG-   run   to + PRON 2SING
       "When the teacher has already punished the child/ after the teacher has punished
       the child for the mistakes which he made, [if] he has (already) beaten the child/
       after he has beaten the child, the child runs to you."

       'Ana   *ka'la*   *'gu-*   *wa.*
       PRON 1SING COMPL   PROG-   go
       "I am already going."

(445) *Kan ka'las*   'uo   za'lan 'mena,   ma'rai ta   'kulu-'kulu.
      if   COMPL PRON 3SING annoyed with +PRON 1PL at once GEN ever-REDUP
      "Once he is annoyed with us, at once, it is forever."

Completion is also expressed by the verb *'kalasu* "finish" followed by
the verb expressing the action that is finished as in (446):

(446) 'Ina   'ma *gi-*   *'kalas* *'karab* ka'lam 'tena   te 'Nubi.
      PRON1PL NEG PROG- finish spoil-Ø   matter PRON POSS 1PL GEN Nubi
      "We do not stop spoiling matter of us, of the Nubi."

There is, however, a difference between the verb *'kalasu* "finish" +
other verb and the construction with the verbal marker *ka'las*. The
verb *'kalasu* "finish" followed by another verb clearly marks the end
point of the action. The action is seen as a whole, without an explicit
starting point, and so is a punctual action. The verbal marker *ka'las*
in combination with a simple verb also refers to the fact that the
action is finished but ignores its end point. *Ka'las* with a *gi-* verb
refers to the starting point of the event or state but ignores its end
point. Its function corresponds more or less to that of the verb *'kala*
"end up" + other verb, which also signals that an event or state has
begun, while nothing is mentioned about its end point.[11] *'Kala* +
verb also differs from *'kalasu* V in that the subject of the following
verb is different as in (448) or that the same subject is repeated as
in (447), while the subject of the verb *'kalasu* is the same as the subject of the following verb.

(447) Ak'wana   lu'far   'tan   *'gu-*   *rwa*   *'kala*
      brother-PL   mouse(mice)   other(s)   PROG-   go   end up-Ø
      'umon   'fadulu   'sita   'bes.
      PRON 3PL   remain-Ø   NUM   only
      "The other mice brothers were going to end up being only six."

(448) 'Ya   bi'niya   'de   *'gu-*   *rwa*   *'kala*
      CONJ   girl   DEF   PROG-   go   end up-Ø
      'lam   'gaba   'de   'abul(u)   'uo.
      meat   forest   DEF   swallow-Ø   PRON 3SING
      "Thus the girl was going to end up the wild animal having swallowed
      her/being swallowed by the wild animal."

---

[11] In a simple clause *'kala* expresses that one is astonished or shocked. In a complement clause, the idea is conveyed that the subject is shocked finding himself in
an unexpected situation; this is rendered here as "end up".

Heine (1982) describes *ka'las* as a perfect marker in Kenyan Nubi. Owens does not regard *ka'las* as a verbal marker but refers to it as a current relevance relater, emphasizing that "some state or action is still relevant, relative to another activity or state" (Owens 1977, 210). According to Pasch and Thelwall (1987,91–165), Nubi *ka'las* marks completion of the action. They discuss whether *ka'las* should be considered a matrix verb or a grammaticalized tense/aspect marker and conclude that *ka'las* is a verb that marks the completion of the action expressed by the dependent verb. In my view, *ka'las* is a verbal marker, although it is a non-core marker. It may co-occur with all other markers, and its position in the sentence is absolutely free.

4.2.1.4.8. *The Non-core Marker 'lisa*

Nubi *'lisa* "still" marks an action or state that is still in progress. However, when it is used as a free constituent, it means "not yet" as in (449):

(449) 'Jina   mis'kin   we'de ...,   bi-   'sul(u) bi'niya   'to
      child   poor man   DEM PROX FUT- take   daughter   PRON POSS 3SING
      ke'fin? A'ta,   'lisa.
      how?   no   not yet.
      "This poor man's child, how will he take his daughter? No, not yet."

'Lisa normally appears in non-punctual contexts, namely nominal contexts with an adjectival or nominal predicate with non-stative verbs marked by the *gi-* prefix or stative verbs in their bare form referring to actions or states that have not yet come to an end and so are still in progress. The position of *'lisa* is not fixed in the sentence as in (450) and (451):

(450) Ba'kan   'lisa   bo'yi.
      Place   still   far
      "The place is still far."

(451) 'Ya   a'buba   'de,   'youm   ta'lata
      CONJ   grandmother   DEF   day   NUM
      'lis(a)   'uo   'g(i)-   *asuru*   nyere'ku   'de.
      still   PRON 3SING   PROG- massage   child   DEF
      "Thus the grandmother, [after] three days, she was still massaging the child."

'Lisa followed by the bare form of non-stative verbs, expresses that something eventually happens, after one or more other events or states as in (452):

(452) 'Wede   ka'man 'ana   'dug(u) 'uo   'fogo
      DEM PROX also   PRON 1SING beat-Ø PRON 3SING for it
      'ladi   'lis(a)   'uo   'sib.
      until   still   PRON 3SING leave
      "This also, I beat him for it until eventually he left."

'Lisa may occur with all verbal core markers. *'Lisa* in combination
with the anterior marker *'kan* implies that the action had not yet
come to an end at a certain time in the past.

(453) 'Lisa 'kan   'an   gi-   'feker   'ruo
      still ANT PRON 1SING PROG- think   go-Ø
      fi   'senior   ta   'arba, 'dukur 'jowju   'ja.
      to   senior lass GEN   NUM   then   marriage come-Ø
      "I was still thinking of going to senior 4, when marriage came."

'Lisa + *'gurwa* V is used in contexts where the speaker indicates that
the agent is first going to conduct the action marked by *'lisa* before
moving to another (requested) action as in (454):

(454) A'santi,   la'kin   'lis(a) 'ana   'gu-   rw(a)   'asadu
      thank you but   still   PRON 1SING PROG- go ask-Ø
      ak'wana   'tai   . . . .
      sister-PL   PRON 1SING
      "Thank you, but still/first I am going to ask my sisters. . . ."

The meaning of *'lisa* in combination with *'gurwa* V is similar to *'lisa
bi-* V. The only difference is that *'gurwa* V refers to an action in the
immediate future, while *bi-* V, even though it marks strong volition,
does not give a clear time indication as in (455):

(455) 'Gasab   'de 'lisa   b(i)-   a'j(u)   aku'lu   gi'dam.
      sugarcane DEF still   FUT- want-PASS eat-PASS-Ø first
      "The sugarcane will have to be eaten first."

I also found that *'lisa* can mark an infinitive form as in (456):

(456) 'Ase, 'ragi ka'la   'jib   ka'lam al   'gow,
      now   man COMPL bring-Ø matter REL tough
      te   'lis(a) 'asrúbu   'chai.
      GEN still   drink-INF   tea
      "Now, the man has brought a tough matter, of still drinking tea."

'Lisa in combination with the negative marker *'ma* signals that the
action has not yet taken place. It typically co-occurs with simple
verb forms or verbs marked by *gi-*:

(457) La'yin min 'ana 'gai
but since PRON 1SING be alive-Ø
'lis(a) 'an(a) 'ainu jahi'liya je na'de 'ma.
still PRON 1SING see-Ø state of ignorance like DEM DIS NEG
"But since I am alive, I have not yet seen a state of ignorance like that
one."

(458) 'Yani 'shida 'tena 'lisa gi- 'kalas 'mafi.
that is problem(s) PRON POSS 1PL still PROG- finish NEG
"That is, our problems have not yet come to an end."

Both 'lisa and the negator 'ma can take any position in the sentence
except with the existential marker *fi* which is obligatorily preceded
by 'ma as in (459):

(459) La'kin 'lisa ma- *fi* 'youm 'wai je 'de, . . .
but still NEG- EXIS day NUM like DEM PROX
"But there has not yet been one day like this, . . ."

When 'kabla "before" precedes 'lisa 'ma, the meaning of 'kabla pre-
vails, and both meanings merge to "before" as in (460):

(460) 'Kabla 'lisa 'tim 'deka 'kamsa 'na'de 'ma,
before still be over-Ø minute(s) NUM DEM DIS NEG
'lufra ka'las afu'ta.
hole COMPL dig-PASS-Ø
"Before those five minutes were over, the hole had been dug."

'Lisa 'ma + future verb, marked by *bi-*, refers to an action/state that
is supposed never to happen:

(461) Ka'lam we'de 'umon 'lisa 'b(i)- aruf' ma.
thing DEM PROX PRON 3PL still FUT- know NEG
"This thing, they will never know."

4.2.2. *Mood*

4.2.2.1. *The Imperative*
The singular imperative consists of the bare verb form, e.g. *jib*
"bring". The imperative of 'rua "go" is 'rua or 'ro. The verb *ja*
"come" forms its imperative with the regular *ja'* or the irregular 'tal.
One final exception is the verb 'alabu "play", which takes 'lib' for
the singular imperative. To form the plural imperative, the subject
suffixes -*kum*, -'tokum or -'takum are fixed to the bare form, e.g. 'gum-
'kum "wake (PL) up!", 'lebis-'takum "get dressed (PL)!", and 'aruf-'tokum

"know(PL)!", respectively. To form the negative imperative, the bare
form is preceded by 'mata for the negative singular imperative and
by 'matakum for the plural imperative, e.g., 'mata 'fata "do not open!"
and 'matakum 'wonus "do(PL) not talk!", respectively. Occasionally, the
negative imperative consists of the positive imperative form followed
by the negative marker 'ma, e.g., 'sul 'ma "do not take [it]!" and
'wonus- 'tokum 'ma "do (PL) not talk!".

In the imperative, the subject is usually not expressed. In verb
chains, all verbs take the imperative form. For the plural imperative, only one verb takes the plural particle -'kum, -'takum or -'tokum,
marking the addressee.

(462) 'Abur   'tal   'gai   fala'ta !!
      try-IMPER   come-IMPER   sit-IMPER   down
      "Try to come and sit down!!!"

(463) 'Arija   'rua-   'takum !!
      return-IMPER   go-IMPER-   ADR-PL
      "Return (PL) and go(PL)!"

Occasionally, the second person pronoun is used. The imperative
clause thus resembles an affirmative sentence with a bare verb form
as in (464):

(464) 'Turuju   'wai   'lad(i)   'ita   'kalas,
      send away-IMPER   NUM   until   PRON 2SING   finish-Ø
      'it(a)   'arij(a)   'abidu   'tan.
      PRON 2SING return-Ø   begin-Ø another.
      "Send one away until you finish [this one], [then] begin another one
      (again)!"

A similar construction is used with the first person plural to express
the hortative 'let us . . .'.

(465) 'Ino   'kutu   'moyo.
      PRON 1PL   put-Ø   water
      "Let us put water."

(466) 'Ino   'rua.
      PRON 1PL   go-Ø
      "Let us go."

The latter is often shortened to 'norwa "let us go". Theoretically, the
progressive marker gi- could be used to express the imperative of a

continuous or iterative action, but no instances of positive imperatives marked by *gi-* occur in my data. The negative imperative, however, may take the progressive marker *gi-* so as to indicate that the
addressee should not conduct a continuous action or that he should
never conduct an action as in (467) and (468):

(467) ʻMa-   ta   gi-   ʃadul   ʻwara   ma   ʻhaya.
      NEG- ADR SING PROG- remain behind with   shame
      "Do not stay behind with shame!"

(468) ʻItokum,   ʻma-   takum   ʻg(i)-   alab   ʻna.
      PRON 2PL NEG- ADR-PL   PROG- play   there
      "You (PL), never play (PL) there!"

I found several instances of imperative forms consisting of an auxiliary verb followed by a main verb. In (469), the combination of
the verb *ʻrua* "go" marked by the auxiliary *ʻgen* + progressive marker
gi- expresses duration. In (470) *ʻgurwa* + V marks an immediate
future. Although the idea of motion is relevant as well, the speaker
wants to emphasize an immediate future time.

(469) ʻBes   ʻgen   ʻgu-   rwa   ʻtu.
      simply   stay-IMPER   PROG- go-Ø   only
      "Simply, keep on going!"

(470) ʻMa-   ta   ʻgu-   rwa   ʻkelem.
      NEG-   ADR-SING   PROG- go   tell-Ø
      "Don 't go to tell."

ʻGidam "first" added to the negative imperative construction expresses
that the addressee should not yet do something as in (471):

(471) ʻMa-   ta   ʻrua   gi'dam.
      NEG-   ADR-SING   go-IMPER   first
      "Do not go yet!"

The position of the negative marker may be important for the meaning of the imperative clause. Consider (472), (473), and (474):

(472) ʻMa-   t(a)   abur   ʻtolu.
      NEG-   ADR-SING try-IMPER   delay-Ø
      "Do not try to delay!".

(473) *'Abur*   *'ma-*   *ta*   *'tolu.*
     try-IMPER NEG-   DR-SING delay-IMPER
     "Try not to delay!".

(474) *'Abur*   *'tolu*   *ma.*
     try-IMPER delay-Ø   NEG
     "Try not to delay!

(472), although grammatically correct, does not make much sense. It was indeed not taken from my recordings but obtained in a discussion on negative imperatives. (474) is rather neutral as to the scope of negation. However, *'ma* logically negates the act of delaying. The imperative meaning may be intensified by means of the suffix *-'ke* as in (475):

(475) *'Nasur,*   *'tala-*   *'ke!*   *'Nasur,*   *'tala-*   *'ke!*
     NPROP come out-IMPER EMPH NPROP   come out-IMPER EMPH
     "Nasur, come out! Nasur, come out!"

4.2.2.2. *The Subjunctive Mood*

The subjunctive mood is expressed by means of the modal marker *ke'de*, or its short form *'ke* followed by a verbal clause generally with a bare verb form as in (476):

(476) *'Kena*   *ni'situ*   *'ma*   *'gal* ....
     SUBJ + PRON 1PL forget-Ø NEG   that
     "We should not forget that. . . ."

If the speaker insists on the durative or recurring character of an event, he may use the non-punctual verb form marked by *gi-* or alternative verb forms such as *'gai gi-* V/ *'gen gi-* V.

(477) *'Uo*   *'kutu fi 'be*   *na*   *ke'de 'gai*   *gi-*   *'chunga*
     PRON 3SING put-Ø in house   there SUBJ stay-Ø PROG- look after
     kala'ma   *'to*   *ta*   *'be*   *'na.*
     thing-PL   PRON POSS 3SING GEN house there
     "He put [him] in the house there in order to keep on looking after his things of the house there."

However, *gi-* marking is not compulsory in subjunctive clauses. The bare verb form may alternate with or take the place of the *gi-* verb form if the context is clear about the non-punctual character of the state or event as in (478):

(478) Ak'wana   ta   'ragi   taki   'aju   'keta
      relative-PL   GEN   husband PRON POSS 2SING   have to-Ø   SUBJ+PRON 2SING
      'g(i)-   ain(u)   'umon   'seme. 'Ragi   'taki   ka'man
      PROG- treat   PRON 3PL   well   husband PRON POSS 2SING also
      ke'de   'ainu   a'nas   'taki   'seme.
      SUBJ   treat-Ø people   PRON POSS 2SING   well
      "The relatives of your husband, you have to treat them well. Your husband should
      also treat your people well."

Other verb forms such as those with the future marker *bi-* (479),
those with the anterior marker *'kan* (480), and the imperative (481)
occur infrequently after the subjunctive marker in the text corpus,
and some of my informants disapproved of them.

(479) 'Ana   'feker   'k(e)   an   bu-   lo'go   'batna 'tan 'gwam 'ma.
      PRON 1SING think-Ø SUBJ PRON 1SING FUT- receive belly other fast   NEG
      "I thought that I should not get another pregnancy fast."

(480) A'ju   ke'de   'kan   hara'gan   'kulu   gi-   kunu's(u)
      must-PASS-Ø SUBJ   ANT   sweat   all   PROG- sweep-PASS
      'neta   mo   ku'nus.
      to + PRON 2SING   with   sweep-GER
      "It is necessary that all the sweat has been swept to you with sweeping./ All the
      sweat must have been swept to you . . ."

(481) 'Ah, aja'ma, 'kena   'gata-   um   'tumur.
      INT people SUBJ + PRON 1PL cut-IMPER- ADR-PL date(s)
      "Ah, people, let us cut the dates."

The two instances in the text material of *ke'de* + imperative were
both from old people. It is possibly an old form that is about to disappear from present-day Nubi.

4.3. *Verbal Derivations*

4.3.1. *The Passive*

Form: The Nubi passive is formed by changing the stress pattern of
the verb. Verbs generally take the stress on the first syllable, e.g.
'kasulu "wash". A small group of verbs like the verb *ni'situ* "forget",
verbs of Swahili origin, such as *ja'ribu* "try", and some Nubi disyllabic verbs, e.g., *we'ri* "show" usually take the stress on the second
syllable. An even smaller group of verbs takes the stress on the last
syllable, e.g. *fata'ran* "be tired", *kisi'lan* "be lazy". In the passive the

stress is shifted to the last syllable.[12] The vowel in the final syllable may be slightly lengthened. This is not obligatory but follows from the stress on that syllable. Likewise, Nubi stress generally co-occurs with high pitch. Therefore, we find high pitch on the final syllable. With regard to Kenyan Nubi, Heine (1982, 42) mentions a movement of "stressed high tone from the first to the last syllable of the verb."

(482) *Ada'ku*   'nas   ku'ra   'to   'de   'kweis.
      brush-PASS-Ø COLL   foot/feet   PRON POSS 3SING   DEF   good.
      "His feet were brushed properly."

As we have seen above, some Nubi verbs already have the stress on the last syllable in the active voice. These are monosyllabic verbs like *ja* "come" and *so* "do" and some disyllabic verbs that take the stress on the second syllable, e.g. *we'ri* "show", *li'go* "find".[13] In the formation of the passive, the stress that can no longer be shifted backwards becomes stronger. The length of the vowel may thus be extended. Passive monosyllabic verbs are marked by a high tone (see also 2.1.4):

(483) *ja* "come" > *já* "there is coming"
      so "do" > *só* "be done"
      we'ri "show" > *we'ri* "be shown"
      li'go "find" > *li'go* "be met"

Approximately an eighth of the Nubi verbs end in a consonant.[14] Different devices may be used in the formation of the passive of these verbs. Most frequently, the stress is put on the last syllable if this was not yet the case, e.g., *'gowgow* "strengthen" becomes *gow'-gow* "be strengthened" as in (484):

(484) *Gi-*   *gow-'gow*   'gelba   ta   a'nas.
      PROG-   strengthen-PASS   heart   GEN   people
      "The heart of the people is strengthened."

Second, a vowel may be attached to the last consonant in accordance with the passivization of verbs ending in a vowel, thus creating

---

[12] According to Owens (1977), Swahili verbs are excluded from the stress shift.
[13] Verbs with stress on the final syllable, which end in a consonant, such as *ta'ban* "bother", will be discussed below.
[14] These are mainly intransitive verbs that can also be used with the passive voice, albeit infrequently.

a new syllable that receives stress and high pitch. The quality of the vowel depends mainly on the vowel of the verb stem as in (485) and (486):

(485) '*zikir* "recite as to praise God" > *ziki'ri* "be recited"
'*chek* "check" > *che'ki* "be checked"
'*nyakam* "confiscate", "capture" > *nyaka'ma* "be confiscated", "capture"

(486) *Gi-* *nyaka'ma* *a'nasi.*
 PROG-capture-PASS people
 "The people were captured."

Speakers of the northern variety of Nubi and educated speakers in general use the passive form of the auxiliary when the main verb is passive as in (487):

(487) . . ., *ari'ja* *se'b(u)* *uo* *fi* '*torof* '*bahar.*
 eturn-PASS-Ø leave-PASS-Ø PRON 3SING in side lake
 ". . . he was left again at the side of the lake."

In the southern part of Uganda, however, only the main verb takes the passive form while the auxiliary retains the active form as in (488):

(488) '*Arija* *fu't(u)* *uo* . . . .
 return-Ø pass-PASS-Ø PRON 3SING
 "He was passed again. . . ."

Use: The non-agent participant or patient generally retains its object position after the verb as in (489):

(489) *Fa'ga* *ena* '*to.* *Ga'ta* '*kasma,* *a'dan.*
 split-PASS-Ø eye(s) PRON POSS 3SING cut-PASS-Ø mouth ear(s)
 "His eyes were split. His mouth and ears were cut."

As a rule, pronouns occur postverbally in passive clauses as in (490):[15]

(490) *Daka'l(u)* '*ita* *fi* *tu'ra.*
 enter-PASS-Ø PRON 2SING in earth
 "You were entered in the earth/ you were buried."

---

[15] The following sentence is exceptional:

'*Ita* '*bes* *lese'gu* '*ya* '*de.*
PRON 2SING only stick-PASS-Ø FOC DEM PROX
"You were just stuck here."

For focus, however, the object may be moved to the sentence-initial position, as in (491):[16]

(491) *Sura*   *'tena*   *'kul* *ga'ta*   fi U'ganda 'in.
umbilical cord(s) PRON POSS 1PL all   cut-PASS-Ø in NPROP here.
"All our umbilical cords were cut here in Uganda."

Animate patients that are placed in sentence-initial position are often referred to by a pronoun following the verb as in (492):

(492) *'Ita 'aju*   *n yere'ku'taki*   *'de* ke'de *ali'm(u)*   *'uo.*
You want-Ø child PRON POSS 2SING DEF SUBJ teach-PASS-Ø PRON 3SING
"You want your child to be educated."

Agent expression in passive clauses occurs neither in Owens' examples (1977, 1996, 125–72) or Heine's texts (1982). I found one counterexample in my material: see (748).

Both the agent and the patient remain unspecified in impersonal passives. The main goal of the speaker is to emphasize the action and not the participants as in (493):

(493) *Aku'lu*   ka'la.
      eat-PASS-Ø COMPL
      "There has already been eaten."

Intransitive verbs like *ja* "come", *'tiri* "fly", and *jere* "run" may also occur in the impersonal passive form. Since they do not have a patient, the emphasis is fully on the action of the verb as in (494):[17]

(494) Fi   'be   ta   a'nas   sati'rin,   *gi-*   *ko're.*
in   house GEN people dominant-PL,   PROG- cry-PASS
Fu 'be   ta   a'nas   ab   da'bara,   *g(i)- ata'ku.*
in   house GEN people REL diplomacy   ROG- laugh-PASS
"In the house of dominant people, there is being cried/they cry. In the house of diplomatic people, there   is being laughed/they laugh."

Transitive/intransitive verbs: Nubi has several verbs that can have both transitive and intransitive meanings without a change of form.

---

[16] In Owens' examples from Kenyan Nubi, the patient usually retains its object position after the verb (Owens 1977), whereas Heine (1982) mentions both preverbal and postverbal patient position.

[17] Owens (1996, 125–72) translates similar clauses with "someone is running", which I do not think conveys the correct sense of the expression. It is the fact that there is 'running' not necessarily by one individual but possibly by more people, which is central.

In the intransitive sense, it is the patient that becomes central in the communication while the role of the agent is ignored. The situation is thought of as a state rather than as an action, unlike in the passive, which focuses on the action as in (495) and (496):

(495)
(a) 'Uo   'kasur   lata.
    PRON 3SING break -Ø   firewood
    "He broke firewood."

(b) Kasu'ru   'bab.
    break-PASS-Ø   door
    "The door was broken."

(c) La'saya   'kasur.
    stick   break -Ø
    "The stick was broken."

(496) Li'mu   a'nasi.   A'nas   'limu.
     gather-PASS-Ø   people   people   gather-Ø
     "The people were gathered. The people were together."

Other verbs that can be both transitive and intransitive are listed in table 18:

Table 18. List of Nubi transitive/intransitive verbs

	Transitive		Intransitive
'abidu	"begin s.th."	'abidu	"begin"
'ainu	"see s.th."	'ain fi	"see into"
'alagu	"hasten s.o."	'alagu	"hurry"
'aminu	"trust s.o.", "believe s.th."	'amin ma	"believe in"
'amula	"fill s.th."	'amula	"be full"
'arija	"send back s.th."	'arija	"return"
'ataku	"ridicule s.o."	'ataku ma	"laugh with"
'badulu	"change s.th."	'badul	"change"
'beredu	"wash s.o."	'beredu	"take a bath"
'bilu	"wet s.th", "moisten s.th."	'bil	"get wet"
'dakalu	"enter s.th."	'dakal fi	"enter into"
'egifu	"stop s.th."	'egif	"stop", "stand up"
'faga	"split s.th."	'faga	"split"
'fata	"open s.th."	'fata	"open"
'fata'ran	"tire s.o.", "exhaust s.o."	'fata'ran	"be tired", "become tired"
'ferteku	"separate s.th."	'ferteku	"be separated"
'furu	"boil s.th."	'furu	"boil"
'futu	"pass s.th."	'futu fi	"pass by"
'gelebu	"defeat s.o."	'geleb	"be difficult"
'genu	"inhabit"	'gen	"sit", "remain"
'geru	"change s.th."	'geru	"change"

Table 18 (*cont.*)

	Transitive		Intransitive
'gesimu	"divide s.th."	'gesim	"be divided"
'gisir	"peel s.th."	'gisir	"loose skin"
'haragu	"burn s.th."	'haragu	"burn"
'hukumu	"govern s.th."	'hukum	"be an authority"
'kabasu	"cheat s.o."	'kabas	"play a game"
'kalasu	"finish s.th."	'kalas	"be finished"
'kasuru	"break s.th."	'kasur	"be broken"
'karabu	"spoil s.th."	'karab	"be spoilt"
'kati	"cover s.th.", "shut s.th."	'kati	"be covered", "be shut"
'kore	"mourn over s.th."	'kore	"cry"
'kosa	"lack s.th."	'kosa	"be lacking"
'kubu	"pour s.th."	'kub	"flow"
'lebis	"dress s.o.", "wear s.th."	'lebis	"get dressed"
'lesegu	"stick s.th."	'lesegu	"be sticky"
'nigitu	"pick s.th."	'nigitu	"ripen"
'nongusu	"reduce s.th."	'nongus	"decrease"
'raba	"raise s.o."	'raba	"mature"
'rada	"breast-feed s.o."	'rada	"be breast-fed"
'rasulu	"send s.th."	'rasul	"arrive"
'rudu	"accept s.th."	'rudu fi	"agree on"
sa'ban	"satisfy s.o."	sa'ban	"be satisfied"
'setetu	"separate s.o.", "scatter s.th."	'setetu	"be separated", "be scattered"
'stenu	"await s.th."	'sten	"wait"
ta'ban	"worry s.o."	ta'ban	"be worried", "be overworked"
'waja	"hurt s.o."	'waja	"be hurt"
'wala	"light s.th."	'wala	"burn"
was'kan	"make s.th. dirty"	was'kan	"be dirty"
'woduru	"lose s.th."	'wodur	"be lost"
'wonusu	"discuss"	'wonus fi	"talk about"
'zidu	"increase s.th."	'zidu	"increase"

4.3.2. *The Stative Passive*

Form: The stative passive verb form is expressed by the simple verb form to which *ma-* is prefixed as in (497):

(497) 'kati "cover" > ma-'kati "(be) covered"
    'kasuru "break" > ma- 'kasuru "(be) broken"
    'agilibu "mix" > ma-'agilibu "(be) mixed"

There are a few exceptional forms as in (498):

(498) 'arufu "know" > ma-a'ruf "(be) known", "be well known"
    'kalagu "create" > ma'klug "(be) created"

The stative passive is generally derived from transitive verbs. An exception is the form *mo-'mutu* "dead" from the intransitive *'mutu* "die" as in (499):

(499) 'Wede,   'ena   'to   mo-   'mutu   'de, ...
      DEM PROX eye(s)   PRON POSS 3SING STAT P-die   DEF
      "This one, [the old woman with] her dead eyes, ... "

Use: The stative passive verb behaves like a predicative adjective and expresses a state resulting from a completed action. The agent is not expressed overtly:

(500) La'yin   ka'lam   'baga   se'b(u)   'omon   ma-   'setetu, ...
      but   because EMPH   leave-PASS-Ø   PRON 3PL   STAT   P-scatter
      "But because they were even left scattered, ... "

(501) 'Ina   'g(i)-   akul   'lam
      PRON 1PL   PROG-   eat   meat
      al   ma-   'haragu   je   'de   'ma.
      REL   STAT P-   burn   like   DEM PROX   NEG
      "We are not eating meat which is grilled like this."

On a total of thirty two instances of stative passive forms, only two functioned as attributive adjectives as in (502) and (503):

(502) 'Ana,   Ibra'him A., nyere'ku mo-   'weledu   to   'Bombo.
      PRON 1SING NPROP   child   STAT P-give birth   GEN NPROP
      "I, Ibrahim A., am a child born in Bombo."

(503) 'Yala 'ina   gi-   'nigitu me   'ena   mo-   'robutu.
      well   PRON 1PL   PROG-   pick   with eye(s)   STAT   P- tie
      "Well, we are picking [fruit] with tied/blindfolded eyes."

According to Owens (1977), the stative passive cannot co-occur with the subjunctive marker *ke'de* or the future marker *bi-*, but it may co-occur with *ka'las*, the marker of completion, the negative marker *'ma*, or *'lisa*. I found similar results. However, in the text corpus there is one instance of a stative passive that is apparently interpreted as a verb after the auxiliary *'gurwa*, denoting immediate future.

(504) Kan   'it(a)   'ajin(u)   'ita,   ka'lam 'taki   'kul
      if   PRON 2SING   harp on-Ø PRON 2SING problem PRON POSS 2SING all
      'gu-   rwa   ma-   'ajin.
      PROG- go   STAT P- harp on
      "If you harp on yourself, your entire problem is going [to be] brought up time and again."

4.3.3. *The Gerund and the Infinitive*

Form: There are two types of verb nominalization in Ugandan Nubi. The stress pattern of the infinitive (INF) corresponds to the stress pattern of the simple verb form. However, the tone on the first and second syllable is high irrespective of stress (see also 2.1.4).[18] In (505), high tone is marked by ´, low tone is unmarked.

(505) 'kuruju "work the soil" > 'kúrúju "working the soil"
      'ataku "laugh" > 'átáku "laughing"
      we'rí "show" > wé'rí "showing"
      ni'situ "forget" > ní'sítu "forgetting"
      ja'ribu "try" > já'ríbu "trying"

The second type that I would like to call the gerund (GER) has been discussed by Owens (1977), Heine (1982), and Pasch and Thelwall (1987, 91–165). With the regular tri- and disyllabic verbs, which take the stress on the first syllable in the simple verb form, the gerund is formed by shifting the stress to the syllable preceding the last consonant, which is usually the penultimate syllable. The stressed syllable has a higher pitch than the unstressed syllables.

(506) 'asrubu "drink" > as'rubu "drinking"
      'atanu "grind" > a'tanu "grinding"
      'kati "cover" > 'kati "covering"

The verb *ni'situ* "forget" and trisyllabic verbs of Swahili origin, which as a rule take stress on the penultimate syllable, do not change their stress pattern as in (507):

(507) ni'situ "forget" > ni'situ "forgetting"
      cha'gua "choose" > cha'gua "choosing"

---

[18] I assume that high pitch on the second syllable should be linked to the phrase structure. I will discuss further on how an infinitive is always followed by its patient in an inalienable-like construction. The tone of the infinitival phrase is similar to that of genuine inalienable possessive constructions, which in turn is different from that of alienable possessive constructions as in:

jéréba 'bágara "a cows' kraal"	><	*jéreba ta 'bágara* "a kraal for cows"
'móyó 'éna "tear(s)"	><	*'móyo ta 'éna* "water for the eyes"
'kúrúju (INF) *'sámba* "working the field"	><	*ku'rúju* (GER) *ta 'sámba* "working the field"

The difference can probably be explained by the fact that inalienable constructions are considered as a whole while alienable constructions or verb phrases are not.

With four syllable verbs, we find interpersonal variation regarding the position of the stress. This depends on whether the vowel preceding the last consonant is analysed as a full vowel or as an epenthetic vowel. The latter is ignored when forming the gerund as in (508):

(508) *jaka'ratu* and *ja'kartu/ja'karatu* "crying in shrill, high voice" > *ja'kar(a)tu* "cry in shrill, high voice"

In the Nubi text material there are a few verbs where final *-u* is turned into *-a* in the gerund form, besides the usual stress changes as in (509):

(509) *'lesegu* "glue" > *le'sega* "glueing", "glue"
'aburu "try", "imitate" > *a'bura* "trying", "imitating", "imitation"
'karabu "destroy" > *ka'raba* "destroying", "destruction"

Some verbs have both gerund forms as in (510):

(510) *'seregu* "steal" > *se'rega* "stealing", "robbery" and *se'regu* "stealing", "robbery"

These forms in *-a* were mainly used by speakers who had been in the southern Sudan for some time, having fled the civil war in Uganda. Some verbs have an irregular nominalized form. However, these irregular forms may co-occur with regular gerund forms, as is shown in table 19:

Table 19. Regular/irregular gerund forms

Verbs	Translation	Regular Gerunds	Translation	Irregular Gerunds	Translation
'agara	"read"	*a'gara*	"studying", "study"	*ga'raya*	"study (N)"
'alabu	"play"	*a'labu*	"playing", "play"	*'libu*	"game"
'arufu	"know"			*ma'arifa* / *ma'rifa*	"knowledge"
'alim	"learn"	*a'lim*	"knowledge"	*'ilim*	"knowledge", "information"
'alimu	"teach"	*a'limu*	"teaching"	*ta'lim*	"training", "teaching", "instruction"
'aminu	"trust"	*a'min*	"trusting", "trust"	*a'man(i)*	"trust (N)"
'amuru	"build"			*a'mara*	"building", "construction"
'doru	"travel"	*'doru*	"travelling", "travel"	*do'riya*	"travel (N)"
'hibu	"love"	*'hibu*	"loving"	*ma'haba*	"love (N)"
'ishi	"live"	*'ishi*	"living", "life"	*ma'isha*	"life"
'kafu	"be afraid"			*k(u)'wafu*	"fear (N)"

Table 19 (cont.)

Verbs	Translation	Regular Gerunds	Translation	Irregular Gerunds	Translation
'kasuru	"break", "damage"			ko'sur	"damage (N)"
'kelemu	"say"	ke'lem	"saying"	ka'lam	"word", "matter"
'lebisi	"dress"	le'bis	"dressing", "clothes"	la'basa	"dressing", "dress"
'nedifu	"clean"	ne'difu	"cleaning"	na'dafa	"cleanliness"
'sadu	"help", "assist"			mu'sada	"assistance"
'sama	"forgive"			mu'sama/ musa'ma	"forgiveness"
'raba	"raise"	'raba	"education"	i'raba	"upbringing", "education
'selemu	"greet"			sa'lam(a)	"greeting"
'wonusu	"talk"	wo'nusu/ we'nusu	"talking"	wa'nasa	"conversation"
'wafiki	"agree"			wa'faka	"agreement"
'zuru	"meet"			zi'yara	"meeting"

Use: Gerund forms may express action nominalizations. In that case, the gerund refers either to the action in its abstract sense or to a specific instance of the verbal action (event noun). Besides action nominalizations, the gerund may express product nominalizations referring to the result of the event described by the verb (result noun) and infrequently patient and agent nominalizations. One form may thus have several meanings. Which one is meant should be inferred from the context as in (511) and (512):

(511) Wo'nusu   'gilib(u)   'itokum
       discuss-GER   be difficult-Ø   PRON 2PL
       "Discussing is difficult for you."

(512) fi   'safa   ta   wo'nus   'wede'de
       at   side   GEN   discussion-GER   DEM PROX
       "on this side of the discussion"

However, we can derive a rough distributional pattern. The irregular gerund forms listed in table 20 often express product/result and patient and agent nominalizations, e.g., ko'sur "damage (N)", ga'raya "study (N)", and le'sega "glue (N)", respectively, or they refer to concrete instances of the verbal action (event noun), such as a'mara "construction", unlike the gerund forms of the same verbs that are in agreement with the regular productive pattern of Nubi gerund formation and tend to refer either to the verbal action in its abstract sense, e.g., *ne'difu* "cleaning", or to event nouns as in (513) and (514):

(513) *'alabu* "play"
(a)   *'Libu*   'ja   'hilu.
        play-GER: game   become-Ø nice
        "The game became nice."

(b)   'Ina   'gen   fi   *a'labu.*
        PRON 1PL   stay-Ø   in   play-GER
        "We continued playing."

(514) *'lebisi* "dress", "get dressed"
(a)   *La'basa*   'toumon   'de, . . . 'umon   'lebis(i) 'uo.
        dress-GER: dress PRON POSS 3PL DEF   PRON 3PL wear-Ø PRON 3SING
        "Their [typical] dress, . . . they wore it."

(b)   'Umon   gi-   'lebis   *le'bis*   'tena   'de.
        PRON 3PL PROG- wear   dress-GER: dress PRON POSS 1PL DEF
        "They are wearing our clothes."

(c)   Ba'na   'aba   *le'bis*   fi   'ajal   ta   ru'jal.
        girl-PL refuse-Ø get dressed-GER in   sake   GEN   man-PL
        "The girls refused to get dressed for the sake of the men."

Infinitives, on the other hand, always refer to concrete instances of verbal actions as in (515):

(515) 'Uo   'ya   fi   *'izábu*   ba'na   'de.
      PRON 3SING FOC in   punish-INF girl-PL   DEF
      "He is punishing the girls."

The gerund and the infinitive are distributed differently. The gerund may occur in the following contexts. First, in intransitive verbs, the gerund is the only possible nominalized form. The agent is optionally expressed with the genitive particle *ta*. The gerundival expression thus acquires the appearance of an alienable possessive construction, the gerund taking the position of the possessed item, while the agent takes the possessor's place.

(516) 'Umon   fu   'moyo. Eh, *a'rija*   'wara   'ma,
      PRON 3PL   in   water INT return-GER back   EXIS NEG
      'rua   gi'dam 'ma.
      go-GER forward EXIS NEG
      "They were in the water. Eh, there was no [chance to] return back, there was no [chance to] go forward."

(517) Wu *da'kul*   *'to,*   'uo   'dakul min 'in, . . .
and enter-GER PRON POSS 3SING PRON 3SING enter-Ø around here
"And his entering, he entered around here, . . ."

Second, the gerund may be formed from transitive verbs whose object
is not expressed. The agent may be expressed with the genitive particle *ta* as in (518) and (519):

(518) 'Ina   lo'go   *i'zabu*   'sei-'sei-'sei-'sei   'de.
PRON 1PL get-Ø   punish-GER   much-REP   EMPH
"We got much, much, much, much punishment."

(519) . . . 'namna al   'kan 'uw(o)   'abidu   fu *a'kulu* *'to,*   . . .
         way   REL ANT PRON 3SING begin-Ø in eat-GER PRON POSS 3SING
". . . the way in which he had begun his eating . . . ."

Third, transitive verbs whose object is explicitly present can either
form a gerund, or an infinitive.[19] In those cases, the gerund obligatorily expresses product/result nominalizations, whereas the infinitive
expresses action/event nominalizations. The patient of a gerund verb
form is introduced by the genitive particle *ta*, whereas the patient of
an infinitive is not.[20] The gerundival expression thus resembles an
alienable possessive construction (520) and (522), whereas the infinitival
expression corresponds to inalienable possessive expressions (521) and
(523):

---

[19] Older speakers of the northern variety of Nubi occasionally use the infinitive
when no patient is present:
'In(a)   aju   'gus(u)   'agili   te   *'wénús*   ma bi'niya 'de.
PRON 1PL want-Ø look for-Ø intelligence GEN talk-INF with girl   DEF
"We want to look for means [by using our intelligence] to talk with the girl".

'Umon   'kabas(u) 'uo   ma   'kila 'namna *'kábásu.*
PRON 3PL cheat-Ø   PRON 3SING INSTR every   way   cheat-INF
"They cheated him in every [possible] way of cheating."
[20] Some of Owens' examples (1977) on the gerund were considered incorrect by
my informants since the patient is not introduced by *ta*:

"ra'kabu 'lam   ta   'mariya ma 'din   'de . . .
your wife's cooking meat with this oil." (Owens 1977, 70)
However, in Ugandan Nubi as well, the gerund form exceptionally occurs in an
inalienable-like construction:
'Toro   'de   'ya *a'bidu*   a'bin   to   U'ganda, ...
NPROP   DEF FOC begin-GER construct-Ø GEN NPROP
"Toro [name of district] is the beginning of the construction of Uganda, ..."
Otherwise, the few examples from Kenyan Nubi in Owens (1996) seem to confirm
the above:

(520) *A'bidu*   *ta*   *ka'lam*   au *a'bidu*   *ta*   *'sokol*, 'yena . . .
      begin-GER GEN   problem   or begin-GER GEN thing   FOC + PRON 1PL
      "The beginning of a problem or the beginning of something, we. . . ."

(521) Ya'la   du'ga   ta   'war(a)   'ana   'je   'gusu
      child-PL   small-PL   GEN   after   PRON 1SING   come-Ø look for-Ø
      'namna to   mu'n(u)?   Ta   *'ábídu*   *ga'raya*.
      way   GEN   who/what?   GEN   begin-INF   study-GER
      "The small children (of) after me [my younger brothers and sisters] began
      to look for a way of what? Of beginning studies."

(522) . . . 'in(a)   'aju   'rua   fi   *ga'raya*   ta   *dini*   'ma.
            PRON 1PL   want-Ø   go-Ø   in   study-GER   GEN   religion NEG
      ". . . we do not want to go to religious studies."

(523) Fu   *ágára*   *Grand Party* *'de*,   'ino   lo'go-lo'go   'fogo
      in   study-INF   NPROP   DEF   PRON 1PL   find-REDUP-Ø   in it
      'shida ta   'doru   fi'lel.
      problem GEN   travel-GER   at night
      "To study the Grand Party, we found problems (in it) in respect of travelling
      at night."

The above is summarized in table 20:

Table 20. Distribution and use of the gerund and infinitive forms

Intransitive verbs and transitive verbs (no object present)	Transitive verbs (overt object)
GER (*ta* AG): abstract actions, event nouns (regular), and product/result noun, event noun, agent and patient nominalizations (irregular)	GER *ta* OBJ: product/result noun
	INF OBJ: event noun

The genitive exponent *ta* does not occur with an infinitive but is used with a gerund to mark either the agent or the patient.[21] The infinitive and the gerund may be combined in one single construction as in (524):

      'Uo   'fi   fi   *ash'rubu*.
      PRON 3SING EXIS   in   drink-GER
      "He is drinking [right now]." (after Owens 1996, 150, 13c)

      Katifu   *'waraga*   'ya   'mariya 'de   'so.
      write-INF   letter   FOC   wife   DEF   do-Ø
      "Write a letter is what my wife did." (after Owens 1996, 151, 17a)

[21] According to Owens (1977), both the agent and patient of the gerund form can be expressed in Kenyan Nubi. The agent position is then marked by the relaters *ta* or *ma*:

(524) *ra'kab*   *ta*   *'ifáde*   *'akili*[22]
      cook-GER   GEN   preserve-INF   food
      "the [way of] cooking of preserving food"

Since the gerund forms are used as nominals, they can be modified
by adjectives, demonstratives, adverbs, and/or the definer *'de* or used
as the object of a preposition to form a noun phrase as in (525),
(526), and (527):

(525) *a'bidu*   *je'didi*
      begin-GER   new
      "a new beginning"

(526) *a'jol*   *ta*   *'ja*   *'leti*
      person   GEN   come-GER   late
      "a person of coming late/ someone who comes late habitually"

(527) *de'retu*   *'de*
      break wind-GER   DEF
      "the breaking of wind"

Adjectives cannot be attributed to an infinitive form, but an infinitive
clause can be modified by a demonstrative or the definer *'de*. In such
a case, the entire clause receives the specification and not just the
infinitive as in (528):

    ... a. ka'tulu (ta) li'fili   ta   'juma
          killing   (of) elephants of Juma   Juma's killing the elephant
        b. ka'tulu (ta) li'fili   ma   'juma (same meaning)
    ... The ta that marks the transitive position is optional. If it does not occur
the position without it will be unambiguously interpreted as transitive. If it does
occur then the position can be interpreted as the actor or the transitive position,
since either sequence, transitive-actor or actor-transitive is allowed. ... If ma marks
the actor ... the actor interpretation is unambiguous. (Owens 1977, 70–71).
    In Ugandan Nubi, the co-occurrence of agent and patient does not exist in nom-
inalized constructions. *ma* may occur, but it does not mark the agent position but
rather the instrument or comitative position.
    [22] The verb *'ifade* "preserve" probably reached Nubi via the Swahili verb *hi'fadhi*
"preserve", "keep", "protect", "save". The stress, which, as a rule, lies on the penultimate syllable in Swahili and which is usually retained when the verb is used in
Nubi, has been shifted exceptionally to the first syllable so that it agrees with the
more usual stress pattern of Nubi verbs. Swahili *hi'fadhi* in turn may have been
derived from Arabic *ḥifāẓ* "preservation" where the stress also lies on the same
syllable.

(528) ʿáláb   do'luka ʿde
     play-INF doluka DEF
     "the doluka dancing"

or as in (529), the demonstrative or definer specifies only the noun following the infinitive.

(529) ʿfikra   ta   ʿgérú   bia'shara   we'de
     idea(s)   GEN change-INF business   DEM PROX
     "ideas for changing this business"

Both gerunds and infinitives may take the subject position (530) and (531) and the object position (532) and (533) in a sentence.

(530) ʿHishma   ʿde   ʿya   ʿadab.
     respect-GER DEF FOC   good behaviour
     "Respect is good behaviour."

(531) ʿÁríja   ma'jib   na nyere'ku 'taki   ʿde
     return-INF   answer to child   PRON POSS 2SING   DEF
     gi-   ʿgeleb   ita.
     PROG- bother PRON 2SING
     "To return an answer to your child is bothering you/It bothers you to answer your child."

(532) To'wil ʿbala   ʿjib   ko'sur.
     length attention bring-Ø damage-GER
     "Long attention brings damage."

(533) Nyere'ku ʿtim   ʿámsúku   mu'lodo.
     child   be old enough-Ø hold-INF hoe
     "The child is old enough to hold the hoe [to work on the field]."

The gerund and infinitive may occur in possessive constructions (534), (535), and (536):

(534) ba'kan   be'redu
     place   wash-GER
     "a bathroom"

535) ka'lam   ta   ke'lem
     thing   GEN say-GER
     "something to say"

(536) 'nia   ta   'árija   'zídú   ga'raya
      intention   GEN   return-INF   increase-INF study-GER
      "the intention of going back to increase studying."

As the object of a preposition both the infinitive and the gerund
may occur in expressions such as (537) and (538):

(537) 'Marya   'de   fi   ku'ruju   'to.
      woman   DEF   in   till-GER PRON POSS 3SING
      "The woman is busy working on the field."

(538) 'Ita   'gum   fi   'kúrúju   ku'ruju   ta   so'bun
      PRON 2SING   get up-Ø in   till-INF   till-GER   GEN   soap
      "You got up for tilling (the field) the working for soap [to get money
      to buy soap]."

This type of construction appears after the verbs 'gen / 'gai "stay",
"remain", 'gum "get up", 'rua "go", 'ja "come", 'kun/'kan "be" and
after the existential marker fi. It emphasizes the purpose of the action
expressed by the first verb as in (539) and (540):[23]

(539) 'Uw(o)   'aba   'gum   fi   'sídú   'bab.
      PRON 3SING   refuse-Ø   get up-Ø   in   close-INF   door
      "She refused to get up to close the door."

(540) 'Umon   'rua   fi   'gaba   fi   'gátá   la'kata.
      PRON 3PL   go-Ø   to   forest   in   cut-INF   wood
      "They went to the forest to cut wood."

Gerunds and infinitives may occur in many other idiomatic expressions:

(541) 'Ana   gu-   'wonusu wo'nus   'tai.
      PRON 1SING   PROG-   discuss discuss-GER PRON POSS 1SING
      "I am discussing my things."

(542) La'kin fi   'shir we'de,   'fi   a'jol   ji'ran   'g(i)-   ain.
      but   in   secret DEM PROX EXIS   person neighbour PROG-   see
      'Fi   a'yin   al   'uo   'g(i)-   ain   'de.
      EXIS see-GER   REL   PRON 3SING   PROG-   see   DEF
      "But (in) this secret, a neighbour was there seeing [it]. There was the view
      which he saw [what he saw was unmistakably true]."

---

[23] A sentence like the following, on the other hand, should be interpreted as
different actions that follow each other subsequently or that occur at the same time
(see 4.5).

      'Uw(o)   'aba   'gum   'sidu   'bab.
      PRON 3SING   refuse-Ø   get up-Ø   close-Ø   door
      "She refused to get up and close the door."

(543) 'Ita   'endis   *ta*   *'ámsúku*   *'ida*   *'to.*
PRON 2SING   have-Ø   to   hold-INF   hand(s)   PRON POSS 3SING
"You have to hold his hands."

(544) *'Pole*   *ma*   *ka'sul!*
sorry   PREP   wash-GER
"Sorry for washing (clothes)! [to express sympathy with a person occupied in
hard labour]."

(545) G(i)-   amru'g(u)   ena   *me*   *'jere.*
PROG-   remove-PASS   PRON 1PL   PREP   run-GER
"We were taken away by running."

(546) La'kin   ka'lam   'de,   a'nas   'de   *gi-*   *ni'situ*   ma   *ni'situ?*
but   matter   DEF   people   DEF   PROG-   forget   INSTR   forget-GER
"But this matter, can people simply forget it?"

4.3.4. *Reduplication*

Form: Reduplicated verbs behave like one verb and are generally
marked for TMA and voice as such as in (547), (548), and (549):

(547) 'Ina   *gi-*   *'kuruju-'kuruju*   *'sia.*
PRON 1PL   PROG-   till the field-REDUP   bit
"We are tilling the field a bit."

(548) Gi-   'ja   li'go   'ras   ta   ba'na 'kul   *ma-*   *gata-'gata.*
PROG-   come   find-PASS-Ø   head   GEN   girl-PL   all   STAT   P-cut off-REDUP
"The heads of all the girls will be found being cut off."

549) fi   *'ágilib(u)-'ágilibu*   soko'lin   'dol'de
in   mix-REDUP-INF   thing-PL   DEM PROX PL
"in mixing these things"

Reduplicated verbs may be passivized in two ways. Either only the
second verb takes the passive form as in (550) or both verbs have
undergone the stress shift as in (551). The latter occurs more often
in the southern than in the northern part of Uganda.

(550) 'Dukur   gi-   'ja   *isab(u)-isa'bu*   ya'la   'de.
then   PROG-   come   count-REDUP-PASS-Ø   child-PL   DEF
"Then the children will be counted."

(551) fi   ju'a   al   *kasu'ru-kasu'ru*   'na   je'de.
in   house-PL   REL   break-REDUP-PASS-Ø   there   EMPH
"in the houses that were broken on all sides there."

They may also form the gerund in two ways, either by reduplicat-
ing the gerund form of the single verb as in (552) or by only forming a gerund of the second verb as in (553):

(552) *Bu'kuru-bu'kuru*   'ita   ka'man . . .
      expose to aromatic smoke-REDUP-GER PRON 2SING   EMPH
      'ita   'ya   gi-   'ja   ma   la'kata   bu'kuru.
      PRON 2SING   FOC   PROG- come with   wood   expose to aromatic smoke-GER
      "The exposure to aromatic smoke, you . . . you come with perfumed wood."

(553) . . . 'kidima 'taki   'ya   *'abur-a'bura* .
            job   PRON POSS 2SING   FOC   imitate-REDUP-GER
      ". . . your job is imitation."

Auxiliaries and the anterior marker *'kan* may also be reduplicated as
in (554) and (555):

(554) 'Motoka   'dol'de   *'kan-'kan*   gi-   na'di   DMC.
      car(s)   DEM PROX PL   ANT-REDUP   PROG- call-PASS   NPROP
      "These cars had been called DMC."

(555) 'Youm 'wai,   ka'lam 'wai   *gi-*   *'ja-'ja*   *we'ri*
      day   INDEF thing   INDEF PROG- come-REDUP   show-Ø
      ja   kala'ma   'de   'kul   a'ta   '(i)t(a)   'endi 'ma.
      as   problem-PL   DEF   all   EMPH NEG   PRON 2SING have-Ø NEG
      "One day, something will show as if [that] you do not have all the problems."

Meaning: Reduplicated verbs express a sense of plurality as in (556)
or diffuseness as in (557) (see also Owens 1977):

(556) La'yin, 'it(a)   'ain,   jira'na   'tai   'in 'kul
      but   PRON 2SING   see-Ø   neighbour   PRON POSS 1SING here all
      'ana   *'kelem- 'kelem*   'noumon   ka'la.
      PRON 1SING say-REDUP-Ø   to + PRON 3PL COMPL
      "But, you see, all my neighbours here, I already told them."

(557) Tu'ra al   *'kubu-ku'b(u)*   'uo   ma   'namn(a)
      soil   REL   pour-REDUP-PASS-Ø PRON 3SING   with   way
      ta   dus'man   'de,   'itokum   *'kum-'kum*   tu'ra.
      GEN fight-GER   DEF   PRON 2PL   collect-REDUP-Ø   soil
      "The soil which was strewn by means of/because of the war, you(PL) collected
      (the soil)."

4.4. *Copulas*

4.4.1. *The Copulas Ø, ʼkan "be" and ʼkun "be"*

Form: Generally, the permanent copula Ø, ʼkan stands for permanent or quasi-permanent states with an emphasis on the real, factual character of the states. Normally, permanent 'be' does not have any surface realization when it indicates present or past states as in (558). To mark a past state before a time in focus, ʼkan may be used as in (559):

(558) ʼUmon   Ø   ʼwai   min   aʼnasi   al   to   ʼjo   ʼbele   weʼde.
      PRON 3PL Ø NUM from people REL GEN inside country DEM PROX
      "They are one of the people who are from within this country."

(559) Zaʼman   ʼkan   ʼuo   misʼkin, . . .
      in the old days be-ANT   PRON 3SING   poor
      "In the old days he was poor, . . ." (This person has always been poor, until recently)

The temporary copula ʼkun in general expresses temporary states. It may add a sense of inchoativeness and/or possibility or contingency for present and future.[24] This implies that all references to the being of someone or something that is not or not yet real or factual, such as an imperative or a subjunctive, is expressed by means of temporary 'be' in Nubi. ʼkun acts like any other non-stative Nubi bare verb form to which all types of marking are added, e.g., *gu- ʼkan, bu-ʼkun*, ʼkan ʼkun, ʼkun-IMPER, and ʼkun-GER.

(560) ʼUmon   ʼkun   aʼnas   al   ʼhak .
      PRON 3PL   be-Ø   people   REL   righteous
      "They became righteous people."

(561) ʼAse,   ʼmoyo   kan   ʼmarya ʼamili . . .   ʼya   ʼmoyo ʼde
      now   water   when   woman   be pregnant-Ø CONJ   water   DEF
      gi-   ʼger(u)   ʼuo,   gi-   ʼkun   ʼdom.
      PROG- change   PRON 3SING PROG- be   blood
      "Now, the water, when the woman is pregnant . . ., then the water changes itself, it becomes blood."

---

[24] Owens (1977, 267) talks about contingent 'be' (my temporary 'be') and stative 'be' (my permanent 'be'). I prefer to use temporary 'be' since its span reaches further than just contingency.

(562) *Kan*   *'kun*   'kweis.
       ANT   be-Ø   good
       "It was good."

(563) *Ma-*   *ta*   *'kun*   Is'lam   ka'man
       NEG-   ADR SING   be-IMPER   Muslim   EMPH
       al   ta   'ábúdu   ka'lam   'tan.
       REL   GEN   worship-INF   thing   other
       "Do not be a Muslim who has [the practice] of worshipping something else."

(564) 'Uo   'gal: eh,   *'kun*   ma   'marya Ø   'seme.
       PRON 3SING say-Ø   eh   be-GER   with   wife   Ø   good
       "He [said] that: eh, being with [having] a wife is nice."

Some Nubi speakers from the Buganda area use the Swahili verb *'kuwa* as an alternative form to temporary *'kun* as in (565):

(565) . . .   'sela   we'de,   'uo   'g(i)-   arufa,
                      luggage   DEM PROX   PRON 3SING   PROG- lift
       gi-   *'kuwa*   'nouo   ke'fifu.
       PROG-   be   to + PRON 3SING   light
       ". . . this luggage, he lifts it, it is light for him."

There is optional number agreement between the subject and the predicate. Human beings/animates are more frequently marked for number than others as in (566) and (567):

(566) *'Ina,*   ka'lam *'kan*   *du'ga* . . . .
       PRON 1PL   because be-ANT   small-PL
       "We, because we were small, . . ."

(567) *A'nas*   *'kun*   *kwei'sin.*
       people   be-Ø   good-PL
       "The people were good."

Use: Besides the equative predicate, *Ø, 'kan, 'kun,* and *'kuwa* may express the location of the subject either spatially or temporally as in (568) and (569):[25]

---

[25] *'Kan* may follow another verb, and introduce an object, a prepositional phrase, a subjunctive phrase, etc. In those cases, the construction expresses that the verbal action took place but that the object is no longer available, that the conditions as expressed in the prepositional phrase no longer exist, or that the expected result as expressed in the subjunctive clause was never obtained and thus belongs to the past. In the following sentences, (a) is taken from the text material and (b) was provided during interviews.

(568) 'Zaidi   ta   a'nas   'kan   fi   'area   'na'de
      many   GEN   people   be-ANT   in   area   DEM DIS
      gi-   na'd(i)   'uo   ma'lim   M'puta.
      PROG-   call   PRON 3SING   teacher NPROP
      "Many people [who] were in that area, called him teacher Mputa (Nile perch)."

(569) 'Youm   ta   ni'ka   'g(i)-   arija   'kuwa   fi   'youm 'sebi 'tan.
      day   GEN   wedding PROG-   return   be-Ø   in   Saturday   another
      "The day of the wedding is again on another Saturday."

Ø, 'kan, 'kun, and 'kuwa plus the preposition ma "with" may denote possession. The possessor takes the subject position, the possessee the object position as in (570) and (571):

(570) 'yal   ba'na ka'man Ø mo   'namna 'toumon   ta   a'sili.
      child-PLgirl-PL EMPH Ø with manner PRON POSS 3PL GEN genuineness
      "the girls are with/ have their genuine manner."

(571) 'Yeta   bi- ja   'kun ma   'suduru ti'nen.
      CONJ + PRON 2SING FUT- come be-Ø with breast(s) NUM
      "Then you will be with/ will have two breasts."

(a) 'Ana   we'di 'neta   'kan   'agil   al   ...
    PRON 1SING give-Ø to + PRON 2SING be-ANT knowledge REL
    "I gave you the knowledge which.... [the knowledge was given. However, 'you' lost it.]"

(b) 'Ana   'kan   we'di 'neta   'agil   al   ...
    PRON 1SING ANT   give-Ø to + PRON 2SING knowledge REL
    "I had given you the knowledge which...."

In (a), the knowledge was given but since then has been lost. If 'kan precedes the main verb as in (b), in which case it should be interpreted as the anterior marker, the speaker intends to say that the action of giving has come to an end before the time in focus, whether clearly referred to or not, without giving any additional information about the state of the knowledge. With the copula 'kan in the postverbal position, we know that the transfer of knowledge took place and that subsequently, before the time in focus, the receiver lost it. The following two sentences differ in that in (a) the house is still demolished, but the war that caused the house to be ruined is over. In (b) with the preverbal anterior marker, however, the war is over, and the house, which was demolished during the war, has been rebuilt.

(a) 'Itokum   'gen   fi 'jua   al   'kasur-'kasur   'kan   te   'vita.
    PRON 2PL stay-Ø in house REL break-REDUP-Ø be-ANT GEN war
    "You (PL) stay in a house that is demolished because of the war [which is finished]."

(b) 'Itokum   'gen   fi 'jua   al   'kan   'kasur-'kasur   te   'vita.
    PRON 2PL stay-Ø in house REL ANT break-REDUP-Ø GEN war
    "You (PL) stay in a house that had been demolished because of the war [but that has been rebuilt]."

Another type of possessive construction may be expressed by 'be', whether Ø/ʿkan, ʿkun, or ʿkuwa and the prepositions ma "with" or na "to" in which the possessor is the complement of the preposition while the possessed item takes the subject position as in (572) and (573):

(572) ʿBal   ʿtaki   ke'de   kun   ʿnana.
      attention   PRON POSS 2SING   SUBJ   be-Ø   to + PRON 1SING
      "Your attention should be to me. / I should have your attention."

(573) ʿSente   Ø   ʿmana   ʿma.
      money   Ø   with + PRON 1SING   NEG
      "Money is not with me. / I do not have money."

Ø, ʿkan, ʿkun, and ʿkuwa may also express existential 'be' as in (574) and (575):

(574) Do'luka,   fi   do'luka   ʿna,   ʿumon   Ø   ma   ba'na.
      dance party   in   dance party   there   PRON 3PL   Ø   with   girl-PL
      "The dance party, on the dance party there, they are [there] with the girls."

(575) La'yin   ʿbesi   school fees   ʿya   je-ʾja   ʿkuwa   ʿma.
      but   only   school fees   FOC   come-REDUP-Ø   be-Ø   NEG
      "But only the school fees did not happen to be there."

ʿKun with future marker bi- or preceded by the verbs ʿagider or ʿweza "be able" with future prefix bi- often expresses modality.[26] The expression is mainly impersonal.[27]

(576) Kan   ʿfi   ʿsokol   ba'tal   al   bi-   ʿsó   na   ji'ran
      if   EXIS   thing   bad   REL   FUT-   do-PASS   to   neighbour
      ʿtaki . . .,   a'j(u)   ita . . .   ʿkun   ʿready.
      PRON POSS 2SING   need-PASS-Ø   PRON 2SING   be-Ø   ready
      Sa'ba   ka'man   bu-   ʿkun   ʿdor   ʿtaki.
      tomorrow   also   FUT-   be   turn   PRON POSS 2SING
      "If there is a bad thing that is done to your neighbour . . ., you should . . . be ready. Tomorrow, it may also be your turn."

---

[26] The adverbs ʿlab(u)da, min ʿaruf, ʿsa ʿtan "maybe", "perhaps", "possibly" express approximately the same meaning:
      Min ʿaruf   ʿuo   ʿb(i)-   awun(u)   ʿina
      maybe   PRON 3SING FUT-   help   PRON 1PL
      fi   ʿshida   ʿtena   al   ʿina   ʿfogo ʿwede'de.
      in   problem   PRON POSS 1PL   REL   PRON 1PL   in it   DEM PROX
      "Maybe he will help us in (this) our problem which we are in."
[27] Owens (1977) talks in this respect about the 'modal contingent'.

(577) Au *'b(i)-*   *agder*   *'kun*   fu   'Kenya.
    or FUT-   be able   be-Ø   in   NPROP
    "Or it might be in Kenya."

4.4.2. *The Copula 'ja "become"*

The copula *'ja* may express an alteration of state as in (578) and (579):[28]

(578) . . . bi'niya, ka'la   'ras   'to   *gi-*   *'ja*   'gow- 'gow.
    girl   COMPL head   PRON POSS 3SING PROG-   become hard- REDUP.
    ". . . the girl, her head already became hard."

(579) 'Ana   *bi-*   *'ja*   'tajir.
    PRON 1SING FUT-   become   rich
    "I will become rich."

Infrequently, the copula *bi'ja* "become" is used (see also Heine (1982) on Kenyan Nubi). In these cases, *bi-* does not carry future meaning but is part of the verb stem as in (580):

---

[28] Other verbs that may function as equative verbs are *'fadul* "remain", *'raba* "grow", *'gai/ 'gen* "stay", *'tim* "be (old) enough", and *'fi* "be (EXIS)" (see 4.4.3):

    'Umon   *'gai*   a'nas   asa'sin   'sei-'sei   'de.
    PRON 3PL   remain-Ø people   beautiful-PL   very-REDUP EMPH
    "They remain to be/are very pretty people."

    'Batna   'jua   *fadulu*   ne'dif.
    inside   house   remain-Ø   clean
    "The inside of the house remains clean."

Owens (1977: 110) also includes transitive verbs like *'kutu* "make", *'so* "make", *'adulu* "prepare", *'alimu* "teach". However, a sentence like:

    'ina   'so   'uwo   'asker
    we   make   him   soldier
    "we made him into a soldier" (see Owens 1977: 110)

would take the verb *'kun* "be" , with or without a subjunctive clause, in Ugandan Nubi:

    'ina   'so   ke'de   uo   'kun   'asker
    PRON 1PL   make-Ø SUBJ   PRON 3SING be-Ø   soldier
    "we made so that he became a soldier."

    'ina   *'kut(u)*   'uo   'kun   'asker
    PRON 1PL   make-Ø PRON 3SING be-Ø   soldier
    "we made him into a soldier."

This fact delimits the discussion on equative verbs in Ugandan Nubi to *'kun/ 'kan* "be", *'ja* "become", *'raba* "grow", *'fadul* "remain", *'gai/ 'gen* "remain", "stay", *'tim* "be (old) enough", and the existential marker *'fi.*

(580) 'Ina   'gai   ma   'ragi   'tai,   'sana *bi'ja*
       PRON 1PL   stay-Ø with husband PRON POSS 1SING year   become-Ø
       ka'lasi 'ashara wu   'sokol.
       COMPL   ten   and   thing
       "I stay with my husband, the years become already ten and something."

4.4.3. *The Existential Marker* 'fi

Form: The existential marker *'fi* may be analysed as a stative verb
denoting a temporary state, even though it has a reduced tense/aspect
system. It may take the progressive marker *gi-*, the future marker *bi-*
, and the anterior marker *'kan*. However, in subjunctive and imperative clauses, the auxiliary verb *'kun* must be added: *ke'de 'kun 'fi*, and
'kun 'fi, respectively. The negative marker *'ma* is prefixed to negate
the existential marker. It becomes *'ma'fi* but may be produced as
'mafi, 'maf, or even *'ma*.

(581) *'Fi*   'warag(a) al   'uw(o)   'aktib? 'Gali: *'ma'fi.*
       EXIS letter   REL   PRON 3SING write-Ø that   EXIS   NEG
       "Is there a letter which he wrote? (He said) that: there is not."

(582) Kan   'ana   'gu-   rwa   fi   sa'fari, 'ragi we'de   'ya
       when   PRON 1SING PROG- go   in   trip   man DEM PROX FOC
       gi-   *'fi*   fi   'be   'tai   'ini ....
       PROG- EXIS in   house PRON POSS 1SING here
       "[Every time] when I go on a trip, this man stays in my house here...."

(583) Ka'man 'aju   'abba 'to   'de   *ke'de* *'kun* *'fi* ...
       also   have to-Ø granny PRON POSS 3SING DEF SUBJ be-Ø EXIS
       "Also his grandmother should be there...."

Use: *'Fi* expressing existence: *'Fi* essentially denotes existence. In that
case, definite subjects, determined by means of the definite article
'de, a demonstrative, or a possessive construction, generally precede
the existential marker as in (584):

(584) *'Abba*   *'tai*   *'kan*   *'fi.*
       granny PRON POSS 1SING ANT   EXIS
       "My granny was there/alive."

Indefinite subjects follow it as in (585):

(585) Za'man   bu'mara   *'kan*   *'fi*   *'rag(i)*   *'wai.*
       previously   very much   ANT   EXIS   man   INDEF
       "A long time ago, there was a man."

When the existential marker is negated, the definite subject generally precedes it as in (586):

(586) 'Yal   ta'lata   'de,   'yal   'de,
      child-PL   NUM   DEF   child-PL   DEF
      ma'ma   'toumon   ka'man   'ma'fi.
      mother PRON POSS 3PL   EMPH   EXIS NEG
      "The three children, the children, their mother was not there/was
      dead."

The indefinite subject either precedes or follows the negated existential marker:

(587) ...,   la'kini   'sente   'ma'fi.
              but   money   EXIS NEG
      "..., but there is no money."

(588) 'Ase'de 'ma'fi   ka'lam.
      now   EXIS NEG   problem
      "Now, there is no problem."

'Fi expressing equation: Existential 'fi may function as an equative
verb, which takes an equative complement. Number agreement is
optional as in (590). 'Fi then refers to a temporary state 'as for now',
contrary to permantent 'kan "be", which marks a more permanent
state. 'Fi, however, differs from 'kun "temporary be" in that the latter conveys the idea of inchoativeness and/or contingency, whereas
'fi lacks any reference of this kind.[29]

(589) ... ta'ra   nyere'ku   to   m'ze   'de   ta a'sil   'fi   'king.
          EMPH   child   GEN   old man DEF   in reality EXIS   king
      "...you see, the child of the old man is in reality a king."

(590) A'nas   'fi   gishe'rin.
      people   EXIS   short-PL
      "The people are short."

'Fi expressing continuation: The existential marker 'fi + preposition
fi followed by a gerund or infinitive construction conveys that the
subject is in the process of conducting an action.[30] Its meaning thus

---

[29] *Pace* Owens (1977) who speaks in this respect of a contingent equational sentence, expressing a state whose inception took place only recently.
[30] The verbal position is not restricted to 'fi. The verbs 'gai/'gen "stay", 'gum "get
up", etc. can as well occur (see 4.3.3)

closely resembles that of the progressive marker *gi-*. Unlike the progressive marker, its function is restricted to expressing continuous action, and excludes the expression of habitual or repeated action (see also Owens 1977). A sentence like (591) would be ungrammatical, since the stative verb *fi* preceded by the progressive marker implies habituality.[31]

(591)   * 'Ana   *gi-*   *fi*   *fi*   *ʾkátífu*   *ʾbuku.*
        PRON 1SING PROG- EXIS in   write-INF   book
        "I am [habitually] writing a book."

More than the progressive marker, *fi fi* + GER/INF emphasizes that the subject is participating in the action at the time in focus. (592)(a) indicates that the people are busy making preparations for the wedding at the time in focus. The fictitious sentence (b) would also mean that the people are in the process of preparing the wedding but not necessarily right now.

(592)
  (a) 'Ase'de,   'youm ju'ma, 'youm   we'de,
       now,   Friday,   day   DEM PROX
       a'nas   *fi*   *fi*   *ádúlu*   *'namna ta*   *'jowju*   'youm 'sebi.
       people   EXIS   in   prepare-INF   way   GEN   marry-GER   Saturday
       "Now, on Friday, this day, the people are busy preparing (the way of) the marriage of Saturday."

  (b) . . . a'nas   *gi-*   *'adulu*   *'namna*   *ta*   *'jowju*   'youm 'sebi.
            people   PROG-   prepare   way   GEN   marry-GER   Saturday
       ". . . the people are preparing (the way of) the marriage of Saturday."

Fi denoting location: When followed by an adverbial phrase of location, the existential marker *fi* expresses the temporary location of the subject as in (593) and (594):

(593)   Li'fili   *'fu*   *'wen?*
        elephant   EXIS   where?
        "Where is the elephant?

(594)   *'Gesi*   *'de*   "debba   *'fi*   *'fogo.*
        grass   DEF   snake   EXIS   in it
        "The grass, there is a snake in it."

---

[31] The aspect of inchoativeness is also barred from the *fi fi* + GER/INF construction (cf. Owens 1977).

'Fi expressing possession: Nubi may use *'fi* + the prepositions *na* "to" or *ma* "with". *Na* denotes that someone or something is close to something or someone else (locative possessive). *Ma* is the comitative marker. There are two types of construction. Either the subject marks the possessed item while the prepositional phrase refers to the possessor (with-possessive) as in (595),

(595) 'uo   ke'de 'ain   kan   *fire ex'tinguisher*   *'fi*   *'nouo.*
      PRON 3SING SUBJ see-Ø if   fire extinghuisher EXIS to + PRON 3SING
      "he should see whether he has a fire extinguisher."

or the subject is the possessor while the preposition *ma* "with" introduces the possessee as in (596):

(596) 'Youm 'tan 'ina   gi-   'ja   li'go nyere'ku 'tena   'de
      day   other PRON 1PL PROG- come find child   PRON POSS 1PL DEF
      'fi   *ma*   'sudur   ti'nin.
      EXIS   with   breast(s)   NUM
      "Another day, we will find our child being with/having two breasts."

The possessee is mainly non-human with the exception of children and personnel, who can be 'possessed'. When the subject is human, *'Fi na* and *'fi ma* indicate that the subject is living together with (an)other person(s).[32]

(597) 'Bes, 'ina   *'kan*   *'fi*   *ma*   kal'ti   'tena.
      well PRON 1PL ANT EXIS with maternal uncle PRON POSS 1PL
      "Well, we were there with our maternal uncle."

(598) Ja'lila   *'fi*   *na*   'ragi   'wai.
      NPROP   EXIS   with   man   INDEF
      "Jalila is there with a [certain] man."

4.4.4. *The Verb 'endi "have"*

Form: Unlike other transitive verbs, *'endi* and its alternative *forms 'endis, 'endisi, 'indi, 'endu, 'andi, 'andis,* and *'andisi* do not have a pas-

---

[32] *'Fi na* also has the idiomatic meaning of "be under the care of...":

'Marya   'de, ...   'ya
woman   DEF   FOC
'ala   'kan   'uo   *'fi*   *'nouo,*   'Aisa.
REL   ANT   PRON 3SING EXIS to +PRON 3SING NPROP
"The woman, ... under whose care she was, Aisa."

sive nor a stative passive verb form (see also Owens 1977). Otherwise, it behaves like any other stative verb. This means that it can take the progressive marker *gi-* when expressing a habit or inchoative-ness, the future marker *bi-*, and the anterior marker *'kan* as in (599), and (600). In interviews, my informants mentioned the possibility of using the verb *'endi* preceded by auxiliaries like *'gurwa* "be going to" to express a near and definite future, or *'ja* "come" to express inchoa-tiveness. In the text material, however, *'gurwa 'endi* was not used, and *'ja 'endi* was apparently replaced by *'(ja) 'kun ma* "be with".

(599) 'Ana   'fekeri   'an(a)   'endu   'sana   'ashara au i'dashar.
      PRON 1SING think-Ø PRON 1SING have-Ø year(s) NUM   or NUM
      "I think I had ten or eleven years/ I was ten or eleven years old."

(600) Kan   ji'yan   'be   'toumon   gi-   'so   'uo,
      when   hunger   home   PRON POSS 3PL   PROG-   do   PRON 3SING
      'dukuru 'uo   'g(i)-   endisi   'namna   'ma.
      then   PRON 3SING PROG- have   means   NEG
      "When homesickness is doing her [when she is homesick], then she doesn 't have means [to go there]."

Use: *'Endi* expressing possession: *'Endi* essentially expresses posses-sion. Above, I discussed the expression of possession by means of *'kun/ 'kan* "be" or the existential marker *fi* followed by either the comitative preposition *ma* or the locative preposition *na*.[33] Although Owens (1977) and Heine (1982) doubt whether a distinction can be made as to the distribution of the different forms, such a distinction does seem to exist. If we distinguish between legal possession, inalien-able possession (like part-whole relations, body parts, characteristics, kinship relations), and temporary possession, we see that all three can be expressed by the Nubi verb *'endi*:

* legal as in (601):

(601) 'An(a)   'endis   'bicycle   'tai.
      PRON 1SING have-Ø bicycle   PRON POSS 1SING
      "I have my bicycle."

---

[33] The following construction including *'endi* and *fi* is not uncommon in Nubi:

'Umon   'endi   'kila   'sokol   'toumon   fi.
PRON 3PL   have-Ø every   thing   PRON POSS 3PL   EXIS
"They have everything of them (being here)."

* inalienable: part-whole relations (602), body parts (603), kin terms
(604), and characteristics (605):

(602) 'Gus(u)   'nana   ku'baya 'chai al   'endi   'tamaga, ...
      find-IMPER for + PRON 1SING cup   tea   REL have-Ø saucer
      "Find for me a tea cup that has a saucer, . . ."

(603) 'Uo   'kan 'indi   'gisim. 'Uo   se'min.
      PRON 3SING ANT have-Ø body   PRON 3SING fat.
      "He had a body. He was fat."

(604) 'Ana   'me 'endi   ma'ma, 'ana   'me 'endi   ba'ba.
      PRON 1SING NEG have-Ø mother PRON 1SING NEG have-Ø father
      "I do not have a mother, I do not have a father."

(605) 'Uw(o)   'endi   'adab.
      PRON 3SING have-Ø   good manners
      "She has good manners."

* temporary: objects (referring to temporary use) as in (606) and
emotions as in (607):

(606) 'Uw(o)   'endis   si'la   to   'in, ...
      PRON 3SING have-Ø gun   PRON POSS 3SING here
      "He has his gun here, . . ."

(607) 'Ya   mar'ba   'de, 'uw(o)   'endis   fu'raha
      CONJ   stepmother   DEF   PRON   3SING have-Ø happiness
      fi   'gelba   'to   'ma   ...
      in   heart   PRON POSS 3SING NEG
      "Thus the stepmother, she does not have happiness in her heart [is not
      happy]. . . ."

The possessive expression POSSESSOR *fi ma* POSSESSEE is used
in the first two domains.

* legal as in (608):

(608) A'nas te   U'gand(a)   'en   'kul,
      people GEN   NPROP   here   all
      'kil(a) a'zol   fi   ma   ma'hal 'to   ka'las.
      every person   EXIS with place PRON POSS 3SING EMPH
      "All the people from Uganda here, everybody has his place."

* inalienable possession: part-whole relations, body parts (609), kinship terms, and characteristics (610):

(609) 'Youm 'tan 'ina   gi-   'ja li'go nyere'ku 'tena   'de
      day   other PRON 1PL PROG- come find child PRON POSS 1PL DEF
      fi   *ma*   'sudur   ti'nin.
      EXIS with breast(s) NUM
      "Another day we will find our child having two breasts."

(610) 'Kena   ende'lea   mo   utama'duni   'tena
      SUBJ + PRON 1PL   continue-Ø   with   civilization PRON POSS 1PL
      ta   za'man al   'kan   'ina   *fi*   'mouo.
      GEN   old days REL ANT   PRON 1PL EXIS with + PRON 3SING
      "Let us continue with our civilization of the old days which we had."

Temporary possession (objects or emotions), however, is generally
not expressed by means of a POSSESSOR *fi ma* POSSESSEE- construction, most likely because *fi* refers to a permanent state that
would conflict with the temporary character of the possession. Instead,
kun ma (and also *'gen/'gai ma*) are found with this type of possession.[34] *Kun ma* adds the idea of inchoativeness or possibility and as
such often refers to (temporary) emotions.[35]

(611) . . . 'itokum   b(i)-   arija   'kun   mo   fu'rai.
             PRON 2PL   FUT-   return   be-Ø   with   happiness
      ". . . you(PL) will again be (with) / have happiness."

The possessive locative constructions POSSESSEE *fi na/ma* POS-
SESSOR cover slightly different domains:

* legal as in (612):

(612) 'Sente   'kan   *fi*   'nana.
       money   ANT   EXIS   to + PRON 1SING
       "I had money."

---

[34] Possession may also be rendered by means of the verbs *'gen/'gai* "stay", "remain"
in combination with the comitative preposition *ma*:

Min   'ita   'gen   ma   'fikra   mi'lan,
from   PRON 2SING   stay-Ø with   thought(s)   many
'to   'num   'seme   'ma,   . . .
PRON 2SING sleep-Ø good NEG
"From the moment that/ because you have many thoughts, you do not sleep
well, . . ."

[35] Although a breast is actually a body part and therefore inalienable, in this
specific context of a girl receiving a missing breast, *kun* "be", even though denoting temporary states, is not out of place.

'Yeta   bi-   'ja   'kun   ma   'suduru   ti'nen.
CONJ + PRON 2SING FUT-   come   be-Ø   with   breast(s) NUM
"Thus you will have two breasts."

* inalienable: characteristics as in (613):

(613) 'Adab te   'súlú-'súlú   soko'lin ta   a'nasi *fi*   'nouo.
      habit GEN take-REDUP-INF thing-PL GEN people EXIS with + PRON 3SING
      "He has the habit of taking things from people/stealing."

POSSESSEE *fi na* POSSESSOR may, besides characteristics, also express temporary possession either of objects or emotions as in (614) and (615), respectively:

(614) 'Baisikil   *fi*   'nana.
      bicycle   EXIS   to + PRON 1SING
      "I had [the use of] a bicycle."

(615) 'Bas 'ini   *fi*   'nena   'ebu   'zaidi.
      well here EXIS to + PRON 1PL shame a lot of
      "Well here we have a lot of shame [are very much ashamed]."

It thus appears that, when expressing legal possession, 'endi and the locative *fi ma/na* constructions are interchangeable except that with 'endi the focus is more on the possessee whereas with the *fi ma/na* constructions the focus is on the possessor. Consider (616):

(616) Ba'ba   'tai   'kan 'endi baga'ra fi Gu'lu.   Baga'ra
      father PRON POSS 1SING ANT have-Ø cow-PL in NPROP cow-PL
      'kan   *fi*   'mouo.
      ANT   EXIS   with + PRON 3SING
      "My father had cows in Gulu. He had cows."

In expressing inalienable and temporary possession, 'endi and the locative possessive constructions, however, have a different distribution, which is summarized in table 21.

Table 21. Nubi expressions of possession

		'endi	*fi ma* POSSee	*fi ma* POSSor	*fi na* POSSor
Legal possession		x	x	x	x
Inalienable possession:	Part-whole	x	x		
	Body parts	x	x		
	Kin relations	x	x		
	Characteristics	x	x	x	x
Temporary possession:	Objects	x			x
	Emotions	x			x

For the locative *ji ma/na* construction, one might expect variants
with the verbs *Ø/'kan* "(permanent) be", *'kun* "(temporary) be", and
'gen/'gai "stay", each with its specific meaning since these verbs are
related to each other on a kind of continuum ranging from permanent *Ø/'kan*, to *ji* and *'gen/'gai* to temporary *'kun*. However, since
the locative possessive construction generally refers to legal and inalienable characteristics, instances of the verbs *'gen/'gai* "stay" and *'kun*
"(temporary) be" with this type of construction are almost non-existent. An exception is (572).[36]

Expressing obligation with *'endi (ta)*: A few speakers use *'endi* (+
an optional element that is homophonous with the genitive particle
ta) to express obligation as in (617) and (618). The utterances were
limited to younger speakers (approximately 35 years) from both the
southern and the northern parts of the country.

(617) Kan 'ragi   'de 'ma'fi,   'it(a)   'endi   ja   'nana, . . .
       if   husband DEF EXIS-NEG PRON 2SING have-Ø come-Ø to+PRON 1SING
       "If [your] husband is not there, you have to come to me, ..."

(618) 'Ita   bi-   'endi to   'rua   na   'awa   'to.
       PRON 2SING FUT- have GEN go-Ø to   aunt PRON POSS 3SING
       "You will have to go to her aunt."

4.5. *Asyndetic Verb Chains*

In 4.2.1.4, we discussed the auxiliary verbs. However, what I considered to be 'auxiliary verbs' may also occur as free verbs. Moreover,
these verbs may occur in asyndetic verb chains preceding another

---

[36] Another type of possession whose number of occurrences is limited consists of
permanent 'be', expressed by *Ø/'kan* followed by the genitive particle *ta* + possessor. The relative marker *al* optionally precedes 'be'. This type of construction only
refers to inalienable possession:

    Nyere'ku 'ya   ta   ke'ni   'na'de.
    child   FOC GEN   co-wife DEM DIS
    "The child is of that wife [is that wife's]."

    'Umon   'sulu   das'turi
    PRON 3PL   take-Ø   habit(s)
    al   'kan   ta   'nas   ji'di   'toumon.
    REL be-ANT GEN   COLL grandfather PRON POSS 3PL
    "They took the habits (which were) of their grandparents."

verb or other verbs (as do the auxiliaries). Unlike the auxiliary verbs, their meaning cannot be combined with tense and/or aspect such as future, duration, and iterativity. The meaning of the free verb is retained. They express different actions following each other or occurring at the same time.

Only a few Nubi verbs occur in an asyndetic verb chain. These are locational-directional verbs, namely:

* verbs of directed motion 'rua "go" expressing motion away from and ja "come" expressing motion towards as in (619) and (620):

(619) 'Ya   umon   bu-   'rua. 'Umon   'bu-   rwa   'kuruju . . . .
      CONJ PRON 3PL FUT- go   PRON 3PL FUT- go   till the soil-Ø
      "Thus they will go. They will go to till the soil. . . ."

(620) 'Kel(i) al   'ingis . . ., al   gi-   'doru   'zaman te 'segete,
      dog   REL   like   REL   PROG- wander about period GEN coldness
      'uo   gi-   ja   num   fi   lu'daya.
      PRON 3SING PROG- come sleep-Ø in   hearth
      "A dog which is like . . ., which is wandering about for some time from the cold,
      he comes to sleep in the   hearth."

* manner direction verbs 'arija "return" and 'gum "get up" as in (621) and (622):[37]

(621) Asker'ya 'kul   'arija   'jere.
      guard-PL all   return-Ø run-Ø
      "All the guards ran back."

---

[37] 'Rua "go", ja "come", and 'arija "return" may also convey the notion of accidentalness:

'Umon   'ro   'ain   ta'gia.
PRON 3PL go-Ø   see-Ø   cap
"They happened to see a head cap."

'Gelba 'to   'kan   je   'kuwa   'tan.
heart   PRON POSS 3SING ANT   come-Ø be-Ø   other
"His heart happened to be different."

Kan   'it(a)   'aju   ke'd(e) 'ow(o)   'rua   fi   'jela,
if   PRON 2SING   want-Ø SUBJ   PRON 3SING go-Ø   to   jail
'ita   'sidu bi'zatu 'ya   'so   su'nu? 'Arija 'rua   fi   'jela.
PRON 2SING REFL REFL   FOC   do-Ø   Q-word return-Ø go-Ø to   jail
"If you wish that he goes to jail, you yourself will do what? (Happen to) go
to jail."

(622) 'Lam   'gaba   *'gum*   *'rua*   na   ku'juru.
      meat   forest   get up-Ø   go-Ø   to   witchdoctor.
      "The wild animal got up and went to the witchdoctor."

* the verbs *'gen/'gai* "sit", "remain" and the existential marker *fi* "be (there)" as in (623) and (624):

(623) Wu   fa'rash   'de   *'gai*   *fi*   *'g(i)-*   *ain*   ka'lam
      and   horse   DEF   sit-Ø   EXIS   PROG-   see   thing
      al   gi-   só.
      REL   PROG-   do-PASS
      "And the horse sat there and watched the thing that was being done."

(624) 'Marya, mu'ze   al   *fi*   *gi-*   *'chunga*
      woman   old person REL   EXIS   PROG-   take care of
      'samba   'to   ta   'mwisho 'nade'de   'lisa   'ma   'weledu.
      field   PRON POSS 3SING GEN   end   DEM DIS   still   NEG   bear-Ø
      "The woman, the old [woman] who is there and takes care of her field of that [plot] at the end, did not yet give birth."

Also the degree verbs *'zidu/'jidu* "increase" and *'tim* "be enough", "suffice" may occur in an asyndetic verb chain as in (625) and (626):[38]

---

[38] Some instances of uncommon verb chains occurred only once. Four of them were uttered by people from the northern part of the country. Two of these people were older than sixty. It may be that, in early Nubi, verbs were combined more freely. In contemporary Nubi, such clauses would normally be expressed by means of the subjunctive marker *ke'de*, the preposition *fi*, or a coordinating conjunction.

'Ma'f(i)   a'jol   al   ke'de   *jer(e)*   *'arija*   *'wara*.
EXIS NEG   person   REL   SUBJ   run-Ø   return-Ø   back
"No one should run back/flee."

Ta   'youm   'da 'na'de,   'fi   gu'masi *gi-*   *kei'tu*   *gi-*   *'kubu*
GEN   a bygone past DEM DIS EXIS cloth(s) PROG- sew-PASS PROG-pour
'yele-'yele   je   gu'mas 'tai   'yele-'yele   we'de.
fringe(s)   like   cloth   PRON POSS 1SING fringe(s)   DEM
"From that bygone past, there were clothes [which were] sewn to fall in fringes like this fringed cloth of   mine."

'Ita   *'gata*   *'amrugu*   'nas   'kilwa.
PRON 2SING   cut-Ø   remove-Ø   COLL   kidney(s)
"You cut and removed the kidneys."

Di'fan   'rasulu   li'go   'nas   'afoyo 'fi   *'g(i)-*   akulu
guest   arrive-Ø   meet-Ø   COLL   rabbit EXIS   PROG-   eat
ma   ya'la   'to   ma   'marya 'kulu ba'kan 'wai
with   child-PL   PRON POSS 3SING   with   wife   all   place NUM
"The guest arrived to meet the rabbit being there and eating with his children and [his] wife all in one place."

(625) 'Umon[1] ka'man *gi-* *'jidu* *gu-* *we'di* 'noumon[2]
    PRON 3PL also PROG- increase PROG- give to + PRON 3PL
    soko'lin al 'umon[1] 'fi 'mouo 'de.
    thing-PL which PRON 3PL EXIS with + PRON 3SING DEF
    "They[1] were also increasingly giving them[1] things which they[1] had."

(626) . . . kan a'nas *bi-* *'tim* *'fikir* au 'kil(a) a'zol 'wai-'wai
    if people FUT- suffice think-Ø or every person NUM-REDUP
    bi- 'feker ma'isha ta . . . 'to ma 'family 'to, . . .
    FUT- think life GEN PRON POSS 3SIGN with family PRON POSS 3SING
    ". . . if people were[reasonable] enough to think or every single person thought about his life and [that] of his family. . . ."

A chain of asyndetic verbs may contain up to three verbs in Nubi as in (627):

(627) 'Abba, 'abba al 'fadul fi'jo 'ju(a) 'en 'de,
    granny granny REL remain-Ø inside house here DEF
    na'fas to *'gúm* *'ró* *'sídú* 'bab we'de,
    opportunity GEN get up-INF go-INF close-INF door DEM PROX
    'uo 'aba.
    PRON 3SING refuse-Ø
    "The granny, the granny who remained inside the house here, the opportunity to get up and go and close this door, she refused [it]."

The first verb of a verb chain generally takes aspect and tense marking by means of prefixes or auxiliaries as in (628):

(628) 'Ya li'wali to 'nus 'umon *'jo* *'gum* *'rua*
    CONJ responsible GEN among PRON 3PL come-AUX get up-Ø go-Ø
    na 'sidu tu'ro we'de 'ase'de al(i) 'ina 'fogo 'de.
    to owner soil DEM PROX now REL PRON 1PL in it DEF
    "Thus the [person]responsible from among them got up to go to the owner of this soil (now) which we were on."

Non-punctual aspect marking by means of the progressive marker *gi-* or any variant form can, however, occur in both verbs as in (629):

. . ., 'uo 'ja 'asuma mu'ze 'wai *gi-* *'wonus gi-* *'dugu* a'dis.
    PRON 3SING came-Ø hear-Ø old man INDEF PROG- talk PROG- beat story
    ". . ., he happened to hear an old man talking and telling a story."

ke'de ka'lam we'de 'ma *'kun* *'waga* nana.
    SUBJ problem DEM PROX NEG be-Ø fall-Ø to + PRON 1SING
    "let this problem not fall on me."

(629) 'An   'g(i)- ain   'fi   a'jol
       PRON 1SING PROG- see   EXIS person
       al   gi-   'ja   gi-   'dakal 'in   'kila 'sa ti'nin te   fi'lel.
       REL   PROG- come PROG- enter here every hour NUM GEN at night
       "I see that there is a person who comes and enters here every [time at] two
       o'clock at night."

It can also appear only in the last verb if the first verb of the chain
is a stative verb and therefore does not need *gi-* marking to express
the non-punctual aspect as in (630):

(630) Wu   ter   'de   *fi*   'gen   gu-   'wonusu.
       and   bird   DEF   EXIS   sit-AUX PROG-   talk
       "And the bird is there talking continuously."

All juxtaposed verbs are usually marked for mood, voice, or nominalization. Consider (627), (631), and (632):

(631) *'Gum*   *'ro*   *'tor(u)*   'umon
       get up-IMPER go-IMPER   wake up-IMPER PRON 3PL
       'k(e)   omon   ja.
       SUBJ PRON 3PL   come-Ø
       "Get up to go and wake them up so that they come."

(632) 'Ya   ka'man *'já*   *paki'y(a)*   ena,   su'l(u)   ina,
       CONJ also   come-PASS-Ø pick up-PASS-Ø PRON 1PL take-PASS-Ø PRON 1PL
       'ró   *ku't(u)*   ina   fi   'India.
       go-PASS-Ø put-PASS-Ø PRON 1PL   in   NPROP
       "Thus we were also (come to be) picked up, we were taken, we were (gone to be) put
       in India."

Only one object is possible in Nubi verb chains as in (623). Similarly,
there is only one negator, whose place is, however, not fixed (see
also 6.3) as in (633):

(633) Bi-   ku't(u) ('i)ta   'gum   'ma   'ro   fi   'ákúl   mai'rungi.
       FUT- cause PRON 2SING get up-Ø NEG go-Ø in   eat-INF qat
       "You will not be forced to get up and go to eat qat."

With imperative forms, the addressee is attached to either the first
or to the second verb.

(634) 'Ro-   'tokum   'alabu.
       go-IMPER-   ADR-PL   play-IMPER
       "Go playing (PL)!".

(635) 'Arija   'rua-   'takum.
      return-IMPER   go-IMPER-   ADR-PL
      "Return and go (PL)!."

4.6. *Conclusion*

A preliminary comparison between Nubi and the characteristics of
creole grammar shows some striking correspondences but also some
obvious differences. Bickerton (1977, 1981) posits three verbal core
markers that are essential in creole grammars: an anterior tense
marker, an irrealis mood marker, and a non-punctual aspect marker.
All markers occur in preverbal position and always in the invariant
order TMA: ANT, IRR, NON-PUNCT. Moreover, Bickerton postulates a distinction between stative and non-stative verbs. Based on
the above, the following paradigm may be set up (table 22):[39]

Table 22. Creole TMA-markers and their functions

	Stative	Non-stative
Ø or zero-marked verb	Non-past	Past
Non-punctual	Temporary states	Durative, habitual or iterative aspect
Irrealis	Unreal time (= future, conditional, subjunctive, modal, etc.)	
Anterior	Past	Past-before-past/ or (remote) past
IRR + NON-PUNCT	Future progressive	
ANT + NON-PUNCT	Non-punctual event in a past-before-past, or during a completed period of time	
ANT + IRR	Unrealized event in the past	
ANT + IRR + NON-PUNCT	Unrealized non-punctual event in the past	

Source: Bickerton (1977, 1981)

The zero-marked or simple verb in Nubi marks the punctual aspect,
which essentially, if no marking for tense is present, refers to the
past for non-stative verbs and the non-past (present resulting states
of past events) for stative verbs. However, the simple verb is neutral with respect to tense (past, present, future) and aspect (punc-

---

[39] See also Bakker, Post and van der Voort (1995, 247–58) .

tual/non-punctual) when tense and aspect are clearly marked otherwise, for instance in previous verbs, with adverbs, the context, or
situation. Holm (1988) states that the normal procedure in creole
languages is one where the simple verb form can refer to any time
if it has clear references in the context. This neutrality is, however,
limited to tense, and moreover only to past and present tenses (see
also Boretzky 1983). Neutrality with respect to tense is thus, according to Holm, common in creoles (see also Givón 1984). The use of
the simple verb form in non-punctual environments, however, seems
to occur only in Nubi and Juba Arabic (see Mahmud 1979). The
progressive marker *gi-* in Nubi refers to the non-punctual aspect
involving the continuative, habitual and/or iterative aspect and is
used mainly with non-stative verbs, in which it indicates present
states/events. However, when marking for tense by other means is
available, any time may be denoted. *Gi-* may mark stative verbs
when indicating the inception of the state, when marking states recurring on a regular basis, and with some speakers with the verbs *'ben*
"look like", *'gen/'gai* "sit", "remain". This may correspond to Bickerton's
locative and other stative verbs marked by the non-punctual marker
when indicating temporary states (Bickerton 1977). However, a sentence like (366) does not really refer to a temporary state. Besides
gi-, Nubi has several other expressions to mark continuation, such
as *fi fi* + GER/INF, *'gen/'gai fi* + GER/INF, and *fi (gi-)* V, *'gen/
'gai (gi-)* V, which are barred from expressing habituality or iterativity. Expressions with the existential marker *fi* generally refer to a
longer state than those referred to by the verb *'gen/'gai* "stay". The
expressions with *fi* GER/INF may also contain the element of
purposefulness.

   Nubi does not have an irrealis marker in the sense meant by
Bickerton. The marker *bi-* indicates strong volition about future events.
It is excluded from subjunctive clauses. It may, however, mark verbs
in conditional clauses and may be involved in the expression of
modality, e.g., *bi-'kun* "it is possible that", in the counterfactual *'kan
bi-* V, etc. *Bi-* also marks habituals of non-stative verbs. Apparently,
it is in the process of being replaced by *gi-* with which it shares
this function. Besides *bi-*V, *gi- 'rua* V also indicates future marking.
Whereas *bi-* V expresses volition on the part of the subject about a
rather general future, *gi- 'rua* V is used when one is sure that the
event will take place more or less instantaneously. Several creoles,
such as Negerhollands and Principe Creole Portuguese, have distinct

markers for expressing general vs. immediate future (see also Boretzky 1983, Holm 1988). The latter as in Nubi, may be formed by prefixing the marker for non-punctuality to a verb with the meaning "go" and/or "come". Nubi has, besides *bi-* V and *'gi- 'rua* V, several additional means of expressing future events by combining the progressive or the future marker with the verb *'rua* "go" or the verb *ja* "come". Every combination conveys a slightly different meaning. The future marker *bi-* co-occurs only infrequently with the progressive marker *gi-* to mark a non-punctual future event.

The Nubi anterior marker *'kan* indicates a past-before-past, a (remote) past, or a perfect aspect both with stative and non-stative verbs. The combination of the anterior marker + the progressive marker *gi-* refers to an event of a non-punctual nature that has come to an end before the time of speaking. The anterior marker *'kan* followed by the future marker *bi-* expresses in particular counterfactuality. The combination of the anterior marker *'kan* + future marker *bi-* + progressive marker *gi-* did not occur in the text material. However, according to Nubi informants, its function corresponds to that of ANT IRR NON-PUNCT as in Bickerton's paradigm.

The order of the Nubi core verbal markers conforms with the order in creole languages. Bickerton (1981, 1977) asserts that the most meaningful elements are closest to the verb. He claims, on the basis of research in neurological processes and children's language acquisition, that the punctual/non-punctual distinction is the most basic one, followed by the realis/irrealis distinction.[40] The distinction past/non-past comes last. The importance of these distinctions is reflected in the order of verbal elements, which in Nubi thus becomes *'kan bi- gi-* V. Givón (1984, 294–95) treats the problem as a matter of scope of application:

> The significance of the rigid order . . . of the Creole TAM markers may be explained in reference to their scope of application:
> (a) The durative/non-punctual has the narrowest, verbal scope;
> (b) The irrealis/modal has a wider, propositional scope;
> (c) The perfect/anterior has the widest, discourse scope.

The wider the scope, the farther away the marker will be placed from the verb.

---

[40] In Nubi, that the bare verb form and the verb with progressive marking express the punctual/ non-punctual distinction neutral as regards tense is further evidence for this.

The marker *ka'las*, whose position in the sentence is entirely free, indicates completion of an action or event. It may co-occur with all of the above mentioned verbal markers, as is the case in a few creoles such as Papiamentu (PROG + COMPL) and Negerhollands (FUT + COMPL) (see Boretzky 1983), unlike many others in which combinations of the completive marker and other markers are ungrammatical or restricted to the anterior marker (see Holm 1988). The verbs *'kalasu* "finish" and *'kala* "end up" convey about the same meaning as the marker *ka'las* but provide nuances as to the starting and end point.

The Nubi verbal system also includes the non-core marker *'lisa* "(not) yet", the auxiliary *'arija* to express 'repetition', and *ja/'gum* V referring to the ingression of the event, among other functions. These and other auxiliaries are reflexes of independent verbs, which may occur as the first element in verbal constructions having undergone semantic bleaching as occurs in many creoles. The singular imperative is formed by the simple verb form, which is a rather universal phenomenon and therefore not restricted to creoles (see also Boretzky 1983). To express a subjunctive, the clause is introduced by a marker *ke'de*, unlike in many creoles that use the irrealis marker. The verb form is either zero-marked or takes the prefix *gi-* to indicate punctual or non-punctual actions respectively.

Productive passive formation as in Nubi does not seem to exist in most creole languages, and if it does, it is treated as a marginal phenomenon (see Bickerton 1981). An alternative construction, in which transitive verbs take the meaning of passive/intransitive verbs, is, however, common in Nubi and in many creoles, such as Haitian Creole French and Papiamentu Creole Spanish (see Holm 1988). In such a construction, the patient is in the subject position. Stative passives are also found in Nubi and in many creoles (see Holm 1988, Boretzky 1983). Nubi has two types of nominalizations, infinitives and gerunds, which are formed by means of a stress shift, and, in the case of infinitives, by tone—a rather unique phenomenon among creole languages. Their form may, however, be related to Arabic source forms, which will be discussed in chapter 7.

Nubi distinguishes between equative 'be' and locative, existential 'be', expressed by *'kun* "(temporary) be" and *'kan*, Ø, "(permanent) be" and *fi*, respectively. However, *'kun/'kan/Ø* may also indicate location and/or existence, although on a rather occasional basis, whereas *fi* may infrequently denote equation. Even if a similar distribution may occur in many creoles, it is definitely not common. Some creoles make no distinction between equative 'be' and locative, existential 'be'. Others do, but then there is no overlap (Holm 1988, Boretzky 1983). Existential *fi* also occurs in expressions of possession in combination with the prepositions *na* "to" or *ma* "with". However, Nubi also developed a verb *'endi* "have", which behaves like other transitive verbs, except that it lacks a passive form. *'Endi* may be used for all types of possession, while other possessive expressions have a limited distribution.

I also discussed verb final *-u* and investigated the correlation between the transitivity of the sentence and the varying occurrence of *-u*. I concluded that *-u* functions as a transitivity marker and therefore corresponds to Tok Pisin *-im*.

CHAPTER FIVE

OTHER WORD CLASSES

5.1. *Prepositions*

The Nubi prepositions with their meaning are listed in table 23:

Table 23. Nubi prepositions

Preposition	Translation	Preposition	Translation
fi	Spatial (definite): "in", "at" Movement towards or away from, the direction is implied in the verb. Temporal (definite) Temporal (indefinite) Goal, purpose: "to" Manner "on", "about" Partitive "among"	*min*	Indefinite location (see also Owens 1977, 49): "in", "at", "around" Movement away from Temporal (indefinite): "in", "at" Temporal "since", "from" Source as in *'abidu min* "begin from", *'gum min* "begin from", *'asadu min* "ask from", *'kalagu min* "create from" Partitive "among" Reason, "because of", "from" *min* is common in comparative constructions and indicates the item with which the subject of the clause is compared (see 3.3.2.4 Comparison).
'ladi	Temporal "until" Spatial "up to"	*jamb*	Spatial "beside"
'fogo[a]	Temporal Spatial "on", "about"	*'ben*	Spatial "near", "around" Temporal "around" Relational "between"
gi'dam	Spatial "in front of"	*'wara*	Spatial "in front of" Temporal "after" Goal "after", "looking for"
'kabla	Temporal "before"	*'bada*	Temporal "after" Goal "after", "looking for"
ma	Comitative "with"	*'bila*	"without"

Table 23. (*cont.*)

Preposition	Translation	Preposition	Translation
	Instrumental "with"[a]		
	ma is also used in certain verbal expressions with gerunds/ infinitives (see 4.3.3)		
na	Benefactive "to" Multi-purpose (only persons), such as in: *'asadu na a'jol* (also *'asadu a'jol*) "ask from s.o." *'kelemu na a'jol* "tell s.o." *'abusu na a'jol* (also *abusu a'jol*) "forbid s.o." *'jere na a'jol* "run to s.o." *'kore na a'jol* "beg s.o.", "complain to s.o." *'gesimu na a'jol* "divide for s.o." *'bio na* "buy from" etc.	*Le*[b]	Benefactive "to" Spatial/directional "to", "towards"
'ila	"except (for)"	*'badul*	"instead of"
za/ja	Expressing equality "similar to", "as", "like"	*'sawa-('sawa)*	Expressing equality
ze/je		*ma*	"similar to"
ja (kan)	"as"	*'jengis*	"as", "like"
'ingis	"as", "like"	*gins*	"as", "like'

Note: Older speakers sometimes omit the preposition, as in:
```
. . . 'uo          'ja      fata'ran ka'la    ku'ruju.
    PRON 3SING come-Ø tired    COMPL work the field-GER
". . . he had become tired [from] working on the field."
```

a. *'Fogo* is normally used as an adverb (temporal or spatial). Three speakers, all of whom had spent some time in Southern Sudan, however, used it as a preposition.

a. In Africa, goods are often transported on the head. The head then both refers to the instrument and the place of the transported goods. Both the instrumental preposition *ma* and the spatial preposition *fi* occur:
```
. . . ka'las   a'nas  'arufa  'sela   ma    'ras.
      EMPH  people lift-Ø  goods  with  head
". . . the people lifted the goods on [their] head."
'sela . . . 'ita            'kutu   fi   'ras.
goods       PRON 2SING put-Ø  on   head
"The goods, . . ., you put it on [your] head."
```

b. *Le* is generally used only by old people and by people from the north.

```
(636) . . .,    'ana             'tala    fi    'samba, . . .
                PRON 1SING leave-Ø  PREP  field
       ". . . ., I left (from) the field, . . . ."
```

(637) . . .   'ita   gi- . . .,   gu-   'so *min*   'sa   'wai
              PRON 2SING PROG-   PROG-   do   PREP   hour   NUM
      'ladi   'sa   ti'nen,   ta'lata,   . . .
      PREP   hour   NUM   NUM
      ". . . you are doing [it] from one o'clock until two, three o'clock, ..."

(638) 'Ine   gi-   'jere   *'ben*   'mutu   wu   'hai.
      PRON 1PL PROG-   run   PREP   death   CONJ   life
      "We are running between life and death."

(639) . . .   'uo   'rua   *'wara*   ba'ba.
              PRON 3SING   go-Ø   PREP   father
      ". . .   he went looking for father."

(640) 'Dukur 'ana   *ja* ma'ma   'to,   'an   'feker
      then   PRON 1SING as mother   PRON POSS 3SING PRON 1SING think-Ø
      'gudra 'tai   'sia   *'fogo*   nyere'ku   *jo*   'wede.
      power   PRON POSS 1SING little   on   child   like   DEM PROX
      "Then I, as its mother, I think that my power is little over a child like this."

Table 24 shows possible combinations of prepositions:

Table 24. Prepositional combinations

Preposition	Translation
min fi	Spatial/directional "from"
	Temporal "since"
'ladi fi	Spatial "up to"
	Temporal "until"
'ladi min	Spatial "up to"
le min	Directional: towards indefinite location
fi gi'dam	Spatial "in front of"

(641)   'ino   'gum   *min*   *fi*   'Mirya, ...
         PRON 1PL   get up-Ø   PREP   PREP   NPROP
         ". . . we left (from) Mirya,. . . ."

(642) 'Yena   'ja   lo'go   'raha   *'ladi* *fi*   'sa   we'de . . .
       FOC + PRON 1PL   come-Ø find-Ø comfort   PREP PREP moment   DEM PROX
       "Then we began to find comfort until this moment,. . . ."

(643) . . . 'ita   gi-   'tala min   'in,   'ita   gu-   'futu
             PRON 2SING PROG- leave PREP here   PRON 2SING PROG-   pass
      fu   'sika,   'ita   'rua *le*   *min*   'na.
      PREP street   PRON 2SING go-Ø PREP PREP there
      ". . . you are leaving from here, you are passing the street, you are going (to) over there."

Constructions such as *fi 'batna 'jua* "inside the house" consist of a preposition *fi* or *min*, followed by a locative noun that stands in an alienable-like or inalienble-like possessive construction. Their meaning resembles that of English prepositions as in (644), (645), and (646):

(644) *fi 'batna (ta)* "in the belly of", "in inside of" > "inside"
ta/fi 'jua/ 'jo (ta) "in the house of", "in inside of" > "inside"
min 'wara (ta) "at the back of" > "behind"
fi 'te (ta) "at the bottom of" > "under"
fi 'ras (ta) "on top of", "about"
fi 'fo (ta) "on top of"
fi 'torof (ta) "at the side of" > "beside"
fi 'safa (ta) "at the side of" > "about"
fi 'ustu (ta) "in the middle of" > "among"

(645) Tom'sa   gi-   'gen   *fi 'batna* 'bahar.
crocodile   PROG- stay   inside   sea
'Yala 'Kako gi-   'gen   *fi 'ras*   'seder.
well   monkey PROG- stay   on top of   tree
"Crocodile stays inside the sea. Well, monkey stays on top of the tree."

(646) 'Na're, 'ana   'gu-   rwa 'wonus ka'lam *fi 'ras*   'tena
today PRON 1SING PROG- go tell-Ø thing   on top of PRON POSS 1PL
ta   'Nubi, ...
GEN   NPROP
"Today, I am going to tell something about us, [about] the Nubi, ..."

In the following cases, listed in (647), the preposition is interpreted as a noun and is followed by *ta*. The prepositional meaning is retained as in (648) and (649):

(647) *gi'dam ta* "ahead of"
'kabla ta "before"
'bada ta "after"
ba'dala ta "instead of"
(fi) 'ben/ 'baina (ta) "among", "between"

(648) Je   'de   'umon   'g(i)- arufu 'ben   'toumon
like DEM PROX PRON 3PL PROG- know   between   PRON POSS 3PL
fi   'kila 'wiki.
PREP every week
"Like this they get to know (among) each other on a weekly basis."

(649) 'Y(a) 'ana   'jo   'rua fi   En'tebbe. 'Kabla   to
FOC   PRON 1SING come-Ø   go-Ø PREP NPROP   before   GEN
'rua   fi   En'tebbe   'wede'de, ...
go-GER PREP NPROP   DEM PROX
"So I set off to go to Entebbe. Before this going to Entebbe, ..."

The noun *ka'bila, 'kabla* "type", "tribe", which is common in inalienable-like constructions, is on the verge of being reanalysed as a preposition. Consider (650) and (651). In (650), *'kabla* is best interpreted
as a noun.

(650) *'Kabla*   *ka'lam*   *wede'de,*   'ita   g(i)-   alim   'fogo
      type   thing   DEM PROX   PRON 2SING   PROG-   teach   in it
      ma   ya'la   fu   'be?
      PREP child-PL   PREP   house
      "This type of thing, are you teaching it to your children at home?"

In (651) *ka'bila*, modified by the proximal demonstrative, is preceded
by a noun in an inalienable-like construction. It can be interpreted
as a preposition meaning "like", "similar to".

(651) 'Adab   *ka'bila* 'wede'de,   'aju   'ita   'seb.
      manners   type   DEM PROX   have to-Ø   PRON 2SING   leave-Ø
      "Manners of this type/manners like this, you have to leave [them]."

5.2. *Adverbs*

Nubi adverbs often consist of a preposition or the genitive marker
ta followed by a noun. Often, the emphasizing element *'de* is attached
to the adverb, e.g. *'ase'de* "now", sometimes even in reduplicated
form, e.g., *'ase'de'de* "now". Most adverbs are sentential modifiers.
Some, such as the adverbs of degree, modify one constituent. Nubi
adverbs include the following categories:
    Adverbs of manner:

(652) *fu ra'isi* "easily"   *ma'rai* "straightaway", "at once"
      'gwam(-'gwam) "quickly"   *ta 'gafla* "by surprise", "surprisingly"
      ma 'gwam "quickly"   *ta 'tab* "problematically"
      bi'ses "slowly"   *'sambala* "anyhow", "by any means"
      ba'rau "alone"   etc.

Adverbs of manner are generally put in the sentence-final position
as in (653):

(653) 'Umon   'kan   'aju   ka'lam   te'gil   'maf,
      PRON 3PL   ANT   want-Ø   problem   tough   NEG
      'umon   'sul   ka'lam   *fu ra'isi.*
      PRON 3PL   take-Ø   thing   easily
      "They did not want a tough problem, they took thing[s] easy."

Adverbs of location/direction:

(654) *'in(i)* "here"   *fi/min gi'dam* "in front"
       ba'kan 'de "here"   *fi/min 'wara* "in the back"
       (i)'na "there"   *fi 'safa 'tan* "at the other side"
       fi ('ida) you'min "on the right hand side" *fala'ta* "down(wards)"
       fi ('ida) sho'mal "on the left hand side"   *ge'ri* "nearby"
       fi/min 'te "underneath"   *bo'yi* "far"
       fi/min 'fo "on top"   *'sambala* "anywhere", "any place"
                                             etc.

Adverbs of location/direction are mainly placed in the beginning of the sentence or at the end. However, they can also be found in any other position in the sentence as in (655):

(655) . . . 'keli   'rasul. Ka'rama 'fi   fi sho'mal, ka'rama 'fi   fi you'min.
             dog   arrive-Ø funeral EXIS on the left funeral EXIS on the right
       'Uo   'sum   min   'in   'hilu, 'uo   'sum   min   'na   'hilu.
       PRON 3SING smell-Ø around here nice PRON 3SING smell-Ø around there nice.
       ". . . a dog arrives. There is a funeral on the left, there is a funeral on the right He
       smells a nice [smell] around here, he smells a nice [smell] over there."

Adverbs of time:

(656) *'ase , 'asa, a'sa* " now"   *gu'bel* "(just) before"
       'ase'de ('de) "now"   *fi'lel* "at night"
       ba'kan 'de "now"   *(ta) min 'subu* "in the morning"
       fi m'wisho "finally", "at last"   *gi'dam* "first"
       'na're "today"   *fi gi'dam ('na)* "in the future"
       you'min'de, yeu'min'de "nowadays"   *(fi) za'man* "long ago"
       'bukra "tomorrow"   *wa'kati 'tan* "another time"
       sa'ba "tomorrow"   *'sambala* "anytime"
       'bad 'bukra "the day after tomorrow" *'in* "now"
       m'bari "yesterday"   *'na* "then"
       waltum'bari "the day before yesterday" etc.
       ba'den "later on"

Adverbs of time may take any position in the sentence but generally occur in the sentence-initial or the sentence-final position as in (657) and (658):

(657) *Za'man*   bu'mara   'kan   'fi   'rag(i) 'wai.
      in the past   very much   ANT   EXIS   man   INDEF
      "A very long time ago, there was a man."

(658) 'Bes   'umon   'abidu   'robutu 'ena 'toumon   gi'dam, gi'dam,
      EMPH PRON 3PL begin-Ø tie-Ø   eye(s) PRON POSS 3PL first   first
      gi'dam, gi'dam ke'de bi'niya 'de   'ain   ta a'sil gi- robu't(u) 'ena.
      first   first   SUBJ girl   DEF   see-Ø truly PROG- tie-PASS   eye(s)
      "Well they started to blindfold their eyes first, first, first, first so that the girl would
      see that [their] eyes are truly blindfolded."

Epistemic adverbs:

(659) min'aruf "maybe"
       'sa 'tan "maybe"
       ta a'sil "truly"
       'mumkin "possibly"
       bi'haki "truly", "really"
       'hassa "especially"
       ma'rai "clearly"
       'ladi "even"
       etc.

'Mumkin always occurs in sentence-initial position and modifies the
whole clause. Min'aruf and 'sa 'tan "maybe" modify either the whole
sentence or one phrase. In the latter case, they precede or follow
the phrase in question as in (661). When they modify a sentence,
they are generally placed in sentence-initial position as in (660). Ta
a'sil "truly" refers to the whole sentence. It may take any position.

(660) 'Sa 'tan 'fi   'to   al   'uw(o)   'aju.
       maybe EXIS PRON POSS 3SING REL PRON 3SING   want-Ø
       "Maybe there is his [girl] whom he wants."

(661) La'kin lo'g(o) 'ita   lipa   ka'las   'kasur 'be,
       but   while PRON 2SING pay-Ø COMPL fine for committing adultery
       'lak 'wai   min'aruf.
       NUM   maybe
       "But while they had already paid the fine for committing adultery, maybe one
       hundred thousand."

Adverbs of frequency:

(662) (le) gi'dam "continually"[1]
       'sa 'tan "sometimes"
       ta ka'waida "usually"

---

[1] Note that gi'dam means "first" or "continually", fi/min gi'dam "in front", fi gi'-
dam "in the future", and le gi'dam "continually".

'zaidi "often", "generally"
ba'rau "only"
'sia "few"
etc.

The position of adverbs of frequency is not fixed. They may occupy
any position in the sentence as in (663) and (664):

(663) 'Kas   'tai   'de,   'office 'tena   'de,
      work PRON POSS 1SING   DEF   office PRON POSS 1PL   DEF
      'uo   'zaidi g(i)-   'ainu   au   gi-   'chunga   ya'la
      PRON 3SING   often   PROG-   watch   or   PROG-   takes care of   child-PL
      al   ba'ba   'toumon   mutu, ati'ma.
      REL   father   PRON POSS 3PL   die-Ø orphan-PL
      "My work, our office, it often watches or takes care of children whose father died,
      orphans."

(664) 'Zaidi   fi   ka'bila   'tena   ta   'Nubi,
      generally PREP   tribe   PRON POSS 1PL   GEN   NPROP
      soko'lin dol'de   gu-   we'di   'youm 'sebi, ...
      Thing-PL DEM PROX PL   PROG-   give-PASS Saturday
      "Generally, in our tribe of the Nubi, these things are given on Saturday, ..."

Adverbs of degree:

(665) *'bi'mara/ bu'mara* "much"
       'sei ('sei) ('de) "much"
       'zaidi "very", "much"
       ka'bisa "completely"
       ba'rau "alone"
       'sia "little (bit)"
       etc.

Adverbs of degree modify an adjective or another adverb and follow the word they modify.

(666) . . ., ma'isha ta   dus'man fi 'batna 'Bombo 'kan   ba'tal *'zaidi.*
              life   GEN   war   inside NPROP be-ANT bad   very much
       ". . ., the life [during] the war in(side) Bombo was very bad."

'Sia "little (bit)" may also modify a verb as in (667):

(667) 'Moyo 'de, 'moyo 'na'de   gi-   'bari-'bari   *'sia,* . . .
      water DEF   water DEM DIS   PROG-   become cold-REDUP   little
      "The water, that water becomes a little cold, ..."

Zi'yada "much" may refer to the entire sentence as in (668):

(668) Mana 'to,   ke'd(e) 'eta   'feker   zi'yada
      that is to say SUBJ PRON 2SING think-Ø   much
      'kabla 'lisa 'ita   'gata   ka'lam   'ma.
      before still PRON 2SING decide-Ø   problem   NEG
      "That is to say, you should think much before (still) you decide on the
      problem."

Two or more adverbs of degree may co-occur as in (669):

(669) . . . afo'yo 'endis   'agil   'zaidi   'sei'sei 'de.
           rabbit   have-Ø   brain   very much   very much
      ". . . the rabbit has a lot, a lot of brains."

The demonstrative adverbs 'ya'de, 'ya'da, and 'yaw are used in particular by elderly people from the northern part of the country.
'Ya'de/'ya'da consists of the focusing particle 'ya followed by 'de when
denoting proximity and by 'da when conveying a sense of distance.

(670) Bi'niya   'fi   'ya'de.
      girl   EXIS   DEM ADV PROX
      "The girl is right here."

(672) As'kari   ta   ba'ba   gi-   'ja   'ya'da.
      guard   GEN   father PROG- come   DEM ADV DIS
      "There comes my father's guard [you see him coming]."

'Ya'de/ 'ya'da may occur more than once in a clause as in (672):[2]

(673) 'Ana   'je   'neta   'ya'de
      PRON 1SING   come-Ø to + PRON 2SING   DEM ADV PROX
      ma   ma'yai   'ya'de.
      with egg(s)   DEM ADV PROX
      "I have come to you right here with the eggs (which are) right here/
      these eggs."

The demonstrative adverbs 'ya'de/'ya'da[3] in a sense verify and emphasize that a referent is at a certain place or time or is about to reach
that place or time. They may best be translated by the French 'voici'
and 'voilà' respectively. Expressing location, the demonstrative adverbs

---

[2] This contradicts Owens' observations that the spatial demonstratives 'ya'de/'ya'da,
as he calls them, can only appear once per clause (Owens 1977, 183).
[3] In elicitation, the following imperative-like forms were mentioned: 'Ya'de! "Have
it!"—'Ya'dekum! "Have (PL) it!", "Here it is for you!".

optionally co-occur with the existential marker *fi* as in (673). In that case, the adverbs *'in* or *'na*, 'here' and 'there' respectively, may also occur as in (674):[4]

(673) Mu'kati 'tai   *fi*   *'ya'de*   al   'abis.
      bread   PRON POSS 1SING EXIS   DEM ADV PROX REL be dry-Ø
      "My bread, which is dry, is right here."

(674) Wa'zeya   'de   *fi*   *'ya'da*   *'na*.
      parent-PL   DEF   EXIS   DEM ADV DIS   there
      "The parents are over there."

The demonstrative adverbs of location appear in approximately half of the cases in verbal sentences as in (675):

(675) 'Ana   gu-   'tub bu'ja fala'ta *'ya'de*.
      PRON 1SING   PROG-   spit saliva down   DEM ADV PROX
      "I am spitting saliva right down here."

The demonstrative adverb mainly occurs with a non-past tense. In the few instances in which it does co-occur with a past tense, it actually denotes the state that the NP is now in as a result of the past action. In that case, it often occurs with the marker of completion *ka'la*.

(676) Ba'na 'de   ka'la   'nesit(u) 'uo   'ya'de.
      girl-PL DEF COMPL forget-Ø PRON 3SING   DEM ADV PROX
      "The girls had already forgotten her."

'Yaw consists of the focusing element *'ya* and the third person pronoun *'uo*. That *'yaw* has a function that is different from that of its source formmay be deduced from (677), where *'yaw* co-occurs with the focus marker *'ya*. The occurrence of *'ya* proves that *'yaw* is no longer related to its origin.

(677) 'Sente   al . . .,   *'ya*   *'yaw*.
      money   REL   FOC   DEM ADV
      "The money which . . ., it is here."

'Yaw does not have the same restrictions as *'ya'de/'ya'da* on tense, since it can co-occur with all tenses. *'yaw* refers to location or time.

---

[4] The adverbs *'in* "here" or *'na* "there" do not co-occur with the demonstrative adverbs in case of a zero copula or when the demonstrative adverb denotes time.

However, while *'ya'de/'ya'da* refers to a specific place (or time), with
'yaw the location or time setting is rather vague: the referent is
around, but it does not really matter where or when exactly as in
(678):

(678) 'Gelba   'de   gi-   'ja   *'yaw.*
       heart   DEF   PROG- come   DEM ADV
       "The heart is coming about now."

5.3. *Conjunctions*

The following words join two or more sentences or two or more
sentence constituents together.
   Coordinating conjunctions:

(679) *ma* "with", "and"   *'yani* "that is to say"
       wu, wa, u "and"   *'mana 'to* "that is to say", "it means that"
       'wala, wa'la "or"   *'yala* "OK", "well"
       au "or"   *'yala, 'ya* "thus" (causal), "then" (temporal)
       'ama, a'ma "or"   *'dukuru* "thus (causal), "then" (temporal)
       la'kin "but"   *'ase ('de)* "well"
       'ila "except", "inevitably"

Ma "with", "and" is homophonous with the comitative marker. It
generally joins together two noun phrases with similar functions.
Occasionally, it joins together two sentences. *Wu, wa, u* "and", on
the other hand, generally join together sentences and only occasionally noun phrases.

(680) 'Ita   'kan   fi   'batna 'be   ma   'nas   ma'ma 'taki
       PRON 2SING be-ANT PREP inside house PREP COLL mother PRON POSS 2SING
       ma   ba'ba 'taki.   *Wu*   ba'ba 'taki   'endis . . .
       CONJ   father PRON POSS 2SING CONJ father PRON POSS 2SING   have-Ø
       "You were at home with (the family of) your mother and your father. And your father
       had. . . ."

In the expression 'either . . . or', a morpheme meaning 'or' is placed
between both constituents as in (681). Occasionally it precedes the
constituent as in (682):

(681) . . . 'ja   'kun   'bakti   ba'tal   *wa'la*   'bakti   'kweis, . . .
              come-Ø   be-Ø   luck   bad   or   luck   good
       ". . . it happened to be bad luck or good luck."

(682) Kan 'ita   gi-   'wonus,   'ita   gi-   'kutu
      if   PRON 2SING PROG- talk   PRON 2SING PROG- put
      'fogo ru'tan: au   ru'tan   Ing'lisi a'ma   ru'tan   Mu'ganda.
      in it language   or   language English   or   language   Luganda
      "If you are talking, you are putting a language in it [Nubi]: either the English language
      or the Luganda language."

The normal position of coordinating conjunctions is at the beginning of the sentence. *La'kin* "but", however, is occasionally placed
in sentence-final position as in (683):

(683) Ka'lam ki'yas 'to   'na'de   'kan   'lisa sa'kar 'zaidi.
      because size   PRON POSS 3SING DEM DIS be-ANT still small very
      'Uw(o)   'agara   la'kin.
      PRON 3SING study-Ø but
      "Because that size of his was still very small. But he studied."

Yani "that is to say" and *'mana 'to* "that is to say" (literally: "its
meaning") generally introduce sentences which elaborate on previously
given information. *Yani* and *'mana 'to* occasionally co-occur as in (684):

(684) 'Ladum 'de   'ya   'to.   Yan(i)   'mana   'to
      bone(s) DEF   FOC PRON POSS 3SING   that is to say that is to say
      kan   'mutu, 'uo   bi-   'dofun 'ladum   'de.
      if   die-Ø   PRON 3SING FUT- bury   bone(s) DEF
      "The bones are his. That is to say, if [it (the child)] dies, he will bury the bones."

The conjunction *'ila* generally expresses that the action expressed in
the clause following *'ila* inevitably will take place with reference to
the action/event of the first clause as in (685):

(685) 'Ase kan 'ita   'b(i)- aj(u)   'jowz(u) 'ana,
      now   if   PRON 2SING FUT- want   marry-Ø PRON 1SING
      'ila   'lad(i) 'it(a)   'asadu a'ku   ba'ba 'tai   'de.
      inevitably until PRON 2SING ask-Ø brother father PRON POSS 1SING DEF
      "Now, if you want to marry me, there is no way until you [will have] asked my
      paternal uncle."

Less frequently, *'ila* is used to exclude events/actions and should be
translated as "except":

(686) . . .   ga'raya   te   'din   'de, ki'boko 'fogo 'na   'zaidi.
                 study-GER GEN   religion DEF beating in it there   much
      La'kin ga'raya   te   Inge'reza,   ki'boko 'to   'sia.
      but   study-GER GEN   NPROP   beating PRON POSS 3SING   little
      'Ila   kan 'ita   'so   'nas   'homework 'mafi, ...
      except if   PRON 2SING do-Ø   COLL homework NEG
      ". . . the study of religion, there is a lot of beating in it. But the study of the Brits, the
      beating is little. Except if you did not do your homework, ..."

Subordinating conjunctions:

(687) *ke'de, 'ke* Subjunctive marker,   *min* "since" (temporal); "because",
      "in order to", "so that"   "since"; "instead of"
   kan, ('gal) "if" (see also 6.7.3)   *'kila kan, kan 'kila* "whenever"
   ja, je "as if", "as"   *'ladi* "until"
   'sala (kan) "although", "even if"[5]   *la'man, na'man* "until"
   wa'kati "while", "when"   *ka'lam* "because"
   ba'kan, kan "while", "when"   *mi'san, mi'sen* "because"
   li'go, lo'go "while" (temporal,   *ala'shan, ala'san* "because"
     absolutive); "because"   *fi a'jil ta* "because"
   'kabla "before"   *'gal* introduction to direct and indirect
   'bada "after"   speech (see 6.7.4.3)

(688) A'jol   'de   gi-   'rasul   'sa   ti'nin.
      person   DEF   PROG- arrive   hour   NUM
      'Ase,   *kan*   'ita   bi-   'dus(u) 'ita,
      now   if   PRON 2SING FUT- hide   PRON 2SING
      wu   *kan*   'uo   'ja   ka'las,   'ana   bi-   'kelem
      and   if   PRON 3SING come-Ø COMPL PRON 1SING FUT- say
      'neta.   La'kin 'ma-   ta   'so   a'raka,
      to + PRON 2SING   but   NEG- ADR SING   do-Ø   hurriedly
      'gal   'keta   'so   su'nu?   'Keta   'tala
      that   SUBJ + PRON 2SING do-Ø Q-word   SUBJ + PRON 2SING leave-Ø
      ma 'gwam,   *'kabla*   'lis(a)   'owo   'beredu   'ma,
      quickly   before   still   PRON 3SING take a bath-Ø NEG
      wa'la   'lis(a)   'uo   'ma   'akul.
      or   still   PRON 3SING   NEG   eat-Ø

"The person arrives at two (= eight) o'clock. Now, if you hide yourself, and if he has come, I will tell you. But do not do [it] hurriedly
in order to do what? In order to leave quickly before he has taken
his bath or before he has eaten."

    Wa'kati and *ba'kan* may express two actions or events that occur
at the same time, or they may express the fact that two actions or
events immediately follow each other. *Li'go* refers exclusively to two
simultaneous actions or events. The time clause with *wa'kati* and
ba'kan comes in the sentence-initial position, while the clause with
li'go takes the second position.

---

    [5] *'Sala* was in one instance used in the expression "either . . . or",
    . . .   'ina   'ma   gu-   'wonus kala'ma 'kulu 'fadi,
            PRON 1PL   NEG   PROG- discuss thing-PL all   openly
    'sal(a)   al   ba'tal   wa'la   'seme.
    even if   REL   bad   or   good
    ". . . we are not discussing all things openly, whether bad or good."

(689) 'Umon   *ba'kan* sa'kari,   ba'ba 'de 'ja   a'yan,
      PRON   3PL   when   small   father DEF become-Ø   ill
      ba'ba 'de 'mutu. *Ba'kan*   ba'ba 'de 'mutu, 'sokol al   ba'ba 'de
      father DEF die-Ø   when   father DEF die-Ø thing REL father DEF
      'sibu   fi 'jua   'noumon,   ri'yal 'tisa.
      leave-Ø in house for + PRON 3PL riyal(s) NUM
      "When they were small, [their] father became ill, [their] father died. When [their]
      father died, the thing which [their] father left in the house for them was nine riyals."

670) ..., 'ana   'gu-   rwa fi   Kam'pala   *lo'go*   we'd(i)
      PRON 1SING PROG- go   to   NPROP   when   give-PASS-Ø
      'ina   fi   'kas   ta   'asker, 'jesh ta   King's African Rifles.
      PRON 1PL in   work   GEN soldier army GEN NPROP
      "..., I went to Kampala, when we were recruited into the soldier's job, [in] the army
      of the King's African Rifles."

Min, li'go, and *ja* mainly express temporal "since", "while", and "as
(if)" (manner) respectively and less frequently "because". For the latter purpose, conjunctions such as *ka'lam, mi'sen*, and *ala'shan* are mainly
used. *Fi a'jil ta* "because" is a rather infrequent form.

(691) *min*   nyere'ku   bu- 'rua   na   'ragi ma'rai al   'me   Isi'lam,
      since   child   FUT- go   to   man   clearly REL NEG   Muslim
      'k(e)   'an(a)   'ain   'bes   a'ku 'wai   al   Isi'lam, ...
      SUBJ   PRON 1SING look for-Ø EMPH relative INDEF REL Muslim
      "Ohoh, because [my] child goes to a man who is clearly not a Muslim, I should
      look for a relative who is a Muslim, ..."

The expression of cause/reason by *min, li'go*, and *ja* is probably a
semantic extension of the temporal meaning of these conjunctions
(temporal "since", "while", and "as (if)" (manner) respectively). For
instance, the conjunction *min* in (692) may be translated in two ways:
as the temporal "since" or as "because".

(692) ... 'ras   'to   te'gil. 'Kan ke'fif, la'kin 'ase'de, min
          head   PRON POSS 3SING heavy be-ANT llight but   now   since/because
      'uo   lo'go 'haya, 'ras 'to   'ja   te'gil.
      PRON 3SING find-Ø shame head PRON POSS 3SING become-Ø   heavy
      "... his head is heavy. It was light, but now, (temporal) since/ because he found shame,
      his head became heavy."

The expression of cause/reason with *min* derives directly from *min*'s
more common and original meaning of "(temporal) since". From the
moment the person became ashamed, his head became heavy as
well. Therefore, the heavy weight of the person's head can be interpreted as the direct result of his shame. The conjunction *li'go*, which

in the first place expresses simultaneity, probably underwent a similar process of extension of meaning because, when an action consistently takes place simultaneously with another action, the meaning of the conjunction may be reanalysed as cause and result. For *ja*, a similar derivation may be postulated: in similar actions, one may be seen as the cause, and the other as the result (cf. English 'as' used both in comparisons with finite verbs, e.g., 'Do as he does', and in adverbial clauses of reason and cause).

Yala/ʾya and *ʾdukuru* often occur in the sentence-initial position referring to the previous sentence or sentences and are best interpreted as "thus", "therefore", "so", establishing a causal relation between the previous sentence and the sentence introduced by *ʾya(la)* or *ʾdukuru*. What the speaker is about to relate in the *ʾya(la)/ʾdukuru-*initial sentence is the consequence or result of what has just been mentioned as in (693) and (694):

(693) ʾIta   ʾma   ʾaju   ʾsokol   ʾtaki   ʾde   ke'de   ʾkarab.
       PRON 2SING NEG   want-Ø thing   PRON POSS 2SING DEF   SUBJ   be spoilt-Ø
       ʾYena   gi-   ʾkelem: ne'gi   fi   ʾhagu.
       CONJ + PRON 1PL PROG- say   keen   on   his thing
       "You do not want your thing to be spoilt. Thus we are saying: keen on his thing."

(694) ʾBes, ʾan(a)   ʾain.   ʾYa   ʾan(a)   ʾaba   ʾmafi.
       well   PRON 1SING understand-Ø CONJ   PRON 1SING refuse-Ø   NEG
       "Well, I understood. Therefore I did not refuse."

A similar causal relationship can be found in conditional clauses where *ʾya* (but not *ʾyala* or *ʾdukuru*) optionally introduces the apodosis as in (695):

(695) Kan   ʾino   lo'go   ʾsente
      if   PRON 1PL   receive-Ø   money
      ʾya   ʾina   ʾb(i)-   arija   fi   ʾkidima.
      CONJ   PRON 1PL   FUT-   return   in   job
      "If we receive money, then we will return to the job."

Ya(la) and *ʾdukuru* may also have a temporal meaning, such as "then" rather than express a logical consequence. In (696), the speaker mentions a list of problems delaying his departure, and he ends by saying:

(696) *Ya*   ʾina   ʾrua,   . . .
       then   PRON 1PL   go-Ø
       "And then we went, . . ."

(697) Ra'd(a)   'uo,   ada'd(a)   a'yan 'to,
      breast-feed-PASS-Ø PRON 3SING nurse-PASS-Ø illness PRON POSS 3SING
      bere'd(u)   'uo.   Je   'de   'lad(i) 'uo   bi- 'tim
      wash-PASS-Ø PRON 3SING like DEM PROX until PRON 3SING FUT- reach
      bi'nadum   ta'mam,   'lad(i) 'uo   bi- 'tim 'sana ti'nin.
      human being full   until PRON 3SING FUT-reach year   NUM
      Yala   wa's(a)   'uo   min   'leben 'de.
      then   take away-PASS-Ø   PRON 3SING from   milk   DEF
      "He was breast-fed, his illness was nursed, he was washed. Like this until he became
      a full human being, until he became two years old. Then he was taken off the milk."

Ya and *'dukuru* often introduce a main clause after an adverbial
clause of time as in (698) and (699):

(698) Ba'kan 'uo   'ja   'seb   'kidima, *'dukuru* na'fas ta   ka'ran 'de
      when   PRON 3SING come-Ø leave-Ø work   then   chance GEN secretary DEF
      ari'jo   we'di   'nana.
      return-PASS-Ø give-PASS-Ø to + PRON 1SING
      "When he happened to leave the job, then the chance of [the job of] secretary was
      given again to me."

(699) 'Dukur ba'kan mas'kin   'je-'ja,   'youo   'kelem: ...
      then   when   poor man come-REDUP-Ø CONJ + PRON 3SING say-Ø
      "Then when the poor man came, he said: . . . ."

Yala, and occasionally also *'ya*, may introduce a new paragraph or
subparagraph and therefore also new information as in (700):

(700) 'Nubi, wa'ze za'man, 'umon   'g(i)-   akul 'luguma   la'jin. . . .
      NPROP elderly long ago PRON 3PL PROG- eat   thick porridge which is kneaded
      Gu-   su'tu   'ladi bi'jo   'luguma   mar'dadi   bi'mara.
      PROG- mingle- PASS   until become-Ø thick porrdige beautiful   very much
      Yala, mu'la 'toumon,   'zaidi 'umon   'g(i)- 'adaku mulu'kiya
      well   sauce PRON POSS 3PL often PRON 3PL PROG- grind kind of herb
      ma   mu'la firin'da, marang'wa al   amru'gu   'girifa 'to
      with   sauce firinda   beans   REL   remove-PASS-Ø peel   PRON POSS 3SING
      'bara.
      outside.
      "Nubi, the old people, long ago, they ate a thick, kneaded porridge. . . . It was mixed until
      it became a very beautiful substance. Well, their sauce, often they ground "mulukiya" with
      "firinda" sauce, beans whose peel is removed [away]."

Yala may also just mean "well", "OK", and as such often introduces direct speech as in (701):

(701) 'Gal: *yala,*   'rua.
       that   OK   go-IMPER
       "[He said] that: OK, go."

The subjunctive marker *ke'de* or *'ke* may combine with the conjunctions *'ladi* "until" and *ka'lam* "because", *'gal* "that", and the relative marker. *'Ladi ke'de/'ke* consists of the conjunction *'ladi* 'until', 'to the extent that' and the subjunctive marker. Two interpretations are possible, depending on the meaning of *'ladi*. First, *'ladi* may indicate the moment or period it takes for an action or state to be performed. In combination with *ke'de*, it denotes a sense of obligation as in (702):

(702) 'Ita   bu-   'rua   je 'de   ka'man - sha'ria   'kelem -
      PRON 2SING FUT-   go   like DEM PROX   EMPH Islamic law say-Ø
      'ladi   ke'de   'rasul   fi 'sana   'saba.
      until   SUBJ reach-Ø in year(s) NUM
      "You will go/continue like this -the Islamic law says/orders—until [he] becomes
      seven years of age. "

Second, *'ladi* carries the meaning of "to the extent of". The combination of *'ladi* and *ke'de* should be interpreted as "in order to", "so that". A time factor is not relevant as in (703):

(703) Bia'shara   we'de,   'ina   bi-   ende'lea mo   ke'fin
      business   DEM PROX   PRON 1PL FUT- continue with it how
      'ladi   ke'd(e) awun(u) 'ina   . . .
      to the extent of SUBJ help-Ø   PRON 1PL
      "This business, we will continue with it how so that it will help us. . . ."

Ka'lam ke'de combines the conjunction *ka'lam* "because" and the subjunctive marker *ke'de*. *ka'lam* seems to be redundant. *Ka'lam ke'de* translates as "in order to", "so that", expressing an intention as in (704):

(704) 'Dukur 'uo   'kutu   'nas   'Fatna 'ke   gi-   'chunga
      then   PRON 3SING order-Ø COLL   NPROP SUBJ PROG- look after
      ga'ya 'to   'de ka'lam ke'de 'ma   sere'gu
      millet PRON POSS 3SING   DEF because SUBJ NEG steal-PASS-Ø
      'Then he ordered Fatna (and her brother) to look after his millet so that it
      would not be stolen.'

Similarly, *'gal* in the expression *'gal ke'de* is more or less superfluous as in (705):

(705) . . . mi'san 'fi   ma'ma al   bu-   'so
            because EXIS   mother REL   FUT- do
      'gal ke'd(e) 'uw(o)   'alim(u) nyere'ku   'to   . . .
      that SUBJ PRON 3SING   teach-Ø child   PRON POSS 3SING
      ". . . because there is a mother who will do [so] in order to teach her child. . . ."

In *al ke'de*, the subjunctive marker *ke'de* is preceded by the relative marker *al*. It marks a relative clause involving potentiality as in (706):

(706) Wu   ma'hal   *al*   'kena   'ro   'fogo,   'ma'fi.
      CONJ   place   REL   SUBJ + PRON 1PL   go-Ø   to it   EXIS NEG
      "And there is no place where we could go to."

5.4. *Question Words*

Nubi question words are listed in table 25:

Table 25. Nubi question words

Question word	Meaning	In-dependent	Position of independent Q-word	Attributive
mu'nu? "who?"	Human, (non-) subject [a]	+	In situ	+
su'nu? "what?"[6]	Non-human, (non-) subject	+	In situ	+
(f)(u)'wen?/we'nu? "where?"	Location	+	Final, occasionally initial	–
mi'ten? "when?"	Time	+	In situ	–
ke'fin?/'kef? "how?"	Manner	+	In situ	–
'le? "why?"	Reason	+	Initial, final	–
ma'lu? "why?"	Reason	+	Initial, medial, final	–
ya'tu? "which?", "what?"	generic	+	in situ	+
'kam? "how many?"	generic	+	in situ	+

a. Occasionally, *mu'nu?* "who?" refers to a non-human entity:
    'Ama   'tom   gi-   'pima   'samaga 'kilos   *mu'nu-mu'nu,*   ya'tu?
    or   PRON 2PL PROG-   measure   fish   kilo-PL   who?-REDUP   which?
    "Or you(PL) are measuring how many kilos?"

(707) . . . 'in(a)   'agara   mad'ras   na   *ma'lim*   *mu'nu?*
      PRON 1PL   study-Ø   Qur'anic school   to   teacher   who?
      ". . . with which teacher did we study [at] the Qur'anic school?"

---

[6] *Su'nu?* "what?" preceded by the noun *ka'lam* "matter", "thing", "problem" is sometimes interpreted as "why?":
    'Ita   gu-   'wonus ma   a'nas   ba'tal je'de   *ka'lam*   *su'nu?*
    PRON 2SING   PROG-   talk   with   people   badly EMPH   matter   what?
    "Why are you talking badly with the people?"

(708) *Su'nu*   'ya   fu   'batna   'to?
      what?   FOC   in   belly   PRON POSS 3SING
      "What is it that is in his belly?"

(709) 'Umon   gi-   'num   *'wen?*
      PRON 3PL   PROG-   sleep   where?
      "Where do they sleep?"

(710) 'It(a)   'aba   'kut(u)   'umon   'g(i)-   akul 'kweis *'le?*
      PRON 2SING   refuse-Ø make-Ø   PRON 3PL   PROG-   eat   well   why?
      "Why did you refuse to make them eat well?"

(711) 'It(a)   'endis   *'sente*   *'kam?*
      PRON 2SING   have-Ø   money   how much?
      "How much money do you have?"

(712) 'Kan   'ita   'baga   nyere'ku   'ingis   *ya'tu?*
      be-ANT   PRON 2SING   EMPH   child   like   what?
      "You were a child like what?/What kind of child were you?"

Question words are often preceded by prepositions that modify the
question word.[7]

(713) 'Ase'de, ma'isa jo 'wede   a'zol   bi-   'gai 'fogo *'ladi* *mi'ten?*
      now   life   like DEM PROX   person   FUT-   stay in it until   when?
      "Now, a life like this one, until when/how long may someone stay in it?"

(714) . . . ak'wana   'tai   'de   'futu   *min*   *'wen?*
             relative-PL   PRON POSS 1SING   DEF   pass-Ø   around   where?
      ". . . where about did my relatives pass?"

The question word may have the meaning of a non-referring adjective, for instance 'any mama', 'any way', 'anything', 'anywhere', or
'in one way or another' as in (715):

(715) Ha, bi'niya we'de,   kan   'ana   bu-   lo'g(o)   'owo
      INT girl   DEM PROX   if   PRON 1SING   FUT-   find   PRON 3SING
      ke'fin,   'ya   'kan   'an(a)   'aju   'jowj(u)   'uo.
      in one way or another CONJ ANT PRON 1SING   want-Ø marry-Ø   PRON 3SING
      "Oh, this girl, if I find her in one way or another, I would like to marry her."

Occasionally, the question word functions as an emphasizer as in
(716):

---

[7] Sometimes, the preposition does not add anything to the meaning of the question word, for instance, *Fi ke'fini?* "How?"

(716) 'Ya   aja'ma,   'ana   'nutu   'de   'baga   'namna 'nutu   ya'tu!!
      VOC people   PRON 1SING   jump-Ø EMPH EMPH manner jump-GER EMPH
      "Oh people, I jumped in a way of jumping [and what kind of!!!]."

5.5. *Focus Markers*

5.5.1. *'ya*

The focus marker *'ya* functions as a contrastive device ranging from
strongly to weakly contrastive.[8] A secondary function of *'ya* associated with the contrastive focus is that of highlighting new or asserted
information (see also Givón 1990). *'Ya* precedes the sentence constituent it focuses on. However, when *'ya* refers to the subject of the
sentence, it comes in second position following the subject.[9] As such,
it may be distinguished from the conjunction *'ya*, which comes before
the subject in sentence-initial position.

(717) 'Ana,   fi   wa'kati al   'kan   'ana   'fi   gi-   'raba,
      PRON 1SIGN   in   time   REL   ANT   PRON 1SING   EXIS   PROG- grow up
      ma'ma 'tai   'me   'endi   'hukum   'fog(o) 'ana.
      mother PRON POSS 1SING   NEG   have-Ø   authority   on   PRON 1SING
      'Kan   *ma'ma 'de,   ma'ma 'wai,   ji'ran,   'bes   je'de   'ya
      ANT   mother DEF   mother INDEF neighbour   EMPH   EMPH   FOC
      gu-   'hukum(u)   'ita   fi   batna   'be   'takum.
      PROG- have authority over   PRON 2SING   in   inside   house   PRON POSS 2PL
      Gi-   'ben   je   'uo   ya   ma'ma   'taki.
      PROG- seem   like   PRON 3SING FOC   mother   PRON POSS 2SING
      'Ita   bi-   'so   ma'kosa   'ini.
      PRON 2SING HAB- do   mistake(s)   here
      Ma'ma 'taki   ya   'ma   gi-   'dug(u) 'ita.
      mother PRON POSS 2SING FOC   NEG   PROG- beat   PRON 2SING
      Ma'ma te   ji'ran   ya   gi-   'ja   'dug(u) 'ita.
      mother GEN   neighbour   FOC   PROG- come   beat-Ø   PRON 2SING
      "I, at the time when I was growing up, my mama did not have authority over me. *It was
      the mama, a mama, the neighbour* who had authority over you inside your (PL) house. It looked
      as if *she* were your mother. [If] you made a mistake here, [then] *it was not your mama* who
      beat you. *It was the mama of the neighbour* who came to beat you."

---

[8] *'Ya* is also the marker for the vocative position:
'Ya   aja'ma,   'ase'de, 'kena   'jere   ka'man.
VOC   people   now   SUBJ + PRON 1PL   run-Ø   also
"Oh people, now, let us also run."

[9] Likewise, if a sentence constituent has been fronted through Y-movement then
the focus marker follows the fronted constituent (see 6.4.2).

The focus marker may refer to any sentence constituent, except the verb.[10] It may, however, focus on the verbal predicate. In the following examples, a verbal predicate (718), an object (719), a prepositional phrase (720), a nominal predicate (721), a relative clause (722), and a subjunctive clause (723) are focused.

(718) Ta'ra   'fi   'marya   'wai   'ya   'seregu   su'nu?   'Ya   'seregu
       you see   EXIS   woman   INDEF   FOC   steal-Ø   what?   FOC   steal-Ø
       nyere'ku   ta   'marya   'wede.
       child   GEN   woman   DEM PROX
       "You see, there is a woman [who] stole what? [Who] stole the child of this woman."

(719) A'ta,   wa'ze   wa'din,
       EMPH NEG   old person-PL   other-PL
       ka'lam   'wede'de,   'kutu   'ya   ga'raya   te   'din
       because of   DEM PROX   make-Ø FOC   study-GER GEN   religion
       euh,   ta   Inge'reza   je'de   'nena   'sia.
       INT   GEN   NPROP   EMPH   to + PRON 1PL   little
       "No, other old people, because of this, made *the study of religion of the English*,
       to be little/infrequent for us."

(720) 'In(a)   'amin   'ma   'ya   'lad(i)   'ina   'ja.
       PRON 1PL   believe-Ø NEG   FOC   until   PRON 1PL   come-Ø
       "We did not believe *until we came*."

(721) 'Yembe   gi-   'ben   'akil   'takum,   ta   'nasi   'kako . . . .
       Mango(s)   PROG-   seem   food   PRON POSS 2PL   GEN   COLL   monkey(s)
       La'kin 'ana,   samaga,   gu'luba . . . ,   'ina,   a'nas   ta   'jo
       but   PRON 1SING   fish   hippopotamus(es)   We   people   GEN   inside
       'moyo, ...   'Akil   'tena   'ya   'ma   yembe.
       water   food   PRON POSS 1PL   FOC   NEG   mango(s)
       "Mangos seem to be your(PL) food, of the monkeys. . . . But I, the fish, hip-
       popotamuses,. . . ., we, the people from inside the water. . . . Our food *is not
       mangos*."[11]

(722) 'Ita   'toru   bi'niya   ta   'kabur
       PRON 2SING   wake up-Ø   girl   GEN   grave
       'ya[1]   [al   'youm   'na'de   gi-   'dugu   'ya[2]   a'disi[2]][1].
       FOC   REL   day   DEM DIS   PROG-   beat   FOC   story
       "You woke up the girl of the grave *who that day told a/the story*."

---

[10] According to Owens (1977, 1996, 125–72), 'ya may operate as focus marker on the fronted verb.
    [11] Contrasting with Owens' findings on Kenyan Nubi (1977), in Ugandan Nubi 'ya may focus on the equative complement, as it may focus on the contingent complement:
       'Umon   'kun   'ya   ka'lasi   kadi'ma   fi   'jua.
       PRON 3PL   be-Ø   FOC   EMPH   servant-PL in   house
       "They became *house servants*."

(723) 'Ase, 'jó   ku'tu   'asker 'wai   'ya   ke'd(e) 'ain   ka'lam 'de
      now come-PASS-Ø   put-PASS-Ø   soldier INDEF FOC SUBJ see-Ø matter DEF
      "Now, a soldier was put *to watch the matter*."

When the second part of a possessive construction is focused on, the focus marker *'ya*, comes between the possessed item and the genitive marker as in (724) and exceptionally between the genitive marker and the possessor item as in (725):

(724) . . . 'uo   'rua   'lad(i) 'uo   'rasul
           PRON 3SING   go-Ø   until PRON 3SING   arrive-Ø
      fi 'bele   'na'de   'ya   ta   'nas   bi'niya   'de.
      in country DEM DIS   REL   GEN   COLL   girl   DEF
      ". . . he travelled until he arrived in that country of the family of the girl."

(725) 'Umon   we'di   'akili fi 'be   ta   'ya   a'rusu 'ragi   al . . .
      PRON 3PL   give-Ø food in house GEN   FOC   bridegroom REL
      "They brought food to the house of the bridegroom who. . . ."

5.5.2. *Sentence Final 'ya, 'yaw, 'ya'de*

Ya, 'yaw and *'ya'de* in the clause-final position may emphasize the entire sentence or question. It is typical for the Nubi variety the of the West Nile District of northern Uganda.

(726) 'Ita   'na're 'katul(u) 'ana   'ya'de!
      PRON 2SING   today   kill-Ø   PRON 1SING   EMPH
      "Today, you certainly killed me!"

(727) 'Jowz(u)   'amur   'yaw.
      marriage   prosper-Ø EMPH
      "Married life gives prosperity, it really does."

(728) Ma'ma,   'jere   'ma   'ya!'
      mama   run-IMPER   NEG   EMPH
      "Mama, certainly do not run!"

5.5.3. *The Emphasizer 'ke/ 'kede*

The use of the emphasizer *'ke* is restricted to people from the northern part of Uganda. *'Ke* always comes in the sentence-final position. It is mainly used in imperative sentences or in direct/indirect speech acts as in (729) and (730):

(729) 'Nasur,   'tala   'ke!
      NPROP   leave-IMPER   EMPH
      "Nasur, leave!"

(730) Ma'ma   'de   'gal   Mo'hamed   'fi   fi   'madrasa   'na   'ke.
      mother DEF   that   NPROP   EXIS in   school   there EMPH
      "The mother said that Mohamed is there at school."

'Kede, too, seems to be a feature of northern Ugandan Nubi. I also
heard it in the dialect of three elderly people from Entebbe. 'Kede
generally highlights the preceding sentence constituent as in (731),
and sometimes the whole sentence as in (732). It is often found in
the expression 'sia 'kede "a little bit" as in (733):

(731) Bi'niya 'toumon   'ja-'ja   'geni
      girl   PRON POSS 3PL   come-REDUP-Ø   stay-Ø
      fi   'be   'toumon   'seme   'kede.
      in   house   PRON POSS 3PL   good   EMPH
      "Their girl came to live in their house in a very good way."

(732) Mu'nu   'b(i)-   aruf(u)   'ana   'kede?!
      Q-word   HAB-   know   PRON 1SING   EMPH
      "Who knows me?"

(733) Kan   'umon   'panda 'sia 'kede,   Al'gul   'gidu.
      when   PRON 3PL   climb-Ø bit EMPH NPROP   turn up unexpectedly-Ø
      "When they had climbed a little bit, Algul turned up unexpectedly."

5.5.4. Other (Contrastive) Focus Markers

This type of emphasizers adds a weak contrastive focus to a sentence or sentence constituent (see Givón 1990, 715–16).

'Bes has several functions. It may modify a noun phrase and stress
the limits of the NP or its insignificance in size, number, or importance as in (734). It mainly precedes the noun phrase but may come
after it as well.

(734) Ma'isha 'tai   'zaidi   'bes   fi   'batna 'Bombo.
      life   PRON POSS 1SING   very much   EMPH   in   belly NPROP
      "My life is very much only inside Bombo."

'Bes can operate at sentence level and expresses the truth of the
event or situation:

(735) Fi   'mwisho, wa'ze   'bes   gu-   'rudu 'so   'jowzu   'de,
      in   end   parent-PL EMPH PROG-   agree do-Ø wedding   DEF
      la'kin lo'g(o)   umon   'ma   fu'rai   ma   ka'lam   we'de.
      but   while   PRON3PL NEG   be happy-Ø   with   matter   DEM PROX
      "In the end, the parents do agree to do the wedding, although they are not happy
      with this matter."

'Tu "only" is used infrequently and always co-occurs with *'bes*, with which it shares its function. Either *'bes* + *'tu* operate at phrase level as in (736) or reinforce the contents of the whole sentence as in (737):

(736) Ru'tan 'tan 'ma. ... *'bes* ka'lam 'Nubi *'tu*.
language other EXIS NEG EMPH language NPROP EMPH
"There is no other language.... only the Nubi language."

(737) 'Mat(a) 'ain 'wara. *Bes* 'gen 'gu- rwa *'tu*.
NEG see-IMPER behind EMPH stay-Ø PROG- go EMPH
"Do not look back. Just keep on going."

Ta'ra has two functions. First, it draws attention to an item or event that comes unexpectedly in view of the preceding events. In this function, it often co-occurs with *la'kin* "but" and comes in sentence-initial position as in (738):

(738) 'Wakti na'de, 'an(a) 'ain je kan kala'ma 'de
time DEM DIS PRON 1SING see-Ø as if problem-PL DEF
'ben je 'gu- rwa 'kalas,
look like-Ø like PROG- go end-Ø
la'kin *ta'ra* gi- 'kalas 'ma, ...
but EMPH PROG- finish NEG
"At that time, (I saw as if) the problems looked like they were going to end, but, on the contrary, they do not finish ..."

Second, the speaker, using *ta'ra*, draws attention to a particular event and says that it takes place without any doubt. The position of *ta'ra* is not fixed as in (739):

(739) Aja'ma, ka'lam 'de *ta'ra* je 'de?
person-PL problem DEF EMPH like DEM PROX
"People, is the problem really like this?"

The emphasizer *'baga* has several meanings with sometimes only small differences. First, in questions, *'baga* comes in the sentence-initial position and stresses the supposed impossibility or insignificance of the request. These must be interpreted as rhetorical questions.

(740) La'kin *'baga* bi'nadum bi- 'so su'nu?
but EMPH human being FUT- do Q-word
"But what can a human being do anyway?"

'Baga may have the same function as *'bes* "only" or *'tu* "only", and delimits the given information as being unique. It may co-occur with *'bes* as in (741):

(741) 'Wedede, 'baga 'kidima 'to   a'sada 'bes.
DEM PROX EMPH job PRON POSS 3SING beg-GER EMPH
"This one [person], his job is only begging."

Third, 'baga strengthens the contents of the sentence or part of the sentence. In this function, it comes close to the focused constituent as in (742):

(742) Ma'ma, mali'ma 'de 'baga ba'tal bi'mara.
mother teacher-PL DEF EMPH bad very much
"Mother, the teachers are indeed very bad."

Fourth, with 'baga, the speaker may express an event which more or less concludes the preceding events as in (743):

(743) Kan ka'las, a'nas 'de bi- 'ja 'wasa, bu- 'rua.
when COMPL people DEF HAB- come leave HAB- go
'Yala, si'b(u) 'uo 'baga ma a'rus 'to.
well leave-Ø-PASS PRON 3SING EMPH with bride PRON POSS 3SING
"When finished, the people set off to leave, they go. Well then, he is left with his wife."

With an imperative, 'baga may intensify the meaning of the command as in (744):

(744) 'Ase, 'baga, 'ita, 'ro 'jib 'taki   'de!
now EMPH PRON 2SING go-IMPER bring-IMPER PRON POSS 2SING DEF
"Now, well, you, go and get yours!"

Ma'lu/'mal was originally a question word, meaning "what is wrong?", "why?" (see 5.4). It is also used in rhetorical questions, in which it can be translated as "why?!", expressing the intensity of the meaning of the clause as in (745). With the latter meaning, it is mainly used in affirmative sentences as in (746).

(745) A'jus we'de *ma'lu* la'dum 'de 'gow je'de?!!
granny DEM PROX why/EMPH bone(s) DEF hard EMPH
"This granny, why are [her] bones so hard?/ [her] bones are so very hard!"

(746) 'Ei, 'akil 'de ma'lu 'hilu!
INT food DEF EMPH nice
"Ei, the food is so good!.

Mus is used, like *ma'lu*, in rhetorical questions as in (747) and in affirmative sentences emphasizing the contents of the sentence, and including a sense of contrast as in (748). In questions, it comes either in the sentence-initial or the sentence-final position or is inserted into the question, whereupon it then comes in a preverbal position. *'Mus* normally precedes the verb in affirmative sentences.

(747) 'Lon 'to 'mus gi- 'ben
     face   PRON POSS 3SING EMPH PROG- look
     je   'lon   'taki   'yaw?
     like   face   PRON POSS 2SING   EMPH
     "His face looks like your face, isn't it?"

(748) Nyere'ku 'mus gu- wele'du me ma'ma me ba'ba!!
     child   EMPH PROG- conceive-PASS with mother with father
     "A child is indeed conceived by a mother and a father!"

'Sei or *se'yi* as well appears in questions as a question word asking for the truth of the aforementioned as in (749):

(749) 'Uo 'sei 'ja 'amrugu, 'uo 'tor?
     PRON 3SING EMPH come-Ø remove-Ø PRON 3SING drive-Ø
     "Did he really come to remove [the bicycle], did he cycle [on it]?"

'Sei is also common in rhetorical questions as in (750):

(750) A'ku yo'wele 'sei gu- 'num ma a'ku 'to bi'niya?!!
     relative boy   EMPH PROG- sleep with relative PRON POSS 3SING girl
     "Does a brother really sleep with/make love to his sister?!!"

Besides this, it occurs in affirmative sentences, emphasizing the authenticity of the sentence.

(751) 'Ya aja'ma, ku'juru 'sei gi- 'kabas 'ana 'ma.
     VOC person-PL witch doctor EMPH PROG- cheat PRON 1SING NEG
     "Oh people, the witch doctor definitely does not cheat on me."

Bi'zatu has a double function in Nubi. First, like *a'gi, 'sidu,* and *bi'-nafsi*, it adds emphasis to the pronoun (see 3.1). Second, *bi'zatu* functions at the sentence level and strengthens the meaning of the sentence as in (752):

(752) 'Ita 'ja bi'zatu lo'g(o) 'ina ka'las 'so ka'lam 'de.
     PRON 2SING come-Ø EMPH while PRON 1PL COMPL do-Ø thing DEF
     "You came of course after we had already done the thing."

Ka'las, which normally operates as the completive marker (see 4.2.1.4.7) functions also as an adverbial emphasizer as in (753):

(753) 'It(a)   'arufu   ko'rofo 'gara   'mus?
       PRON 2SING   know-Ø   leave(s) pumpkin   EMPH
       Ka'las   'it(a)   arufu   ko'rofo   'gara.
       EMPH   PRON 2SING   know-Ø   leave(s)   pumpkin
       "You know pumpkin leaves, don't you? Of course, you know pumpkin leaves."

In nominal clauses, *ka'las* emphasizes the meaning of the adjective
as in (754):

(754) 'Moyo   al   *ka'las*   ke'bir   'ya   'kan   al   'uo   'b(i)-   agider
       water   REL   EMPH   big   FOC   ANT   REL   PRON 3SING FUT- be able
       'adi   'ma   'de,   'yal(a) a'nasi 'de   'gata 'mo   'seri....
       cross-Ø   NEG   DEF   well   people DEF   cut-Ø with+ PRON 3SING shore
       "The water which is very wide, and which he therefore would not have been able to
       cross, well the   people crossed it with him."

Ka'man, besides its usual meaning of "also", may be interpreted as
a kind of emphasizer. It may modify the sentence as in (755) or a
noun phrase as in (756):

(755) Eh,   'uo   'gai   fu   'fom   je'de   fu   'torofu 'jua   je'de.
       INT   PRON 3SING   stay-Ø   in   opening   EMPH   in   side   house EMPH
       'Uo   'gai   *ka'man* fu   'fom   'de.
       PRON 3SING   stay-Ø   EMPH   in   opening   DEF
       "Eh, he stayed in the opening at the side of the house. He, indeed, stayed in the
       opening."

(756) 'Bas, 'youm 'wai,   'uo   'ja   lo'go   bi'niya 'wai   *ka'man* a'sas.
       well day   INDEF PRON 3SING   come-Ø meet-Ø girl   INDEF EMPH   beautiful
       "Well, one day, he happened to meet a very beautiful girl."

'Ladi "even" suggests that what follows is rather surprising as in (757):

(757) Wu   'Salim 'Bey   'de   bi'zatu, 'uo   'mutu   'na.
       CONJ   NPROP   DEF   self   PRON 3SING   die-Ø   there
       'Lad(i) dofu'n(u)   'uo   'na.
       EMPH   bury-PASS-Ø PRON 3SING   there
       "And Salim Bey himself, he died there. He was even buried there."

'De, which is homophonous to the definite article and the proximal
demonstrative, may act as an emphasizer adding extra stress to
adverbs and demonstratives. It follows the word it modifies as in *'sei
'sei 'de* "very", *'asede 'de* "now", *'wede 'de* DEM PROX.

A'ta, which normally acts as a morpheme of negation (see 5.6),
may also emphasize the negation. In general, *a'ta* accompanies a
negative particle as in (758):

(758) Mi'sen gi- 'ben 'nana je *a'ta* bi- 'ja 'ma.
because PROG- seem to + PRON 1SING as EMPH NEG FUT- come NEG
"Because it seems to me as if it will not come."

Exceptionally, *a'ta* does not imply any sense of negation but rather strenghtens the affirmative context as in (759):

(759) Min 'na, ka'man 'umon 'arija 'doru 'wiki ge'ri ti'nin,
from there also PRON 3PL return-Ø walk-Ø week nearly NUM
'gu- rwa a'ta fi 'shar.
PROG- go EMPH to month
"From there, also they walked again nearly two weeks, it was even going to be a month."

Je'de, which is a combination of *ja* "like", "as" and the proximal demonstrative *'de*, has a slighly emphatic effect on the clause. It often reinforces the function of other emphasizers.

(760) Kan 'itokum 'ja, 'bes 'itokum 'rasul *je'de*
when PRON 2PL come-Ø EMPH PRON 2PL send-Ø EMPH
'shef to Mu'hammad.
sword GEN NPROP
"When you(PL) come, you(PL) [will] indeed send the sword of Muhammad."

Finally, *'kan* in sentence-final position may be used as an emphasizer as in (761):

(761) 'Ita, . . . mu'nu 'ya 'akul nyere'ku 'tai *'kan?*
PRON 2SING who FOC eat-Ø child PRON POSS 1SING EMPH
"You, . . ., who is it who has eaten my child?"

5.6. *Morphemes of Denial*

'Ma and *'mafi/'maf* serve as "no" as in (762) and (763). *A'ta*, besides functioning as an emphasizer, may do the same as in (764):

(762) 'Umon 'kelem: *'Ma,* 'akil al 'in(a) 'aju 'de,
PRON 3PL say-Ø no food REL PRON 1PL want-Ø DEF
ke'd(e) aku'l(u) 'taki 'de gi'dam.
SUBJ eat PRON POSS 2SING DEF first
"They said: No, the food that we want, let yours be eaten first."

(763) 'Bas, 'uo 'kelem 'gal: *'Mafi,* 'awun(u) 'ana.
well PRON 3SING say-Ø that no, help-IMPER PRON 1SING
"Well, he said that: No, help me."

(764) *A'ta*, 'marya je 'na'de 'in 'ma'fi.
      no   woman like DEM DIS here EXIS NEG
      "No, a woman like that is not here."

5.7. *Conclusion*

Some of these elements have been discussed in creole linguistics. Most creoles have two types of prepositions (Holm 1988, Boretzky 1983). The first type consists of direct derivations of superstrate prepositions. The others are more complex constructions resembling possessive phrases such as the Sranan Creole English *na baka* "behind" from English "back" and Príncipe Creole Portuguese *ubásu sé* "under him". The Nubi prepositions include both the simple prepositions derived directly from Arabic in particular and the more complex structures consisting of a preposition + noun (+ genitive exponent *ta*) or of a preposition + genitive exponent.

Holm (1988) and Boretzky (1983) discuss the general locative preposition *na* and its equivalents, which occur in several Atlantic creoles. Their translation depends on the context and is closely related to the meaning of the verb. It is the verb that determines whether location or motion toward or from is meant. Similarly, Nubi *fi* (as spatial preposition) is neutral as regards location or movement (toward or from) and depends much on the meaning of the accompanying verb.

In Nubi, the coordinating conjunction for joining together two noun phrases is homophonous to the comitative preposition *ma*. There are other words – *wa*, *wu*, or *u* – for linking sentences. Holm (1988) and Boretzky 1983) discuss a similar feature in some of the Atlantic creoles.

CHAPTER SIX

CLAUSE STRUCTURE

6.1. *Constituent Order*

6.1.1. *Constituent Order in Main Clauses*

Nubi is essentially an SVO language as in (765):

(765)	Fi'lel,	'it(a)		'afuta	'lufra ke'biri.	'Ito		'kubu	la'kata	'de	'kulu
	ADV	S		V	DO	S		V	DO		
	at night	PRON 2SING		dig-Ø	hole big	PRON 2SING		throw-Ø	firewood	DEF	all
	fi	'lufura	'de	'na.	'Ito		'kub	'fogo	dikin'ta		ti'yari.
	ADV CL				S		V		DO		
	in	hole	DEF	there	PRON 2SING		pour-Ø	in it	kerosine		ready

"At night, you dug a big hole. You threw all the firewood in the hole there. You poured kerosine in it [so that it was] ready."

Several other constituents take the postverbal position:
* oblique as in (766):

(766)	La'siy(a)		'youm	'wai	a'ku	'de	'rua	*fi*	*'samba.*
	evening		day	INDEF	brother	DEF	go-Ø	to	field
	'Uo		'tala	*min*	*'samba.*				
	PRON 3SING		leave-Ø	from	field				

"The evening of one day, the brother went to the field. He left (from) the field."

* object complement: complement clause as in (767):

(767)	. . .	'bag(a)	'etokum	'aruf	*'gal*	*Mo'hamadi*	*'mutu*	*ka'las.*
		EMPH	PRON 2PL	know-Ø	that	NPROP	die-Ø	COMPL

". . . you(PL) do know that Muhammad has died already."

* object complement: complement clause as in (768):

(768)	. . .	'in(a)	'aju	*'ro*	*'gata*	*ma'tunda*	*'fo.*
		PRON 1PL	want-Ø	go-Ø	pick-Ø	passion fruit(s)	up

". . . we want to go and pick passion fruit up [there]."

* object complement: subjunctive as in (769):

(769)	'Bas,	'uo		gi-	'kelem	na	Al'gul	*ke'de*	*'sten(u)*	*'uo*	*'in.*
	well	PRON 3SING		PROG-	say	to	NPROP	SUBJ	await-Ø	PRON 3SING	here

"Well, he says to Algul that he should wait for him here."

* adjectival predicate as in (770):

(770) Wu   fi   'hali   bi'niya   'de   'kan   *a'sasi*   *'zaidi.*
      and   in   situation girl   DEF   be-ANT beautiful   very
      "And with [her] situation the girl was very beautiful."

* nominal predicate as in (771):

(771) Bi'niya we'de   al   'ita   gi-   'kelem 'wede'de,
      girl   DEM PROX   REL   PRON 2SING   PROG-   say   DEM PROX
      'wede   *nyere'ku* ta   sul'tan ta   sulta'na   ta   ba'kan 'na'de.
      DEM PROX child   GEN   sultan   GEN   sultan-PL   GEN   place   DEM DIS
      "This girl that you are talking [about], this is a child of one of the sultans of that place."

The beneficiary or indirect object, introduced by the preposition *na*, is normally placed after the direct object as in (772):

(772) . . .,   'ina   'ya   'sa 'tan   gu-   we'di   *'kabar*
                PRON 1PL   FOC   sometimes   PROG-   give   news
      na   *akwa'na*   *'tena.*
      to   brother(PL)   PRON POSS 1PL
      ". . ., we sometimes give the news to our brothers."

(773) 'Bes,   'umon   'kutu   *'sum*   *na*   *Mo'hamadi.*
      well   PRON 3PL   put-Ø   poison   to   NPROP
      "Well, they put poison for Mohamad."

(774) 'Ito   we'd(i)   'ana   'nouo.
      PRON 2SING   give-Ø   PRON 1SING   to + PRON 3SING
      "You gave me to him."

However, when the indirect object is expressed pronominally and the direct object is not, then the indirect object precedes the direct object as in (775):

(775) . . .   ma'ma 'de   we'di   'nouo   'dawa   fu   'akili.
               mother DEF   give-Ø   to + PRON 3SING   medication   in   food
      ". . . the mother gave him medication in [his] food."

Adverbial clauses, especially adverbial clauses of time, may take any position in the sentence. The most frequent position is, however, after the verb as in (776):

(776) *'Youm*   *'wai,*   'umon   'ja   'amsuku 'sika.   'Umon   'rua
      day   INDEF   PRON 3PL   come-Ø   catch-Ø road   PRON 3PL   go-Ø
      fi   *'gaba*   *fi*   *'gata*   *la'kata.*
      to   forest   to   cut-Ø   firewood
      "One day, they happened to catch the road/ to go out. They went to the forest to cut firewood."

The word order may be reversed with passive verbs (4.3.1), in conditional clauses (see below), and with focus attracting devices such as left dislocation, Y-movement, and strategies for introducing new information (see below). Questions do not normally have a deviant word order (see below). The position of the non-core markers *ka'las* and *'lisa* 'still' and of the negative marker is not fixed. Their presence, however, does not result in a change of word order (see 4.2.1.4.7, 4.2.1.4.8., and 6.3. respectively). Still there are numerous examples of sentences that do not sound acceptable. Generally, they are not to be considered incorrect since the basic word order SVO is retained. In these cases, basically, too many words have been inserted between the subject and the verb as in (777), between the verb and the object as in (778), or between the anterior marker *'kan* and the verb as in (779), so the sentence becomes quite unclear.

(777) 'Ija   'de   ka'man   'in   je'de   'koma.
       story   DEF   EMPH   here   EMPH   finish-Ø
       "The story indeed finishes here."

(778) 'Yal(a)   'an(a)   'aj(u)   'asrub   'de   gi'dam   'chai, ...
       well   PRON 1SING   want-Ø   drink-Ø EMPH   first   tea
       "Well, first I want to drink tea, ..."

(779) La'kin 'kan 'haki   za'man   gi-   'só   je   'de.
       but   ANT   EMPH   a long time ago   PROG-   do-PASS   like   DEM PROX
       "But truly, a long time ago, it was done like this."

Most of them are unique in their composition and are probably due to rapidity of speech, since all these texts were transmitted orally.

6.1.2. *Constituent Order in Subordinate Clauses*

The order of constituents in subordinate clauses is virtually the same as that in main clauses (see below) except that, in the subjunctive clause, the subjunctive marker *ke'de* may stand between the subject and the verb (see 6.7.2).

6.2. *Subject-Predicate Agreement*

Similar to number agreement within the noun-phrase (see 3.4.2), agreement across the predicate is optional as in (780) and (781):

(780) A'nas   'kun   kwei'sin.
      people-PL   be-Ø   good-PL
      "People are good."

(781) 'Umon   mis'kin
      PRON 3PL   poor-SING
      "They are poor."

6.3. *Negation*

6.3.1. *Negation with* 'ma *or* 'mafi, 'maf

Nubi employs two different elements for negating sentences or clauses:
the marker 'ma, which may take any place in the sentence, and 'mafi
or 'maf. The markers 'mafi and 'maf mainly occur in sentence-final
position as in (782). If not, they follow the verb and may precede
a prepositional phrase as in (783):

(782) A'ta,   'ina   gi-   'dusman   'mafi.
      no   PRON 1PL   PROG- fight   NEG
      "No, we are not fighting."

(783) 'De   li'go   'lisa   Ingi'lis 'lisa   'rasul   'mafi
      DEF   when   still   English   still   arrive   NEG
      mo   'ukum   'to.
      with   government   PRON POSS 3SING
      "This was when the English had not yet arrived with his[their]
      government."

Sentences like (784), in which the negative marker 'mafi, 'maf precedes an object, are exceptional, except when the object is expanded
such as by a relative clause. Consider for instance (785):

(784) 'Umon   'agara 'mafi   ga'raya   te   Ingi'lis.
      PRON 3PL   study-Ø NEG   studies   GEN   English
      "They did not study the studies of the English."

(785) 'Ina   'lisa   li'go   'maf(i) a'zol
      PRON 1PL   still   meet-Ø   NEG   person
      al   'agder   'so   re'search   a'dil   . . . .
      REL   be able-Ø   do-Ø   research   straightforward
      "We did not yet meet a person who can do straightforward
      research. . . ."

The negator 'ma may take any position in the sentence, although the sentence-final position is the most frequent one. The varying positions can generally be ascribed to sentence rhythm and not to differences in scope. Instead, it is the context which distinguishes the difference in scope. In (786), the people did come, albeit not like slaves. The negative marker, however, precedes the verb and not the prepositional phrase 'like slaves'.

(786) 'Umon   'ma   'ja   ja   la'bi.
      PRON 3PL   NEG   come-Ø like slave(s)
      "They did not come like slaves."

The same applies to the negative marker in equational sentences as in (787) and (788):

(787) 'Be   'toumon   'kweis   'ma.
      house   PRON POSS 3PL   good   NEG
      "Their house is not good."

(788) Ka'lam 'de   'ma   'gow.
      problem DEF   NEG   tough
      "The problem is not tough."

Differences in scope, however, do exist in more complex sentences consisting of more than one clause. The negative marker only affects one part of the clause. Consider the difference between (789) and (790):

(789) 'An(a)   'aju   'ma   'keta   che'lewa   'na.
      PRON 1SING   want-Ø NEG   SUBJ + PRON 2SING   delay-Ø   there
      "I do not wish you to delay there."

(790) 'Uw(o)   'aju
      PRON 3SING   want-Ø
      'keta   'wonus   'fogo nyere'ku 'to   'ma.
      SUBJ + PRON 2SING   talk-Ø   about child   PRON POSS 3SING   NEG
      "He wishes you not to talk about his child."

In some cases, it is not possible to assess formally which clause falls under the scope of the negator as in (791). The negative marker 'ma is in between the main clause and the complement clause. The sentence-final position is the most common. From this, we could derive that 'ma refers to the verb 'ain "see". However, from the context it can be inferred that the man was not working the field properly, at least not like he used to do every day.

(791) 'Uw(o)   'ain   'ma   'uo   'kuruju
      PRON 3SING   see-Ø   NEG   PRON 3SING   work the field-Ø
      je   te   'kila   'youm   'de   . . . .
      like   GEN   every   day   DEF
      "He saw that he did not work the field like every day. . . ."

A sentence-initial negative marker normally focuses on the initial
phrase, which is usually the subject as in (792):

(792) 'Ma   'marya   bi-   'wasa.
      NEG   wife   FUT-   leave
      "Not the wife will leave [but somebody else]."

As was mentioned in 4.4.3, the negative existential marker is 'ma'fi,
which may be realized as 'mafi, 'maf, and even 'ma.

(793) 'Ma'fi   'sokol   al   gu-   'rud(u)   'ase'de.
      EXIS NEG   thing   REL   PROG-   answer   now
      "There is no one who answers now."

(794) 'Uw(o)   'endis 'marya 'to   'wai.
      PRON 3SING   have-Ø wife   PRON POSS 3SING   NUM
      'Marya, . . .   nuswa'na   'to   'de   ti'nin   'ma.
      wife   wife-PL   PRON POSS 3SING   DEF   NUM   EXIS NEG
      "He has his one wife. Wife . . ., his two wives are not there."

It could be argued that the latter 'ma is not the negated existential
marker, but rather the negative particle of a Ø-copula, meaning
"(permanent) be" and denoting existence (see 4.4.1). Ø, 'kan "be" is,
however, used infrequently for expressing existence, whereas 'ma referring to existence is not at all uncommon. In (795), the non-existence
of the field is expressed by means of the existential marker 'fi and
sentence-final negator 'ma. This is one of the exceptional cases where
the negator 'ma and the existential marker 'fi are separated.

(795) . . . 'plot   'fi   'fogo   'shamba 'ma.
            plot   EXIS   in it   field   NEG
      ". . . the plot, there is no field in it/it has no field."

6.3.2. Double Negation

A few instances of double negation were recorded. The verb and
both definite subjects are negated as in (796), or the verb and both
nondefinite subjects as in (797):

(796) ... 'dunia ta you'min'de 'ma je
        world GEN nowadays NEG like
'dunia ta za'man ta wa'ze 'tena 'de 'ma.
world GEN bygone days GEN parent-PL PRON POSS 1PL DEF NEG
"... the world (of) today is not like the world of the bygone days of our parents."

(797) 'Bad(a) 'uo ne'bi 'tan 'ma'fi
     after PRON 3SING prophet other EXIS NEG
al 'gal bi- 'ja rasu'lu ke'de 'ja me 'dini 'tan
REL that FUT- come send-PASS-Ø SUBJ come-Ø with religion other
au 'je 'zidu fi ka'lam fi 'dini te Is'lam 'mafi.
or come-Ø increase-Ø in matter in religion GEN NPROP NEG
"After him, there is no other prophet of whom it is said that he will be sent so that he comes with another religion or [so that he] will add to the matter of the religion of Islam."

6.3.3. *Expressions with Negative Marker*

Nubi has some idiomatic expressions containing the negative marker.

(798) 'Nade'de 'dugu 'ma.
      DEM DIS beat-GER NEG
      "That is not beating. [It is much worse than that]."

(799) 'Dunia 'de 'dunia 'mafi.
      world DEF world NEG
      "The world is not a world/ is no world. [to express that the situation is extremely chaotic]."

(800) 'Tan 'só 'kidima 'ma.
      other do-PASS-Ø work NEG
      "No other work was done."

In clauses introduced by *bila* "without", the negative particle optionally adds emphatic force as in (801):

(801) Za'man, 'umon gi- 'seregu ba'na min 'batna 'be.
     in times past PRON 3PL PROG- abduct girl-PL from inside house
'Uo 'sulu bi'niya je'de, ... 'bila wa'ze 'arufu 'ma.
PRON 3SING take-Ø girl EMPH without parent-PL know-Ø NEG
"In times past, they were abducting the girls from inside the house. He took the girl, ... without the parents knowing."

After verbs of prohibition, the subjunctive clause is optionally negated in Ugandan Nubi. Compare the following two examples, which have the same meaning even if (802) has the negative marker and (803) does not.

(802) Kuba'rin   'g(i)-   ab(a)   'ana   ke'd(e)   ana   'rua   'ma.
      elder-PL   PROG- forbid   PRON 1SING   SUBJ   PRON 1SING   go-Ø   NEG
      "The elder people forbid me to go."

(803) 'Uw(o)   'ab(a)   a'nas   'de   ke'de   'sulu   'meiti ta   'marya   'de.
      PRON 3SING   forbid-Ø   people   DEF   SUBJ   take-Ø   body   GEN   woman   DEF
      "He forbade the people to take the body of the woman."

6.4. Focus and Topicalization

6.4.1. Existential Marker *fi* + Indefinite Subject

In 3.3.1.1.1, I discussed how the indefinite article *'wai* typically introduces new information that is pragmatically referential. Another syntactic device that serves this same purpose is the existential marker
fi followed by a zero-marked noun or a noun marked by the indefinite
article. The normal SVO order is thus reversed as in (804) and (805):

(804) *'Fi*   *'marya*   'dofuru   'biris   'to   'seme.
      EXIS   woman   weave-Ø   mat(s)   PRON POSS 3SING   good
      "There is a woman who weaves her mats well."

(805) 'Ase'de,   *fi*   'sultan   'wai.
      now   EXIS   sultan   INDEF
      "Now, there was a sultan."

Verbs that operate similarly to the existential marker *fi* are *'gen,'gai*
"stay", "remain", *'fadul* "remain", *'ja* "come", etc. as in (806):

(806) Ba'kan   *'ja*   'nouo   te'lim, . . .
      when   come-Ø   to + PRON 3SING   dream
      "When there came to her a dream/When a dream came to her, ..."

6.4.2. *Y-movement*

Y-movement or contrastive topicalization (see also Givón 1990) involves
the movement of a sentence constituent to the sentence-initial position, which has a contrastive effect, albeit a weak one on the sentence constituent in question. Y-movement in Nubi in general does
not apply to new or asserted information but operates on referents
that have been cited in previous discourse. All the sentence constituents as well as the second part of the possessive phrase can be

subjected to this type of movement, but it operates primarily on the
direct object. The focus marker *'ya* comes between the moved constituent and the main clause. A resumptive pronoun can be placed
optionally in the object position and is obligatory in the prepositional
and/or possessive phrase. *'Fogo* "in it" is an obligatory reference to
the adverbial phrase of location or purpose. It optionally refers to
the adverbial phrase of time and manner. Similar patterns of co-reference are found in the formation of the relative clause (see 3.3.7).

(807) *Ya'la*   *lu'far*   *'dol'de*   *du'ga-du'ga-du'ga*   *'dol'de*
       child-PL   mouse/mice   DEM PROX PL   small-PL-REP   DEM PROX PL
       'ya   *'yal*   *'bura*   *'g(i)-* *akul(u)*   *'lad(i)*   *'umon*   *gi-*   *'so*   *su'nu?*
       FOC   child-PL   cat(s)   PROG-   eat   until   PRON 3PL   PROG- do   Q-word
       "It is these small, small, small baby mice that kittens eat until they do what?"

(808) *Nyere'ku*   *'ya*   a'dan   *'to*   *'ma.*
       child   FOC   ear(s)   PRON POSS 3SING   EXIS NEG
       "The child, its ears are not there."

(809) *'Ma*   *'ye*   *'uw(o)*   *'aju*   *'jowju*   bi'niya.
       NEG   FOC   PRON 3SING   want-Ø   marry-Ø   girl
       "It is not that he wants to marry a [specific] girl."

(810) *Min*   *fu*   *wa'kati*   *ta*   *A'min*   *'de,*   *te*   *O'bote*   *ja*   *ta*   *A'min*
       from   in   time   GEN   NPROP   DEF   GEN   NPROP   like   GEN   NPROP
       'yena   *'ja*   *'ral(u)*   *'in.*
       FOC + PRON 1PL   come-Ø   move-Ø   here
       "From [in] the time of Amin, of Obote, like [that] of Amin, we came to move here."

When a subject is fronted, it is generally repeated pronominally. The
focus marker follows the pronoun as in (811):

(811) A'nas   al   *'jowju-jow'ju*   *'de*
       people   REL   marry-REDUP-PASS-Ø   DEF
       'umon   *'ya*   *gi-*   *'so*   *kun'gu*   *we'de.*
       PRON 3PL   FOC   PROG-   do   song   DEM PROX
       "The people who got married, they do this song."

I have no data on the fronting of verbs in a Y-movement-like device.
Owens, however, gives the following examples. The verb is replaced
by the verb *'so* "do" in the original position.

'gata   *'laam*   ma   *se'kin*   *'de*   *'ya*   a'zol   *'nade*   *'arija*   *'so*
cut   meat   with   knife   this   ph emph   person   that   return   do
"it was cut meat with this knife that that person did again." (Owens 1977, 283)

Kátifu wáraga   yá   máriya   dé   só.
Write   letter   FOCUS   wife   the   did
"Write a letter is what the wife did." (Owens 1996, 151)

6.4.3. *Left-dislocation*

Left-dislocation, unlike Y-movement, does not have a contrastive function. Its function is to re-introduce a referent in discourse after a considerable gap (see also Givón 1990).[1] As with Y-movement, the sentence constituent in question is fronted. Unlike Y-movement, this sentence constituent is not followed by the focus marker *'ya* but by an optional pause. The same rules on co-referentiality in the clause apply as with Y-movement.[2] In (812), (813), and (814), the referents have been mentioned in previous discourse, sometimes leaving quite some distance between the two occurrences. In this respect, left-dislocation also differs from Y-movement in that, in the latter, the referents usually occur within a span of two or three clauses.

(812) *'Kidima*   *ta*   *'hatar*   *je*   *'de,*
       job   GEN   danger   like   DEM PROX
       'aju   'ket(a)   'aba   'maf.
       must-Ø   SUBJ + PRON 2SING   refuse-Ø   NEG
       "A dangerous job like this, you should not refuse it."

(813) *A'nas*   *'na'de,*   ru'tan   *'toumon*   'kul ba'rau.
       people DEM DIS PL   language(s) PRON POSS 3PL all   different
       "Those people, their languages are all different."

(814) *Ba'kan*   *'de*   *'kulu,*   ku'tu   *'fogo*   aya'nin.
       place(s)   DEF   all   put-PASS-Ø   in it   sick people
       "All the places, sick people are put in it."

---

[1] A fronted verb that is repeated in its original position rather than re-introducing old information functions as a mere emphasizer strenghtening the meaning of the verb.

'Gus,   *'ito*   *bi-*   *'gusu*   'wen?
look for-GER   PRON 2SING   FUT-   look for   where
"To look for (it), where will you look for (it)?"

[2] Left dislocated noun phrases are occasionally repeated in full:

Fu *'volunteer 'work,*   *'ina*   'kul 'dakul 'moumon   'sawa
in   volunteer work   PRON 1PL   all   enter-Ø with + PRON 3PL   together
fi *'kas*   *ta*   *'volunteer.*
in   work   GEN   volunteer
"In the volunteer work, we all entered together with them in the volunteer work."

During the dislocation sequence, the involved sentence constituent may be neutralized. The result may be that a prepositional phrase loses its preposition as in (815):

(815) 'Sente   'de,   'fadul   'asa   'shiling 'mia. < min 'sente 'de
money   DEF   remain-Ø   now   shiling NUM
"From the money, there remain now hundred shilings."

Occasionally, the resumptive pronoun is omitted in the main clause as in (816):

(816) 'Gari   'takum,   'tammam-   kum   'moyo.
vehicle   PRON POSS 2PL   check-IMPER-   ADR PL   water
"Your vehicle, check(PL) [its] water."

6.4.4. Cleft and Pseudo-cleft Constructions

Pseudo-clefts consist of a noun phrase followed by the focus marker 'ya and a headless relative clause as in (817) and (818). They function contrastively. In Nubi, the copula is often not marked overtly (cf. 4.4.1).
    * NP   'ya   Ø   REL   headless RC

(817) Wu   'asker   'uo   'na'de,
and   soldier   PRON 3SING   DEM DIS
'uo   'ya   al   'youm 'na'de, . . ., li'go   fi   'bab   gate.
PRON 3SING   FOC   REL   day   DEM DIS   find-PASS-Ø   in   door   gate
"And that soldier, he is [the one] who on that day . . . was found at the gate./ it is him who on that day"

(818) 'Ana   'ya   ab   'asuru ku'ra 'tai   'de.
PRON 1SING   FOC   REL   tie up-Ø leg   PRON POSS 1SING   DEF
"I am [the one] who tied up my leg./It is me who tied up my leg."

Nubi cleft constructions have much contrastive strength. They are introduced by 'de and consist of the following three subtypes. The focus marker 'ya is optional.
    * 'de   ('ya)   Ø   REL   RC

(819) 'De   'ya   ka'las   'sabab
DEF   FOC   EMPH   reason
al   'kutu   'ana   'lim(u)   'etokum   fi   'be   'in   'de.
REL   make-Ø   PRON 1SING   gather-Ø   PRON 2PL   in   house   here   DEF
"It is the reason that made me gather you(PL) in the house here."

* 'de   ('ya¹)   Ø   NP   ('ya²)   no   REL   RC

(820) 'De   wa'zeya   gi-   'j(a)   'aki
       DEF   old person-PL   PROG-   come   tell-Ø
       'nena   kala'ma   'dolde'de.
       to + PRON 1PL thing-PL   DEM PROX PL
       "It is the old people who happen to tell us these things."

(821) 'De   'ya¹   'Ahmed 'ya³   omon   'atan.
       DEF   FOC   NPROP FOC   PRON 2PL   wear down-Ø
       "It is Ahmed who is the one whom they wore down."

(822) 'De   'Rabana   'ya   'kutu   je   'de.
       DEF   God   FOC   put-Ø   like   DEM PROX
       "It is God who is the one putting it like this."

The following subtype that involves 'de is a bit dubious. It consists
of 'de + 'ya + clause. At surface-level, there is no relative clause.
The presence of introductory 'de and optionally the focus marker 'ya,
however, argues for listing them among the cleft constructions.
Moreover, their only possible interpretation is that of a cleft construction, since there are two verbs, a hidden copula joining 'de and
the main clause, and the verb of the clause. However, a relativizer
and a relativized noun phrase are absent.[4]
    * 'de   'ya   Ø   clause

(823) La'yin kan   'ita   'bu-   rwa   we'ri   'nouo,
       but   if   PRON 2SING FUT-   go   show-Ø to + PRON 3SING
       'de   'ya   ka'las   'ita   bi-   'kosa   'marya   'de.
       DEF   FOC   EMPH   PRON 2SING FUT-   lose   wife   DEF
       "But if you are going to show [it] to her, it is [then that] you will lose [your] wife."

---

[3] The focus marker 'ya, which is between 'Ahmed and 'omon 'atan, marks the object
after it has been fronted (Y-movement, see above).
    [4] Occasionally, similar sentences occur without the focus marker 'ya, for instance:
'De   'uo   gu-   'rua   'dakal   'sumuku   fi   'dongo   'in.
DEF   PRON 3SING   PROG- go   enter-Ø hair slide   in   hairdo   here
"It is [the moment that] he is going to place the hair slide in the hairdo here."
(wedding custom).
    Instead of being regarded as a cleft, this type of sentence may be considered to
be merely introduced by 'de, a construction that is reminiscent of sentences introduced
by the sentence-introduction particle dâ or dî, for instance, in Egyptian. However,
if we take a look at some examples from the Egyptian Arabic dialect, such as those
in Fischer (1959, 182), we note that they also have a contrastive meaning. This
type of Nubi sentence may be related to the Egyptian sentence, or to similar sentences in other Arabic dialects. The occurrence of 'ya in similar sentences is most
likely a Nubi innovation, since Nubi 'ya typically expresses contrast. The above Nubi
sentence is taken from a text of my oldest informant, a woman who was close to
eighty years of age. Her speech was definitely closer to the Arabic source language.

(824) 'De   'ya   nyere'ku ab   'kweis gi-   'raba 'ingis we'de   je'de
      DEF FOC child   REL   good PROG- grow like   DEM PROX   EMPH
      "It is [the way that] a good child grows so."

6.4.5. *Relative Complements*

Nubi speakers often use the following construction: a verb in its gerund or infinitive form is followed by a relative clause whose verb is a repetition in the finite form of the verbal head noun. There are two types. In the first type, the verbal noun, whether gerund or infinitive (see 4.3.3), is repeated in the relative clause as a finite verb. No other information is added. This type of clause merely serves to strengthen the meaning of the verb.[5]

(825) 'Ase'de, 'ja   al   'ana   'ja   'de,
      now   come-GER   REL   PRON 1SING   come-Ø   DEF
      'ana   'kan   'aju   'jowj(u) 'ita.
      PRON 1SING   ANT   want-Ø   marry-Ø PRON 2SING
      "Now, the coming that I came/the reason why I came, [its purpose is that I want to tell you that] I would like to marry you."

In the second type, extra information is added to the verb in the relative clause by means of, for example, an object, a quantifier, or and adverbial clauses that specifies and restricts the meaning of the verb as in (826):

(826) Ba'kan 'ja   'nouo   te'lim, te'lim 'na'de   'kelem ja
      when   come-Ø to + PRON 3SING dream dream DEM DIS   tell-Ø as
      kan   'kore   'to   al   'uo   'kore   'zaidi   'de,
      if   cry-GER   PRON POSS 3SING REL PRON 3SING cry-Ø a lot   DEF
      'Raban(a) 'asma 'zulum   al   zulu'm(u)   'uo   'fogo 'nade'de
      God   hear-Ø injustice REL treat unjustly-PASS-Ø PRON3SING in it DEM DIS
      "When a dream came to her, that dream told as if (through) her cry which she cried very much, God heard that injustice with which she was treated unjustly."

6.4.6. *Question-Answer*

The question-answer device used to focus on asserted information is common in Uganda, the rest of Eastern Africa, and the Arabic world.

---

[5] A similar strenghtening of the meaning of the verb is established by repeating the verb in its gerund or infinitive form after the preposition *ma*:

'keta   'g(i)-   'angulu 'nouo   'akili *ma a'ngulu*
SUBJ + PRON 2SING PROG- carry to + PRON 3SING food with carry-GER
"you must carry food to her."

The speakers formulate their assertion as a question that asks for
the information to be focused on and subsequently answer it as in
(827) and (828):

(827) 'Youm   ta   maski'nin   'je   'tim
      day   GEN   poor man-PL   come-Ø   be present-Ø
      lo'go   'ragi   'de   ka'man   'so   su'nu?   'Safir.
      when   man   DEF   also   do-Ø   Q-word   travel-Ø
      "The day of the poor people came to be there when the man also
      did what? Travelling."

(828) 'Kulu   'sawa,   'itokum   gi-   'sten   sa'uti   *ta*   *mu'nu?*
      all   same   PRON 2PL   PROG-   wait for sound   GEN   Q-word
      Ta   *lun'gara*   *'na'de.*
      GEN   drum   DEM DIS
      "All together, you(PL) are waiting for the sound *of what? Of that drum.*"

6.4.7. *Changes in Word Order*

Attention is drawn to a sentence constituent referring to new or
given information by either putting it in the sentence-initial or, less
frequently, the sentence-final position. It is only the word order that
is reversed. There is no pause or any other marking in the dislocated
constituent, and no co-referential pronouns occur. In (829), the adverbial clause of time is fronted. This is a very common device. In
(830), the subject is placed in final position. Moreover, part of the
subject undergoes left-dislocation. The second part of the genitive
construction is fronted, and is repeated pronominally in the main clause.

(829) *Za'man*   *bu'mara*   'kan   'fi   'rag(i)   'wai.
      long ago   very   ANT   EXIS   man   INDEF
      "A very long time ago, there was a man."

(830) 'Ragi   'taki,   'gelib(u) 'ita   *'chunga*   *'to*
      husband PRON POSS 2SING   worry-Ø PRON 2SING   take care-GER   PRON POSS 3SING
      'Marya   'taki,   'gelib(u) 'ita   *'chunga*   *'to.*
      wife   PRON POSS 2SING   worry-Ø PRON 2SING   take care-GER   PRON POSS 3SING
      "Your husband, taking care of him worries you. Your wife, taking care of her worries you."

6.5. *Questions*

6.5.1. *Yes-no Questions*

Yes-no questions are formed by raising the intonation. There is no change in word order. Answers are given in full or are introduced by *'ai* or *'aiwa* (for an affirmative answer) and by *'ma(f)(i)* or *a'ta* (for negative answers) as in (831) and (832):

(831) . . .	'gal:	Eh,	ba'ba	'taki			'de,	'uo		'ja
	that	INT	father	PRON	POSS	2SING	DEF	PRON	3SING	come-Ø
	'in	'de.	'Sei	'ita		'rakab	'nouo		'nas	'chai?
	here	DEF	EMPH	PRON	2SING	cook-Ø	for + PRON	3SING	COLL	tea
	'Gal:	'Ai,	ma'ma.							
	that	yes	mama							
	'Uo		'beredu?	'Gal:	'Uo		'beredu.			
	PRON	3SING	take a bath-Ø	that	PRON	3SING	take a bath-Ø			
	'Uw(o)		'akulu?	'Gal:	'Ai.					
	PRON	3SING	eat-Ø	that	yes					

". . . [she said] that: Eh, your father, he came here. You really cooked tea for him? [You said] that: Yes, mama. He took a bath? [You said] that: He took a bath. He ate? [You said] that: Yes. "

(832) 'K(e)	'ana		'ro	'metokum?		
SUBJ	PRON	1SING	go-Ø	with + PRON 2PL		
'Gal:	'Ma,	'ito		was'kan.	'Gen	'in.
that	NEG	PRON	2SING	be dirty-Ø	stay-IMPER	here

"Shall I go with you(PL)? [They said] that: No, you are dirty. Stay here."

The answer to negative questions is usually in full in order to avoid misunderstandings.

(833) Tom'sa		'ataku	'gal:	'Akil	'tai			'de,
crocodile		laugh-Ø	that	food	PRON	POSS	1SING	DEF
'it(a)		'arufu	'ma?	'Gal:	'An(a)		'arufu	'ma.
PRON	1SING	know-Ø	NEG	that	PRON	1SING	know-Ø	NEG

"Crocodile laughingly [said] that: My food, you don't know [it]? [He said] that: I don't know [it]."

(834) Wu		'ragi	'taki			'ya	'g(i)-	aju	'sokole	'ma?
and		husband	PRON	POSS	2SING	FOC	PROG-	want	thing	NEG
'G(i)-	aju		'marya	'bara	'mafi?					
PROG-	want		woman	outside	NEG					
'Gal:	Ah,	'baga,	'uo			'to		'g(i)-	aju.	
that	INT	EMPH	PRON	3SING	PRON	POSS	3SING	PROG-	want	

"And doesn't your husband want something? Doesn't [he] want a woman outside? [She said] that: Ah, he wants."

The tag *'mus(u)* in the sentence-initial or sentence-final position converts a sentence into a question as in (835):

(835) 'Yal   ba'na   'fi   ta'lata.   Ta'lata,   'musu?
      child-PL   girl-PL   EXIS   NUM   NUM   isn't it?
      "The daughters, there are three [of them]. Three, isn't it?"

6.5.2. *Q-word Questions*

Question words and their position in the sentence have been mentioned above (5.4). Generally, questions retain the word order of declarative sentences, which is SVO. The question words *mu'nu?* "who?", *su'nu?* "what?", *ya'tu?* "which?", *'kam?* "how many?", *ke'fin?*, *'kef?* "how?", and *mi'ten?* "when?" remain in situ depending on whether they function as the subject, the object, or part of a prepositional phrase, etc. as in (836), (837), and (838). *(f)(u)'wen?*, *we'nu?* "where?" usually takes the sentence-final position but may be found in other positions in an interrogative sentence. *'Le?* and *ma'lu?* "why?" may take any position as in (839). The tone is raised towards the end of the sentence.

(836) 'Marya   'de   ka'man gi-   'kafu   'marya *to*   *mu'nu?*
      woman   DEF   EMPH   PROG-   be afraid of wife   GEN   who
      "The woman is afraid of whose wife?"

(837) Ta'ra,   ta'r(a),   'ragi 'endis *su'nu?*
      EMPH   EMPH   man   have-Ø what?
      "You see, you see, what does the man have?"

(838) Ma'ma ta   Fai'za,   difa'na   kan   gi-   'ja
      mother GEN   NPROP   guest-PL   if   PROG-   come
      fi   'be   'taki   'de, karibi'sh(a)   'omon   *ke'fin?*
      in   house   PRON POSS 2SING   DEF   welcome-PASS-ØPRON 3PL   how?
      "Mama of Faiza, guests, if [they] come to your house, how are they welcomed?"

(839) Bi'niya 'de   *ma'lu* gi-   'gen fi   sa'raya   'fo?
      girl   DEM PROX   why?   PROG- stay in   appartment   high
      Ma'lu 'uo   'ma   gi-   'doru   mo   ak'wana?
      why?   PRON 3SING   NEG   PROG- walk around   with friend-PL
      "This girl, why is she staying high in [her] appartment? Why isn't she walking around with friends?"

The anterior marker *'kan* was discussed 4.2.1.3 and often occurs in questions, where it may function as a kind of highlighter or emphasizer as in (840):

(840) 'Jé   rasu'l(u)   'ita   ge'ri 'kan   'sa   'kam?
      come-PASS-Ø send-PASS-Ø   PRON 2SING   nearly ANT   hour how many?
      "You were sent at nearly, it was at what time?"

'Kan usually comes immediately in front of the question word. Occasionally, however, it occurs in the sentence-initial position and is thus separated from the question word.[6]

(841) Gi-   ziki'ri   'kan   ke'fin-ke'fini?   'Kan   ko'ru
      PROG- recite-PASS   ANT   how?-REDUP   ANT   sheep
      'to   gi-   da'ba   ke'fin-ke'fini?
      PRON POSS 3SING   PROG-   slaughter-PASS   how?-REDUP
      "There was being recited, it was how? His sheep was being slaughtered, it was how?"

6.6. *Coordination*

6.6.1. *Coordination at Phrase Level*

Two NPs may be joined together to become one noun phrase by means of the conjunctions *ma* "with", "and", *au* "or", *'wala, wa'la* "or", *'ama, a'ma* "or", and occasionally *wu, wa, u* "and", or by simple juxtaposition but divided by pauses and/or intonational separation. The joined constituents participate in the same event or share the same function in the event.

(842) 'Ija   'de   *fu 'ras* *ta*   *sul'tan*   *ma*   *nuswa'na 'to*   *ti'nin.*
      story DEF   about   GEN   sultan   and   wife-PL PRON POSS 3SING   NUM
      "The story is about a sultan and his two wives."

(843) 'Umon   a'nas   al   a'ta . . .,   'umon   a'nas
      PRON 3PL   people   REL   EMPH NEG   PRON 3PL   people
      al   a't(a)   'arufu 'dini   'ma   wa'la   su'nu 'ma.
      REL   EMPH NEG   know-Ø religion NEG   or   what   NEG
      "They are people who, no . . ., they are people who do not know religion nor anything else."

---

[6] Occasionally, *'kan* seems to serve as a question marker in questions which lack a question word. This use of *'kan* is restricted to the language of old people.
      'Kan   gi-   da'ba   fu   'gaba?
      ANT   PROG-   slaughter-PASS   in   forest
      "Was it [the sheep] slaughtered in the forest?"

6.6.2. *Coordination at Sentence Level*

Wu, wa, u "and", *au* "or", *wa'la, 'wala* "or", *'ama, a'ma* "or", *'ila*[7] "except", "inevitably", and *la'kin* "but" join two or more sentences as in (844) and (845):

(844) . . .   'uw(o)   'endis   kuba'niya   'ma
              PRON 3SING   have-Ø   friend(s)   NEG
       wu   fu'raha   'to   'sia.
       and   happiness   PRON POSS 3SING   little
       ". . . he does not have friends and his happiness is low."

(845) We'le   'g(i)-   agara, *la'kin* 'itokum,   ba'na,   'yal   ba'na   'g(i)-   agara
      boy-PL PROG- study but PRON 2PL girl-PL child-PL girl-PL PROG- study
      su'kulu   'ma.
      school   NEG
      "The boys studied, but you(PL), the girls, the girl children did not study [at] school."

(846) 'It(a)   'aju   'k(e) ana   'ya   'gus   'neki
      PRON 2SING   want-Ø SUBJ PRON 1SING FOC look for-Ø   for + PRON 2SING
      bi'niya   *wa'la* 'fi   'tak(i)   al   'it(a)   'ain   ka'la?
      girl   or   EXIS   PRON POSS 2SING REL   PRON 2SING see-Ø   COMPL
      "Do you want me to look for a girl for you or is there yours which you have already seen?"

6.7. *Subordination*

6.7.1. *Adverbial Clauses*

Adverbial clauses of time: To express that one event precedes another event, Nubi uses the temporal conjunction *'kabla 'lisa ('ma)* "before" or *'kabla* "before". The verb in the adverbial clause generally takes the zero form. When the verb in the main clause is marked by the anterior marker *'kan*, the entire sentence refers to consecutive events in the past as in (847). When it takes a marker other than the anterior marker, then the sentence refers to present or near future events as in (848):

---

[7] Occasionally, *'ila* "except", "inevitably" refers to words instead of sentences:
       . . . ,   *'ila*   'bes   'shida,   *'ile*   fi   'tabu,
                 inevitably   only   problem(s)   inevitably   in   trouble
       'ita   bi-   'kun   'mo.
       PRON 2SING   FUT-   be   with it
       ". . . , only problems, in trouble, inevitably, you will be with them."

(847) ...   *'kabla*   'ita   'sulu   'badu   ma   'sheik,
             before   PRON 2SING   take-Ø   RECIP   with   sheik
      'kan   'ita   'fi   fi   ba'kan   ya'tu?
      ANT   PRON 2SING   EXIS   in   place   Q-word
      "... before you came together with the sheikh, in which place were you?"

(848) La'yin *'kabla* *'lisa*   'ina   'gata   'youm 'ma,
      but   before still PRON 1PL   decide-Ø   day   NEG
      'k(e)   'ena   'lim(u)   akwa'na   'tena   'de.
      SUBJ PRON 1PL   bring together-Ø relative-PL   PRON POSS 1PL   DEF
      "But before we decide on a day, we should gather our relatives."

'Bada "after" expresses the fact that an event follows another event.
The verb in the adverbial clause is either the simple verb form, a
verb marked by the anterior marker *'kan*, or a verb marked by *ka'las*.
The verb in the main clause may be marked by any TMA marker.

(849) 'Gari   'takum,   'tamam- kum   'moyo. 'Bad(a) 'itokum
      car   PRON POSS 2PL   check-Ø ADR-PL   water   after   PRON 2PL
      'tamam 'moyo ka'las,   'aju   'k(e)   'etokum   'tamam 'oil.
      check-Ø water COMPL   have to-Ø   SUB   PRON 2PL   check-Ø oil
      "Your(PL) car, check(PL) [its] water. After you(PL) have checked the water, you(PL)
      have to check the oil."

There are no restrictions on tense and aspect marking in time clauses
with the conjunctions *'ladi* "until", *la'man* "until", *na'man* "until", *ba'kan*
(kan) "when", "while", *wa'kati* "when", "while", and *li'go* "while" as
in (850) and (851).

(850) 'Bes,   'itokum   gu-   'futu   *la'man* 'itokum   bi-   'rasul
      EMPH   PRON 2PL   PROG-   continue until   PRON 2PL   FUT-   arrive
      ka'man   'fogo   'takum.
      EMPH   in   PRON POSS 2PL
      "Well, you(PL) continue until you(PL) arrive in yours(PL)/(your rooms)."

(851) *Wa'kat(i)*   'uo   ma'lim 'tena,   'g(i)- alim(u) 'ina,
      while   PRON 3SING   teacher PRON POSS 1PL PROG- teach   PRON1PL
      'uo   'kan   tiki'yan 'zaidi.
      PRON 3SING   be-ANT irritated much
      "While he was our teacher, [while he] taught us, he was much irritated."

Li'go "while" often co-occurs with *'lisa 'ma* "not yet" in expressing
that an action/event is taking place while at the same time another
event did not yet occur, even if it was expected.

(852) ...   'ita   'je   *li'go* 'lisa m'ze   'de   'ja   'ma.
             PRON 2SING   come-Ø while   still old man DEF   come-Ø NEG
      "... you came while the old man had not yet come."

Min "since" generally co-occurs with a simple verb. The main clause often contains *'lisa 'ma* "not yet", and expresses that from a certain moment on, an action or event has not yet taken place as in (853):

(853) La'yin *min*   'ana   'gai,   *'lis(a)* 'an(a)   'ainu
      but   since PRON 1SING stay-Ø still PRON 1SING see-Ø
      jahi'liya   je   'na'de   *'ma.*
      state of ignorance   like   DEM DIS NEG
      "But since I am staying/since I am alive, I did not yet see a state of ignorance like that one."

The verb in the time clause with *'kila kan, kan 'kila* "whenever" either takes the bare verb form or the progressive marker *gi-*. The verb in the main clause normally takes the simple verb or a verbal prefix expressing habit or repetition as in (854):

(854) *'Kila kan*   'ino   'gu-   rwa   fi'lel,
      whenever PRON 1PL   PROG- go   at night
      'yal(a)   'uo   bi-   'ja   'turuj(u)   'ina   je'de-je'de.
      well PRON 3SING FUT- come send away PRON 1PL EMPH-REDUP
      "Whenever we go at night, well he comes to send us away."

Adverbial clauses of location: These are expressed with *ba'kan* "where" as in (855):

(855) 'Ya   *ba'kan* 'ina   'gai,   *'lis(a)* 'ina   'gai 'ladi 'na're,....
      CONJ where PRON 1PL stay-Ø still PRON 1PL stay until today
      "Thus where we stay (the place that we stay in), we have stayed [there] until today,...."

Adverbial clauses of manner: These are introduced by *ja* "as", *ja (kan)* "as if".

(856) 'Ita   'g(i)-   asma   fi   'muku 'taki   'na
      PRON 2SING PROG- feel   in   brain PRON POSS 2SING there
      je   'it(a)   'aju   'mutu.
      as if PRON 2SING want-Ø die-Ø
      "You felt in your brain there as if you were about to die."[8]

---

[8] Nubi use the expression *'aju* "want" + V to express that someone is on the verge of doing or undergoing an action or event. Thus, when someone is about to fall, Nubi say: 'It(a)   'aju   'waga.
      PRON 2SING want-Ø fall-Ø
      "You are about to fall."
In this particular case, it is also implied that the speaker feels sorry for the hearer. It is therefore rude not to say it.

(857) 'So-   'takum   *je*   'ana   gi-   'so,. . . .
      do-   ADR PL   as   PRON 1SING   PROG-   do
      "Do(PL) as I am doing, . . ."

Adverbial clauses of reason: The conjunctions *ka'lam, mi'sen, ala'shan, min, li'go, ja, fi a'jil ta* "because", "since", "as" introduce adverbial clauses of reason as in (858) and (859):

(858) La'kin   'fijo   'chalo   'na,   'ana   'kafu   a'kul   'na,
      but   inside   village   there   PRON 1SING   be afraid of-Ø   eat-GER there
      mi'sen   a'nas   'na'de   jahi'liya.
      because people   DEM DIS PL   ignorant
      "But inside the village there, I was afraid of eating there, because those people were ignorant."

(859) 'Uo   'kelem   'gal   nyere'ku   'de   wele'du
      PRON 3SING   say-Ø   that   child   DEF   give birth to-PASS-Ø
      fu   ni'ka   'to,   fu 'ras   si'da   'to,
      in   marriage   PRON POSS 3SING   on   bed   PRON POSS 3SING
      lo'go   'marya   'de   'to, ...
      since   woman   DEF   PRON POSS 3SING
      "He says that the child is born in his marriage, on his bed, since the woman is his,. . . ."

Substitution: It is expressed by *min* "instead of" followed by a clause with a finite verb. The clause following the substitutive clause is often introduced by the subjunctive marker *ke'de* as in (860):

(860) 'Sa   we'de   ka'las   'sa   'ashara. Ka'las *min*   'ita
      moment   DEM PROX   COMPL   hour   NUM   EMPH instead of   PRON 2SING
      li'go   'badu   ma   a'ku   bi'nadum   fi   'sika,   a'ker   ke'de
      meet-Ø   RECIP   with   brother   human   in   street   it is better   SUBJ
      ita   li'go   'badu   ma   'lam   'gaba, ...
      PRON 2SING   meet-Ø RECIP   with   meat   forest
      "At this moment it is already 4 o'clock. Instead of you meeting a human being in the street, it is better that you meet a wild animal,. . . ."

6.7.2. *Subjunctive clauses*

The subjunctive clause is introduced by the marker *ke'de* or *'ke* (see also 4.2.2.2. and 5.3). It "codes the target event performed—or to be performed—by the manipulee." (Givón 1990, 518). When an argument of the subjunctive clause is extracted, it is referred to in the subjunctive clause by means of a referential pronoun or *'fogo*. Formal co-reference is compulsory with possessive and prepositional phrases and in adverbial phrases of location and purpose as in (861):

(861) 'Marya,   'sente   we'de,   'kena   'jowju   'mo   'marya.
      wife   money   DEM PROX   SUBJ + PRON 1PL   marry-Ø   with it   woman
      "Wife, this money, let us marry with it [another] woman."

However, co-reference is optional in objects and adverbial phrases
of manner and time (see also 6.4.2. and 3.3.7) as in (862):

(862) Bi'nadum   'tan   kan   'Rabana 'ke   'jib   'nana   'in, . . .
      human being   other   if   God   SUBJ   bring-Ø   to + PRON 1SING   here
      "Another human being, if God could only bring me [one] here, . . . "

The subjunctive marker has three functions, for the subjunctive clause
may occur after verbs of manipulation, and the marker may also
express a hortative or a goal or intention.

6.7.2.1. Subjunctive Clauses after Verbs of Manipulation
First, a subjunctive clause may follow a manipulative verb. With
manipulative verbs, the object or indirect object of the main clause
is identical to the subject of the subjunctive clause and can be referred
to as the manipulee. The complement clause expresses the event to
be performed by the manipulee (see also Givón 1990). The act of
manipulation itself is expressed in the main clause. Nubi verbs of
manipulation are listed in table 26:

Table 26. Nubi verbs of manipulation

Implicative verbs	Translation	Non-implicative verbs	Translation
'kutu	"cause"	'aju	"want"
'so	"make", "cause"	'aba	"forbid"
'dugu	"make", "cause"	'kelemu	"tell", "order"
'awunu	"help"	'gal	"tell", "order"
'sadu	"help", "assist"	am'risha	"order"
sai'dia	"help", "assist"	'asadu	"ask", "beg"
'sebu	"let"	'kore	"beg"
'abusu	"stop", "prevent"	'gata	"decide", "order"
'kabasu	"deceive into doing s.th."	'rudu	"allow", "permit"
		'rasulu	"send"

The first group consists of implicative verbs, which imply that, if the
manipulative verb is a fact, the complement is also a fact (see Givón
1984, 123). The subjunctive marker is optionally present. The use
of the subjunctive marker is compulsory with the other verbs. These

are non-implicative verbs: "neither success nor failure of the manipulation is strictly implied by the truth of the main verb/clause"
(Givón 1984, 124). The verb *'aju* "want", "wish", although it belongs
to the group of non-implicative verbs, may occur with or without
the subjunctive marker.

Let us first consider the *non-implicative verbs*. The subject of the subjunctive clause either follows or precedes the subjunctive marker *ke'de*.
Therefore, if the object position, direct or indirect, of the main clause
is the subject of the subjunctive clause, it appears either in the main
clause and not in the subjunctive clause, or it does not appear in
the main clause but is present in the subjunctive clause, or it is realized in both clauses. In the first scenario, the manipulee precedes
the subjunctive marker *ke'de*. It thus appears as the object of the
main clause, while it does not occur overtly in the subjunctive clause
as in (863):

(863) 'Dukur   'uo   'rudu   bi'niya 'wai   'de   ke'de   'nyenjili.
      then   PRON 3SING   allow-Ø girl   NUM   DEM PROX   SUBJ   descend-Ø
      "Then he allowed this one girl to descend."

In the second case, the manipulee is not mentioned in the main
clause. It follows the subjunctive marker and so is part of the subjunctive clause as in (864):

(864) Ba'kan sul'tan   'asma   ka'lam   'de,   'uo   'kelem
      when   sultan   hear-Ø   problem DEM PROX   PRON 3SING   tell-Ø
      ke'de   wa'zir   'to   'de   'sulu . . ., 'amsuku ka'lam 'de 'kweis.
      SUBJ   minister PRON POSS 3SING   DEF   take-Ø   take-Ø   matter DEF well
      "When the sultan heard this problem, he suggested that his minister would take . . .,
      treat the problem well."

The difference between the two types of sentence is that, in the former, where the manipulee is the object of the main clause, the
manipulator has more impact on the manipulee than in the latter.
The chances that the act to be performed will take place are thus
more realistic in the former type. In the latter, the chance that the
manipulative act is successful is reduced. In a third type of sentence
with non-implicative manipulative verbs, which occurs only infrequently, the manipulee is expressed both in the main clause and in
the subjunctive clause. In the few examples from the text corpus,
the manipulee is the indirect object of the main clause. This type
of sentence seems to be a variant of the first type.

(865) . . .   'an(a)   'arija   'kore   *na* 'Rabana
               PRON 1SING   return-Ø beg-Ø   to   God
     ke'd(e) *uw(o)*   'awun(u)   'ana   . . . .
     SUBJ   PRON 3SING   help-Ø   PRON 1SING
     "I again begged God to help me. . . ."

With the implicative verbs, a similar difference in scope is shown
between clauses where the manipulee precedes or follows the subjunctive marker. However, the third type, a variant of the first, occurs
more frequently with implicative than with non-implicative verbs.
Whether as a direct or indirect object of the main clause, we find
a co-referent for the manipulee in the subjunctive clause.

(866) . . .   *ke'd(e)* *ow(o)*   'awun(u)   *'ana*
               SUBJ   PRON 3SING   help-Ø   PRON 1SING
     'k(e)   *ana*   *'raba*   'dol'de   *gi'dam.*
     SUBJ   PRON 1SING   raise-Ø   DEM PROX PL   first
     ". . . he should help me to raise these [children] first."

However, with implicative verbs the problem of the occurrence and
non-occurrence of the subjunctive marker surfaces and has possible
consequences for meaning. When the subjunctive clause of implicative manipulative verbs is introduced by *ke'de*, there is not necessarily co-temporality between the manipulative act and the action to
be performed as in (867):

(867) 'Dukur 'an   *gi-*   *'seb(u)* 'uo   *ke'de* *'rua.*
      then   PRON 1SING   PROG-   let   PRON 3SING SUBJ   go-Ø
      "Then, I let him go [any time]."

This co-temporality, is, however, assured when no subjunctive marker
occurs as in (868):

(868) 'Ana   *seb(u)*   ak'wana   wa'din
      PRON 1SING   leave-Ø   relative-PL   other-PL
      gi-   *'so*   bia'shera   'toumon, ...
      PROG- do   business   PRON POSS 3PL
      "I let the other relatives continue doing their business, . . . [now]."

The non-implicative verb *'aju* "want", "wish" may occur both with
and without the subjunctive marker *ke'de* similar to the implicative
verbs. From the presence of *ke'de* in (869), it is inferred that the crocodile wants his friend Kako to come over to his place. The agent
exerts quite some manipulative force so that the action is performed,

but not necessarily at this very moment. The crocodile and Kako still have to arrange a day for the visit. In (870), the agent wants the act of shaving to be performed immediately.

(869) Ak'we, 'Kako, 'an(a) *'aj(u)* *'ita*
    my brother NPROP PRON 1SING want-Ø PRON 2SING
    ke'de 'ja 'ro 'ainu 'be ta'yi.
    SUBJ come-Ø go-Ø see-Ø house PRON POSS 1SING
    "My brother, 'Kako, I wish that you would come and see my house [one day]."

(870) ... 'ana *'aj(u)* 'ita 'jenu 'ras 'tai.
    PRON 1SING want-Ø PRON 2SING shave-Ø head PRON POSS 1SING
    "... I want you to shave my head [now]."

To negate manipulative sentences, Nubi has the following patterns. In all cases, they are aimed at the non-performance of a certain action. However, there is a difference in scope. When the negator occurs in the main clause, the manipulative act is negated. The manipulator does not want or does not agree on the action to be performed as in (871):

(871) Ka'lam mi'san 'uw(o) *'aju* *'ma* *ke'd(e)* 'asma 'to
    because because PRON 3SING wish-Ø NEG SUBJ name PRON POSS 3SING
    'ben je 'Nubi.
    resemble like Nubian
    "Because he does not wish his name to resemble a Nubi [name]."

When the subjunctive clause contains the negative marker, the speaker expresses his wish or his intention that the action should not be performed as in (872):

(872) 'Uw(o) *'aju* *'keta* 'wonus
    PRON 3SING wish-Ø SUBJ + PRON 2SING talk-Ø
    'fogo nyere'ku 'to *'ma.*
    about child PRON POSS 3SING NEG
    "He wishes you not to talk about his child."

(873) is rather exceptional, since the most logical interpretation would be the negation of the main clause, even if it is the subjunctive clause that is negated.

(873) Wu ka'man 'uo *bu-* *'rudu* *ke'de* a'ku 'na'de 'zulum
    CONJ also PRON 3SING FUT- agree SUBJ brother DEM DIS harm-Ø
    nyere'ku fi'lan *'ma.*
    child certain NEG
    "And also she does not accept that that brother harms a certain child."

Infrequently, double negation may occur as in (874):

(874) 'It(a)   'aju   'ma
      PRON 2SING   wish-Ø NEG
      'ke   a'ku   'taki   'de   abu'su   'ma.
      SUBJ   brother PRON POSS 2SING   DEF   arrest-PASS-Ø NEG
      "You wish that your brother would not be arrested."

The complement verb may be passive unlike the manipulative verb
as in (875):

(875) 'Simba 'kutu   turu'ju   'ragi.
      lion   cause-Ø   chase off-PASS-Ø   man
      "The lion caused the man to be chased off."

6.7.2.2. *Subjunctive Clauses Expressing a Hortative*

The subjunctive marker may express a hortative. This is done either
by means of a subjunctive marker + a subjunctive clause without a
main clause or by means of a subjunctive clause preceded by *afa'zal*
"it is better", *a'ker* "it is better", impersonal *'aju* "need", "have to"
expressing external obligation or the impersonal passive form *a'ju* "be
needed", "must", expressing obligation as imposed by the speaker.
With *afa'zal* and *a'ker* meaning "it is better" the subjunctive marker
is always present as in (876) and (877):[9]

(876) ...   *a'ker*   *ke'd(e)* 'uo   'mutu   'na   min
             it is better   SUBJ   PRON 3SING   die-Ø   there   than
      'uo   'ja   'kelem fi 'be   'in   'gal
      PRON 3SING   come-Ø   say-Ø   in house   here   that
      sin'g(a)   'owo,   au   turu'j(u)   'owo.
      defeat-PASS-Ø   PRON 3SING   or   send back-PASS-Ø   PRON 3SING
      "... it is better that he dies there than that he comes and tells here at home that he was
      defeated or that he was sent back."

(877) *Afa'zal*   'ke   ja'da   a'nas   wa'din   'de   'kulu.
      it is better   SUBJ   throw-PASS-Ø   people   other-PL   DEF   all
      "It is better that all the other people are thrown [aside]."

---

[9] One speaker used *'lazima* "it is necessary" followed by the subjunctive marker.
Normally it occurs without.

'ana   'lazima   ke'de   'nigitu   'sokol al   'nigitu ...
PRON 1SING   it is necessary SUBJ   select-Ø   thing   REL   be ripe-Ø
"It is necessary that I pick the thing that is ripe ..."

The impersonal verb *'aju (ke'de)* expresses external and moral authority while its passive form *a'ju (ke'de)* is used when authority is imposed by the speaker. The use of the subjunctive marker is not compulsory. *Ke'de* is generally omitted when addressing the hearer.

(878) A'ju   ke'd(e) ow(o)   'arija   'wara   ma   nyere'ku   'de.
      must-PASS-Ø SUBJ   PRON 3SING return-Ø backwards with child   DEF
      "He must go back with the child."

(879) 'Kil(a) a'jol   'aju   ke'd(e)   'amsu(ku)   'sika   'to.
      every person have to—Ø SUBJ   take-Ø   way   PRON POSS 3SING
      "Every person has to take his way/ has to make his [own] way."

The subjunctive marker is, however, present when talking about a third person. There seems to be no correlation between the presence/absence of *ke'de* and the temporal settings.

(880) La'kin fi   'be   'tai   'na, kan   'ito   'gu-   rwa,
      but   in   house   PRON POSS 1SING there if   PRON 2SING PROG-   go
      a'j(u)   'ita   'ro   ma   'akil   'taki,   ka'lam
      must-PASS-Ø PRON 2SING go-Ø   with food   PRON POSS 2SING   because
      'akil   al   te   'be   'tai   'de   'ma   gi-   'tim.
      food   REL GEN   house PRON POSS 1SING DEF   NEG PROG-   be enough
      "But at my place there, when you are going, you must go with your food, because the food
      that [is] of my house is not enough."

(881) Ka'lam nyere'ka, kan 'ita   fi   'be   ta   ba'ba   'taki,
      because child-PL if   PRON 2SING in   house   GEN   father   your
      ma'ma 'taki,   min   'subu,   'lata   gi-   'saba,
      mother PRON POSS 2SING at around   morning   weather PROG- become morning
      'aj(u)   'ita,   nyere'ku,'ita 'ya   'gum   gi'dam.
      have to-Ø   PRON 2SING child   you   FOC wake up-Ø   first
      "Because, children, if you are in the house of your father, your mother, in the morning,
      [when] it is becoming morning, you have to, child, you [have to] wake up first."

The advice may as well consist of the subjunctive marker + the subjunctive clause without a main clause. The subject of the subjunctive clause precedes or follows the subjunctive marker. When the subject of the subjunctive clause precedes the subjunctive marker, it seems that there is more pressure (moral or external) on it than when it follows the subjunctive marker.

(882) 'Gal: 'Ai,   'k(e)   ana   'kalas   kala'ma to   jo'kon   'de
      that   yes   SUBJ   PRON 1SING   finish-Ø thing-PL GEN   kitchen DEF
      gi'dam. 'Ana   ke'de   'ja.
      first   PRON 1SING SUBJ   come-Ø
      "[She said] that: Yes, let me finish the things of the kitchen first. [Then] I should come."

However, in (883), it is possible that the length of the subject, which consists of several elements, is the reason why the subject has moved to sentence-initial position.

(883) *A'yan*   *'to*   *al*   *fi*   ke'de   *'pona.*
       illness   PRON POSS 3SING   REL   EXIS   SUBJ   get better-Ø
       "Let his illness which is there, get better."

6.7.2.3. *Subjunctive Clauses Expressing Goal or Intention*
Ke'de followed by a subjunctive clause can be used after any verb to express the goal or intention of the action conveyed in the first verb as in (884) and (885):

(884) A'ku   ba'ba   'de   'ja   'fata   du'kan 'sia   je'de
       brother father   DEF   come-Ø   open-Ø   shop   small   EMPH
       ke'de   bi'niya 'de   *'gen*   *gu-*   *'uza.*
       SUBJ   girl   DEF   stay-Ø   PROG-   sell
       "The paternal uncle opened a small shop so that the girl could (continuously) sell."

(885) 'Fi   a'nas   al   gi-   rasu'l(u)
       EXIS   people   REL   PROG-   send-PASS
       ke'd(e)   *abur*   *'rua*   *'ain*   ta'biya   ta   bi'niya   'de.
       SUBJ   try-Ø   go-Ø   see-Ø   habit(s) GEN   girl   DEF
       "There are people who are being sent in order to try to find out about the habits of the girl."

6.7.3. *Conditional Clauses*

Conditional sentences in Nubi basically consist of two types: the simple or probable conditional sentences and the counterfactual ones. In the former, the chance that the event/state expressed in the main clause will happen is real, since the condition, posed in the if-clause, is not unlikely to occur. The latter, however, refers to a supposition that is contrary to known or expected facts and that, therefore, is not true. This implies that the state or event expressed in the main clause cannot be true either. An additional third type, which formally resembles the counterfactual type, involves the hypothetical conditional sentences.[10] The if-clause expresses a state or event that

---

[10] Givón (1990: 832) mentions in this respect: "Quite often the very same markers (*perfective* and *irrealis*) used to code counter-fact conditionals are also used to code low-likelihood conditionals."

could be possible but whose realization is judged to be improbable.

In all types, the if-clause is introduced by *kan* "if".[11] The conditional marker *kan* differs from the anterior and/or modal marker *'kan* in that it is not stressed.[12] The main clause is optionally introduced by the conjunction *'ya*, and infrequently by the conjunction *'dukuru* "then" as in (886):

(887)	Kan	'uo		'kutu	ku'ra	'to		je	'de,
	if	PRON 3SING		put-Ø	foot(feet)	PRON POSS 3SING		like	DEM PROX
	'yo	'uo		'g(i)-	arija	je	'de, . . .		
	CONJ	PRON 3SING		PROG-	return	like	DEM PROX		

"If he puts his feet like this, he returns like that,. . . ."

The if-clause generally comes first. However, this is a matter of frequency rather than a strict rule, since the if-clause may also follow as in (887):

(887) . . .	'umon		'kun	'wara	'sei-'sei		'de	
	PRON 3PL		be-Ø	behind	very-REDUP		EMPH	
kan	'ita		com'pare	me	'ini	fi	U'gand(a)	'en.
if	PRON 2SING		compare-Ø	with	here	in	NPROP	here

". . . they are very much behind, if you compare [it] with here, in Uganda here."

6.7.3.1. *Simple or Probable Conditional Clauses*

The verb in the protasis of the simple conditional sentence is either unmarked or marked by progressive *gi-* or future *bi-* or a variation on these forms. The verb in the apodosis generally belongs to one of the irrealis categories whether future as in (888), subjunctive,

---

[11] *'Ja/je kan* and *kan ja/je* whose original meaning is "as if", "like if" are occasionally used to express conditionality

A'rus[1]	'de	je	kan	gi-	daka'l(u)		'uo[1]	
bride	DEF	as	if	PROG-	enter-PASS		PRON 3SING	
'fijo	'jua	je'de,	'uo[2]		'ya	'g(i)-	arufa.	
inside	house	EMPH	PRON 3SING		FOC	PROG-	lift	

"The bride, (as) if she is brought in inside the house, he is the one who carries [her]."

[12] *Kan* may function as a temporal conjunction, corresponding to the more usual temporal conjunction *ba'kan*:

Kan	'marya	'wai	'de	'jo	'weledu		
when	woman	NUM	DEF	come-Ø	bear-Ø		
nyere'ku	'to		'wai,	'asma	to	nyere'ku	'de	Ma'nara.
child	PRON POSS 3SING		NUM	name	GEN	child	DEF	NPROP

"When the one woman happened to bear her one child, the name of the child was Manara."

imperative as in (889), modal, verbs expressing intent, ability or disposition as in (890), or verbs of certainty as in (891) (see also Givón
1990):

(888) ... kan   'it(a)   'aju   'ke   ana   'sul(u)   'ita,
         if   PRON 2SING want-Ø SUBJ PRON 1SING take-Ø PRON 2SING
         'ana   *bi-*   *ja-ja.*
         PRON 1SING FUT-   come-REDUP.
         "... if you wish me to take you, I will come."

(889) Kan   'itokum   'b(i)-   atan   'shef   'de,   'shef   'de   'lesegu,
       if   PRON 2PL   FUT-   draw   sword   DEF   sword   DEF   stick-Ø
       'aruf-'tokum   ja   a'ku   'de   'mutu.
       know-IMPER-PL   as   brother   DEF   die-Ø
       "If you(PL) draw the sword, [and] the sword sticks, know(PL) that [your] brother died."

(890) Kan 'gelba 'to   'ja   'ain   'gai   'tena
       if   heart   PRON POSS 3SING   come-Ø   see-Ø   stay-GER   PRON POSS 1PL
       'gai   'kweis,   'uw(o)   *'aju*   'ja.
       stay-GER   good   PRON 3SING   want-Ø   come-Ø
       "If his heart happens to see that our stay/[way of living] is a good way of living, he
       will like to come."

(891) 'Uo   'gal: Kan   'an   bi-   'jib(u)   'fogo   'marya,
       PRON 3SING   that   if   PRON 1SING   FUT-   bring   in it   wife
       'ben   je   'b(i)-   awun(u)   'ana.
       seem-Ø   as   FUT-   help   PRON1SING
       "He [said] that: If I will bring a wife in it, it seems that it will help me."

Occasionally, a simple verb form or a zero form is attested in the
main clause. This is not so exceptional in view of the neutral character of the unmarked forms (see 4.2.1.1).

(892) Ter   'de   kan   'b(i)-   arija   'ja   'gai
       bird   DEF   if   FUT-   return   come-Ø   sit-Ø
       fi   'ras   ta   nyere'ku   'de,   'kuris   'de   ta   nyere'ku   'de.
       on   head   GEN   child   DEF   chair   DEF   GEN   child   DEF
       "The bird, if it will come back and sit on the head of the child, the chair/throne will
       be of the child."

The progressive marker *gi-*, though it has not been mentioned above
as one of the categories of the apodosis, may be used to emphasize
the habitual character of the entire sentence. Progressive *gi-* usually,
but not obligatorily, occurs both in the if-clause and in the main
clause.

(893) ‘Kila   ‘ragi   ‘to   kan   ‘gu-   rwa   fi   sa’fari,
      every   husband   PRON   POSS   3SING   if   PROG-go   on   trip
      ‘uo   ‘g(i)-   amrugu   ‘tím-’tím   ‘resin
      PRON   3SING   PROG- take out be enough- REDUP-INF   ration
      al   g(i)-   usi’ana   ma   ‘youm
      REL   PROG-   corresponds   with day(s)
      al   ‘uo   ‘gu-   rwa   ‘gen   ‘fogo.
      REL   PRON 3SING   PROG-   go   remain-Ø   in it
      “Every husband [of theirs], if he is going on a trip, he will take out enough rations which
      correspond to the days he is going to remain [out].”

6.7.3.2. *Counterfactual and Hypothetical Conditional Clauses*
In the counterfactual and hypothetical type of conditional clauses,
the verb in the protasis always contains the anterior marker ’kan in
one of the following combinations: ’kan V, ’kan gi-V, or ’kan bi-V.
The verbs in the apodosis in my data are one of the following:

– ’kan V as in (894)
– ’kan bi-V, typically encoding counterfactuality as in (895)
– a future tense, either bi- V, or ’gurwa V as in (896)
– a subjunctive
– a non-finite verb, either gerund or infinitive as in (897)
– a verb expressing intention, ability, disposition
– a cognition-utterance verb, e.g. ’feker “think”

(894) Kan   ‘kan   ‘ana   ba’ra,   ‘kan   ba’kan   ‘de   ‘sia.
      if   be-Ø   PRON 1SING   alone   be-ANT place   DEF   small
      “If I had been alone, the plot would have been small [but now I am not alone]”
      (counterfactual)

(895) Kan   ‘kan   ‘an   bi-   lo’go a’jol   ‘de   ‘na’re,
      if   ANT   PRON 1SING   FUT-   meet   person   DEF   today
      ‘kan   ‘ana   bi-   ‘katul(u) ‘uo.
      ANT   PRON 1SING   FUT-   kill   PRON 3SING
      “If I were meeting this person today, I would kill him.” (hypothetical)

(896) Kan   ‘kan   ‘ita   gi-   saka’ran   fi   ‘sir,   ‘youm ‘tan,
      if   ANT   PRON 2SING   PROG- be drunk   in   secret day   other
      ‘ita   ‘gu-   rwa   ‘kal(a)   ‘ita   saka’ran
      PRON 2SING   PROG- go   end up-Ø   PRON 2SING be drunk-Ø
      gi’dam   a’nas.
      in front of   people
      “If you were getting drunk secretly, another/one day, you would end up being drunk
      in front of [other] people.” (hypothetical)

(897) Kan   'kan 'youm 'de   'uo   'ro   'rudu   'ragi
      if   ANT   day   DEF   PRON 3SING go-Ø   accept-Ø   husband
      ka'bila jo   'wede   'ma,   eh,   'kore-'kore-'kore-'kore.
      type   like DEM PROX   NEG   INT   cry-GER-REPET
      "If the other day, she had not accepted a husband of this type, eh, [it would have been]
      crying, crying, crying, crying." (counterfactual)

6.7.3.3. *Concessive Conditional Clauses*

Concessive conditional clauses are introduced by *'sala (kan)* "even
if". The verbs in the protasis and apodosis behave like verbs in sim-
ple/probable conditional clauses.

(898) 'Sala kan   nyere'ku 'taki   'so   ma'kosa,
      even if   child   PRON POSS 2SING   make-Ø mistake(s)
      'bes 'ita   'ya   'aruf   'uo   'so   ma'kosa 'ma, ...
      only PRON 2SING FOC   know-Ø PRON 3SING do-Ø   mistake(s) NEG
      "Even if your child makes a mistake, you just know that he did not make a mistake, ..."

(899) 'Marya 'de,   'sala 'ana   bi-   'seb(u), bi-   'gen 'moumon.
      woman DEF   even if PRON 1SING FUT- leave,   FUT- stay with + PRON 3PL
      "Even if I will leave, the woman will stay with them."

6.7.3.4. *Disjunctive Conditional Clauses*

'Whether . . ., or . . .' clauses are expressed by repeating *kan* 'if' or
'sala kan 'even if' before every new proposition as in (900) and (901):

(900) Kan   'laki 'wai, kan   'elf tama'nini, kan   'elf kam'sin,
      if   NUM   if   NUM   if   NUM
      bi-   'kuwa fi 'kweis   ta   a'nas   'na'de.
      FUT- be   in goodness   GEN   people   DEM DIS PL
      "Whether one hundred thousand, or eighty thousand, or fifty thousand, it
      will be good for those people."

(901) 'Kila 'sokol al   'kan 'ita   'hibu bi'mara, 'sala kan 'marya
      every thing REL   ANT PRON 2SING   love-Ø very   even if wife
      'sala kan   'pesa, 'sala kan   'jua, ...
      even if   money even if   house
      "Every thing that you would like very much, whether a wife, or money, or
      a house,. . . ."

The second proposition may be introduced by *'wala* "or" as in (902):

(902) 'An(a)   'aruf   'ma 'de i'raba   kan al   'ja   je'didi,
      PRON 1SING know-Ø NEG DEF   raise-GER if REL come-Ø new
      wa'la ke'fin?
      or   Q-word
      "I do not know whether this is an upbringing that developed recently, or how?"

Alternatively, and less frequently, *'sala . . .*, *'wala . . .*, can be interpreted as "whether. . . ., or . . .".

(903) 'Ina   'ma   gu-   'wonus kala'ma   'kulu 'fadi,   'sal(a)   al   ba'tal
      PRON 1PL   NEG   PROG- discuss matter-PL all openly   even   REL   bad
      wa'la   'seme.
      or   good
      "We are not discussing all matters openly, whether bad or good."

6.7.3.5. *Negative Conditional Clauses*
The negative conditional is expressed by means of *kan* + negative
marker or by means of *'ila kan* "except if ", "unless" as in (904) and
(905):

(904) Mo'hamed   'de,   kan   ba'ba 'de   'ma'fi   je'de,
      NPROP   DEF   if   father DEF   EXIS NEG   EMPH
      gi-   'gai   fi   'be,   'g(i)- agara 'ma.
      PROG- stay   in   house PROG- study NEG
      "Unless father is there, Mohammaed stays at home, he does not study."

(905) La'kin ga'raya   te   Inge'reza,   ki'boko   'to   'sia.
      but   schooling   GEN   NPROP   punishment   PRON POSS 3SING   few
      'Ila   kan   'ita   'so   'nas   'homework   'mafi,. . . .
      except if   PRON 2SING do-Ø   COLL homework   NEG
      "But the schooling of the English, its punishment is little. Unless you did not do
      homework,. . . ."

6.7.4. *Complement Clauses*

Complement clauses are a type of clause combination in which a
sentence contains two verbs or more that either share the same subject or take different ones. Complement clauses function as an argument (whether subject of object) of another clause. Syntactically, the
sentence consists of two separate clauses, the first referring to the
act expressed by the first verb and the second referring to the contents of the second verb.

Many Nubi verbs are part of a matrix clause that has another
clause that functions as one of the matrix clause's arguments (subject or object). A complement clause functioning as a subject is very
rare in Nubi, unlike object complement clauses, which are common.
The matrix verbs of complement clauses fall into three categories:
modality verbs such as "begin", "try", and "be able to", cognition-
utterance verbs such as "know", "say", and "think", and verbs of

manipulation, such as "cause", "allow", and "want". Only modality verbs show constraints on the subject: the subject of the main clause and of the complement clause are obligatorily the same (see also Givón 1990: 533).

6.7.4.1. *Complement Clauses after Verbs of Modality*

This type of verb codes "inception, termination, persistence, success, failure, attempt, intent, obligation or ability—vis-à-vis the complement state/event." (Givón 1990, 533). In Nubi, this group includes *'abidu* "begin", *'kalasu* "finish", "stop", *ni'situ* "forget", *'alimu* "get used to", *'aju* "intend to", *'aburu* "try", *ja'ribu* "try", *'rudu* "agree", *'weza* "be able", *'agider* "be able", *'arufu* "be able", "have the knowledge to", *'tim* "be old enough to", *'aba* "refuse", *'kafu* "be reluctant to", *'fadul* "remain", "continue". As mentioned above, the subject of the complement verb has to be identical to that of the main verb. The complement verb is finite. Its tense, aspect, and mode are more constrained here than with the manipulative and cognition-utterance verbs.

(906) 'Ana   ni'situ   'bio   'nena   mu'kati fi 'sika 'na.
      PRON 1SING   forget-Ø buy-Ø   for + PRON 1PL bread   on   road   there
      "I forgot to buy bread for us on the road there."

(907) . . .   kan   'ita   'ja   'alim   gi-   'doru
              if   PRON 2SING come-Ø get used to-Ø PROG- go
      fi   'madrasa,
      to   Qur'an school
      'skul   'je   'neta   ra'isi fi 'din.
      school become-Ø for + PRON 2SING easy   in   religion
      ". . . if you begin to get used to going to the Qur'anic school, then [day] school becomes easy for you concerning religion."

If the modality verb is passive, the complement verb is passive as well as in (908):

(908) Abi'du   tayiri'sha.
      begin-PASS-Ø   prepare-PASS-Ø
      "It was begun to be prepared."

Instead of a finite verbal complement, modality verbs can take a gerundival complement. There is, however, a pragmatic difference. With gerundival complements, the information is presupposed rather than asserted new information. There is usually a reference to previously-mentioned information, for instance *a'kulu 'to* "his eating" and not just "eating", *be'redu* '*to* "his bath" and not just "a bath". A complement verb, on the contrary, gives new information. Moreover, with gerundival complements, it is more likely that the complement event has been carried out successfully than with a verbal complement. It is not surprising therefore that a gerundival complement often occurs after implicative verbs like *'abidu* "begin" and especially after *'kalasu* "finish".[13]

(909) 'Uo   'beredu.   'Uo   'kalas   be'redu   'to
      PRON 3SING take bath-Ø. PRON 3SING finish-Ø take bath-GER PRON POSS 3SING
      "He took a bath. He finished (taking) his bath."

6.7.4.2. *Complement Clauses after Verbs of Manipulation*
This has been discussed extensively above (see 6.7.2. Subjunctive clauses).

6.7.4.3. *Complement Clauses after Cognition-Utterance Verbs*
The complement clause of cognition-utterance verbs behaves entirely independently. The subjects are different, and there are no constraints on the verb as to tense, aspect, mode, voice, etc. Nubi cognition-utterance verbs are *'arufu* "know", *'ainu* "understand", "perceive", "see", "understand", *'alimu* "learn", *li'go* "find", "meet", *'kala* "find out (shockingly)", *'stenu* "expect, *kum'buka* "remember", *ni'situ* "forget", *'kabas* "lie", *'feker* "think", "believe", "assume", "suppose", *'zan* "think", *'aminu* "believe", *'kelemu,* "say", "claim", "disclose", "propose", *we'ri* "show", "disclose", *'alimu* "teach", "disclose", *'asadu* "ask", *'kafu* "be afraid of".[14]

---

[13] We see a correspondence with English where verbs like "finish" and "stop" can only take the nominal *-ing* form of the verb (see Givón 1990, 534).

[14] There are several Nubi verbs which may belong to more than one category:

	Modality verbs	Manipulative verbs	Cognition-Utterance verbs
'aba	"refuse"	"forbid"	
'aju	"intend"	"want"	
'alimu	"get used to"		"learn; "teach", "disclose"
'asadu		"ask"	"ask"
'kabas		"deceive into"	"lie"
'kafu	"be reluctant to"		"be afraid of"
'kelemu		"tell", "order"	"say", "claim", "disclose"
ni'situ	"forget"		"forget"
'rudu	"agree"	"allow", "permit"	

The complement clause is either a direct quote complement, an indirect quote complement, or an embedded question complement. Direct quote complements may be introduced by *'gal* "that" as in (910):[15]

(910) A'jol   'de   'kelem   'gal: 'Ai,   kan 'it(a)   'aju,
      man   DEF   say-Ø   that   yes,   if   PRON 2SING   want-Ø
      'ana   bi-   'kelem   'neta.
      PRON 1SING FUT-   say   to + PRON 2SING
      "The person said that: Yes, if you want [it], I will tell you."

An indirect quote complement is either introduced by *'gal* "that" as in (911), *ja* "as", or *ja kan, kan ja* "as if", "that", or by zero-marking as in (912):[16]

(911) ... ke'd(e) 'umon   'aruf *'gal* 'fi   difa'na   al   gi-   'ja.
          SUBJ PRON 3PL   know-Ø that EXIS guest-PL   REL PROG-   come
      "... so that they know that there are guests who are coming."

(912) 'Uo   'ro   lo'go   aku'lu   ga'ya 'de   'safa 'wai.
      PRON 3SING   go-Ø find-Ø eat-PASS-Ø   millet DEF   side   NUM
      "He happened to find the millet having been eaten at one side."

Embedded question complements are introduced by a question word as in (913) or by kan "if", "whether", if the verb is one of negative certainty as in (914):

(913) We'ri   'nena
      show-PASS-Ø   to + PRON 1PL
      'nas   ma'ma ta   'marya 'tai   'de   'ya   mu'nu.
      COLL   mother GEN   wife   PRON POSS 1SING   DEF   FOC   Q-word
      "We were shown who the mother of my wife and her relatives were."

(915) 'An(a)   'arufu 'mafi kan 'uo   bu-   'rudu.
      PRON 1SING   know-Ø NEG   if   PRON 3SING   FUT-   agree
      "I don't know whether he will agree."

---

[15] *'Gal* "that" may also introduce a direct quote and may occur without a preceding verb:

'Gal: 'Ai, sa'ba   min   'sub,   'umon   'b(i)- arija   'rua.
that   yes   tomorrow   from morning PRON 3PL   FUT-   return go-Ø
"[He said] that: Yes, tomorrow morning, they will go again."

[16] In the Ugandan Nubi text material, *je kan* only occurs after the verbs *'aminu* "believe", *'arufu* "know", *'kelemu* "say", "disclose", *'fahamu* "understand", *we'ri* "show", "disclose", *'ainu* "understand", "perceive", "see".

6.8. *Conclusion*

SVO is the normal word order both in Nubi and in most creoles. Interrogative clauses are distinguished from declarative clauses by intonation rather than by a change in the word order. This applies also to Nubi and most creoles. Nubi question words remain generally *in situ* except for *'wen, we'nu?* "where?" and *'le, ma'lu?* "why?", which take sentence-final and any position, respectively. In many creoles, fronting of the Q-word is common.

As in most creoles, the Nubi negative marker is identical with the morpheme of denial. In many creoles, the negator takes position between subject and negated verb phrase (generally the preverbal position) (Bickerton 1977, 1981, Holm 1988). In other creoles, the negator comes in the sentence-final position (Boretzky 1983 , Holm 1988). In Nubi, the negator *'ma(f)(i)* can take any position in the sentence although the final position is dominant. Double negation is not a common phenomenon in Nubi. In this respect, Bickerton (1981, 65) argues: "In creoles generally, nondefinite subjects as well as nondefinite VP constituents must be negated, as well as the verb, in negative sentences." In Nubi this is rather an exception. Moreover, not only nondefinite constituents are negated, Nubi definite subjects may also be treated as such.

In most creoles focusing is achieved by fronting the sentence constituent in question. It is often preceded by a highlighting particle (see Holm 1988, Boretzky 1983, Veenstra and den Besten 1995: 303–15, Byrne, Caskey and Winford 1993, ix–xvi). This particle is generally homophonous with the copula, for instance Krio *na*, or a with a demonstrative, such as Negerhollands *da* (Boretzky 1983, 22 1–22). Nubi cleft constructions introduced by the determining element *'de* share their most common features with this type of focusing device. In several creole languages, the fronted sentence constituent is attached to the rest of the sentence by a relativizing element, for instance, *ki* on Principe. In Nubi, fronting can be used as a focusing device. The fronted sentence constituent is attached to the sentence by means of *'ya*, which is, however, not a copula, a demonstrative, or a relative particle. In that sense, Nubi is unique. Nubi also seems to be unique in that a pro-copy is left in the main clause, unlike in most creoles.

CHAPTER SEVEN

NUBI, FROM A DIACHRONIC AND
COMPARATIVE PERSPECTIVE

7.1. *Introduction*

This chapter will deal with two issues: the reconstruction of some Nubi features and the matter of the source language: which Arabic dialect or dialects are involved in Nubi's development? Both issues are of course related. Any comparison between Nubi and Arabic should take Kaye's remark into account that "a comparison between Nubi and WSA (Owens 1985a, 229–71) . . ., ignores the fact that the origin of EAN could not be WSA directly, but rather an older Sudanese pidgin or creole Arabic." (Tosco and Owens 1993, 220). Like Kaye, I assume that even before 1820 a pidginized Arabic was used in the Sudanese belt, especially as a trade language. Probably, this pidgin, which was far from stable, was characterized by many regional varieties, that have undergone a certain degree of levelling through mutual contacts of the speakers. Several authors writing on the origins of p/c Arabic in East Africa, such as Owens (1985a, 229–71, 1996, 125–72), and Kaye (1985, 201–30), propose a proto-p/c, for which they take WSA as the main source, considering the many similarities between the two groups of languages. An alternative possibility is, however, that the similarities between Nubi, Turku, and WSA are to be attributed to parallel, independent developments.

The discussion of the socio-historical background of Nubi and its speakers (chapter 1) is relevant to discerning the source/lexifier language of Nubi as are other possible language influences (adstrate, substrate) and the other two Arabic p/cs of the area, Juba Arabic and Turku. They will be mentioned briefly. The first aim of this chapter is to examine a selection of aspects of Nubi phonology, vocabulary, morphology, and syntax and to compare them with available material on the possible source dialects, whether EA, SA, or WSA. Similarities between Nubi and these dialects will be evaluated as to their possible impact, and Nubi (and Juba Arabic) will be compared with

Turku. Differences between Turku and Nubi (and Juba Arabic) may point to different evolutions and to different language inputs. The information provided on the Arabic dialects, the African languages of the area, and Turku (and Juba Arabic) features will be used to reconstruct the evolution of some Nubi features, which is the second aim of this chapter. A certain circularity can, however, not be avoided. The reconstruction can be valid only when we are certain about the nature of the source language of languages. However, the source language or languages cannot be identified unless we have a valid reconstruction.

7.1.1. *Language Influences*

7.1.1.1. *Adstrate Influences*
All Nubi are multilingual. The second language for most of the Nubi, in both Kenya and Uganda, is, without doubt, Swahili (see also Heine 1982). Heine adds that "among the Nubi, the number of Swahili speakers is roughly identical within the male and female population and within different age groups. It is only Nubi children of pre-school age who have a relatively low percentage of Swahili speakers" (Heine 1982, 16). Khamis (1994), who did research on multilingualism among pre-school children in Bombo, came to roughly the same conclusion. In northern Uganda and in Kenya, Swahili is the lingua franca. Nubi from southern Uganda may learn it during visits to relatives living in those areas. English is the official language in Uganda and Kenya and the language of education. Knowledge of it is limited to people who have had the chance to go to school. Women, therefore, are often barred from this knowledge. In southern Uganda, the Baganda often know only of their mother tongue, Luganda. Nubi in the Buganda area are generally fluent in this language. Knowledge of other languages varies according to the area in which the Nubi reside and their tribal areas, for instance Lugbara, Kakwa, Alur in West Nile Province, Acholi in and around Gulu, and Lango in the neighbourhood of Lira. The influence of these languages is mainly restricted to vocabulary and phonology. The surrounding languages may affect the accent of the Nubi speakers. For instance, the articulation of *r* is extremely close to *l* in the Luganda area.

7.1.1.2. Substrate Influences
The tribes that the recruits and women were accepted from were many: Nuba, Shilluk, Nuer, Acholi, Luo, Ndogo, Shuli, Yangwara, Dinka, Madi, Bari, Shefalu, Fajulu, Baka, Avukaya, Mundu, Niamniam, Bongo, Kreish, Makraka, Monbuttu, Lur, Lendu, Lugbara, Kakwa, and Moru (see Mounteney-Jephson 1890, Meldon 1907, 123–46, Nasseem and Marjan 1992, 196–214, Gray 1961). These languages belong to the African-language group (according to Greenberg 1966) and can be divided into the Niger-Kongo-Kordofan group and the Nilo-Saharic group. Most of them belong to the second group (see table 27).

Table 27. Classification of the substrate languages of Nubi
(italics: *languages*)

I. Niger-Congo-Kordofan group:			
	Niger-Congo languages: Adamawa-Eastern: Eastern:		*Mundu*
	Kordofanian: Koalib-group:		*Nuba*
II. Nilo-Saharic language group:			
	Chari-Nile: Eastern Sudanic:		*Nubian*
		Nilotic: Western:	*Shilluk, Acholi, Lur, Luo, Dinka, Nuer*
		Eastern:	*Bari, Fajulu, Kakwa*
	Central Sudanic:		*Bongo, Baka Kreish Moru, Avukaya, Lugbara, Madi Mamvu Lendu*

Source: Greenberg 1966

Substrate and adstrate influences are mainly apparent in the fields of vocabulary and phonology. Whether Nubi morphology and syntax are also affected by substrate and adstrate grammars will be discussed below.

7.1.1.3. Lexifier Influences
Several authors have discussed the question of the Arabic colloquial from which the Arabic pidgin evolved. Heine (1982, 17) suggests that the ancestor of Nubi "was a dialect closely linked to modern Egyptian and modern Khartoum Arabic". In this respect, I refer to

the military training camps in Aswân, the Egyptian and Khartûm merchants in the *zarîba*, and the Egyptian recruits and officers among Emin
Pasha's men. Owens (1985a, 229–71) argues that Nubi's ancestor
was essentially a Sudanese Arabic dialect and, more specifically, a
Western Sudanese Arabic one that had some features of Egyptian
and Khartûm Arabic.[1] Owens finds evidence in the vocabulary such
as the presence of words of Sudanese Arabic origin, in phonology
such as the lack of pharyngealization, which Nubi shares with Western
Sudanese Arabic, and to a much lesser extent in morphology and
syntax such as the Nubi word order, which corresponds to WSA
word order. These will be discussed below.

From an historical viewpoint, there were probably contacts between
the Mediterranean, the eastern and the western Sudan. Gray (1961,
4–5) writes:

> These caravan routes, leading west and east to Kordofan, Sennar and
> the Red Sea, and northwards to Egypt across either the Bayuda steppe
> or the Nubian desert, were but the eastern extension of the ancient
> network of trade-routes linking the coast lands of the Mediterranean
> with Africa south of the Sahara. Islam had given this network both
> unity and exclusiveness, so that it was possible, though sometimes dan-
> gerous, for a Muslim to travel throughout its length and breadth for
> trade and the pilgrimage.

Nachtigal (1967, vol. 2 and 3) alludes to commercial contacts between
Bornû and Wadaï, on the one hand, and Dâr Fûr and Egypt, on the
other. Schweinfurth (1922, 91) lists Dâr Fûrians among the *jallâba* of
the Ghattas *zarîba* on the river Jur in Bahr al-Ġazâl. Therefore, it
is possible that elements of Western Sudanese Arabic were relevant
in the establishment of the Arabic pidgin(s) of the area. Kaye (1991,
4–16) emphasizes the importance of the Western Sudanese Arabic
dialects for the development of Nubi. But he also illustrates the influences of Egypt in the trade and cultural life of Dâr Fûr with the
Darb al-arba'în, i.e., the forty-day path from Upper Egypt to al-Fashâr,
passing west of Dunqula.

---

[1] Owens comments on the Western Sudanese Arabic dialects relevant here: "The
Arabic dialects of the western sudanic region- Nigeria, N. Cameroun, Chad and
the W. Sudan are more notable for their similarities than for their differences, and
sharp dialectical boundaries are rare. . . . comparative data indicate that some structures exist in Chadian Arabic, and in some ways in a dialect of the north-central
Sudan, further underscoring the point that one is dealing with a pan-sudanic Arabic
structure, an areal feature." (Owens 1991b, 1172)

7.1.2. *Other Arabic Pidgins in the Twentieth Century*

Apart from Nubi, there are two other Arabic p/cs in the Sudan.[2] In the southern Sudan, a pidgin Arabic, called Juba Arabic, is still spoken as a lingua franca. It has recently been creolized. Near Lake Chad, another pidgin Arabic was used, namely Turku, which by now, however, has become extinct. Both Juba Arabic and Turku will be discussed briefly below.

7.1.2.1. *Juba Arabic*

Juba Arabic, whose name derives from the name of the capital of the southern Sudan, is used in the entire area (see Miller 1985–86, 155–60, Owens 1996, 125–72). Its speakers may be descendants of people who stayed behind when Emin and his troops left for the Lake Albert area of people who deserted from Emin's troops to join the Mahdists. The similarities between Nubi and Juba Arabic suggest that they share the same ancestor. Juba Arabic, as the lingua franca of the area, has long been a second language for its speakers. Only in the last two decades has Juba Arabic been nativized to an extent because of the growing number of interethnic marriages. Whereas in rural environments, Juba Arabic remains predominantly a pidginized variety, according to Miller (1985–86, 155–60), it has become the mother tongue of about forty percent of the inhabitants of the town of Juba. At the same time, increasing contacts mainly with the Kharṭûm Arabic colloquial have generated decreolization processes (Mahmud 1979, Miller 1986, 296–306, 1987, 1–23, Versteegh 1984, 1990). The result is a continuum going from basilectal to acrolectal varieties. Therefore, Juba Arabic is not a static entity. Several features of the development and variation in Juba Arabic have been described by Miller (1985–86, 155–60, 1986, 296–306, 1987, 1–23, 1994, 225–46), Mahmud (1979), and Tosco (1995, 426–59).

7.1.2.2. *Turku*

We have noted above (1.1.2.3) that Rabîh, one of Sulaimân's commanders, after the latter's defeat in 1879, managed to flee with his troops and followers to the Chari-Logone River Basin to the south

---

[2] Thomason and Elgibali (1986, 317–49) describe a small text of pidginized Arabic of the eleventh century A.D. They call it Maridi Arabic and locate it in present-day central Mauritania. Some small pidginized varieties probably remain in other small towns in southern Sudan, for instance Wau Arabic, Amadi Arabic.

east of Lake Chad. Estimates of the number of people following Rabîh range from 700 slave-soldiers to 7,500 people in all (Tosco and Owens 1993, 177–267). The group introduced their pidgin Arabic in the area, which subsequently was heavily influenced by the Chadian Arabic dialects. The name Turku is probably derived from the term *Turk* or *Turuk*, which in the southern Sudan was used to refer to the non-Arab Sudanese black population that was involved in the military. Emin and his troops were often called Turks (see 1.1.4., n. 25). The only written account of Turku is by Muraz (1926), a physician in the French colonial troups. According to Prokosch (1986) and Tosco and Owens (1993, 177–267), Turku was a stable pidgin. Turku no longer exists, but it may have influenced present-day Arabic-based Chadian pidgins.

In order to view Nubi from a diachronic perspective, I will link it to the regional varieties of Arabic and Turku.

7.2. *Phonology*

7.2.1. *Phonological segments*

7.2.1.1. *Consonants*

bilabials

$b < b$ UN *'bele* "country" < EA *balad* "town"/SA *balad* "town", "country"
      UN *ba'kan* "place" < EA (Asyûṭ and Aswân)/SA *bakân* "place"
$m < m$ UN *'matara* "rain" < EA *maṭar* "rain"/SA *matar* "rain"
      UN *'zambi* "offence" < EA/SA *zamb* "offence"
$w < w$ UN *'waraga* "paper" < EA *waraq*/SA *warag* "paper"
      UN *'sawa* "together" < EA/SA *sawa* "together"

labiodentals

$f < f$ UN *'fata* "open" < EA /SA *fataḥ* "open"

alveolars

$t < t$ UN *tu'ra* "soil" < EA/SA *turâb* "soil"
      UN *'tani* "other" < EA/SA *tânî* "other"
$t < ṭ$ UN *ta'ma* "greedy" < EA/SA *ṭammâ'* "greedy"

Velarized/emphatic consonants, like *ṭ*, *ḍ*, *ṣ*, and *ẓ*, are absent in Nubi. Owens (1985a, 229–71) reports that these consonants are also

absent in certain Western Arabic dialects, such as Bagirmi and
Ndjamena Arabic (Tosco and Owens 1993, 177–267). Emphatic
sounds do not seem to occur in Abbéché Arabic (Roth 1979) either.
I assume that emphasis, which is a highly marked feature, was lost
during the development of the Arabic p/cs, parallel to processes in
these dialects.

t < d   UN *'aseti* "lion" < EA/SA *asad* "lion"

d has been devoiced to *t*. According to Owens (1985a, 229–71), this
fits in a more general trend of devoicing final obstruents in the
Western Sudanese Arabic dialects and even in the entire Sudanic belt.
It may be a universal tendency in languages (Aitchison 1991, Tosco
and Owens 1993, 177–267). In this example, devoicing of the last
consonant must have taken place before the final vowel was attached.

d < d   UN *de'biba* "snake" < EA/SA *de'bib, da'bib* "snake"
              UN *'danab* "tail" < EA/SA *danab* "tail"

Reflexes of the Old Arabic interdental fricative *dh* [ð] are *d* in the
dialects and *z* in Classical Arabic loans. Generally, those words that
have *d* in SA (Hillelson's list) have *d* in Nubi, and those that have
z in SA take *z* in Nubi, e.g., UN *'zikir* < SA *zikr* < OA *dhikr* "devotional exercise" (see below).[3]

d < ḍ   UN *'ardi* "land", "soil" < EA/SA *arḍ* "land", "soil"

See remark above on the loss of emphatic sounds.

n < n   UN *ni'ka* "marriage" < EA *nikâh*/SA *nikâh* "marriage"
r < r   UN *ma'raya* "mirror" < EA/SA *mirâya* "mirror"
           UN *'rada* "breast-feed" < *raḍa'* EA "suckle"/SA "suck (of infant)", "breast-feed"
s < s   UN *'sabab* "cause", "reason" < EA/SA *sabab* "cause", "reason"
s < sh   UN *sa'ban* "be satisfied" < EA/SA *shab'ân* "be satisfied"
s < ṣ   UN *'asli* "origin" < EA/SA *aṣl* "origin"

---

[3] An exception is Nubi *'dahab*/*'zahab* from OA *dhahab* "gold". EA/SA *dahab* is
most likely the source form of *'dahab*, whereas the varieties of *zahab* may have to
be linked to Qur'anic influence (one speaker: *'zahab*), or to influence from Luganda
(another speaker: *za'habu* from Luganda *zaabù*).

See the remark above on emphatic sounds.

z < *ẓ*   UN *'zaman, za'man* "old days" < EA/SA *zaman, zamân* "old days"
       UN *bi'zatu* "himself" < EA *bizât(u)*/SA *be zâto* "himself"
z < *ẓ*   UN *'zuluma* "injustice" < EA *ẓulm*/SA *zulum* "injustice"

This fits into the general tendency of the loss of emphatic sounds.

l < *ḷ*   UN *'leben* "milk" < EA *laban*/SA *leben* "milk"

postalveolars

sh < *sh*   UN *'shukuru* "thank" < EA/SA *shakar (u)* "thank"
j < *j*   UN *'jebel* "hill", "mountain" < SA *jebel, jabal* "hill", "mountain"
j < *z*   UN *a'zol/a'jol* "man", "person" < EA/SA *zôl* "man", "person"

palatals

y < *y*   UN *'yôm* "day" < EA/SA *'yôm* "day"

y < *ʿ*   UN *bo'yi* "far" < EA/SA *baʿîd* "far"
       UN *ji'yan* "hungry" < EA/SA *jiʿân* "hungry"

Owens (1985a, 238) mentions that /ʿ/ "frequently corresponds to /y/, e.g. NA gaayid ~ gaaʿid *seated*, Abbeche (Roth 1979, 53) gaid *seated*, so for many words the /y/ forms were probably taken intact by Nubi and are not innovative." Parallel developments may, however, also be responsible for the correspondence.

velars

k < *k*   UN *'kulu* "every", "all" < EA/SA *kull* "every", "all"
       UN *'katulu* "kill" < EA(between Suhâj and Idfu)/SA *katal* "kill"
k < *g*   UN *'kabri* "grave" < SA *gabr* "grave"
       UN *'kidif* "vomit" < SA *gadhaf, gidhif* "vomit"
       UN *kur'baba, gur'baba* "nether garment" < SA *gurbâb* "nether garment"

It is possible that the above words were derived from Arabic words with *k* instead of *g*. However, I could not find a dialect where these specific words occur with *k*. Swahili influences may perhaps be responsible for the *k* < *g* change.

k < *kh* [x]   UN *'kabar* "information", "news" < EA/SA *khabar* "tale", "information", "news"
k < *ḥ* [h]   UN *luku'mar* "donkey" < EA/SA *al-ḥumâr* "the donkey"
        UN *'aksen* "better", "best" < EA/SA *aḥsan* "better", "best"

According to Owens (1985a, 229–71), *ḥ* does not occur in Western Sudanese dialects and is replaced by *kh*, which results in a regular

Arabic-Nubi correspondence *kh-k*. It is, however, also possible that
the Nubi development is a parallel one.

k < *ḡ* [ɣ]   UN *'sokol* "thing" < EA *shuḡl* "occupation", "work"/ SA *shoḡol* "thing", "matter"
           UN *'kasulu* "wash" < EA/SA *ḡasal, ḡassal* "wash"
           UN *ke'sim* "stupid" < SA *ḡashîm* "clumsy", "crude"
           UN *'kati* "cover" < EA/SA *ḡaṭṭâ* "cover"
           UN *'kettis* "sink" < SA *ḡaṭas* "sink"
           UN *'kafir* "watch", "guard" < SA *ḡafar (i)* "watch", "guard"

Owens (1985a, 236) states that:

> in Chad there are two main areas where Arabic /ḡ/ is /x/,
> Ndjamena ... and the area around Abbeche, e.g., ... xarb *west* rather
> than ḡarb, shuxul rather than shuḡul. Assuming the Nubi forms derive
> from the /x/ WSA dialects there is no need to assume a /k/—/ḡ/
> correspondence.

However, Owens (1985a, 268, n. 13) adds that there are also *g–ḡ* correspondences, which is why he assumes that WSA dialects that have
ḡ are also involved. I would rather suggest that both the *ḡ–g* and
the *g–k* correspondences occur in Nubi, given a word like SA *ḡana-
maya* "goat", which is either realized as *gala'moyo* or *kala'moyo* in Nubi,
the former being the more usual (see also below). Also in Turku, we
find that *ḡ* has *g* and *k* reflexes, for instance in Turku *gazal* "gazelle"
< SA *ḡazâl* "gazelle" and Turku *kalbann* "pregnant" < SA *ḡalbâna*
"pregnant" respectively.[4]

g < *g*   UN *'gasab* "sugar cane" < EA (Upper Egypt)/SA *gaṣab* "cane" (< OA *q*)
       UN *'gelba* "heart" < EA (Upper Egypt)/SA *galb, gelb* "heart" (< OA *q*)
       UN *'gifir* "bad talking" < EA *gafr* "fortune telling" (< OA *j*)
       UN *'ragi* "man" < EA *râgil* "man" (< OA *j*)
       UN *'masgit* "mosque" < EA *masgid* "mosque" (< OA *j*)
       UN *'gism* "body" < EA *gism* "body" (< OA *j*)
       UN *'gesma* "shoe" < EA *gazma* "shoe", "pair of shoes" (< OA *j*)
       UN *'giriba* "deep leather bag" < EA *agriba* (PL of *girâb* "small bag", "pouch")

---

[4] I adhere to the orthography of Muraz (1926), the only written account of
Turku. Tosco and Owens (1993, 188) write: "... Muraz's orthography. While it
appears to be largely phonetically based, there are a number of conventions and
variations which render a straightforward interpretation impossible." Besides the
inconsistency of Muraz' orthography, one of the main problems is that of the double consonants, which do not seem to indicate geminates but which may have to
be interpreted as markers of stress. Double *nn* may have served to keep the French
reader from reading a V*n*-sequence as a nasalized vowel, as is usual in French. The
reader should keep in mind that *di, dj,* and *dji* probably correspond to /ʃ/; *tch* and
ti to /c/; *ch, chi,* and *sh* to /ʃ/; *ni* to /ɲ/; *ou* to /w/ or /u/; and *eu* to /ə/ (see
also Tosco and Owens 1993, 177–267).

About one quarter of the Nubi words whose ultimate OA source form is with *jîm* contain *g* as a reflex of OA *jîm*, which implies that the source forms of these words must be Egyptian, since in Egyptian Arabic: OA *jîm* > *g*. However, I suggested above that the source forms of Nubi words with *j* should be sought in a dialect where OA *jîm* > *j*, which is true for the Sudanese Arabic dialects.[5]

g < *ḡ*   UN *gala'moyo* (also *kala'moyo*) "goat" < SA *ḡanamâya* "goat"
            UN *'gaba* "forest" < SA *ḡâba* "forest"
            UN *'gar* "cave", "cavity", "depth" < EA/SA *ḡâr* "cave"

glottals

h < *h*   UN *mu'him* "important" < EA/SA *muhimm* "important"
h < *ḥ*   UN *'bahar* "sea", "lake" < EA/SA *baḥr* "river", "sea"

According to Owens (1985a, 229–71), pharyngeal *ḥ* and glottal *h* have merged into *h* in several WSA dialects. Hillelson (1930) mentions that *ḥ* has been substituted by *h* in the dialects of the sedentary tribes of Kordofân. Therefore, Owens assumes Nubi to have been derived from such a dialect. I tend to attribute the lack of pharyngeal *ḥ* to parallel developments in those WSA dialects and in Nubi, rather than positing a direct link between both.

---

[5] A few words have both alternatives *g* and *j* in Nubi. These are:
    UN *'gili* ~ *'jili* "skin", "hide"
    UN *'lager* ~ *'lajer* "stone"
    UN *'gins* ~ *'jins* "sort", "kind"
    UN *'ragi* ~ *'rajil* "man"

Among these words, with known variation, the *g*-forms are the ones used most. The pair *'gili/'jili* "hide", "skin", "body" was uttered 8 times and once, respectively. *'jili* was used in variation with *'gili* by an old woman residing in Kigumba, a town in the central part of Uganda. She was born in the north and had stayed for some time in exile in southern Sudan. In the pair *'lager/'lajer* "stone", *'lajer* is used only once, whereas *'lager* is the common form. The man who used *'lajer* in co-variation with *'lager*, is well-educated. He knew, among other languages, Swahili and Juba Arabic, and had some passive knowledge of (Qur'anic) Arabic. The pair *'gins/'jins* "class" wais uttered by the same speaker. He had stayed in Kenya and Tanzania for quite some time. Of the pair *'ragi/'rajil* "man" the first is the common one, whereas *'rajil* was used only in one instance by a 40-year old man. He was married with two Sudanese wives, one of Madi and the other of Kuku descent, who spoke basilectal Juba Arabic, which may explain the form *'rajil*. In all the above cases, the *g*-form is the basic one and the *j*-word an alternative form. As Kaye (1991, 4–16) suggested, the variation has to be attributed to decreolization, either through knowledge of the *Qur'ân*, or through knowledge of a variety of Arabic that takes *j* for OA *jîm*, such as the Sudanese Arabic dialects or Juba Arabic.

Ø < *h*   UN *'uo* PRON 3SING < EA/SA *huwa* PRON 3SING
            UN *'na're* "today" < EA/SA *an-nahâr-dâ* "today"

Except for the deletion of word initial *h*, which is probably a Nubi
innovation, similar developments took place in WSA. I assume these
developments took place independently rather than consider the WSA
words to be the source forms of the Nubi forms.

Ø < *ḥ*   UN *a'buba* "grandmother" < SA *ḥabôba* "grandmother"
            UN *'amer* "red" < EA/SA *aḥmar* "red"
            UN *'fata* "open" < EA/SA *fataḥ* "he opened"
Ø < *y*   UN *a'tim* "orphan" < EA/SA *yatîm, atîm* "orphan"

y > Ø is attested in some Sudanese Arabic dialects.

Ø < ʿ   UN *'libu* "play", "dance" < EA/SA *liʿib/ liʿb* "play", "dance"

The consonants *p, v, ch* and *ng*[6] only occur in words of non-Arabic
origin as in (915):

(915) *p* in *'lipa* "pay" (from Swahili), in *'camp* (from English)
       v in *'vita* "war" (from Swahili), in *'memvu* "banana" (from Luganda
            amaenvu (PL) "bananas", and in *'yellow 'fever* (from English)
       ch in *'chai* "tea", *cha'ran* "sewing machine" (both from Swahili)
       ng in *'bang-bang* "mentally deprived", "fool" (from Acholi *abaŋbaŋ*), in
            'rungu-rung "be wrinkled" (Nubi innovation), in *'ning(i)-ning* "complain"[7]

The consonant *ny* is found in general in words of non-Arabic origin as in (916):

(916) UN *nyere'ku* "child" from Dinka *nyárkuk* (Yokwe 1985, 328)/Bari *nyereku*
       "child" (Owens 1985a, 238) (possibly via *nyarkúk* "child" (known in
       Khartûm Arabic (Nhial 1975, 89)/ Shuwa *nyirku* "child")
       UN *'nyekem* "chin" (from Bari)
       UN *'nyanya* "tomato" (from Swahili)

The data on Turku have been extracted from Tosco and Owens (1993,
177–267). In general, the consonant changes in Turku are similar to

---

⁶ *ng* [ŋ] is also an allophone of *n* before velars as in UN *'dengiri* "bend" and *lu'n-
gara* "drum".
⁷ *'ning(i)-ning* "complain" is possibly a reflex of the Acholi question word *niŋniŋ*
"how?" (Kitching n.d.). *Wu 'ita gi-'ning-ning su'nu?* could be interpreted as "And what
are you asking how? how?" Cf. also *néŋneŋ* "be a nuisance", which exists also in
KA (see Nhial 1975).

those in Nubi. There are only a few exceptions as in (917), they apply to individual words and not to groups of words. These can be treated as unique cases.

(917) UN *bo'yi* / Turku *béhid* "far" < SA *ba'îd* "far"
       UN *gaf'lan* "suddenly" / Turku *kaffalann* "surprised" < SA *ḡaflan* "suddenly"
       UN *'kamsa* / Turku *kamza* "five" < SA *khamsa* "five"
       UN *'ena* / Turku *henn* "eye" < SA *'ên* "eye"

Most of the exceptions are linked to rare cases of consonant changes as in (918):

(918) UN *'turuju* / Turku *tourdou* "chase" < SA *aṭrudu* "chase him!"
       UN *li'fil* / Turku *pfil* "elephant" < SA *fil* "elephant"
       UN *'gusu* / Turku *koussou* "look for" < SA *kûs-u* "look for it!"
       UN *'arnam* / Turku *arnab* "rabbit" < SA *arnab* "rabbit"

Consonant changes, such as *s* < *sh* and *j* < *z*, occur less frequently in Kenyan Nubi and in Turku than in Ugandan Nubi. The change *s* < *sh* occurs in Kenyan Nubi and in Turku, on a less regular basis than in Ugandan Nubi. In Uganda itself, the change is far more widespread in the southern varieties than in the northern varieties of Nubi. The same holds for the change *j* < *z*, which is common in southern Uganda, while less frequent in northern Uganda and Kenya (see also Owens 1985a, 229–71). Turku has only one *j* < *z* alternation: *zamann* "long ago" vs. *diamann* "recently", "in previous days" (Muraz 1926), which both derive from SA *zamân* "in old times". Other differences between Nubi and Turku may be attributed to different source forms, which may imply that they have different lexifier languages. Consider the forms in (919):

(919) UN *'wakti* "time" < SA *wakt* "time" and Turku *ouaguitt* "time" < SA *wagt* "time"
       UN *'ragi* "man" < EA *râgil* "man" and Turku *radjel, radjiel* "man" < SA *râjil* "man"
       UN *mal'yan* "full" < SA *malyân* and Turku *malann* "full" < SA *malân* "full"

Substrate and adstrate influences may have interfered in the following Nubi sound changes:

n < *d*   UN *ru'man* "ashes", "grey" < EA/SA *rumâd* "ashes"
r < *l*   UN *bra'ngiti* "blanket" < English *blanket* , Luganda *bulangiti* "blanket"
l < *r*   UN *'leja-'leja* "work on a free-lance basis" < SWAH *rejareja* "returnable"
l < *n*   UN *'lengil* "offload", "descend" < SA *nangil* "we remove"

In many African languages, apicals such as *d, l, r,* and *n* are related
and are used as allophones (Holm 1988). It may be that the presence of this phenomenon in substrate languages of Nubi influenced
similar sound changes both diachronically, and synchronically (consider *jeber* < *jebel* "mountain", *charo* < *chalo* "village" (from Luganda
ekyalo)). In Luganda and in some words in Bari, *l* and *r* are interchangeable (Chesswas 1954, Spagnolo 1933). In Luganda *l* and *r* are
in complementary distribution: *r* is found after the vowels *e* and *i,*
while in all other cases *l* is used (Chesswas 1956). However, in allegro
forms, these sounds are used interchangeably by mother-tongue speakers of Luganda as well as by non-native speakers. The variation even
seems to influence the distribution of both sounds in Nubi, especially
in the southern variety of Nubi spoken in the Buganda area.

s < *sh*   UN *'sheder/ 'seder* "tree" < SA *shadar* "tree"

Owens (1991a, 1–30) attributes the change from *sh* to *s* in Ugandan
Nubi to Bari influence, since in Bari, *sh* does not occur (Spagnolo
1933). However, neutralization of the dichotomy *sh—s* is common
in pidginization processes (see Mühlhäusler 1986, Heine 1973). Some
remarks are in order here. First, Owens (1996, 125–72) claims that
all words with *sh* in Ugandan Nubi have variants in *s.* Although
many do have the double pronunciation, there are words that lack
a variant in *s,* for instance *sha'ria* "Islamic law", *'shukuru* "thank".
For the latter, *s/sh* is even contrastive, *'sukur* meaning "snore". Second,
the postalveolar fricative is absent not only in Bari but in other sub-
strate/adstrate languages as well, for instance, in Dinka (Nebel 1948),
in Mamvu (Stoks 1988, Owens 1991a, 1–30), and probably and more
importantly, in Luganda. It is very likely that the change from *sh* to
s was instigated through the lack of *sh* in some of the substrate languages, which would also explain why the alternation occurs as well
in Kenyan Nubi, although not on a very large scale. Moreover,
Turku, too, has the alternation *sh/s,* for instance *shufu / sufu* "see"
(Muraz 1926). However, the lack of *sh* in Luganda probably has a
much greater impact, since it is especially in the Luganda-speaking
area that *sh* is replaced by *s.* Third, a few words in Ugandan Nubi
no longer have the *sh*-variant as in (920):

(920) UN *soro'muta* "prostitute" < SA *shermûta* "prostitute"
      UN *'sela* "luggage", "burden" < SA *shêl* "burden"
      UN *'sia* "a little" < SA *shwiyya* "a bit"
      UN *bi'ses* "slowly" < SA *bi shesh* "slowly"[8]

Fourth, most words that retain *sh*, whether as the unique form or not, are also present in Swahili, where they invariably occur with *sh* as in (921):

(921) UN *shan'ga/san'ga* "(be) surprised"—SWAH *shangaa* "surprised"
      UN *'ashara/'asara* "ten"—SWAH *ashara* "ten"
      UN *'ishma/'isma* "respect"—SWAH *heshima* "respect"

This may be an additional reason why, for Kenyan Nubi, the *sh*—*s* alternation is less frequently attested than in UN, Swahili being much more common in Kenya than in Uganda. Finally, *sh* is retained in words of Swahili origin, such as *'shamba* "field", *m'wisho* "at last", *kari'bisha* "welcome".[9]

j < *z*   UN *za'lan/ja'lan* "angry" < EA/SA *zaʿlân* "angry"
             UN *bi'zatu/bi'jatu* "self" < EA *bizâtu*/SA *be zâto* "himself"

It is not unlikely that substrate languages interfered in the change from *z* to *j* in Nubi and in Juba Arabic (Miller 1994, 225–46), since in several Nilotic languages such as Bari, Acholi, Shilluk, Dinka, and Mamvu the phoneme *z* is infrequent, while they do have *j*. In Bari, *z* is an allophonic variant of *j* (Spagnolo 1933).

k < *kh*
g < *ḡ*

Most Nubi words that are reflexes of Arabic *ḡ*-words, have equivalents in Swahili in *gh*. It is possible that, in the creolization phase of Nubi, both forms in *g* and *k* (*g* < *ḡ*, *k* < *ḡ*) were present but that, through reinforcement by Swahili words in *gh* [gʰ], their Nubi equivalents in *g* were retained whereas the forms in *k*, which were probably the most common ones (consider also the Turku words) were preserved for the others. For instance, *gaflan* and *kaflan** "suddenly" (from SA

---

[8] Those Ugandan Nubi words, which Owens (1985a, 229–71) lists as exclusive *s*-words, namely *'semsi* "sun", *su'nu* "what?", *'asurubu* "drink", *'gesi* "grass" all have *sh*-variants in my Ugandan Nubi data.

[9] An exception is *bia'shara* "business", which in Nubi may be realized *bia'sara*.

ḡaflân "suddenly") may have co-existed in Nubi. However, owing to Swahili influence (*ghafula*) during the creolization phase, the *g*-form may have been kept. Consider the Turku form in *k*, which is *kaffalann*. See also the forms in (922):

(922) UN *ɡalatu, ga'latu* "error"—SWAH *ghalati* "error" < SA *ḡalaṭ* "error"
      UN *ɡeru* "change"—SWAH *ghairi* "change" < SA *ḡayar* "change"
      UN *ɡelebu* "defeat"—SWAH *ghalibu* "defeat" < SA *ḡalab (i)* "defeat"
      UN *ɡali* "expensive"—SWAH *ghali* "scarce", "expensive" < SA *ḡâli* "rare", "scarce"

The *k* < *kh*-change probably took place irrespective of developments in Swahili where we find that most words of Arabic origin with *kh* have now become *h*-initial words (Johnson 1989 [1939]a).

(923) UN *ʼkidima* "work", "service" < EA/SA *khidma* "work", "service" vs. SWAH *hu'duma* "service"
      UN *ʼkabar* "news" < EA/SA *khabar* "news" vs. SWAH *ha'bari* "news"

The change itself, which is common in pidginization processes (Tosco and Owens 1993, 177–267) is possibly reinforced by the absence of *kh* in many of the substrate languages, such as Shilluk (Westermann 1912), Dinka (Nebel 1948), Acholi (Kitching n.d.), Bari (Spagnolo 1933), and in Swahili or Luganda (Chesswas 1954). *ḡ* occurs in Dinka and Shilluk but not in the other languages.

k < *g*

Many words in which the Arabic *g* has become *k* have equivalents in *k* in Swahili. It is thus likely to assume Swahili influence. Some, originally Arabic words, may have entered Nubi via Swahili, such as UN *ki'sudi* "intention" from Arabic *qaṣd* "intention" (EA/SA *gaṣd*) via SWAH *ku'sudi* "intention", or, through influence of the Swahili form, the original Nubi *g* changed into *k as in* UN *ɡoho/ ʼkoho* "cough" (KN *goho*, Turku *goho*) from SA *goḥḥa*, where *g* may have changed into *k*, influenced by SWAH *kohoa* "cough". For others, Swahili influence cannot be assumed, since there is no Swahili equivalent. Consider also the forms in table 28.

A few words have variants with *g* and *k*, such as *gur'baba/ kur'baba* "undergarment", *ɡoho/ ʼkoho* "cough", and *ɡawa/ ʼkawa* "coffee". The variation is interpersonal. The *g*-forms are used by old people and by an uneducated young woman I recorded. The use of the *k*-forms cannot be explained by one single reason. The *k*-forms are used by a younger generation. For the word *ʼkawa*, influence from Swahili

Table 28. UN, Swahili words in *k*

SA	UN	KN	Turku	Swahili
gabl "before"	*'kabla* "before"		*gobel*	*'kabla*
gabr "grave"	*kabri* "grave"			*ka'buri*
gabîla "tribe"	*ka'bila* "tribe"	*gabila/kabila*		*ka'bila*
gurṭâs "paper"	*kar'tas* "paper"			*kara'tasi*
gissa "tale", "story"	*'kisa* "tale", "story"			*'kisa*
magâṣṣ "scissors"	*ma'kas* "scissors"	*ma'gas*		*ma'kasi*
gifl "lock"	*'kuful* "lock"			*ku'fuli*
gahwa "coffee"	*gahwa, kahwa* "coffee"	*gahawa*	*gaoua*	*ka'hawa*
giyâs "measure"	*ki'yas* "measure"			*ki'asi*
gawâ'id "base"	*ka'waida* "habit"			*ka'waida*

and/or Luganda may play a role. However, *kur'baba* is used mainly by speakers who have resided in southern Sudan, for whom Kaye (1991, 4–16) mentions *korbaba*.

7.2.1.2. *Vowels*

My data on vowel changes reflect more or less Owens' analysis (1985a, 229–71). In Nubi, the contrast between long and short vowels has been neutralized. Therefore, vowel length, which is distinctive in Arabic, will not be treated here. Moreover, since Nubi tends towards a CV structure, epenthetic vowels may be added between two consonants. The quality of the vowel depends on the quality of the other vowels in the word. Excluding the vowel in the last syllable, front vowels co-occur with front vowels while back vowels co-occur with back vowels. *a* being neutral to both of them. *a* tends to be inserted in the vicinity of other *a*'s, although there are many exceptions to this (see below).

a < a   in the vicinity of velars and bilabials. With bilabials, often in free variation with *o*:
   UN *ka'lam* "word", "matter", "problem" < EA/SA *ka'lâm* "word"
   UN *'wakti/'wokti* "time", "period" < SA *wakt* "time"
   UN *'batna* "belly" < EA/SA *baṭn* "belly"

a < u   UN *'dakal* (via old UN *'dakul*) "enter" < SA *adkhul* "enter!"

e < e   UN *'kef?/ke'fin?* "how?" < EA/SA *kêf? kefin?* "how?"
   UN *'ges* "grass", "weeds" < SA *'geshsh* "grass", "weeds"

e < i   in the vicinity of alveolars, especially *l* or *r*:
   UN *'gelebu* in free variation with *'gilibu, 'gelibu* (via UN *'agilibu*) "win"
        < SA *aḡlibu* "win it!"
   UN *'werim* "swell" < SA *wirim* "it swelled"

e < *a*   before stressed syllable *Cî*, except initially or after *h* or ʿ (then *a* < *a*), also attested in
SA dialects:
UN *neʾdif* "clean" < SA *nadîf/naḍîf* "clean"
UN *jeʾdid* "new" < SA *jadîd/jeʾdid* "new"

but: UN *toʾwil* "long" (influenced by bilabial *w*) < SA *ṭawîl* "long"

e < *a*   in the vicinity of alveolars. Also attested in SA dialects, especially with *l* or *r*:
UN *ʿsemsi* "sun" < SA *shams/shems* "sun"
UN *jebel* "mountain" < SA *jabal/jebel* "mountain"
UN *ʿberedu* "wash" < SA *barrad/berred* "wash!"

However, in the vicinity of *l* or *r*, if in the initial position or after *h* or ʿ:
UN *arnam* "rabbit" < SA *arnab* "rabbit"

However: UN *ʿelfu* "one thousand" < SA *alif/alf* "one thousand"

And other exceptions, such as:
UN *taʾlata* "three" < SA *taʾlâta/telâta* "three"
UN *ʿfikir* in free variation with *ʿfeker* "think" < SA *fekker* "think"

o < *o*   UN *ʿmoyo* "water" < SA *moya* "water"
UN *ʿkore* "shout" < SA *kôrak* "shout"

o < *u*   also attested in some SA dialects:
UN *ʿsokol* "thing" < SA *shuḡl/shogol* "thing"
UN *tomʾsa* "crocodile" < SA *tumsa* (also *timsâh)* "crocodile"

o < *a*   in the vicinity of bilabials, especially *w*:
UN *yoʾwele* "boy" < SA *ya ʿwalad* "oh boy"
UN *galaʾmoyo* "goat" < SA *ḡanamaye* "goat"

o < *a*   in the vicinity of *u* or *o* (vowel assimilation) and especially when close to velars and
bilabials but seldom in the vicinity of emphatic/pharyngeal consonants or *h*, or
in word-initial position
UN *doʾluka* "dance" < SA *dallûka* "drum", "dancing drum", "dance"
UN *ʿdofunu* "bury" (via *ʿdafunu)* < SA *adfunu* "bury it"

o < *e*   in the vicinity of *u*, (and bilabials?):
UN *ʿwenusu/ʿwonusu* (via *ʿwenesu* (*a* ~ *e* near alveolars)) "talk" < SA *wanasu*
            "they talked"
UN *soroʾmuta* "prostitute" < SA *shermûta* "prostitute"

o < *i*   in the vicinity of labials:
UN *tomʾsa* "crocodile" < EA/SA *timsâh* "crocodile"
UN *shoʾmal* "left" < EA/SA *shimâl* "left"

u < *u*   UN *ʿdufur* "finger nail" < SA *ḍufur* "finger nail"
UN *ʿkura* "ball" < SA *kûra* "ball"

u < *au*   UN *ʿrua* "go" < SA *ra(u)wah* "go"
UN *ʿso* "do" < SA *sau, sow* "do"

u < a in the vicinity of alveolars (and labials):

        UN *'awunu* "help", "assist" < SA *'awwanu* "help him"

        UN *'badul* "instead of" < SA *badal* "instead of"

u < i also a synchronic feature in UN:

        UN *'kuful* "(pad)lock" < SA *'gifl* "(pad)lock"

        UN *'sulu*, in free variation with *'shilu* "take" < SA *shîl-hu* "take it!"

i < i UN *'kidima* "work", "employment" < SA *khidma* "labour", "work", "employment"

        UN *'biris* "grass mat" < SA *'birish* "grass mat"

The following data on Turku are given by Tosco and Owens (1993, 177–267). As for the consonants, the changes in Nubi and Turku are approximately the same. However, different words have undergone different changes as in (924):

(924) UN *'batna* "belly"/Turku *botonn* "belly" < EA/SA *baṭn* "belly"

     UN *su'nu?* "what?"/Turku *chenou?/chonou?* < SA *shinu?* "what?"

     UN *'ashrubu* "drink"/Turku *cherbou/cheurbou* "drink", "smoke" < SA *sharab* "drink"

     UN *'ferteku* "be scattered", "scatter"/Turku *fartakou, fartaka* "be scattered",

           "scatter" < SA *fartak* "scatter"

     UN *'woduru/ weduru* (via *'wederu* (*e < a* near alveolars)) "lose"/Turku *ouodeur, ouaddar,*

     ouodourou "forget", "lose" < SA *waddaru/wadderu/wedderu* "lose"

Turku must have been influenced by WSA dialects, more than Nubi, which has consequences for the phonology of both p/cs. Moreover, while Turku always remained a pidgin, Nubi was creolized.

7.2.2. *Syllable Types*

Although syllables of the type V, CVC, VC, and C and, to a lesser extent, CCVC and CVCC, occur, Nubi, in general, tends towards a CV structure (see also Owens 1985a, 229–71, Pasch and Thelwall 1987, 91–165). A CV structure is generally established in four ways: vowel insertion in consonant clusters, degemination, loss of a consonant, and addition of a final vowel. The tendency towards open syllables is more common in Ugandan than in Kenyan Nubi and Turku (see also Owens 1991, 1–30), while it is inconsistently applied in Juba Arabic (Miller 1994, 225–46).

    * Insertion of a vowel in a consonant cluster: In rapid casual speech, these vowels are often elided and so not heard. Vowel epenthesis is not unfamiliar in Sudanese Arabic dialects (see also Tosco and Owens 1993, 177–267, Roth 1979). The quality of the Nubi vowel depends on rules of vowel harmony and is usually *u* or *i*, although

other vowels can occur as well. Excluding the final vowel, a morpheme has either only front or back vowels, *a* being neutral between
the two. The quality of the epenthetic vowel is partly linked to the
quality of the other vowels. Back vowels and the semi-vowel *w* attract
u or occasionally *o*. Front vowels and the semi-vowel *y* attract *i* or
sometimes *e* as in (925). The quality of the epenthetic vowel is sometimes rather obscure in allegro forms and resembles a central schwa
as in *'arufu* "know" [ˈaːrəfu].

(925) UN *'bikir* "virgin", "first born" < EA/SA *bikr* "virgin", "first born"
       UN *'kidima* "work", "employment" < EA/SA *khidma* "work", "employment"
       UN *'rukuba* "knee" < EA/SA *'rukba* "knee"
       UN *kutuba* "sermon" < EA/SA *khutba* "oration"
       UN *muju'nun* "crazy" < SA *maj'nûn* "insane", "lunatic", "mad"

If the vowel(s) in the word is/are *a*, the consonant context affects
the quality of the epenthetic vowel. *i* tends to occur before dentals
and alveolars, while *u* occurs before labial consonants (see also Owens
1985a, 229–71) as in (926):

(926) UN *'agili* "intelligence" < SA *'agl* "intelligence"
       UN *'arija* "return" < SA *arja'* "return"
       UN *'abidu* "begin" < SA *abda'* "begin!"
       UN *'aruba* "four" < SA *arba'* "four"
       UN *'asuma* "hear" < SA *asma'* "hear"

Some exceptions are listed in (927):[10]

(927) KN/UN *'amula/ 'amla* "fill" (*u* before alveolar *l*) < SA *amla* "fill!"
       UN *wasa'kan* "dirt", "dirty" (*a*) < SA *waskhân* "dirt"
       UN *fala'ta* "down" (*a*) < SA *falta* "down"
       UN *'madarasa* "school" (*a*) < SA *madrasa* "school"

Vowel harmony plays a role in the choice of the epenthetic vowel
in many creoles as well, which could be attributed to a universal
tendency (Holm 1988). Synchronically, the epenthetic vowel has
become a full vowel. Consider the formation of the gerund of *'arija*

---

[10] The vowel *u* in *mu'ze* "old man" should be related to Bantu morphology. The
Bantu prefix *mu-* (in Swahili *m(w)-* (Ashton 1944); in Luganda *(o)mu-* (Ashton 1954)
is used in words referring to human beings. The same applies to words like *mu'chele*
"rice" and *mu'kati* "bread", which are part of the class referring to, *inter alia*, living
but non-human things. In Swahili, this class is marked by the prefix *m(w)-* in the
singular (Ashton 1944), in Luganda by *mu-* (Ashton 1954). Therefore, the atypical
vowel is to be explained by adstrate morphology.

"return", which is *a'rija* "returning" (see also Owens 1985a, 229–71). In nominal allegro forms, however, the epenthetic vowel is often obscured as in (928):

(928) UN *'gezima/ 'gezma* "shoe"
       UN *'gudura/ 'gudra* "power"
       UN *dulu'gan/ dul'gan* "rag"
       UN *'suluba/ 'sulba* "waist"

Not all words with CC are affected by vowel epenthesis. Consider the words in (929):

(929) *'hafla* "feast"
       jins "like"
       'halwa "sweet"
       'gelba "heart"

Kenyan Nubi, which in more than one way seems more conservative than Ugandan Nubi, may reflect an intermediate stage between the input forms and Ugandan Nubi, which underwent a more drastic change. For instance, EA *'gazma* "shoe", "boot" is found in KN as *gíizma, géézma.*[11] In UN, *i* has been inserted between the two successive consonants in order to create an open syllable structure: *'gezima* "shoe". Miller (1994, 225–46) adds that insertion of an epenthetic vowel to create open syllables in JA is less frequent in urban environments, whereas it seems to be a characteristic of more pidginized varieties. Vowel epenthesis does not occur frequently in Turku as in (930):

(930) UN *'bahar*—Turku *bahr* "sea"
       UN *'biris*—Turku *birss, birch* "mat"
       UN *'mutufa*—Turku *moutfa* "canon", "bomb"

* degemination: geminates in source forms have been degeminated as in (931):

(931) UN *'kelemu* "say" < EA/SA *kallim* "speak to someone"
       UN *'ita* PRON 2SING < SA *itta* PRON 2SING

It is difficult to evaluate the Turku data since Muraz often writes double consonants, which are most likely not geminates in view of the Arabic source forms. Consider (932):

---

[11] Source: Heine (1982, 80). The transcription is Heine's.

(932) Turku *toumssa* < SA *timsâḥ* "crocodile"
       Turku *botonn* < SA *baṭn* "stomach", "belly"
       Turku *koussou* "look for" < SA *kûs-u* "look for it!"

Possibly, the double consonants indicated stress rather than gemination (see also Tosco and Owens 1993, 177–267, and see above
7.2.1.1, n. 4).

    * Third, through the loss of a consonant, an otherwise closed syl-
lable may become open. Final consonants are especially affected as
in (933):

(933) UN *'keli* "dog" < SA *kelib* "dog"
       UN *'bele* "country" < EA/SA *'balad* "village"
       UN *'waja* "ache", "hurt" < SA *waja‘* "it hurts"

Word-medially, especially ', ‘, h, ḥ, and *kh* are elided. In words that
have incorporated the Arabic article, this may result in an open syllable structure as in (934):

(934) UN *'lager* "stone" < EA *al-ḥagar* "the stone"
       UN *la'bi* "slave" < EA/SA *al-‘abîd* "the slaves"

The loss of final consonants occurs far less frequently in Turku.
Consider the pairs in (935):

(935) UN *'abya*—Turku *abiett* "white"
       UN *(yo)'wele*—Turku *ouled* "boy"
       UN *de'gi*—Turku *daguig* "dough"
       UN *'di*—Turku *dik* "cock"
       UN *ge'ri*—Turku *guérib* "nearby"
       UN *tu'ra*—Turku *tirap, trap* "soil", "earth"
       UN *'ragi*—Turku *radjel, radjiel* "man"

    * the addition of a final vowel:[12] An open syllable structure is also
obtained by the addition of a final vowel, where the Arabic source

---

[12] The source forms of many Nubi words may be V-final words, such as:

UN verb < Arabic verb + object suffix:

   UN *'ashrubu* "drink" < SA *ashrub-u* "drink it!"
   UN *ni''situ* "forget" < SA *nisit-u* "I forgot it"
   UN *'nongusu* "reduce" < SA *nanguṣ-u* "we reduce it"

UN noun < Arabic N (generally body parts and kin terms) + pronominal suffix:

   UN *'gildu* "skin" < EA *gild-hu* "his skin"
   UN *sa'bi* "my friend" < SA *ṣâḥib-î* "my friend"

form has a consonant ending.[13] Vowels have been attached to all
types of consonants. Since *k, g, d,* t, *j, ch, z, ny,* and *h* never occur
word-finally, the addition of a vowel after these consonants is obligatory. These vowels cannot be elided in allegro forms as in (936),
as can word-final vowels in other contexts.

(936) UN *'muku* "brain" < EA/SA *mukhkh* "brain"
    UN *'rizigi* "wealth", "livelihood" < SA *rizg* "livelihood"
    UN *'hadi* "extent", "border" < EA/SA *ḥadd* "border"
    UN *'waji* "face" < SA *wajh* "face"
    UN *'roho* "spirit", "soul", "breath" < EA *rôḥ* /SA *rûḥ* "spirit", "soul"

The question that remains is the quality of the final vowel. Owens
(1985a, 229–71) contrasts verb final *-u* with nominal final vowel *-i*,
which would be a characteristic of nominals. It is true that final *i*
is common in nominals whereas final *-u* is common in verbals since
it is the marker of transitivity.[14] But in Ugandan Nubi, the quality of
the paragogic vowel does not seem to be linked to the function of
the word, be it nominal or verbal. Similar to the quality of the epenthetic vowel, the quality of the vowel depends on the quality of the
other vowels of the word and on the quality of the final consonant.
i tends to occur with dentals and alveolars, while *u* occurs with labial
consonants as in (937):

 Derivation from possessive suffixes may explain the quality of the final vowel,
which would otherwise not fit in the vowel and consonant context.
 [13] In the following, I ignore the verbal transitive marker *-u,* which is treated below.
 [14] Apart from being an additional vowel, final *-i* is part of the stem if it is from
the following categories:
 – of non-Arabic origin as in *bwangiri* "cheeck" from Bari *gwangiri* "cheeck"
 – ending in *-i* in the Arabic source form, as in:
   UN *'dafi* "(luke)warm" < SA *dâfi* "warm"
   UN *sa'bi* "friend" < SA *ṣâḥib-î* "my friend", "my companion"
 – final *-i* resulting from final consonant deletion, as in:
   UN *'ragi* "man" < EA *râgil* "man"
   UN *bo'yi* "far" < SA *ba'îd* "far", "distant"
Next to nominals, however, there are also some verbs ending in *-i* in Nubi. They
are derived from Arabic source forms whose third consonant is either *w* or *y,* or
from Arabic derived stems II with an object suffix as in:
  UN *'kati* "cover" < SA *ḡatti* "cover!" from SA *ḡatta* (II) "cover"
  UN *we'ri* "show" < SA *warri-hi* "show it!" IMPER + OBJ SUFF from *warra* (II)
  "show"

(937) UN *'tajiri* "rich" < SA *tâjir* "trader", "merchant"
　　　UN *'feker(i)* "think" < EA/SA *fakkir* "think!" IMPER
　　　UN *a'rusu* "bride" < EA/SA *'arûs* "bride"
　　　UN *a'nasi* "people" < EA/SA *an-nâs* "the people"
　　　UN *'tabu* "problem", "trouble" < SA *ta'b* "trouble", "discomfort"

In Turku, the consonants *k, g, d, t, j, ch, z, ny*, and *h*, may occur in word-final position, but I found no instance of a word-final *j* or *ny*, and the word-final *h* occurs only in the words *Allah* "God", *usbah* "finger", and *sabah* "east". However, according to Tosco and Owens (1993, 177–267), the final *h* is rather a sign of stress than a segmental phoneme. Other Turku examples are listed in (938):

(938) *ouélik* "lightening"
　　　azreg, azrag "deep blue", "black"
　　　béhid "far"
　　　djild "skin"
　　　bett "house"
　　　siritch "saddle for horses"
　　　baz "falcon"

The tendency towards a CV structure through final vowel addition is thus more firmly established in Nubi than in Turku and may thus be considered a Nubi feature. Consider also the examples in (939):

(939) UN *'fogo*—Turku *fok* "above", "on top of"
　　　UN *'libu*—Turku *lip* "play", "dance"
　　　UN *'nusu*—Turku *nouss* "half"
　　　UN *'muku*—Turku *mouk* "brain"

This type of paragogue may have been influenced by substrate/adstrate languages such as Swahili and Luganda. In Swahili and Luganda, no syllable can end in a consonant (Tucker 1946, 854–71, Pilkington 1901).[15] In Bari, words usually end in a vowel (Spagnolo 1933), while in Shilluk there cannot be two consecutive consonants without an intervening vowel. When two words follow each other, the one ending in a consonant, the other beginning in one, then a paragogic vowel is inserted if the first consonant is other than a liquid or a nasal (Westermann 1912).

---

[15] In borrowings with a final consonant, Swahili adds a final vowel: "the vowel -i is usually added, unless the consonant is a labial one, in which case the vowel -u is added." (Tucker 1946, 856).

Owens (1985a, 248) states with respect to the Nubi tendency towards a CV-structure:

> In most Arabic dialects closed syllables are very common, and there is in fact, a nearly universal tendency to shun series of open syllables. Interestingly, one of the few areas to resist the tendency is the sudanic one. . . . The Nubi affinity for open syllables can thus be seen as a continuation of a SA tendency to keep open syllables, though it carries the tendency much further.

Owens, thus, uses the disposition to open syllables in Sudanic Arabic dialects to explain the tendency for a CV structure in Nubi. However, the tendency towards open syllables is attested in language-changing processes worldwide (see Aitchison 1991). It is also attested in Nubi, in some pidginized varieties of JA, and, to a lesser extent, in Kenyan Nubi and Turku. However, in urban varieties of Juba Arabic and in rapid Ugandan Nubi, the CV structure does not seem to be significant. In rapid speech, Ugandan Nubi speakers tend to drop epenthetic and paragogic vowels so that the CV-syllable structure is partly obscured. In Juba, increasing contacts with the Arabic dialect of Khartûm in particular may have influenced the urban variety of Juba Arabic so as to abandon the CV structure wholly or partly in favour of a closed syllable structure.

7.2.3. *Stress and Tone*

Stress in Nubi words is lexically determined and is a reflex stemming from the stress patterns of the Arabic or other source forms as in (940):

(940) UN *'ragi* "man" < EA *'râgil* "man"
      UN *ru'jal* "men" < SA *ru'jal* "men"
      UN *kari'bisha* "welcome" < Swahili *kari'bisha* "welcome"

In a few instances, a slight movement of the stress has taken place during the development from Arabic to Nubi forms, especially when Arabic material, whether vowels or consonants have gone lost or have been moved as in (941):

(941) UN *'kunusu* "sweep" (via *'akunusu*) < SA *'aknus-u* "sweep it!"
      UN *'na're* "today" < EA *an-na'hâr dâ* "today"

Variants such as *'masgit—mas'giti* "mosque" may be the result of varying stress rules in the Arabic and/or other source dialects, such as *'madrasa* "Qur'an school", which is similar to the Omdurman Arabic stress (Worsley 1925), while *mad'rasa* conforms to the Cairene Arabic stress rules (Behnstedt and Woidich 1985, vol. 2, 60). *'Zaman* and *za'man* "time", "period" are synonyms in Sudanese Arabic (Hillelson 1930, 306). Of the pair *'masgit*—*mas'giti* "mosque", the first is common in EA. *Mas'giti* may be a Nubi innovation affected by Swahili *msi'kiti* "mosque". UN *fitna* "mischief" is derived from EA/SA *fitna* "conspiracy", "riot", while *fi'tina* is the Swahili form.

Tone is present in Nubi only in a few cases, namely in the formation of the infinitive and in monosyllabic verbs, which have high tone in the infinitive and passive verb form. Heine analyses the KN suprasegmental stucture as based on tone rather than on stress, since he finds "instances of unstressed high tone syllables which are never pronounced with a low tone" (Heine 1982, 27). According to him, the first high tone unit in a word carries stress. For Juba Arabic, Yokwe (1985, 323–28) reanalyses the stress pattern of the source forms based on two elements. First, stress is replaced by tone, and, subsequently, the words are subjected to the tone pattern of the native languages of JA speakers. Miller (1993, 137–74, 1994, 225–46) does not mention tone in JA nor does tone seem to be of any relevance in Turku.

7.2.4. *Conclusion*

Table 29. Common features in p/cs and certain Arabic dialects / features unique to p/cs in phonology

Common features in p/cs and (certain) Arabic dialects	Features unique to Arabic p/cs
	Qualitative 5-vowel system
	Vowel length: non-distinctive
Assimilation and vowel harmony in several dialects, especially in WSA, however limited by grammatical criteria	Vowel harmony/vowel assimilation
	e < *a* in context of alveolars, especially *l* and *r*
Old Arabic *jîm*: *g* in EA, *j* in SA, both in p/cs, especially in Nubi	
	Tendency to replace *sh* by *s*/free variation *sh-s*

Table 29 (*cont.*)

Common features in p/cs and (certain) Arabic dialects	Features unique to Arabic p/cs
	Tendency to replace *z* by *j*/free variation *j* < *z*, especially in southern UN (substrate influences?)
Loss of emphatics, especially in WSA: variably attested, no emphasis in Bagirmi, Njamena	
Loss of pharyngeals: *ḥ* > *h*/ Ø/*kh*, *ʿ* > Ø/*y* (especially in WSA, however variably attested: no pharyngeals in Nigeria and Chad)	
h > Ø, especially in WSA, e.g. NA, while variably attested in AA.	
kh < *ḡ*, in WSA	*k* < *kh*
	k < (WSA *kh* ?) < *ḡ*, *ḥ*
Epenthesis (in most SA dialects)	Tendency for open syllables: • through degemination • through insertion of epenthetic vowel (pidginized variety of JA, Turku, Nubi) • through loss of internal consonant • through loss of final plosives and dentals (although less regular in JA and KN than in UN)
	Morphological role of stress in Nubi and JA (but applying only to a limited range of words, and mostly fossilized remnants of Arabic source forms, which have become productive)
Final devoicing	

Sources: Miller (1994, 225–46), Tosco and Owens (1985a, 229–71, 1993, 177–267, 1996, 125–72).

As we can see in table 29, compared to Arabic, Nubi has a reduced sound system. It lacks emphatic sounds, for instance. On the other hand, *p*, *ch*, and *v*, which do not exist in Arabic, have entered Nubi

via African substrate and adstrate languages. Most of these Arabic
pidgin and creole features may be attributed to more general phenomena operating in languages worldwide or in pidginization and
creolization processes. Thus, it is difficult or even impossible to say
whether these features should be linked to specific dialect influences,
such as WSA (as is especially advocated by Owens 1985a, 229–71,
1996, 125–71), or to more general tendencies of language change. When
we compare the etymology of phonological segments in Nubi and
Turku and look at the phonological changes that have taken place,
we find many parallels, which, however, are not applied to the same
words. They have the phonological processes in common but not
the individual results of these processes. On this basis, I consider
parallel processes to be responsible for the changes in Nubi rather
than direct influence from (W)SA. The phonological differences
between Nubi and Turku are minimal. Consider table 30:

Table 30. Nubi-Turku distinctions in phonology

Nubi	Turku
Egyptianisms: *g* pronunciation in OA *j*- words	No Egyptianisms, no *g* in OA *j*- words
j < *z*: especially in southern UN	*j* < *z*: not in Turku
Vowel assimilation: common	Vowel assimilation: less applied
Tone is relevant in infinitives and monosyllabic passive verbs	Tone: most likely absent in Turku

7.3. *Lexicon*

7.3.1. *The Etymology of Words*

Typical words of EA origin are some UN words in *g* such as ʿgildu
"skin", ʿragi "man" (EA *g*, whereas OA, SA *jim*) and some adverbs of
time such as ʿnaʾre "today" (from EA *an-nahâr dâ*), and ʿbukra "tomorrow" (from EA *bukra*). The bulk of UN words, however, seem to be
reflexes of SA source forms, which points to a pan-Sudanese origin
as in (942). The SA data are from Hillelson (1930):

(942) UN *ba'kan* "place" < SA *bakân* "place"
       UN *'sheder/'seder* "tree" < SA *shadar* "tree"
       UN *a'buba* "grandmother" < SA *habôba* "grandmother"
       UN *'kore* "cry" < SA *kôrak* "cry"
       UN *'dengir* "bend down" < SA *dangar* "bend down"
       UN *sin'gi* "hunchback" < SA *sinkît* "hump"
       UN *dulu'gan* "rag" < SA *dul'gân* "rag"

In Turku, Egyptianisms are extremely rare (Owens 1996, 125–71). However, there are two words with *g*, corresponding to OA *j*-words: *guidad* "chicken" and *guiniss* "colour" (Muraz 1926, see also Tosco and Owens 1993, 177–267). Words of typical WSA origin are rare in Nubi. A UN word, such as *'homa* "fever", "malaria", which may be linked to WSA *homa* (as opposed to Sudanese *humma*), may also be related to Swahili *homa* "fever" (Johnson 1989 [1939]a). A word of WSA origin is probably UN *fala'ta* "down" resembling Shuwa *falta*. It is striking that words of WSA origin in Turku are non-existent in Nubi (Tosco and Owens 1993, 177–267). Moreover, Nubi reflexes of Arabic feminine words are in -*a*, whereas in WSA they are often in -*e*. In Turku, we also find instances of final -*e* as in (943):

(943) UN *'libira*—Turku *ibré* "needle"
       UN *me'dida*—Turku *madidé* "porridge"
       UN *me'risa*—Turku *mérissé* "alcoholic beverage"
       UN *'sana*—Turku *sané* "year"
       UN *'tisa*—Turku *tissé* "nine"

7.3.2. *Processes of Word Formation: a Reanalysis of Morphological Material*

Most noun formation processes in Nubi are common in pidginization processes (Holm 1988):

* N(PL): A few Nubi nouns are derived from reanalysed Arabic plurals (see also Owens 1985a, 229–71) as in (944):

(944) UN *di'fan* "guest" < SA *dêfân* "guest(PL)"
       UN *su'nun*, in free variation with *'sin* "tooth" < SA *sinûn* "teeth" (in Turku: *senounn* "tooth")

* N + POSS SUFF: incorporation of possessive suffix: in particular with kin terms and body parts, since kinship and body parts are often referred to in relation to their "owner" as in (945):[16]

---

[16] POSS SUFF 1SING: -*î* in EA, KA, Shuwa, and AA (Behnstedt and Woidich 1985, vol. 2, Worsley 1925, Lethem 1920, Roth 1979).

(945) UN *ama'ti* "sister of husband", "sister-in-law" < SA *ʿammat-î* "my
       paternal aunt"
      UN *sa'bi* "friend" < SA *ṣâḥib-î* "my friend"
      UN *ʾgildu* "skin" < EA *ʾgild-u* "his skin"
      UN *ʾbatna* "stomach" < SA *baṭn-a* "his stomach"
      UN *zam'bi* "offense", "sin" < SA *zamb-î* "my offense"
      UN *ʿebu* "shame" < SA *ʿêb-u* "his shame"

Owens links POSS 3SING -*a* to WSA dialects. However, it also
occurs in EA, in the area between Asyûṭ and Gina, and around
Luxor (Behnstedt and Woidich 1985, vol. 2, 154–56) and is not
exclusively a WSA feature. The incorporation of possessive suffixes
may explain -*t*- in words such as *ama'ti* "sister-in-law", -*t*- being part
of the feminine marker *a(t)* that is present only in possessive forms.
I found only two instances of possessive suffix incorporation in Turku,
namely *sabi* "friend" (from SA *ṣâḥib-î* "my friend"), and *nassipti*
"mother-in-law" (from SA *nasîbat-î* "my mother-in-law"). Some words
that have an incorporated possessive pronoun in UN have equivalents without it in Turku as in (946):

(946) UN *ʿebu* "shame"—Turku *hepp* "shame"
      UN *ʾbatna* "stomach"—Turku *botonn* "stomach"
      UN *ʾgildu* "skin"—Turku *djild* "skin"

* VOC + N: incorporation of the vocative marker: the Arabic vocative marker *ya* is included in a few cases in the Nubi noun as in
(947). I found no instances in Turku.

(947) UN *ʾyaba* "(old) man" < SA *ya ab* "oh father"
      UN *yo'wele* "boy" < SA *ya walad* "oh son", "oh boy"

* DEF + N: incorporation of the definite article:

(948) UN *ʾlarda* "termites" < SA *al-arḍa* "the termite"
      UN *luku'mar* "donkey" < SA *al-ḥumâr* "the donkey"
      UN *ʾlibira* "needle", "injection" < SA *al-ibra* "the needle"
      UN *la'ris* "bridegroom" < SA *al-ʿarîs* "the bridegroom"
      UN *Al'gul* < EA/SA *al-ġûl* "the demon", "the vampire"
      UN *lar'ba/ ʾlarba* "spear" (*lakarba* in JA) < SA *al-ḥarba* "the spear"

POSS SUFF 3SING: -*u* after C, -*a* after C between Asyûṭ and Gina, and around
Luxor (Behnstedt and Woidich 1985, vol. 2), -*u* after C in KA, (Worsley 1925),
-*hu*, -*ah* in Shuwa (Lethem 1920), -*a* in AA (Roth 1979).

In Turku, several words contain an incorporated article as in (949):

(949) *al-hadji* "pilgrim" (however UN *'haji*)
almé "water" (however UN *'moyo*)
larba "Wednesday" (cf. UN *'yom lar'ba*)
letinenn "Monday" (cf. UN *'yom leti'nin*)

However, except for names of weekdays, those words that have an incorporated article in UN occur without this morphological material in Turku as in (950):

(950) UN *'labil*—Turku *abil, habil, hébil* "rope"
UN *la'siya*—Turku *achouya* "evening"
UN *'larda*—Turku *arda* "termite"
UN *lu'far*—Turku *far* "mouse"
UN *lun'gara*—Turku *nougar* "drum"
UN *a'nas*—Turku *nass* "people"
UN *la'bi*—Turku *habitt* "slave"
UN *la'didi*—Turku *hadid* "iron"
UN *'libira*—Turku *ibré* "needle"
UN *luku'mar*—Turku *oumar* "donkey"
UN *li'fil*—Turku *pfil* "elephant"

The compounds in (951) are reflexes of Arabic genitival constructions, since the Arabic article *al-* is included in the compounded noun:

(951) UN *'beiti'raha* "toilet" < *bet ir-râḥa* "house of comfort"
UN *'sabal'hikma* "expert", "specialist" < *ṣâḥib al-ḥikma* "companion of wisdom"
UN *'sabal'bele* "native" < *ṣâḥib al-balad* "companion of the country"

A similar phenomenon exists in Turku with the noun *sidal* (from SA *sîd al-* "owner of the . . .") in compounds such as *sidal dérib* "guide", *sidal djidam* "leper", *sidal kett* "tailor", etc.

  * PREP + N: Prepositions may be incorporated in nouns to form nouns, adverbs, prepositions, etc. as in (952):

(952) UN *fi'lel* "night" (cf. Turku *fillel* "night") < SA *fi lêl* "at night"
UN *bi'zatu* "himself" < SA *be zâto* "himself"
UN *'ladi* "to the extent of", "until" < SA *li ḥadd* "to (the) extent"

  * other incorporated material:

(953) UN *iza'zul* "earthquake" < OA *iḏa zul(zilat)* . . . "when the earth is shaken . . ." (first line of the Qur'ânic sûra 99 (*Zilzâl*)
UN *'jengis* "like" < EA *zayy gins* "like the type" (via metathesis, *j* < *z*, and *e* < *a*)

UN *binadu'miya* "humaneness", "humanity" < SA *ibn âdam* "human
being"/*âdamiya* "humanity"

* reduplication: In Turku, there are only a few reduplicated words,
and these are generally fixed forms derived from the Arabic dialect
source (Tosco and Owens 1993, 177–267). In Nubi and JA, however, reduplication is, at least partially, a productive process affecting
nouns, adjectives, numerals, verbs, and adverbs. Miller (1993, 137–74)
points to Bari, where reduplication is highly productive and functions as a grammatical device.

7.3.3. *Conclusion*

The Nubi lexicon contains elements from the Sudanese Arabic belt
and from Egypt, whereas hardly any vocabulary items from WSA
occur. On the other hand, Egyptianisms hardly occur in Turku,
whereas WSA lexical items are common. Similar processes of morphological reanalysis, such as article incorporation, have operated in
Nubi and in Turku. These are not productive anymore in the Arabic
p/cs. Nubi and Turku are different in some respects as in table 31:

Table 31. Nubi-Turku distinctions in the lexicon

Nubi	Turku
Egyptianisms, such as:	Egyptianisms: rare
UN*'na're* "today" < EA *an-nahâr dâ* "today"	Turku *alyoum* "today" < SA *el yôm*
'bukra "tomorrow" < EA *'bukra* "tomorrow"	*am baker* "tomorrow" < SA *bâkir*
Words of WSA-origin: rare	Words of WSA-origin, like feminine words in *-e*
Incorporation of vocative particle	No instances
Reduplication: productive process	Reduplication: only fossilized forms

7.4. *The Noun Phrase*

7.4.1. *Pronouns*

The tables 32 and 33 compare the pronouns in the Arabic p/cs and
dialects respectively.

Table 32. Pronouns in Arabic p/cs

		UN	KN	JA (Tosco)	JA (Mahmud)	JA (Nhial)	Turku
SING	1	'ana	'aana	'ana	ana	'ana	ana
	2	'ita	'ita	'ita	ita	'inta ('ita)	innté, tou
	3m	'uo	'uo	'uo	uwa, hu, u	'uwa	hou, ou
	3f						hi
PL	1	'ina	'ina	'inna	nna, nina	a'nina	anina
	2	'itokum ('itakum) 'tokum	'ita-kum, 'ito-kum	'itakum	itakum	'in'takum ('itakum)	inntoukoum, inntokoum, inntékoum
	3	'umon	'umon	'umon	hum, uman	'umen	oumann

Sources: UN: my data, KN: Heine (1982), JA: Tosco's data in (Kaye and Tosco 1993: 269–306), Mahmud (1979), and Nhial (1975, 81–93), Turku: Tosco and Owens (1993, 177–267).

Table 33. Pronouns in Arabic dialects

		UDA	EA	KA	SA	AA	Shuwa
SING	1	ana	ana	'ana[17]	ana	'ana, ana	ana
	2m	inta	anta, inta	'inta	inta, itta, itt	inta, itta, anta, enta	inta
	2f		anti, inti	'inti	intî, ittî	inti, itti, anti, enti	inti
	3m	hûa	huwwa, hûwa, hû	'huwa	hû, hûwa	hu, hûwa	hu
	3f	hîa	hiyya, hîya, hî	'hiya	hî, hîya hi, hîya		hi
PL	1	nîna	ahna, ihna nahna, nihna	'nihna 'nahna	nihna, ihna, anihna	anîna	anihna
	2m	entû	antu, intu	'intu	intû, ittû	intu, ittu, antu, entu	intu
	2f			'intan	intan, ittan	/	intan
	3m	hûma	humma, humman	'hum	hum, hun	humma, huma, humman	hum
	3f			'hin	hin	/	hunna

Sources: UDA: Kaye and Tosco (1993, 269–306), KA: Trimingham (1946), and Worsley (1925), SA: Hillelson (1930), AA: Roth (1979), Shuwa dialect: Lethem (1920), EA: Behnstedt and Woidich (1985, vols. 1 and 2), Khalafallah (1969).

The reduction in comparison to the Arabic dialects is not restricted to Arabic p/cs. The above Arabic p/c paradigms correspond to the paradigms of many pidgins and creoles and of other languages worldwide since no distinction is made for gender and number (see Holm 1988). Probably Nubi 'ina developed from Arabic 'iḥna (Upper Egypt, SA) through the loss of ḥ. The other possibility that 'ina developed out

---

[17] Stress in this and other tables is only indicated when stress is marked in the sources.

of Arabic (SA) *anîna* via *a'nina* → *'nina* → *'inna* → *'ina* is less likely. The second person plural *'itakum/'itokum* is probably a pidgin inno- vation, since it is nowhere attested in the Arabic dialects. It consists of the independent second personal pronoun followed by the Arabic pronominal suffix for the second person plural *-kum*. In Turku, we find a related form: *inntoukoum, inntokoum,* or *inntekoum* (Tosco and Owens 1993, 177–267). The final *-n* of the third person plural form *'umon* is common in all three Arabic p/cs (Turku *oumann,* JA *uman, umon, umen*). It is only attested in Upper Egypt and in Abbéché Arabic *humman* (Roth 1979). In the latter, it was elicited only in a para- digm, not in spontaneous speech. Juba Arabic *hum* is probably the result of decreolization.

Unlike the Arabic dialects in which pronominal subjects are incor- porated into the verb and pronominal objects are suffixed to the verb, the Arabic p/c subject and object pronouns are always expressed as independent pronouns.

The tables 33 and 34 list the possessive pronouns in the Arabic p/cs and dialects respectively.

Table 34. Possessive pronouns in Arabic p/cs

		UN	KN (Heine)	JA (Tosco)	JA (Mahmud)	JA (Nhial)	Turku[a]
SING	1	*'tai, ta'yi*	*ta'i*	*(bi)ta'ai*	*tai, bita-i*	*tai*	*anaï, anahi*[b]
	2m	*'taki*	*'taki*	*(bi)'tak*	*taki*	*'taki*	*anaki*
	2f						*anaki*
	3	*'to*	*to*	*(bi)'to*	*to, bitau*	*'tou*	*anahou*
PL	1	*'tena*	*'tinna* *'tenna*	*(bi)ta'anna*	*tai-na, bitana*	?	*anina*
	2	*'takum*	*'takum ('tokum)*	*(bi)'takum*	?	?	*anakoum*
	3	*'toumon*	*to-'umon*	*(bi)'tomon*	*to-um, bitauman*	?	*anahoumann, anahoum, anam*[c]

Sources: UN: my data, KN: Heine (1982), JA: Tosco's data in Kaye and Tosco (1993, 269–306), Mahmud (1979), Nhial (1975, 81–93), Turku: Muraz (1926), Tosco and Owens (1993, 177–267).

a. Muraz (1926) also gives pronominal suffixes for the singular persons: 1: *-i*, 2m: *-k, -ak*, 2f: *-ki*, 3: *-hou*.
b. I quote Tosco and Owens (1993, 258, n. 39) on the PRON POSS 1SING: "Muraz fre- quently writes the first person pronoun *anahi*. Considering the general tendency of *h* to dis- appear in Turku, we think the *h* could have indicated some sort of syllable break. If unstressed, *ana + i* would have yielded a form like *anay, ...*, so the *h* in *anahi* can be taken indirectly to indicate a stressed final *i* (as in WSA *hanaayi* mine."
c. Tosco and Owens (1993, 177–267) mention *ana-hum/anam* for the PRON POSS 3PL in Turku. *Anam* derives from *ana-hum* via *ana-um*. *-Um* is, according to them, common in WSA dialects as an alternative of *-hum*.

Table 35. Possessive pronouns in Arabic dialects

		UDA	EA	KA	SA	AA	Shuwa
SING	1	*bitai*	*bitâᶜ-î*	*bi'tâᶜî*	*ḥagg-i, hana-i, betâᶜ-i*	*hanâyi*	*hanai*
	2m	*bitak*	*bitâᶜ-ak*	*bi'tâᶜak*	*hana-/ betâᶜ- ak, (-ku)*	*hanâk*	*hanâk*
	2f		*bitâᶜ-ik, -uk, -ki*	*bi'tâᶜik*	*hana-/ betâᶜ-?*		*hanâki*
	3m	*bitau*	*bitâᶜ-u, bitâᶜ-a*	*bi'tâᶜu*	*hana-/ betâᶜ-ho*	*hanâhu*	*hanahu*
	3f		*bitâᶜ-ha*	*bi'tâᶜâ*	*hana-/ betâᶜ-?*	*hanâha*	*hanaha*
PL	1	*bitatina bitanîna*	*bitâᶜ-na*	*bi'tâᶜna*	*hana-/ betâᶜ-?*	*hanâna*	*hanana*
	2m	*bitakom*	*bitâᶜ-kum, -ku*	*bi'tâᶜkum (bi'tâᶜkun)*	*hana-/ betâᶜ-kun, -kum*	*hanâku, -ko, -kum*	*hanaku*
	2f			*bi'tâᶜkan*	*hana-/ betâᶜ-kan*		*hanakan*
	3m	*bitahom*	*bitâᶜ-hum*	*bi'tâᶜum (bi'tâᶜun)*	*hana-/ betâᶜ-hun, -hum*	*hanâhum, -um, -m*	*hanahum*
	3f			*bi'tâᶜin*	*hana-/ betâᶜ-hin*		*hanahin*

Sources: UDA: Kaye and Tosco (1993, 269–306), KA: Trimingham (1946), Worsley (1925), EA: Behnstedt and Woidich (1985, vol. 2), Fischer and Jastrow (1980), AA: Roth (1979), Carbou (1913), Shuwa dialect: Lethem (1920).

Considering the above forms, we can conclude that the possessive pronouns consisting of suffixed forms following the genitive exponent are fossilized forms of Arabic forms. The same applies to Juba Arabic and Turku. The genitive exponent, which is *(bi)ta* in Nubi and JA, and *ana* for Turku clearly points to an eastern source for Nubi/JA and to a western source for Turku.[18] With regard to the form of the pronominal suffixes, we see that the suffixes are quite similar in all three p/cs. Tosco and Owens (1993, 177–267) suggest that the final *-i* of 2SING *-ki* is derived from the feminine pronominal suffix, which is always *-ki* in WSA. However, feminine 2SING is highly marked. Moreover, it seems that the feminine 2SING suffix is not common at all in the Sudanese dialects. Therefore, I doubt that this is the source

---

[18] It is difficult to say at which stage *bi-* in Nubi/Juba Arabic *bita-* was lost. Considering the JA data where *bita-* co-occurs with *ta-*, one might suggest that the loss occurred at a rather recent stage. However, Kaye and Tosco (1993, 269–306) believe that *bi-* was reintroduced via recent decreolization rather than being a remnant of a previous stage. Concerning the loss of *bi-*, they suggest either the evolution *bi-* → **pi-* → **p-* → Ø, or the interpretation of *bi-* as a separate morpheme that had been deleted. Devoicing *bi-* into *pi-* seems to be a feature of present-day JA as well.

of the pronominal part of *(bi)taki* (or Turku *hanaki*). Probably, the
-i is just a paragogic vowel after *k-*. The pronominal suffix for 2PL is
invariably *-kum* in all three p/cs, which links the p/cs to eastern varieties of Arabic dialects rather than to WSA dialects, which generally
have *-ku*. The final nasal *-n* in 3PL suggests a general Sudanese source.
According to Owens (1985a, 229–71), stress on the last syllable in
Nubi PRON POSS 1SING *ta'yi* should be attributed to the influence
of certain WSA dialects. However, a similar stress pattern occurs in
some Egyptian Arabic dialects and in Kharṭûm Arabic as well (Behnstedt and Woidich 1985, vol. 2, Tosco and Owens 1993, 177–267).

7.4.2. *Nouns*

The tables 36 and 37 compare number formation of nous in the
Arabic p/cs and the Arabic dialects respectively.

Table 36. Number in Arabic p/cs

	UN	KN	JA	Turku
Internal (suppletion, ablaut)	Fossilized forms	Fossilized forms	Fossilized forms	Fossilized forms
Stress shift	Yes	Yes	No	?
Suffixation	-'in	-'in	-'in	-în
	-'a	-'a	-'at	
	-'iya			
	-'an	-'an		
		-ti		
		-z		
		-'ka[a]		
			-jin	
Prefixation	Bantu loans	Bantu loans	?	No
Mixed forms	Yes	Yes	Yes	Yes
Other means	Yes	Yes	Yes	Yes
Number agreement	Optional	Optional	Regular (not systematic)	Minimal

Sources: UN (own data), KN: Heine (1982), JA: Miller (1993, 137–74, 1994, 225–46),
Turku: Tosco and Owens (1993, 177–267).

a. About the only Nubi word that forms its plural in -'ka is *nyere'ku- nyereku-'ka* "children". However, I think that *nyereku'ka* is a more regular plural in -'a of the word
nyer'kuk "child", which occurs as such in JA.

Table 37. Number in Arabic dialects

	UDA	EA	KA	SA	Shuwa	AA[a]
Dual	No	Yes, but adjectives: plural	Yes, but adjectives: plural	Yes	Yes	Only fixed forms
Broken/ internal	Yes	Yes	Yes	Yes	Yes	Yes
Internal + -*ân*	?	Yes	Yes	Yes	Yes	Yes
Suffixation	-*în*	-*în*	-*în*	-*în*	-*în*	-*în*
	(-*ât*)	-*ât*	-*ât*	-*ât*	-*ât*	-*ât*
					-*ên*	-*ên*
					-*îya*	-*a*
Mixed forms	?	Yes	?	?	?	Yes
Other means	Yes		?	?	?	No
Number agreement	No?, optional?	Yes	Yes	Yes	Yes	Yes

Sources: UDA: Kaye and Tosco (1993, 269–306), EA: Fischer and Jastrow (1980), KA: Trimingham (1946), SA Hillelson (1930), Shuwa: Lethem (1926), Shukriyya Arabic: Reichmuth (1983), AA (Roth 1979).

a. The suffix -*în* is generally used for masculine nouns and -*ât* for feminine nouns. However, in Shuwa and in Abbéché Arabic, there is a tendency to mark masculine plurals with -*ât*. -*în* and -*ât* are the main means for marking the plural of masculine and feminine adjectives, respectively (beside a limited number of broken plurals). In Abbéché Arabic, however, -*în* is especially favoured for marking plural adjectives.

Whereas nouns in most pidgin/creole languages are not inflected for number (see Holm 1988), plural marking is optional in Arabic p/cs. Plural is often indicated by inference from the context, separate quantifiers, numerals, or plural demonstratives. Nubi differs in this respect from the Arabic dialects where number marking on the noun is compulsory as is number agreement. Consider also the Turku example in (954):

(954) *Chili rangaye lâm ouaïdinn ana pokteur anina.* "Take some pots of meat for our porters." (Muraz 1926, 276)
       Nass mardaninn ma-badoroum. "Sick people, we do not want them." (Muraz 1926, 291)

Arabic p/c nouns may receive number marking, but this is not a frequent feature. The Arabic p/c internal plurals (suppletion and ablaut) are generally frozen forms of Arabic plurals. The Nubi suffix -'*a* is to be traced to Arabic feminine plural -'*ât*, which lost its final consonant.[19] *-ât* takes the stress which accounts for the stress shift towards Nubi *-'a* as well (see also Owens 1985a, 229–71). Plural marking by means of a stress shift of Nubi nouns ending in other than *-a* may have originated by analogy with those in *-a*. Nubi plural forms by stress shift or by suffixation can be explained in part by Arabic source forms as the result of a productive process.

Table 38 opposes the Nubi fossilized plural forms to the Nubi innovative plurals.

Table 38. Fossilized forms vs. Nubi innovations of plural marking

	Fossilized forms	Nubi innovations
Stress shift	UN *la'bi* "slaves" < SA *al-ʿabîd*	*ju'a* "houses"
-'in	UN *aya'nin* "sick people" < SA *ʿaiyân*	*soko'lin* "things"
-'a	UN *ruta'na* < SA *ruṭânât* "languages"	*difa'na* "guests"
-'iya	UN *hara'miya* "thieves" < SA *ḥarâmîya*	*binadu'miya* "human beings"
-'an	*sab(i)'yan* "friends" < AA *subiyân*	*ke'lan* "dogs"
mixed	?	*kubari'na* "directors", "leaders"

Apparently, fossilized plurals are found in nouns that occur commonly or that refer to human beings. Other nouns, however, are subjected to rules of plural formation that operate independently but that are based on common Nubi plurals (frozen forms of Arabic plurals). These rules may be a feature of a creolization process.

The Nubi collective marker *'nas* is a reflex of the noun *nâs* "people". In Ugandan Nubi and in JA (see Miller 1993, 137–74), *'nas* is not restricted to human beings but may occur with all quantifiable nouns, whether human or non-human, e.g., *'nas 'dufur* "the nails". For Kenyan Nubi, however, Heine (1982) mentions that *nas* is limited to human beings. Shuwa Arabic seems to be the only other dialect where the collective word *nâs* occurs referring only to human beings. The development from a count noun to a pluralizer is attested in many Indian Ocean Creoles. For instance, French *bande* "bunch", "troop", "group" developed into the pluralizer *ban* (Mühlhäusler 1986).

---

[19] *mahlu'kati* "creature(s)" is probably the only noun in Nubi where the Arabic plural morpheme *-'at* is retained. In Juba Arabic, the most productive and most frequent means of plural marking is by suffixation of *-at*, including for nouns of non-Arabic origin, such as *nyer'kuk* "child"—*nyerku'kat* "children", *molodo* "hoe"—*molo'dat* "hoes".

7.4.3. *Modifiers*

7.4.3.1. *Articles and Demonstratives*

The tables 39 and 40 compare the articles and demonstratives in the Arabic p/cs and dialects respectively.

Table 39. Articles and demonstratives in the Arabic p/cs

	UN	KN	JA	Turku
INDEF	'wai	'wai	'wahid	(ouaïd)?
DEF	'de	'de	de, da	da
Zero-marking	Yes	Yes	Yes	Yes
DEM PROX SING	'de, ('u)we'de(ATTR), (u)'wede (PRED)	'de, 'we'de	de, da, di	da
DEM PROX PL	'dol'de	'dol'de	de, del	doll da
DEM DIS SING	'na'de	'na'de	de, dak	?
DEM DIS PL	'na'de, 'na 'dol'de	'na'de	del	?
N DEM or DEM N?	N DEM	N DEM	N DEM, but 'wahid N	N DEM

Sources: UN: own data, KN: Heine (1982), JA: Miller (1988–89, 23–58), Mahmud (1979), Tosco (1995, 423–59), Turku: Muraz (1926), Tosco and Owens (1993, 177–267).

Table 40. Definite article and demonstratives in the Arabic dialects

	UDA	EA	KA	SA	Shuwa	AA
INDEF	?	wâhid N	?	wâhid	N wâhid	N wâhid
DEF	el (al, ul, l)	al-, el-	al-, el-	al-, el-	al-, el-	al-, (da)
DEM PROX SING m	dei	dâ	da	dâ	dâ	da
DEM PROX SING f		dî	di	dî	dî	(di)
DEM PROX PL m	dôl	dôl	dêl	dôl, dêl	dôl(a)	dôl
DEM PROX PL f		/	/	/	dêl(a)	/
DEM DIS SING m	dak	dak(ha)	dâk ('dâka)	dâk	dâk(a)	dâk
DEM DIS SING f		dik(ha)	dîk	dîk	dîk(a), dîke	dîk
DEM DIS PL m	dâl	duk(hum) dak dôl	dê'lâk	dêlâk	dôlâk(a)	dôlak
DEM DIS PL f		dik dôl	/	dêka	dêlâk(a)	/
N DEM or DEM N	?	N DEM	N DEM	N DEM	N DEM	N DEM

Sources: UDA: Kaye and Tosco (1993, 269–306), EA: Behnstedt and Woidich (1985, vol. 2), Fischer (1959), KA: Worsley (1925), SA: Hillelson (1930), Shuwa: Lethem (1920), AA: Roth (1979).

The indefinite article in Nubi is homophonous with the numeral 'one', and is most likely derived from it. I found only one instance of indefinite marking in JA by means of 'wahid. 'wahid precedes the noun as in (955):

(955) *wáhid rájil*   gum túruju jemús   de, . . .
          one   man   *gum* chase buffalo DET . . .
          "A man set out to chase the buffalo,. . . ." (Tosco 1995, 440)

In general, however, no marking seems to be available in Juba Arabic
to express an indefinite, referential noun as in (956):

(956) fi   zól   nadi . . .
          EXIS   person call-PASS-Ø
          "There was someone who was called. . . ." (after Miller 1979–84, 31)

Several instances of *ouaïd* occur in Muraz's data on Turku. It is
unclear whether to interpret these as the numeral "one" or as the
indefinite article as in (957). The French translation is not of much
assistance since in French the numeral "one" and the indefinite article are also homophonous.

(957) *Amchi bî rass-saboun ouaïd.* "Go and buy a/one piece of soap." (Muraz
          1926, 267)
          Soultan djibou bed-guidad ma guidad ouaïd. "The sultan brings eggs
          and a/one chicken." (Muraz 1926, 271)

The development of an indefinite article from the numeral "one",
in Nubi is a feature found in languages worldwide (Givón 1984). A
similar development is also present in some Arabic dialects such as
Syrian Arabic (Fischer and Jastrow 1980). In the Chadian Arabic
variety, spoken by people with Maba roots, there is a tendency to
omit the definite article. To mark indefiniteness, *wâhid* is postposed
to the noun in order to distinguish it from the zero-marked definite
(Roth 1979). In Shuwa Arabic, too, *wâhid* following the noun may
function as an indefinite article (Lethem 1920).

The definite article in the Arabic p/cs is either *da* or *de*.[20] *Da/de*
derives from the EA/SA demonstrative. Muraz (1926) mentions that
the definite article is non-existent in Turku, which is contradicted
by the texts, where *da* is translated with a definite article or a demonstrative (proximal/distal?).[21] In JA, *de/da* functions as a definite article
and as a demonstrative. The development of demonstratives into
definite articles corresponds to the evolution in creole and other languages (see also Greenberg 1978, Harris 1980, Holm 1991). For Arabic,

---

[20] The phonological change from *da* to *de* may be related to similar changes in
other word categories, where *a* changed into *e* in the vicinity of alveolars.
[21] See also the discussion in Tosco and Owens (1993, 177–267).

this is attested in Abbéché Arabic (Roth 1979), Nigerian Arabic (Owens 1985a, 229–71), and in Palestinian and Syrian-Lebanese dialects (Fischer 1959). The form *da* has undergone a process of semantic bleaching with respect to its demonstrative meaning while at the same time another demonstrative system has emerged (see below). Unlike in Arabic dialects where the article precedes the noun, the p/c article follows the noun it determines, a feature that corresponds to other pidgins and creoles (see Holm 1988). The normal position of the EA/SA demonstrative is also after the noun.

While in most creole and other languages the definite article derives from a distal demonstrative (see Givón 1984, Bruyn 1995b, Holm 1991), in Nubi it derives from the proximal demonstrative *da*.[22] This feature is not restricted to Nubi. Similar observations were made for several Arabic dialects. Roth (1979) noticed in AA that the normal form in slow, careful speech is to have the noun, marked by the definite article *al-*, followed by the demonstrative *da*, but in spontaneous varieties of AA, the article *al-* is omitted, so that only *da* remains. The demonstrative meaning of *da* is weakened, which is why Roth considers it a substitute for the definite article. Owens (1985a, 229–71) observed a parallel development in Nigerian Arabic.

None of the Arabic p/cs has obligatory marking of the noun either for definite or for indefinite reference. In some varieties of Abbéché and Nigerian Arabic, too, the definite article may be omitted. In Arabic, it is common for 'indefiniteness' not to be marked by means of an article (except for some varieties of Chadian Arabic, which have N *wâhid*).

The UN demonstrative system is far more elaborate than that of the other Arabic p/cs. All Arabic p/cs and dialects are similar in that they distinguish between two categories of demonstratives, one proximal and one distal, which may be used attributively and predicatively. The central element of the Nubi (and Turku?) demonstrative is *da/de*. The UN proximal singular demonstrative consists of the personal pronoun 3SING + *'de*: *'uo 'de*. In creolized Nubi, *'uo 'de* has been reinterpreted as one form and underwent a minor phonological change (fronting of *o*). The distal demonstrative in Nubi is distinguished

---

[22] Harris (1980, in accordance with Greenberg 1977) assumes that it is the remote member within a demonstrative system that serves as the unmarked form and thus as the marker of definiteness. Givón (1984) claims that what is close to the speaker and thus removed from the hearer is probably less well known to the hearer and should therefore be related to 'indefiniteness'. Conversely, what is far from the speaker and thus near to the hearer is better known to the hearer and thus 'definite'.

from the proximal demonstrative by the addition of the deictic particle *'na* 'there', expressing remoteness.[23] For Turku, there is no mention of a separate demonstrative expressing distance. It is, however, possible that *da* expressed both proximity and distance, leaving it to the hearer to understand from the context whether "near" or "far" was meant. Consider *fi yom da* "(since) that day" (Muraz 1926, 282) clearly referring to a day, (more or less) remote in the past.[24]

The plural demonstrative is *'dol'de* in Nubi and *doll da* in Turku. It is very likely that *'dol* lost its deictic force in Nubi and Turku and was reinterpreted as a mere marker of plurality. More evidence for this assumption can be inferred from the demonstratives *do'linde*, and *'na 'dol'de*. *Do'linde* consists of *'dol* + *'in* + *'de*. *'In* "here" is the deictic adverb denoting proximity, which is added to the proximal, plural demonstrative to assert its sense of nearness. *'Na 'dol'de*, consisting of *'na* "there" + *'dol'de*, is one of the allomorphs of the plural distal demonstrative. *'Dol* is added to the distal demonstrative, otherwise neutral with respect to number, to mark it for plurality. Roth (1979) recorded a similar development in AA. The plural demonstrative *dol* is occasionally followed by the element *da*. Likewise, in Nigerian Arabic, plural demonstratives are sometimes followed by the masculine singular form *da* (Owens 1993a). It is thus possible that an evolution, similar to the one in AA and in NA, is taking place in Nubi: *da*, whose function as a deictic marker has been established, became accepted as the demonstrative marker in the form *dol da* as well, while *dol* is reinterpreted as the marker for plurality (Roth 1979). The latter development is also attested in some creoles. Cape Verde Creole

---

[23] Nubi *'na'de*, which consists of the adverb *'na* "there" + demonstrative, has parallels in Afrikaans. Versteegh (1984, 109, n. 35) mentions "the generalized use of the Dutch demonstrative *die* as definite article in Afrikaans, where an extended form of this form, *hierdie* and *daardie*, is used as a new demonstrative." Dutch *hier* and *daar* means "here" and "there" respectively.

[24] In Nubi, two instances of forms with *da* occur: *'youm 'da* referring to a day in the past and *'ya'da* "be overthere". We find *al yaum da* "today" in the Shuwa dialect (Lethem 1920) and *al yôm da* "today" in Sudanese Arabic (Hillelson 1930). This implies that in these forms, *da*, which reflects proximity in Arabic colloquials, has been reinterpreted in Nubi to denote distance in space and/or time. At the same time, opposite forms developed in Nubi with *'de*, namely *you'min'de* "nowadays" and *'ya'de* "be here", respectively, which convey a sense of proximity. Tosco and Owens include *ine/ ine da* "here" among the Turku adverbs, where the marker *da* is related to an adverb expressing proximity (Tosco and Owens 1993, 177–267). On the other hand, *fi yom-da* "(since) that day" (Muraz 1926, 282) refers to a day in the past. The notions 'distance'-'proximity' have been blurred here.

Portuguese and Lesser Antillean Creole French use pluralizers that are derived from plural determiners of the source languages (Holm 1988).

Nubi and Turku show many similarities in their demonstrative system even if the data on latter are incomplete. The AA and NA demonstrative systems seem to have undergone parallel developments. The Juba Arabic demonstratives, on the other hand, correspond to those of Sudanese Arabic dialects, which is probably the result of decreolization.

7.4.3.2. *Adjectives*
Like Nubi, Turku, and JA express comparison with the adjective + *futu/min* (Tosco and Owens 1993, 177–267, Miller 1993, 137–74). The verb *futu* "pass" has been reanalysed as a marker of comparison. The use of the verb meaning "pass" in a serialized construction is a typical pidgin/creole feature (Sebba 1985, 155–33, Muysken and Veenstra 1995, 289–301). There is a similar expression in Nigerian and in Bagirmi Arabic (Tosco and Owens 1993, 177–267). Comparison through 'X (sur)passes Y, regarding quality Z' is restricted to Nubi, and does not occur in JA or Turku. A similar use of a verb meaning "surpass" is attested in Abbéché Arabic (Roth 1979) and in Nigerian Arabic (Owens 1993a). It occurs also in Bantu languages, in Swahili (Ashton 1947), and in some of the substrate languages (Spagnolo 1933 on Bari, Westermann 1912 on Shilluk).

7.4.3.3. *The Possessive Phrase*
In Turku, possessive phrases either consist of N *ana* N/PRON, e.g., *koura ana diamouss* "foot of the buffalo", *mâl-ana-akitt* "money of wedding", "dowry", and *sandouk anahou* "his box" (Muraz 1926) or of mere juxtaposition of the possessed item and the (pro)nominal possessor as in *mardann-noum* "sickness of sleeping", "sleeping sickness", and *pokteur anina* "our porters" (Muraz 1926). Only owner-possessed relationships are generally expressed by N *ana* N. Usually, other possessive relationships occur in a N-N form, although some of these sometimes occur with *ana*. Compare the pairs in (958):

(958) *ouarga ragab* "amulet for the neck" >< *ouarga ana hid* "amulet for the hand" (Muraz 1926, 165) *ako ana hia* "maternal uncle" >< *act hia* "maternal aunt" (Muraz 1926, 114–15)

Many of the N-N expressions may be treated as compounds, i.e. a combination of two nouns, whose meanings differ from the meanings of the two separate elements as in *ial chiadar* "children of the tree"

> "fruit", *bourma toumbak* "pot for tobacco" > "pipe" (Muraz 1926, 125, 147). According to Tosco and Owens (1993, 177–267), some compounds consist of a noun/adjective + (negative) existential marker *(ma)fi*, such as *tchitann fi* "possessed (by the devil)", *gassi mafi* "difficult NEG", "easy" (Muraz 1926, 84, 139). These forms occur, however, only in Muraz's lexical listing and not in the text data. In Nubi, the opposite is expressed by negating the whole sentence without marking the adjective itself. Strings of possessive phrases occur both in Nubi and in Turku, like the < Turku *nass mardann ana hillé anaki* "the sick people of your village" (Muraz 1926, 284). The position of Turku modifiers is not fixed. In the clauses in (959), the modifier refers to the first 'possessed' noun. The modifier in the first clause immediately follows the noun, while it comes in the final position in the second example.

(959) *aouïnn katir ana hillé* "many women of the village" (Muraz 1926, 282)
     Nassara ana France koulou "all the Christians/white people of France" (Muraz 1926, 294)

Muraz' data contain an occasional synthetic possessive, such as *zob el-oumar* "penis of the donkey" > "champignon" (Muraz 1926, 185), which may, however, be a fossilized form. For JA, Miller (1993, 137–74) only mentions that there are compounds alongside analytic constructions with *ta*.

In Kharṭûm Arabic, the synthetic *'iḍâfa* construction occurs along with the analytic Noun GEN Noun construction. The latter is the most frequent one in colloquial speech, although it cannot be applied to body parts and kinship terms (Trimingham 1946). In Shuwa Arabic, the basic possessive construction seems to be the *'iḍâfa* construction, although the analytic possessive does occur expressing, for example, the material from which something is made. Compound nouns, often with *abu* "father", *umm* "mother", *sîd* "master", or *ṣâḥib* "owner" (see also below), are very frequent; these are treated as one word (Lethem 1920). In Abbéché Arabic, the synthetic genitive is limited to the written language, while in the spoken language there is a tendency to use the analytic construction (Roth 1979). Thus, in most Arabic dialects, the synthetic and the analytic construction co-occur. It seems that there are pragmatic arguments for their use, namely their distribution in written and spoken language, respectively, or their distribution among literate versus illiterate speakers. Moreover, Versteegh (1984, 94) postulates on the basis of a survey conducted by Harning (1980), that:

wherever the analytical and the synthetic genitives are competing constructions, the analytical genitive tends to be used for concrete possession, or for qualifications (contents, material, etc), whereas the synthetic genitive is always used—even in those dialects where the analytical genitive was highly successful—for the expression of abstract relations, such as periods of time, intimate relations of kinship, partitive relations, and for parts of the body.

Although the distributional pattern is not entirely the same in Nubi, there are some striking similarities, such as the use of the analytic construction in both native Arabic and Nubi/Turku for concrete possession and qualification, while kinship terms, part-whole relations, and body parts are expressed by a non-analytic construction, namely by the synthetic genitive in Arabic and by juxtaposition in Nubi and Turku. The semantic distinction between alienable and inalienable possession is a very common one worldwide and results in different formal strategies (Croft 1990), alienable possession including at least ownership of worldly goods while inalienable possession involves kinship terms, body parts, etc. (Payne 1997).

7.4.3.4. *Numerals*

The Nubi numeral system is a decimal one. The cardinal numerals 1–10, the tens, 100, and 1,000 are fossilized Arabic forms, as they are in Turku and in Juba Arabic, with the exception of Nubi *'lak* "hundred thousand", which is a Swahili loan. The order in the numerals above ten in Turku differs from the JA/Nubi order (see table 41):

Table 41. Numeral formation in Turku and JA/Nubi

Turku (Muraz 1926)		JA/Nubi	
achara ouaï	"11" (10 + 1)	*i'dashar*	"11" (1 + 10)
achara tinenn	"12" (10 + 2)	*it'nashar*	"12" (2 + 10)
issirinn ouaïd	"21" (20 + 1)	*'waid ishi'rin*	"21" (1 + 20)
mihia kamza	"500" (100, 5 times)	*'kamsa 'mia*	"500" (5 times 100)
?		*'elf ta'lata*	"3,000" (1,000 times 3)
N NUM		N NUM	
Plural marking on N:	Rare	Plural marking on N:	Optional

The JA/Nubi (no data for Turku) thousands are expressed *'elf ta'lata* "3,000", etc.

Table 42 lists the numerals in the Arabic dialects.

Table 42. Numerals in Arabic dialects

	KA	SA	Shuwa Arabic	AA
11	*ḥadā'shar* (1 + 10)	*iḥdâshar* (1 + 10)	*'ashara wâḥid* (10 + 1)	*(w)adâsher* (1 + 10) (also *ashara wâḥid*)
12	*itnā'shar* (2 + 10)	*itnâshar* (2 + 10)	*'ashara tanîn* (10 + 2)	*atnâsher* (2 + 10) (also *ashara tinên*)
21	*wâḥid wa 'ashrîn* (1 + 20)	*wâḥid u 'ishrîn* (1 + 20)	*'ashrin wa wâḥid* (20 + 1) / *wâḥid wa 'ashrin* (1 + 20)	*wâḥid u ishirîn* (1+ 20) (also *ishirîn (u) wâḥid*)
500	*khamsa miya* (5 times 100)	*khumsumîya* (5 times 100)	*khams mi'ât* (5 times 100)	*khumsumîye* (5 times 100)
3,000	*talat alâf* (3 times 1,000)	*telâta alâf* (3 times 1,000)	*talâtat alâf* (3 times 1,000)	*talâte alâf* (3 times 1,000)
Order	NUM N		N NUM (NUM N)	N NUM or NUM N
Plural marking?	Plural marking on N from 1–10		Plural marking on N	Optional plural marking on N

Sources: Roth (1979), Worsley (1925), Lethem (1920), Hillelson (1930).

The Turku system resembles the one in Shuwa Arabic (Lethem 1920). However, it is unique in counting the hundreds. We find correspondences in the neighbouring languages, Sara-madyinngaye and Saram'baye, described by Muraz, except that the two Sara languages use a particle to bind the unit and the ten whereas Turku does not. The JA/Nubi system corresponds to the Sudanese Arabic, except for thousands, which in Arabic are expressed as 'x times thousand'. The Nubi and Turku numerals follow the noun they modify (Muraz 1926), unlike KA, where the numeral precedes the head noun (Worsley 1925). In Shuwa and Abbéché Arabic, both orders co-occur (Lethem 1920, Roth 1979). In KA, the numerals 3–10 yield plural head nouns while from eleven onwards the noun is singular (Trimingham 1946). In Shuwa Arabic, the noun is generally marked for plural (Lethem 1920), and in Abbéché Arabic there seems to be a tendency to weaken the rules on number agreement (see Roth 1979). In Nubi, nouns sometimes take plural markers, but the numeral itself is a common device for marking plurality in Nubi.

The Turku ordinal numerals are homophonous with the cardinal numerals and behave like adjectives (Muraz 1926). Nubi uses an analytic construction with *ta* uniting the head noun and the numeral, such as *nyere'ku ta ti'nen* "the second child", except for *aw'lan* "first", which is a fossilized form of Arabic. The Arabic ordinals 1–10 undergo internal morphological changes and follow the head noun immediately. In Shuwa and Abbéché Arabic, the ordinal numerals from eleven onwards consist of the cardinal numeral preceded by the article (Lethem 1920, Roth 1979). The Arabic p/c-features of N-Num order and the formation of the ordinal numerals are present in at least the Shuwa and AA dialects, which suggests either direct influence or parallel processes.

7.4.4. *Conclusion*

In table 43 the NP features unique to Arabic p/cs are singled out.

Table 43. Features common to p/cs + certain Arabic dialects and features unique to p/cs in NP

Features common to (some) Arabic dialects and p/cs	Features unique to Arabic p/cs
	Pronouns: no gender and number distinction Subject/object pronouns: no distinction Distinguished from pronominal possessors (fossilized forms of Arabic genitive exponent + suffix pronoun) Subject and object, when expressed pronominally: independent pronouns PRON POSS 2SING in -*ki*: *ta-ki* (Nubi), *(bi)ta-ki* (JA), *ana-ki* (Turku)
PRON POSS 2PL: -*kum* in eastern SA KA, EA)	PRON 2PL: in -*kum*: *itokum, itakum, intokum, inntoukoum*
PRON 3PL: *humman* (Upper Egypt)	PRON POSS 2PL: *ta-kum* (Nubi), *(bi)ta-kum* (JA), *ana-koum* (Turku) PRON (POSS) 3PL in final -*n* Loss of dual, however (limited) plural marking Only fossilized forms of broken plurals Other means of number marking: context, adverbs Optional/minimal number agreement Number marking through stress shift (UN)
Collectivity marked by *nas* (WSA)	Collectivity marked by *nas* (Nubi, JA) Three-way division of articles: DEF: definite, pragmatically Referential NPs; INDEF: indefinite, pragmatically referential NPs; Ø-marking: non-referential NPs

Table 43 (*cont.*)

Features common to (some) Arabic dialects and p/cs	Features unique to Arabic p/cs[a]
Demonstrative *da* used as definite article, beside *el* (AA, NA)	Definite article: *de/da* < Arabic demonstrative
DEM PROX: least marked form (AA, EA)	DEF *de/da* < Arabic DEM PROX
	Order: N + DEF (>< Arabic DEF + N)
Numeral *wâḥid*: used as indefinite article in some dialects (Shuwa/AA: N *wâḥid*)	Indefinite article: *wai, wahid* (Nubi, JA) from numeral "one"
Indefinite marking: optional	Indefinite marking: not compulsory Definite marking: not compulsory Core part of demonstrative: *de/da* (Nubi, Turku)
AA DEM PROX: PRON + *da* Reinterpretation of Arabic PL DEM *dol* as plural marker: in AA, (and NA?) (Nubi, Turku)	Nubi DEM PROX: PRON + *'de*
	Addition of adverbs "here", "there"
Comparison: ADJ + *fuut* + complement: NA, Bagirmi Comparison: ADJ + *min* + complement: KA, AA, NA Comparison: X surpasses Y in quality Z: in AA, NA, Shuwa comparative/superlative	Comparison: ADJ + *futu* + complement (*futu* < verb with meaning "pass") Comparison: ADJ + *min* Comparison: X surpasses Y in quality Z (UN)
Possession: replacement of synthetic by analytic constructions Analytic possessive constructions: concrete possession, qualifications Synthetic constructions: kin terms, part-whole relations	Possession: analytic constructions and juxtaposition Analytic possessive constructions: concrete possession, qualification Juxtaposition: kin terms, part-whole relations
	Numerals: thousands: *'elf ta'lata* (Nubi, JA)
Word order: NUM N/ N NUM (Shuwa, AA)	Word order: N NUM (Nubi, JA, Turku)
	Numeral functions as plural marker

a. See also Tosco and Owens (1993, 177–267).

In the above table, features unique to Nubi, JA, and Turku are contrasted with those that result from developments in both the Arabic dialects and the p/cs. Parallel developments occurred in all the possible source dialects, in the eastern dialects (EA, KA), or in the dialects of Abbéché, Nigeria, and Shuwa (WSA).

Several developments seem to have been more firmly established in Nubi than in Turku. This may be because the only description of Turku dates from the beginning of the previous century, around 1926, while Nubi has gone through several stages since then. Morever, Muraz' data are limited. There are, however, some clear distinctions between Nubi and Turku, which are linked to influences from regional Arabic dialects (see table 44):[25]

Table 44. Nubi-Turku differences in NP

	Nubi	Turku
PRON 1PL	*'ina* (< EA/SA *ihna*)	*anina* (< WSA *anina*)
PRON 2SING/PL	*'ita* / *'itokum*	*innté*/ *inntoukoum*
DEM PROX	*'de*, *('u)we'de*, *(u)'wede*	*da*
GEN	*ta* (< EA/SA *bitâ'*/ *betâ'*)	*ana* (< SA/WSA *hanâ*)
NUM 11–99	*i'dashar*, *it'nashar* (cf. EA, SA)	*achara ouaï*, *achara tinenn* (cf. Shuwa, AA)
Ordinals	*ta* + NUM	Ordinals = cardinals, adjectives

7.5. *The Verb Phrase*

7.5.1. *The Nubi Verb Form*

Can Nubi and Turku basic verbs be linked to Arabic source forms? The following tables (45, 46, 47) bring together the basic forms of Ugandan Nubi and Turku verbs, their equivalents in Shuwa and Sudanese Arabic, the inflected Arabic source form, whether imperative, perfect, or imperfect, etc. I chose to refer to Shuwa verbs (and not to Sudanese Arabic) because of the explicitness of the material. However, I do not mean to imply that the Nubi and Turku verbs are derived from Shuwa source forms. According to Owens (1985a, 177–267), most of the Nubi verbs, approximately two thirds, are most likely derived from Arabic imperative forms. In SA, the imperative of regular and V-final verbs are formed with *a-* + verb stem, which explains verb initial *a-* in many Nubi verbs. Even if the imperative is not the simplest morphological form, it is likely to have been

---

[25] See also Owens (1996, 125–71).

used frequently in direct interpersonal contact, especially in a military context where a strict hierarchy reigns (see also Owens 1985a, 177–267). In table 45 I try to make a reconstruction of probable inputs for the Nubi verb based on the Shuwa and SA verb forms and on the form of the Nubi verb itself.

Table 45. Nubi/Turku verbs deriving from imperatives

Nubi	Turku	Shuwa Lethem (1920)	SA Hillelson (1930)	Imperative[a]	Translation
a.					
ʿadi	addou	ʿaḍḍ	ʿaḍḍ (u)	ʿuḍḍ-u, ʿaḍḍ-u	"bite"
ʿakulu	akoul	akal	akal (u)	akul-u	"eat"
ʿalasu	alass/ alssou	laḥas, liḥis	liḥis (a)	alḥas-u	"lick"
ʿaskutu	asskoutt	sakat	/	askut	"be quiet"
ʿasuru	asserou	ʿaṣar	ʿaṣ(s)ar	aʿasur-u	"massage"
b.					
ʿmofuku	amfoukou	nafakh	nafakh (u)	anfukh-u	"blow up"
ʿrobutu	arbottou	rabaṭ	rabaṭ (u)	arbuṭ-u	"tie"
ʿtala	atala	ṭalaʿ (a)	ṭalaʿ (a)	aṭlaʿ-Ø	"ascend"
ʿdofunu	dafounou, dafana	dafan	dafan (i)	adfin-u, adfun-u u	"bury"
ʿdofuru	/	ḍafar	ḍafar	adfur-u	"plait", "weave"
ʿgelebu, ʿgilibu, ʿgelibu (Old UN: ʿagilibu)	/	ḡalab	ḡalab (i)	aḡlib-u	"win", "defeat"
ʿakitibu, ʿkatifu	aktoubou, kétéfou	katab	katab (u)	aktub-u, (EA: aktib-u)	"write"
ʿlebisi, (KN: also albis)	/	libis, labas	labas (a)	albas, albis	"wear", "get dressed"
c.					
ʿlim(u)	loumou	lamm	lamm (i)	limm-u, lumm-u	"gather", "collect"
ʿdugu	dougou	dagg	dagg (u)	dugg-u	"hit"
ʿrudu	ridi	radd	radd (u)	rudd-u	"answer", "accept"
ʿmidu	/	madd	madd (i)	midd-u	"extend"
ʿsidu	siddi	sadd	sadd	sidd-u	"close"
ʿgum	goum	gâm	gâm (u)	gum	"get up"
ʿkutu	koutou	ḥaṭṭ	khaṭṭ, khatt (u)	ḥuṭṭ-u	"put"
ʿsulu, ʿshilu	silli, chilli, choulou	shâl	shâl (i)	shîl-u	"take"
ʿfutu	foutt	fât	fât (u)	fut(-u), fût(-u)	"pass"

Table 45 (*cont.*)

Nubi	Turku	Shuwa Lethem (1920)	SA Hillelson (1930)	Imperative[a]	Translation
'hum	houm	'âm	'âm (u)	'um/ 'ûm	"swim"
'zidu	zidi	zâd	zâd (i)	zîd-u	"increase"
d.					
'sten(u)	/	istanna (X)	istannâ (X)	istanna	"wait"
'kati	/		ḡatta (II)	ḡatti-(hi)	"cover"
'alimu	alloumou	'allam (II)	'allam (II)	'allim-u	"teach", "show"
'badul(u)	badelou, badilou, bodolou, badolou	baddal	baddal (II)	baddil-u	"change"
'awunu	aounou	'awwan (II)	'âwan (III)	'awwin-u, 'âwin-u	"help", "assist"
'so	sao, so	sawwa (II)	sau	sow-u	"do"

a. Lethem (1920) claims that the vowel after the second consonant in the Shuwa imperfect and/or imperative is either *a, i, e,* or *u*. Except for some verbs where the vowel is fixed, the speaker is free to choose. Hillelson (1930), however, generally lists the imperfect vowel together with the verb.

Remarks:

* The final vowel -*u* which is added will be discussed below.
* In Turku and/or Nubi, we find verbs without the initial *a-*. It is, however, possible that these verbs too were derived from Arabic imperatives. The CV sequence may be attributed to processes of vowel epenthesis and subsequent deletion of a stressed syllable. For the Nubi verb *'kunusu* "sweep", we also find the form *'akunusu* "sweep" with the stress on initial *'a-*, as is the case in the SA source form *'aknus-u*. It is likely that an epenthetic vowel *u* was inserted between *k* and *n* to arrive at the Nubi CV-structure. Subsequently, the initial stressed syllable *'a-* may have been dropped. If we consider an imperative form to be the source form of Nubi verbs, this could explain the vowel sequences *o-u-u*, or *u-u-u* in several cases.[26] Consider also the forms in (960):

---

[26] Pasch and Thelwall (1987, 91–165) also suggested a derivation of CVCVC-V verbs from Arabic imperatives, through metathesis of the first vowel/consonant. This is refuted by Tosco and Owens (1993, 258, n. 46), since vowel-consonant metathesis is not a common process in the area, neither in the Arabic dialects nor in the Arabic p/cs.

(960) UN *'dofuru* "weave" < *'adufuru/'adofuru* < SA *adfur-u* IMPER + OBJ
      SUFF "plait it"
      UN *'turuju* "chase" < *'aturuju* < SA *aṭrud-u* IMPER + OBJ SUFF
      "chase him!"
      UN *'mofuku* "blow" < *'amufuku/'amofuku* < *'amfuku* < SA *anfukh-u*
      IMPER + OBJ SUFF "blow it"

* The verbs in (c) are most likely reflexes of imperatives of Arabic
verbs where one of the consonants is the weak *y* or *w* or of verbs
with two identical consonants. These do not form their imperative
with the usual initial *a-*.

* As in (c), the source forms of the Nubi and Turku forms in (d)
do not have an imperative in *a-*. Regressive vowel assimilation is a
common phenomenon in Nubi/Turku: the vowel in the penultimate
syllable changes into a back vowel, influenced by the final back *-u*
as in Turku *alloumou* "teach" < SA *'allim-u*, Nubi/Turku *awunu/aounou*
"help" < SA *'awwin-u, 'âwin-u*.

The second most important group of source forms for the Nubi/
Turku verbs consists of Arabic perfects (see table 46):

Table 46. Nubi and Turku verbs derived from Arabic perfects

Nubi	Turku	Shuwa	SA	Perfect	Translation
'fadul	*fadal, fadel*	*faḍal*	*faḍal (a)*	*faḍal* (3SING)	"remain"
'negetu	*néguitt*	*najaḍ*	*nijiḍ (a)*	*nijiḍ* (3SING)	"get ripe"
'talagu	*tallak*	*ṭallag*	*ṭallag*	*ṭallag-û* (3PL)[27]	"divorce"
'waga	*ouaka, ouaga*	*waga'*	*waga'*	*waga'* (3SING)	"fall"
'waja	*ouodjia*	*waja'*	/	*waja'* (3SING)	"hurt"
/	*simitt*	*sami'*	*simi' (a)*	*sami't* (1SING)	"understand"
ni'situ	/	*nisi/nasi*	*nisa, nisi (a)*	*nisît* (1SING)	"forget"
/	*niss*	*nisi/nasi*	*nisa, nisi (a)*	*nisi, nisa* (3SING)	"forget"

Nubi and Turku verbs that derive from an Arabic imperfect are less
frequent:[28]

---

[27] That the third radical is voiced in the Nubi form suggests that the third radical in the Arabic source form did not occur in final position but was followed by
a vowel. Otherwise, it would be devoiced, as is the case in SA *nijiḍ* "it got ripe",
which developed into *'negetu* "get ripe" in Nubi.
[28] Tosco and Owens (1993, 177–267) link the p/c imperfect forms to WSA verb
sources, since, according to them, both lack the prefix *bi-, be-*, indicating especially
habituality but also futurity. However, imperfect forms are used either with or without this prefix both in the eastern and in the western Arabic dialects. Moreover,
Turku (western) contains many more *b-* forms than Nubi (eastern).

(961) UN *'nongusu* "reduce" < Shuwa *nanguṣ-hu* "we reduce it" IMPERF
         1PL + OBJ SUFF from *nagaṣ*   "reduce"
         UN *'telim* "dream" < Shuwa *taḥlim* "you dream" IMPERF 2SING
         MASC from *ḥilim* "dream"
         UN *'aba* "refuse" < Shuwa *âba* "I refuse" from *aba* "refuse"/ SA *âbâ*
         "I refuse" from *abâ* "refuse"
         UN *'agider* "be able" < Shuwa/SA *agdar* "I can" from *gadar* "be able"

(962) Turku *baba* "refuse" < Shuwa *be'âba* "I refuse" *b*-IMPERF 1SING
         from *aba* "refuse"
         Turku *bagdeur* "be able" < Shuwa *bagdar* "I can", "he can" *b*-IMPERF
         1/3SING from *gadar* "be able"
         Turku *bassman* "understand", "listen" < Shuwa *basma'an* "they (FEM)
         understand" *b*-IMPERF 3PL FEM from *sami'* "understand", "hear"
         Turku *batak* "laugh" < Shuwa *baḍḥak* "I laugh", "he laughs" *b*-IMPERF
         1/3SING from *ḍaḥik* "laugh"

A few Nubi and Turku verbs originate from Arabic participles as in
(963):

(963) UN *'mashi/* Turku *machi* "go", "walk" < SA *mâshî* "walking" PART
         ACT from *mashâ (i)* "walk"
         UN *'azu/'aju* < EA *âwiz-u* "wanting it" PART ACT + OBJ SUFF
         from *'az* "want"[29]
         UN *'arufu/* Turku *arfou* "know" < *ârif-u* "knowing it" PART ACT +
         OBJ SUFF from SA *'araf (i)* "know"
         Turku *zourtou* "swallow" (through regressive vowel assimilation) <
         Shuwa *zarit-u* "swallowing it" PART ACT + OBJ SUFF from
         zarat/zarad "swallow"

A few verbs probably derive from adjectives as in (964). These are
part of what I would call 'verbal adjectives' in Nubi. When in the
Ø form, they indicate a state, but when marked by the progressive
marker, they express inchoativeness:

(964) UN *za'lan/ja'lan* "be angry" < SA *za'lân* "angry" ADJ
         UN *hara'gan* "be sweating" < SA *'argân* "sweating" ADJ
         UN *ji'an/* Turku *diânn* "be hungry" < SA *ji'ân* "hungry" ADJ

There are only very few instances of Nubi verbs deriving from a
noun.[30]

---

[29] Turku has *doro* "want", "like", which is reminiscent of Sudanese Arabic *dâr*,
dawwar "want".
[30] Pasch and Thelwall (1987, 91–165) also include the verbs *doluka* "dance",
"drum", *huri* "be civilized", and *hara'gan* "sweat" among the verbs to derive from
nouns. The two first verbs do not occur in Ugandan Nubi, whereas for *hara'gan*,
there is an adjectival equivalent *'argân* "sweating" in Sudanese Arabic.

(965) UN *'tomburu* "do the man's part at the dolûka-dance" < SA *ṭambûr*
      "vocal accompaniment to dance", "long-necked stringed instru-
      ment", "drum" (Turku: *sao tambour* "do a military exercise")
      UN *'saba* "become morning" in *'lata 'saba/ 'lata gi-'saba* "it is morn-
      ing" < UN *sa'ba* "tomorrow" cf. SA *el-waṭa aṣbaḥat* "it is morning"
      (Hillelson 1930, 195)
      UN *'rutan* "speak" < SA *ru'ṭana* "foreign language"/UN *ru'tan* "lan-
      guage"[31]
      UN *'isabu* "count" < SA *ḥisâb* "calculation"/UN *i'sab*

P/c verbal allomorphs may have more than one grammatical source
form as in (966) and (967):

(966) Turku *apki/ tapki* "cry", "weep":
      apki < Shuwa *abki* "cry!" IMPER SING from *baka* "cry"
      tapki < Shuwa *tabki* "you cry IMPERF 2SING MASC/FEM", or
      "she cries" IMPERF 3SING FEM from *baka* "cry"
(967) UN *'wegif(u)/ 'yegif(u)/ 'agif(u)* "stop s.th.", "come to a halt":
      UN *'wegif(u)* < Shuwa/SA *wagaf* "he stopped" PERF 3SING from
      wagaf "stand", "stop"
      UN *'yegif(u)* < Shuwa *yagif* "he stops" IMPERF 3SING from *wagaf*
      "stand", "stop"
      UN *'agif(u)*/Turku *aguif* < Shuwa *agif* "stop!" IMPER from *wagaf*
      "stand", "stop"

The Nubi and Turku verbs in table 47, although derived from one
Arabic lexical form, have different grammatical source forms:

  Forms that probably derive from imperative source forms are fairly
frequent in Nubi,[32] in view of the many verbs beginning in *a-* (remnant of Sudanese Arabic imperatives) and the large number of verbs
whose vocalic pattern resembles that of the sound pattern of Arabic
imperatives. The question that yet needs to be tackled is why imperatives should serve as such an important input for the p/c forms.

---

[31] Owens (1985a, 229–71) states that *'rutan* "speak" originates from the noun *ru'-
tan* "language". Hillelson (1930) lists the verb *raṭan* "speak a foreign language". This
means that there is a verb with similar consonants and similar meaning, which at
first sight is a more likely and more direct source form of the Nubi verb *'rutan*. However, Owens is probably correct in deriving verbal *'rutan* from nominal *ru'tan* since
the sequence of the verbal vowels, if derived from the verb *raṭan*, would be *a-a* or
a-u, and not *u-a*. The latter vowel sequence directly leads to the SA/Nubi noun
ru'tan "(foreign) language". For similar reasons, Nubi *i'sabu* "count" is probably
derived from Nubi *i'sab*/SA *ḥisâb* "calculation" and not from the verb *ḥasab (a)* "count".
[32] Owens (1985a, 177–267) assumes that about two thirds of Kenyan Nubi verbs
are derived from imperatives.

Table 47. UN and Turku verbs derived from different source forms

UN	Grammatical source form	vs.	Turku	Grammatical source form	From Shuwa/SA	Translation
ʻaba	IMPERF 1SING	vs.	baba	b-IMPERF	aba, abâ	"refuse"
ʻashrubu	IMPER	vs.	cherbou	PERF	sharab	"drink", "smoke"
ʻasma	IMPER	vs.	simitt	PERF	samiʿ	"understand", "hear"
ʻataku	IMPER	vs.	batak	b-IMPERF	ḍaḥik	"laugh"
ʻagider	IMPERF 1SING	vs.	bagdeur	b-IMPERF	gadar	"be able"
ʻtelim	IMPERF 2SING	vs.	hilim	PERF 3SING	ḥilim	"dream"
niʻsitu	PERF 1SING	vs.	niss	PERF 3SING	nisi	"forget"
liʻgo	PERF 3PL	vs.	légui	PERF 3SING	ligi	"get", "obtain", "find"
weʻri	IMPER	vs.	ouorou	PERF 3SING	warra	"show", "explain"
ʻja	PERF 3SING	vs.	bedji	b-IMPERF	jâʼ	"come", "become"

On the one hand, the input of the native speaker of the source language is relevant. He adjusts his speech level to the assumed level of the non-native speaker so as to make himself comprehensible resulting in so-called 'foreigner talk'. One feature of importance in the present discussion is the reduction of inflections, which is compensated for by the retention of one or two 'all-purpose' forms (Ferguson and DeBose 1977, 99–128). The communities in the military and trade camps were hierarchic ones in which the use of imperatives must have been frequent. Moreover, in foreigner-talk registers, the personal pronoun "you" often co-occurs with the imperative (Ferguson and DeBose 1977, 99–128), which facilitates the analysis of the form as an inflected verb. Besides, the non-native speaker only acquires those forms that are characterized by saliency and frequency of utterance. Presumably commands, and therefore imperative forms, were common in the interaction between the native Arabic speaking officers and the non-native Arabic speaking subordinates, thus fulfilling the requirements of saliency, namely frequency and stress.

According to Owens, the final vowel *-u*, which is found with approximately half of the Nubi verbs, is derived in most cases from the Arabic suffix for the masculine plural, which is used in the perfect and in the plural imperative, e.g., *katabû* "they wrote" and *uktubû* "write(PL)", respectively. Final *-u* does not seem to follow the com-

mon vowel harmony rule in Nubi according to which front and back
vowels normally do not co-occur within morpheme boundaries (see
2.2.2.1). This implies that historically *-u* occurred across the morpheme
boundaries of verbs and, therefore, that it has morphemic status
instead of just being a paragogic vowel, such as *'seregu* "steal" (Owens
1985a, 229–71). But why should the Nubi verb be derived from a
masculine plural imperative and not from any other form? In Owens'
opinion (1985a, 229–71), the non-native speaker of Arabic chooses
from among the forms he hears and extracts the one which fits best
his internal grammar of the language. Nubi obviously tends towards
a CV structure. The Arabic masculine plural and the feminine singular imperative forms conform to this pattern. Since the latter is
highly marked, predictably, the masculine plural imperative remains.

Versteegh (1984) and Pasch and Thelwall (1987, 91–165), like
Owens, try to find a system in the occurrence or non-occurrence of
-u with verbs and go back to the origin of the verb stem. As mentioned above, the most important group of Arabic verb forms from
which Nubi verbs are derived are imperatives. Unlike Owens, Versteegh
and Pasch and Thelwall regard singular imperatives as the most
likely source form. Versteegh (1984, 124) speculates that:

> In Nubi the suffix *-u* could be derived from the personal pronoun
> suffix of the 3rd ps masculine singular which in most dialects becomes
> *-u* after consonants and Ø after *a*. In accordance with the last rule we
> find in Nubi transitive verbs such as *'gata* "to cut", *'agara* "to read"
> without the *-u*.

By analogy with the suffix *-im* in Tok Pisin, *-u* is treated as a transitive marker and is thus linked to the inherent lexical transitivity of
the verb. Versteegh (1984) cites the existence of inherently intransitive verbs like *'num* "sleep" and *'gum* "get up" that lack the final *-u*
or any other vowel, as additional support. I agree with Versteegh
and Pasch and Thelwall in regarding the Nubi verbs as derivatives
of singular imperatives with or without an object suffix.[33] Native
speakers choose one or two multi-purpose forms in foreigner-talk

---

[33] The object suffixes 3SING are *-hu* after V, *-u* after C in Kharṭûm Arabic
(Trimingham 1946), *-hu* after V, *-u* after C in Shuwa Arabic (Lethem 1920), final
vowel length, attracting stress after *-V* in Sudanese Arabic (Owens 1985a, 229–71),
-u or *-a* after C and Ø after a vowel in Egyptian Arabic (Behnstedt and Woidich
1985, vol. 2, Khalafallah 1969).

registers to compensate for the loss of inflections. Evidently, imperatives are one of these. It is difficult to believe that speakers of a foreigner-talk register, aiming at paradigmatic analogy, would use singular and plural forms as co-existing forms. Still, this is what Owens posits when he regards -*u* final verbs as the remnants of plural imperatives while forms ending in a consonant or another vowel have other sources. Consider the verbs in (968):

(968) UN *'agara* "read", "study", "recite" < SA *agra* "read!" IMPER SING
       from SA *gara* "read"
       UN/Turku *'gata* "cut" < SA *agṭaʿ(-ah)* "cut it" IMPER SING (+ OBJ
       SUFF) or *gaṭaʿ-ah* "he cut (it)" PERF 3SING (+ OBJ SUFF) from
       gaṭaʿ "cut"
       UN *'gum* "wake up", "get up" < SA *gûm* "rise!" IMPER SING from
       gâm "rise"
       UN *'num* "sleep" < SA *nûm* "sleep!" IMPER SING from *nâm* "sleep"

The above SA verb forms, if plural imperative or perfect, would be *agrû* "read(PL)!", *agṭaʿû* "cut(PL)!" and *gaṭaʿô* "they cut", *gumû* "rise(PL)!", and *numû* "sleep(PL)!" respectively. There is no doubt that the Nubi verbs were not derived from these source forms. Apart from the more regular Nubi verbs with stress on the first syllable, some disyllabic verbs take the stress on the second or last syllable, which suggests that the stress fell on the final syllable in the input form. Owens explains these forms as imperative forms of Arabic derived verbs with an object suffix attached to it, which may pull the stress backwards (see Owens 1985a, 177–267) as in (969):

(969) UN *we'ri* "show" < SA *warr-î* "show it!" IMPER + OBJ SUFF from
       warra (II) "show"[34]
       UN *na'di*/Turku *nadi* "call" < SA *nâd-î* "call him" IMPER + OBJ
       SUFF from *nâda* (III) "call"

If we assume that final -*u* is a remnant of plural imperative forms, these verbs are exceptions to a more general system of p/c verb derivation of plural imperatives. But if we accept that -*u* originates

---

[34] According to Hillelson (1930), however, verbs with geminated middle consonant insert *â* before the pronominal suffixes in PERF 3SING, e.g. *daggâho* "he beat him". PERF 3SING + OBJ SUFF for *warra* "show" would then be *warrâho* "he showed him", which can be the source form of Turku *woru*, but not of Nubi *we'ri*. This certainly argues in favour of Egyptian Arabic influences on Nubi.

from an object suffix, the above verbs are regular examples.[35] The masculine object suffix *-u* may also explain the final *-u* in forms derived from active participles as in UN *'arufu/*Turku *arfou* "know", UN *'azu, 'aju* "want", Turku *zourtou* "swallow", and Turku *hartou* "cultivate", "clear with a hoe". The plural active participle would end in *-în*, which is not attested in the p/c verb forms. Moreover, with plural perfect forms, another problem is encountered. In WSA dialects, such as Shuwa, the suffix is *-ô* and not *-û*. Owens (1985a, 229–71) tackles the problem himself by assuming that, in spite of a Western Sudanese Arabic origin of the Arabic p/cs, there was Egyptian and Kharṭûm Arabic interference with respect to the perfect plural endings, or alternatively that, by aiming at analogous forms, only *-u* forms were yielded instead of co-occurring *-o* and *-u* forms since the imperative *-u* forms were the most frequent ones.

Pasch and Thelwall (1987, 91–165) deal with the problem of counterexamples in Kenyan Nubi, namely either intransitive verbs with the *-u* ending or transitive verbs lacking final *-u*. With respect to the first type of verbs, they suggest that in some of these cases the plural imperative is, after all, the most likely source form of the Nubi verb as in (970):

(970) *'askutu* "be quiet" < *(sakat/yaskut) askut-u* "be(pl) quiet!" (Pasch and Thelwall 1987, 154)

I would suggest, however, that this verb was derived from a singular imperative, after which a paragogic vowel *-u* was attached to avoid a final plosive alveolar, which is virtually non-existent in Nubi (see 2.1.3). Conversely, Pasch and Thelwall suggest that some Nubi transitive verbs occur mainly without *-u* because they were intransitive at an earlier stage or because, according to them, it is unlikely that the Arabic transitive verb was used with an object pronoun. They analyse these verbs as being derived from singular imperative forms that were not followed by the object pronoun and argue that

---

[35] An exception is the Nubi verb *li'go* "find", "meet" which probably derives from a plural perfect + object suffix. The Turku verb *leggui*, on the other hand, may originate from a singular perfect form:
Nubi *li'go* "find" <Shuwa *ligô(-hu)* "they obtained (it)" PERF 3PL + OBJ SUFF from *ligi* "obtain", "get"
Turku *leggui* "meet", "find" < Shuwa *ligi-(hi)* "he obtained (it)" PERF 3SING + OBJ SUFF from *ligi* "obtain"

this is the reason why the resulting verb in Nubi does not have final
-*u* as in (971):

(971) KN *'rasul* "arrive", "send" < SA *rassil* "send!" IMPER from *rassal* (II)
"send"
KN *'awun* "help" < SA *'âwin* "help!" IMPER from *'âwan* (III) "help"
(after Pasch and Thelwall 1987, 154–155)

Pasch and Thelwall use Heine's data, which are insufficient to draw
proper conclusions. *'rasulu* and *'awunu* with final -*u* occur frequently
in Ugandan Nubi with the meanings "send" and "help", respectively.
Moreover, there is no reason why *rassal* "send" and *'âwan* (III) "help"
should occur in native Arabic speech without an object suffix. I
assume that not all verb forms (either with or without final -*u*) should
be treated as deriving from the source directly but that some verbs
are the result of a productive process within the language. There
are cases of Nubi verbs (from an intransitive verb in the lexifier language) with an individuated object which take -*u*. Consider, for
instance (972) with the transitive verb *'wonusu* "tell s.th.". To my
knowledge, no Arabic dialect has a transitive verb with this root.
Still, in Nubi, both a transitive and an intransitive verb occur, *'wonusu*
"tell s.th." and *'wonus* "talk", "converse", respectively.

(972) 'Ana   'gu-   rwa   *'wonusu*   *'ja.*
PRON 1SING   PROG-   go   tell-Ø   story
"I am going to tell a story."

In the Turku word list, there is an obvious correlation between
intransitive verbs and absence of final -*u* on the one hand, and transitive verbs and presence of final -*u* on the other hand. In table 48,
-*u* final verbs are contrasted with C-final verbs.[36] Verbs ending in
other vowels are not taken into consideration here.
   Consider also the pairs in (973), (974), (975), and (976):

(973) *delli* "come down" >< *dellou* "bring down"
Ana doro delli fi diouad fichann pont gohoui mafi. "I want to descend from
[my] horse because the bridge is not strong." (Muraz 1926, 131)
Dellou kommomm titt. "Make the convoi come down.", "Stop the convoi." (Muraz 1926, 270)

---

[36] See also the discussion in Tosco and Owens (1993, 177–267).

Table 48. Transitive *u*-final verbs and intransitive
C-final verbs in Turku

Transitive		Intransitive	
amfoukou	"blow up"	*batak*	"laugh"
asserou	"massage"	*hilim*	"dream"
arbottou	"tie"	*houm*	"swim"
dougou	"hit"	*asscoutt*	"be quiet"
loumou	"collect"	*bagdeur*	"be able"
kétéfou	"write"	*goum*	"get up"
addou	"bite"	*noum*	"sleep"
cherbou	"drink"	*fadel, fadal*	"remain"
ouorou	"explain", "show"	*néguitt*	"get ripe"
arfou	"know"	*tallak*	"divorce"
dafounou	"bury"	*boul*	"urinate"
fartakou	"scatter"	*tir*	"fly"
alloumou	"teach"	*nik*	"make love"
aounou	"help"	*temtiemm*	"stammer"
koutou	"put"	*gahed*	"stay"
djibou	"bring"	*djom*	"take a rest"
foukou	"untie", "open"	*temeuss, tameuss*	"dive"
djourou	"pull"	*nafass*	"breath"
tér(é)bou	"plant"	*kor*	"cry", "scream"
fatéchou	"look for"	*gobel*	"come back"
choufou	"see"	*akout ma*	"marry with"
fartou	"vaccinate"	*gassar*	"lack"
dossou	"attack"	etc.	
badelou	"change"		
tourdou	"chase", "follow"		
gobolou	"bring back"		
toussou	"put"		
etc.			

(974) *chokoleb* "turn" >< *chokolbou* "turn s.th."
      Ri chokoleb.[37] "The wind has turned." (Muraz 1926, 275)
      Oro-lé pokteur-da chokolbou sandouk anahou "Tell (to) the porter to return
      his case." (Muraz 1926, 272)

(975) *gobel* "come back" >< *gobolou* "give back" (Muraz 1926, 140)
      . . . , *inntoukoum gobel fi dar anakoum.* "You(PL) will return to your(PL)
      country." (Muraz 1926, 293)

---

[37] Muraz (1926) mentions *chokolbou* as an alternative form.

Gobolou mâl-ana-akitt ana mara-da lé radjiéla ... "Return the dowry of that woman to [her] [ex-] husband. ..." (Muraz 1926, 288)

(976) *soub* "fall" >< *sobou* "pour"
Mattra soub "It rains" (Muraz 1926, 158)
Sobou almé "Pour water" (Muraz 1926, 176)

and the sentences in (977):

(977) *Pokteur anahi ouaïd mardann. Badelou* "One of my porters is ill. Change him." (Muraz 1926, 271)
Yaoda ourar anahou. Foukou è lamoussou. "Here are its faeces. Open *them* and touch *them*." (Muraz 1926, 274)
Gousou boundouk è dousou dihn katir. "Clean the weapons and put much grease." (Muraz 1926, 277)

In sentences as in (978), the verb (with no final *-u*) appears to take an object (noun phrase, no preposition). However, the phrase refers to the location where the action takes place, and may therefore be interpreted as an adverbial phrase, and the verbs as intransitive or reduced in transitivity.

(978) *Mata oumann bedji schreub bouta-da?* "When did they come to drink [from] the pool?" (Muraz 1926, 275)
Orini kann anina ouassal nouss dérib. "Tell me when we will have reached halfway." (Muraz 1926, 269)

Exceptions are the verbs in (979):

(979) transitive, no final *-u*:   *simitt* "understand", "hear"
                                           niss "forget"
                                           bassman "listen"
                                           akoul "eat"
                                           tar "circumcise"
                                           dafok, dafouk "pay"
intransitive, final *-u*:   *ballou* "get wet"
transitive/intransitive,
one form, no final *-u*:   *tamann* "cost", "evaluate"
transitive, both forms: *tellef, tellfou* "destroy"
                                             alass, alssou "lick"

and the sentences in (980) and (981):

(980) *Kan doktor fut ine, rujal kulu, awin kulu, yal dugag kulu, inte lumu gidam anahu.* "If the doctor passes here, all the men, all the women, all the small children, you will gather in front of him." (Muraz 1926, 289)

(981) *Sersas nasara ana compagnie anakum baktubu le nas anakum. . . .*"The white
       sergeants of your regiment will write to your people. . . ." (Muraz
       1926, 292)

There are also some transitive verbs with final *-i*. The Nubi equivalents have final *-u as in* (982):

(982) *siddi* "close" cf. UN *'sidu*
       zidi "increase" cf. UN *'zidu*
       ridi "like", "accept" cf. UN *'rudu*
       chiri "buy"

I have no explanation for these cases. If we take final *-i* to be the
result of progressive vowel assimilation, then these verbs are actually counterexamples for the transitivizing function of the vowel *-u*.
However, there are a few verbs that Muraz lists that end in *-i*,
whereas in the texts in a transitive context they end in *-i* or *-u*, which
implies that these forms are not fixed as in (983), (984), and (985):

(983) *leggui* "find", "meet"
       Anina leggui abou gueurn araï gahilé "We will find the rhino at around
       midday." (Muraz 1926, 279)
       . . . , inntoukoum leggou penchon kann sané achara kamza kalass. ". . ., you(PL)
       will get leave when the fifteen years are over" (Muraz 1926, 293)
(984) *nadi* "call"
       Nadi soultann "Call the sultan" (Muraz 1926, 270)
       Nadou kuznié "Call the cook" (Muraz 1926, 266)
(985) *shili* "take"
       *Koulioum yom achara kamza inntoukoum chili serfi. Kann tou choulou mandat
       ana silgui, . . .*
       "Every fifteen days you take [your] payment. If you take a mandate
       at the post . . ." (Muraz 1926, 292)

Roth discusses verb final *-a* in Abbéché Arabic, which she treats as
a possible remnant from the third person singular object pronoun
of Arabic. Although the contexts in which *-a* is used are rather
difficult to establish, Roth concludes that *-a* has been reanalysed as
a marker of transitivity and modality of the verb. As in Nubi *-u*,
-a seems to be conditioned both phonetically and syntactically.
Phonetically, *-a* is always found with CC final verbs, while with VC
verbs the use of *-a* seems to depend on other factors. Regarding the
perfect of VC verbs, Roth (1979, 65) says that:

> . . . -a ne peut s'adjoindre qu'aux verbes transitifs directs. Les verbes intransitifs l'excluent. *katab* et *kataba* "écrire"; *libis* et *libisa* "revêtir"; . . . , mais on ne relève que *lataf* "être aimable", *gidir* "pouvoir". . . . L'élement -a peut donc fonctionner comme un morphème indice de transitivité.

Thus, -a does not occur with intransitive verbs but it may occur with transitives. In the imperfect, the distribution pattern of -a is less transparent. When contrasting the '*présent général*' to the '*présent actualisé*', -a seems to mark the latter, although in combination with other elements. The use of -a seems to be determined also by the occurrence of the particle *le*, which is used to introduce an individuated direct object. "Il y a cumul de marques pour l'expression de la notion de procès actualisé, la présence de -a étant liée à l'usage de la particule *le* pour introduire le complément" (Roth 1979, 66). The distinctions between perfect and imperfect and between the '*présent général*' (non-punctual) and '*présent actualisé*' (punctual), and the importance of an individuated direct object in Abbéché Arabic can be related to the parameters that Hopper and Thompson (1980) introduce in their discussion of transitivity (see also 4.1).

In Juba Arabic, Miller recognizes a pattern in which -u marks verbal trisyllabic forms and Ø /-a nominal trisyllabic forms:

> A l'alternance vocalique interne de l'arabe se substitue donc une suffixation vocalique. Le suffixe -u n'est plus une marque de personne (3e pers. pluriel) comme dans la langue source mais une marque de catégorie (classe?) verbale, le suffixe -a n'est plus une marque de féminin ou de nom unité (par opposition au collectif, au nom d'espèce) mais une marque de catégorie (classe?) nominale. (Miller 199, 153–154)

According to Miller, this derivational process is productive in Juba Arabic. She refers to verbs derived from nouns/adjectives through the replacement of the final -a/ or Ø of the noun by -u as in (986):

(986) *se'tima* "insult (N)"   vs.   *'setimu* "insult (V)"
      'gisir "peel (N)"   vs.   *'gisiru* "peel (V)"
      ne'dif "clean (ADJ)"   vs.   *'nedifu* "clean (V)" (after Miller 1993, 153)

Miller mentions similar productive patterns in other creoles as in the French creoles of the Antilles and the Indian Ocean. If her analysis is correct, this development would differ from the one in Nubi. In the decreolizing urban variety of Juba Arabic -u has been lost in the verbal forms (Miller 1993, 137–74).

7.5.2. *TMA-marking*

7.5.2.1. *The Bare Verb Form*

In Nubi, the zero form of the verb may express all tenses and aspects if tense and aspect are marked otherwise in the text. About the unmarked form in pidgins/creoles, Holm (1988, 150) notes that "The simple form of the verb without any preverbal markers refers to whatever time is in focus, which is either clear from the context or specified at the beginning of the discourse." Nubi thus resembles other p/cs, at least for tense. In discussing Turku based on Muraz' description, Tosco and Owens (1993, 177–267) note that in many sentences no verbal suffixes or adverbial elements indicating either tense or aspect are used. Whether a verb refers to the past, present or future must be inferred from the context.

7.5.2.2. *The Progressive Marker gi-*

The progressive marker *gi-* is probably a JA and Nubi innovation since it is not attested in Sudanese Arabic dialects. Turku has *gaed/gahed*, which marks continuous or recurrent action as in several SA dialects (Tosco and Owens 1993, 177–267, Roth 1979, Worsley 1925, Trimingham 1946). Therefore, Nhial (1975), Mahmud (1979), Owens (1985a, 229–71) and Tosco (1995, 426–59) suggest that the active participle *gaed/gâ'id* is the source form of *ga/ge/gi*, through deletion of the last consonant. Kaye (in Kaye and Tosco 1993, 269–306), however, considers *ge* to be a remnant of the p/c verb *genib* "sit" (< *gannib* "sit down!" IMPER of SA *gannab* "sit down") via the intermediary stage of *'gen*. The *gâ'id*-source form seems, however, more likely, since parallels occur in the Sudan. *qâ'id*, *gâ'id* or *jâ'id* "sitting" may express an imperfective aspect in the Sudan (Fischer and Jastrow 1980), while in Shâygiyya Arabic in northern Sudan, the verbal prefix *ga'-* yields the same meaning (Reichmuth 1983). Moreover, final C deletion and monophtongization are common processes in the Arabic p/cs, while the loss of a full syllable is attested less frequently. The future/irrealis marker *bi-* may have influenced the vowel of *ga-/ge-* thus making it change into *gi-* in front of front vowels, and *gu-* in front of back vowels. Both *'gai* "sit" and *'gen* "sit" occur in current JA and Nubi, complementing the progressive marker *gi-*, to mark continuity. Holm (1988) links the fact that verbs with a semantic notion of position or location often express a progressive aspect to a language universal.

Similar to Nubi, the stative/non-stative distinction is found in JA

(Tosco 1995, 426–59). In Turku, it is not possible to assess the existence of a stative/non-stative distinction since the neutral zero form may express the past, present, and future tense, and both a punctual and non-punctual aspect. In the few instances with *gahed* V, however, the verb is non-stative (*beji* "come" and *jibu* "bring") as in (987):

(987) *Yaoda mattra gahed bedji.* "Here, the rain is on its way coming" (Muraz 1926, 270)
    Tchar al gahed bedji-da, ana machi rouk fi canton anaki. "The month which will be coming, I will go to your county" (Muraz 1926, 289)
    Fi inak bodjéni katir gahed djibou mardann- noum le nass. "Over there there are many tse-tse-flies,   which bring the sleeping sickness to the people" (Muraz 1926, 288)

Kaye and Tosco (1993, 269–306) note that the stative/non-stative distinction was probably productive in Ugandan Pidgin Arabic (see 1.2.2.2). A similar distinction is attested in Abbéché Arabic (Roth 1979). In Nubi, some stative verbs may be marked by the progressive marker *gi-* to indicate habituality, to indicate inchoativeness of stative verbs and verbal adjectives (for a similar phenomenon in Sranan Creole English and Haitian Creole French, see Holm 1988). Bickerton (1975) mentions thatn in Guyanese Creole, the progressive marker may be used with predicate adjectives, when a process is referred to, rather than a state. In JA as well, the progressive marker may occur with stative verbs, although according to Mahmud (1979) this is because the *gi-* marker is, more than anything else, the marker of duration, which is exactly the aspect conveyed in stative verbs. According to Tosco (1995, 426–59), however, stative verbs in JA conform to Bickerton's paradigm in that they convey present meaning when no marking appears. In Kenyan Nubi as in Ugandan Nubi, stative verbs may occur with the progressive marker *gi-* when denoting habitual meaning (see texts in Heine 1982).

7.5.2.3. *The Future Marker bi-*
In Egyptian Arabic, the prefix *bi-* marks duration (Mitchell and al-Hassan 1994), but in many SA dialects it marks future[38] and habituality

---

[38] Lethem is not clear about the reasons for the presence or absence of *b-* + imperfect in Shuwa Arabic. He notes, however, that "Some Shuwas distinguish this use of *b* as indicating immediate present, while the ordinary form indicates future. In general, however, no such distinction is observed." (Lethem 1920, 106) *b-* is especially common with 1SING, but uncommon with 1PL in Shuwa Arabic.

(Trimingham 1946, Worsley 1925, Reichmuth 1983), and it is in
this sense that it is used in JA and Nubi. In Jenkins' material on
Ugandan Pidgin Arabic, there is only one instance of *bi-* indicating
a non-past: *ma bidûru* "I don't like him" (Kaye and Tosco 1993,
280). In Turku, *bi-* marks futurity (Tosco and Owens 1993, 177–267).

Functions and meaning of *bi-* and *ge-* in JA have been discussed
extensively by Miller (1985–86, 155–66), Mahmud (1979), and Tosco
(1995, 423–59). According to Miller (1985–86), the verbal prefixes
bi- and *ge-* in Juba Arabic have different functions, when used in
the countryside or in town (Juba). In the countryside, the use of *bi-*
is that of futurity and iterativity/habituality. The use of *ge-* is restricted
to marking continuation. In the capital Juba, however, the function
of *ge-* has been expanded to that of iterativity, habituality, and the
generic, besides its common use as the progressive. In Juba, *bi-*
retained its function of marking futurity but has partly lost its function of marking the iterative and the generic. Miller (1985–86, 165)
concludes that:

> La relation entre Fbi et Fge s' est donc totalement modifiée. Il ne
> s'agit plus d'une opposition entre un inaccompli général (Fbi) et un
> progressif (Fge), mais d' une opposition entre un modal (Fbi) et un
> non modal (Fge).

Mahmud (1979), however, states that *ge/gi* has all conceivable functions,
including the perfective and imperfective, the progressive and habitual, and the future. Mahmud argues that *gi-* is the most basic JA
marker, and that it is *bi-* that gradually takes over the functions of
ge-/gi- in the acrolectal varieties of Juba Arabic, influenced by Khartûm
Arabic. Tosco (1995, 423–59) views the JA verbal system as a more
stable entity and claims that differences in the use of *ge/gi-* and *bi-*
are not sociolinguistically but semantically determined. *bi-* and *gi-*
normally express the future and non-punctuality respectively, while
they share the ability to mark habituality. *gi-*, however, denotes an
actual habitual while *bi-* expresses a more general and thus virtual
habitual. Considering the synchronic data on Nubi, namely the higher
frequency of *gi-* with habituals and the use of *gi-* and not *bi-* with
stative verbs for expressing habituality, I assume that there is a development in Nubi similar to the one in JA, as noted by Miller (1985–86),
in which *gi-* is partially taking over the functions of *bi-* (see 4.2.1.2).

7.5.2.4. *The Anterior Marker 'kan*

'Kan occurs in most Arabic dialects as an auxiliary indicating past tense. As in the Arabic dialects, Nubi *'kan* is both the past tense of the verb "be", while at the same time it is the auxiliary marking anteriority. The position of Nubi *'kan* in pre- or post- subject position could be a reflection of its position in SA dialects (see Owens 1991b). *'Kan* can be combined with the markers *gi-* to express a past progressive and with the marker *bi-* to express counterfactuality. In theory, it can co-occur with both markers *gi-* and *bi-* to express a non-punctual counterfactual. However, in practice, this combination rarely occurs. If it does, the order of markers is *'kan bi- gi-*, thus ANT FUT/IRR PROG, which conforms to the general pattern as posited by Bickerton (1977). In the Arabic dialects, too, *kân* precedes the other markers and/or auxiliaries. However, since *bi-* is always attached to the verb in Arabic dialects, *gâ'id* naturally precedes *bi-* as in (988):

(988) *kunta qâ'id barqûṣ* "I went on dancing" (Worsley 1925, 50)

Tosco and Owens (1993, 177–267) make no mention of an anterior marker in Turku. Anteriority is marked by means of adverbs. According to Jenkins, *'kan* was used in order to express continuous action in the past in Ugandan Pidgin Arabic (Kaye and Tosco 1993, 269–306).

The Nubi marker *'kan*, apart from marking anteriority, may be interpreted as a marker of modality (cf. above 4.2.1.3). While modal *'kan* followed by the simple verb rather seldom expresses counterfactuality and seems to be disappearing, the use of modal *'kan* + future marker *bi-* is increasing. Bickerton (1977) claims that the combination of anterior + irrealis referring to an unrealized condition in the past occurs in all creole languages. Nubi would thus tend towards a more 'normal' creole system. Owens (1991b, 1169–79) wonders whether the *'kan bi-* construction in Nubi should be ascribed to universal processes or to a source language influence. He argues that a similar construction, consisting of modal *kân* + (*bi-*) imperfect, occurs in some Sudanese Arabic dialects, namely Nigerian Arabic, Abbéché Arabic and possibly Shukriyya Arabic, in conditional and non-conditional contexts, conveying a rather diffuse meaning, including contingency, vagueness, and conditionality,[39] Comparing the Sudanese Arabic data with Nubi, he concludes that:

---

[39] A similar construction (anterior + irrealis) also occurs in Egyptian Arabic, e.g. *kân ḥayi'mil* "he was going to do" (see Versteegh 1984).

> The Nubi counterfactual, though not itself a conditional, has an inher-
> ent meaning of conditionality in it: "would have done x (if y had not
> happened)." It would thus not have been a large step for Nubi kan
> bi- to have developed the very precise meaning of "counterfactuality"
> out of a more general meaning of kan/kaan (bi-) "conditionality, vague-
> ness", etc. (Owens 1991b, 1177)

Whether or not influence of source languages or of universal processes
is assumed, the fact is that *'kan* plus the zero form of the verb may
convey contingency, vagueness, conditionality, and even counterfactuality in Nubi. Both forms *'kan* V and *'kan bi-* V were possibly introduced in Nubi from native Arabic. However, *'kan bi-* V tends to
survive, while *'kan* V is on the verge of disappearing. *'Kan* V is far less
frequent than *'kan bi-* V in expressing counterfactuality, and its users
are mainly old people and people from the northern part of Uganda,
which implies that the construction is not being transmitted from
older to younger people or from the north to the south. Tosco (1995,
423–59) does not mention the modal function of *'kan* for JA. He
argues that the two functions of the *'kan bi-* combination, namely the
future perfective and the counterfactual, are to be explained by the
double function of *bi-*, which expresses both the future and irrealis.

In Nubi, both temporal and modal *'kan* may follow the main verb.
Roth (1979) mentions a few examples of conditional clauses in
Abbéché Arabic where the protasis is introduced by conditional *kân*.
A particle *kân* is repeated in the apodosis in pre- or postverbal position. This particle probably marks the past or the irrealis. Roth
ascribes the construction in which the particle *kân* follows the main
verb to poor knowledge of Arabic.

7.5.2.5. *The Auxiliary 'gurwa + V*
Nubi is far from unique in deriving an auxiliary marking future from
a free verb meaning "go" or "come". It shares this feature with many
languages worldwide, including many pidgin and creole languages
(Payne 1997, Bickerton 1981), and, at least for the verb "go", with
several Arabic dialects. Roth (1979) mentions for Abbéché Arabic
the verbal combination *mâša* "go", "walk" + perfective/imperfective,
which is used to refer to an immediate future but describes it as a
serial verb (semi-auxiliaire). She also discusses *dahâba* "go", which
denotes an action taking place in either a near future or a near past,
depending on the aspect of the verb it precedes. Reichmuth (1983)
gives one example of Shukriyya Arabic *maša* + participle without
further discussion: /imši nâgiṣ/ "er nimmt ab (Mond)". In Egyptian

Arabic, verbs of motion may indicate the same meaning, for instance, the active participle *râyih* "going", which has been grammaticalized into the marker *ha-* via *rah-*, indicating proximate intention (Mitchell and al-Hassan 1994).

In the town variety of JA, *ge+ ruwa* V expresses an imminent future, alternating with *bi-V* (Miller 1985–86, 155–66), while *gi- 'ja* V expresses an uncertain future (Tosco 1995, 423–59). Mahmud (1979) deals with the use of *masha* "go" as a tense/aspect marker in JA but is not clear as to its exact use.

7.5.2.6. *The Imperative*

The Nubi imperative whose form is identical to the zero form has parallels in Ugandan Pidgin Arabic (Kaye and Tosco 1993, 269–306) and in Turku (Tosco and Owens 1993, 177–267). This resembles imperative formation in languages worldwide (Boretzky 1983). It differs, however, from the SA imperative, which is inflected. The Nubi plural imperative, which consists of the verb + *-kum*, is an Arabic p/c innovation. There has been some discussion of the structure of the Nubi negative imperative which consists of *'mata*(SING)/ *'matakum*(PL) + imperative. Pasch and Thelwall (1987, 91–165) suggest two possibilities. The first one (supported by Tosco 1995, 455, n. 3) is that the negative marker *'ma* conjoins with the 2nd person pronouns *'ita* for the singular and *'itokum/'itakum* for the plural to become *'mata* and *'matakum*, respectively. However, Pasch and Thelwall (1987, 138–139) argue that:

> ... it is much more likely that the 2nd person pronoun prefix *ta-* of Arabic imperfective (and negative imperative) form has been reanalyzed as one valid only for negative imperative forms:

má	ta	rúa	f(i)	tááun	'Don't go into town (Heine 1982, 43)
NEG	ADR	go	to	town	
má	ta	já			'Don 't come.' (ibid.)
NEG	ADR	come			

cf. SCA   *maa*   *ta-jiy*

By analogy with the formation of the plural form of the absolute pronoun of the 2nd person, the plural of the addressee is formed by suffixing -kum. The final -u, the second part of the Arabic discontinuous 2nd pl pronoun has been dropped from the verb:

má	ta-kum	rúa	f(i)	tááun	'Don't (pl) go to town (ibid.)
NEG	IMP-2pl	go	to	town	
má	ta-kum	já			'Don't (pl) come.' (ibid.)
NEG	IMP-2pl	come			

If our analysis is right, it would mean that Nubi, which has lost the possessive and object personal pronouns, has developed a series of addressees, *ta* (sg) and *ta-kum* (pl), just for the negative imperative.

This is a very interesting line of thought. A few considerations should be presented here. First, the derivation of *'mata* from *'ma ta*-V would provide an explanation of the Nubi irregular imperatives, such as *'tal* "come!" and *'lib*! "play!" whose negative counterparts are *'mata 'ja*! "don't come!', *'mata 'alab* "don't play", respectively, which cannot derive from **'mata 'tal* and **'mata 'lib*, respectively. Second, in addition to the more usual *'mata/ 'matakum* V- forms, Nubi has an alternative set of negative imperative forms consisting of the bare verb form (to which *-'tokum* is attached for plural forms) followed by the negative marker *'ma*, albeit it is infrequently used. Below, I will argue that negative formation in Nubi takes place along two lines, either by a preverbal negator or by a sentence-final negator, which evolved from different inputs. Whereas in indicative clauses the most common position of negative markers is sentence-final, in imperative clauses it is in preverbal position. Let us now assume that the negative imperative was not derived from *mâ ta-V*, and take the imperative verb as a starting point. In that case, parallel to indicative clauses, the negator is put in the clause-final position, and we get a form such as *'rua 'ma* "do not go", lacking any pronominal traces. These forms exist in Nubi, although they occur rather exceptionally. This implies that for the more common negative imperative, we do have to turn to an input that involved at least a reflex of a pronoun. Such a reflex is present in the form which Pasch and Thelwall have suggested.

In Muraz's data on Turku, I found only one instance of a negative imperative, namely: *kalam mafi* "do not talk" (Muraz 1926, 277) with the sentence-final negator. Tosco and Owens (1993, 248) also discuss a small text excerpt quoted after Junker (1891, 472):

(989) "hathab   emsik   dalwagti mafish
         wood   take   now   not"

Junker interpreted *emsik* as a verbal noun, but, as Tosco and Owens point out, an imperative interpretation is much more likely, and one should translate the sentence as "don 't take the wood now", which makes it a p/c Arabic negative imperative with again a sentence-final negator. These two imperatives can be seen as proof of a very early existence of sentence-final negation. This implies that *mâ ta*-V

was certainly the source form, but that it must have been reinterpreted as *mâ 'ita* V. One last remark deals with those p/c verbs that
are not derived from Arabic imperatives. Kaye and Tosco (1993,
269–306) contrast the Ugandan Dialect Arabic *ma tinsash* with the
Ugandan Pidgin Arabic *ma nessîtu* ~ *ma nassîtu*, all meaning "do not
forget". From the occurrence of *ma nessîtu*, to be interpreted as a
negative imperative, we may observe that, since the *ta*-reflex was not
heard in the input, it was probably not expressed in the negative
imperative until later. Again, this supports Pasch and Thelwall's suggestion about a *mâ* IMPER 2SING input.

7.5.3. *Verbal Derivations*

7.5.3.1. *Passivization*

In Nubi, the passive is formed by a stress shift to the last syllable
of the verb (cf. above 4.3.1). Miller (1993, 137–74) sketches a similar
pattern for the formation of intransitive/passive verbs from transitive verbs in JA, and suggests that this morphological process is productive. In her opinion, the stress shift can be traced to the Arabic
dialectal third-person plural, which ends in a long *û (-ûh)*. It seems
more likely that the Nubi (and the JA?) passive evolved along the
following lines: initially, the agent was deleted, while the patient was
retained. The verb itself remained unchanged. Instances of impersonal clauses with an active verb still occur infrequently in contemporary Nubi as in (990) and (991):

(990) 'Juru   'youm.
      pull-Ø   day
      "[It] pulled the day/ The day was pulled forward./The day proceeded."

(991) 'Badulu-'badulu   ru'tan   'toumon.
      change-REDUP-Ø   language   PRON POSS 3PL
      "[They] changed their language/Their language was altered."

For reasons of emphasis, the patient is topicalized leaving a resumptive pronoun *'uo* (PRON 3SING) at the extraction site. Consider the
fictitious example in (992):

(992) *. . . nyere'ku   'de   kan   'durubu uo   ka'la
         child   DEF   when   shoot-Ø it   already
      ". . . the child when [they] had already shot it./when it had already
      been shot."

A similar construction with a topicalized patient occurs in Arabic. The patient is referred to in its former position with an object pronoun agreeing in gender and number. Subsequently, the last vowel of the verb is absorbed by the first vowel of the pronoun *'durub(u)'uo* and takes the main stress (and consequently high pitch) at the expense of the stress on the first syllable of the verb. Item 993 is taken from my field work material.

(993) ... nyere'ku   'de   kan   duru'b(u)   uo   ka'la.
         child   DEF   when   shoot-PASS-Ø   it   COMPL
      "... when the child has already been shot."

During creolization, the pronoun is reduced to stressed -*u*, while verb + attached resumptive pronoun are reinterpreted as a new verb form. The formation of the passive thus became a productive process involving a stress shift towards the last syllable (expressed with high pitch) regardless of the quality of the last vowel.

Except for one case (748) that introduces the agent with *me*, there are no passive clauses with an expressed agent in my text material. Miller's text corpus, however, contains a few examples where the agent is expressed after the preposition *ma* "by" as in (994):

(994) *a'di a'ku ta'e ma du'ban asel* "my brother has been bitten by a bee"
      (Miller 1993, 157)

As far as I know, similar developments (stress shift and/or patient replacement) did not occur in any other Arabic dialect. The above may thus describe an independent development in Nubi (and in JA).

In Muraz' Turku text material, I found several instances of intransitive verbs with transitive counterparts in the lexical list. The intransitive verbs are marked by the absence of final -*u*, while stress is shifted to the second/last syllable, marked by Muraz by doubling of the final consonant (see also Tosco and Owens 1993, 177–267) as in (995), (996), and (997):

(995) *diéboutou* "pull", "bring" (Muraz 1926, 131) > *djiéboutt* "be pulled"
      Baleinière djiéboutt mafi. "The sloop is not pulled [forward]" > "The sloop does not proceed" (Muraz 1926, 272)

(996) *rabotou* "tie" (Muraz 1926, 169) > *raboutt* "be tied"
      Ana doro koutou fi dabra anaki daoua samé, batann raboutt ma farda. "I want to put good medication on your wound, again tied with a piece of cloth." (Muraz 1926, 283)

(997) *lobodou* "hide" (Muraz 1926, 34) > *loboutt* "be hidden"
       Kann ouaïdinn loboutt. . . . "If there are some that are hidden . . ." (Muraz
          1926, 289)

These 'passives' are formed differently than Nubi three-consonant
verbs. The stress shift is common to both. However, in Nubi, the
stress is shifted towards the final syllable, which ends in -*u*, while in
Turku, the stress lies on the penultimate syllable, and the final -*u*,
present in the active verb, is dropped. The Turku passive forms
resemble those Turku adjectives that are derived from SA adjectives
as in (998):

(998) Turku *térinn, tarinn* "sharp", "sharpened" < SA *ṭarîn* "sharp"
       Turku *amlass* "polished", "smooth" < SA *amlas* "smooth"
       Turku *afinn* "rotten", "spoilt" < SA *ʿafin* "stinking"
       Turku *néguitt* "ripe" (ADJ), "ripen" (V) < SA *najîḍ* "ripe"

The equative verb "be" is not expressed overtly in Arabic or in Turku.
Therefore, it is possible that Sudanese Arabic/Turku adjectives, with
the stress on the second syllable, were reinterpreted as intransitive,
passive verbs. Whereas the SA adjectives refer to the result of a
process, Muraz' translations of the Turku forms refer both to the
process and the result. Consequently, passivization via a stress shift
to the penultimate/second syllable with loss of the final vowel may
have become a productive process in Turku.[40]

7.5.3.2. *Nominalization*
The formation of gerund forms by a stress shift to the penultimate
syllable is partly productive in Nubi (cf. above 4.3.3). Some Nubi
gerunds are reflexes of Arabic nominalized forms. Although Arabic
nominalized forms have different structures, many have the pattern
CvCvvC(-a): the vowel in the second syllable is long, which attracts
stress as in SA *ʿamâra/ʿimâra* "building work". Reinterpreting such a
nominalization for Nubi, we get *Cv'CvC(-a)* with the stress on the
second syllable: *a'mara* "construction". This must have become a

---

[40] I tried to reinterpret the above sentences as gerunds because then these verbs
would fit without problem into the Nubi/JA system. This is, however, only possible for (996). *Raboutt* could with some effort be interpreted as "in an attachment
with some cloth". The nominal translation corresponds better to Muraz' translation "un pansement". The stress pattern, but not the vowel sequence, resembles the
SA nominal *rubâṭ* "bandage".

productive process for the formation of gerunds by shifting the stress
to the syllable preceding the third consonant. The Nubi vowels, however, did not undergo changes. This explanation covers gerund forms
of trisyllabic verbs that were derived from Arabic imperative forms,
such as *'amrugu* "remove"—*am'rugu* "removing", "removal". They cannot be interpreted as being derived in one way or another from
Arabic nominalized forms, since imperative verbs are not the basic
forms for nominalization in Arabic. Miller (1993, 154–155) observes
parallel processes in JA.

> La place de l'accent [in nominals (I.W)] en Juba-Arabic ou en Ki-
> Nubi est souvent l'indice d'une syllabe lourde étymologique (CVV ou
> CVVC) qui s'est abrégée. La place de l'accent semble donc reproduire
> les règles d'accentuation de la langue source (et cible). Mais l'accent
> joue également un rôle morphologique, non attesté dans la langue
> source: *le déplacement accentuel peut marquer une distinction verbo-nominale d'une*
> *part, et une distinction entre forme verbal transitive et intransitive-passive d'autre*
> *part.* Ainsi on relèvera les oppositions:
> *ásrubu* "boire" / *asrúbu* "fait de boire" / *asrubú* "être bu"
> *ábinu* "construire"/ *abínu* "construction" / *abinú* "être construit"
> *rásulu* "envoyer" / *rasúlu* "fait d' envoyer" / *rasulú* "être envoyé"

The Nubi infinitive is probably the result of a similar derivational
process. At an earlier stage, other Nubi nominalized forms were
reflexes of Arabic nominalized forms of verbs with pattern CvCvC,
CvCC as in (999):

(999) SA *zikr* "devotional exercise" from *zakar* "mention" (Roth-Laly 1969b,
       206)
       SA *kasr* "fracture", kas(i)r "breaking", "fragmentation" from *kasar*
       "break" (Roth-Laly 1972, 418–19, Reichmuth 1983, 224)
       SA *katal* "slay", *katl* "murder", *kâtal* "fight" from *katal* "kill" (Roth-
       Laly 1972, 407)
       ShA *libis* "clothes" from *libis* "dress", "put on (garment)" (Reichmuth
       1983, 227)
       ShA *faham* "understanding" from *fihim* "understand" (Reichmuth 1983,
       225)
       SA *katib* "writing" from *katab* "write" (Lethem 1920, 79)

These nominalizations are not marked by vowel lengthening or stress
shift and are actually very similar to the Arabic citation verb form
(PERF 3SING). I assume that some nominalized forms were introduced in the Arabic p/cs in this way. I chose the above examples
in part because of their resemblance to the Ø-form of the Nubi verb,

assuming common Nubi phonological processes such as vowel assimilation and vowel epenthesis in order to obtain a CV structure.
However, precisely because of their formal similarity with the zero
form of the verb, they have become indistinguishable from verbs. I
suppose that this second type of nominalization also became productive in Nubi, producing nominalized forms (which I termed
infinitives, cf. 4.3.3) that are more or less homophonous with the
bare form of the verb. Both types of nominalization occur in JA as
well, as is clear from Miller's remark that nominalization through
stress shift is apparently not systematic in view of examples of the
following type:

(1000) *kásuru ta báb* "breaking of the door"
        móya ta ásurubu "water for drinking" (Miller 1993, 155)

I assume that, initially, both types of Nubi nominalizations were used
concurrently. Above (4.3.3., n. 19, 20) I noted that, in particular,
my older informants and informants from the northern part of the
country, contrary to my other observations, occasionally used the
infinitive form in an alienable-like construction with *ta* and in constructions in which no agent or patient was expressed, while they
sometimes used the gerund in an inalienable-like construction.[41] This
variation could be attributed to a previous stage of the language
where a distinction was still in the making. In (1001), the speaker,
an 80–year old woman, uses first the gerund and afterwards the
infinitive of the verb *'zikiri* "recite", "conduct a devotional exercise".

(1001)	Fi	Li'ra,	'kan	'ina	gi-	'zikiri.	*Zi'kiri*	'kan
	in	NPROP	ANT	PRON 1PL	PROG-	recite	recite-GER	ANT
	fi	'be	ta	'sheik.	'Ana		'marya	ta	'sheik.
	in	house	GEN	sheikh	PRON 1SING	woman	GEN	sheikh
	'Zikiri		'kan	'zikiri.				
	recite-INF		be-ANT	recite-INF				

"In Lira, we were reciting. The recitation was in the house of the
sheikh. I was the wife of the sheikh. A recitation was a recitation."

Consider also the JA clauses in (1000). However, the question that
yet remains to be answered is why and how the distinction was

---

[41] I claimed that gerund forms occur in alienable-like constructions with the
agent/patient, marked by the genitive exponent *ta*, whereas infinitive forms are
found in inalienable-like constructions with the patient not linked by *ta*. When neither the agent nor the patient is expressed, the gerund is used (cf. 4.3.3).

made. As for the reason, I do not see any parallels, except maybe in Bari. Bari distinguishes between a simple and an emphatic gerund with the following characteristics (see table 49):

Table 49. Features of gerunds in Bari

Simple gerund GEN noun	Emphatic gerund GEN noun
Passive meaning	Active meaning
Noun = patient	Noun = agent or patient
Emphasis on noun	Emphasis on verb (emphatic gerund)
Cannot stand alone	Can stand alone or as object of verbs of motion, introduced by a preposistion *to*, *into*, or *with*

Source: Spagnolo (1933).

Note: I guess that by active and passive Spagnolo (1933) means that for 'passive' the noun is passive as to the action. Therefore, it is the patient of the action, whereas with 'active' the noun conducts the action and is, therefore, the agent. Consequently, for the passive meaning, the emphasis is on the patient (or noun), whereas for the active meaning, the emphasis is on the action itself, or on the verb. This would imply that the noun of a simple gerund is the patient, and that the noun of the emphatic gerund is the agent. However, in Spagnolo's examples, the noun of both the simple and the emphatic gerund may co-occur with a noun-agent and a noun-patient. For the emphatic gerund, this could more or less be explained. Since the emphasis is on the verb, it may not really matter whether the patient or the agent of the verbal action is expressed. However, for the simple gerund, in my opinion the noun, which is the centre of the construction, cannot be other than the patient, considering Spagnolo's remarks. There is only one example in his grammar of an agentive noun co-occurring with a simple gerund: *ta ayiŋ jama nikaŋ* "Did you hear our speaking?". *Jama* is the simple gerund. Possibly, Spagnolo means "our being spoken to", in which case this example does not contradict his other findings. For the discussion of the Nubi INF/GER, I assume that the Bari simple gerund can only co-occur with a patient, and not with an agent.

Except for both the simple and the emphatic gerund being found in constructions marked by a genitive exponent, there are some similarities between the Nubi infinitive/gerund and the Bari simple/emphatic gerund, respectively. The infinitive always co-occurs with a patient, which has the emphasis. The gerund, by contrast, which may or may not co-occur with an agent or a patient, always has the emphasis itself. Unlike in Bari, both the infinitive and the gerund may be used in a prepositional phrase after a verb. The question remains as to why there is no genitive exponent with the infinitive, while with the gerund genitive *ta* is present. In the INF N construction, the emphasis is on the patient, which is subjected to the action expressed by the infinitive. Both may thus be regarded as impossible to divide and thus as inalienable. In this case, *ta* is not expressed. On the other hand, the central part of a gerundive construction is the gerund. The agent or patient are less relevant to the entire construction and so are marked by the genitive exponent.

A similar distinction is apparently made in JA. Miller talks about a productive process of stripping the verb of its stress in order to nominalize it. In (1002), a gerund-like form is followed by the genitive particle *ta* + noun or it stands alone, while in (1003) and in (1004), a non-accentuated verb is immediately followed by its nominal patient.

(1002) *rakábu ta laám* "cooking of the meat"
       kurúju dé sókol ta náse jídu ta nina "agriculture is a traditional activity"

(1003) *dúgu* "hit" >< *dugu* "hitting"
       dugu báb dé sáab "knocking on a door is difficult"

(1004) *gáta* "cut" >< *gata* "cutting"
       gata gís dé sógol ta muzáre "cutting the grass is the work of the peasants"

The infinitives (or what Miller calls '*formes désaccentuées*') are presumably not without stress. Miller's examples are all bisyllabic verbs, and, in combination with a following noun, their stress may be reduced but does not disappear.

For Turku, I found only one minimal pair where the verb and the nominal were clearly distinguished, namely *dafounou, dafonou* "bury" >< *dafana* "funeral" (Muraz 1926, 48, 53). For other pairs, Muraz does not distinguish formally between the verb and the noun as in (1005) and (1006):

(1005) Turku *asserou* "massage" (V) >< *asserou* "massage" (N) < SA *'aṣṣar*
       "massage"
       Turku *assbour* "forgive", "wait" >< *assbour* "pardon" < SA *ṣabar* "be
       patient", "wait"

(1006) Turku *lip* "dance" (V) >< *lip* "dance" (N) < SA *lïʿib* "dance", "game"
       Turku *mal* "inherit" (V) >< *mal* "inheritance" < SA *mâl* "property",
       "wealth"
       Turku *sidal* "possess" (V) >< *sidal* "possessor" (N) < SA *sîdu (a)l-*
       . . . "owner of the . . .'

In (1005), the Turku verb is probably basic, whereas the noun is derived. In (1006), however, the verb is derived from the noun, since

there is no verb similar to the Turku ones in Sudanese Arabic. In
(1007), I assume that the phrase *zourtou daoua* is the dislocated object of
the clause, which consists of the infinitive *zourtou* plus its patient *daoua*.

(1007)   . . . fichan   *zourtou*   *daoua*   ana   niss   mafi.
        so that   swallow-INF   medication   PRON 1SING   forget-Ø   NEG
        ". . . so that I will not forget the swallowing of [my] medication/to swallow
          [my] medication."
        (Muraz 1926, 280)

Consider also (1008):

(1008)   Doktor bedji chouf inntoukoum fichann *sao daoua*. Hou bedji fichann
        koutoulou inntoukoum mafi. "The doctor comes to see you for making
        medication. He does not come for killing you." (Muraz 1926, 289)

7.5.4. *The Verb ʿendi "have"*

Neither in the Arabic dialects or in the substrate and adstrate languages
is there a verb expressing possession. To express "have", Arabic
dialects use an expression "(there is) with /for . . .". In KA, the preposition *ʿind* "with", "by" is the commonest, e.g., in *ʿindi marabba wa
zibda* "with-me are jam and butter/I have jam and butter" (Trimingham 194, 54). Its use is not limited, unlike *maʿa* "with", which can
only be used to express possession of small articles on a person or
in the hand, and unlike *lê* "for", "to", which is used to express possession of big property or for periods of time. The preposition *ʿind/ʿand*
"with", "by" is, therefore, the most logical input for the Nubi verb
ʿendi/ʿendis "have". In KA, the possessor may be placed in the sentence-initial position while being copied pronominally after the preposition to emphasize the possessor as in (1009):

(1009)   ana   ʿind-i   ʿênên   w-   inta   ʿind-ak   ʿênên
        PRON 1SING   with me   eye-DUAL   and   PRON 2SING   with you   eye-DUAL
        "I have two eyes and you have two eyes". (Trimingham 1946, 42–43)

Similar topicalization structures exist in EA as in (1010) with the
preposition *ʿand* "with":

(1010)   al-ʿarîs   ʿandu   ʿarabiyya
        the bridegroom   with him   cart
        "The bridegroom has a cart." (after al-Tonsi and al-Sawi 1986, 109)

From there it requires only a small step to reanalyse the erstwhile locative possessive with Ø copula as a 'have'-possessive with SVO order repositioning the subject properties from the possessed item to the possessor and reinterpreting the erstwhile preposition as a verb. A similar development took place in Maltese Arabic (see Comrie 1985).

The Nubi form *'endis* or *'endisi* must probably be traced to the negated form of the locative possessive that occurs with the negative marker *mâ* and final *-sh* in EA: *mâ 'andîsh* "not with me", *mâ 'andûsh* "not with him" (al-Tonsi and al-Sawi 1986, Pasch and Thelwall 1987, 91–165, Kaye and Tosco 1993, 269–306). In SA, the final *-sh* does not occur often, so that it could be disconnected from its negative meaning. In present-day Nubi *'endis* and *'endisi* are used as allomorphs of *'endi*. Several forms of different dialects have served as inputs for the ultimate Nubi forms for "have", namely, *'indi, 'endi, 'andi*, including *'indi* from *'ind* (Aswân, and area above Minya, Omdurman Arabic), or *ind* (Abbéché Arabic) *'andi, 'endi* from *'and* (between Minya and Aswân) (see Behnstedt and Woidich 1985, vol. 2, Worsley 1925, Trimingham 1946, Roth 1979).

The introduction of a verb meaning "have" is probably a more recent pidgin/creole innovation in which Turku does not seem to have shared. Turku has *mal* "have money" "inherit", and *sidal* "possess". Generally, however, possession is expressed by means of the existential marker as in (1011):

(1011) kanamaye   achra   fi   bakann   ana
        goats   ten   exist place/with me
        "There are ten goats at my place." (after Muraz 1926, 16)

In JA, the normal way of expressing possession seems to be with the verb *índu* "have".

(1012) "ínna   ma   índu   múskil   ma   étakum
        we   NEG   have   problem   with   you-P
        "We have nothing against you." (Tosco 1995, 426)

However, Tosco (1995, 426) states that "One of my informants often used this verb with Arabic pronominal affixes (e.g. *índi* "I have", *índana* "we have"). Likewise, he also used *fi* "be-there" before *ind +
pronoun*, thus reproducing the colloquial Arabic construction. . . ." as in (1013):

(1013) *híni   de   tában   fi   índana   munazzamát*
       here   DET of-course be-there have-we organizations
       "Of course, we have organizations here." (Tosco 1995, 426)

Watson (1984, in Tosco and Owens 1993, 244) gives (1014) for Juba
Arabic, where existential *fi* and the preposition *le* serve to express
possession:

(1014) fi   le   ána   míle
       exist at   me   salt
       "I have salt"

Therefore, it seems that in JA both types of possessive constructions
co-occur. It is possible that JA is still in a transitory stage in which
preposition *ind* + pronoun is reinterpreted as the verb *ind* "have".
It is, however, more likely that the verb *ind* has been established
firmly in JA and that forms with *ind* + pronoun are due to influence
from the Khartûm Arabic dialect. From the speech of the informants
in Miller (1988–89, 23–58), we learn that the basilectal and mesolec-
tal speakers use the verb *indu* "have", while in the acrolectal speech
variety we find the preposition *ind* + pronominal affix. This implies
that the preposition *ind* + pronoun has indeed been reintroduced
through decreolization.

From the above it may be concluded that Nubi and JA follow a
universal tendency in introducing a special verb "have" by gram-
maticalizing an existing construction and that this verb receives most,
and in the case of Nubi, even all functions.

7.5.5. *Conclusion*

In table 50 the features unique to the Arabic p/cs are singled out.

Table 50. Arabic p/c features and common features of
Arabic dialects and p/cs in VP

Common features of (some) Arabic dialects and p/cs	Arabic p/c features
	One verbal stem form: no person/number marking on the verb, no distinction perfect/imperfect Ø expressing all tenses and aspects, if TA is marked by other means

Table 50 *(cont.)*

Common features of (some) Arabic dialects and p/cs	Arabic p/c features
gâʿid / *qâʿid*: continuous, recurrent actions (SA)	*gi-* (Nubi, JA): progressive marker
	gaed/*gahed* (Turku): continuous, recurrent actions
Stative/non-stative distinction (AA, UDA)	Stative/non-stative distinction (Nubi, JA) *gi-* + stative verbs: to mark habituality, inchoativeness, verbal adjectives (Nubi, JA)
bi-/*be-*: future/habituality (SA)	*bi-*: future marker (Nubi, Turku), future/habituality (JA)
kân: pre-or postsubject position (SA)	
kan: temporal and modal (NA, AA, (ShA))	*kan bi*-V: counterfactuality (Nubi) *kan bi-gi*-V order (Nubi) , unlike SA *kân gâʿid bi*-V
AUX FUT from verb "go" (EA, AA, ShA)	AUX FUT from verb "go", "come" (Nubi, JA, (Turku)) AUX ingressive/resultative from verb "come" (Nubi, JA)
AUX ingressive from verb "get up" (AA, EA, ShA) AUX repetition from verb "return" (AA, EA) AUX continuity/duration from verb "sit" (AA, EA, KA)	
	Completive marker *ka'las* (Nubi, JA) IMPER SING: Ø-form (Nubi, JA, Turku) IMPER PL: V-*kum* (Nubi) Nubi negative imperative: *ʻmata* V < Arabic *mâ* IMPERF 2SING Passive formation through stress shift on last/ (third) syllable) (Nubi, JA), on second syllable (Turku) Nominalized forms: reflexes of Arabic infinitive forms (Nubi, JA, Turku) Nubi: productive process, distinction gerunds/infinitives
	Verb "have" through reanalysis of ' Arabic preposition (Nubi, JA)

Except for the temporal/modal use of *kân*, there are no typical WSA features in both the Arabic p/cs and in some WSA dialects. Most p/c features are innovations that are characterized by the reinterpretation of morphological material of the Arabic dialects (either of the eastern or western part). Similar developments are attested in languages worldwide. Differences between Nubi and Turku are listed in table 51.

Table 51. Nubi-Turku distinctions in VP

Nubi	Turku
Marker *gi-*	Auxiliary *gahed/gaed*
bi-gi- V	No co-occurrences *be* and *gaed* (however limited data)
Negative imperative: *'mata* V	Negative imperative: V *mafi*
Passive: stress shift to last (mainly third syllable): reanalysis of V + OBJ PRON	Stress shift to second syllable: corresponding to Arabic adjectives
Verb for "have"	No verb for "have"

Note: See also Owens (1996, 125–72).

7.6. *Other Word Classes*

7.6.1. *Conjunctions*

The UN conjunction *yâ* has no obvious source form in SA. It seems, however, to occur in AA as in (1015):

(1015) *ana gâid negeri yâ fransa jo* "j'" étais en train à lire et à écrire (quand?) les Français sont arrivés"
fî Dambe (lieu) yâ n-nâr ôgodôha "à Dambe où le feu a été mis". (Roth 1979, 219)

Roth (1979) also discusses the form *hîya*, which occurs in the sentence-initial position in both nominal and verbal sentences. Its function resembles the function of UN sentence-initial *'ya* indicating temporal modality or introducing a sentence that more or less sums up the foregoing as in (1016):

(1016) *xalli nijibu le almi wa hîya na'addîki* "allons chercher l'eau et alors (ou ensuite) je te (les) donnerai." (Roth 1979, 199)

It is thus possible that AA *hîya* and *yâ* are allomorphs and that there is a link between both forms and the UN conjunction *'ya*. The Nigerian Arabic *yé* also seems to function as a conjunction introducing the apodosis of a conditional clause similar to UN *'ya* as in (1017):

(1017) kán   ad-dáwaka   jó   yé   bǝssaww-úu-a   lée-na
       if   def-musicians   come   ye   do-pl-it   for us
       "If the musicians come, they play it for us." (Owens 1993a, 100)

A parallel is found in the substrate language Alur. Alur *ya*, which does not seem to have a fixed position, expresses a causal relation between two sentences (Vanneste 1940, Ukoko, Knappert and Van Spaandonck 1964).

The Nubi subjunctive marker *ke'de* is probably related to eastern Sudanese *kadi*, Egyptian *kide* or *kede* (dialect of Asyût). In Omdurman Arabic, *kadi* means "then", "consequently", and *'ale kadi* "so that", whereas *kida* means "so", "in this way", "like this" (Fischer 1959, Trimingham 1946). The latter functions more or less as a demonstrative adverb, the former as a subjunctive marker.

Conditional *kan* seems to be a typical element of the Sudanic belt. It occurs also in Upper Egypt. Conditional *kan* exists in Nigerian Arabic (Owens 1991b, 1169–79, Owens 1993a), in Abbéché Arabic (Roth 1979), and among other markers, in Sudanese Arabic (Trimingham 1946, Worsley 1925, Reichmuth 1983). JA *kan*, like UN *kan*, may mean both "if" and "when" (Mahmud 1979, Miller 1979–84, 295–315, Tosco 1995, 423–59). "If" in JA is also expressed by *lo* (Mahmud 1979, Tosco 1995, 423–59) and by the Egyptianism *izakan* (Miller 1979–84, 295–315). Conditional "if" in Turku is also expressed by *kan*. In Nubi, JA, and Turku *kan*, apart from its function in conditional clauses is also used in temporal contexts. In Abbéché Arabic as well, *kân* is used in certain contexts to express temporal value (Roth 1979). Consider also Givón (1990), who mentions that simple conditionals, or in his terminology irrealis conditionals, and irrealis when-clauses are expressed similarly in many languages.

The conjunction introducing direct and indirect speech has been discussed extensively in the p/c literature. Typically, a reflex of a verb meaning "say" introduces a sentential complement after verbs of speaking, telling, and other cognition-utterance verbs (Sebba 1985, 115–33, Versteegh 1984, Holm 1988). The Arabic verb *qâl* "say" was reanalysed as the UN conjunction *'gal* that introduces direct and indirect quotations.

7.6.2. *The Focus Marker* 'ya

The origins of the focus marker *'ya* are quite difficult to assess. Focusing UN *'ya* has parallels in contemporary Abbéché Arabic and in Nigerian Arabic.[42] In Nigerian Arabic, according to Owens (1993a), the NP-final *yé* marks a pre-predicate constituent, which is mainly an NP and most commonly a subject. In some cases, the marked constituents are topics in the narrow sense.

(1018) "*al-aǫlla   ye   biyaakǝl-úu-a*
        def-grain ye   eat-m/pl-it
        "As for the grain, they eat it". (Owens 1993a, 100)

(1019) *ma lammáa-k   fi šáy,   ha l-yóom ye jǔ-na   fi l-bírni*
        not gather-you in thing   and today ye came-we in def-city
        "Nothing bothered us, yet today here we've come to the city."
        (Owens 1993a, 100)

(1018) and (1019) are examples of Y movement in NA, where the moved constituent is marked by *yé*. In this sense, UN *'ya* functions similarly to NA *yé*. According to Roth (1979, 219), AA *yâ* is "une modalité d' insistance. . . . C'est en quelque sorte une marque par laquelle le locuteur souligne la véracité ou l'authenticité des propos qu'il tient ou des faits qu' il relate."

---

[42] According to Miller (1987, 1–23), *yaú* is very frequent in Juba Arabic, where it functions as an emphasizer or topicalizer.

yala   baga   taab   tani   yau   ge   jibu   fi   dula   tou
voilà   devenir   fatigue   autre   TOP   ge+   apporter dans côte de   lui
Il va y avoir un autre problème avec cette personne. (Miller 1985–86, 163)

fi   karánga   yaw   ínna kan rúa fi gába, . . .
in   dry-season TOP   we   kan go   in bush
"In the dry season we went into the bush" (Tosco 1995, 441)

JA *yaú* is a compulsory element in nominal predicates, functioning more and more as a copula:

kalam   de   yaú   batál
word   DET   COP   bad
"These are bad words." (Miller 1987, 19)

(1020) *bahasba al-humâr yâ waga' fî bîr* "il pensait que l' âne était bel et bien tombé dans le puits" (Roth 1979, 219)

(1021) *ad-dûd bu-gûl: tôrî yâ wilid; al ba'ašôm bu-gûl: bagarti yâ wildat.*
"le lion dit: c'est mon beuf qui a mis bas; le chacal dit: c' est ma vache qui a mis bas." (Roth 1979, 219)

However, in (1020), AA *yâ* seems to function as a focus marker or it seems to mark a cleft-like construction as in (1021). For Roth (1979), the origin of *yâ* remains obscure. According to her, it is mainly used by the elite or by native speakers of Arabic. From this, it could be inferred that the origins of Abbéché *yâ* and Nubi *ya* should be sought in Arabic dialects and not in the substrate languages. *ya/yâ* occurs in several Arabic dialects, and, apart from its meaning of vocative particle, it has very different functions.[43]

The clue to the etymology of UN *ya* may, however, lie in the SA clause in (1022)

(1022) *yâ hû r râjil be zâto el ja elbârih* "this is the same man who came yesterday" (after Hillelson 1930, 257)

It is difficult to interpret *yâ* here correctly, since the clause is taken out of its context. It is not unlikely that *yâ* serves as an adverb, meaning "really!", "indeed", and thus acts merely as an emphasizing particle. In allegro forms, *yâ hû* is pronounced *yaw* and interpreted as one form, which is reanalysed as a focusing particle, leaving the sentence devoid of a subject, which consequently is reintroduced. The form *yaw* has been retained in JA and in the Turku compound form *yaoda*, while in UN, in AA, and in Nigerian Arabic, it has been monophthongized to *ya*, *yâ*, and *yé*, respectively. The above may have been reinforced by substratal features. In some of the possible substrate languages *ya*-like forms function as a copula or a relativizer. Bickerton (1993) states that worldwide focusing markers can generally be traced to copulas and sometimes to relativizers. In Shilluk, *ya* is used as a

---

[43] Fischer (1959) links the vocative particle in Arabic dialects to the sentence-introducing particle. He writes that in the Arabic dialects in Sudan/Jezîra, besides *yâ*, *hâ* and *'â* are found as vocative particles. "Demnach ist es nicht erstaunlich, daß neben *hâ* auch *'â* as Satzeinleitungspartikel vorkommt." (Fischer 1959, 167). If this is correct, it is not too difficult to assume an extension towards the use of vocative *yâ* as a sentence-introducing particle.

copula "be" but only if the predicate is an adverb (Westermann 1912). In Bari, the so-called relative adjectives may be preceded by the copula when used predicatively. A sentence like "my daughter is small" can then be interpreted as "my daughter is she who is small" (Spagnolo 1933, 61). In Lango and other Luo dialects, clefts are formed by means of the relative particle *àmê* or *àyé* alternatively, which follows its head noun (Noonan 1992, Crazzolara 1955). Dinka *ye* functions as an interrogative auxiliary (Nebel 1948).

7.6.3. *Conclusion*

In table 52 the features that are unique for the Arabic p/cs are singled out.

Table 52. Common features of Arabic dialects and p/cs vs.
unique Arabic p/c features in other word classes

Common features of Arabic dialects and Arabic p/cs	Features unique to Arabic p/cs
Conjunction *hîyâ, yâ, yé* (NA, AA) (UN *ʾya*)	
Conditional *kân* (SA)	
Conditional *kan* also temporal value (AA)	
	Nubi complementizer from verb "say"
UN subjunctive marker *ke'de*, cf. OA *kadi?*	
ya/ ye: focusing element (AA, NA)	Nubi *ʾya* focus marker (JA *yau:* copula)

7.7. *Clause Structure*

7.7.1. *Constituent Order*

The normal word order in Nubi as in Turku, JA, and most creole languages, is SVO, which corresponds to the normal word order in the Arabic dialects (Versteegh 1984). The direct object precedes the indirect object. Consider the Turku sentence in (1023):

(1023) *Gobolu mâl ana akit ana mara-da lé rajiéla jaman,*. . . . "Return the dowry of this woman to her ex-husband, . . ." (Muraz 1926, 288)

However as in Nubi, the normal word order in Turku may sometimes be altered. In (1024), the object follows the adverbial phrase.

(1024) *Ana doro koutou fi dabra anaki daoua samé,. . . .* "I want to put good med-
ication on your wound, . . ." (Muraz 1926, 283)

7.7.2. *Subject-Predicate Agreement*

According to Versteegh (1984), agreement across the predicate in JA
is the result of Arabic dialect influence, and is thus a feature of
decreolization. He is, however, wrong in asserting that this type of
agreement does not occur in Nubi, which would imply that Nubi
preserves more archaic forms. There is optional agreement both in
the Kenyan and Ugandan variety of Nubi, and I assume that in
Juba Arabic and in Nubi agreement has always been optional. It is,
however, very likely that agreement in JA is more common owing
to Arabic influence.

7.7.3. *Negation*

In Ugandan Nubi, sentences are negated either by *'ma*, which may
take any position in the sentence, or by *'maf(i)*, which is generally
found in the sentence-final position. In Kenyan Nubi, the negative
particle is in a preverbal position (Khamis 1994, Kaye and Tosco
1993, 269–306, Tosco and Owens 1993, 177–267). However, Heine
(1982, 39) gives several examples of sentence-final *ma* in Kenyan Nubi.
Tosco and Owens (1993, 258, n. 53) refer to more mutual contact
between the two Nubi groups (in Kenya and Uganda) after the fall
of Amin in 1979, which may have led to fewer restrictions on the
position of *ma* in Kenyan Nubi. In JA, negation seems to be restricted
to constructions with preverbal *ma*. In Turku, three types of negation occur. Sentence-final *mafi* is most common. Occasionally, the
preverbal negator *ma* occurs. The third type is only attested in Muraz's
texts with the first person singular pronoun in clauses such as (1025):

(1025)   Ma-   na-   doro innté   koutoulou kanamaye mara.
         NEG- PRON 1SING- want PRON 2SING kill-Ø   goat(s)   woman
         "I do not want you to kill female goats." (after Muraz 1926, 288)

Jenkins mentions three forms of negation for Ugandan Nubi at around
the turn of the century (in Kaye and Tosco 1993, 269–306), namely
mâ . . . sh [. . .], *mûsh* [. . .], and *ma* [. . .]. These are Egyptianisms and

could be consigned to the category of Arabic dialect influence in Uganda. Only *ma* [. . .] is also a Ugandan Pidgin form, and always occurs preverbally.

The preverbal negator *ma* is obviously a reflex of Sudanese Arabic *ma* (Lethem 1920, Trimingham 1956, Hillelson 1930, Owens 1993a, Roth 1979). To explain sentence-final *'mafi*, we turn to Bickerton (1981), who reconstructs the development of negative constructions by drawing parallels between children's acquisition of negation and creolization-decreolization. Generally, in a child's language acquisition and in creoles, in the first stage, the morpheme of denial (*no*, and only occasionally *not* for children acquiring English, or English-based creoles) is placed at the beginning or end of the utterance. In the Sudanese Arabic dialects, this morpheme is generally *la*. In Nigerian Arabic, it may also be *'mâfi* (Owens 1993a). "not-being-there" is, however, generally expressed in the Sudanese dialects by *mâfî* (or *mâfîsh*) (Trimingham 1946), which is placed in sentence-final position to negate the preceding sentence. Pasch and Thelwall (1987, 91–165) interpret *'ma'fi* as:

> . . . an expression used to express the non-availability of something that has been requested and constitutes a clause where the subject can be deleted because it has already been mentioned before. . . . maa fii is to be interpreted as an expression negating the preceding clause. It is now conceivable that ma fii was interpreted monolexemically having the meaning 'not'. . . .

The stress on the second part of the negative existential is less strong than on the first: *'ma fi*. Consequently, the vowel or even the whole syllable may have been dropped (see also Pasch and Thelwall 1987, 91–165). It is, however, difficult to judge whether the sentence-final negator *'ma* is the result of an extreme reduction of the original sentence-final negator *'ma'fi*, or whether it is the negator *'ma*, whose position is no longer restricted to the preverbal position in present-day Ugandan Nubi. Even if sentence-final *mafi* is in competition with (preverbal) *'ma* in Ugandan Nubi, it has not yet disappeared. Tosco and Owens (1993, 177–267) attribute this to the influence of substrate languages (Central Sudanic languages), where sentence-final negation occurs. However, Nigerian Arabic, besides the more common preverbal negator *ma* sometimes uses sentence final *máfi* (Owens 1993a) while, according to Tosco and Owens (1993, 177–267), a sentence final negator *mafi* is attested in Arabic dialects of Western Chad and Northern Cameroon as well.

In creoles, negation is generally conveyed by means of a preverbal negative element (Holm 1988, Romaine 1988). Yet there are several creoles with sentence-final negation sometimes co-occurring with preverbal negation such as Principe Creole Portuguese, Palenquero Creole Spanish (Holm 1988), Shaba Swahili (De Rooij 1995, 179–90), Fa d'Ambu (Post 1995, 191–204), and Berbice Dutch (Kouwenberg 1995, 233–43). Interestingly, these are pidgins and creoles that allow double negation, as does Nubi (see below). In the Shaba-Swahili example in (1026) (from the Zairean copperbelt), the sentence-final *apana* is a clear reflex of the Swahili morpheme of denial *hapana*.

(1026) *A*-i-kuwa   fura(h)a ya   famille   apana
       NEG-it-COP   joy   CONN family   NEG
       "It was no joy for the family at all." (de Rooij 1995, 189)

Turku and Ugandan Nubi employ both types of negation. JA has only preverbal *'ma*. In the Kenyan Nubi variety, only the negator *'ma* is retained, whether in preverbal position or placed more freely. Neither Owens (1977) nor Heine (1982) mention any instances of the negator *'mafi/'maf*. The question remaining is how it is possible that *'mafi* survived in Ugandan Nubi and not in JA, since the substrate languages that might have affected the sentence-final negative construction are more or less the same. Influence of the Arabic source language may, however, have played a role in Juba Arabic in restricting negation to the use of preverbal *'ma*. Likewise, one might ask how it is possible that sentence-final *'mafi* was lost in Kenyan Nubi while it is a common method of negation in Ugandan Nubi. However, both Kenyan Nubi sentence-final *'ma* and Ugandan Nubi sentence-final *'maf(i)* are remnants of sentence-final *'ma'fi*. The difference is only that the second part of the negated existential marker has been dropped entirely in Kenyan Nubi while its consonant *-f-* has been retained in Ugandan Nubi.

After verbs of prohibition, the subjunctive clause may be negated in Ugandan Nubi, while the negation is compulsory in Kenyan Nubi (Owens (1977). Substrate influence may play a role. For instance, in Dinka, similar negative constructions are employed with verbs expressing feelings of fear, repugnance, prohibition or impossibility (Nebel 1948).

7.7.4. *Conclusion*

In table 53 the features unique to the Arabic p/cs are singled out.

Table 53. Common features of Arabic dialects and p/cs and features
unique to Arabic p/cs in clause structure

Common features of Arabic dialects and p/cs	Features unique to Arabic p/cs
SVO	
	Subject-predicate agreement: optional and rather rare (except for JA: decreolization)
Preverbal negator *ma* (SA) Sentence final negator *mâfî* (NA, Western Chadian Arabic, Northern Cameroon Arabic)	

7.8. *Conclusion*

In this chapter, I tried to link Arabic p/cs and especially Nubi with
the Arabic dialects of the area, going from Egypt via Eastern Sudanese
Arabic (KA) and the Arabic of the Sudanese belt to Western Sudanese
Arabic (Abbéché Arabic, Shuwa Arabic, and Nigerian Arabic). My
aim was to reconstruct the development of Nubi (and JA/Turku)
and to investigate the nature of the source language or languages.
At first, I approached the problem from an historical point of view.
I assumed that several pidgin varieties existed before 1820 in the
area. Through contacts between speakers of different areal varieties,
some degree of levelling may have taken place. From 1820 onwards,
however, the influence of varieties with an eastern Arabic input may
have increased through the Egyptian military and the impact of
Egyptian and Kharṭûm traders. In travellers' diaries we also read
about Western Sudanese traders in the *zarîbas*. The historical sources
thus suggest a pan-Sudanese origin for the Arabic p/cs. For the purpose of investigating the linguistic sources of the Arabic p/cs and
especially Nubi, I reorganized the dialect features that parallel the
Nubi features discussed above in table 54 according to their geographical distribution.

Table 54. Areal distribution of common features of Arabic dialects and p/cs

Developments in all source dialects, or in some dialects, including however eastern and western varieties	Typical for eastern Arabic dialects	Typical for western Arabic dialects
Phonology	EA *g* < Old Arabic *jīm*	Assimilation and vowel harmony in several dialects, especially in WSA, but limited by grammatical criteria Loss of emphatics, especially in WSA: variably attested, no emphasis in Bagirmi, Njamena
Ø < h , especially in WSA, e.g. NA, while variably attested in AA (Tosco and Owens 1993: 232–233 Roth 1979: II).		Loss of pharyngeals: *ḥ* > *h*/Ø/*kh*, ʿ > Ø/*y* (especially in WSA, but variably attested no pharyngeals in Nigeria and Chad)
epenthesis (in most SA dialects)		
final devoicing		
Vocabulary	Egyptianisms in Nubi, not in Turku	WSA words in Turku, however not in Nubi
Noun phrase	PRON 1PL: Nubi ʿina < *iḥna* PRON POSS 2PL: -*kum* PRON 3PL final -*n*: *huṃṃan*	PRON 1PL: Turku *anina* < *anîna*
		Collectivity marked by *nâs* (Shuwa)
DEM PROX: least marked form (EA, AA) (>< generally in languages: DEM DIS: least marked) numeral 'one' used as indefinite article		*da* used as definite article, beside *el* (AA, NA)
		DEM PROX < PRON + *da* (AA) Reinterpretation of Arabic PL DEM *dol* as plural marker: in AA, (and NA?)

Table 54 (cont.)

Developments in all source dialects, or in some dialects, including however eastern and western varieties	Typical for eastern Arabic dialects	Typical for western Arabic dialects
optional marking of indefiniteness comparison: ADJ + min + complement		Comparison: ADJ + fuut + complement (NA, Bagirmi) Comparison: X surpasses Y in quality Z (AA, NA, Shuwa)
possession: analytic and synthetic constructions N GEN N-constructions: concrete possession, qualifications, while synthetic constructions: kin terms, part-whole relations	genitive exponent: Nubi ta, JA (bi)ta < bitāʕ-	Turku genitive exponent ana < hana Word order N NUM/NUM N (AA, Shuwa)
Verb phrase gāʕid / gāʕud: continuous, recurrent actions from verb "sit", "stand" bi-/be-: future/habituality in SA kān: pre-or postsubject position: SA		Stative/non-stative distinction kān: temporal and modal (NA, AA, Shukriyya)
Other word classes Conditional kān (SA)		Conjunction hiyâ, yâ, ye (NA, AA) ya/ye: focusing element (AA, NA) from SA yâ "indeed" Conditional kan also temporal value (AA)
Clause structure SVO Preverbal negator ma		Sentence-final negator māfi (NA, Western Chadian Arabic, Northern Cameroon Arabic)

In the above table, we see that most source forms for the Arabic
p/cs are common to the entire area or that they are found at least
in one dialect in the eastern Sudan and at the same time in at least
one dialect in the western Sudan. If we now look at the features
that occur either in the western dialects or in the eastern dialects,
we see that the typically WSA features are much more frequent than
the typically eastern Arabic features. According to Owens (1985a,
229–71), these parallels point to the WSA origin of the Arabic p/cs.
However, most, if not all, of these developments, such as the loss of
emphatics and pharyngeals, the loss of gender marking/agreement,
the expression of comparison with ADJ *fut(u)* complement, the verbal stative/non-stative distinction, the sentence-final negator *mâfî*, are
general tendencies in languages and/or pidgins/creoles worldwide.
It is, therefore, not possible to state whether the p/c developments
are the result of direct influences from WSA or that they result from
parallel but independent developments taking place both in the WSA
dialects and in the Arabic p/cs. Only the vocabulary and morphological
markers, such as the genitive exponent may give some indication of
the source of the Arabic p/cs. For Nubi and Juba Arabic, the vocabulary points to a pan-Sudanese origin but not to WSA sources. In
Turku, which lies in the WSA area, we find some words of exclusively WSA origin. Nubi, on the other hand, contains some typically
Egyptian words. Their presence can easily be explained on historical grounds, since there were still native Egyptians among Emin's
troops. The Nubi developments and structure may show many similarities with those in western Sudanese Arabic dialects, but the fact
that the Nubi vocabulary indicates Egyptian sources, apart from its
general Sudanese origin, suggests that direct influence from WSA should
be excluded, and the similarities should rather be attributed to parallel developments. I, therefore, support Miller (1994, 227, n. 4),
when she says:

> Je suis également favorable a cette hypothese "pan-soudanaise", mais
> la similitude entre le nubi et les dialectes de l'ouest parlés par des non
> arabes ne signifie pas forcement que les seconds sont a l' origine du
> premier (comme le postule Owens), mais que tous ces parlers ont subi
> les mêmes processus de restructuration.

Several times, I mentioned similarities between Nubi and substrate
and adstrate languages. As with the issue of the source language, it
is not possible to see clearly whether to attribute them to direct

influence or to more universal tendencies. I would opt, therefore, for an explanation in terms of universal strategies, which may have been reinforced by substrate influence. Even if a feature is present in one substrate language, it may be absent in another, so that direct influence from that one language may not be a plausible explanation. Parallels occur especially between Nubi and Bari among the above-mentioned substrate and adstrate languages. This might be the case because Bari is one of the few languages of the region that is described in detail while the descriptions of the other grammars remain insufficient. However, it may also be that Arabic p/c speakers of Bari origin were frequent at one stage or another.

To conclude, in table 55, I compare the features of the different regional varieties of the Arabic p/cs, namely Ugandan Nubi, Kenyan Nubi, Juba Arabic, and Turku. Only those features are mentioned in which disagreements occur between one or more of the regional varieties. Features not mentioned here are similar in all Arabic p/cs. Regarding these common features, it is again not possible to establish whether they originate from a feature present in an early pidgin stage or whether they are the result of parallel but independent developments in all Arabic p/cs.

Table 55. Areal distribution of features of Arabic pidgins/creoles

	Ugandan Nubi	Kenyan Nubi	Juba Arabic	Turku
Phonology				
s < sh	Frequent, especially in southern Uganda	Less frequent	Less frequent	Less frequent
j < z	Frequent, especially in southern Uganda	Less frequent	Less frequent	Rare
Tendency towards CV-structure	Common	Less common	Inconstant	Less common
CV-structure through epenthesis, final vowel addition	Frequent (however, more frequent in southern than in northern Uganda)	Frequent	Frequent in pidginized variety, less in urban JA	Frequent
CV-structure through loss of final plosives/dentals	Frequent	Less frequent	Less frequent	Less frequent
Vowel assimilation	Common (however more general in southern than in northern Uganda)	Common	Common	Less common
Vocabulary				
Reduplication	Productive	Productive	Productive	Fossilized forms
Egyptianisms	Yes	Yes	Yes	No
WSA-words	Rare	Rare	Rare	Yes, e.g. feminine words in -e
Incorporation of vocative particle	Yes	Yes	?	No

Table 55 (cont.)

	Ugandan Nubi	Kenyan Nubi	Juba Arabic	Turku
Noun phrase				
PRON 2SING/PL	ʿita/ ʿitokum	ita/ itakum	Ita (inta)/ itakum (intakum)	imté/ imntoukoum
PRON 1PL	ʿina	ina	ina/ anina	amina
GEN	ta	ta	ta	ana
Plural marking through stress shift	Yes	Yes	No	?
Number agreement	Optional	Optional	Regular	Minimal
Collective marker nas	Also non-humans	Only humans	Also non-humans	?
DEM PROX SING	ʿde, (ʿu)weʿde, (u)ʿwede	ʿde, ʿweʿde	de, da, di	da
DEM PROX PL	ʿdolʿde	ʿdolʿde	de, da, del	doll da
DEM DIS	ʿnaʿde (SING + PL)	ʿnaʿde (SING + PL)	de, dak (SING), del (PL)	?
Comparison: X surpasses Y in Z	Yes	?	No	No
Numerals 11–19	1, 2, 3,... + 10	1, 2, 3,... + 10	1, 2, 3, ... + 10	10 + 1, 2, 3, ...
Ordinals	ta + NUM	ta + NUM	?	Ordinals = cardinals, adjectives
Verb phrase				
Verb final -u	Transitive marker Yes	Transitive marker Yes	Verbal marker ? Yes	Transitive marker ?
Stative/non-stative distinction	Aspect marker gi-	Aspect marker gi-	Aspect marker gi-	Auxiliary gaed/ gahed

gi-stative verb	Habituality, ingression of verbal adjectives, some verbs	?	Duration	?
bi- marker	Future, habitual *gi*- replaces *bi*- for indicating habituality	Future, habitual	Future, habitual *gi*- replaces *bi*- for indicating habituality in town, not in countryside	Future
gi-/*bi*-		?	?	/
Anterior marker ʼkan	Yes	Yes	Yes	?
ʼkan: anterior and modal marker	Yes	Yes	?	?
Negative imperative	ʼmata IMPER/ IMPER ʼmafi	ʼmata IMPER	ʼmata IMPER	IMPER mafi
Passive of trisyllabic verbs	Stress shift to third syllable	Stress shift to third syllable	Stress shift to third syllable	Stress shift to second syllable, loss of third syllable
Nominal forms	Productive through stress shift	Productive through stress shift	Urban variety: productive: final vowel -a/Ø	Fossilized forms?
Verb 'have'	Yes	Yes	Yes, (in variation with PREP *ind* + pronoun)	No verb "have"
Other word classes Focus marker ʼya	Yes	Yes	Functions more and more as a copula	?
Clause structure Negation	Preverbal ʼma, sentence-final ʼma(f)(i)	Preverbal, sentence-final ʼma	Preverbal ʼma	Preverbal ʼma, sentence-final ʼma(f)(i)

APPENDIX: TEXTS

H.M.[1]

1. | 'Ija | 'de | | fu | 'ras | ta | sul'tan |
   |------|-----|--|-----|------|-----|---------|
   | fairy tale | DEM PROX | | in | head | GEN | sultan |

ma	nuswa'na	'to		ti'nen.	Nuswa'na		'to
and	wife-PL	PRON POSS 3SING		two	wife-PL		PRON POSS 3SING

ti'nen,	'wai	'de	ma'ma	ta	Mu'hamad	ma	'Fatna,	u	'wai	'de
two	one	DEF	mother	GEN	NPROP	AND	NPROP	and	one	DEF

ma'ma	ta	A'li.	Ma'ma	ta	'Fatna	'ya	'mary(a)	al	ma-	'aju.
mother	GEN	NPROP	mother	GEN	NPROP	FOC	woman	REL	STAT P-	want

5. | Ma'ma | ta | 'Fatna | ma | A'li, | 'marya | 'na'de | | 'jo | 'mutu. |
   |--------|-----|--------|-----|-------|--------|--------|--|------|--------|
   | mother | GEN | NPROP | and | NPROP | woman | DEM DIS | | come-Ø | die-Ø |

'Sa	al	'marya	'de	'mutu,	ma'ma	ta	A'li	'ya	'fadul
hour	REL	woman	DEF	die-Ø	mother	GEN	NPROP	FOC	remain-Ø

fi	'be	'de	'na.	Wu	'Fatna	'de	a'gi	'to,	
in	house	DEF	there	and	NPROP	DEF	self	PRON POSS 3SING	

'uo		bi'niya	al	'ja . . .,		'uo		abo'bo	je'de.
PRON 3SING		girl	REL	(be)come-Ø		PRON 3SING		mute	EMPH

'Uo		ka'man	bang-'bang	je'de.	'Dukuru	Mu'hamad	'de,	'uo
PRON 3SING		also	mentally deprived	EMPH	then	NPROP	DEF	PRON 3SING

10. | 'ya | yo'wele | al | fi | 'batna | 'be | ta | ba'ba | 'to | | 'na |
    |-----|---------|-----|----|--------|-----|-----|-------|-----|--|-----|
    | FOC | boy | REL | in | inside | house | GEN | father | PRON POSS 3SING | | there |

nyere'ku		al	a'sas	ka'mani.	'Uo		yo'wele	al	ka'man	ka'janja	je'de.
child		REL	beautiful	EMPH	PRON 3SING		boy	REL	also	energetic	EMPH

'Ya	mar'ba		'de,	'uw(o)		'endis	fu'raha			
FOC	stepmother		DEF	PRON 3SING		have-Ø	happiness			

fi	'gelba	'to		'ma	mo	nyere'ku		ta	ke'ni
in	heart	PRON POSS 3SING		NEG	with	child		GEN	co-wife

'to		'na'de.	Ba'ba	'de	ka'man	gi-	'gai		
PRON POSS 3SING		DEM DIS	father	DEF	also	PROG-	stay		

---

[1] H. M. is a 24-year old woman, living in the northern Ugandan town of Arua. During the civil war, she stayed for some time in Congo. She studied up to Secondary 4 and works at home. Besides Nubi, she knows some English, Kiswahili, and Lugbara.

15.
a'gi	'to		fi	'be	'ma.	Ba'ba	'de	gi-	'gai
self	PRON POSS 3SING		in	house	NEG	father	DEF	PROG-	stay

'bara-'bara.	'Sa 'tan	fi	'wiki	'uo		gi-	'ja	fi	'be
outside-REDUP	sometimes	in	week	PRON 3SING		PROG-	come	in	house

sa'far	ti'nen	'ama	'maf-'maf	'de	'mara	ta'lata.	U	ba'ba	'de
time(s)	two	or	NEG-REDUP	DEF	time(s)	three	and	father	DEF

'endis	fa'rash	'to		fi	'be	'na	ka'man.
have-Ø	horse	PRON POSS 3SING		in	house	there	also

'Uo	'kutu	fi	'be	na	ke'de	'gai	gi-	'chunga
PRON 3SING	put-Ø	in	house	there	SUBJ	stay-Ø	PROG-	look after

20.
kala'ma	'to		ta	'be	'na.	Fa'rash	'to		'fi.
thing-PL	PRON POSS SING		GEN	house	there	horse	PRON POSS 3SING		EXIS

'Ya	yo'wele	A'li	'de,	ma'ma	'to,		'uo		'kutu
CONJ	boy	NPROP	DEF	mother	PRON POSS 3SING		PRON 3SING		cause-Ø

M.	'de	gu-	we'di		fi 'skul	'ma.	A'li	'de	'ya	nyere'ku
NPROP	DEF	PROG-	give-PASS		in school	NEG	NPROP	DEF	FOC	child

'to		ta a'sil	'de,	'yowo		'kutu	'g(i)-	agara.	Mu'hamad
PRON POSS 3SING		truly	EMPH	CONJ + PRON 3SING		make-Ø	PROG-	study	NPROP

'de,	kan	ba'ba	'de	'ma'fi	je'de,	gi-	'gai	fi	'be,	'g(i)-	agara
DEF	when	father	DEF	EXIS NEG	EMPH	PROG-	stay	in	house	PROG	study

25.
'ma.	A'li	'de	'ya	gu-	we'di	fi	ga'raya.	Wu	A'li	'de
NEG	NPROP	DEF	FOC	PROG-	give-PASS	in	study-GER	and	NPROP	DEF

'aju	a'ku	'to		Mu'hamad	'de	'sei-'sei'de.
like-Ø	brother	PRON POSS 3SING		NPROP	DEF	very-REDUP

'Bile	Mu'hamad,	ah,	A'li	gi-	'gai	'bile	was'was.
without	NPROP	INT	NPROP	PROG-	stay	without	doubt(s)

Kan	Mu'hamad	'fi	je'de,	A'li	'endis	was'was	'tan	'ma.
when	NPROP	EXIS	EMPH	NPROP	have-Ø	doubt(s)	other	NEG

Kan	Mo'hamad	'ma'fi	je'de,	A'li	'endis	was'wasi	'zaidi.
when	NPROP	EXIS NEG	EMPH	NPROP	have-Ø	doubt(s)	a lot of

30.
'Ya	ma'ma	'de,	'ita		'ja	'kutu	asker'ya	'taki,
CONJ	mother	DEF	PRON 2SING		come-Ø	make-Ø	soldier-PL	PRON POSS 2SING

ta	sul'tan	'de	ke'de	'kasur	la'kata.	Aja'ma		we'de	'kasur	la'kata
GEN	sultan	DEF	SUBJ	cut-Ø	firewood	person-PL		DEM PROX	cut-Ø	wood

fi	'gaba	mi'lan,	'jibu	la'kata	'in.	'Sa	al	ji'bu
in	forest	many	bring-Ø	firewood	here	hour	REL	bring-PASS-Ø

la'kata,	ma'ma	'de,	'ita		'ja	'afuta	'lufura.	Fi'lel,	'it(a)
firewood	mother	DEF	PRON 2SING		come-Ø	dig-Ø	hole	at night	PRON 2SING

'afuta	'lufra	ke'biri.	'Ito		'kubu	la'kata	'de	'kulu
dig-Ø	hole	big	PRON 2SING		throw-Ø	firewood	DEF	all

35.

fu	'lufura	'de	'na.	'Ito	'kub	'fogo	dikin'ta	ti'yari.
in	hole	DEF	there	PRON 2SING	pour-Ø	in it	kerosine	ready

'Ase'd(e)	A'li	'de	gaf'lan	a'gi		'to		'g(i)-	alabu.
now	`NPROP	DEF	surprisingly	self		PRON POSS 3SING		PROG-	play

'Uo		'g(i)-	alab	ma	ak'wana	'de	a'gi	'to
PRON 3SING		PROG-	play	with	friend-Ø	DEF	self	PRON POSS 3SING

m'pira	min	'bara	'na.	Ma'ma	'de,	'ita		na'di	A'li	'de
football	from	outside	there	mother	DEF	PRON 2SING		call-Ø	NPROP	DEF

lo'go	ka'las	'ita		'dugu	'nar	gu-	'wala.	'Ito		'dugu
when	COMPL	PRON 2SING		beat-Ø	fire	PROG-	burn	PRON 2SING		beat-Ø

40.

ka'las	'nar	'amsuku	'te		'na.	Gu-	'wala.	La'kata	'de	gu-	'wala
COMPL	fire	catch-Ø	underneath		there	PROG-	burn	firewood	DEF	PROG-	burn

'sei-'sei	'de.		'Dukur	'ita		'kati	ma	'birisi
very much-REDUP	DEF		then	PRON 2SING		cover-Ø	with	mat(s)

lo'g(o)	eta		'dugu	ma	tu'ra	'de.	'Ita		'sidu	ba'kan	'de
while	PRON 2SING		beat-Ø	with	soil	DEF	PRON 2SING		close-Ø	place	DEF

'kweis.	'Ita		'kati	ma		'biris	'ma'rai	'kweis.	A'ta	je	ba'kan
good	PRON 2SING		cover-Ø	with		mat(s)	at once	good	no	like	place

al	'lufra	'in	je'de	'ma.	'Ito		'kutu	'kuris	'tak(i)
REL	hole	here	EMPH	EXIS NEG	PRON 2SING		put-Ø	chair	PRON POSS 2SING

45.

min	'wara.	'Ita		'kutu	'biris	'en	min	gi'dam	'de.
from	behind	PRON 2SING		put-Ø	mat(s)	here	from	front	DEF

Ita		na'di	Mu'hamad	'de.	'Ita		'kelem	ke'd(e)owo
PRON 2SING		call-Ø	NPROP	DEF	PRON 2SING		say-Ø	SUBJ PRON 3SING

'jib	'neta		'moyo ta	ásrúb.		'Ya	Mu'hamad,
bring-Ø	to + PRON 2SING	water	GEN	drink-INF		CONJ	NPROP

'sa	al	'ita		'ja	mo	'moyo	'de,	'it(a)	'aju
hour	REL	PRON 2SING		come-Ø	with	water	DEF	PRON 2SING	want-Ø

'midu	'kan	fi	'dar	ta	mar'ba	'taki		'de.
pass-Ø	be-ANT	in	back	GEN	stepmother	PRON POSS 2SING		DEF

50.

Mar'ba	'de	'gal:	" 'Ita	gi-	'midu	'nana
stepmother	DEF	that	PRON 2SING	PROG-	pass	to + PRON 1SING

'moyo	'de	fi	'dar	'tai		ke'fin?	'Futu,
water	DEF	in	back	PRON POSS 1SING		how?	pass-IMPER

'midu	'nana		'moyo	'de	min	gi'dam	'in."	Mu'hamad
pass-IMPER	to + PRON 1SING	water	DEF	in	front	here	NPROP

gi-	'gata	'corner.	'Bes	je	'uo	'gu-	rwa	'ja
PROG-	cut	corner	EMPH	as	PRON 3SING	PROG-	go	come-Ø

gi'dam	ma'ma	'de	'jede'de,	'uo	'meles	fu	'lufra	'de.
in front of	mother	DEF	EMPH	PRON 3SING	slip-Ø	in	hole	DEF

55. 'Jowo   gi-   'meles fu   'lufra de,   'ma'rai, ma'ma   'de,
    as + PRON 3SING PROG-   slip   in   hole   DEF   at once mother   DEF

    'it(a)   'amrugu   'biris 'de.   Ita   'kati   ba'kan 'de
    PRON 2SING   remove-Ø   mat(s) DEF   PRON 2SING   cover-Ø place DEF

    'sa   we'de.   'Ras   ba'kan 'de   'ita   'kati   ma   tu'ra
    hour   DEM PROX   head   place   DEF   PRON 2SING   cover-Ø with   soil

    'seme 'ma'rai.   'It(a)   'arija   'adul   ba'kan 'de   ja   ba'kan
    good   at once   PRON 2SING   return-Ø   prepare-Ø   place   DEF   like   place

    al   'kan   afu'ta   'ma.   Wu   fa'rash 'de   'gai   'fi   'g(i)- ain
    REL   ANT   dig-PASS-Ø   NEG   and   horse   DEF   sit-Ø EXIS   PROG-   watch

60. ka'lam al   gi-   'só.   Robu't(u)   uo.
    thing   REL   PROG-   do-PASS   tie-PASS-Ø   PRON 3SING

    La'kin 'uo   'fi   'g(i)- ain   kala'ma   al   'fi   gi-   'só
    but   PRON 3SING   EXIS   PROG-   watch thing-PL   REL EXIS   PROG-   do-PASS

    'uo.   'Uo   'g(i)-   ain.   'Fatna   'de   a'gi   'to
    PRON 3SING   PRON 3SING   PROG-   watch NPROP   DEF   self   PRON POSS 3SING

    a'wiri, bang-'bang   je'de.   Gi-   turu'j(u)   'uo   min   'in
    stupid   mentally deprived   EMPH   PROG-   chase-PASS   PRON 3SING   from   here

    je'd(e). 'Uo   'gu-   rw(a)   a'gi   'to   min   'na
    EMPH   PRON 3SING   PROG-   go   self   PRON POSS 3SING   from   there

65. 'ladi   'sa   al   bi-   na'd(i)   'owo   ka'man 'fo.
    until   hour REL   FUT-   call-PASS   PRON 3SING   EMPH   upstairs

    'Ya   A'li   'sa   al   'ja   min   ga'raya,   A'li   'asadu:
    CONJ   NPROP   hour   REL   come-Ø   from   study-GER   NPROP   ask-Ø

    "Ma'ma,   Mu'hamad   f(u)   we'ni   'ya?"   Ma'ma   'de   'gal:
    mother   NPROP   in   where   EMPH   mother   DEF   that

    "Mu'hamad   'fi   fi   'madrasa   'na   'ke."   'Gal: "Mu'hamad
    NPROP   EXIS   in   Qur'anic school   there   EMPH   that   NPROP

    'maf.   Madra'sa   'sia.   Ma'ma,   Mu'hamad   f(u)   'wen?"
    EXIS NEG   Qur'anic school-PL few   mother   NPROP   in   where

70. Ma'ma 'de   'je   'har(i). 'Uo   'turuju A'li   'd(e).   'Uo
    mother DEF   (be)come-Ø   hot   PRON 3SING   chase-Ø NPROP DEF   PRON 3SING

    'je   'hari. A'li   'de   gi-   'kaf(u)   'ase'de-'ase'de
    (be)come-Ø   hot   NPROP   DEF   PROG-   fear   now-REDUP

    ma'ma   'to   ma   a'ku   'de,   ma'ma   'de   min   'ja
    mother PRON POSS 3SING   with   brother   DEF   mother   DEF   from   come-GER

    'hari. 'Ya   'futu   'fogo   'youm   ta'lata. 'Gu-   rwa   fi   'youm   ta   'arba.
    hot   CONJ   pass-Ø   in it   day(s)   three   PROG-   go   in   day   GEN   four

    Sul'tan 'ja.   'Sa   al   sul'tan   'ja,   'uw(o)   'asadu: " 'Ah, 'Mohamed
    sultan   come-Ø   hour   REL   sultan   come-Ø   PRON 3SING   ask-Ø   INT   NPROP

75.
fu	'weni?	"Ma'ma	'de	'gal:	"Mu'hamad	'rua	fi	'madrasa."
in	where	mother	DEF	that	NPROP	go-Ø	in	Qur'anic school

"Mu'hamad	f(u)	'wen?"	"Mu'hamad	'rua	fi	'madrasa."
NPROP	in	where	NPROP	go-Ø	in	Qur'anic school

'Uo	'sten	'sa	al	ya'la	ta	'madrasa	gi-	'tala.
PRON 3SING	wait for-Ø	hour	REL	child-PL	GEN	Qur'anic school	PROG-	leave

Ya'la	'tala.	Mu'hamad	'fogo	'ma.	"Ah,	ka'lam	'de	su'nu?
child-PL	leave-Ø	NPROP	in it	EXIS NEG	INT	matter	DEF	what?

Mu'hamad	f(u)	'wen?"	'Gal:	"Mu'hamad	fi	'madrasa.	Mu'hamad
NPROP	in	where?	that	NPROP	in	Qur'anic school	NPROP

80.
you'min'de	'g(i)-	aju	'gai-'gai	fi	'be	'in	'ma.	Mu'hamad
nowadays	PROG-	want	stay-REDUP-Ø	in	house	here	NEG	NPROP

gi-	'gai-'gai	'bara-'bara	'ladi	gu-	r'wá	ji'b(u)
PROG-	stay-REDUP	outside	until	PROG-	go-PASS	bring-PASS-Ø

'uo	ma	'jibu.	Bi-	'kun	'sa	we'de	'uo
PRON 3SING	with	bring-GER	FUT-	be	hour	DEM PROX	PRON 3SING

'fi	'g(i)-	alab	fi	ji'ran	'na."	Ba'ba	'de	'kelem:	" 'Ma."
EXIS	PROG-	play	in	neighbourhood	there	father	DEF	say-Ø	no

'Youm	ta aw'lan	'de	'futu.	Ah,	nyere'ku	'de	'ben	'ma.	'De ke'fini?
day	first	DEF	pass-Ø	INT	child	DEF	appear-Ø NEG	DEF	how?

85.
'Youm	ta	ti'nen,	ba'ba	'de,	'ito	'gum.	'Ito	'rua
day	GEN	two	father	DEF	PRON 2SING	wake up-Ø	PRON 2SING	go-Ø

na	fa'rash	'de	min	'sub(u).	'It(a)	'alab-'alab	ma	fa'rash	'de.
to	horse	DEF	in	morning	PRON 2SING	play-REDUP-Ø	with	horse	DEF

'Gal:	"Mu'hamad	f(u)	'wen?"	Fa'rash	'de	'abidu	'kore.	'Sa
that	NPROP	in	where?	horse	DEF	begin-Ø	neigh-Ø	hour

al	fa'rash	'de	'abidu	'kore,	fa'rash	'de	gu-	we'ri	ba'kan 'ya
REL	horse	DEF	begin-Ø	neigh-Ø	horse	DEF	PROG-	show	place FOC

al	'ya . . .,	al	'ya	Mu'hamad	'kettis	'fogo	'de.
REL	FOC	REL	FOC	NPROP	sink-Ø	in it	DEF

90.
Ba'ba	'de	'gal:	"Ah,	ka'lam	'de	ta a'sili?"	Uw(o)	'asadu	fa'rash	'de
father	DEF	that	INT	matter	DEF	truly	PRON 3SING	ask-Ø	horse	DEF

ge'ri	'mara	ti'nen,	ta'lata.	Fa'rash	'de	'bes	gu-	we'ri	ba'kan
nearly	time(s)	two	three	horse	DEF	EMPH	PROG-	show	place

'wai-'wai	'de.	Ba'ba	'de,	'ita	'rasul(u)	asker'ya	'taki
one-REDUP	DEF	father	DEF	PRON 2SING	send-Ø	soldier-PL	your

ke'de	'ja	'gwam	'sei-'sei	'de.	Asker'ya	'ja.	'It(a)
SUBJ	come-Ø	fast	very much-REDUP	DEF	soldier-PL	come-Ø	PRON 2SING

'asadu	ma'ma	'de.	Ma'ma	'de	'aju	we'ri	'ma.	'It(a)	'asadu
ask-Ø	mother	DEF	mother	DEF	want-Ø	show-Ø	NEG	PRON 2SING	ask-Ø

95.
ma'ma	'de.	Ma'ma	'de	'aju	we'ri	'ma.	'Ita		'fiku	'labil
mother	DEF	mother	DEF	want-Ø	show-Ø	NEG	PRON	2SING	untie-Ø	rope

min	fa'rashi	'de.	'Ito		'dugu	fa'rash	'de	kur'bai	'aruba.
from	horse	DEF	PRON	2SING	hit-Ø	horse	DEF	whip(s)	four

Fa'rash	'de	'jere,	'ro	'gai	ma'rai	fi	ba'kan	al	'ya	Mu'hamad
horse	DEF	run-Ø	go-Ø	stay-Ø	at once	in	place	REL	FOC	NPROP

'kettis	'fogo.	'Ite		gi-	'dugu	fa'rash	'de.	Fa'rash	de	'agder
sink-Ø	in it	PRON	2SING	PROG-	beat	horse	DEF	horse	DEF	be able-Ø

'gum	'ma	min	ba'kan	'de.	Fa'rash	'de	'bes	'g(i)-	adaku	'ras
get up-Ø	NEG	from	place	DEF	horse	DEF	EMPH	PROG-	press	head

100.
'to		'in	je'de.	Gi-	'kore.	Ah,	'ya	ba'ba	'de,	'ita
PRON	POSS 3SING	here	EMPH	PROG-	neigh	INT	VOC	father	DEF	you

'arufu	'maf(i)	a'jol	al	'so	ka'lam	'de	fi	'batna	'be	'na.
know-Ø	NEG	person	REL	do-Ø	thing	DEF	in	inside	house	there

'De	'bes	'ya	bu-	'kun	mar'ba		'de	ka'lam	mar'ba		'de
DEF	EMPH	FOC	FUT-	be	stepmother		DEF	because	stepmother		DEF

'ya	a'jol	al	fi	'batna	'be	'na	mo	ya'la	'de.	'Ita	'rasul
FOC	person	REL	in	inside	house	there	with	child-PL	DEF	you	send-Ø

'gwam	ke'de	'ró	ji'bu		ma'ma	ta	bi'niya	'de
quickly	SUBJ	go-PASS-Ø	bring-PASS-Ø		mother	GEN	girl	DEF

105.
ma	ba'ba	'to		ma	family	'to		'tan.
with	father	PRON	POSS 3SING	with	family	PRON	POSS 3SING	other

'Gwam	'ró		ji'bu		a'nasi		'de.	Ka'man	'uo		na'di
quickly	go-PASS-Ø		bring-PASS-Ø		person-PL		DEF	also	PRON	3SING	call-Ø

ke'ya	'to		'ja	ti'yari	'mara	'wai.	'Kul	gi-	'sten
army	PRON	POSS 3SING	come-Ø	ready	at once		all	PROG-	wait for

'kan	'nas	ma'ma	'de.	Je	'nas	ma'ma	'de	gi-	'rasul	'de,
be-ANT	COLL	mother	DEF	as	COLL	mother	DEF	PROG-	arrive	DEF

'uo		'aki	kala'ma	'de.	'Uo		'kelem	nyere'ku
PRON	3SING	tell-Ø	thing-PL	DEF	PRON	3SING	say-Ø	child

110.
'to		'de,	'marya	'de	'jada	ma	'jada	fi	'lufra.
PRON	POSS 3SING	DEF	woman	DEF	throw-Ø	with	throw-GER	in	hole

Ka'lam	al	'fi,	'uw(o)		'aju	ke'd(e)	afu'ta	nyere'ku
matter	REL	EXIS	PRON	3SING	want-Ø	SUBJ	dig-PASS-Ø	child

'to	'de.	'Bada	de'kika	'kamsa	nyere'ku		'de	ke'de	'tala	'bara.
his	DEF	after	minute(s)	five	child		DEF	SUBJ	leave-Ø	outside

'Kan	a'nas	'de	'zat(u)	'afuta	bi'sesi.	A'nas	'ya	al	'g(i)-	afuta	'de,
ANT	people	DEF	EMPH	dig-Ø	slowly	people	FOC	REL	PROG-	dig	DEF

'uo		we'di	'noumon	de'kika	'kamsa.	Kan	'umon		'afuta	'ma,
PRON	3SING	give-Ø	to + PRON 3PL	minute(s)	five	if	PRON	3PL	dig-Ø	NEG

115. ke'de   katu'l(u)   umon   'bara.   'Gái   ti'yari. Gi-   ste'nu.
     SUBJ   kill-PASS-Ø   PRON 3PL   outside   stay-PASS-Ø ready   PROG-   wait for-PASS

     Bi-   daka'l(u)   'sa   ya'tu?   'Uo   bi-   'tala   'sa   ya'tu?
     FUT-   enter-PASS   hour   which?   PRON 3SING   FUT-   leave   hour   which?

     'Ya   abi'd(u)   afu'ta.   'Kabla   'lisa   'tim   'dekka   'kamsa
     CONJ   begin-PASS-Ø   dig-PASS-Ø   before   still   be over-Ø   minute(s)   five

     'na'de   'ma,   'lufra ka'las afu'ta.   Fa't(a)   owo,
     DEM DIS PL   NEG   hole   COMPL   dig-PASS-Ø   open-PASS-Ø   PRON 3SING

     size   al   je'de   nyere'ku   gi-   'ben   min   'jua.   'Nar   'ya
     size   REL   EMPH   child   PROG-   appear from   inside fire   FOC

120. al   'kan   'ya   'marya   'de   'kasur   la'kata,   al   'uo   'kasur,
     REL   ANT   FOC   woman   DEF   cut-Ø   firewood   REL   PRON 3SING   cut-Ø

     'yo   'uo   'kub   'fogo   'dikin   'sa   al   'uo
     FOC   PRON 3SING   pour-Ø   in it   kerosine   hour   REL   PRON 3SING

     gi-   'jada   nyere'ku   'de,   'yo   'uo   'to   'feker
     PROG-   throw   child   DEF   FOC   she   PRON POSS 3SING   think-Ø

     nyere'ku   'de   'haragu   ka'las   min   'jua.   'na,   ta'ra,   'sokol,
     child   DEF   burn-Ø   COMPL   in   there   on the contrary thing

     agili'b(u)   'uo   'bahar,   agilli'b(u)   'uo   'bahar
     change-PASS-Ø   PRON 3SING   sea   change-PASS-Ø PRON 3SING   sea

125. min   'jua   'na.   'Dukur   'bes   'jina   'lager   sa'kar   je'de   nyer'eku   'de
     in   inside   there   then   EMPH   smallness   stone   small   EMPH   child   DEF

     'gai   fi   'ras   'to.   'Sokol   ta   a'kulu   'ma
     stay-Ø   in   head   PRON POSS 3SING   thing   GEN   eat-GER   EXIS NEG

     fi   'jua   'moyo   'ma.   La'kin   'Rabana   'jibu   'sokole   'de,
     in   inside   water   EXIS NEG   but   NPROP   bring-Ø   thing   DEF

     'Rabana   'jibu   fruits   ta   'yembe.   'Kan   ma-   'nigitu   'Bes,   'g(i)-   alab-'alab
     NPROP   bring-Ø   fruits   GEN   mango   be-ANT   STAT P-   be ripe   EMPH   PROG-   dance-REDUP

     fi   'moyo   ge'ri   ma   nyere'ku   'de.   'Ya   nyere'ku   'de   'g(i)-   akul.
     in   water   near   with   child   DEF   CONJ   child   DEF   PROG-   eat

130. 'Bes,   'sa   al   g(i)-   afu'ta   'lufra   'de   'nusu   'bes,
     EMPH   hour   REL   PROG-   dig-PASS   hole   DEF   half   EMPH

     'sia   je'de,   ba'ba   'de   'ain(u)   nyere'ku   'to   gi-   'ben
     a bit   EMPH   father   DEF   see-Ø   child   PRON POSS 3SING   PROG-   appear

     min   'jua   'na.   Ba'ba   'de,   'ito   'nutu   min   'jua   'na.
     in   inside   there   father   DEF   PRON 2SING   jump-Ø   in   inside   there

     Ka'las,   'de   gu-   r'wá   zi'du   fa'ta   'lufra   'de   lo'g(o)
     COMPL   DEF   PROG-   go-PASS   increase-PASS-Ø open-PASS-Ø   hole   DEF   while

     'owo   'sul(u), . . . 'uw(o)   'amuta   nyere'ku   'to   ka'las.
     PRON 3SING   take-Ø   PRON 3SING   remove-Ø   child   his   COMPL

135. 'Uo 'sul(u) fi 'ida fi 'jua 'moyo 'na. A'nas 'de
     PRON 3SING take-Ø in arm in inside water there person-PL DEF

     'fata. 'Dukur 'uo 'tala. 'Sa al 'uo 'tala,
     open-Ø then PRON 3SING leave-Ø hour REL PRON 3SING leave-Ø

     'uo we'ri kala'ma 'de 'ke 'nas ba'ba ta bi'niya 'de
     PRON 3SING show-Ø thing-PL DEF SUBJ COLL father GEN girl DEF

     'fadi ma family ta bi'niya 'de 'ain ka'lam al bi'niya 'de
     openly with family GEN girl DEF see-Ø thing REL girl DEF

     'so 'fogo nyere'ku 'to. 'Uo 'ja ka'las
     do-Ø on child PRON POSS 3SING PRON 3SING come-Ø COMPL

140. 'youm ta'lata 'na're. 'Uo 'g(i)- asadu nyere'ku 'to
     day(s) three today PRON 3SING PROG- ask child PRON POSS 3SING

     f(i) 'wen? 'Gal: "Nyere'ku 'de fi 'madrasa."
     in where that child DEF in Qur'anic school

     "Nyere'ku 'to f(i) 'wen?" 'Ladi fa'rash 'de 'ya
     child PRON POSS 3SING in where? until horse DEF FOC

     'jo we'ri 'nouo ma'hal al nyere'ku 'de ku'tu 'fogo,
     come-Ø show-Ø to + PRON 3SING place REL child DEF put-PASS-Ø inside

     'ya 'ladi 'uo 'kutu afu'ta 'ya 'ladi nyere'ku 'de
     CONJ until PRON 3SING make-Ø dig-PASS-Ø FOC until child DEF

145. 'tala 'yaw. 'Uw(o) we'di 'dekka 'kamsa ke'de katu'lu 'marya 'de.
     leave-Ø EMPH PRON 3SING give-Ø minute(s) five SUBJ kill-PASS-Ø woman DEF

     A'nas ta 'marya 'de ka'man 'wonus 'ma. Duru'bu 'marya 'de.
     person-PL GEN woman DEF EMPH talk-Ø NEG shoot-PASS-Ø woman DEF

     Katu'lu 'marya 'de. 'Lufra al afu'ta 'nade'de, 'ya
     kill-PASS-Ø woman DEF hole REL dig-PASS-Ø DEM DIS FOC

     ari'ja dofu'n(u) 'fogo. Ari'ja ja'da 'fogo 'marya 'de.
     return-PASS-Ø bury-PASS-Ø in it return-PASS-Ø throw-PASS-Ø in it woman DEF

     Ka'ti. 'Uw(o) 'ab(a) a'nas 'de ke'de 'sulu 'meiti
     cover-PASS-Ø PRON 3SING forbid-Ø person-PL DEF SUBJ take-Ø body

150. ta 'marya 'de. 'Ya 'in je'de 'sa al ka'la katu'lu
     GEN woman DEF CONJ here EMPH hour REL COMPL kill-PASS-Ø

     'marya 'de 'ya sa'fari. 'Kila 'wai 'amsuku 'sika 'to,
     woman DEF FOC journey every one take-Ø road(s) PRON POSS 3SING

     'arija 'wara. 'Nas ba'ba 'de 'amsu(ku) 'sika 'toumon. 'Umon
     return-Ø back COLL father DEF take-Ø road(s) PRON POSS 3PL PRON 3PL

     'arija fi 'be 'toumon 'wara. Asker'ya 'to 'de
     return-Ø in house(s) PRON POSS 3PL back soldier-PL PRON POSS 3SING DEF

     'arija fi 'kazi 'toumon ka'man. 'Uo 'fadul ma nyere'ka
     return-Ø in work PRON POSS 3PL also PRON 3SING remain-Ø with child-PL

155. | 'to | | | fi | 'batna | 'be | 'to | | | 'na | 'baga |
|-----|---|---|-----|--------|------|-----|---|---|------|-------|
| PRON POSS 3SING | | | in | inside | house | PRON POSS 3SING | | | there | EMPH |

'bile	'marya.	'Ya	'ija	'de	ta	aw'lan	'de	'kalas	'in.
without	wife	CONJ	fairy tale	DEF	GEN	first	DEF	finish-Ø	here

Translation:

1. This fairy tale is on (top of) a sultan and his two wives. His two wives, the one is the mother of Muhammad and Fatna, and the one [the other] is the mother of Ali. The mother of Fatna is the woman who is beloved.

5. The mother of Fatna and (Ali) [Muhammad], that woman happens to die. The moment that the woman dies, the mother of Ali remains at the house there. And Fatna herself, she is a girl who became . . ., she is mute. She is also mentally deprived.

10. Then Muhammad, he is [the] boy who inside the house of his father there, is a very beautiful child. He is also a very energetic boy. Thus the stepmother, she does not have happiness in her heart with the child of that co-wife of hers. The father also he does not stay at home himself.

15. The father stays outside. Sometimes he comes two times in a week or [if] not three times. And the father also has his horse in the house there. He put [it] in the house there to keep on looking after his things of the house there.

20. His horse is there. Thus the boy, Ali, his mother, she made Muhammad not to be brought to school. Ali is her child (truly)/Ali is her real child. Well she makes [him] study. Muhammad, when the father is not there, stays at home, [he] does not study.

25. Ali is given for studies. And Ali likes his brother, Muhammad very much. With(out) Muhammad, ah, Ali stays without doubts. When Muhammad is there, Ali does not have other doubts. When Muhammad is not there, Ali has a lot of doubts.

30. Thus the mother, you begin to make your soldiers, the sultan's, cut firewood. The people cut a lot of firewood in the forest, [they] bring the firewood here. The moment that the firewood is brought, the mother, you begin to dig a hole. At night, you dig a big hole. You throw all the firewood in the hole there.

35. You pour kerosine ready in it. Now, (Ali) [Muhammad] surprisingly himself is playing. He himself is playing football with (the) friends outside there. The mother, you call (Ali) [Muhammad] when you have already made the fire burn.

40. You have made the fire catch underneath there. It is burning. The firewood is burning very much. Then you cover [it] with a mat while you throw (with the) soil [on it]. You close the place well. You cover [it] at once good with a mat. No, like a place where there is no hole (here).

45. You put your chair at the back. You put the mat here in front. You call Muhammad. You tell him to bring (to) you water for drinking. So Muhammad, the moment that you come with the water, you want to pass at the back of your stepmother.

50. The stepmother [says] that: "How do you pass (to) me the water at my back? Pass, pass (to) me the water here in front. Muhammad cuts the corner. As he is going to come in front of the mother, he slips into the hole.

55. As he slips into the hole, at once, the mother, you remove the mat. You cover the place this moment/instantly. The top of the place, you cover [it] at once well with soil. You prepare the place again like a place that has not been dug. And the horse sits there and watches the thing that is being done.

60. It is tied up. But it is there watching the things that are being done. It is watching. Fatna herself is stupid, mentally deprived. She is chased from here. She goes [away] herself from there until the moment that she will be called upstairs.

65. Thus Ali, the moment that he comes from studies/school, Ali asks: "Mama, where is Muhammad?" The mother [says] that: "Muhammad is at the Qur'anic school there." [Ali says] that: "Muhammad is not there. Qur'anic schools are few. Mama, where is Muhammad?"

70. The mother becomes furious. She chases Ali off. She becomes furious. Ali now fears his mother for his brother, his mother for becoming furious. Thus there pass three days over it. It is going to the fourth day. The sultan comes. The moment/when the sultan comes, he asks: "Ah, (in) where is Muhammad?"

75. The mother [says] that: "Muhammad went to the Qur'anic school." "Where is Muhammad?" "Muhammad went to the Qur'anic school." He waits for the moment when the children of the Qur'anic school are leaving. The children leave. Muhammad is not in it/among them. "Ah, what is the problem? Where is Muhammad?" [The mother says] that: "Muhammad is at the Qur'anic school.

80. Nowadays, Muhammad does not want to stay at home here. Muhammad stays outside until he is going to be brought with bringing. It is possible that at this moment he is there playing in the neighbourhood there." The father says: "No." The first day passes. Ah, the child does not turn up. How is that [possible]?

85. The second day, the father, you get up. You go to the horse in the morning. You play with the horse. [You say] that: "Where is Muhammad?" The horse begins to neigh. When the horse begins to neigh, the horse is showing the place that Muhammad sank into.

90. The father [says] that: "Ah, is the matter true?". He asks the horse nearly two, three times. The horse just shows the same place. The father, you send [for] your soldiers to come very quickly. The soldiers come. You ask the mother. The mother does not want to show [anything]. You ask the mother.

95. The mother does not want to show [anything]. You untie the rope

from the horse. You hit the horse [with] four whip[lashes]. The horse runs, [it] goes to stay straightaway at the place that Muhammad sank into. You are beating the horse. The horse cannot get up from the place. The horse is only pressing [down] its head.

100. It is neighing. Ah, the father, you do not know someone inside the house there who does the/[such a] thing. It can only be the stepmother because the stepmother is the person who is inside the house there with the children. You send quickly [for] the mother of the girl to be brought with her father and her other family.

105. The people are brought quickly. He also calls his army to come and be ready at once. They are all waiting for the mother and her family. As the mother and her family arrive, he [the father] tells the things. He says [that]

110. his child, the women threw [it] with throwing in the hole. The matter that is there [is that] he wants his child to be dug [out]. His child should come out in five minutes. The people (have) dug only slowly. It are the people who are digging [whom] he gives five minutes (to them). If they do not dig, they should be killed (outside)/instantly.

115. There is stayed. There is being waited. At what time will there be entered? At what time will he come out? Thus there is begun to be dug. Before those five minutes are over, the hole has already been dug. It is opened [at a] size that the child appears inside.

120. The fire [for] which the woman (had) cut the firewood, that she (had) cut, that she (had) poured kerosine on it the moment that she threw the child [in it], that she thinks that the child has already burnt inside on the contrary, the thing, it [the fire] has been changed into a sea, it has been changed into a sea inside there.

125. Then a small stone, the child sits on top of it. There is nothing to eat inside the water. But God brought the thing, God brought mango fruits. They are ripe. They are dancing on the water near (with) the child. Thus the child [can] eat.

130. The moment that the hole is dug half[way], a bit, the father sees his child appearing inside there. The father, you jump inside there. Already, the hole is going to be opened more when he has already taken, removed his child.

135. He takes [it] in [his] arms inside the water there. The people open [the hole]. Then he gets out. The moment that he gets out, he shows the things so that the father of the girl and his people and the family of the girl will see openly the thing that the girl did on his child.

140. He has come already [for] the third day today. He is asking where his child is? [She says] that: "The child is at the Qur'anic school." "Where is his child?" Until it was the horse who came to show him the place in which the child was put, thus until he made [it] to be dug until the child got out.

145. He gives five minutes for the woman to be killed. The people of the woman do not talk. The woman is shot. The woman is killed. That hole which was dug, she is (again) buried in it. The woman is (again)

thrown in it. It is covered. He [the father] forbids the people to take the body of the woman.

150. Thus here the moment that the woman has already been killed, it is [time for the] journey. Everyone takes his way, goes back. The people of the father take their ways. They go back to their houses. His [the father's] soldiers also return to their work.

155. He [the father] remains inside his house there with his children without a wife. Well the first fairy tale finishes here.

K. and R.[2]

mother—friend

1. | Ma'ma | ta | 'Faiza, | 'an(a) | | 'endi | ka'lam | 'tai | | 'je | 'ase'de. |
|---|---|---|---|---|---|---|---|---|---|---|
| mother | GEN | NPROP | PRON 1SING | | have-Ø | problem | PRON POSS 1SING | | come-Ø | now |

Nyere'ku		'tai		yo'wel(e)		'aju	'jowju.	'Wede		'an(a)
child		PRON POSS 1SING		boy		want-Ø	marry-Ø	DEM PROX		I

'arufu	'ma —	bu-	'só	ke'fini?
know-Ø	NEG	FUT-	do-PASS	how?

Fi	*ke'fini?*
in	how?

5. | 'Ma | 'ye | 'uw(o) | 'aju | 'jowju | bi'niya. | 'Uo | | 'gal | 'ke | gu's(u) |
|---|---|---|---|---|---|---|---|---|---|---|
| NEG | FOC | he | want-Ø | marry-Ø | girl | PRON 3SING | | that | SUBJ | look for-PASS-Ø |

'nouo			bi'niya.	La'kin	'an(a)	'arufu	'ma,	'ana		'ye	'endi
for + PRON 3SING			girl	but	I	know-Ø	NEG	I		FOC	have-Ø

te . . .
GEN

'Marya	*al*	*'itokum*	*'gu-*	*rwo*	*'gusu*	*ñouo*		*'de,*	*'uo*
woman	REL	PRON 2PL	PROG-	go	search-Ø	for + PRON 3SING		DEF	he

'gu-	*rwo . . .,*	*'uo*		*'gu-*	*rwo*	*'aju*	*'ma.*	*'Aju*	*wa'faka*	*ke'd(e)*
PROG-	go	PRON 3SING		PROG-	go	want-Ø	NEG	need-Ø	agree-GER	SUBJ

---

[2] K. was, at the time of the interview, a 29-year old woman from Bombo. She was born there and always lived there except for one year (1978) in Toro. Nubi is her mother tongue. She also speaks some Luganda and some English. She went to school up to secondary 3 and now works as a housewife. She is married to a Nubi man and has five children.
    R. was a 33-year old woman from Bombo. She was born in Bombo and lived there until the family went into exile in southern Sudan in 1979. They returned to Bombo in 1985. R. studied up to primary 4. She was a housewife with three children and was married to a Nubi man from Bombo. Her mother-tongue was Nubi, and she spoke some Swahili, some Luganda, and some Juba Arabic.

10. 'owo 'ya 'gusu 'marya 'to. 'Umon 'wafiki ma
PRON 3SING FOC look for-Ø wife his PRON 3PL agree-Ø with

'marya 'to. 'Yala, 'uo 'jibu 'kabar. Mi'san ab '(i)to
wife his well PRON 3SING bring-Ø news because REL PRON 2SING

'gu- rwa 'gusu 'nouo 'de, 'uo gu- r'w(a) aju 'ma.
PROG- go search-Ø for + PRON 3SING DEF PRON 3SING PROG- go want-Ø NEG

'Taki, '(i)to gu- r'w(a) aju 'adab. 'To,
PRON POSS 2SING PRON 2SING PROG- go want-Ø good manners his

'uo gu- r'w(a) aju a'sas.
PRON 3SING PROG- go want-Ø beauty

15. La'kin 'ja 'to al 'uo 'ja 'nan(a)
but come-GER his REL PRON 3SING come-Ø to + PRON 1SING

'en, 'ben je 'ow(o) 'aju 'kana 'so su'nu?
here seem-Ø as if PRON 3SING want-Ø SUBJ + PRON 1SING do-Ø what?

'Kana 'ya 'gusu 'nouo. 'Il(a) 'ase'de 'j(e) eta
SUBJ + PRON 1SING FOC search-Ø for + PRON 3SING except now like you

'kelem 'nana 'gali ya'la te you'min'de ma'tata, 'an(a)
tell-Ø to + PRON 1SING that child-PL GEN nowadays weird PRON 1SING

'endi to 'row(a) 'asad(u) 'uo gi'dam.
have-Ø GEN go-Ø ask-Ø PRON 3SING first

20. Kan 'uo 'kelem 'neta 'keta 'ya 'gusu
when PRON 3SING tell-Ø to + PRON 2SING SUBJ + PRON 2SING FOC search-Ø

'nouo, 'ase 'ita bi- 'endi to 'rua
for + PRON 3SING now PRON 2SING FUT- have GEN go-Ø

na 'awa 'to. 'Ito 'gu- rwo 'wonus
to paternal aunt PRON POSS 3SING PRON 2SING PROG- go talk-Ø

ma 'awa 'to. 'Tokum 'b(i)- ain 'nouo 'marya.
with aunt his You(PL) FUT- see to + PRON 3SING wife

Kan 'uo bu- 'rudu 'marya 'de 'ma, yal(a) 'uo bu- 'gus(u)
if he FUT- accept woman DEF NEG well he FUT- look for

25. ab 'to al 'gelba 'to 'aju.
REL PRON POSS 3SING REL heart PRON POSS 3SING want-Ø

mother—son

'Ase, ak'we, nyere'ku yo'wele, 'an(a) 'g(i)- asad(u) 'ita. 'Ita 'ja
now my friend child boy I PROG- ask you you come-Ø

'nana. 'It(a) 'aju 'kana 'ya 'gus 'neki
to + PRON 1SING you want-Ø SUBJ + PRON 1SING FOC search-Ø for + PRON 2SING

bi'niya wa'la 'fi 'tak(i) al 'it(a) 'ain ka'la?
girl or EXIS PRON POSS 2SING REL PRON 2SING see-Ø COMPL

Ka'lam 'tokum ma'tata. 'Ana bi- 'jo 'ro 'gusu,
problem PRON POSS 2PL weird PRON 1SING FUT- come go-Ø search-Ø

30. 'ita 'gal: " 'Wede a'sas ma. 'Wede 'kan ke'fini?" 'Ase,
    you that DEM PROX beautiful NEG DEM PROX EMPH how? now

    'an(a) 'aju 'keta 'kelem 'nana 'fi 'tak(i)
    PRON 1SING want-Ø SUBJ + PRON 2SING say-Ø to + PRON 1SING EXIS yours

    al 'it(a) 'ain ka'la wa'la 'it(a) 'aju ke'de gu'su
    REL PRON 2SING see-Ø COMPL or PRON 2SING want-Ø SUBJ search-PASS-Ø

    'neta?
    to + PRON 2SING

    'An(a) *'aju* *'keto* *'gus* *'nana.*
    PRON 1SING want-Ø SUBJ + PRON 2SING search-Ø for + PRON 1SING

35. 'Ase, kan 'it(a) 'aju 'ke gu's(u) 'neta, 'an(a)
    now when PRON 2SING want-Ø SUBJ search-PASS-Ø for + PRON 2SING I

    'gu- rwa 'kelem na 'awa 'taki.
    PROG- go tell-Ø to (paternal) aunt PRON POSS 2SING

    mother—*paternal aunt*

    'Ase, 'awa te yo'wele. A'ku nyere'ku 'ja 'nana. 'Uw(o) 'aju
    now aunt GEN boy brother child come-Ø to me PRON 3SING want-Ø

    'nana . . ., 'uw(o) 'aju 'kana 'gus 'nouo 'marya.
    to + PRON 1SING he want-Ø SUBJ + PRON 1SING search-Ø to + PRON 3SING wife

    'Uw(o) 'aju lo'go 'be. La'yin 'ana 'kelem: " 'An(a) 'agder
    PRON 3SING want-Ø find-Ø house but PRON 1SING say-Ø PRON 1SING can-Ø

40. 'gus 'neta 'ma. 'Kana 'ja na 'awa." 'Ase'de, 'awa,ke'fini?
    search to + PRON 2SING NEG SUBJ + I come-Ø to aunt now aunt how?

    'Sei 'fi bi'niya al 'it(a) 'agder lo'go no yo'wele 'tena 'de?
    EMPH EXIS girl REL PRON 2SING can-Ø find-Ø to boy our DEF

    'Ai, *'in(a)* *'agder* *'gusu.* *'In(a)* *'agder* *gusu* *nyere'ku* *te* *fi . . .*
    well PRON 1PL can-Ø look for-Ø we can-Ø search-Ø child GEN in

    te ji'ran 'tena al 'fi min 'fo 'na'de. 'Ita
    GEN neighbour PRON POSS 1PL REL EXIS from up DEM DIS you

    bu- *'aburu we'ri* *'nouo,* *kan* *'uo* *bu-* *'rudu* *nyere'ku* *'na'de. . . .*
    FUT- try show-Ø to + PRON 3SING whether he FUT- accept child DEM DIS

45. 'Kan ben nyere'ku al 'seme. 'Uw(o) 'endi adab. *Kan* *'uo*
    ANT seem-Ø child REL good PRON 3SING have-Ø good manners if he

    bu- *'rud(u)* *'uo,* *'seme.* *Ka'man* *kan* *'uo* *'b(i)-* *aba,*
    FUT- accept PRON 3SING good also if PRON 3SING FUT- refuse

    'ina 'b(i)- abur 'ain ba'kan 'tan.
    PRON 1PL FUT- try see-Ø place another

    Ta're, 'ita 'feker je 'ana. 'Ana, ka'man, bi'niya 'na'de
    you see PRON 2SING think-Ø like I I also girl DEM DIS

    'ya 'kan su'nu? 'Ya 'kan 'an(a) 'ainu. 'Ase, 'kan(a)
    FOC ANT what? FOC ANT PRON 1SING see-Ø now SUBJ + PRON 1SING

50.
'aburu	'kelem	'nouo		'sa	'de.	'Ana	'b(i)-	arije	'je	'neta.
try-Ø	tell-Ø	to + PRON 3SING		hour	DEF	I	FUT-	return	come-Ø	to + you

'Yala.
OK

mother—*son*

Ak'we	yo'wele,ke'fini?	Bi'niya,	'ina		lo'go	'neta		ka'las,	bi'niya	fi'lan.
my friend boy	how?	girl	PRON 1PL		find-Ø	to + PRON 2SING		already	girl	X

'It(a)		'ain	ke'fini?	'Ken(a)		'adul		'neta?
PRON 2SING		see-Ø	how?	SUBJ + PRON 1PL		arrange-Ø		for + PRON 2SING

Ya'tu?
which one?

55.
Al	te	ji'ran	'tena	min	'fo	'na'de,		ta	ma'ma	'Amina 'de.
REL	GEN	neighbour	our	from	up	DEM DIS		GEN	mother	NPROP DEF

Ma'ma,	*a'ta*	*'ana*		*'ya*	*'aju*	*'na'de*		*'ma.*
mama	EMPH	PRON 1SING		FOC	want-Ø	DEM DIS		NEG

'Ase,	'it(a)		'aju	ke'fin?	'Mus,	'youm	'na'de,		'ita	'kelem
now	PRON 2SING		want-Ø	how?	EMPH	day	DEM DIS		PRON 2SING	tell-Ø

'nana		'kana		'gus	'neta?		'Mal	bi'niya	'de
to + PRON 2SING	SUBJ + PRON 1SING		search-Ø	to + PRON 2SING		EMPH	girl		DEF

'ben	je	'seme!	'Mal	bi'niya	'de	'endis	'adabu.
seem-Ø	like	good	EMPH	girl	DEF	have-Ø	good manners

60.
'Ena	*'to*			*a'sas*	*'ma.*
eye(s)	PRON POSS 3SING			beautiful	NEG

'It(a)		'aju	'de	a'sasi,	wa'la	'it(a)		'aju	'de	'adab?
PRON 2SING		want-Ø	DEF	beauty	or	PRON 2SING		want-Ø	DEF	good manners

'An(a)	*'aju*	*al*	*a'sasi,*	*mi'san*	*kan*	*'an*		*gi-*	*'ja*	*'mas*
PRON 1SING	want-Ø	REL	beautiful	because	when	PRON 1SING		PROG-	come	walk-Ø

'mouo	*fi*	*'sika*	*je'de,*	*gi-*	*kele'm(u)*	*'gal:*	*"'Marya*		*te*	*fi'lan*
with + she	in	street(s)	EMPH	PROG-	say-PASS	that	woman		GEN	X

ya'da."
DEM ADV DIS

65.
A'sasi	'bes	'ye	'it(a)		'aju	fi	'sika?	Ka'lam	'marya	te		fi'lan
beauty	EMPH	FOC	PRON 2SING		want-Ø	in	street	because	wife	GEN		X

lo'go	'adab		'nouo		'ma, kan	'ite		'je	'jib
when	good manners		to + PRON 3SING		NEG when	PRON 2SING		come-Ø	bring-Ø

'nena		'marya al	gi-	'lim(u)		'ina		'ma.
to + PRON 1PL		woman REL	PROG-	bring together		PRON 1PL		NEG

'Ase,	ma'ma	'it(a)		'aju	'kan(a)	'jib		'marya	al	kan	a'nas
now	mother	PRON 2SING		want-Ø	SUBJ + I	bring-Ø		woman	REL	when	people

gi-	'j(a)	ain	je'de,	'bes	'g(i)-	ain	'marya:	'De	'an	gi-	'kaf(u)
PROG-	come	see-Ø	EMPH	well	PROG-	see	woman	DEF	I	PROG-	be afraid

70. 'owo   'mara 'wai."?!! 'An(a) 'tai,   'an(a) 'aju 'marya
  PRON 3SING instantly I   PRON POSS 1SING I   want-Ø wife

  al a'sas.
  REL beautiful

  Eeh nyere'ku   ta'yi, a'sas a'ta 'b(i)- awun(u) 'ita   'ma. A'sas
  INT child   of mine beauty EMPH FUT- help PRON 2SING   NEG beauty

  yeu'min'd(e) 'endis a'yan. A'sas yeu'min'de gi- 'katul(u) a'nasi.   'Ai,
  nowadays have-Ø disease beauty nowadays PROG- kill person-PL yes

  a'sas 'de 'kan 'in(a)   'aba 'ma. Ta a'sil 'aju   a'jol 'sulu
  beauty DEF ANT PRON 1PL   refuse-Ø NEG really have to-Ø   person take-Ø

75. 'marya al a'sasi, la'kin lo'go 'uw(o)   'endis 'adab.
  wife REL beautiful but when PRON 3SING have-Ø good manners

  'Ase, 'marya 'na'de   'yeta   ku'sima nana   la'kin
  now woman DEM DIS   FOC + PRON 2SING admire-Ø for + PRON 1SING but

  ma'l(u) 'uo   a'sas 'ma.
  EMPH PRON 3SING beautiful NEG

  'Ase, 'tak(i)   'kan 'ite   'feker ya'tu?
  now PRON POSS 2SING ANT PRON 2SING think-Ø which?

  'Ke gu'su   al   a'sasi. Ke'd(e) abu'ru   gu'su   gi'dam.
  SUBJ look for-PASS-Ø REL beautiful SUBJ try-PASS-Ø   look for-PASS-Ø first

80. 'Ase'de, 'na'de 'kan 'in(a) 'ain(u) ma 'awa 'taki.
  now DEM DIS ANT PRON 1PL see-Ø with aunt PRON POSS 2SING

  'Ken(a)   'abur 'ro 'gus 'tan je 'ite 'kelem 'de?
  SUBJ + PRON 1PL try-Ø go-Ø look for-Ø another like you say-Ø DEF

  'Ah.
  yes

  Ka'man kan 'ine bi- 'je 'kelem 'neta,   'gal 'ita 'kelem:
  EMPH when we FUT- come tell-Ø to + PRON 2SING that   you say-Ø

  "A'ta a'sa 'ma", 'ase 'bag(a) 'ita 'ro 'jib(u) 'taki   'de.
  EMPH beautiful NEG now EMPH you go-Ø bring-Ø PRON POSS 2SING DEF

85. 'Yala 'baga 'ina   bi- 'ja 'so su'nu? 'Ina bi- 'ja 'dakal
  well EMPH PRON 1PL FUT- come do-Ø what? we FUT- come enter-Ø

  'fogo? La'kin kan bu- lo'go   ka'man al 'ita 'jibu 'de 'gal
  in it but when FUT- find-PASS also REL you bring-Ø DEF that

  ne'siya 'ma, 'ita bi- 'j(a) 'afin(u)   'ito   'fogo.
  good NEG PRON 2SING FUT- come smell-Ø PRON 2SING in it

  'Yala.
  OK

  mother—(paternal) aunt

  'Ase, 'awa te bi'niya. Ke'fini? Ka'lam al 'youm 'da 'ana 'ja
  now aunt GEN girl how? problem REL the other day I   come-Ø

90. 'mo   'neta   'de, 'an(a) 'asadu yo'wele 'tayi,
    with + PRON 3SING to + PRON 2SING DEF I   ask-Ø   boy   PRON POSS 1SING

    'ana   'kelem 'nouo   'fogo, la'kin yo'wel(e)   'aba.
    PRON 1SING   tell-Ø to + PRON 3SING on it   but   boy   refuse-Ø

    'Gal   bi'niya 'de   a'sas   'ma.   'Uw(o)   'aju   a'gi   'to
    that   girl   DEF   beautiful NEG PRON 3SING   want-Ø   self   PRON POSS 3SING

    bi'niya al   a'sasi. 'An   'kelem 'nouo: "Bi'niya 'de   a'sasi.
    girl   REL   beautiful PRON 1SING tell-Ø to + PRON 3SING girl   DEF   beautiful

    Bi'niya 'de   'endis 'adab."   'Gal: "A'ta   a'sasi 'ma." 'An(a) 'aju 'jib
    girl   DEF   have-Ø good manners that EMPH   beautiful NEG   I   want-Ø bring-Ø

95. 'nouo   'marya al   a'nas   kan   gi-   'j(a) ayin je'de,
    to + PRON 3SING wife   REL   person-PL   when   PROG- come   see-Ø EMPH

    gi-   'jere? Uw(o)   'aju   a'jol al   a'sasi,   al   kan   'uo
    PROG- run   PRON 3SING want-Ø person REL   beautiful REL   when   PRON 3SING

    gi-   'mas   'mouo   fi   'sika, 'ke   kele'm(u)   'gal: " 'Ain,
    PROG- walk   with + she in   street SUBJ   say-PASS-Ø   that   see-IMPER

    'marya te   fi'lan 'ya'da. 'Sei 'wede   'haki? La'kin 'mal bi'niya 'de
    wife   GEN   X   DEM ADV EMPH DEM PROX right   but   EMPH girl   DEF

    'kan   'endis 'adabu. Wu   a'nas   'to   'kul
    ANT   have-Ø good manners and   person-PL   PRON POSS 3SING all

100. a'nas   ta   'fakhma.
     person-PL   GEN   understanding

     'Ase, 'it(a) 'ain ke'fini? 'Bes, 'kena,   'kena   'so
     now   you   see-Ø how   EMPH   SUBJ + PRON 1PL   SUBJ + PRON 1PL   do-Ø

     'wede'de, wa'la 'keno   'ro   'gus   'tan?
     DEM PROX or   SUBJ + PRON1PL   go-Ø   look for-Ø   other

     'Uo   'kelem 'kena   'gus   'nouo   tan. 'Ana
     PRON 3SING   say-Ø SUBJ + PRON 1PL search-Ø for + PRON 3SING   other I

     'kan   'kelem 'now(o):   " 'Ase'de ke'fin?" Ke'de 'yal(a) 'uo   'jib(u)
     ANT   say-Ø   to + PRON 3SING now   how?   SUBJ   well   PRON 3SING bring-Ø

105. 'to,   al   'endis 'adab   'to.   'Uo 'gal
     PRON POSS 3SING   REL   have-Ø good manners PRON POSS 3SING   he   that

     ah'ah, 'ken(a)   'arija   'gus   'nouo   tan.
     nono   SUBJ + PRON 1PL   return-Ø search-Ø for + PRON 3SING other

     'Ase'de, kan   'ino   'ro   'gus   'nouo   tan, 'uo
     now   when PRON 1PL   go-Ø   search-Ø for + PRON 3SING   other PRON 3SING

     bu-   'rudu? Wa'la 'besi, 'kena   'seb   'nouo,   ke'd(e)
     FUT-   accept or   EMPH   SUBJ + PRON 1PL   leave-Ø to + PRON 3SING   SUBJ

     'uo   'ro   'gus,   'yala ke'd(e) uo   'jib(u)
     PRON 3SING   go-Ø   look for-Ø   well   SUBJ   PRON 3SING bring-Ø

110. 'nena   'marya   'to   al   'gelba   'to   'aju?
     to + PRON 1PL woman   PRON POSS 3SING   REL   heart   PRON POSS 3SING   want-Ø

     Mi'san 'ase'de 'sala   'ina   'gu- rwo 'gus   'tani   al
     because now   even if PRON 1PL   PROG- go   search-Ø other   REL

     bi-   ji'bu   'nouo   'de,   'uo   bu-   'rudu   'ma.
     FUT-   bring-PASS   for + PRON 3SING DEF   PRON 3SING   FUT-   accept NEG

     'Sa 'tan 'fi   'to   al   'uw(o)   'aju.
     mayb EXIS PRON POSS 3SING   REL   PRON 3SING   want-Ø

     'Mus 'ya   ka'man 'an   'kelem 'now(o)?   'An   'gal: " 'Ase'de,
     EMPH FOC   also   PRON 1SING   say-Ø to + PRON 3SING I   that   now

115. 'it(a)   'endi   ab   'it(a)   'ayin ka'la? 'Ito 'gu-   rwa 'jib
     PRON 2SING   have-Ø   REL   PRON 2SING   see-Ø COMPL you   PROG- go bring-Ø

     'kena   'so   'sokole 'de?   Wa'la 'kena   'ro   'gus? "
     SUBJ + PRON 1PL   do-Ø   thing   DEF   or   SUBJ + we   go-Ø   look for-Ø

     'Gal   'ken(a)   'arija   'gus   'nouo   tan. 'Ana   'kelem
     tha   SUBJ + PRON 1PL   return-Ø search-Ø to + PRON 3SING other PRON 1SING say-Ø

     'now(o):   " 'Ase,   kan   'ino bu-   'gusu,   ka'man kan   'ina
     to + PRON 3SING   now   when we   FUT- look for also   when PRON 1PL

     bi-   'jib,   'ita   'b(i)-   aba,   'ite   bi-   'so   'sokole 'de,
     FUT-   bring   PRON 2SING FUT-   refuse PRON 2SING FUT-   do   thing   DEF

120. 'ita   'gu-   rwa 'jib(u) ab   'taki.   'Yala 'baga 'ina
     PRON 2SING PROG- go   bring-Ø REL   PRON POSS 2SING well EMPH   we

     'ja   'dakal fu kala'ma."
     come-Ø   enter-Ø in matter-PL

     'Ase'de, ke'd(e) abu'ru   asa'du   'nouo   te   ma'ma 'Hawa 'de?
     now   SUBJ   try-PASS-Ø ask-PASS-Ø to + PRON 3SING GEN   mother NPROP DEF

     Kan 'uo   bu-   'rudu, ke'd(e) owo   'sul(u) 'uo. Ka'man kan
     when PRON 3SING   FUT-   accept SUBJ   PRON 3SING   take-Ø   her   also   when

     'uw(o)   'aba,   ke'd(e) owo   'ro   'jib(u) ab   su'nu? Ab   'to
     PRON 3SING   refuse-Ø SUBJ   PRON 3SING go-Ø   bring-Ø REL   what   REL his

125. al   'uw(o)   'aju   'de.   Mi'san gi-   'ben   'nana   jo   'fi
     REL   PRON 3SING   want-Ø DEF   because PROG- seem   to + PRON 1SING   as if EXIS

     'to   al   'uw(o) 'aju, la'kin ke'lem 'to   'ya
     PRON POSS 3SING   REL   he   want-Ø but   tell-GER PRON POSS 3SING   FOC

     'gow 'nouo.
     tough to + PRON 3SING

     'Uo   'fi   fi   dere'b(e)   'en.   'Kan(a)   'abur na'd(i)
     PRON 3SING EXIS   in   back of house here   SUBJ + PRON 1SING   try-Ø call-Ø

     'owo,   'an(a)   'kelem 'now(o).
     PRON 3SING PRON 1SING   say-Ø to + PRON 3SING

mother—*son*

130. A.,   'abur   'tal   'ya'de.   Ak'w(e) asa ke'fin? Bi'niya 'na'de
    NPROP try-IMPER come-IMPER DEM ADV PROX friend now how? girl   DEM

    ka'las   'it(a)   'aba.   'Ina 'seb   'badu   'mouo.   'Ase   'fi
    COMPL PRON 2SING refuse-Ø we leave-Ø together with + PRON 3SING now EXIS

    ta   ma'ma 'Hawa 'de.   '(I)t(a)   'ayin   ke'fin?
    GEN   mother NPROP DEF PRON 2SING see-Ø   how?

    Oh, ma'ma 'ahah. Bi'niya na'de   a'ta   a'sas   'ma.   A'ta 'ana   'ya
    INT   mother nono   girl   DEM DIS   EMPH beautiful NEG EMPH I   FOC

    'aju   bi'niya 'na'de 'ma.   Bi'niya 'de   gi-   'sitim(u) a'nas. 'Yala ka'man
    want-Ø girl   DEM   NEG   girl   DEF   PROG   insult person-PL well also

135. 'uw(o)   'endi 'fi   'asma 'to   al   'yal   we'le 'kutu
    PRON 3SING have-Ø EXIS name PRON POSS 3SING REL child-PL boy-PL put-Ø

    'now(o).   'Euh, gi-   'já   saka'l(a)   'ana.
    for + PRON 3SING INT PROG- come-PASS tease-PASS-Ø PRON 1SING

    'Asma 'de   ka'bila 'asma ya't(u) al   gi-   'já   saka'l(a)   eta
    name(s) DEF type   name(s) which? REL PROG- come-PASS tease-PASS-Ø you

    'mo   'de?
    with + PRON 3SING DEF

    A'ta, 'bes   a'nas 'bes   'kutu-'kutu 'nouo   'asma-'asma je'de.
    no   EMPH people EMPH put-REDUP-Ø to + PRON 3SING name(s)-REDUP EMPH

140. *Ah,* a'ta   'ana   'ya   'aj(u) 'uo   'ma.
    INT   EMPH PRON 1SING FOC want-Ø PRON 3SING NEG

    'Asma 'de,   'kan 'uo   'seregu? 'Uo   'so   su'nu al   'ya
    name(s) DEF ANT PRON 3SING steal-Ø PRON 3SING do-Ø what? REL FOC

    ku'tu   'nouo   'asma al   'ita   gi-   'kaf   'gal
    put-PASS-Ø to + PRON 3SING name(s) REL PRON 2SING PROG- be afraid that

    ka'lam 'asma 'de. G(i)- a'ju   a'jol ka'lam 'asma wa'la 'adab
    because name(s) DEF PROG- want-PASS person because name(s) or   good manners

    'to?   'Mus 'wede   'ya   ka'lam al   'youm   'da 'an
    PRON POSS 3SING EMPH DEM PROX FOC problem REL the other day I

145. gi-   'kelem 'de?
    PROG- say   DEF

    'Mm, 'ana   'tai   'an(a) 'aju   bi'niya al   'ameri.
    INT   PRON 1SING PRON POSS 1SING I   want-Ø girl   REL red

    Al   'amer 'ye   'it(a)   'aju?!!
    REL red   FOC PRON 2SING want-Ø

    Mmm.
    INT

    Al   'aswe 'de   'it(a)   'aju   'ma?
    REL black DEF PRON 2SING want-Ø NEG

150. *Mmm.*
INT

'It(a)   'aju   al   a'sasi?
PRON 2SING want-Ø REL beautiful

'An(a)   'aju   al   a'sas.
PRON 1SING want-Ø REL beautiful

'Yala, 'ro   'jib(u)   al   'taki 'de   'kena
well   go-IMPER bring-IMPER REL yours DEF SUBJ + PRON 1PL

'ja   'ayin. 'Ase, 'kan 'it(a)   'ayin mu'nu?
come-Ø see-Ø now ANT PRON 2SING see-Ø who?

155. 'An(a)   'aju . . . fi bi'niya, fi Mar'yam. . . .
PRON 1SING want-Ø EXIS girl EXIS NPROP

Translation:

mother—*friend*

1. Mama of Faiza, I have my problem [that] came now. My son wants to marry. This—I do not know—how it will be done?
How?
5. It is not that he wants to marry a [specific] girl. He [says] that a girl should be searched for him. But I don't know, it is me who has to . . . *The woman whom you(PL) are going to search for him, he is not going . . ., he is not going to like [her]. It needs*
10. *an agreement so that it is him who looks for his wife. [Let] (them)/him agree with his wife.*
[Let] him bring the news. Because the one you are going to search for for him, he is not going to want. Yours, you are going to want good manners. His, he is going to want beauty.
15. But his coming that he came [with] here to me, it seems as if he wants that I do what? That I am the one searching for him. Except now like you tell me that the children (of) nowadays are weird, I have to go and ask him first.
20. *When he tells you that it is you to search for him, now you will have to go to his (paternal) aunt. You are going to talk to his (paternal) aunt. You(PL) will find a wife for him. If he is not going to accept the woman, well he will look for his,*
25. *whom his heart wants.*

mother—*son*

Now, my (friend) son, I am asking you. You came to me. Do you want that I look for a girl for you or is there yours whom you have already seen? Your (PL) problem is weird. I will search, [and]
30. you [will say] that: "This [one] is not beautiful. How is this one?"

Now, I want you to tell me [whether] there is yours whom you have seen already or do you want that there is searched for you?
I want that you look for me.

35. Now, when you want that there is searched for you, I am going to tell your aunt.

mother—*paternal aunt*

Now, aunt of the boy. [The] boy came to me. He wants for me . . ., he wants that I will search for him a wife. He wants to find a home. But I told him:

40. "I cannot look for you. Let me come to auntie." Now, auntie, how? Is there really a girl whom you can find for our boy?
Yes, we can search. We can (search)/ask the child of in . . ., of our neighbour who is up there. You may try to show him whether he will accept that child. . . .

45. *[She] seems [to be] a good child. She has good manners. If he will accept her, [then it is] good. Also if he will refuse. We will try to look for another place.*
You see, you think like me. I, also, what was that girl? [It was her] that I had seen.

50. Now, let me try to tell him now. I will come back to you.
OK

mother—*son*

My [dear] boy, how [are you]? A girl, we have already found [one] for you, girl X. How do you see [her]? Shall we arrange [her] for you?
Which one?

55. Of our neighbour up there, of mama Amina.
Mama, I definitely do not want that one.
Now, how do you want [it]? The other day, you told me to look for you, isn't it? The girl seems to be good! The girl seems to have good manners!

60. *Her eyes are not beautiful.*
Do you want (it is) beauty, or do you want (it is) good manners?
I want a beautiful one because when I am going to walk with her in the streets, [that] there is said that:
"The wife of X is over there."

65. Beauty, you just want [it] [for] in the streets? Because the wife of X, when she does not have good manners, when you will bring a wife to us, who does not bring us together.
Now, mama, do you want me to bring a wife whom, when the people see her, well [when they] see the woman, [they will say that]: "I am afraid of her instantly"?!!

70. *I, for me, I want a beautiful wife.*
Eeh, my child, beauty, it won't help you at all. Beauty nowadays has disease. Beauty nowadays kills people. Yes, beauty, we would not refuse [it]. Really, a person should take a wife who is beautiful,

75. but when she has good manners.
     Now, that woman whom you admire for me, but she is not beautiful.
     Now, yours, whom would you think of?
     A beautiful one should be looked for. Let [such one] be tried to be looked for first.
80.   Now, that one we had seen with your aunt. Shall we try to go and
     look for another one like you say?
     Yes.
     When we will come to tell you, [and] (that) you [will] say [that]: "Not
     beautiful", now [then] you will bring yours.
85.   Well, what will we do? We will enter into it?. But when will be
     found [out] that also the one whom you brought, that [she] is not
     good, you yourself will smell in it/you will be in for it
     OK.

mother—*aunt*

     Now, aunt of the (girl)/[boy]. How [are you?] The problem that the
     other day I came with (it) to you,
90.   I asked my boy, I told him about it, but the boy refused. [He says]
     that the girl is not beautiful. He himself wants a beautiful girl. I told
     him: "The girl is beautiful. The girl has good manners." [He said]
     that: "[She] is not beautiful at all."
95.   Do I want to bring him a wife whom when the people see [her],
     [they] will run? He wants a beautiful person about whom, when she
     walks with him in the street, it is said that: "Look, the wife of X is
     over there."
     Is this right? But the girl has good manners. And all her people are
     understanding people.
100. *Now, how do you see [it]? Should we just, should we do this, or should we go
     and look for another [one]?*
     He said that we should look for another [one] for him. I have told
     him: "Now, how?" Well let him bring his who has (her) good manners.
105. He [said] that, no no, we should again look for him for another [one].
     *Now, when we go and look for another [one] for him, will he accept [her]? Or
     should we just leave it to him so that he goes and searches,*
110. *well so that he brings his woman to us, whom his heart wants. Because now
     even if we are going to look for another one, who will be brought for him, he
     will not accept [her]. Maybe, there is his, whom he wants.*
     Didn 't I also told him as such? I [said] that:
115. "Now, you have [one] whom you have seen already? Are you going
     to bring [her] so that we do the thing? Or should we search? " [He
     said] that we should look for another [one] for him. I told him: "Now,
     when we will look, [and] when we will bring [one], and you will
     refuse, [then] you will do the thing,
120. you are going to bring yours. Well, we will enter into the matters."
     *Now, let the one of mama Hawa be tried and asked for him? When he will
     accept, let him take her. Also when he [will] refuse, let him go and bring what?*

125. *His, whom he wants. Because it seems to me as if there is his, whom he wants,*
but his telling/to tell is tough for him.
He is here at the back of the house. Let me try to call him, [and]
(I) tell him.

mother—*son*

130. Abdallah, try and come here. My friend, how [are you] now? That
girl, you have already refused [her]. We have left her (together). Now,
there is [the one] of mama Hawa. How do you see [her]?
Oh mama, no no. That girl is not beautiful at all. I definitely do not want that
girl. That girl insults people.

135. *Well also she has her names that the boys give her. Euh, I am going to be teased.*
The names are what type of names, which you are going to be teased
with?
No, people just give her names.

140. *Ah, I definitely do not want her.*
The names, has she stolen? What did she do that names are given
to her that you are scared because of the names. Is someone liked
because of [his] names or [because of his] good manners? This is the
thing that I said the other day, isn 't it?

145. *Mm, I myself, I want a red/light skinned girl.*
A light skinned [one] it is that you like?!!
Mmm.
The black [ones] you do not want?

150. *Mmm.*
You want a beautiful one?
I want a beautiful one.
Well, go and bring yours so that we see [her]. Now, whom did you
see?

155. *I want . . . there is a girl, there is Maryam. . . .*

M.K.[3]

1.	Wa'nasa	ta	'mana				
	talk-GER	GEN	meaning				
	A'nas	ta	za'man	'kelem . . . Ta	aw'lan: ne'gi	fi	'hagu.[4]
	person-PL	GEN	old days	say-Ø	GEN	NUM keen	on	his thing

---

[3] M.K. was a 54-year-old male. He was born in Mbarara in the western part
of Uganda from a Nubi father and mother. As an adult he lived mainly in Bombo
and Kampala and spent 8 years in exile in southern Sudan. His mother tongue
was Nubi, but he also spoke English, Swahili, Luganda, the related languages
Runyankole-Rutoro-Ruchiga-Runyoro, and Juba Arabic and had some passive knowledge of Arabic. M.K. finished high school, non-university level.

[4] Sudanese Arabic *ḥagg* functions as a particle that expresses possession. It is fol-

Mana   'to,   'kil(a)   a'zol   ne'gi   fi   'sokol
meaning PRON POSS 3SING   every   person keen   on   thing

'to.   'Ite   ne'gi   fi   nyere'ku   'taki.
PRON POSS 3SING   PRON 2SING   keen   on   child   PRON POSS 2SING

5. 'Ite   ne'gi   fi   'jua   'taki.   'Ite   ne'gi
    PRON 2SING   keen   on   house   PRON POSS 2SING   PRON 2SING   keen

    fi   'kila   'haja   'taki.   'Mana 'to,   'ita   'ma
    in   every   thing   PRON POSS 2SING   it means that   PRON 2SING   NEG

    'aju   'sokol   'taki   'de   ke'de   'karab.
    want-Ø   thing   PRON POSS 2SING   DEF   SUBJ   be spoilt-Ø

    'Yena   gi-   'kelem: ne'gi   fi   'hagu.
    CONJ + PRON 1PL   PROG-   say   keen   on   his thing'

    'Sala   kan   nyere'ku   'taki   'so   ma'kosa,   'bes   'ita
    even   if   child   PRON POSS 2SING   do-Ø   mistake   EMPH   PRON 2SING

10. 'ya   'arufu   'uo   'so   ma'kosa 'ma,   ka'lam 'ite   ne'gi
    FOC   know-Ø   PRON 3SING   do-Ø   mistake NEG   because PRON 2SING   keen

    fu   nyere'ku   'taki.
    on   child   PRON POSS 2SING

    Te   ti'nen: za'man 'ma   li'go.   'Mana 'to,   a'jol   al   gi- 'gem(u)
    GEN   two   old days NEG   find-PASS-Ø   it means that   person REL   PROG- pride

    'uo   kan   'uo   lo'go   'mali,   'yena
    PRON 3SING   when   PRON 3SING   receive-Ø   wealth   FOC + PRON 1PL

    gi-   'kelem   'gal   za'man   'kan   'uo   mis'kin, 'uo   'me
    PROG-   say   that   old days be-ANT   PRON 3SING   poor   PRON 3SING   NEG

15. 'endu.   'Ase'de, min   'uo   lo'go,   'dukur 'bag(a)   'owo
    have-Ø   now   since   PRON 3SING   receive-Ø then   EMPH PRON 3SING

    'ja   'gem.
    come-Ø   boast-Ø

    'Namba   ta'lata gi-   'kelem: ku'wafu 'raba   a'tim.   'Mana 'to,   a'tim
    number   three   PROG-   say   fear   raise-Ø   orphan   it means that   orphan

    'raba   fu   'be   ta   a'zol   'tan.   'Uo   'gai
    grow up-Ø   in   house   GEN   person   other   PRON 3SING   stay-Ø

    ma   ku'waf(u).   'Uo   'ma   'gai   ma   ha'gar.
    with   fear   PRON 3SING   NEG   stay-Ø   with   meanness

---

lowed by a pronominal suffix or by a noun expressing the possessor (see Roth-Laly
1969b: 121). *ḥagg* + -*u* (Sudanese Arabic pronominal suffix for the third person singular masculine) is reinterpreted as one word in Nubi and could best be translated
as 'his thing', 'his possession'.

20. | Mi'sen | bi'ses-bi'ses, | 'sa | al | 'uo | lo'go | 'tabu, |
|---|---|---|---|---|---|---|
| because | slowly-REDUP | hour | REL | PRON 3SING | get-Ø | trouble(s) |

'uo		'bes	'gen	mo	ku'waf(u)	'to.
PRON 3SING		EMPH	stay-Ø	with	fear	PRON POSS 3SING

Je	'de.		'Lad(i)	'owo	'raba,		'uo	'ma
like	DEM PROX		until	PRON 3SING	grow up-Ø		PRON 3SING	NEG

'so	ha'gar.	'Ya	'Nubi	gi-	'kelem	'gal	ku'wafu	'raba	a'tim.	Ka'lam
do-Ø	meanness	CONJ	NPROP	PROG-	say	that	fear	raise-Ø	orphan	because

a'tim	'de	'raba	ka'las.	'Uo		'je	ke'bir
orphan	DEF	grow up-Ø	COMPL	PRON 3SING		become-Ø	big

25. | 'Namba | 'arba | gi- | 'kelem: | 'sifa-sifa | | je'resa. | 'Mana | 'to, | a'jol |
|---|---|---|---|---|---|---|---|---|---|
| number | four | PROG- | say | praise-REDUP-GER | | shame | it means | that | person |

al	gi-	'sifa-sifa	'nafsi	'to		fu	'sokol	fila'niya,
REL	PROG-	praise-REDUP	soul	PRON POSS 3SING		for	thing	any

kanu	ka'lam	'de,	'sokol	'na'de		'uo	'ja	'karab,
when	thing	DEF	thing	DEM DIS		PRON 3SING	come-Ø	spoil-Ø

gi-	'jibu	'nouo		'haya.	'Ya	'mana	'to		je'resa.	'Ita
PROG-	bring	to + PRON 3SING		shame	CONJ	meaning	PRON POSS 3SING		shame	you

gi-	'sifa-'sif(a)	'eta		'gal	'ita	'abu	'guwa,
PROG-	praise-REDUP	PRON 2SING		that	PRON 2SING	possessor of	force

30. | au | 'it(a) | ab | du'ra. |
|---|---|---|---|
| or | PRON 2SING | possessor of | biceps |

La'kin	'ita		'jo	lo'go	a'jol	'wai	'amsuk(u)		'ita,
but	PRON 2SING		come-Ø	meet-Ø	person	INDEF	take-Ø		PRON 2SING

'arim(u)	'ita		fala'ta.	'Dukur	'ito		lo'go	je'resa.
throw-Ø	PRON 2SING		down	then	PRON 2SING		find-Ø	shame

'Yala,	'youm	'kul	'ita		gi-	'sifa-'sif(a)		'eta
well	day(s)	all	PRON 2SING		PROG-	praise-REDUP		PRON 2SING

'gal	'ita		'ya	a'jol	to	'gudra.
that	PRON 2SING		FOC	person	GEN	strength

35. | 'Namba | 'kamsa | 'kelem: | 'mutu | ke'tiri | 'fara. | 'Wede | wa'nasa | | ta |
|---|---|---|---|---|---|---|---|---|---|
| number | five | say-Ø | die-GER | many | joy | DEM PROX | talk-GER | | GEN |

wa'ze		za'man	al	gu-	we'di	'guwa	'noumon
old person-PL		old days	REL	PROG-	give	strength	to + PRON 3PL

ke'd(e)	'omon		'dusman	dus'man	ta	aske'riya.	'Ma
SUBJ	PRON 3PL		fight-Ø	war	GEN	soldier-PL	NEG

gi-	si'bu	a'k(u)	'wai	ke'd(e)	'ow		'mutu	'uo
PROG-	leave-PASS	brother	one	SUBJ	PRON 3SING		die-Ø	PRON 3SING

ba'rau.	'Umon		gi-	'lim(u)	'umon		'kul	ke'd(e)	umon
alone	PRON 3PL		PROG-	gather	PRON 3PL		all	SUBJ	PRON 3PL

40.
'ro	ba'kan	'wai.	'Fara	'de,	'mana 'to	je	'hafla	ke'bir.
go-Ø	place	one	joy	DEF	it means that	like	party	big

Kan	'uo		'mutu	ba'kan	'wai,	gu-	we'ri	'gal
when	PRON 3SING		die-Ø	place	one	PROG-	show-PASS	that

'umon		'mutu	'sawa	'bil(a)	'umon		'kaf.	'De	'ya
PRON 3PL		die-Ø	together	without	PRON 3PL		be afraid-Ø	DEF	FOC

wa'nasa	'toumon		ta	za'man	al	gu-	we'di	'gudra,	'gal:
talk-GER	PRON POSS 3PL		GEN	old days	REL	PROG-	give	strength	that

" 'Ro-	tokum	'na,	'dusman-		'itakum.	Kan	'ina		'mutu,	'ina
go-IMPER-	ADR PL	there	fight-IMPER-		ADR PL	when	PRON 1PL		die-Ø	we

45.
'mutu	'kul."	'Ma'f(i)		a'jol	al	ke'de	'jer(e)	'arija	'wara.
die-Ø	all	EXIS NEG		person	REL	SUBJ	run-Ø	return-Ø	back

'Namba	'sita	gi-	'kelem:	ne'siba	'kati	'semsi.	'Mana	'to	kan
number	six	PROG-	say	relative	cover-Ø	sun	it means	that	when

'it(a)	'endi	ne'siba		'taki,		kan	'uw(o)		'awun(u)
PRON 2SING	have-Ø	relative		PRON POSS 2SING		when	PRON 3SING		help-Ø

'ita	fi	'shida,		'de	'ya	'sems(i)	al	'uo
PRON 2SING	in	problem(s)		DEF	FOC	sun	REL	PRON 3SING

'kati	me	sem'siya.	Kan	'semsi	gi-	'harag(u)		'ita,
cover-Ø	with	parasol	when	sun	PROG-	burn		PRON 2SING

50.
'uo	'jib	shem'shiya,	'uo	'kutu	fi	'ras
PRON 3SING	bring-Ø	parasol	PRON 3SING	put-Ø	on	head

'to,		fi	'ras	'taki,		'mana 'to,
PRON POSS 3SING		on	head	PRON POSS 2SING		it means that

'uw(o)	'awun(u)	'ita	min	'hari	ta	'sems.
PRON 3SING	help-Ø	PRON 2SING	from	heat	GEN	sun

Au	kan	'shida	'waga	'neta,		ne'siba	'taki
or	when	problem(s)	fall-Ø	to + PRON 2SING		relative	PRON POSS 2SING

bi-	'jere,	'uo	'ja	'awun(u)	'ita		fi	'shida
FUT-	run	PRON 3SING	come-Ø	help-Ø	PRON 2SING		in	problem(s)

55.
'de.	'Yena		'gi-	'kelem	ne'siba	'kati	'sems.
DEF	CONJ + PRON 1PL		PROG-	say	relative	cover-Ø	sun

Ta	'saba	gi-	'kelem:	'keli	'akul	ka'sara.	'Mana	'to,	kan
GEN	seven	PROG-	say	dog	eat-Ø	(at a) loss	it means	that	if

'it(a)	'endi	'kel(i)	al	'ma	gi-	'kore,	wu	'keli	'ma
PRON 2SING	have-Ø	dog	REL	NEG	PROG-	bark	and	dog	NEG

'g(i)-	amrugu	'moyo,	'keli	'ma	gi-	'so	'kidima,	'yal(a)	'ito
PROG-	remove	water	dog	NEG	PROG-	do	work	well	PRON 2SING

gu-	we'di	'nouo		'akil	'kulu	'youm,	'ita
PROG-	give	to + PRON 3SING		food	all	day	PRON 2SING

60. gi-   'kelem 'gal 'kel(i) 'de 'akul ka'sara. 'Mana   'to   a'dil
    PROG-   say   that dog   DEF eat-Ø (at a) loss meaning PRON POSS 3SING   real

    gu-   we'ri a'jol   al   gi-   'gai   'meta,   'uo
    PROG-   show   person REL PROG-   stay   with + PRON 2SING   PRON 3SING

    'ma   gi-   'kuruju, 'uo   'ma gi-   'so   'kidima   'kulu-'kulu,
    NEG   PROG-   till field PRON 3SING   NEG PROG-   do   work   all-REDUP

    'bes   'kidima 'to,   'sa   'tim,   'uo   'ja
    only   work   PRON POSS 3SING   hour be there-Ø   PRON 3SING   come-Ø

    'akul,   'sa   'tim,   'uo   'ja   'akul,   'wede
    eat-Ø   hour   be there-Ø   PRON 3SING   come-Ø   eat-Ø   DEM PROX

65. 'ina   'kelem 'gal   a'zol   al   'g(i)-   akul ka'sara. Wu   nyere'ku
    PRON 1PL   say-Ø that   person   REL PROG-   eat   (at a) loss and   child

    ka'man al   kan   'so   'neta   'kidima, 'uo   'ro
    also   REL when do-Ø   for + PRON 2SING   work   PRON 3SING   go-Ø

    'angulu 'moyo 'uo   'kasur 'lata,   kan   'uo   'jibu   'lata
    carry-Ø water PRON 3SING   cut-Ø   firewood when PRON 3SING   bring-Ø   firewood

    'de   au   'moyo 'de,   'ite   gi-   'kelem 'nouo
    DEF   or   water DEF   PRON 2SING   PROG-   say   to + PRON 3SING

    'gal   'kel(i) 'akul   ka'sara. 'Mana 'to,   'ita,   nyere'ku
    that   dog   eat-Ø   at a loss it means that   PRON 2SING   child

70. 'tai,   'sala   'ita   'g(i)-   akul,   'ita
    PRON POSS 1SING   even when   PRON 2SING   PROG-   eat   PRON 2SING

    'g(i)-   akul lo'go 'ita   gi-   'so   'nana   'kidima.
    PROG-   eat   while PRON 2SING   PROG-   do   for + PRON 1SING   work

    Ta   ta'manya   'kelem: 'kel 'num fi lu'daya, au   'it(a)
    GEN   eight   say-Ø   dog   sleep-Ø in hearth   or   PRON 2SING

    'agider 'kelem: 'kel 'aswe 'num fi lu'daya. 'Mana   'to
    be able-Ø say-Ø dog   black sleep-Ø in hearth meaning PRON POSS 3SING

    min   'jua   gi-   'kelem 'youm 'na'de   fi   lu'daya 'na,
    from   inside PROG-   say   day   DEM DIS   in   hearth there

75. wa'la   'nari   'ma. Wa   kan   wa'la   'fogo   'nari   'ma,
    light-PASS-Ø   fire   NEG   and when light-PASS-Ø   in it   fire   NEG

    'kel(i) al   'ingis . . ., al   gi-   'doru-'doru   'zaman,
    dog   REL like   REL PROG-   wander about-REDUP   for a long time

    te   'segete, 'uo   gi-   'jo   'num   fi   lu'daya -ka'lam 'nar
    GEN   cold   PRON 3SING   PROG-   come   sleep-Ø   in   hearth because fire

    'fogo   'ma- ke'd(e) 'o(w)   lo'go   'lata   hari. 'Mana
    in it   NEG   SUBJ   PRON 3SING   find-Ø   air   warm   meaning

    'to   'tan   gi-   'kelem fu   'be   'de
    PRON POSS 3SING   other   PROG   say   in   house   DEF

80. lo'go — aku'l(u) — 'akili — 'ma. — Kan — wa'la — 'nari — 'ma,
find-PASS-Ø — eat-PASS-Ø — food — NEG — when — light-PASS-Ø — fire — NEG

'mana 'to — raka'b(u) — 'akili — 'ma. — Kan — raka'b(u) — 'akili — 'ma,
it means that — cook-PASS-Ø — food — NEG — when — cook-PASS-Ø — food — NEG

a'nas — 'num — ma — ji'an. — 'Ya — a'jol — kan — 'kelem — 'gal — 'keli
person-PL — sleep-Ø — with — hunger — CONJ — person — when — say-Ø — that — dog

'num — fi — lu'daya, — 'mana 'to — a'nas — 'de — fi — 'be — 'de
sleep-Ø — in — hearth — it means that — person-PL — DEF — in — house — DEF

'num — ma — ji'an. — 'Umon — 'akulu — 'ma. — Wa'la — 'nari — 'ma.
sleep-Ø — with — hunger — PRON 3PL — eat-Ø — NEG — light-PASS-Ø — fire — NEG

85. 'De — 'ya — 'mana — ta — ka'lam — 'de.
DEM PROX — FOC — meaning — GEN — proverb — DEM PROX

Ah, — ta — 'tisa — 'kelem — 'sika — ti'nen — 'gelib — 'keli — au — 'sa 'tan
INT — GEN — nine — say-Ø — road(s) — two — defeat-Ø — dog — or — sometimes

'umon — gi — 'kelem — 'gal — ka'rama — ti'nin — 'gelib — 'keli.
PRON 3PL — PROG- — say — that — funeral(s) — two — defeat-Ø — dog

'Mana 'to — 'keli — 'rasul. — Ka'rama — 'fi — fi — sho'mal. — Ka'rama — 'fi — fi
it means that — dog — arrive-Ø — funeral — EXIS — in — left — funeral — EXIS — in

yau'min. — 'Uo — 'sum — min — 'in — 'hilu. — 'Uo — 'sum — min
right — PRON 3SING — smell-Ø — around — here — nice — he — smell-Ø — around

90. 'na — 'hilu. — 'Bes — 'uo — 'fadul — fu — 'ustu. — 'Sika — 'ma'f(i)
there — nice — EMPH — PRON 3SING — remain-Ø — in — middle — road(s) — EXIS NEG

al — 'uo — 'bu- — rwa — 'fogo — 'de. — 'Mana 'to — 'uo
REL — PRON 3SING — FUT- — go — in it — DEF — It means that — PRON 3SING

gu- — we'ri — 'neta, — bi'nadum: " — 'Ma- — ta
PROG- — show — to + PRON 2SING — human being — NEG- — ADR SING

ka'man — gi- — 'turuju — soko'lin — ti'nen. — 'Turuju — 'wai — 'lad(i)
EMPH — PROG- — send away — thing-PL. — two — send away-IMPER — one — until

'ita — 'kalas, — 'it(a) — 'arij(a) — 'abidu — 'tan,
PRON 2SING — finish-Ø — PRON 2SING — return-Ø — begin-Ø — another.

95. 'ita — 'kalas."
PRON 2SING — finish-Ø

Ta — 'ashara — gi- — 'kelem: — 'dunia — 'amuru, — 'ferteku. — 'Mana 'to,
GEN — ten — PROG- — say — world — prosper-Ø — split up-Ø — it means that

kan — 'dunia — ḥilu, — a'nas — 'gen — ba'kan — 'wai — fi — 'raha.
when — world — nice — person-PL — stay-Ø — place — one — in — rest

'Umon — 'g(i)- — ataku. — 'Umon — gi- — fu'rai. — La'kin — 'youm — fu'rai
PRON 3PL — PROG- — laugh — PRON 3PL — PROG- — be happy — but — day(s) — happiness

we'de — 'karab, — je — 'zaman — ta — 'vita. — 'Zaman — to — dus'man,
DEM PROX — be spoilt-Ø — like — time — GEN — war — time — GEN — war

100.

a'nas	'ferteku	'wai-'wai.	'Ya	ba'kan	al	'Nubi
person-PL	split up-Ø	one by one	FOC	place	REL	NPROP

gi-	'kelem	'dunia	'amur,	'ferteku.	'Ina	'kan
PROG-	say	world	prosper-Ø	split up-Ø	PRON 1PL	be-ANT

fu	a'mara	'tena.	'Ina	gi-	fu'rai.
in	prosperity	PRON POSS 1PL	PRON 1PL	PROG-	be happy

'Ina	'g(i)-	ataku.	'Ina	'g(i)-	akulu.	'Ase'de,	'ino
PRON 1PL	PROG-	laugh	PRON 1PL	PROG-	eat	now	PRON 1PL

gu-	'num	ma	ji'an.	'Ino	gu-	'num	fi	'segete.
PROG-	sleep	with	hunger	PRON 1PL	PROG-	sleep	in	cold

105.

'Dunia	'amuru,	'ferteku.
world	prosper-Ø	split up-Ø

I'dashar	'kelem:	da'bara	'gelib	sa'tara.	'Mana	'to	a'jol	al
eleven	say-Ø	coax-GER	defeat-Ø	bravado	it means	that	person	REL

gi-	'dabara	'wara	'sokol,	'uo	'g(i)-	asadu	bi'ses,	'uo
PROG-	coax	after	thing	PRON 3SING	PROG-	ask	slowly	PRON 3SING

'gu-	rwa	'war(a)	'aw(o)	ma	'ḥikima,	'uw(o)	'aksen
PROG-	go	after	PRON 3SING	with	respect	PRON 3SING	better

min	a'jol	al	'gu-	rwa	'wara	'sokol	'de	mo	'guwa,
than	person	REL	PROG-	go	after	thing	DEF	with	power

110.

mo	'dus.	'Uo	'gal	'uw(o)	ab	du'ra,
with	force	PRON 3SING	that	PRON 3SING	possessor of	biceps

'uo	'lazima	bi-	li'go.	La'kin	a'jol	al	gi-	'dabara
PRON 3SING	inevitably	FUT-	receive	but	person	REL	PROG-	coax

'de,	'ya	kele'm(u)	'gal	a'jol	te	'ḥikma.
DEF	FOC	say-PASS-Ø	that	person	GEN	respect

'Uo	'ya	'aḥsen	min	a'jol	ta	sa'tara.	'Ya	kele'm(u)
PRON 3SING	FOC	better	than	person	GEN	bravado	CONJ	say-PASS-Ø

'gal	fi	'be	t(a)	a'nas	sati'rin,	gi-	ko're.
that	in	house	GEN	person-PL	daring-PL	PROG-	cry-PASS

115.

Fi	'be	ta	a'nas	ab	da'bara,	g(i)-	ata'ku.
in	house	GEN	people	GEN	coax-GER	PROG-	laugh-PASS

'Tan	gi-	'kelem:	'ukum	Na'sara	fi	ki'tab.	'Mana 'to
other	PROG-	say	authority	Christian-PL	in	book	it means that

'kila	'sokol	ta	Na'sara,	'mana 'to	'kila	'sokol	te
every	thing	GEN	Christian-PL	it means that	every	thing	GEN

Ingi'lis,	'kulu	gi-	ku'tu	fala'ta,	gi-	kati'fu.
English-PL	all	PROG-	put-PASS	down	PROG-	write-PASS

'Ita	kan	gi-	'so	'ahadi	au	'ita	'so
PRON 2SING	when	PROG-	do	promise	or	PRON 2SING	do-Ø

120. 'ahadi   ma   a'zol,   'ita   'jo   'sul   min   'uo
     arrangement   with   person   PRON 2SING come-Ø   take-Ø   from   PRON 3SING

     'den,   kala'ma 'de   gi-   kati'f(u)   fala'ta.   Kan   'ita   'ma
     loan   thing-PL DEF   PROG-   write-PASS   down   when   PRON 2SING   NEG

     'lipa,   sa'ba   gi-   fa'ta   'waraga. La'kin 'tena
     pay-Ø   tomorrow   PROG-   open-PASS   letter   but   PRON POSS 1PL

     'de,   'bes   'an   'gal: "A'ku,   'we   'nan(a)
     DEF   only   PRON 1SING   that   brother give-IMPER   to + PRON 1SING

     'elf 'ashara."   We'di   'neta.   'Ito   'rua.
     ten thousand   give-PASS-Ø   to + PRON 2SING   PRON 2SING   go-Ø

125. Kati'fu   'ma.   'Ya   wa'ze   ta   za'man   'kelem   'gali
     write-PASS-Ø NEG   CONJ   old person-PL   GEN   old days   say-Ø   that

     'hukum   Na'sara   fi   ki'tab. 'Kila   'sokol   gi-   kati'f(u)   fala'ta.
     authority Christian-PL   in   book   every   thing   PROG-   write-PASS   down

     Tala'tashar: 'átán   li'fili fi   'dulu.   'Mana 'to,   'wede
     thirteen   crush-INF   elephant in   shade   it means that   DEM PROX

     wa'nasa   ta   mata'na.   I'tom   'wonus   'fogo   a'jol
     talk-GER   GEN   indirect way of talking evil PRON 2PL   talk-Ø   on   person

     lo'g(o)   'owo   'fi   'jamb   'itokum   'in,   la'kin   i'tom
     while   PRON 3SING   EXIS   beside PRON 2PL   here   but   PRON 2PL

130. gi-   'wonus   fi   'torof-'torof-'torof-'torof.   'Mana 'to,   i'tom
     PROG-   talk   in   side-REPET   it means that   PRON 2PL

     'g(i)-   atan   'dul   ta   li'fil.   Li'fil   ya'da,   la'kin   i'tom
     PROG-   crush   shade   GEN   elephant elephant   DEM ADV DIS   but   PRON 2PL

     'g(i)-   atan   'dul   'to   min   'in.   'Asa   a'zol
     PROG-   crush   shade   PRON POSS 3SING   around   here   now   person

     'na'de   'ya   gi-   na'di   li'fil.   I'tom   gu-   'wonus
     DEM DIS   FOC   PROG-   call-PASS   elephant   PRON 2PL   PROG-   talk

     'fog(o)   'owo   ke'd(e)   'owo   'faham   'ma.   'Mana 'to,
     on   PRON 3SING   SUBJ   PRON 3SING   understand-Ø   NEG   it means that

135. i'tom   'g(i)-   atan   li'fil   'de   fu   'dul   'to.
     PRON 2PL   PROG-   crush   elephant DEF   in   shade   PRON POSS 3SING

     'Ya   'Nubi   ta   za'man   kelem: 'átán   li'fil   fi   'dulu.
     CONJ   NPROP   GEN   old days   say-Ø   crush-INF   elephant in   shade

     A'mara   'gasi,   ka'raba   'hain.   'Mana   'to
     construct-GER   difficult   destroy-GER   easy   meaning   PRON POSS 3SING

     min   'jua   gi-   'kelem   'ábín   'sokol   gu-   'kun   'gow,
     from   inside   PROG-   say   build-INF   thing   PROG-   be   tough

     je   'ábín   'jua   gi-   'sul   'youm   mi'lan.   La'yin   kan
     like   build-INF   house   PROG-   take   day(s)   many   but   if

     kele'm(u)   'gal: "   'Kasur-   kum   'jua   'de! ",   'youm   'wai   ba'ra
     say-PASS-Ø   that   break-IMPER-   ADR PL   house   DEF   day   one   only

140. 'jua   'kasur.   Je   'wakti   to   dus'man,   'bes   'youm   'wai
     house   be broken-Ø   like   time   GEN   war   only   day   one

     kan   ja'da   'mutufa,   ju'a   'kul   fu   'bele   'kasur.
     when   throw-PASS-Ø   bomb(s)   house-PL   all   in   country   be broken-Ø

     A'nas   mi'lan   'mutu.   La'kin   we'ledu   ta   a'nas   'na'de
     person-PL   many   die-Ø   but   bear-GER   GEN   person-PL   DEM DIS PL

     ma   'ábín   ju'a   'dol'de   ma   'nas   du'kan   lo'go
     and   build-INF   house-PL   DEM PROX PL   and   COLL   shop(s)   find-PASS-Ø

     'sulu   'youm   mi'lan.   'Ya   'Nubi   'kelem   ta   za'man   'gal   a'mara
     take-Ø   day(s)   many   CONJ   NPROP   say-Ø   GEN   old days   that   construct-GER

145. 'gasi,   'ábínu   soko'lin   'dol'de   'gow,   la'kin   ka'raba
     difficult   build-INF   thing-PL   DEM PROX PL   tough   but   destroy-GER

     'to,   ka'rab   'hain.   'Hain   'de,   'mana   'to
     PRON POSS 3SING   destroy-GER   easy   easiness   DEF   meaning   PRON POSS 3SING

     'gwam.
     quickness

     Ta   kamis'tashar   'kelem: ke'ni   'weledu   'marya.   'Mana   'to,   'rag(i)   'wai
     GEN   fifteen   say-Ø   co-wife   bear-Ø   wife   it means   that   man   one

     'endis   nus'wan   ti'nen.   U   nus'wan   'de   'gen   fi   'jua   'wai.
     have-Ø   wife-PL   two   and   wife-PL   DEF   stay-Ø   in   house   one

150. 'Kila   'marya   'endis   sabu'len   'to   ma   mi'dan
     every   wife   have-Ø   living room   PRON POSS 3SING   and   yard

     'to.   'Wai   min   nus'wan   'dol'de   'weledu   nyere'ku   bi'niya
     PRON POSS 3SING   one   from   wife-PL   DEM PROX PL   bear-Ø   child   girl

     Bi'niya   'de,   kan   'gum   min 'subu,   'uo   kan
     girl   DEF   when   wake up-Ø   in morning   PRON 3SING   when

     'gu-   rwa   'kunusu   mi'dan,   'uo   gu-   'kunusu   mi'dan   ta   'safa
     PROG-   go   sweep-Ø   yard   PRON 3SING   PROG-   sweep   yard   GEN   side

     ta   ma'ma   'to.   'Safa   ta   'marba
     GEN   mother   PRON POSS 3SING   side   GEN   stepmother

155. 'to,   'uo   gi-   'kunusu   'ma.   'Ya   'dukur
     PRON POSS 3SING   PRON 3SING   PROG-   sweep   NEG   CONJ   then

     ma'ma   'na'de   ab   'endi   nyere'ku   bi'niya   'ma   'de,   'uo
     mother   DEM DIS   REL   have-Ø   child   girl   NEG   DEF   PRON 3SING

     gi-   kelem   'gali: "Ke'ni   'tai   'de,   'uo   'weledu
     PROG-   say   that   co-wife   PRON POSS 1SING   DEF   PRON 3SING   bear-Ø

     'marya   'tan.   Ase'd(e)   'umon   'fi   nus'wan   ti'nen   al
     wife   other   now   PRON 3PL   EXIS   wife-PL   two   REL

     gi-   'dusman   'mana.   'Mana 'to,   'umon   gi-   'so
     PROG-   fight   with + me   it means that   PRON 3PL   PROG-   do

160. | 'tyel | 'fog(o) | 'ana, | | a'nas | ti'nen. | " 'Ya | 'ase'de, | kele'm(u) |
|---|---|---|---|---|---|---|---|---|
| | rivalry | on | PRON 1SING | | person-PL | two | CONJ | now | say-PASS-Ø |

'gal	ke'ni	'weledu	'marya.	'Mana 'to,	nus'wan		'de,	fu	'be
that	co-wife	bear-Ø	wife	it means that	wife-PL		DEF	in	house

'de	ta'lata.
DEF	three

Translation:

1. Talking of meaning/proverbs.
   The people of the old days said . . . The first [one]: keen on his thing.
   Its meaning is [that]/it means [that] every person is keen on his thing.
   You are keen on your child.

5. You are keen on your house. You are keen on everything of yours. It
   means that you do not want your thing to be spoilt. Thus we say: keen
   on his thing. Even if your child made a mistake, you know that he
   did not make a mistake,

10. because you are keen on your child.
    The second [one]: in the old days it was not found. It means that it
    is [about] a person who prides himself when he receives wealth, then
    we say that he was poor before, he did not have/possess [anything].

15. Now, since he received, (well then) he began to boast.
    The third [one] says: fear raises the orphan. It means that an orphan
    grows up in the house of another person. He stays with fear. He does
    not stay with meanness.

20. Because slowly-slowly, the moment that he receives problems, he just
    stays with his fear. Like this. Until he grows up, he does not do mean
    [things]. Thus the Nubi are saying that fear raises the orphan. Because
    the orphan has already grown up. He has become big.

25. The fourth [one] says: extensive praise is shame. It means that a per-
    son who praises himself extensively for everything, when he spoils the
    thing, that thing, it is bringing shame to him. Thus its meaning is
    shame. You are praising yourself extensively that you are tough, or
    [that] you are strong.

30. But you happen to meet someone [who] takes you, [who] throws you
    down. Then you find shame. Well, every day, you are praising your-
    self (extensively) that you are a person of strength.

35. Number five says: dying [with] many is joy. This is a proverb of the
    old people of the old days that gave strength to them so that they
    would fight a soldiers' war. A brother was not left behind to die alone.
    They were all gathering (themselves) to go to one place.

40. It means that the joy was like a big party. When he/[they] died in
    one place, it was shown that they died together without (them) being
    afraid. It was their expression of the old days that gave strength, that:
    "Go(PL) there, fight(PL). When we die, we all die."

45. No one should run back/flee.

Number six says: a relative covers/hides the sun. It means that when you have your relative, [and] when he helps you in problems, it is the sun which he covers/hides with a parasol. When the sun is burning you, [and]

50. he brings a parasol, he puts it on his head, on your head, [then] it means that he helps/protects you from he heat of the sun. Or when problems fall on you, your relative will run, he will come to help you in the problems.

55. Thus we say [that] a relative hides the sun.
The seventh [one] says: a dog eats at a loss. It means that, if you have a dog who does not bark, and the dog does not remove water, [and] the dog does not do [any] work, well, [and] you give him food every day, [then] you say that

60. the dog eats at a loss. Its real meaning shows [that] a person who stays with you, [and] he is not working the field, he is not doing any work, [and] his work is only [that] he comes to eat [when] the time is there, he comes to eat [when] the time is there,

65. [for] this we say that [he is] a person who is eating at a loss. And also a child (that), when he is doing work for you, [and when] he goes to carry water, [and when] he cuts firewood, when he brings the firewood or the water, [then] you say to him that a dog eats at a loss. It means that you, my child,

70. even when you are eating, you are eating while your are working for me. The eigth [one] says: a dog sleeps in the hearth, or you can say: a black dog sleeps in the hearth. Its inner meaning says [that] that day, in the hearth there,

75. no fire was lit. And when no fire was lit in it, a dog that was like . . ., that was wandering about for a long time from the cold, he came to sleep in the hearth—because there was no fire in it—to find warm air. Its other meaning says [that]

80. in the house it was found/the situation was such that no food was eaten. When no fire is lit, it means that no food is cooked. When no food is cooked, the people sleep with hunger. Thus when a person says that a dog sleeps in the hearth, it means that the people in the house sleep with hunger. They did not eat. No fire was lit.

85. This is the meaning of this proverb.
Ah, the ninth [one] says [that] two roads defeat a dog, or sometimes, they say that two funerals defeat a dog. It means that a dog arrives. There is a funeral on the left. There is a funeral on the right. It smells [a] nice [smell] around here. It smells [a] nice [smell] around there.

90. It just remains in the middle. The road is not there/there is no road that it will go into. It means that it s hows to you, human being: "Do not send away two things. Send one away until you finish [this one], [then] begin another one (again),

95. [and] (you) finish."
The tenth [one] says: the world prospers, [and] splits up. It means that when the world is nice, the people stay in one place in peace. They

are laughing. They are happy. But the days of this happiness are spoilt, like at the time of the war. At the time of the war,

100. the people split up one by one. It is where the Nubi say [that] the world prospers, and splits up. We were in our prosperity. We were happy. We were laughing. We were eating. Now, we are sleeping with hunger. We are sleeping in the cold.

105. The world prospers, [and] splits up.
The eleventh [one] says: diplomacy defeats bravado. It means that a person who is coaxing after something, he is asking slowly, he is going after it with respect, [well] he is better than a person who is going after the thing with power, with force.

110. He [says] that he is a strong one, [that] he will inevitably receive [it]. But the person who is persuading gently, it is said that [he is] a person of respect. He is better than a person of bravado. Thus, it is said that in the house of daring people, there is being cried/they cry.

115. In the house of diplomatic people, there is being laughed/they laugh. Another [one] says: the authority of the Christians is in the book/in writing. It means that everything of the Christians, it means that everything of the English (Europeans), everything is put down, it is written. When you are making a promise or

120. you make an arrangement with someone, you have come to take a loan from him, [then] the things are written down. When you do not pay, tomorrow a/the letter is opened. But for us, I just [say] that: "Brother, give me ten thousand." It is given to you. You go.

125. It is not written. Thus the old people of the old days said that the authority of the Christians is in the book. Everything is written down. The thirteenth: crushing the elephant in the shade. It means that this is a proverb of talking evil indirectly. You(PL) talk on a person while he is there beside you(PL) here,

130. but you(PL) are talking at the side/indirectly/with hidden remarks. It means that you(PL) are crushing the shade of an elephant. The elephant is over there, but you(PL) are crushing its shade around here. Now, that person is called an elephant. You(PL) are talking on him so that he does not understand.

135. It means that you(PL) are crushing the elephant in its shade. Thus the Nubi of the old days said: rushing an elephant in the shade.
Construction is difficult, destruction is easy. Its inner meaning says [that] building a thing might be tough like building a house takes many days. But if there is said that: "Break(PL) the house!", in only one day, the house is broken.

140. Like at the time of the war, when bombs were thrown, all the houses in the country were broken in only one day. Many people died. But the giving birth of those people and the building of these houses and shops were found to take many days. Thus the Nubi of the old days said that

145. construction is difficult, building these things is tough, but its destruction, destruction is easy. The easiness, its meaning is quickness. The

fifteenth [one] says: the co-wife bears a wife. It means that one man has two wives. And the wives stay in one house.

150. Every wife has her living room and her yard. One of these wives gives birth to a baby girl. The girl, when she wakes up in the morning, when she is going to sweep the yard, she sweeps the yard on the side of her mother. The side of her stepmother,

155. she does not sweep. Thus that mother, who does not have a daughter, she says that: "My co-wife, she gave birth to another wife. Now, they are two wives who are fighting with me.

160. It means that they are doing rivalry on me, two people. "Thus now, it is said that the co-wife gave birth to a wife. It means that the wives in the house are three/there are three wives in the house.

N.[5]

1.
'Ana,	ma'ish	'tai			ta'mam,	'an	'kan	mu'zuluwe,[6]
PRON 1SING	life	PRON POSS 1SING			entire	PRON 1SING	be-ANT	born person

mo'weleda	to	Gu'lu.	Min	sa'kar	'tai,	'an	'gu-	rwa
born person	GEN	NPROP	from	childhood	of me	PRON 1SING	PROG-	go

'rasul	'tai			fi	'sana	ta	ar'bein,	'sana ar'bein	'ma,
reach-Ø	PRON POSS 1SING			in	year(s)	GEN	forty	year(s) forty	NEG

'an	'wosul	'sana	'kamsa wu tele'tin,		'ase,	'dukur	'an		'je	'tala.
I	reach-Ø	year(s)	thirty five		now	then	PRON 1SING		come-Ø	leave-Ø

5.
'An	'rua	fi	'Lira.	Do'riya	ta	'tabu		ka'bisa.		'Asa,
I	go-Ø	in	NPROP	travel-GER	GEN	problem(s)		completely		now

'an(a)	'aju	'gum.	'An		'rua	fi	Kabara' maide.	Ma'ishe
PRON 1SING	want-Ø	get up-Ø	PRON 1SING		go-Ø	in	NPROP	life

'tai		'na . . .	'an	gi-	'so	'kazi,	'an		gi-	'so
PRON POSS 1SING		there	I	PROG-	do	work	PRON 1SING		PROG-	do

'kidima	ta	'carpenter,	'lad(i)	'ana		'ja	'sebu.	'An(a)	'arij(a)
work	GEN	carpenter	until	PRON 1SING		come-Ø	leave-Ø	I	return-Ø

'abidu	'kazi ta. . . .	'kidima	ta	'samaga	muchu'ruzi.	'Ana	'so,	lo'go	'tabu.
begin-Ø	work GEN	work	GEN	fish	type of fish	I	do-Ø	meet-Ø	problem

---

[5] N. was born in 1930 in Gulu in northern Uganda. At the time of the interview he was 68 years old. He lived, as described in the text, in Gulu, Lira, and Kabaramaide. In 1979, he went into exile in Yei in southern Sudan. He returned to Uganda and lived for a short period in Ombachi, Arua, and subsequently in Mirya, Masindi. Finally, he moved to Masindi Port. N. had Qur'anic education and went to school up to primary 4. He worked as a carpenter and a trader. Besides his mother-tongue Nubi, he spoke Swahili, Acholi and Kuman.

[6] *mu'zuluwe* is a contraction of the words *a'zol* 'person' and *mo'weledu* STAT PASS of *'weledu* 'be born', and means 'person who is born', 'descendant'.

10. 'Tega-'tega,   'ina   gi-   'so   'kazi   ta   'tega   me   'himba.
    catch-REDUP-GER   we   PROG-   do   work   GEN   catch-GER   with net(s)

    'Ine   'gu-   rwa   fi   'bahar   fi   je'jira.   'Ino   'gu-   rwa
    PRON 1PL   PROG-   go   in   lake   in   island   PRON 1PL   PROG-   go

    'gai   'na.   'Ine   gi-   'so,   'ine   gi-   'so   tu'jar   ta   ba'kan
    stay-Ø   there   we   PROG-   do   PRON 1PL   PROG-   do   business GEN   place

    'uo 'na'de   'ladi   'hadi   'ana   'je   'sebu.   'An(a)   'arij(a)   'abidu
    DEM DIS   until   stage   PRON 1SING   come-Ø   leave-Ø I I   return-Ø   begin-Ø

    'kidima ta   tu'jar   ta   'túndá tolo'bun,   'túndá ga'ya,   'túndá   'sim-'sim,
    work   GEN   business GEN   sell-INF (red) millet   sell-INF millet sell-INF sesame

15. 'túndá 'nas   'fulu.   'Ina   gi-   'sil(u)   'in.   'Ina   'gu-   rwa
    sell-INF COLL   groundnut(s)   PRON 1PL   PROG-   take   here   we   PROG-   go

    fi   So'roti. 'Ine   gi-   'jibu. 'Ine   gi-   'jib   fi   Li'r(a)   'en.
    in   NPROP   PRON 1PL   PROG-   bring   we   PROG-   bring   in   NPROP   here

    'Ine   gi-   'so   'kidima 'to.   'Kazi   ta   'tabu.   La'kin
    we   PROG-   do   work   PRON POSS 3SING   work   GEN   problem(s) but

    'wakhti 'ten(a)   'na'de,   'sente 'tena   mi'lan, te'gili.
    time   PRON POSS 1PL   DEM DIS   money   PRON POSS 1PL   many   heavy

    'Ite   bi-   'so   'sente   'sia. . . . 'ite   bi-   'so   'kidima 'sia,
    PRON 2SING   FUT-   do   money   little   PRON 2SING   FUT-   do   work   little

20. gi-   'jib   'neta   'sente ke'tiri 'ladi   'ina   'ja   'gai,
    PROG-   bring   to + PRON 2SING   money   many   until   PRON 1PL   come-Ø   stay-Ø

    'ine   'je   li'go   du'kan. 'Baga   'wakhti ta   A'min,   'ine   'je
    PRON 1PL   come-Ø   receive-Ø   shop   EMPH   time   GEN   NPROP   we   come-Ø

    li'go   du'kan. 'Ana   'je   li'go   du'kan ma   'nas   'tai,
    receive-Ø   shop   PRON 1SING   come-Ø   receive-Ø   shop   with   people   PRON POSS 1SING

    ma   'family 'tai,   ma   'nas   'tai,
    with   family   PRON POSS 1SING   with   people   PRON POSS 1SING

    ma   aja'ma   'tai.   'Ine   'ja   'dakal   fi   du'kan,
    with   people   PRON POSS 1SING   PRON 1PL   come-Ø   enter-Ø   in   shop

25. 'so   bia'shara   mo   'kweis. 'Ine   gu-   'so   tu'jar   'tena
    do-Ø   business   with   quality we   PROG-   do   business PRON POSS 1PL

    'kweis 'ladi   'ino   'wosul   fu   'hadi   te   'jere.   'Bas,   'ya   'ini
    good   until   PRON 1PL   reach-Ø in   stage   GEN   run-GER well   FOC   here

    'jé   turu'j(u)   ina.   'Ino   'rua.   'Ina   'tala
    come-PASS-Ø   chase off-PASS-Ø   PRON 1PL   PRON 1PL   go-Ø   PRON 1PL   leave-Ø

    min   'ini,   'dakal   fi   'Lira.   'Dakal   fi   'Lira.   'Ina   'jo   'ro
    from   here   enter-Ø in   NPROP   enter-Ø   in   NPROP   we   come-Ø   go-Ø

    'dakal fi   Gu'lu.   Gu'lu,   'ahah,   'dákál,   'tálá   fi   'Lira,   'ino
    enter-Ø in   NPROP   NPROP   nono   enter-INF   leave-INF   in   NPROP   we

30. 'ro 'kun 'dukur fu 'Arua. 'Arua, 'ino 'ro 'dakal fi Su'dan,
go-Ø be-Ø then in NPROP NPROP we go-Ø enter-Ø in NPROP

fi 'Yei. 'Ase, 'ine 'ro 'gai 'na 'gai ta 'shida.
in NPROP now we go-Ø stay-Ø there stay-GER GEN problem(s)

'Bes 'ina 'gai 'gai ta 'tabu ze'de, ta 'tabu
EMPH we stay-Ø stay-GER GEN problem(s) EMPH GEN problem(s)

ze'de, ta 'tabu ze'de. 'Bes, 'ladi 'Rabana 'ja 'awun(u) 'ina.
EMPH GEN problem(s) EMPH well until NRPOP come-Ø help-Ø we

Ji'bu 'nena 'namna ta 'akili ma- shara'fi, 'gal
bring-PASS-Ø to + PRON 1PL way GEN food PART PASS- distribute that

35. gi- shara'f(i) ina 'mo. Bes, 'ina ka'man 'gai
PROG- distribute-PASS we with + PRON 3SING well PRON 1PL EMPH stay-Ø

'mo 'kweis 'ladi 'Rabana 'ja 'awun(u) 'ina. 'Já
with + PRON 3SING well until NPROP come-Ø help-Ø PRON 1PL come-PASS-Ø

ari'ja amru'g(u) 'ina min 'in. We'd(i) ina
return-PASS-Ø remove-PASS-Ø PRON 1PL from here give-PASS-Ø PRON 1PL

fi 'kambi. 'Ino 'ro 'gai fi 'kambi. 'Ina 'gai ma 'namn(a)
in camp we go-Ø stay-Ø in camp we stay-Ø with way

ab 'kweis fi 'kambi 'na. La'kini 'kweis 'to 'ma.
REL good in camp there but quality PRON POSS 3SING NEG

40. 'Bes 'tabu-'tabu. 'Ita 'kan fi 'bele te 'wakhid 'zol.
EMPH problem(s)-REDUP PRON 2SING be-ANT in land GEN one person

'Ila 'bes 'shida, 'ile fi 'tabu, 'ita bi- 'kun
except EMPH problem(s) except in problem(s) PRON 2SING FUT- be

'mo. 'Bas, 'ya 'tabu 'na'de, 'shida-'shida
with + PRON 3SING well FOC problem(s) DEM DIS PL problem(s)-REDUP

'ina 'sidu 'mo 'gelba, 'ladi 'ja 'akhir 'to.
we close-Ø with + PRON 3SING heart(s) until come-Ø end PRON POSS 3SING

'Já amru'g(u) ina min Su'dan. 'Ya 'ina 'ja
come-PASS-Ø remove-PASS-Ø PRON 1PL from NPROP CONJ we come-Ø

45. 'gum min 'Yei. Ze'de 'ina 'dakal fi 'Arua, fi Omba'chi.
get up-Ø from NPROP EMPH we enter-Ø in NPROP in NPROP

'Ina 'gai fi Omba'chi. 'Ine 'je 'tala min Omba'chi.
PRON 1PL stay-Ø in NPROP we come-Ø leave-Ø from NPROP

'Jé ji'b(u) 'ina fi 'kambi 'ten(a) 'in
come-PASS-Ø bring-PASS-Ø PRON 1PL in camp PRON POSS 1PL here

fi 'Mirya. 'Bes 'ina 'gai fi 'Mirya 'ini ge'ri 'sana 'arba.
in NPROP EMPH PRON 1PL stay-Ø in NPROP here nearly year(s) four

'Ya gover'menti ta 'Mirya, ta Ma'sindi 'ya 'amrug(u) 'ina,
FOC government GEN NPROP GEN NPROP FOC remove-Ø we

50. ʼjib(u)   ʼine   fi   Ma'sindi P.   ʼLad(i)   ʼase'de   ʼina   ʼfi   ʼini,   ʼyani
    bring-Ø   we   in   NPROP   until   now   we   EXIS   here   it is to say

    ʼshida   ʼtena   ʼlisa   gi-   ʼkalas   ʼmafi   min   ʼábídu   ʼjere
    problem(s)   of us   still   PROG-   finish   NEG   from   begin-INF   run-GER

    ʼlad(i) ʼase'de.   ʼIna   ʼma   ʼkun   fi   ista'rabu   je   ʼkan   min   ʼbedir
    until   now   we   NEG   be-Ø   in   civilization   like   be-ANT   from   before

    ʼine   ʼfi   ʼmouo.   ʼBes   ʼina   ʼfi   ma . . .   ʼbes   ma
    PRON 1PL   EXIS   with + PRON 3SING   EMPH   we   EXIS   with . . . EMPH   with

    gal'gal   ze'de.   Ma'ish ah,   ma'isha ʼtena   ta   ʼtabu.   ʼÁkúl
    disturbance(s)   EMPH   life . . . INT   life   PRON POSS 1PL   GEN   problem(s)   eat-INF

55. ʼtena   ta   ʼtabu.   ʼNum   ʼtena   te   ʼtabu.
    PRON POSS 1PL   GEN   problem(s)   sleep-GER   PRON POSS 1PL   GEN   problem(s)

    Bia'shera   ʼmaf.   ʼBes   tu'jar ʼma   kan   ʼkan   je   ʼina
    business   EXIS NEG   EMPH   business EXIS NEG   when   be-ANT   like   we

    gi-   ʼso   min   ʼyoum ʼda   ʼbedir   ʼina   ʼfi   ʼmow(o).
    PROG-   do   from   old days   before   PRON 1PL   EXIS   with + PRON 3SING

    ʼGai   ʼtena   ʼkan   ʼgai ʼtena,   ʼingis   za'man   ʼina
    stay-GER   PRON POSS 1PL   be-ANT   stay-GER PRON POSS 1PL like   old days   PRON 1PL

    gi-   ʼgai   min   ʼbediri.   ʼKul   ʼma'fi.   ʼBes   ʼlad(i)   ʼase'de   ʼbes   ʼlis(a)   ʼina
    PROG-   stay   from   before   all   EXIS NEG EMPH   until   now   EMPH   still   we

60. ʼfi   ze   ʼde.   ʼYa   ʼasa,   ʼina   fi   Ma'sindi Port   ʼen.
    EXIS   like   DEM PROX   CONJ   now   PRON 1PL   in   NPROP   here

    ʼAna   fi   Ma'sindi Port   ʼeni   ma   a'nas   ʼtai.   ʼIna
    I   in   NPROP   here   with   person-PL   PRON POSS 1SING   we

    ʼgai.   ʼAn(a)   gi-   ʼso   bia'sher(a)   ʼini   ta   tu'jar   sia-ʼsia:
    stay-Ø   PRON 1PL   PROG-   do   business   here   GEN   business   little-REDUP

    ʼtúndá   so'bun,   ʼtúndá   maran'gwa,   ʼtúndá   ʼsim-sim,   ʼtúndá   ʼfulu,   ʼtúndá
    sell-INF   soap   sell-INF   bean(s)   sell-INF   sesame   sell-INF   groundnut(s)   sell-INF

    soko'lin-soko'lin.   ʼAn   gi-   ʼtunda.   ʼYa   ʼhal   al   ʼina   ʼfi
    thing-PL-REDUP   I   FUT-   sell   CONJ   situation   REL   PRON 1PL   EXIS

65. ʼmouo   ʼini,   ʼnamn(a)   al   ʼina   ʼfi   ʼmouo
    with + PRON 3SING   here   way   REL   we   EXIS   with + PRON 3SING

    ʼini   ʼya   ʼwede.   ʼAse'de   ʼana   fi   ka'lam. . . .
    here   FOC   DEM PROX   now   PRON 1SING   in   matter

    ʼRaba   ʼtai   al   ʼan   ʼraba   ʼmo
    grow up-GER   PRON POSS 1SING   REL   I   grow up-Ø   with + PRON 3SING

    fu   Gu'lu,   ʼwakht   al   ʼlis(a)   ʼina   duga'gin,   ba'ba   ʼtai
    in   NPROP   time   REL   still   we   small-PL   father   PRON POSS 1SING

    ʼkan   ʼendi   baga'ra fu   Gu'lu.   Baga'ra   ʼkan   ʼfi   ʼmouo.   Gala'moyo
    ANT   have-Ø   cow-PL in   NPROP   cow-PL   ANT   EXIS   with + he   goat(s)

70. 'kan 'fi 'mouo.   Wu 'kas 'to   kan 'bes
    ANT EXIS with + PRON 3SING and work PRON POSS 3SING be-ANT EMPH

    to 'kúrúju. Wu 'uo   gi- 'so . . . 'kidima 'to   'de
    GEN work the field-INF and he PROG- do work PRON POSS 3SING DEF

    'wakhti al 'lisa fi 'hai 'tai   'ana 'fi 'mouo.
    time REL still in life PRON POSS 1SING I EXIS with + he

    Ka'las 'ana gi- 'faham. 'Uo 'gusu 'kidima 'to
    COMPL I PROG- understand he look for-Ø work PRON POSS 3SING

    ta bia'shera 'to al 'uo gu- lo'go 'ma
    GEN business his REL he PROG- find with + PRON 3 SING

75. 'sente 'to.   La'kin 'uw(o) 'endi baga'ra 'to.
    money PRON POSS 3SING but PRON 3SING have-Ø cow-PL PRON POSS 3SING

    'Ina 'kan gi- 'sara baga'ra. 'Ase 'ine gi- 'sara baga'ra.
    PRON 1PL ANT PROG- herd cow-PL now we PROG herd cow-PL

    Ase, 'lis(a) 'ine duga'gin, gi- 'sara baga'ra 'to.
    now still PRON 1PL small-PL PROG- herd cow-PL PRON POSS 3SING

    Baga'ra 'tena, 'ina gi- 'sara. La'siya ze'de 'ine
    cow-PL PRON POSS 1PL PRON 1PL PROG- herd evening EMPH PRON 1PL

    gi- 'jib baga'ra fi 'be. 'Ana 'je-'ja 'tim, 'tosha
    PROG- bring cow-PL in house I come-REDUP-Ø be enough-Ø be enough-Ø

80. ga'raya, 'kalwa. 'Bas, 'ya 'ja. 'Ina 'ja, 'ana 'ja
    study-GER religious school well FOC come-Ø we come-Ø I come-Ø

    'rua. We'd(i) an fi 'kalwa. 'In(a) 'abidu 'g(i)- agara 'kalwa,
    go-Ø give-PASS-Ø I in school we begin-Ø PROG- study school

    'kalwa ta 'sheik 'Musa 'Fere. 'In(a) 'agara mo 'kweis. 'An(a) 'agara
    school GEN sheik NPROP we learn-Ø with quality PRON 1SING learn-Ø

    'lad(i) 'ana 'khitma al-Qur'an. Ak'wana tai wa'din
    until I conclude-Ø the Qur'ân brother-PL PRON POSS 1SING others

    'fadul 'sara baga'ra. 'Bas, 'ya 'ini 'wakhti ka'las 'ana 'je ke'biri 'sia.
    remain-Ø herd-Ø cow-PL well FOC here time COMPL I come-Ø big little

85. Ari'ja si'l(u) 'an, ah, daka'l(u) 'an
    return-PASS-Ø take-PASS-Ø PRON 1SING INT enter-PASS-Ø PRON 1SING

    fi 'skulu. 'An(a) 'abidu 'g(i)- agara 'skul. La'kin 'hai 'tena
    in school I begin-Ø PROG- study school but life PRON POSS 1PL

    ta'mam je'de, 'ine 'tena 'kan 'fi 'kweis.
    entire EMPH PRON 1PL PRON POSS 1PL ANT EXIS good

    'Ina 'g(i)- 'akul 'akil ta 'kúrúju, 'kila 'sokol te 'shamba.
    we PROG- eat food GEN work the field-INF every thing GEN field

    'Maf 'sokol al 'ina gi- bio, mi'san ba'ba 'tai
    EXIS NEG thing REL we PROG- buy because father PRON POSS 1SING

90. 'kan a'zol ta 'kúrúju. | 'Uw(o) a'zol ta ma'isha
be-ANT person GEN work the field-INF | PRON 3SING person GEN life

to 'kweisi. 'Tab 'to | 'ma'fi. 'Shida 'nouo
GEN quality problem(s) PRON POSS 3SING | EXIS NEG problem(s) to + he

'maf 'mara 'wai, 'mara 'wai, 'gal 'kena | 'so su'nu?
EXIS NEG straightaway straightaway that SUBJ + PRON 1PL | do-Ø what?

'Kena 'ya 'ro 'bio 'akil wa'la 'kena | 'jere-'jere.
SUBJ + we FOC go-Ø buy-Ø food or SUBJ + we | run-REDUP-Ø

'Ahah, 'maf. 'Bas, 'ladi 'ana 'jo 'wosul fi 'hadi 'tai.
nono NEG well until I come-Ø reach-Ø in stage PRON POSS 1SING

95. 'Ana 'seb ak'wana wa'din gi- 'so bia'shera 'toumon,
I leave-Ø brother-PL other-PL PROG- do business PRON POSS 3PL

gi- 'shara galamo'ya ma 'nas baga'ra ta ba'ba. 'Ana 'tala (. . .)
PROG- herd goat-PL with COLL cow-PL GEN father I leave-Ø

'Ama 'gai 'tena 'wakht(i) al 'lis(a) 'ino we'le,
or stay-GER PRON POSS 1PL time REL still PRON 1PL boy-PL

'ina 'gai-'gai ta 'raha ka'bisa. 'In(a) 'endi 'tabu 'mafi
we stay-REDUP-Ø GEN peace entirely PRON 1PL have-Ø problem(s) NEG

je 'wakhti 'takum, 'wakhti ta 'ase'de, ta we'le ta 'ase'de,
like time PRON POSS 2PL time GEN now GEN boy-PL GEN now

100. 'takum, 'yal ta 'ase'de 'de. I'tom gi- 'ish 'ish
PRON POSS 2PL child-PL GEN now DEF PRON 2PL PROG- live live-GER

ta 'tabu bi'mara. 'Ish 'takum a'ta ta 'raha
GEN problem(s) very live-GER PRON POSS 2PL EMPH GEN peace

'saki 'de 'ma. 'Ma je 'tena ta aw'lan, ta 'awal
nothing DEF NEG NEG like PRON POSS 1PL GEN first GEN first

'ina 'fi 'mouo fi 'bele 'tena fi Gu'lu.
PRON 1PL EXIS with + PRON 3SING in land PRON POSS 1PL in Gulu

'Ina 'kan a'nas ta 'raha ka'bisa. 'Ine gu- 'wafik 'ben
PRON 1PL be-ANT person-PL GEN peace entire we PROG- agree among

105. 'tena. 'Ine gi- 'dor-'dor, 'ine gi- 'dor
PRON POSS 1PL PRON 1PL PROG-travel-REDUP PRON 1PL PROG- travel

fi 'ben 'tena. 'Ina 'g(i)- akul 'kul ba'kan 'wai
between PRON POSS 1PL PRON 1PL PROG- eat all place one

ma wa'ze 'tena. 'Ina, 'ina . . . 'kan ajusi'ya
with old person-PL PRON POSS 1PL PRON 1PL PRON 1PL be-ANT old person-PL

'tena, wa'ze 'tena 'dol'de, kan 'umon
PRON POSS 1PL old person-PL PRON POSS 1PL DEM PROX PL when PRON 3PL

'fi ze'de, bi- na'd(i) ita, 'ita bi- 'ja 'gai
EXIS EMPH FUT- call-PASS PRON 2SING PRON 2SING FUT- come stay-Ø

110. 'moumon ba'kan 'wai. 'Umon gu- 'wonus a'dis 'toumon
with + PRON 3PL place one PRON 3PL PROG- talk story(s) PRON POSS 3PL

ta za'man, kala'ma 'toumon ta za'man. I'tom 'gai fala't(a) 'en,
of old days thing-PL PRON POSS 3PL GEN old days PRON 2PL stay-Ø down here

i'tom 'g(i)- asuma mo 'kweisi. I'tom gi- 'faham.
PRON 2PL PROG- hear with quality PRON 2PL PROG- understand

G(i)- adi'b(u) 'ina ma a'daba 'kweisi. Wu 'ina ka'man
PROG- educate-PASS we with good manners good and we also

'indi 'faham. 'Ino gu- 'rudu ma kala'ma 'toumon.
have-Ø intelligence PRON 1PL PROG- agree with thing-PL PRON POSS 3PL

115. Kan 'gal: " 'Gai fal'ta!", 'gái. Kan 'gal: " Yo'wele, 'gum!
if that sit-IMPER down sit-PASS-Ø if that boy get up-IMPER

'Ro 'jib 'nana 'sokole ba'kan . . ., 'ro 'bio
go-IMPER bring-IMPER to + I thing place go-IMPER buy-IMPER

'nana 'sokole ba'kan fi'lan", 'ite gi- 'jere fi 'sa we'de.
to + PRON 1SING thing place X you PROG- run in hour DEM PROX

'Ito 'gum, 'ite 'jib 'sokol uo 'na'de 'mara 'wai. 'Uo
you get up-Ø PRON 2SING bring-Ø thing DEM DIS straightaway PRON 3SING

bi- 'shukur 'neta: " 'Ana gu- 'tub bu'ja fala'ta 'ya'de.
FUT- thank to + PRON 2SING I PROG- spit saliva down DEM ADV PROX

120. 'Ana gu- 'tub bu'ja fala'ta 'ya'de. Kan 'ita 'seb bu'ja
PRON 1SING PROG- spit saliva down DEM ADV PROX when you leave-Ø saliva

'de, 'abis, 'ite bi- 'je li'go la'saya." 'Ana 'ja 'ain
DEF dry-Ø PRON 2SING FUT- come meet-Ø stick PRON 1SING come-Ø see-Ø

ta 'ase'de. Wu 'haki 'ma. 'Ino gu- 'gum, 'ino
GEN now and right EXIS NEG PRON 1PL PROG- get up PRON 1PL

'gu- rwa. 'Ino 'gu- rwa fi 'sa 'uo 'na'de. 'Ita 'bio
PROG- go we PROG- go in hour DEM DIS PRON 2SING buy-Ø

'sokol 'taki to m'ze 'na'de. 'Ita 'ja, 'ite
thing PRON POSS 2SING GEN old man DEM DIS you come-Ø PRON 2SING

125. 'jo 'wosul 'now(o) 'ini, 'ite we'di 'sokol 'to
come-Ø reach-Ø to + PRON 3SING here you give-Ø thing PRON POSS 3SING

'de. " 'Gai fal'ta!" 'Gái. " 'Ro 'jib 'sokol fi'lan!" 'Ito
DEF stay-IMPER down stay-PASS-Ø go-Ø bring-Ø thing X PRON 2SING

'rua. " 'So 'sokol fi'lan!" 'Ito 'rua.
go-Ø do-IMPER thing X PRON 2SING go-Ø

Kan 'uo 'gal: " 'Num fal'ta, 'kan(a)
when PRON 3SING that sleep-IMPER down SUBJ + PRON 1SING

'dug(u) 'ita", du'gu 'ita. Kan 'só ma'kosa,
beat-Ø PRON 2SING beat-PASS-Ø PRON 2SING if do-PASS-Ø mistake(s)

130. 'ite | gi- | 'jere. | 'Ite | 'ro | na | a'ku | 'wai | 'na. | A'ku | 'de
PRON 2SING | PROG- | run | you | go-Ø | to | brother | one | there | brother | DEF

ka'man | 'g(i)- | amsuku | la'saya, | gi- | 'dug(u) | 'ita. | 'Ite | gi- | 'jere,
also | PROG- | take | stick | PROG-beat | PRON 2SING | PRON 2SING | PROG- | run

'it(a) | 'aju | 'rua | na | ma'ma | 'na'de. | Ma'ma | 'jad(a) | 'eta | fal'ta,
PRON 2SING | want-Ø | go-Ø | to | mother | DEM DIS | mother | throw-Ø | you | down

'agurus(u) | 'ita. | 'Bas, | 'dukur | 'kan | 'wakhti | 'na'de | 'ino | 'kun
pinch-Ø | PRON 2SING | well | then | be-ANT | time | DEM DIS | we | be-Ø

ma | 'adab | 'kweis | ka'bisa al | 'it(a) | 'endis | 'shaka | 'wai | 'kede | 'ma.
with | good manners | good | entirely REL | you | have-Ø | doubt(s) | one | EMPH | NEG

135. Ka'man | kala'ma | ta | 'nas | sa'ra . . ., | 'sara | 'de | 'kul | 'kan | 'ma'fi.
also | thing-PL | GEN | COLL | witch(es) | witch(es) | DEF | all | be-ANT | NEG

'Khusu | me | 'khusu | 'de | 'kun | 'kul | 'ma'fi. | A'yan | 'samba-samba'la
meanness | with | meannes | DEF | be-Ø | all | EXIS NEG | disease(s) | any-REDUP

'de | ka'man | gu- | so'w(o) ena | 'mafi | 'ladi | 'hadi | al | 'ino
DEF | also | PROG- | do | PRON 1PL | NEG | until | stage | REL | PRON 1PL

'ja | 'kun | 'mow(o). | La'kin | 'ase'de | 'hadi | al | i'tom | 'fi | 'fogo,
come-Ø | be-Ø | with + PRON 3SING | but | now | stage | REL | you(PL) | EXIS | in it

we'le | ta | 'ase'de | we'de, | kala'ma | 'takum | 'gilibu | 'ras | 'tena
boy-PL | GEN | now | DEM PROX | matter-PL | your(PL) | defeat-Ø | head | our

140. 'ina, | wa'ze | 'de. | 'Gilib(u) | 'ina | ka'bisa. | Nyere'ku, | 'ita
we | old person-PL | DEF | defeat-Ø | PRON 1PL | entirely | child | you

'b(i)- | aju | 'rasul(u) | 'uo, | 'uw(o) | 'aju | 'mafi. | Nyere'ku, | 'it(a)
FUT- | want | send | PRON 3SING | PRON 3SING | want-Ø | NEG | child | you

'aju | 'so | 'nouo | ka'lam | fi'lan | ze'd(e), | 'uw(o) | 'azu | 'mafi.
want-Ø | do-Ø | to + PRON 3SING | matter | X | EMPH | PRON 3SING | want-Ø | NEG

'It(a) | 'aju | 'kelem | 'nouo | 'sokol | je'd(e), | 'uw(o) | 'aju | 'mafi.
PRON 2SING | want-Ø | tell-Ø | to + PRON 3SING | thing | EMPH | PRON 3SING | want-Ø | NEG

'Dukuru | 'asa | 'ine | 'sebu | 'wede | fi | 'ida | 'takum. | 'Bag(a)
then | now | we | leave-Ø | DEM PROX | in | hand(s) | PRON POSS 2PL | EMPH

145. 'itokum, | we'le | ta | 'ase'de | ma | 'hadi | 'takum | al | 'Rabana | 'jibu
PRON 2PL | boy-PL | GEN | now | with | stage | PRON POSS 2PL | REL | NPROP | bring-Ø

'netokum, | al | 'itokum | 'fi | 'mouo | fi | 'zaman | 'takum
to + your (PL) | REL | you(PL) | EXIS | with + PRON 3SING | in | period | your (PL)

ta | 'ase'de, | 'ya | 'bes, | 'ina | ka'man | 'seb(u) | 'itokum | 'mouo.
GEN | now | FOC | EMPH | we | EMPH | leave-Ø | PRON 2PL | with + PRON 3SING

'Ina | min | 'ma | bi- | 'kelem | mi'san | 'gilib(u) | 'ina | ka'las.
PRON 1PL | INT | NEG | FUT- | say | because | defeat-Ø | PRON 1PL | COMPL

'In(a) | 'aj(u) | 'adul(u) | i'tom | fi | 'sik(a) | al | a'dil. | 'Itokum
PRON 1PL | want-Ø | prepare-Ø | youçPL) | in | way(s) | REL | straight | PRON 2PL

150.

'aju	'ma.	'In(a)	'aj(u)	'adul(u)		we'le	ta	'ase'de	fi		'sik(a)	al
want-Ø	NEG	we	want-Ø	prepare-Ø		boy-PL	GEN	now	in		road(s)	REL

a'dil.	'Umon	gi-	'ja	'ma.	'Bas,	'ya	'zaman	ta	'ase'de	'wosul
straight	they	PROG-	come	NEG	well	CONJ	period	GEN	now	reach-Ø

fi	'hadi	jo	'wede.	'Ita		bi-	'kelem	ka'lam,	'ita
in	stage	like	DEM PROX	PRON 2SING		FUT-	say	thing	PRON 2SING

bi-	ta'ban.	A'yan	'sambal-samba'la		'youm 'da	'nen(a)	'en	'ma.
FUT-	become annoyed	disease	any-REDUP		other day	to + we	here	NEG

Wu	kala'ma	ta	'nasi	ha'rami ke'tir,	se'regu	ke'tir	'kan	'fi
and	problem-PL	GEN	COLL	thief(es) many	steal-GER	many	ANT	EXIS

155.

'nena	'ma.	La'kin	'ase'de	ka'lam	we'de	'je	je'didi	min	'ten(a)
to + we	NEG	but	now	matter	DEM PROX	come-Ø	new	since	our

al	'kan	'ine	'fi	'mo.		'Ana		'feker	ka'lam	ke'tir
REL	ANT	we	EXIS	with + PRON 3SING		PRON 1SING		think-Ø	thing(s)	many

'ma'f(i)		al	'an(a)		bu-	'wonusu.
EXIS NEG		REL	PRON 1SING		FUT-	talk

Translation:

1. I, my entire life, I have been a descendant, a descendant of Gulu. From my childhood, I myself was not going to reach (in) forty years., I reached thirty five years, now, then I left.

5. I went to Lira. A trip full of problems. Now, I wanted to get up. I went to Kabaramaide. My life there . . . I was doing the work . . ., I was doing the work of carpenter, . . . until I left. I again began the work of . . ., the work of fish. I did [it], found problems.

10. Catching, we were doing the work of catching with nets. We went into the lake on an island. We were going to stay there. We were working, we were doing business of that place until the stage that I left. I began again the work of business of selling (red) millet, selling millet, selling sesame, selling groundnuts.

15. We were taking [them] here. We were going to Soroti. We were bringing [them]. We were bringing [them] to Lira here. We were doing its work. A work of problems. But in that time of ours, our money was much, heavy. You would make a little money . . ., you would do a little work,

20. it brought you much money until we came to stay, we came to get a shop. Well at the time of Amin, we got a shop. I got a shop with my people, with my family, with my people, with my people. We entered the shop,

25. [we] did business with quality. We were doing our business good until we reached at the stage of running. Well, it was here that we were chased off. We went. We left here, [we] entered Lira. [We] entered

Lira. We went and entered in Gulu. Gulu, nono, entering, leaving from
Lira,

30. we went to be then in Arua. [From] Arua, we went and entered in
Sudan, in Yei. Now, we stayed there a stay of problems. We just stayed
a stay of problems, of problems, of problems. Well, until God came
to help us. We were brought means of distributed food, that we were
given (with) it.

35. Well, we stayed well with it until God came to help us. We were again
taken away from here. We were brought to a camp. We went and
stayed in a camp. We stayed with good means in the camp there. But
its quality was not good.

40. Just problems. You were on the land of one person. Only with problems, only with problems we were with. Well, it were those problems,
[those] troubles that we closed [our] heart with (them) until its/their
end came. We were taken away from Sudan.

45. Thus we got up from Yei. We entered Arua, in Ombachi. We stayed
in Ombachi. We left Ombachi. We were brought to our camp here
in Mirya. We stayed in Mirya here nearly four years. Then it was the
government of Mirya, of Masindi that took us away,

50. brought us to Masindi Port. Until now, we are here, that is to say,
our problems have not yet finished since the beginning of [our] flee
until now. We are not with civilization like before we were with. We
are just here with . . ., just with disturbances. Life . . ., ah, our life is
problematic.

55. Our eating is problematic. Our sleep is problematic. There is no business. There is just no business [as] when we were working before in
the old days we were with. Our stay was our stay like before in the
old days we were staying with. All [that] is not there. Just until now,

60. we are still here like this. Thus now, we are in Masindi Port here. I
am here in Masindi Port with my people. We stay. I am doing business here of small business: selling soap, selling beans, selling sesame,
selling groundnuts, selling things. I am selling.

65. Thus the situation that we are with here, the way that we are with
here is this [one]. Now, I am in a matter. . . . My growing up, which
I grew up with in Gulu, the time that we were still small, my father
had cows in Gulu. He had cows.

70. He had goats. And his work was [that] of working the field only. And
he was doing . . . his work, the period of my life that I was still with
him. I had already understood. He looked for his work of his business,
with which he got his money.

75. But he had his cows. We were herding the cows. Now, we were herding the cows. Now, we were still small, [we] were herding his cows.
Our cows, we were herding [them]. In the evening, we were bringing
the cows home. I became old enough, old enough for studying, [for]
religious school.

80. Well it came. We came, I went. I was brought to religious school. We
began to study [at] school, the school of sheik Musa Fere. We studied

with quality/very good. I studied until I concluded the Qur'ân. My other brothers continued to herd the cows. Well, here was the time that I had already become a little big.

85. I was again taken, ah, I was taken to school. I began to study school. But [during] our entire life, we, for us, were in good conditions. We were eating the food/products of tilling the field, everything of the field. . . . There was nothing that we were buying,

90. because my father was a person of working the field. He was a person of a life of quality. He did not have problems. He did not have any problems at all, not at all, so that we should do what? That we should go and buy food or that we should flee. No no, not. Well, until I came to reach my stage.

95. I left my brothers doing their business, herding the goats and the cows of [our] father. I left. . . . Or our stay at the time that we were still boys, we stayed in complete peace. We did not have problems like in your (PL) time, the time of now, of the boys of now, yours (PL), the boys of now.

100. You (PL) are very much living a life of problems. Your (PL) life is not peaceful and nothing else. [It is] not like ours that we were with first, first, in our land in Gulu. We were people of complete peace. We agreed among ourselves.

105. We were travelling, we were travelling between ourselves/among each other. We were all eating in one place with our old men. We, we . . . our elderly, these old people of ours, when they were there, you would be called, you would come to stay with them in one place.

110. They were telling their stories of the old days, their things of the old days. You(PL) stayed down here, you(PL) were listening well. You(PL) understood. We were educated with good manners. And we also had intelligence. We agreed on their things.

115. If [there was said] that: "Sit down!", there was sat. If [there was said] that: "Boy, get up! Go and bring me something [from that] place . . ., go and buy me something [from] a certain place!", you ran on this moment/instantly. You got up, you brought that thing straightaway. He would thank you: "I am spitting saliva down here.

120. I am spitting saliva down here. When you leave the saliva dry, you will get the stick." I came to see [the situation] of now. And there is no right. We were getting up, we were going. We were going on that moment/instantly. You were buying your thing of that old man. You came,

125. you reached him here, you gave his thing. "Sit down!" There was sat. "Go and bring a certain thing!" You went. "Do a certain thing!" You went. When he [said] that: "Sleep down, so that I beat you", you were beaten. If a mistake was done,

130. you ran. You went to a brother there. The brother also took a stick, [he] beat you. You ran, you wanted to go to that mama. The mama threw you down, pinched you. Well, then at that time, we were with very good manners, [about] which you did not have one single doubt.

135. Also the things of the witches, all the witches were not there/none of the witches was there. Meanness with meanness was all not there. All the diseases also were not doing/threatening us up to the stage that we came to be with (them). But now, the stage that you(PL) are in, the boys of now, your(PL) matters defeat our head, us, the old people.

140. [They] defeat us completely. A child, you want to send him, he does not want. A child, you want to do to him a certain thing, he does not want. You want to tell him a thing, he does not want. Then now, we leave this in your(PL) hands.

145. You(PL), the boys of now with your(PL) stage which God gave you(PL), which you(PL) are with in your(PL) time of now, we just leave you(PL) with it. We will not say [anything] because it has already defeated us. We want to prepare you(PL) in a straight way. You(PL) do not want.

150. We want to prepare the boys of now in a straight way. They do not come. Well thus the period of now reached (in) a stage like this. You will say something, you will become annoyed. We did not have all the diseases here in the old days. And we did not have problems of many thieves, of much stealing.

155. But now this matter came new since ours, which we were with. I think that there are not many things that I will talk [about].

S.[7]

1.
'Ana	'ja	fi	'safa	ta	ha'dis.	'An(a)	'endi	'ija	'wai
PRON 1SING	come-Ø	in	side	GEN	story(s)	PRON 1SING	have-Ø	fairy tale	INDEF

'sia	'ali	'an(a)	'asma	'bediri	na	mu'ze	'tai,		
small	REL	PRON 1SING	hear-Ø	before	from	old man	PRON POSS 1SING		

a'ku	ba'ba	'tai.		Ha'dis	'to		furayi's(a)	'ana	
brother	father	PRON POSS 1SING		story	PRON POSS 3SING		make happy-Ø	I	

'zaidi.	Ha'dis	'de	'g(i)-	amsuku	'badu	'fogo	Tom'sa	ma	sa'bi	'to,
very	story	DEF	PROG-	touch	together	with	Crocodile	with	friend	his

5.
'kan	'fi	K.	T.		gi-	'gen	fi	'jua	'bahar.	Kala'maya
ANT	EXIS	Goat	Crocodile		PROG-	stay	in	inside	lake	Goat

gi-	'gen	'fo	fi	'aridi.	'Ase	Tom'sa fi	'be	'to	'na,	
PROG-	stay	up	in	earth	now	Crocodile in	house	his	there	

'kila	'youm,	'uo	'g(i)-	asma	Kala'maya	kan	'rasul	la'siya	je'de
every	day	PRON 3SING	PROG-	hear	Goat	when	reach-Ø	evening	EMPH

[7] S. Was a son of N. He was 35 years old at the time of the interview. As a child, he lived in several towns in northern Uganda. During the war, he stayed in Yei in the South of Sudan. After his return to Uganda, he lived in Kampala for some time. At the time of the interviews, he lived in Kigumba in Central Uganda. He had finished his O-levels (three years), secondary school. Nubi was his mother-tongue. He also spoke English, Swahili, Acholi, and Lango. He had two wives, both of them Nubi. At home, however, both Nubi and Lango were used.

gi-   'kore-'kore   'zaidi,   gi-   'dugu   ki'lele.   'Uo,   Tom'sa   'kelem
PROG-   cry-REDUP   very   PROG-   beat   noise   he   Crocodile   say-Ø

na   'marya: "Eh   'marya,   ma'lu   ji'ran   'tai   'de   je   'de?
to   wife   INT   wife   why   neighbour   my   DEF   like   DEM PROX

10. 'Be   'to   'g(i)-   askutu   'ma.   Ki'lele   'kila   'youm,   ki'lele   'kila   'youm."
     house   his   PROG-   be quiet   NEG   noise   every   day   noise   every   day

'Ya   'youm   'tan,   'uo   'gal: "   'Marya,   'ana   ke'de   'ro   'abur   'ainu
CONJ   day   other   he   that   wife   PRON 1SING   SUBJ   go-Ø   try-Ø   see-Ø

ji'ran   'tai   'de.   'Sa 'tan, 'fi   a'nas   al   gi-   'taban
neighbour   my   DEF   maybe   EXIS   person-PL   REL   PROG-   annoy

'uo."   'Ya   'uo   'robutu   sa'fari   'to.   'Uo   'ro
PRON 3SING   CONJ   PRON 3SING   tie-Ø   trip   PRON POSS 3SING   he   go-Ø

'ainu   sa'bi   'to,   Kala'maya.   'Uo   'rasul   na   Kala'maya,
see-Ø   friend   his   Goat   PRON 3SING   reach-Ø   to   Goat

15. 'so: " As-sa'lam a'leikum."   K.   'rudu: "Wu a'leikum us-sa'lam. It'fadal."
     do-Ø   Islamic greeting   Goat   answer-Ø   Islamic greeting   please [come in]

Ah,   sa'bi   'to,   Tom'sa 'dakal.   'Ya   'uo   'rakab   'chai.
INT   friend   PRON POSS 3SING   Crocodile enter-Ø   CONJ   PRON 3SING   cook-Ø   tea

Tom'sa   'asrubu.   'Gal: "Ah,   Tom'sa, 'ita   'kan   'kila   'youm gi-   'ja
Crocodile   drink-Ø   that   INT   Crocodile you   ANT   every   day   PROG-   come

'nana   'ma   'ke.   'Nare,   ke'fin?"   'Gal: "   'Ai,   'sokol   al   'jib(u)   'ana
to + PRON 1SING   NEG   EMPH   today   how?   that   yes   thing   REL   bring-Ø   I

'neta,   sa'bi   'tai,   'ana   'ja   'asad(u)   'ita
to + PRON 2SING   friend   PRON POSS 1SING   PRON 1SING   come-Ø   ask-Ø   PRON 2SING

20. 'tab   'taki   'de   su'nu?"   Kala'maya   'gal: " 'Ana 'ma   'eindu
     problem   PRON POSS 2SING   DEF   what?   Goat   that   I   NEG   have-Ø

'tabu."   'Gal: "Ah,   'kila   'youm,   'ana   'g(i)-   asm(a)   'eta   gi-   'dugu
problem   that   INT   every   day   PRON 1SING   PROG-   hear   you   PROG-   beat

ki'lele.   'Kila la'siya 'ita   gu-   'dugu   ki'lele."   'Ya   Kala'maya   'gali: "Ki'lele
noise   every evening you   PROG-   beat   noise   CONJ   Goat   that   noise

'tai   'de,   'ya   sa'bi   Tom'sa,   'de   'gúsú   we'ledu.   'It(a)
PRON POSS 1SING   DEF   VOC   friend   Crocodile   DEF   search-INF   give birth-GER   you

'aruf   'ina,   kala'maya,   kan   'gu-   rwo   'weledu,   'ino   gi-   'dugu
know-Ø   we   goat(s)   when   PROG-   go   bear-Ø   PRON 1PL   PROG-   beat

25. ki'lele."   'Ya   'gal: " 'Dinya ki'lele   'de   'kul,   'ito   'gus   'wélédu?!!
     noise   CONJ   that   enormity noise   DEF   all   you   look for-Ø   give birth-INF"

'Ita   gu-   'weledu 'kam   fi   'sana?   "Kala'maya   'gal: " 'Ana,
PRON 2SING   PROG-   bear   how many?   in   year   Goat   that   I

fi 'sana, 'an   gu-   'weledu 'wai,   au   kan   'ma   ti'nin."   'Gal: "We'ledu
in year   I   PROG-   bear   one   or   if   NEG   two   that   bear-GER

'yeta			'dugu	'fogo	ki'lele.	'Dukur	'ita	'weledu	'wai,	ti'nin	'bes?
FOC + PRON 2SING			beat-Ø	in it	noise	then	you	bear-Ø	one	two	only

'An(a)		al	gu-	'wonus	'meta		'de,	'ana	gi-	'weledu
PRON 1SING		REL	PROG-	talk	with + you		DEF	I	PROG-	bear

30. se'bein. La'kin sa'uti 'tai, 'ita 'g(i)- asma 'ma. 'Aya, Abu 'gada

se'bein.	La'kin	sa'uti	'tai,	'ita	'g(i)-	asma	'ma.	'Aya,	Abu	'gada
seventy	but	voice	my	you	PROG-	hear	NEG	INT		Turtle

min	'jua	'moyo	'na	gu-	'weledu	ma'yai	'ladi	si'tin.	'Gonyo	waltum'bari
inside	water	there		PROG-	bear	egg(s)	until	sixty	Frog	day before yesterday

'weledu	'yal	'na.	'Uo	'faga	ge'ri	'elf	'wai	wu	mi'ten.	'Ase'de,
bear-Ø	child-PL	there	she	split-Ø	nearly	thousand	one	and	200	now

'ya	Kala'maya,	'taki		'de	'ena		'wai	ti'nin	'yeta	
VOC	Goat	your		DEF	eye(s)/unit(s)		one	two	FOC+ PRON 2SING	

'dugu	'fogo	ki'lele	je	'de?!! "		'Ya	ha'dis	'tai		'de
beat-Ø	on it	noise	like	DEM PROX		CONJ	story	PRON POSS 1SING		DEF

35. 'koma 'ini, wu ha'dis 'de 'g(i)- alim(u) 'ina 'gali 'ma kan

'koma	'ini,	wu	ha'dis	'de	'g(i)-	alim(u)	'ina		'gali	'ma	kan
end-Ø	here	and	story	DEF	PROG-	teach	PRON 1PL		that	NEG	when

'ita		'gu-	rwa	'so	'sokol	ke'd(e)	'eta		'sif(a)	'eta	'fogo
PRON 2SING		PROG-	go	do-Ø	thing	SUBJ	PRON 2SING		praise-Ø	you	in it

gi'dam.	'Ite		'feker	'gal	'ita		'ya	'agider.	Ta'ra	'fi	'nas
first	PRON 2SING		think-Ø	that	PRON 2SING		FOC	be able-Ø	you see	EXIS	people

al	'fut(u)	'ita. . . .
REL	surpass-Ø	PRON 2SING

Translation:

1. I came at the side of [the] stories. I have one small fairy tale which I
   heard before from my old man, the brother of my father. His story
   made me very happy. The story touches (together) upon Crocodile and
   his friend,

5. (there was) Goat. Crocodile stayed inside the lake. Goat stayed up on
   the earth. Now, Crocodile in his house there, every day, he heard Goat
   crying very much, making a lot of noise, when evening arrived. He,
   Crocodile, said to [his] wife: "Eh wife, why is my neighbour like this?

10. His house is not quiet. Noise every day, noise every day." Thus the
    other day, he [said] that: "Wife, let me go and try to see my neigh-
    bour. Maybe, there are people who are annoying him." Thus he
    tied/arranged his trip. He went to see his friend, Goat. He reached
    (to) Goat,

15. [he] did: "As-salâm aleikum". Goat answered: "Wu aleikum us-salâm.
    Please [come in]." Ah, his friend, Crocodile, entered. So he prepared
    tea. Crocodile drank. [Goat said] that: "Ah, Crocodile, you did not
    come to me every day. How about today?" [Crocodile said] that: "Yes,
    the thing that brought me to you, my friend, [is that] I came to ask you

20. what your problem is?" Goat [said] that: "I do not have a problem."
[Crocodile said] that: "Ah, every day, I hear you making noise. Every
evening you are making noise." Thus Goat [said] that: "My noise, oh
Crocodile friend, it is searching reproduction. You know [that] we,
goats, when we are going to mate, we are making noise."

25. Thus [Crocodile said] that: "All this noise, you are attempting to
breed/you are mating?!! How many [young] do you bear a year?" Goat
[said] that: "I, in a year, I bear one, or if not, two." [Crocodile said]
that: "It is mating that you are making noise for. Then you bear one,
two only? I, who is talking to you, I am bearing seventy.

30. But my voice, you do not hear [it]. Well, Turtle (from) in(side) the
water there bears up to sixty eggs. The day before yesterday, Frog
bore children [there]. Se split nearly one thousand two hundred [eggs].
Now, oh Goat, yours, it are one or two young that you are making
noise for like this?!!" Thus my story finishes here,

35. and the story teaches us that when you are going to do something,
you should not first praise yourself on it. You think that you are able.
But you see, there are people who surpass you. . . .

REFERENCES

Anon. [possibly Alice Werner]. 1910. Review of *An English-Arabic vocabulary, with grammar and phrases*, by Jenkins. JAS 9. 328–29.

Adams, William Y. 1977. *Nubia: Corridor to Africa*. London: Allen Lane.

Aitchison, Jean. 1991. *Language change: Progress or decay?* Cambridge: University Press.

Al-Sayyid Marsot, Afaf Lutfi. 1984. *Egypt in the reign of Muhammad Ali*. Cambridge: University Press.

al-Tonsi, Abbas and Laila al-Sawi. 1986. *An intensive course in Egyptian colloquial Arabic*: part I. Cairo: American University.

Arends, Jacques. 1989. Syntactic developments in Sranan: Creolization as a gradual process. Ph.D. diss., Nijmegen University.

Arends, Jacques, Pieter Muysken and Norval Smith, eds. 1995. *Pidgins and creoles: An introduction*. Amsterdam/Philadelphia: John Benjamins.

Arends, Jacques and Adrienne Bruyn. 1995. "Gradualist and developmental hypotheses," in *Pidgins and creoles: An introduction*. Edited by Jacques Arends, Pieter Muysken and Norval Smith. Amsterdam/Philadelphia: John Benjamins. 111–20.

Arkell, A.J. 1955. *A history of the Sudan: From the earliest times to 1821*. London: Athlone Press.

Ashton, E.O. 1944. *Swahili grammar*. Essex: Longman.

Ashton, E.O., E.M.K. Mulira, E.G.M. Ndawula, and A.N. Tucker. 1954. *A Luganda grammar*. London-New York-Toronto: Longmans, Green and Co.

Baer, Gabriel. 1969. *Studies in the social history of modern Egypt*. Chicago: The University of Chicago Press.

Bakker, Peter. 1995. "Pidgins," In *Pidgins and creoles: An introduction*. Edited by Jacques Arends, Pieter Muysken and Norval Smith. Amsterdam/Philadelphia: John Benjamins. 25–39.

Bakker, Peter, Marike Post and Hein van der Voort. 1995. "TMA particles and auxiliaries," In *Pidgins and creoles: An introduction*. Eidted by Jacques Arends, Pieter Muysken and Norval Smith. Amsterdam/Philadelphia: John Benjamins. 247–58.

Beachey, R.W. 1967. The East African ivory trade in the nineteenth century. JAH. VIII 2. 269–90.

Behnstedt, Peter and Manfred Woidich. 1985a. *Die ägyptisch-arabischen Dialekte*. Band 1: Einleitung und Anmerkungen zu den Karten. Wiesbaden: Dr. Ludwig Reichert Verlag.

—— 1985b. *Die ägyptisch-arabischen Dialekte*. Band 2: Dialektatlas von Ägypten. Wiesbaden: Dr. Ludwig Reichert Verlag.

—— 1994. *Die ägyptisch-arabischen Dialekte*. Band 4: Glossar Arabisch-Deutsch. Wiesbaden: Dr. Ludwig Reichert Verlag.

Besten, Hans den. 1985. "Die doppelte Negation im Afrikaans und ihre Herkunft," In *Akten des 1. Essener Kolloquiums über "Kreolsprache und Sprachkontakte"*. Edited by Norbert Boretzky, Werner Enninger, Thomas Stolz. Bochum: Brockmeyer. 9–42.

Bickerton, Derek. 1975. *Dynamics of a creole system*. New York: Cambridge University Press.

—— 1977. "Pidginization and creolization: Language acquisition and language universals," In *Pidgin and creole linguistics*. Edited by Albert Valdman. Bloomington and London: Indiana University Press. 49–69.

—— 1979. "The Status of *bin* in the Atlantic creoles," In *Readings in creole studies*. Edited by Ian F. Hancock. Ghent: Story-Scientia. 309–14.

—— 1981. *Roots of language.* Ann Arbor: Karoma.

—— 1993. "Subject focus and pronouns," In *Focus and grammatical relations in creole languages.* Edited by Francis Byrne and Donald Winford. Amsterdam/Philadelphia: John Benjamins. 189–212.

Bickerton, Derek and Pieter Muysken. 1988. "The linguistic status of creole languages: Two perspectives," In *Linguistics: The Cambridge survey II. Linguistic theory: Extensions and implications.* Edited by Frederick J. Newmeyer. Cambridge: University Press. 267–306.

Boretzky, Norbert. 1983. *Kreolsprachen, Substrate und Sprachwandel.* Wiesbaden: Harrassowitz.

—— 1987. "Zur Grammatischen Struktur des Nubi," In *Beiträge zum 4. Essener Kolloquium über Sprachkontakt, Sprachwandel, Sprachwechsel, Sprachtod.* Bochum: Brockmeyer. 45–88.

Braukämper, Ulrich. 1993. Notes on the origin of Baggara Arab culture with special reference to the Shuwa. Sprache und Geschichte in Afrika 14: 13–46.

Bruyn, Adrienne. 1995a. "Noun phrases," In *Pidgins and creoles: An introduction.* Edited by Jacques Arends, Pieter Muysken and Norval Smith. Amsterdam/Philadelphia: John Benjamins. 259–70.

—— 1995b. *Grammaticalization in creoles: The development of determiners and relative clauses in Sranan.* Ph.D. diss., Amsterdam University.

Bühler, Karl. 1982. "The deictic field of language and deictic words," In *Speech, place, and action: Studies in deixis and related topics.* Edited by Robert J. Jarvella and Wolfgang Klein. New York: Wiley. 9–30.

Bureng Vincent, George. 1986. "Juba Arabic from a Bari perspective," In *Current approaches to African linguistics.* Edited by Gerrit Dimmendaal. Dordrecht: Foris. 71–78.

Byrne, Francis. 1988. Deixis as a noncomplementizer strategy for creole subordination marking. Linguistics 26–3: 335–64.

Byrne, Francis and Donald Winford, eds. 1993. *Focus and grammatical relations in creole languages.* Amsterdam/Philadelphia: John Benjamins.

Byrne, Francis, Alexander F. Caskey and Donald Winford. 1993. Introduction: Focus and grammatical relations in creole languages, To *Focus and grammatical relations in creole languages.* Edited by Francis Byrne and Donald Winford. Amsterdam/Philadelphia: John Benjamins. ix–xvi.

Carbou, Henri. 1913. *Méthode pratique pour l' étude de l'arabe parlé au Ouaday et à l'est du Tchad.* Paris: Geuthner.

Chesswas, J.D. 1954. *The essentials of Luganda.* Nairobi/Kampala/Dar es Salaam: The Eagle Press.

Cohen, David. 1963. *Le dialecte arabe Hassânîya de Mauritanie.* Paris: Klincksieck.

Collins, Robert. 1971. *Land beyond the rivers: The southern Sudan, 1889–1918.* New Haven/London: Yale University Press.

Comrie, Bernard. 1989. *Language universals and linguistic typology: Syntax and morphology.* Oxford: Basil Blackwell.

Crabtree, W.A. 1913. The languages of the Uganda Protectorate. African Affairs 13: 152–66.

Crazzolara, J.P. 1955. *A study of the Acooli language: Grammar and vocabulary.* London: Oxford University Press.

Croft, William. 1990. *Typology and universals.* Cambridge: University Press.

Crowley, Terry. 1992. *An introduction to historical linguistics.* Oxford: University Press.

Crystal, David. 1992. *An encyclopedic dictionary of language and languages.* Cambridge, Mass.: Blackwell.

Decorse, Dr. Gaston Jules, and Maurice Gaudefroy-Demombynes. 1906. *Rabah et les Arabes du Chari: Documents arabes et vocabulaire.* Paris: Guilmoto.

Derendinger, R. 1923. *Vocabulaire pratique du dialecte arabe centre-africain.* Paris: Tournon.

de Rooij, Vincent. 1995. "Shaba Swahili," In *Pidgins and creoles: An introduction.* Edited by Jacques Arends, Pieter Muysken and Norval Smith. Amsterdam/Philadelphia: John Benjamins. 179–90.

Ehlich, Konrad. 1982. "Anaphora and deixis: Same, similar, or different?," In *Speech, place, and action: Studies in deixis and related topics*. Edited by Robert J. Jarvella and Wolfgang Klein. New York: John Wiley and Sons Ltd. 315–38.

Emin Pasha. 1916. *Die Tagebücher von Dr. Emin Pascha*. Herausgegeben mit Unterstützung des Hamburgischen Staates und der Hamburgischen Wissenschaftlichen Stiftung von Dr. Franz Stuhlmann. Vol. 1. Hamburg: Georg Westermann Verlag.

—— 1919. *Die Tagebücher von Dr. Emin Pascha*. Herausgegeben mit Unterstützung des Hamburgischen Staates und der Hamburgischen Wissenschaftlichen Stiftung von Dr. Franz Stuhlmann. Vol. 2. Hamburg: Georg Westermann Verlag.

—— 1922a. *Die Tagebücher von Dr. Emin Pascha*. Herausgegeben mit Unterstützung des Hamburgischen Staates und der Hamburgischen Wissenschaftlichen Stiftung von Dr. Franz Stuhlmann. Vol. 3. Hamburg: Georg Westermann Verlag.

—— 1922b. *Die Tagebücher von Dr. Emin Pascha*. Herausgegeben mit Unterstützung des Hamburgischen Staates und der Hamburgischen Wissenschaftlichen Stiftung von Dr. Franz Stuhlmann. Vol. 4. Hamburg: Georg Westermann Verlag.

Fage, J.D. 1969. *A history of West Africa: An introductory survey*. Cambridge: University Press.

Faraclas, Nicholas G. 1989. Review of *Pidgins and creoles. Vol. I: Theory and structure*, by John A. Holm. JALL 11–1: 103–10.

—— 1996. *Nigerian pidgin*. New York: Routledge.

Ferguson, Charles. 1959. The Arabic koine. Language 35: 616–30.

Ferguson, Charles and Charles E. DeBose. "Simplified registers, broken language, and pidginization." In *Pidgin and creole linguistics*. Edited by Albert Valdman. Bloomington and London: Indiana University Press. 99–128.

Fischer, Wolfdietrich. 1959. *Die demonstrativen Bildungen der neuarabischen Dialekte: Ein Beitrag zur historischen Grammatik des Arabischen*. The Hague: Mouton.

Fischer, Wolfdietrich and Otto Jastrow. 1980. *Handbuch der arabischen Dialekte*. Wiesbaden: Harrassowitz.

Furley, O.W. 1959. The Sudanese troops in Uganda. African Affairs 58: 311–28.

Givón, Talmy. 1984. *Syntax: A functional-typological introduction*. Vol. 1. Amsterdam/Philadelphia: John Benjamins.

—— 1990. *Syntax: A functional-typological introduction*. Vol. 2. Amsterdam/Philadelphia: John Benjamins.

Glubb, John Bagot. 1969. *A short history of the Arab peoples*. London/Melbourne/New York: Quartet Books.

Goodman, Morris. 1986. Review of *Pidginization and creolization: The case of Arabic*, by Kees Versteegh. Journal of pidgin and creole languages 1–1: 165–70.

Gray, Richard. 1961. *A history of the southern Sudan: 1839–1889*. Oxford: University Press.

Greenberg, Joseph. 1966. *Languages of Africa*. The Hague: Mouton.

—— 1974. *Language typology: A historical and analytic overview*. The Hague/Paris: Mouton.

Greenberg, Joseph, ed. 1978. *Universals of human language. Vol. 1: Method and theory*. Stanford: University Press.

Grotzfeld, H. 1965. *Syrisch-Arabische Grammatik (Dialekt von Damaskus)*. Wiesbaden: Harrassowitz.

Hagège, Claude. 1973. *Profil d'un parler arabe du Tchad*. Paris: Geuthner.

Hall, Robert A. Jr. 1983. Review of *Russenorsk: Et pidginspråk i Norge*, by Ingvild Broch and Ernst Håkonjahr. Oslo: Novus. 1981. Language 59–3: 668–70.

Hancock, Ian F. 1971. "A map and list of pidgin and creole languages." In *Pidginization and creolization of languages*. Edited by Dell Hymes. Cambridge: University Press. 509–23.

—— 1977. "Repertory of pidgin and creole languages." In *Pidgin and creole linguistics*. Edited by A. Valdman. Bloomington: Indiana University Press. 362–91.

—— 1981. "Répertoire des langues pidgins et créoles." In *Les langues dans le monde ancien et moderne. Les langues de l'Afrique Subsaharienne: pidgins et créoles.* Vol. 1. Texte. Edited by Jean Perrot. Paris. CNRS. 631–47.

Hancock, Ian F., ed. 1979. *Readings in creole studies.* Ghent: Story-Scientia.

Hansen, Holger Bernt. 1991a. "The pride and decline of a migrant community: The Nubians in Uganda and the military profession." In *Agrarian Society in History.* Edited by M. Lundahl and Th. Svensson. London: Routledge. 318–42.

—— 1991b. Pre-colonial immigrants and colonial servants: The Nubians in Uganda revisited. African Affairs 90: 559–80.

Harning, Kerstin Eksell. 1980. *The analytical genitive in the modern Arabic dialects.* Göteborg. Orientalia Gothoburgensia 5. [non vidi]

Harris, Martin B. 1980. "The marking of definiteness: A diachronic perspective." In *Papers from the 4th international conference on historical linguistics.* Edited by Elisabeth Closs Traugott, Rebbeca Labrum and Susan Shepherd. Amsterdam: John Benjamins. 75–86.

Headly, J.T. and W.F. Johnson. 1890. *H.M. Stanley's wonderful adventures in Africa.* Excelsior Publishing Co.

Heine, Bernd. 1970. *Status and use of African lingua francas.* München: Weltforum Verlag.

—— 1973. *Pidgin-Sprachen im Bantu-Bereich.* Kölner Beiträge zur Afrikanistik. Vol. 3. Berlin: Reimer.

—— 1979. "Some linguistic characteristics of African-based pidgins." In *Readings in creole studies.* Edited by Ian F. Hancock. Ghent: Story-Scientia. 89–98.

—— 1982. "The Nubi language of Kibera, an Arabic creole: grammatical sketch and vocabulary." In *Language and dialect atlas of Kenya.* Vol. 3. Berlin: Reimer.

Herzog, Rolf. 1957. *Die Nubier: Untersuchungen und Beobachtungen zur Gruppengliederung, Gesellschaftsform und Wirtschaftsweise.* Berlin: Akademie-Verlag.

Hill, Richard. 1959. *Egypt in the Sudan: 1820–1881.* London: Oxford University Press.

Hillelson, S. 1930. *Sudan Arabic: English-Arabic vocabulary.* 2nd ed. London. Published by the Sudan Government.

Holm, John A. 1988. *Pidgins and creoles I: Theory and structure.* Cambrige: University Press.

—— 1989. *Pidgins and creoles II: Reference survey.* Cambridge: University Press.

Holt, Peter M. 1958. *The Mahdist state in Sudan: 1881–1898: A study of its origins, developments, and overthrow.* Oxford: Clarendon Press.

—— 1961. *A modern history of the Sudan: From the Funj sultanate to the present day.* London: Weidenfeld and Nicolson.

—— 1966. *Egypt and the fertile crescent 1516–1922: A political history.* Ithaca: Cornell University Press.

Holt, Peter M. and Martin W. Daly. 1988. *The history of the Sudan: from the coming of Islam to the present day.* London: Weidenfeld and Nicolson.

Hopper, Paul J. and Sandra A. Thompson. 1980. Transitivity in grammar and discourse. Language 56–2: 251–99.

Johnson, Douglas H. 1988. "Sudanese military slavery from the eighteenth to the twentieth century." In *Slavery and other forms of unfree labour.* Edited by L. Archer. London: Routledge. 142–56.

Johnson, Frederick. 1989 [1939]a. *A standard Swahili-English dictionary.* Nairobi/Dar es Salaam: Oxford University Press.

—— 1989 [1939]b. *A standard English-Swahili dictionary.* Nairobi/Dar es Salaam: Oxford University Press.

Junker, Wilhelm. 1891. *Reisen in Afrika.* Vienna: Hölzel. [non vidi]

—— 1928. *Bei meinen Freunden den Menschenfressern.* Leipzig: F.A. Brockhaus.

Kampffmeyer, Georg. 1899. Materialien zum Studium der arabischen Beduinendialekte Innerafrikas. MSO 2: 143–221.

Kaye, Alan S. 1976. *Chadian and Sudanese Arabic in the light of comparative Arabic dialectology.* The Hague: Mouton.

—— 1985. On the importance of pidgins and creoles for historical linguistics. Diachronica 2–2: 201–30.

—— 1987. Ki-Nubi etymologies. JALL 9: 157–59.

—— 1991. Peripheral arabic dialectology and Arabic pidgins and creoles. Languages of the World 2: 4–16.

Kaye, Alan S. and Mauro Tosco. 1993. Early East African pidgin Arabic. Sprache und Geschichte in Afrika 14: 269–306.

Keesing, Roger M. 1991. "Substrates, calquing and grammaticalization in Melanesian pidgin." In *Approaches to grammaticalization. Vol. 1: Focus on theoretical and methodological issues.* Edited by Elisabeth Closs Traugott and Bernd Heine. Amsterdam/ Philadelphia: John Benjamins. 315–42.

Khalafallah, A. Abdelghany. 1969. *A descriptive grammar of Sai:di Egyptian colloquial Arabic.* The Hague/Paris: Mouton.

Khamis, Cornelia. 1994. *Mehrsprachigkeit bei den Nubi: Das Sprachverhalten viersprachig aufwachsender Vorschul- und Schulkinder in Bombo/Uganda.* Münster/Hamburg: LIT Verlag.

Kieffer, Charles. 2000. "The Arabic speech of Bactria (Afghanistan)." In *Arabic as a minority language.* Edited by Jonathan Owens. Berlin/New York: Mouton de Gruyter. 181–98.

Kitching, A.L. n.d. *An outline grammar of the Acholi language.* London: Sheldon Press.

Knappert, Jan. 1983. Persian and Turkish loanwords in Swahili. Sprache und Geschichte in Afrika 5: 111–43.

Kokole, Omari H. 1985. The "Nubians" of East Africa: Muslim club or African "tribe"? The view from within. Journal of the Institute of Muslim Minority Affairs 6–2: 420.

Kouwenberg, Silvia. 1995. "Berbice Dutch." In *Pidgins and creoles: An introduction.* Edited by Jacques Arends, Pieter Muysken and Norval Smith. Amsterdam/Philadelphia: John Benjamins. 233–43.

Labov, William. 1990. "On the adequacy of natural languages: I. The development of tense." In *Pidgin and creole tense-mood-aspect systems.* Edited by J.V. Singler. Amsterdam/Philadelphia: John Benjamins. 1–58.

Ladefoged, Peter, Ruth Click and Clive Criper. 1972. *Language in Uganda.* London: Oxford University Press.

Ladefoged, Peter. 1975. *A course in phonetics.* New York: Harcourt Brace Jovanovich.

Ladefoged, Peter and Ian Maddieson. 1996. *The sounds of the world's languages.* Oxford: Blackwell.

Lass, Roger. 1984. *Phonology: An introduction to basic concepts.* Cambridge: University Press.

Le Page, Robert. 1977. "Processes of pidginization and creolization." In *Pidgin and creole linguistics.* Edited by Albert Valdman. Bloomington and London: Indiana University Press. 222–58.

Lepsius, Richard. 1852. Briefe aus Aegypten, Aethiopien und der Halbinsel des Sinai. Berlin: Willem Herz.

Lethem, G.J. 1920. *Colloquial Arabic, Shuwa dialect of Bornu, Nigeria and of the region of Lake Chad.* London: Crown Agents for the Colonies.

Lloyd, Albert B. 1906. *Van Oeganda naar Khartoum: Leven en avonturen aan den Boven-Nijl.* Amsterdam: De maatschappij voor goede en goedkope lectuur.

Lyons, J. 1968. *Introduction to theoretical linguistics.* Cambridge: University Press.

Lugard, Frederick D. 1968a. *The rise of our East African empire: Early efforts in Nyasaland and Uganda.* Vol. 1. London: Frank Cass and Co.

—— 1968b. *The rise of our East African empire: Early efforts in Nyasaland and Uganda.* Vol. 2. London: Frank Cass and Co.

Lukas, J. 1936. The linguistic situation in the Lake Chad area of central Africa. Africa 9: 322–49.

MacMicheal, H.A. 1967 [1912]. *The tribes of northern and central Kordofan*. London: Frank Cass and Co.

Mahmud, Ushari Ahmad. 1979. *Linguistic variation and change in the aspectual system of Juba Arabic*. Unpublished Ph.D. thesis, Georgetown University.

Mazrui, Ali A. 1977. Religious strangers in Uganda: From Emin Pasha to Amin Dada. African affairs, Vol. 76: 21–38.

Meldon, J.A. 1907. Notes on the Sudanese in Uganda. JAS 7: 123–46.

Miller, Catherine. 1983. Aperçu du système verbal en Juba Arabic. Comptes rendus du GLECS XXIV–XXVIII.

—— 1979–84. Vol. 2. Paris: Geuthner. 295–315.

—— 1985–86. Un exemple d'évolution linguistique: Le cas de la particule "GE" en "Juba Arabic". Cahiers du MAS-GELLAS 3: 155–66.

—— 1986. Analyse des usages de l' arabe dans une communauté non arabophone: Le cas du tribunal coutumier de Juba. 4ème colloque international sur l'acquisition d'une langue étrangère. Aix-en-Provence: 296–306.

—— 1987. De la campagne à la ville: Évolution fonctionelle de l'arabe véhiculaire en Équatoria (Sud-Soudan). Bulletin du centre d'étude des plurilinguismes et des situations pluriculturelles 9: 1–23

—— 1988–89. Kelem kalam bitak: Langues et tribunaux en Equatoria. Matériaux Arabes et Sudarabiques—GELLAS 2. 23–58.

—— 1990. Substrat ou superstrat en Juba-Arabic: Problématique de l'autonomisation d'une variété ou d' un système. 20th Colloquium on African Languages and Linguistics, Leiden.

—— 1993. Réstructuration morpho-syntaxique en Juba-Arabic et ki-Nubi: À propos du débat universaux/substrat et superstrat dans les études créoles. MAS-GELLAS 5: 137–74.

—— 1994. « Créolisation et acquisition: Quelques phénomènes observés à propos de l'arabe du Soudan. » In *Créolisation et acquisition des langues*. Edited by Daniel Véronique. Aix-en-Provence: Université de Provence. 225–46.

Mitchell, T.F. 1978 [1956]. *An introduction to Egyptian colloquial Arabic*. Oxford: Clarendon.

Mitchell, T.F. and S.A. al-Hassan. 1994. *Modality, mood and aspect in spoken Arabic, with special reference to Egypt and the Levant*. London/New York: Kegan Paul International.

Mounteney-Jephson, A.J. 1890. *Emin Pasha and the rebellion at the Equator*. London: Sampson Low, Marston, Searle and Rivington.

Mufwene, Salikoko S. 1981. "Stativity and the count/mass distinction." In *Papers from the 17th regional meeting of the Chicago Linguistic Society*. Edited by Roberta A. Hendrick, Carrie S. Masek and Mary Frances Miller. 221–38. [non vidi]

—— 1984. *Stativity and the progressive*. Bloomington: Indiana University Linguistics Club.

—— 1986a. "The universalist and substrate hypotheses complement one another." In *Substrate versus universals in creole genesis*. Edited by Pieter Muysken and Norval Smith. Amsterdam/Philadelphia: John Benjamins. 129–62.

—— 1986b. Restrictive relativization in Gullah. Journal of Pidgin and Creole Languages 1–1: 1–31.

Mühlhaüsler, Peter. 1979. *Growth and structure of the lexicon of New Guinea pidgin*. The Australian National University: Pacific Linguistics.

—— 1980. "Structural expansion and the process of creolization." In *Theoretical orientations in creole studies*. Edited by A. Valdman. New York: Academic Press. 19–55.

—— 1986. *Pidgin and creole linguistics*. Oxford: Basil Blackwell.

Muraz, Gaston. 1926. *Vocabulaire du patois arabe tchadien ou "tourkou" et des dialectes sara-madjinngaye et sara-m'baye*. Paris: Charles Lavauzelle.

Musa-Wellens, Inneke. 1994. *A descriptive sketch of the verbal system of the Nubi-language, spoken in Bombo, Uganda*. Unpublished M.A. thesis, Nijmegen University.

Muysken, Pieter. 1981. "Creole tense/mood/aspect systems: The unmarked case?" In *Generative studies on Creole languages*. Edited by Pieter Muysken. Dordrecht: Foris. 181–99.

Muysken, Pieter and Norval Smith. 1995. "Reflexives." In *Pidgins and creoles: An introduction.* Jacques Arends, Pieter Muysken and Norval Smith. Amsterdam/Philadelphia: John Benjamins. 271–88.

Muysken, Pieter and Tonjes Veenstra. 1995. "Serial verbs." In *Pidgins and creoles: An introduction.* Edited by Jacques Arends, Pieter Muysken and Norval Smith. Amsterdam/Philadelphia: John Benjamins. 289–301.

Nachtigal, Gustav. 1967a [1879–1881]. *Sahara und Sudan* I. Graz: Akademische Druck- und Verlagsanstalt.

—— 1967b [1879–1881]. *Sahara und Sudan* II. Graz: Akademische Druck- und Verlagsanstalt

—— 1967c [1879–1881]. *Sahara und Sudan* III. Graz: Akademische Druck- und Verlagsanstalt

Nasseem, Zubairi B. and Doka Wahib Marjan. 1992. The 'Nubians' of East Africa: A discussion. Journal Institute of Muslim Minority Affairs 13–1: 196–214.

Nebel, P.A. 1948. *Dinka grammar (Rek-Malual dialect), with texts and vocabulary.* Verona: Missioni Africane.

Nhial, Abdon Agaw Jok. 1975. "Ki-Nubi and Juba Arabic: A comparative study." *Directions in Sudanese linguistics and folklore.* Edited by Sayyid Hamid Hurreiz and Herman Bell. Khartoum: University Press. 81–93.

Noonan, Michael. 1992. *A grammar of Lango.* Berlin/New York: Mouton de Gruyter.

Owens, Jonathan. 1977. *Aspects of Nubi grammar.* Ph.D. thesis, London School of Oriental and African Studies.

—— 1980. Monogenesis, the universal and the particular in creole studies. Anthropological Linguistics 22–3: 97–117.

—— 1984. *A short reference grammar of eastern Libyan Arabic.* Wiesbaden: Harrassowitz.

—— 1985a. The origins of East African Nubi. Anthropological Linguistics 27–3: 229–71.

—— 1985b. Arabic dialects of Chad and Nigeria. Zeitschrift für arabische Linguistik 14: 45–61.

—— 1989. Zur Pidginisierung und Kreolisierung im Arabischen. Afrika und Übersee 72: 91–107.

—— 1991a. Nubi, genetic linguistics and language classification. Anthropological Linguistics 33–1: 1–30.

—— 1991b. "Local and universal sources of a creole verbal construction." In *Semitic studies.* Edited by Alan Kaye. Wiesbaden: Harrassowitz. 1169–79.

—— 1993a. *A grammar of Nigerian Arabic.* Wiesbaden: Harrassowitz.

—— ed. 1993b. Arabs and Arabic in the Lake Chad region. Sprache und Geschichte in Afrika 14. Rüdiger Köppe.

—— 1993c. Nigerian Arabic in Comparative Perspective. Sprache und Geschichte in Afrika 14. 85–176.

—— 1996. "Arabic-based pidgins and creoles." In *Contact languages: A wider perspective.* Edited bt Sarah G. Thomason. Amsterdam/Philadelphia: John Benjamins. 125–72.

—— 1999. Review of *L'Arabe tchadien: Émergence d'une langue véhiculaire*, by Patrice Jullien de Pommerol. 1997. Paris: Karthala. Antropological Linguistics 41–2: 278–79.

—— 2000. Arabic as a minority language. Berlin/New York: Mouton de Gruyter.

Pasch, Helma and Robin Thelwall. 1987. "Losses and innovations in Nubi." In *Bochum-Essener Beiträge zur Sprachwandelforschung* Vol. 3. Edited by Norbert Boretzky, W. Enniger and Th. Stolz. Bochum: Brockmeyer. 91–165.

Payne, Thomas E. 1997. *Describing morphosyntax: a guide for field linguists.* Cambridge: University Press.

Perkins, Revere D. 1992. *Deixis, grammar and culture.* Amsterdam/Philadelphia: John Benjamins.

Pilkington, G.L. 1901. *A hand-book of Luganda.* London: Society for Promoting Christian Knowledge.

438 REFERENCES

Post, Marike. 1995. "Fa d'Ambu." In *Pidgins and creoles: An introduction*. Edited by Jacques Arends, Pieter Muysken and Norval Smith. Amsterdam/Philadelphia: John Benjamins. 191–204.

Prokosch, Erich. 1986. *Arabische Kontaktsprachen (Pidgin- und Kreolsprachen) in Afrika*. Graz: Institut für Sprachwissenschaft der Universität Graz.

Reichmuth, Stefan. 1983. *Der arabische Dialekt der Šukriyya im Ostsudan*. Hildesheim: Georg Olms.

Rifaat Bey, M. 1947. *The awakening of modern Egypt*. London: Longmans, Green and Co.

Romaine, Suzanne. 1988. *Pidgin and creole languages*. London/New York: Longman.

Roth-Laly, Arlette. 1969a. *Lexique des parlers arabes Tchado-Soudanais: An Arabic-English-French lexicon of the dialects spoken in the Chad-Sudan area* Vol. 1.

—— 1969b. *Lexique des parlers arabes Tchado-Soudanais: An Arabic-English-French lexicon of the dialects spoken in the Chad-Sudan area* Vol. 2.

—— 1971. *Lexique des parlers arabes Tchado-Soudanais: An Arabic-English-French lexicon of the dialects spoken in the Chad-Sudan area* Vol. 3.

—— 1972. *Lexique des parlers arabes Tchado-Soudanais: An Arabic-English-French lexicon of the dialects spoken in the Chad-Sudan area* Vol. 4.

Roth Arlette. 1979. *Esquisse grammaticale du parler arabe d'Abbéché (Tchad)*. Atlas Linguistique du Monde Arabe. GLECS Supplément 8. Paris: Geuthner.

Rouchdy, Aleya. 1980. Languages in contact: Arabic—Nubian. Anthropological Linguistics 22–8: 334–44.

—— 1991. *Nubians and the Nubian language in contemporary Egypt: A case of cultural and linguistic contact*. Leiden: Brill.

Schweinfurth, Georg. 1922. *Im Herzen von Afrika: Reisen und Entdeckungen im Zentralen Äquatorial-Afrika während der Jahre 1868–71*. Leipzig: F.A. Brockhaus.

Sebba, Mark. 1985. "Arguments for serial verbs." In *Akten des 1. Essener Kolloquiums über "Kreolsprache und Sprachkontakte"*. Edited by Norbert Boretzky, Werner Enninger, Thomas Stolz. Bochum: Brockmeyer. 115–33.

—— 1987. *The syntax of serial verbs: An investigation into serialisation in Sranan and other languages*. Amsterdam/Philadelphia: John Benjamins.

Singler, J.V, ed. 1990. *Pidgin and creole tense-mood-aspect systems*. Amsterdam/Philadelphia: John Benjamins.

Slatin, Rudolf C. Pasha. 1896. *Fire and sword in the Sudan: A personal narrative of fighting and serving the Dervishes. 1879–95*. London/New York: Edward Arnold.

Smart, J.R. 1990. Pidginization in Gulf Arabic: A first report. Anthropological Linguistics 32–1, 2: 83–119.

Soghayroun, Ibrahim El-Zein. 1981. *The Sudanese Muslim factor in Uganda*. Ph.D. thesis, Khartoum. University

Spagnolo, A. 1933. *Bari grammar*. Verona: Missioni Africane.

Spitta-Bey, Wilhelm. 1880. *Grammatik des arabischen Vulgärdialectes von Aegypten*. Leipzig: Hinrichs'sche Buchhandlung.

Stoks, Hans. 1988. *Kleines philologisches Wörterbuch der Lese- und Mamvu-Sprachen*. Saarbrücken: Homo et Religio.

Stuhlmann, Franz. 1916. Introduction to *Die Tagebücher von Dr. Emin Pascha*, by Emin Pasha. Herausgegeben mit Unterstützung des Hamburgischen Staates und der Hamburgischen Wissenschaftlichen Stiftung von Dr. Franz Stuhlmann. Vol. 1. Hamburg: Georg Westermann Verlag.

Sulaiman, Habib. 1972. *Bombo, centre for the Nubians in Uganda*. Kampala.

Thomason, Sarah.G. and Alaa Elgibali. 1986. Before the lingua franca: Pidginized Arabic in the eleventh century AD. Lingua 68: 317–49.

Thorburn, D. Hay. 1924. Sudanese soldiers' songs. JAS 24: 314–21.

Todd, L. 1974. *Pidgins and creoles*. London/Boston: Routledge/Kegan.

Tosco, Mauro. 1995. A pidgin verbal system: The case of Juba Arabic. Anthropological Linguistics 37–4: 423–59.

Tosco, Mauro and Jonathan Owens. 1993. Turku: A Descriptive and Comparative study. Sprache und Geschichte in Afrika 14. 177–267.

Traugott, Elizabeth Closs. 1977. "Pidginization, creolization, and language change." In *Pidgin and creole linguistics*. Edited by Albert Valdman. Bloomington and London: Indiana University Press. 70–98.

Trimingham, J. Spencer. 1946. *Sudan colloquial Arabic*. London: Oxford University Press.

—— 1964. *Islam in East Africa*. Oxford: Clarendon.

Tucker, Alfred, R. 1911. *Eighteen years in Uganda and East Africa*. London: Edward Arnold.

Tucker, A.N. 1934. The linguistic situation in the southern Sudan. Africa 7: 28–36.

—— 1940. *The eastern Sudanic languages*. Vol. I. London: Oxford University Press.

—— 1946. Foreign sounds in Swahili. Bulletin of the School of Oriental and African Studies 11–4: 854–71.

—— 1947. Foreign Sounds in Swahili. Bulletin of the School of Oriental and African Studies 12: 214–32.

Twaddle, Michael. 1988. "Slaves and peasants in Buganda." In *Slavery and other forms of unfree labour*. Edited by L. Archer. London: Routledge. 118–29.

Ukoko, Joseph, Jan Knappert and Marcel Van Spaandonck. 1964. *Proeve van Dho Alur woordenboek*. Gent.

Valdman, A., ed. 1977. *Pidgin and creole linguistics*. Bloomington: Indiana University Press.

Vanneste, P.M. 1940. *Woordenboek van de Alur-taal Mahagi*. Boechout: Seminarie der Witte Paters.

Vatikiotis, P.J. 1969. *The modern history of Egypt*. London: Weidenfeld and Nicolson.

Veenstra, Tonjes and Hans den Besten. 1995. "Fronting." In *Pidgins and creoles: An introduction*. Edited by Jacques Arends, Pieter Muysken and Norval Smith, Amsterdam/Philadelphia: John Benjamins. 303–15.

Versteegh, Kees. 1984. *Pidginization and creolization: The case of Arabic*. Amsterdam/Philadelphia: John Benjamins.

—— 1990. *Over taal en verandering*. Inaugural speech, Nijmegen University.

—— 1992. The debate concerning Latin and Early Romance. Diachronica 9–2: 259–85.

—— 1993. Leveling in the Sudan: From Arabic creole to Arabic dialect. International Journal of the Sociology of Language 99: 65–79.

—— 1993. Esperanto as a first language: Language acquisition with a restricted input. Linguistics 31: 539–55.

Watson, R. with L. Ola. 1984. *Juba Arabic for beginners*. Juba. [non vidi]

Werner, Roland. 1987. *Grammatik des Nobiin (Nilnubisch)*. Hamburg: Buske.

Westermann, Diedrich. 1912. *The Shilluk people: Their language and folklore*. Berlin: Dietrich Reimer.

—— 1940. "Sprache und Erziehung." In *Völkerkunde von Afrika*. Edited by Hermann Baumann, Richard Thurnwald and Diedrich Westermann. Essen: Essener Verlagsanstalt. 375–433.

Wilson, C.T. and R.W. Felkin. 1883a. *Uganda und der Aegyptische Sudan*. Vol. 1. Stuttgart: Cotta'sche Buchhandlung Verlag.

—— 1883b. *Uganda und der Aegyptische Sudan*. Vol. 2. Stuttgart: Cotta'sche Buchhandlung Verlag.

Worsley, Allan. 1925. *Sudanese grammar*. London: Society for Promoting Christian Knowledge.

Yokwe, Eluzai M. 1985. "The diversity of Juba-Arabic." In *Studies in African linguistics*. Supplement 9. Edited by R.G. Schuh. 323–28.

INDEX

STUDIES IN SEMITIC
LANGUAGES AND LINGUISTICS

6. Bravmann, M.M. *Studies in Semitic Philology*. 1977. ISBN 90 04 04743 3
8. Fenech, E. *Contemporary Journalistic Maltese*. An Analytical and Comparative Study. 1978. ISBN 90 04 05756 0
9. Hospers, J.H. (ed.). *General Linguistics and the Teaching of Dead Hamito-Semitic Languages*. Proceedings of the Symposium held in Groningen, 7th-8th November 1975, on the occasion of the 50th Anniversary of the Institute of Semitic Studies and Near Eastern Archaeology of the State University at Groningen. 1978. ISBN 90 04 05806 0
12. Hoftijzer, J. *A Search for Method*. A Study in the Syntactic Use of the H-locale in Classical Hebrew. With the collaboration of H.R. van der Laan and N.P. de Koo. 1981. ISBN 90 04 06257 2
13. Murtonen, A. *Hebrew in its West Semitic Setting*. A Comparative Survey of Non-Masoretic Hebrew Dialects and Traditions. Part I. *A Comparative Lexicon*.
    Section A. *Proper Names*. 1986. ISBN 90 04 07245 4
    Section Ba. *Root System: Hebrew Material*. 1988. ISBN 90 04 08064 3
    Section Bb. *Root System: Comparative Material and Discussion*. Sections C, D and E: *Numerals under 100, Pronouns, Particles*. 1989.
        ISBN 90 04 08899 7
14. Retsö, J. *Diathesis in the Semitic Languages*. A Comparative Morphological Study. 1989. ISBN 90 04 08818 0
15. Rouchdy, A. *Nubians and the Nubian Language in Contemporary Egypt*. A Case of Cultural and Linguistic Contact. 1991. ISBN 90 04 09197 1
16. Murtonen, A. *Hebrew in its West Semitic Setting*. A Comparative Survey of Non-Masoretic Hebrew Dialects and Traditions. Part 2. *Phonetics and Phonology*. Part 3. *Morphosyntactics*. 1990. ISBN 90 04 09309 5
17. Jongeling K., H.L. Murre-van den Berg & L. van Rompay (eds.). *Studies in Hebrew and Aramaic Syntax*. Presented to Professor J. Hoftijzer on the Occasion of his Sixty-Fifth Birthday. 1991. ISBN 90 04 09520 9
18. Cadora, F.J. *Bedouin, Village, and Urban Arabic*. An Ecolinguistic Study. 1992. ISBN 90 04 09627 2
19. Versteegh, C.H.M. *Arabic Grammar and Qurʾānic Exegesis in Early Islam*. 1993. ISBN 90 04 09845 3
20. Humbert, G. *Les voies de la transmission du Kitāb de Sībawayhi*. 1995. ISBN 90 04 09918 2
21. Mifsud, M. *Loan Verbs in Maltese*. A Descriptive and Comparative Study. 1995. ISBN 90 04 10091 1
22. Joosten, J. *The Syriac Language of the Peshitta and Old Syriac Versions of Matthew*. Syntactic Structure, Inner-Syriac Developments and Translation Technique. 1996. ISBN 90 04 10036 9
23. Bernards, M. *Changing Traditions*. Al-Mubarrad's Refutation of Sībawayh and the Subsequent Reception of the *Kitāb*. 1997. ISBN 90 04 10595 6
24. Belnap, R.K. and N. Haeri. *Structuralist Studies in Arabic Linguistics*. Charles A. Ferguson's Papers, 1954-1994. 1997. ISBN 90 04 10511 5
25. Talmon R. *Arabic Grammar in its Formative Age. Kitāb al-ʾAyn and its Attribution to Ḫalīl b. Aḥmad*. 1997. ISBN 90 04 10812 2

26. Testen, D.D. *Parallels in Semitic Linguistics*. The Development of Arabic la- and Related Semitic Particles. 1998. ISBN 90 04 10973 0

27. Bolozky, S. *Measuring Productivity in Word Formation*. The Case of Israeli Hebrew. 1999. ISBN 90 04 11252 9

28. Ermers, R. *Arabic Grammars of Turkic. The Arabic Linguistic Model Applied to Foreign Languages & Translation of 'Abū ayyān al-'Andalusī's* Kitāb al-'Idrāk li-Lisān al-'Atrāk. 1999. ISBN 90 04 113061

29. Rabin, Ch. *The Development of the Syntax of Post-Biblical Hebrew*. 1999. ISBN 90 04 11433 5

30. Piamenta, M. *Jewish Life in Arabic Language and Jerusalem Arabic in Communal Perspective*. A Lexical-Semantic Study. 2000. ISBN 90 04 11762 8

31. Kinberg, N. ; Versteegh, K. (ed.). *Studies in the Linguistic Structure of Classical Arabic*. 2001. ISBN 90 04 11765 2

32. Khan, G. *The Early Karaite Tradition of Hebrew Grammatical Thought*. Including a Critical Edition, Translation and Analysis of the *Diqduq* of 'Abū Ya'qūb Yūsuf ibn Nūḥ on the Hagiographa. 2000. ISBN 90 04 11933 7

33. Zammit, M.R. *A Comparative Lexical Study of Qur'ānic Arabic*. ISBN 90 04 11801 2 (in preparation)

34. Bachra, B.N. *The Phonological Structure of the Verbal Roots in Arabic and Hebrew*. 2001. ISBN 90 04 12008 4

35. Åkesson, J. *Arabic Morphology and Phonology*. Based on the Marāḥ al-arwāḥ by Aḥmad b. 'Alī b. Mas'ūd. Presented with an Introduction, Arabic Edition, English Translation and Commentary. 2001. ISBN 90 04 12028 9

36. Khan, G. *The Neo-Aramaic Dialect of Qaraqosh*. 2002. ISBN 90 04 12863 8

37. Khan, G., Ángeles Gallego, M. and Olszowy-Schlanger, J. *The Karaite Tradition of Hebrew Grammatical Thought in its Classical Form*. A Critical Edition and English Translation of *al-Kitāb al-Kāfī fī al-Luġa al-'Ibrāniyya* by 'Abū al-Faraj Hārūn ibn al-Faraj. 2 Vols. 2003. ISBN 90 04 13272 4 (*Set*), ISBN 90 04 13311 9 (*Vol. 1*), ISBN 90 04 13312 7 (*Vol. 2*)

38. Haak, M., De Jong, R., Versteegh, K. (eds.). *Approaches to Arabic Dialects*. A Collection of Articles presented to Manfred Woidich on the Occasion of his Sixtieth Birthday. 2004. ISBN 90 04 13206 6

39. Takács, G. (ed.). *Egyptian and Semito-Hamitic (Afro-Asiatic) Studies in Memoriam W. Vycichl*. 2004. ISBN 90 04 13245 7

40. Maman, A. *Comparative Semitic Philology in the Middle Ages*. From Sa'adiah Gaon to Ibn Barūn (10th-12th C.). 2004. ISBN 90 04 13620 7

41. Van Peursen, W.Th. *The Verbal System in the Hebrew Text of Ben Sira*. 2004. ISBN 90 04 13667 3

42. Elgibali, A. *Investigating Arabic*. Current Parameters in Analysis and Learning. 2004. ISBN 90 04 13792 0

43. Florentin, M. *Late Samaritan Hebrew*. A Linguistic Analysis of Its Different Types. 2004. ISBN 90 04 13841 2

44. Khan, G. *The Jewish Neo-Aramaic Dialect of Sulemaniyya and Ḥalabja*. 2004. ISBN 90 04 13869 2

45. Wellens, I. *The Nubi Language of Uganda*. An Arabic Creole in Africa. 2005. ISBN 90 04 14518 4

46. Bassiouney, R. *Functions of Code-Switching in Egypt*. Evidence from Monologues. 2006. ISBN 90 04 14760 8

47. Khan, G. *Semitic Studies in Honour of Edward Ullendorff*. 2005. ISBN 90 04 14834 5